THE VAN DE WALLE PROFESSIONAL MATHEMATICS SERIES

VOLUME TWO

Teaching
Student-Centered
MATHEMATICS
Grades 3–5

JOHN A. VAN DE WALLE
Virginia Commonwealth University

LOUANN H. LOVIN
James Madison University

PEARSON

Boston | New York | San Francisco
Mexico City | Montreal | Toronto | London | Madrid | Munich | Paris
Hong Kong | Singapore | Tokyo | Cape Town | Sydney

Series Editor: Traci Mueller
Development Editor: Sonny Regelman
Editorial Assistant: James P. Neal, III
Marketing Manager: Jen Armstrong
Senior Editorial-Production Administrator: Donna Simons
Composition and Prepress Buyer: Linda Cox
Manufacturing Buyer: Andrew Turso

Cover Designer: Kristina Mose-Libon
Permissions Coordinator: William Walsh
Permissions Researcher: Renee Nicholls
Editorial-Production Service: Omegatype Typography, Inc.
Interior Designer: The Davis Group, Inc.
Illustrations: Omegatype Typography, Inc.
Electronic Composition: Omegatype Typography, Inc.

For related titles and support materials, visit our online catalog at www.abprofessionaled.com.

Library of Congress Cataloging-in-Publication Data

Van de Walle, John A.
    Teaching student centered mathematics. Grades 3–5 / John A. Van de Walle, LouAnn H. Lovin.
      p. cm. — (Volume 2 of The Van de Walle professional mathematics series)
    Includes bibliographical references and index.
    ISBN 0-205-40844-3
    1. Mathematics—Study and teaching (Elementary)—United States.   I. Lovin, LouAnn H.
  II. Title.

QA13. V34 2006
372.7—dc22

                        2005042919

Printed in the United States of America

10 9 8   VHP   10 09 08 07 06

BRIEF CONTENTS

CONTENTS

PREFACE

And once I had a teacher who understood. He brought with him the beauty of mathematics. He made me create it for myself. He gave me nothing, and it was more than any other teacher has ever dared to give me.

—Cochran (1991, pp. 213–214)

Math makes sense! This is the most fundamental idea that an elementary teacher of mathematics needs to believe and act on. It is through the teacher's actions that every child in his or her own way can come to believe this simple truth and, more importantly, believe that he or she is capable of making sense of mathematics. Helping students come to this belief should be a goal of every teacher.

The title of this book, *Teaching Student-Centered Mathematics,* reflects our belief in the best way for students to develop this confidence and understanding of mathematics. We believe that teachers must create an environment in which students are trusted to solve problems and work together using their ideas to do so. Instruction involves posing tasks that will engage students in the mathematics they are expected to learn. Then, by allowing students to interact with and struggle with the mathematics using *their* ideas and *their* strategies—a student-centered approach—the mathematics they learn will be integrated with their ideas; it will make sense to them, be understood, and be enjoyed.

Our Goals for the Book

For many teachers, the idea of allowing students to struggle with mathematics is sometimes difficult to accept. *How and why should I allow students to wrestle with problems and not show them the solutions? Where can the right kinds of tasks be found? Where can I learn the mathematics content information I really need in order to be able to teach in this way?* With these and other questions firmly in mind, we have three main objectives for this book:

1. To help teachers understand what it means to teach in a student-centered, problem-based manner. This is a theme that runs throughout the book. We have also tried to help teachers understand why this is the best method available for helping students understand mathematics.
2. To provide a reference book for all the mathematics content found in third to fifth grades and the best information available concerning how children learn this mathematics. We have tried to provide this information in a readable, useful manner, completely integrated with instructional strategies.
3. To provide a resource of simple, problem-based activities or tasks that can engage students in the mathematics that is important for them to learn.

These are also goals of my larger book, *Elementary and Middle School Mathematics: Teaching Developmentally (EMSM)*. Written primarily as a textbook for college courses about teaching mathematics, *EMSM* has, over the years, also become popular as a resource book for classroom teachers. Therefore, it made sense to use that larger text as the basis for this series of books.

My first decision was to ask Dr. LouAnn Lovin to assist me in adapting *EMSM*. Together, we decided to use it as the foundation for each of the books in this series of three grade-banded books. In many instances we have used both text and activities exactly as they appear in the college text. Those of you familiar with that book will undoubtedly see overlap as we included much of the material, both text and activities, from *EMSM*. However, we also quickly found that in order for the books to be more useful for the classroom teacher at the prescribed grade level, there were gaps to be filled, material to be rearranged, and language to be focused. As a result, we wrote new activities, expanded the mathematics, and in a few cases wrote almost completely new chapters. Unlike *EMSM,* this book is designed expressly for the classroom teacher at the third- to fifth-grade level. We hope you will find that this is a better resource for your purposes.

What You Will Find in This Book

We view this book as a primary resource for teachers. It is not simply a book of activities—although it has nearly 150 good, practical activities. It is not a book about content—although it addresses a deep understanding of mathematics and how children learn it. Nor is it a book about constructivist views of teaching—although it is firmly based on a constructivist view of how children learn. Rather, we have attempted to bring together all of these aspects of teaching student-centered, problem-based mathematics and integrate them in a manner that we hope is most helpful to you, the classroom teacher.

Foundations of Student-Centered Instruction

Chapter 1 is the only "general" chapter in the book. It describes four core ideas for effective mathematics teaching: knowledge of how children learn, an explanation of teaching mathematics through problem solving, suggestions for planning student-centered lessons, and strategies for assessment in a student-centered environment. We strongly believe that this is the most important chapter of the book. The remaining eleven chapters are based on these core ideas. We encourage you to read this chapter thoughtfully.

Big Ideas in Mathematics

Much of the literature espousing a student-centered approach suggests that teachers plan their instruction around "big ideas" rather than individual skills or concepts. At the start of every chapter after the first one, you will find a list of the key mathematical ideas associated with the chapter. Teachers find these lists beneficial because they focus thinking on the broader goals of a mathematics unit and, thus, keep both instruction and assessment on target.

Activities

Throughout Chapters 2 to 11, you will find numerous activities that can be directly adapted to lessons in your classroom. Most of the time you will find these set off from the text with a number and a title. Other ideas are described directly in the text or in the illustrations. Each of these is a problem-based task as described in Chapter 1.

It is important that you see these activities as an integral part of the text that surrounds them. The activities are inserted as examples to support the development of the mathematics being discussed and how children can be helped to learn that content. Therefore, we hope that you will not take any activity as a suggestion for instruction without reading carefully the full text in which it is embedded.

Following the table of contents, you will find the Activities at a Glance chart, a list of all the named and numbered activities with a short statement of the mathematical goal for each. You may occasionally find that a topic you are teaching is not in the list. Whole-number computation is an example, even though all of Chapter 4 is devoted to this large curricular area. The format of a boxed activity did not lend itself to the topic. Keep in mind that although this book addresses all of the big mathematical ideas in grades 3 to 5, it is not an activity book in the traditional sense.

Assessment Notes

We believe that in a student-centered environment, assessment should be integral to instruction rather than an interruption or a test at the end of a unit. To teach in a student-centered manner demands "listening" carefully to the thinking of students (with attention to what they do and write) so that you can plan tomorrow's lesson, assist students, and communicate with parents. To aid in your listening, you will find assessment ideas located throughout Chapters 2 to 12.

Stop and Reflect

Reflective thinking is the key to effective learning. This is true not only for students but also for all learners. Throughout the book, you will run across stop signs with questions that ask you to pause in your reading and reflect on some aspect of what you have read. These stop-and-reflect sections do not signal every important idea, but we have tried to place them where it seemed natural and helpful for you to slow down a bit and think.

Expanded Lessons

The activities in the book are written in a very brief format so as not to detract from the flow of ideas. Details of how an activity should be implemented in the classroom are generally left to you, with the assumption that your class is unique. The process of designing a good student-centered, problem-based lesson requires careful thought regardless of where the idea for the lesson comes from. By way of example, we selected one activity in each chapter and expanded it into a complete lesson plan, following the structure described in Chapter 1. We included lesson elements such as mathematical goals, notes on preparation, specific expectations for the students, and notes on assessment. Clearly, any lesson should be modified to suit the special needs of your class. We offer these examples as suggestions for making the many decisions involved in lesson planning. These Expanded Lessons are located at the end of Chapters 2 to 12.

NCTM Standards Appendix

NCTM's *Principles and Standards for School Mathematics* (2000) has been a guiding force for the reform in school mathematics and we feel that this book is reflective of that document. In Appendix A, you will find a copy of the appendix to the *Standards,* listing all of the content standards and goals for each of the four grade bands: pre-K–2, 3–5, 6–8, and 9–12.

Blackline Masters

Throughout the book are references to Blackline Masters that are useful for conducting the activities being discussed. In Appendix B, you will find a small thumbnail version of all of the Blackline Masters so that you will be able to see what they look like. A PDF version of each Master is available on the website for the book: www.ablongman.com/vandewalleseries. We have found that this method of providing the masters is actually much more useful to teachers than having to copy pages from the book. Each time you download a master, remember to keep a copy on your computer. That way they will always be at your fingertips. You may copy these masters freely for use in your classroom.

Acknowledgments

This series of books began as a straightforward and seemingly simple project: adapt *Elementary and Middle School Mathematics* to suit the needs of classroom teachers in three grade bands, K–3, 3–5, and 5–8. It was not nearly as simple as it initially seemed. I am indebted to a number of people who have helped to make the books a reality.

Two people at Allyn & Bacon have been truly indispensable. Our editor, Traci Mueller, has offered encouragement from start to finish. She has answered questions and helped with many big decisions. Our development editor, Sonny Regelman, is a master of detail and a font of good judgment. Her constant prodding and careful editing have become my safety net. Throughout the development of these books, and also *EMSM*, we have become close professional friends. It has been a pleasure to continue my association with these and all of the people at Allyn & Bacon.

I would especially like to take this opportunity to offer a huge thank-you to my coauthor, Dr. LouAnn Lovin. In addition to contributing manuscript, LouAnn brought to this project a valuable second viewpoint on issues of mathematics and how best to help students learn. Without LouAnn's able collaboration, this series would probably not exist. More importantly, the books are significantly better for her efforts. Thanks, LouAnn!

To all of the teachers throughout the United States and Canada who have encouraged me and expressed their appreciation of the *EMSM* book, a special thanks. We hope that this book will be of even more help to you as you work with your students. Remember always to believe in kids. Allow them to think and to make sense of mathematics daily.

—John Van de Walle

ACTIVITIES AT A GLANCE

This table lists all of the named and numbered activities in the book. In addition to providing an easy way to find an activity, the table provides the main mathematical goal or objective for each activity, stated as succinctly as possible. We hope this will be useful.

Rather than a book of activities, this is a book about teaching mathematics. Many practical and effective activities are used as examples. Every activity should be seen as an integral part of the text that surrounds it. Therefore, it is extremely important not to take any activity as a suggestion for instruction without reading carefully the full text in which it is imbedded.

In addition to the named and numbered activities, the book is also full of ideas for problem-based instruction that are found within the text and in the illustrations but without an activity name and number. While we know you will find the activities in this table useful, we are confident that each chapter has much more to offer than the numbered activities.

Chapter 2   Developing Early Number Concepts and Number Sense

	Activity	Mathematical Goal	page number
2.1	Ten-Frame Tell-About	Develop benchmarks of 5 and 10	41
2.2	Ten-Frame Flash	Practice benchmarks of 5 and 10 for numbers to 10	41
2.3	Build It in Parts	Develop part-whole concepts for numbers to 12	42
2.4	Who Am I?	Develop relative magnitude of numbers to 100	45
2.5	Who Could They Be?	Develop relative magnitude of numbers to 100	45
2.6	Close, Far, and in Between	Explore relative differences between numbers	45
2.7	Is It Reasonable?	Develop real-world referents for numbers	46
2.8	What Comes Next?	Develop the continuing pattern in the place-value system	48
2.9	Collecting 10,000	Develop an understanding of the size of large numbers	50
2.10	Showing 10,000	Develop an understanding of the size of large numbers	50
2.11	How Long?/How Far?	Develop an understanding of the size of large numbers	50

Chapter 3   Helping Children Master the Basic Facts

Chapter 4   Strategies for Whole-Number Computation

Chapter 5   Developing Fraction Concepts

Chapter 6 Fraction Computation

Chapter 7 Demical and Precent Concepts and Decimal Computation

Chapter 9   Developing Measurement Concepts

Chapter 10   Algebraic Reasoning

ACTIVITIES AT A GLANCE

ABOUT THE AUTHORS

John A. Van de Walle is Professor Emeritus at Virginia Commonwealth University. After 30 years with his university, Dr. Van de Walle continues to work with teachers at the K–8 level as a mathematics education consultant. He has taught mathematics to children at all levels, K–8. He is a coauthor of a mathematics series for K–6 (Scott Foresman) and the author of *Elementary and Middle School Mathematics: Teaching Developmentally,* the market-leading text and resource book on which this series is based.

LouAnn Lovin is a former classroom teacher and is currently an assistant professor in mathematics education at James Madison University, where she teaches mathematics methods and mathematics content courses for Pre-K–8 prospective teachers and has been involved in the mathematical professional development of teachers in grades 4–8. She is actively involved with NCTM and is also President of the Valley of Virginia Council of Teachers of Mathematics (V^2CTM). Her research interests are in the area of teacher knowledge, in particular, exploring the nature of the mathematical knowledge needed for effective teaching.

FOUNDATIONS OF STUDENT-CENTERED INSTRUCTION

What is basic in mathematics is as simple as this: *Math makes sense!* Every child in his or her own way can come to believe this. More important, every child can come to believe that he or she is capable of making sense of mathematics.

Students have to develop this understanding themselves. Their understanding and, thus, their confidence grow as a result of being engaged in doing mathematics. To teach effectively means to engage students at their level so they can create or develop new ideas to use and understand so they can make sense of mathematics.

The fundamental core of effective teaching of mathematics combines an understanding of how children learn, how to promote that learning through problem solving, and how to plan for and assess that learning on a daily basis. Information to help you with these four foundational components—children learning constructively, teaching with problems, planning lessons, and assessing where students are—are discussed in the next four sections of this chapter.

The remaining chapters of the book are designed to help you apply these core ideas to the content that you teach.

HOW CHILDREN LEARN AND UNDERSTAND MATHEMATICS

To put it simply, *children construct their own knowledge.* This is the basic tenet of the theory of learning called *constructivism.* In fact, not just children, but all people, all of the time construct or give meaning to things they perceive or think about. As you read these words, you are giving meaning to them. You are constructing ideas.

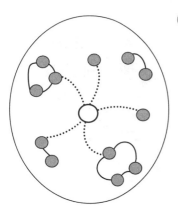

FIGURE 1.1 • • • • • • • • • • •

We use the ideas we already have (gray dots) to construct a new idea (white dot), developing in the process a network of connections between ideas. The more ideas used and the more connections made, the better we understand.

Constructing Ideas

To construct or build something in the physical world requires tools, materials, and effort. Constructing ideas can be viewed similarly. The tools we use to build understanding are our existing ideas, the knowledge that we already possess. The materials may be things we see, hear, or touch—elements of our physical surroundings. Sometimes the materials are our own thoughts and ideas—existing ideas and thoughts used to modify other ideas. The effort that must be supplied is active and reflective thought. If minds are not actively engaged in thought, no effective learning occurs.

To get a notion of what it means to construct an idea, consider the diagram in Figure 1.1. Imagine that it represents a small portion of a student's knowledge concerning a collection of related ideas. The gray dots represent ideas that the student already has developed. The lines joining these dots represent connections between and among the ideas. Every idea or bit of knowledge that a person has is connected in at least some way to some other idea. No idea exists in complete isolation.

Now suppose that this person is trying to understand or learn or give meaning to a new idea, the one represented by the white dot in the diagram. The tools that are available to construct this idea are precisely the related ideas that the person already owns. As the existing ideas give meaning to the new idea, new connections are formed—the dotted lines in the diagram—between the new idea and the existing ones. The more existing ideas that are used to give meaning to the new one, the more connections will be made. The more connections made, the better the new idea is understood.

Understanding

It is possible to say that we know something or we do not. That is, knowledge is something that we either have or don't have. In contrast, *understanding* can be defined as a measure of the quality and quantity of connections that an idea has with existing ideas. Understanding is never an all-or-nothing proposition. It depends on the existence of appropriate ideas and on the creation of new connections (Backhouse, Haggarty, Pirie, & Stratton, 1992; Davis, 1986; Hiebert & Carpenter, 1992; Janvier, 1987; Schoeder & Lester, 1989). For example, most students in grade 4 or 5 know something about fractions. Given the fraction $\frac{6}{8}$, nearly all students at this level will be able to read the fraction correctly and identify the 6 and 8 as the numerator and denominator, respectively. They may or may not be able to explain what the 6 and the 8 tell us about the fraction. Many students will know that this fraction is more than $\frac{1}{2}$. Some will think that it is a "big" fraction because the numbers are both somewhat big compared to the numbers in $\frac{1}{2}$ or $\frac{2}{3}$. That the fraction is equivalent to $\frac{3}{4}$ is also a reasonably common connection for fifth-grade students to make. However, different students may have different understandings of what it means to be equivalent. They may know that $\frac{6}{8}$ can be reduced to $\frac{3}{4}$ but not understand that $\frac{3}{4}$ and $\frac{6}{8}$ are identical numbers. Some may think that reducing $\frac{6}{8}$ makes it a smaller number. Those with a better understanding will be able to explain using a variety of models how $\frac{6}{8}$ and $\frac{3}{4}$ are the same quantities. You could easily expand on the range of ideas that students often connect to their individualized concept of fraction—some things correct, others not so. Each of your students brings a different set of dots to his or her knowledge of fraction. Each "understands" fractions in a different way.

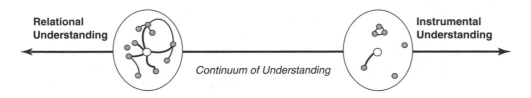

FIGURE 1.2 • • • • • • • • •

Understanding is a measure of the quality and quantity of connections that a new idea has with existing ideas. The greater the number of connections to a network of ideas, the better the understanding.

Another way to think about an individual's understanding is that it exists along a continuum (see Figure 1.2). At one extreme is a very rich set of connections. The understood idea is associated with many other existing ideas in a meaningful network of concepts and procedures. Hiebert and Carpenter (1992) refer to "webs" of interrelated ideas. Clearly, our goal for children is that each new mathematical idea be well understood—that it be imbedded in as rich a web of related mathematical ideas as possible.

At the other end of the continuum, ideas are completely isolated or nearly so. Here we find ideas that have been rotely learned. Due to their isolation, poorly understood ideas are easily forgotten and are unlikely to be useful for constructing new ideas.

For instance, consider the concept of "division" as constructed by a student in the fourth grade. Most likely there is some connection to multiplication and the student may, therefore, know to use multiplication to check a division computation. This connection may be meaningful or conceptual, or it may simply be something recalled because the teacher told students to use multiplication to check their division. In a conceptual connection, $42 \div 6$ supplies the blank in both of these equations: $\square \times 6 = 42$ (how many sixes make 42) and $6 \times \square = 42$ (6 sets of how many make 42). These same ideas can connect division to addition and/or subtraction. That is, $42 \div 6$ tells how many sixes must be added to make 42 or, similarly, how many sixes can be subtracted from 42. These noncontextual ideas can also be connected to real-world situations such as those that are typically found in story problems: If balloons cost 19 cents each, how many can Sam buy for $2.50? Because multiplication can take on other forms, so can division. For example, if the ice cream store can make 42 different ice cream sundaes using 6 toppings, how many different flavors of ice cream are used? This question is again answered with $42 \div 6$. Division can also be connected to fractions. The fraction $\frac{42}{6}$ is simply another way of expressing $42 \div 6$. As an understanding of fractions grows, the connections to division can also grow.

When computation is considered, even more connections are possible. The traditional algorithm of divide-multiply-subtract-bring down can be connected to the ideas of multiplication as well as place value. The algorithm for $367 \div 8$ is based on finding out: 8 sets of what size are close to 367? But other strategies use different ideas. An informal process for dividing 367 by 8 might go this way: 10 eights are 80. Since 4×80 is 320, 40 eights are 320. That means that there are 47 left. Six times 8 is 48—one too many. It must be 5 with 7 left over. In all, that is 40 and 5 or 45 remainder 7. Here the connections with place value and other computational strategies are obvious.

Of course, we cannot "see" a student's understanding. We can only make inferences about what it may be. When students are given problems without directions for solving them, the assumption is that students use the ideas they have, whatever those ideas may be. In the case of traditional computational rules, the danger is that we may see students using the rules correctly but have limited or no understanding of why the rules work. In this case, our inference about student understanding may be incorrect.

Classroom Influences on Learning

The theory of constructivism suggests that we cannot teach students by telling. Rather, we must help them construct their own ideas using the ideas that they already own. This does not mean that we simply let students play around and hope that they will magically discover new mathematical ideas. On the contrary, the manner in which you conduct your class plays an enormous role in what is learned and how well it is understood. Let's examine three factors that influence learning:

- student reflective thinking
- social interaction with other students in the classroom
- use of models or tools for learning (manipulatives, symbolism, computer tools, drawings, and even oral language)

Each factor impacts what and how well students learn. Each one is significantly influenced by you, the classroom teacher.

Reflective Thought

 Stop for a moment and see if you can come up with a good definition of reflective thinking. What does that phrase mean to you?

Whatever your description of reflective thinking, it almost certainly involves some form of mental activity. It is an active, not a passive, endeavor. You may have said that it involves figuring something out or trying to connect ideas in your head. You may have used the words *ponder* or *consider*. What you just did to try to come up with a definition of reflective thinking almost certainly involved reflective thinking.

If we assume that constructivist theory is correct, then we want students to be reflective about the ideas they need to learn. For a new idea you are teaching to be interconnected in a rich web of interrelated ideas, students must be mentally engaged. They must find the relevant ideas they possess and bring them to bear on the development of the new idea. In terms of the dots in Figure 1.1, we want to activate every gray dot a student has that is related to the new white dot we want him or her to learn. The more relevant gray dots used—the more reflective thinking—the better the new ideas will be constructed.

But we can't just hold up a big THINK sign and expect students to ponder the new thought. The challenge is to get them to be mentally engaged. As you will see later in this chapter and throughout this book, the key to getting students to be reflective is to engage them in problems that force them to use their ideas as they search for solutions and create new ideas in the process. Two other related activities are also encouraged: writing about solutions to problems and having discussions with the rest of the class. Each is a method of promoting reflective thinking. Each should be built into most of your lessons.

Students Learning from Others

Reflective thought and, hence, learning are enhanced when the learner is engaged with others working on the same ideas. Students reside in classrooms. An interactive, thoughtful atmosphere in a classroom can provide some of the best opportunities for learning.

A worthwhile goal is to transform your classroom into what might be termed a "mathematical community of learners," or an environment in which students interact with each other and with the teacher. In such an environment students share ideas and results, compare and evaluate strategies, challenge results, determine the validity of answers, and negotiate ideas on which all can agree. The rich interaction in such a classroom significantly raises the chances that productive reflective thinking about relevant mathematical ideas will happen.

The Interaction of Students' Ideas with the Ideas of Others

Piaget helped us to focus on the cognitive activity of the child and to begin to understand how an individual uses ideas in a reflective manner to construct new knowledge and understanding. Vygotsky focused on social interaction as a key component in the development of knowledge. Vygotsky viewed the ideas that exist in the classroom, in books, and those shared by teachers and other authorities as distinct from the ideas constructed by the child. The well-formulated ideas that are external to the child, Vygotsky called *scientific concepts,* whereas those developed by the child (in the manner described by Piaget) he called *spontaneous concepts.*

Vygotsky talked about these two types of concepts as working in opposite directions, as shown in Figure 1.3. The scientific concepts work downward from external authority. As such, they impose their logic on the child. The spontaneous concepts bubble upward as a result of reflective activity. In Vygotsky's *zone of proximal development,* the child is able to meaningfully work with the scientific concepts from outside. Here the child's own conceptual understanding is sufficiently advanced to begin to take in the ideas from "above."

It is not necessary to choose between a social constructivist theory that favors the views of Vygotsky and a cognitive constructivism that is built on the theories of Piaget (Cobb, 1996). In a classroom mathematical community of learners, students' learning is enhanced by the reflective thought that social interaction promotes. At the same time, the value of the interaction for individual students is determined to a large extent by the ideas that each individual brings to the discussions. When, for any given child, the conversation of the classroom is within his or her zone of proximal development, the best social learning will occur.

Classroom discussion based on students' own ideas and solutions to problems is absolutely "foundational to children's learning" (Wood & Turner-Vorbeck, 2001, p. 186).

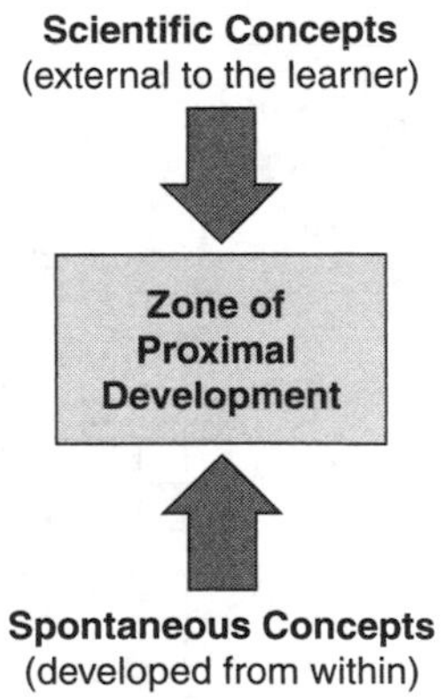

Mathematical Communities of Learners

In the wonderful book *Making Sense* (Hiebert et al., 1997), the authors describe four features of a productive classroom culture for mathematics, in which students can learn from each other as well as from their own reflective activity.

1. Ideas are important, no matter whose ideas they are. Students can have their own ideas and share them with others. Similarly, they need to understand that they can also learn from the ideas that others have formulated. Learning mathematics is about coming to understand the ideas of the mathematical community.
2. Ideas must be shared with others in the class. Correspondingly, each student must respect the ideas of others and try to evaluate and make sense of them. Respect for the ideas shared by others is critical if real discussion is to take place.

Scientific Concepts
(external to the learner)

Zone of Proximal Development

Spontaneous Concepts
(developed from within)

FIGURE 1.3 • • • • • • • • • •

Vygotsky's zone of proximal development is the place where new external ideas are accessible to the learner with those ideas already developed.

CLASSROOM INFLUENCES ON LEARNING

3. Trust must be established with an understanding that it is okay to make mistakes. Students must come to realize that errors are an opportunity for growth as they are uncovered and explained. All students must trust that their ideas will be met with the same level of respect whether they are right or wrong. Without this trust, many ideas will never be shared.

4. Students must come to understand that mathematics makes sense. As a result of this simple truth, the correctness or validity of results resides in the mathematics itself. There is no need for the teacher or other authority to provide judgment of student answers. In fact, when teachers routinely respond with "Yes, that's correct," or "No, that's wrong," students will stop trying to make sense of ideas in the classroom and discussion and learning will be curtailed.

Classrooms with these characteristics do not just happen. The teacher is responsible for creating this climate. It happens over time in two ways. First, there must be some direct discussion of the ground rules for classroom discussions. Second, teachers can model the type of questioning and interaction that they would like to see from their students.

Tools for Learning

It would be difficult for you to have become a teacher and not at least heard that the use of manipulatives, or a "hands-on approach," is the recommended way to teach mathematics. There is no doubt that these materials can and should play a significant role in your classroom. Used correctly they can be a positive factor in students' learning. But they are not the cure-all that some educators seem to believe them to be. It is important that you have a good perspective on how manipulatives can help or fail to help children construct ideas.

Models Are Not the Same as Concepts

Conceptual knowledge of mathematics consists of logical relationships constructed internally and existing in the mind as a part of a network of ideas. It is the type of knowledge Piaget referred to as *logico-mathematical knowledge* (Kamii, 1985, 1989; Labinowicz, 1985). By its very nature, conceptual knowledge is knowledge that is understood (Hiebert & Carpenter, 1992). Ideas such as three-fourths, rectangle, tens—hundreds—thousands, product, and percent are all examples of mathematical relationships or concepts.

Figure 1.4 shows the three blocks commonly used to represent ones, tens, and hundreds. By second grade, most children have seen pictures of these or have used the actual blocks. Nearly all third-grade children are able to identify the rod as the "ten" piece and the large square block as the "hundred" piece. Does this mean that they have constructed the concepts of ten and hundred? All that is known for sure is that they have learned the usual names typically assigned to them. The mathematical concept of a ten is that *a ten is the same as ten ones*. Ten

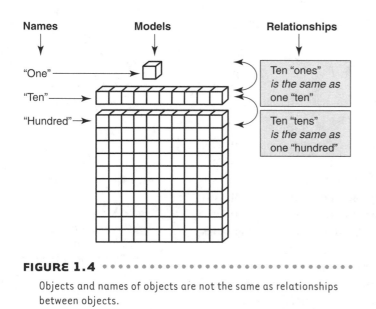

FIGURE 1.4

Objects and names of objects are not the same as relationships between objects.

is not a rod. The concept is the relationship between the rod and the small cube. It is not the rod or a bundle of ten sticks or any other model of a ten. This relationship called "ten" must be created by children in their own minds. The blocks can help students "see" the relationships and talk about them, but what they see are blocks, not concepts.

The same blocks used in the primary grades for whole numbers are often used in the fourth and fifth grades to represent decimals. Now students have to use the idea that any of the blocks can represent the units or ones. A collection of 3 flats, 7 longs, and 4 small cubes represents 374. However, the same collection can also represent 3.74 if the flat pieces are designated as the unit or 37.4 if the longs or sticks are the units. Students who have only attached names to the pieces without constructing the ten-to-one relationships among the different shapes will have great difficulty understanding these decimal representations. In our adult minds, because we already understand decimal relationships, the blocks appear to be excellent models. But the difficulty students have making this shift to decimals indicates that the concepts are not in the blocks but in the relationships imposed on the blocks.

With this understanding we can define a model as follows: A *model* for a mathematical concept refers to any object, picture, or drawing that represents the concept and onto which the relationship for that concept can be imposed. In this sense, any set of objects can be a model of the concepts "tenth" and "hundredth" as long as we can impose the 10-to-1 and 100-to-1 relationships on the objects. For example, there is a set of base-ten materials called *Digie Blocks*™ that look nothing at all like the usual wooden base-ten blocks. With *Digie Blocks,* ten of a small piece fit into a container that is the same shape but ten times as large as the smaller piece—a 10-to-1 relationship. These and any model for whole numbers can also be used for decimal numbers.

It is incorrect to say that a model "illustrates" a concept. To illustrate implies showing. That would mean that when you looked at the model, you would see an example of the concept. Technically, all that you actually see with your eyes is the physical object; only your mind can impose the mathematical relationship on the object (Thompson, 1994). For a person who does not yet have the relationship, the model does not illustrate the concept *for that person.* In contrast, when you see a bicycle, what you see is in fact an example of the physical concept of *bicycle.* But unlike physical concepts, there are no physical examples of mathematical concepts. Mathematical concepts are relationships constructed in a person's mind.

Models and Other Tools for Learning

Hiebert and his colleagues (1997) argue that the concept of model should be expanded to include oral language, written symbols for mathematics, and any other tools that can help students think about mathematics. Certainly, calculators can and should be included in this broad definition of mathematical tools. For example, the automatic constant feature of a calculator can assist students in the development of the idea that the decimal 0.01 is a relatively small quantity. If students press 1 ⊞ 1 ⊟ ⊟ . . . they can quickly make the calculator count to 100. However, if the constant is changed to 0.01—that is, press .01 ⊞ .01 ⊟ ⊟ . . . —then one hundred presses counts only to 1 and it requires ten thousand presses to count to 100.

The calculator's auto-constant feature is also useful for illustrating multiplication as repeated addition. Pressing 67 ⊞ ⊟ ⊟ ⊟ ⊟ adds 67 to itself 4 times. Pressing 4 ⊠ 67 gives the same result.

CLASSROOM INFLUENCES ON LEARNING

Although students do not see concepts by seeing mathematical models or by handling manipulative materials, these various tools can help them learn important mathematical ideas in several important ways:

- Ideas that students are in the process of developing can be tested to see if they "fit" or work correctly when applied to a model that the teacher or other students have suggested represents that idea.

- It is often easier for students to think through a problem or task by use of an appropriate model or tool.

- Tools are especially helpful in communicating ideas that are otherwise difficult for students to talk about or write about.

- Simple drawings of counters, base-ten blocks, number lines, or fraction pieces can help students who are trying to record their ideas.

As students use a tool to represent an idea, their work or reflective activity can help develop meaning for the tool in their own minds. As these meanings for tools are developed, they also become more useful as a tool for further learning. That is, students must both develop meanings *for* tools and meaning can be developed *with* tools.

Procedural Knowledge as a Tool

Procedural knowledge of mathematics is knowledge of the rules and the procedures that one uses in carrying out routine mathematical tasks and also of the symbolism that is used to represent mathematics. Procedural knowledge of mathematics plays a very important role both in learning and in doing mathematics. For example, algorithmic procedures help do routine tasks easily and, thus, free children's minds to concentrate on more important tasks. Symbolism is a powerful mechanism for conveying mathematical ideas to others and for "doodling around" with an idea as students do mathematics. But even the most skillful use of a procedure will not help develop conceptual knowledge that is related to that procedure (Hiebert, 1990). Doing 15 products involving a two-digit multiplier will not help students understand why they put a zero in the ones place before multiplying by the tens digit. Nor will it help them understand why the carried digits should be added after you multiply and not before. In fact, students who are skillful with a particular procedure are very reluctant to attach meanings to it after the fact. It is generally accepted that procedural rules should never be learned in the absence of a concept, although, unfortunately, that happens far too often.

Using Models in the Classroom

Mathematical concepts that students are in the process of constructing are formulated little by little over time. As children actively reflect on their new ideas, they test them out through as many different avenues as we might provide. This is where the value of student discussions and a mathematical environment comes in. Talking through an idea, arguing for a viewpoint, listening to others, and describing and explaining are all mentally active ways of testing an emerging idea against external reality. As this testing process goes on, the developing idea gets modified, elaborated, and further integrated with existing ideas. When there is a good fit with external reality, the likelihood of a correct concept being formed is good.

Models and mathematical tools in the more general sense can play this same role, that of a testing ground for emerging ideas. Tools can be thought of as "thinker toys," "tester toys," and "talker toys." It is difficult for students (of all ages) to talk about and test out abstract relationships using words alone. Models give learners something to think about, explore with, talk about, and reason with.

Introducing Models and Making Them Available

We can't just give students a set of Cuisenaire rods or fraction pie pieces and expect them to develop the mathematical ideas that these materials potentially represent. When a new model or new use of a familiar model is introduced into the classroom, it is generally a good idea to explain how the model is used and perhaps conduct a simple activity that illustrates this use.

For example, suppose that you begin working on fraction concepts with your third- or fourth-grade students. You may begin by using circular pie pieces and have students identify the fraction that each different-sized piece represents. On other days you may use a geoboard and pose tasks in which students have to find fractional parts of various regions. To introduce the idea of fractional parts of a set, you pass out two-color counters. As an introductory activity with this model, you pose problems similar to this: If 12 counters is one whole, how many counters is $\frac{2}{3}$? How many is $1\frac{1}{4}$? On another day you introduce the use of Cuisenaire rods to model fractions. Designating different colors of rods as the whole, students have to find rods that represent various fractional parts and explain their reasoning. By doing a few introductory activities with these various models, you can feel reasonably comfortable that students understand how each can be used as a model for fractions. Later, when you begin to add fractions with unlike denominators, you can pose tasks such as $\frac{3}{4} + \frac{2}{3}$ and suggest that students may want to use a model of their choice to figure out the answer. Students should feel free to use any model or perhaps no model at all. All that is required is that they are able to give an explanation for their results.

With many tasks, the choice of using a model or not should be left to the students. In the area of fractions, many good tasks are tied to models whereas others work best when no model is used at all. For example, the following task cannot be done without Cuisenaire rods. *If the dark green rod is $\frac{2}{3}$ of the whole, what rod represents the whole?* In contrast, comparison tasks generally work best if no models are permitted. In the task *Which is greater, $\frac{3}{4}$ or $\frac{2}{3}$?*, the use of a model can allow students to get an answer without any real reasoning being involved.

Although the free choice of models should generally be the norm in the classroom, you can often ask students to use a model to show their thinking. This will help you find out about a student's understanding of the idea and also his or her understanding of the models that have been used in the classroom.

The following are simple rules of thumb for using models:

- Introduce new models by showing how they can represent the ideas for which they are intended.

- Allow students (in most instances) to select freely from available models to use in solving problems.

- Encourage the use of a model when you believe it would be helpful to a student having difficulty.

Assessment Note

Lesh, Post, and Behr (1987) talk about five representations for concepts, two of which are manipulative models and pictures. (See Figure 1.5.) Their research has found that students who have difficulty translating a concept from one representation to another are the same students who have difficulty solving problems and understanding computations. As students move between and among these representations of concepts, there is a better chance of a concept being formed correctly and integrated into a rich web of ideas.

Translation activities can be used for lessons or for diagnosis. For example, students may be given a ten-by-ten grid with 75 squares shaded. Their task may be to write the percent of the square that is shaded (symbols), to locate the same percentage on a number line (a different model), and describe a real situation in which that percentage is used and makes sense (real world). They could also be asked to write the percentage as both a fraction and a decimal (translations within symbols).

Think about the translation tasks when you want to do a short interview with a student to find out more about his or her thinking. How a student represents ideas in various forms and explains why these representations are similar or different can often provide you with valuable information about what misconceptions he or she may have and what type of activity to use to help.

Incorrect Use of Models

The most widespread error that teachers make with manipulative materials is to structure lessons in such a manner that students are being directed in exactly how to use a model, usually as a means of getting answers. There is a natural temptation to get out the materials and show students exactly how to use them. Students will blindly follow the teacher's directions, and it may even look as if they understand. A rote procedure with a model is still just that—a rote procedure (Ball, 1992; Clements & Battista, 1990).

A natural result of overly directing the use of models is that students begin to use them as answer-getting devices rather than as thinker toys. When getting answers rather than solving problems becomes the focus of a lesson, students will gravitate to the easiest method available to get the answers. At the third- to fifth-grade level, fractions are a common concept for which models are used inappropriately. In the comparison task mentioned earlier (*Which is greater, $\frac{2}{3}$ or $\frac{3}{4}$?*), a student using pie pieces or fraction bars can simply create each fraction and compare the models for size. This does not help to develop fraction sense because the student does not have to reason about the size of fractions, only compare the models.

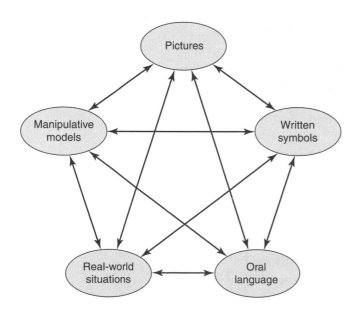

FIGURE 1.5 •

Five different representations of mathematical ideas. Translations between and within each can help develop new concepts.

TEACHING WITH PROBLEMS

Understanding should be a goal for all of the mathematics we teach. This message of NCTM's *Principles and Standards for School Mathematics* (2000) is a goal with which it is difficult to argue. For many years and continuing today, didactic, top-down, do-as-I-show-you instruction has been the norm in the United States. The results have not been positive except for our brightest students and those who memorize rules well. There must be a better method of teaching.

The single most important principle for improving the teaching of mathematics is to *allow the subject of mathematics to be problematic for students* (Hiebert et al., 1996). That is, students solve problems not to apply mathematics but also to learn new mathematics. When students engage in well-chosen problem-based tasks and focus on the solution methods, what results is new understanding of the mathematics embedded in the task. When students are actively looking for relationships, analyzing patterns, finding out which methods work and which don't, justifying results, or evaluating and challenging the thoughts of others, they are necessarily and optimally engaging in reflective thought about the ideas involved. The appropriate dots in their cognitive structure are acting to give meaning to new ideas. *Most, if not all, important mathematics concepts and procedures can best be taught through problem solving.*

Problem-Based Tasks

A *problem* is defined here as any task or activity for which the students have no prescribed or memorized rules or methods, nor is there a perception by students that there is a specific correct solution method (Hiebert et al., 1997).

A problem for learning mathematics also has these features:

- *The problem must begin where the students are.* The design or selection of the task should take into consideration the current understanding of the students. They should have the appropriate ideas to engage and solve the problem and yet still find it challenging and interesting. In other words, it should be within their zone of proximal development.

- *The problematic or engaging aspect of the problem must be due to the mathematics that the students are to learn.* In solving the problem or doing the activity, students should be concerned primarily with making sense of the mathematics involved and thereby developing their understanding of those ideas. Although it is acceptable and even desirable to have contexts or external conditions for problems that make them interesting, these aspects should not overshadow the mathematics to be learned.

- *The problem must require justifications and explanations for answers and methods.* Students should understand that the responsibility for determining if answers are correct and why rests with them. Students should also expect to explain their solution methods as a natural part of solving problems.

It is important to understand that mathematics is to be taught *through* problem solving. That is, problem-based tasks or activities are the vehicle through which your curriculum can be developed. Student learning is an outcome of the problem-solving process.

Teaching with problem-based tasks is student centered rather than teacher centered. It begins with and builds on the ideas that children have available—their dots, their understandings. It is a process that requires faith in children, a belief that all children can create meaningful ideas about mathematics.

Learning Through Problem Solving: A Student-Centered Approach

Let's look into a hypothetical fourth-grade class in the first part of the year. The teacher has already reviewed addition and subtraction computation and has been working on multiplication concepts and facts. The students have mastered many of their multiplication facts and a few know them all. As part of their exploration of multiplication concepts and facts, the teacher has used the idea of area of a rectangle to show how repeated addition can be related to an array of squares in a rectangle.

These experiences and those that have occurred in the third grade have provided most students with a collection of ideas about tens and ones (from their work with addition and subtraction), an understanding of the meaning of multiplication as related to addition, a variety of number strategies for mastering multiplication facts, and they are beginning to connect multiplication to arrays and area concepts. These are their gray dots—their ideas related to multiplication and place value that they can bring to a development of multiplication computation. Each child's unique collection of ideas is connected in different ways. Some ideas are well understood, others less so; some are well formed, others still emerging. Some students are more reliant on the use of models, others less so.

The lesson begins with a task that is designed to set the stage for the main portion of the lesson. On the overhead, the teacher shows a 6 × 8 rectangle of squares. The bottom row of 8 squares is shaded. The students quickly agree that adding up 6 eights will tell how many squares are in the rectangle. The teacher asks, "But if we didn't remember that 6 sets of 8 is 48, could we slice the rectangle into two smaller pieces where we know the multiplication fact and use that to get the total in our heads?" Students are given a few minutes to think of at least one way to slice the rectangle, share the idea with a partner, and prepare to share with the class. Four ideas are offered:

- *Slice one row off the bottom. The top part is 5 by 8 or 40; 40 and the 8 on the bottom is 48.*
- *We cut it in half top to bottom. Each side is 6 × 4; 24 and 24 is 48.* (The teacher asks how the two 24s were added. These students used double 25 and took 2 off. Another student offers that you could add 20 and 20, and 4 and 4.)
- *You can also slice it in half the other way and get 3 × 8 = 24, doubled.*
- *If you take two columns of 6, that's 12. Then double that will give you four columns, or 24. And then double 24 is 48.*

The teacher passes out some centimeter grid paper. On the board she sketches a large rectangle and labels the dimensions 24 and 8. "I want you to sketch a rectangle on the grid paper that is 24 by 8. Your task is to figure out how many squares are in the rectangle. But since we are very lazy, I don't want you to count the squares. Instead, slice the rectangle into two or more parts—sort of like we did with the 6 by 8 example—and use the smaller parts to figure out the whole thing. See if you can find ways that make it really easy to calculate." As is the norm in the class, the students are told that they are to prepare words and numbers as well as the drawing to explain their reasoning.

The students work in pairs for about 15 minutes. The teacher listens to different students talk about the task and offers a hint to a few who are stuck for an idea. Soon the teacher begins a discussion by having students share their ideas and answers. As the students report, the teacher records their ideas on the board. Sometimes the teacher asks questions to help clarify ideas for others. She makes no evaluative comments, even when a student is in error. Although this is a hypothetical class, the following solutions are not unusual for classes such as this.

> **STOP** Before reading further, see how many different ways you can think of to solve this problem (24 × 8) without using the traditional algorithm. Draw a sketch for each way you can think of.

Group 1: *We know that 8 times 8 is 64, so we made three squares that took up the 24. We added 64 + 64 + 64.* (There is a brief discussion of adding the 64s mentally.)

Group 2: *We used tens. We sliced two sections of 10 and then there were 4 left at the end. Ten times 8 is 80. That makes 160 in the two big sections and then the last section is 8 × 4. We added 160 and 32 in our heads.*

Group 3: *Our method was sort of like that but we just used 20 times 8. Since 2 times 8 is 16, you can add a zero and get 160. Then you add the 32 at the end.*

Group 4: *We didn't really slice the rectangle. Instead, we added a row at the end and made it 25 by 8. Then we knew that 4 rows of 25 is like a dollar, or 100. That makes 200 squares in all. But then we had to take off the 8 in the row that we added.*

Figure 1.6 shows three of these methods. You may have thought of other ways as well.

The objective is to begin development of computational strategies for multiplication with two-digit numbers. The teacher wants students to use their own strategies and to be flexible in their methods depending on the numbers. These are the white dots the class will be working on in the next few class periods. By allowing students to solve the problem in their own way, each student is essentially required to use his or her own particular set of dots to give meaning to the solution strategy.

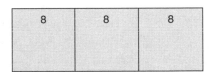

8 × 8 = 64. Add 64 + 64 + 64.

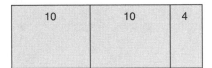

10 × 8 is 80. 80 + 80 + 32 = 192.

25 × 4 is 100. Double is 200. Take off 8.

FIGURE 1.6 • • • • • • • • • • • • • • •

Slicing a rectangle into parts can make it easy to figure the area.

What ideas did you learn from those shared in this example? Try using some of these new ideas to find the product of 38 × 6. These numbers may make you think of a method that was not used in the task just discussed.

During the discussion periods of classes such as this one, ideas continue to grow. Students may hear and understand a clever idea that they could have used but that did not occur to them. Other students actually begin to create new ideas to use as they hear (usually after numerous lessons) the strategies used by their classmates. Perhaps earlier they had simply not been able to use or understand these ideas. Some in the class may hear excellent ideas from their peers that do not make sense to them. These students are simply not ready or do not have the prerequisite concepts to construct these new ideas. For example, in this lesson one or more students may have counted all the squares or perhaps counted them in sets of ten. On subsequent days there will be similar opportunities for all students to grow at their own pace based on their own understandings.

In classrooms such as the one just described, teachers begin *where the children are*—with *their* ideas. They do this by allowing children to solve problems or approach tasks in ways that make sense to them. The children have no other place to turn except to their own ideas.

Show and Tell: A Teacher-Directed Approach

In contrast to the student-centered class just described, let's consider how a lesson with the same basic objective might look using a teacher-directed approach.

In this lesson students use centimeter grid paper as well. They begin by drawing the 24 by 8 rectangle on the paper. On the board the teacher also draws a rectangle and writes the multiplication problem beside it.

The students are directed to count over 20 squares and draw a vertical line in the rectangle as the teacher demonstrates on the board. Then a series of questions is asked as students are directed through the steps of the traditional algorithm. All record the steps on their own paper at the same time.

- *What is 8 × 4?* (Points to small section of the rectangle.)

- *We want to record the 32 in our problem.* (The teacher demonstrates how to write 2 beneath the line in the problem and "carry" the 3. She also writes "32" in the small portion of the rectangle.)

- *What is 8 × 2?* (Attention is directed to the 8 by 20 portion of the rectangle.) *So here we are really multiplying by 20 or by 2 tens. Eight times 2 tens is 16 tens.* (The teacher writes "16 tens" in the large portion of the rectangle.)

- *We already have 3 more tens. How much is 16 and 3?*

- *We record the 19 tens below the line. The final answer is 192.*

When this step has been completed, students are given five similar multiplication problems. For each they are to sketch a small rectangle on their paper and show how it is divided between the tens and the ones. Then they record the two products in the rectangle and complete the computation to the side. The teacher circulates and helps students having difficulty by guiding the students through each of the steps and the recording procedure.

STOP **Think about what you like and do not like about this lesson. How is it different from the earlier example? What ideas will the students be focusing on?**

In this lesson the teacher and students use an area model on centimeter grid paper in a conceptual manner. The rectangle is divided into parts that correspond to the two digits in 24 and each partial product is recorded accordingly.

The follow-up exercises continue the connection to the rectangle. After several lessons similar to this one, most of the class will learn how to multiply a two-digit number. This is a typical example of what often is viewed as an excellent lesson.

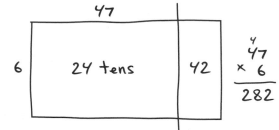

But let's examine this lesson more closely. The teacher tells students how to divide the rectangle. Only one way is suggested and with little rationale provided. The teacher receives no information about the ideas that individual students may have. She can only find out who has and who has not been able to follow the directions. The assumption is that those students who solve the problems correctly also understand. However, many students (including some of those who do the problems correctly) will not understand and will be reinforced in their belief that mathematics is a collection of rules to be learned. Everyone in the class must do the problem the way that makes sense to the teacher rather than the way that makes sense to him or her. Students are not given the opportunity to find out that their own personal ideas count or that there are numerous good ways to solve the problem. This disenfranchises the student who needs to continue working on the development of multiplication concepts and the student who could easily find one or more ways to do the problem mentally if only asked to do so. Rather, students are likely to use the same tedious method to multiply 4 × 51, which should certainly be done mentally at this level. The errors that students typically make with the multiplication algorithm are well known. For example, students often add the carried digit before multiplying. Others do not carry at all. For the problem 6 × 47 these students will write 2,442 as the answer.

The Value of Teaching with Problems

There is no doubt that teaching with problems is difficult. Tasks must be designed or selected each day, taking into consideration the current understanding of your students and the needs of your curriculum. It is hard to plan more than a few days in advance. If you are using a traditional textbook, modifications will need to be made. However, there are excellent reasons for making the effort.

- *Problem solving focuses students' attention on ideas and sense making.* When solving problems, students must necessarily reflect on the mathematics inherent in the problems. Emerging ideas are more likely to be integrated with existing ones, thereby improving understanding. In contrast, no matter how skillfully you explain ideas and offer directions, students will attend to the directions but rarely to the ideas.

- *Problem solving develops the belief in students that they are capable of doing mathematics and that mathematics makes sense.* Every time you pose a problem-based task and expect a solution, you say to students, "I believe you can do this." Every time the class solves a problem and students develop their understanding, confidence and self-esteem are enhanced.

- *Problem solving provides ongoing assessment data.* As students discuss ideas, draw pictures or use manipulatives, defend their solutions and evaluate those of others, and write reports or explanations, they provide a steady stream of valuable information. That information can be used for planning the next lesson, helping individual students, evaluating their progress, and communicating with parents.

- *Problem solving is an excellent method for attending to a breadth of abilities.* Good problem-based tasks have multiple paths to the solution, ranging from simple or inefficient to clever or insightful. Each student gets to make sense of the task using his or her own ideas. Furthermore, students expand on these ideas and grow in their understanding as they hear and reflect on the solution strategies of others. A teacher-directed approach ignores diversity to the detriment of most students.

- *Problem solving engages students so that there are fewer discipline problems.* For most students, the process of solving problems in ways that make sense to them is intrinsically rewarding. There is less reason to act out or to cause trouble. Real learning is engaging, whereas following directions is often boring.

- *Problem solving develops "mathematical power."* Students solving problems will be engaged in all five of the process standards described in the NCTM *Principles and Standards* document: problem solving, reasoning, communication, connections, and representation. These are the processes of doing mathematics.

- *It is a lot of fun!* After experiencing teaching in this manner, very few teachers return to a teach-by-telling mode. The excitement of students developing understanding through their own reasoning is worth all the effort. And, of course, it is fun for the students.

A Three-Part Format for Problem-Based Lessons

It is useful to think of problem-based lessons as consisting of three main parts: *before, during,* and *after.* (See Figure 1.7.)

If you allot time for each before, during, and after segment, it is quite easy to devote a full period to one seemingly simple problem. The same three-part structure can be applied to small tasks, resulting in a 10- to 20-minute mini-lesson. A mental mathematics activity is a good example of such a mini-lesson.

The Before Phase

You have three tasks to accomplish here: get students mentally prepared for the task, be sure the task is understood, and be certain that you have clearly established your expectations beyond simply getting an answer.

Get Students Mentally Prepared

You want to be sure that whatever ideas students have about the mathematics in the task for the day are "up and running" in their heads. There are several possible strategies you might consider.

- Begin with a simple version of the task you intend to pose. Slicing the 6 × 8 rectangle in preparation for the 24 × 8 rectangle is a good example. If you want students to explore area and perimeter relationships on dot grids, you might have them make a rectangle with a specific perimeter, such as 12. As students share examples, the class will realize that there can be more than one rectangle with a given perimeter and will be better prepared for the coming task.

- You might begin a lesson by posing the task right away and then brainstorming solution strategies. For example, if the task involves gathering data, you might ask students to think about the graphing techniques that they have learned recently and briefly discuss what each can tell us about the data. What would a circle graph tell us? What would a bar graph tell us? Brainstorming works best when the task has multiple solution paths that students may not necessarily think of without some prompting.

- For tasks involving a single computation such as 13.4 + 2.76, you can have students think about the size of the answer. Is it more than 20? Why or why not? You may even have students tell what they think the answer is because many will be able to compute mentally. This does not spoil the task for others or "give away the answer." Remember, students must explain the reasoning they use to get the answer. It is helpful for students to hear ideas before they are left completely on their own.

Be Sure the Task Is Understood

You must always be sure that students understand the problem or task before setting them to work. Remember that their perspective is different from yours.

Discuss briefly what information is provided in the problem and help students clarify what the problem is asking. Go over vocabulary that may be troublesome. Having students restate the problem in their own words forces them to think about the problem in a more complete manner.

Establish Expectations

Every task should require more of students than simply the answer. Minimally, students should be prepared to explain their thinking to the class. Whenever possible, some form of writing that shows how students have solved the problem should be included as part of the task. Whatever the expectations, written work, or preparation for discussion, they must be made clear at the outset.

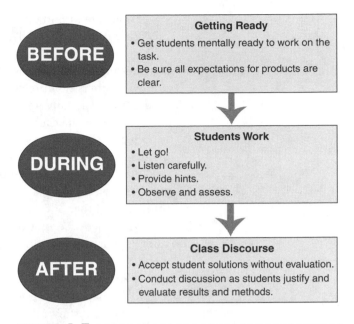

BEFORE

Getting Ready
- Get students mentally ready to work on the task.
- Be sure all expectations for products are clear.

DURING

Students Work
- Let go!
- Listen carefully.
- Provide hints.
- Observe and assess.

AFTER

Class Discourse
- Accept student solutions without evaluation.
- Conduct discussion as students justify and evaluate results and methods.

FIGURE 1.7 •

Teaching through problem solving suggests a simple three-part structure for lessons.

A THREE-PART FORMAT FOR PROBLEM-BASED LESSONS

There are important reasons for requiring more than just answers. Students preparing to explain and defend their answers will spend time reflecting on the validity of their results and will often make revisions even before sharing them. They will have a greater interest in the class discussion because they will want to compare their solution with others' solutions. When an explanation is included as part of what is required by the task, especially if it is in the form of writing and drawings, students will have "rehearsed" for the class discussion and be ready to participate. Students should be expected to show the ideas and the work that they have considered even when they are unable to fully solve a problem.

Requesting students to use words, pictures, and numbers to explain their thinking also has the effect of placing an emphasis on process. Students need to know that their thinking and that of their classmates are at least as important as answers.

As students become more accustomed to writing, consider replacing "Show how you got your answer" with "Explain why you think your answer is correct." With the former direction, students may simply record their steps ("First we did . . . , and then we . . ."). The focus needs to shift to justification and reasoning rather than simply a record of what was done, especially if students are apt to use a traditional algorithm.

Figure 1.8 shows the work of three fourth-grade students. They had not been taught the traditional method of multiplication. The teacher encouraged all sorts of

There were 35 dogsleds. Each sled was pulled by 12 dogs. How many dogs were there in all?

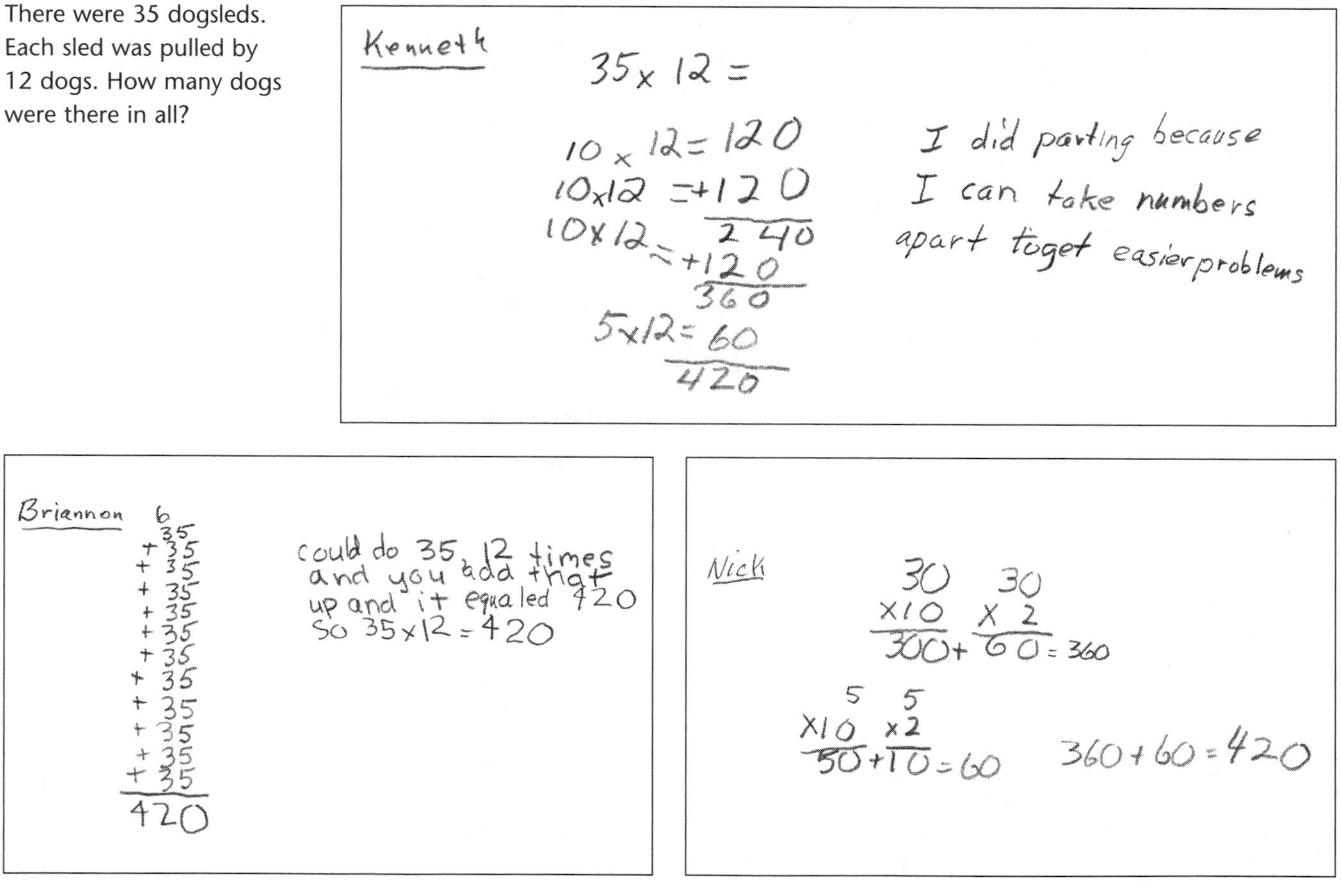

FIGURE 1.8

Three fourth-grade students solve a multiplication problem using their own invented strategies. Their explanations are minimal but what they did is clear.

strategies. These students make it very clear what they did even though there are minimal words. Kenneth's "parting" refers to *partitioning,* a strategy label that was provided earlier by the teacher. Many students in the room used labels for their methods but not always correctly. Notice how close Nick's strategy is conceptually to the traditional method involving four partial products. In the same class, many students used adding strategies such as Briannon's addition method. Here we know *what* the students did but they need more help in explaining why they did it.

In Figure 1.9, third-grader Crystal provides a clear explanation of what she did in a way that matches the problem. Crystal's work is a good model for the class because she is connecting what she did with the drawing and her work.

For some tasks you may decide to forgo written work. If so, strongly consider using a "think-pair-share" approach, requiring students to reflect on results before sharing. This causes students to defend their ideas to a peer and prepares them to talk to the class.

Each day Jim writes down what page of his book he is on. Yesterday he was on page 12. Today, after reading some more, he finished on page 26. How many pages did Jim read today?

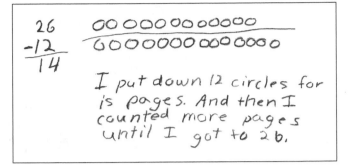

FIGURE 1.9 ●

The work of this third-grade student indicates clearly her connection between what she did (drawing and computation) and the context of the story problem.

The During Phase

The most important thing for you to do here is to *let go!* Give students a chance to work without your guidance. Give them the opportunity to use *their* ideas and not simply follow directions. Your second task is to *listen.* Find out how different students or groups are thinking, what ideas they are using, and how they are approaching the problem.

You must demonstrate confidence and respect for your students' abilities. Set them to work with the expectation that they will solve the problem. Students must deeply believe that the teacher does not have a predetermined or preferred method for solving the problem. If they suspect otherwise, there is no reason for them to take risks with their own ideas and methods.

Provide Hints but Not Solutions

How much help to give students is always an issue. Should you let them stumble down the wrong path? Do you correct errors you see? Always keep in mind that as soon as students sense that you have a method of solving the problem, they will almost certainly stop searching for their own methods because they are convinced that your way must be best.

Before being tempted to help or provide a suggestion, first find out what ideas the student or group has. Try to construct any hints on ideas that you hear them considering. "If you think an equivalent fraction might help, then go ahead and try it and see how that turns out." Notice that a phrase such as this does not suggest that the student's idea is right or wrong, only that he or she needs to continue with it rather than wait for sanction from you.

You might suggest that students try using a particular manipulative or drawing a picture, if that seems appropriate. For example, if students cannot decide how to solve a decimal subtraction problem, suggest that they use base-ten models to show each number.

Encourage Testing of Ideas

Students will look to you for approval of their results or ideas. Consistently avoid being the source of "truth" or of right and wrong. When asked if a result or method is correct, ask, "How can you decide?" or "Why do you think that might be right?" or "I see what you have done. How can you check that somehow?" Even if not asked for an opinion, asking, "How can we tell if that makes sense?" reminds students that answers without reasons are not acceptable.

Listen Actively

This is one of two opportunities you will get in the lesson (the other is in the discussion period) to find out what your students know, how they think, and how they are approaching the task you have given them. You might sit down with a group and simply listen for a while, have the students explain what they are doing, or take notes. If you want further information, try saying, "Tell me what you are doing," or "I see you have drawn a number line. Can you show me how you are using it?" You want to convey a genuine interest in what students are doing and thinking. This is *not* the time to evaluate or to tell students how to solve the problem.

The After Phase

Plan ample time for this portion of the lesson and then be certain to *save* the time. It is not necessary to wait for every student to finish. Often this is when the best learning will take place. Twenty minutes or more is not at all unreasonable for a good class discussion and sharing of ideas. This is not a time to check answers but for the class to share ideas. Over time, you will develop your class into a community of learners who together are involved in making sense of mathematics. This atmosphere will not develop easily or quickly. You must teach your students about your expectations for this time and how to interact with their peers politely, attentively, and critically.

Engage the Full Class in Discussion

You may want simply to list answers from all of the groups and put them on the board without comment. Following that, you can return to one or more students to get explanations for their solutions or to explain their processes.

When there are different answers, the full class should be involved in the discourse concerning which answers are correct. Allow those responsible for the answers to defend them and then open the discussion to the class. "Who has an idea about this? George, I noticed that you got a different answer than Tomeka. What do you think of her explanation?"

One of your functions is to make sure that all students participate, that all listen, and that all understand what is being said. Encourage students to ask questions. "Pete, did you understand how they did that? Do you want to ask Mary a question?"

A second suggestion is to begin discussions by calling first on the students who tend to be shy or lack the ability to express themselves well. Rowan and Bourne (1994) note that the more obvious ideas are generally given at the outset of a discussion. When asked to participate early and given sufficient time to formulate their thoughts, these reticent students can more easily participate and, thus, be valued.

Make it a habit to ask for explanations to accompany *all* answers. Soon the request for an explanation will not signal an incorrect response, as students initially believe. Many incorrect answers are the result of small errors in otherwise excellent thinking. Likewise, many correct answers may not represent the insightful thinking you might have assumed. A student who has given an incorrect answer is very likely to see the error and correct it during the explanation. Try to support students' thinking without evaluating responses. "Does someone have a different idea or want to comment on what Daniel just said?" All children should hear the same teacher reactions that only the so-called "smart kids" used to hear.

Use Praise Cautiously

Be an attentive listener to all ideas, both good and not so good. Praise offered for a correct solution or excitement over an interesting idea suggests that the student did something unusual or unexpected. This can be negative feedback for those who do not get praise.

In place of praise that is judgmental, Schwartz (1996) suggests comments of interest and extension: "I wonder what would happen if you tried . . ." or "Please tell me how you figured that out." Notice that these phrases express interest and value the student's thinking. They also can and should be used regardless of the validity of the responses.

Teachers' Questions About Problem-Based Teaching

A problem-based approach to teaching is a new idea to many teachers. Even for those who have been working at it for some time, there are stumbling blocks and doubts that arise. Here are a few questions that are often raised by teachers and our answers to them.

> **STOP** After reading each of the following questions, pause first to consider your personal response. Then compare your thoughts with the ideas suggested.

What Can I Tell Them? Should I Tell Them Anything?

When teaching through problem solving, one of the most perplexing dilemmas is how much to tell or not to tell. To tell too little can sometimes leave students floundering and waste precious class time. A good rule of thumb is that you should feel free to share relevant information as long as the mathematics in the task remains problematic for the students (Hiebert et al., 1997). That is, "information can and should be shared as long as it does not solve the problem [and] does not take away the need for students to reflect on the situation and develop solution methods they understand" (p. 36).

According to Hiebert et al., three specific types of information can and should be shared:

1. *Mathematical conventions.* Students must be told about the social conventions of symbolism and terminology that are important in mathematics. For example, placing a decimal point to the right of the units followed by digits representing tenths, hundredths, and so on is a convention. That the top number is called the numerator and indicates the number of fractional parts being considered are conventions. All definitions and labels are conventions.

2. *Clarification of students' methods.* You should help students clarify or interpret their ideas and perhaps point out related ideas. Discussion or clarification of students' processes focuses attention on ideas you want the class to learn. Care must be taken that attention to one student's ideas does not diminish those of other students or suggest that one method is the preferred approach.
3. *Alternative methods.* You can, with considerable care, suggest to students an alternative method or approach for consideration. You must be very cautious in not conveying to students that their ideas are second best. Nor should students ever be forced to adopt your suggestion over their own approach. In contrast, try this: "The other day I saw some students in another class solve a problem this way. (Show the method.) What do you think of that idea?"

How Will I Be Able to Teach All of the Basic Skills?

There is a tendency to believe that mastery of the basics is incompatible with a problem-based approach or that drill is essential for basic skills. However, the evidence strongly suggests otherwise. First, drill-oriented approaches in U.S. classrooms have consistently produced poor results (Battista, 1999; Kamii & Dominick, 1998; O'Brien, 1999). Short-term gains on low-level skills may possibly result from drill, but even state testing programs require more.

Second, research data indicate that students in constructivist programs based on a problem-solving approach do as well or nearly as well as students in traditional programs on basic skills as measured by standardized tests (Campbell, 1995; Carpenter, Franke, Jacobs, Fennema, & Empson, 1998; Hiebert & Wearne, 1996; Silver & Stein, 1996). Any deficit in skill development is more than outweighed by strength in concepts and problem solving.

Finally, traditional skills such as basic fact mastery and computation can be effectively taught in a problem-solving approach (for example, see Campbell, Rowan, & Suarez, 1998; Huinker, 1998).

Why Is It Okay for a Student to "Tell" or "Explain" but Not for Me?

There are three answers to this question. First, students will question their peers when an explanation does not make sense to them, whereas explanations from the teacher are nearly always accepted without scrutiny—even when they are not understood. Second, when students are responsible for explaining, class members develop a sense of pride and confidence that *they* can figure things out and make sense of mathematics. Third, having to explain forces the student who is doing the explaining to clarify his or her thoughts.

This Approach Takes More Time. How Will I Have Time to Cover Everything?

The first suggestion is to teach with a goal of developing the "big ideas," the main concepts in a unit or chapter. Most of the skills and ideas on your list of objectives will be addressed as you progress. If you focus separately on each item on the list, big ideas and connections—the essence of understanding—are unlikely to develop. Second, with a traditional approach far too much time is spent reteaching because students don't retain ideas. Time spent up front to help students develop meaningful networks of ideas drastically reduces the need for reteaching, thus creating time in the long term. You must have faith that time invested in concept development will create time later.

Do I Need to Use a Problem-Based Approach Every Day?

Yes! Any attempt to mix problem-based methods with traditional teaching by telling will cause difficulties. Consider the response of Mokros, Russell, and Economopoulos (1995):

> In classrooms where both approaches are used to teach a skill, children become confused about when they are supposed to use their own strategies for figuring out a problem and when they are supposed to use the officially sanctioned approach. Children get the sense that:
>
> * Their own approach to problem-solving is merely "exploration," and they will later learn the "right way."
> * Their own approach isn't as good as the one the teacher shows.
> * The teacher didn't really mean it when he or she said there were lots of good strategies for solving problems like 34 × 68. (p. 79)

Is There Any Place for Drill and Practice?

Yes! However, the tragic error is to believe that drill is a method of developing ideas. Drill is only appropriate when (a) the desired concepts have been meaningfully developed, (b) students already have developed (not mastered) flexible and useful procedures, *and* (c) speed and accuracy are needed. Watch students drilling basic facts who are counting on their fingers or using some other inefficient method. What they may be improving is their ability to count quickly. They are not learning their facts.

If you consider carefully these three criteria for drill, you will likely do much less of it than in the past.

My Textbook Is a Traditional Basal. How Can I Use It?

Traditional textbooks are designed to be teacher directed, a contrast to the approach you have been reading about. But they should not be discarded. Much thought went into the content and the pedagogical ideas. Your book can still be used as a prime resource if you think about translating units and lessons to a problem-oriented approach.

Adopt a *unit perspective*. Avoid the idea that every lesson and idea in the unit require attention. Examine a chapter or unit from beginning to end and identify the two or three *big ideas*, the essential mathematics in the chapter. (Big ideas are listed at the start of each of the remaining chapters in this book. These may be helpful as a reference.) Temporarily ignore the smaller subideas that often take up a full lesson.

With the big ideas of the unit in mind, you can now do two things: (1) Adapt the best or most important lessons in the chapter to a problem-solving format and (2) create or find tasks in the text's teacher notes and other resources that address the big ideas. The combination will almost certainly provide you with an ample supply of tasks.

What Do I Do When a Task Bombs or Students Don't "Get It"?

There may be times when your class simply does not solve the problem during the class period, but not as often as you might suspect. When it does happen, do not give in to the temptation to "show 'em." Set the task aside for the moment. Ask yourself why it bombed. Did the students have the ideas they needed? How did students attempt the task? Occasionally we need to regroup and offer students a simpler related problem that gets them prepared for the one that proved difficult. When you sense that a task is not going anywhere, listen to your students and you will know where to go next. Don't spend days just hoping that something wonderful might happen.

PLANNING IN A PROBLEM-BASED CLASSROOM

Teaching with a problem-based approach requires more time for planning lessons than simply following the pages in a traditional text. Every group of students is different and each day is best built on the actual growth of the previous day. Choices of tasks must be made daily to best fit the needs of your students.

Planning Problem-Based Lessons

The outline in Figure 1.10 illustrates suggested steps for planning a lesson. The first four steps involve the most thought and are the most crucial. The next four steps follow from these initial decisions and will assure that your lesson runs smoothly. Finally, you can write a concise lesson plan that will be easy to follow.

Step 1: **Begin with the Math!** Articulate clearly the ideas you want students to learn as a result of the lesson. Think in terms of mathematical concepts, not skills. Describe the mathematics, not the student behavior.

But what if a skill is the intended outcome? Often state or local objectives are written in procedural terms (for example, "The student will be able to. . . ."). Perhaps you want students to master their multiplication facts. Rather than drill facts, work on partitioning numbers and use story problems that lead to strategies. Instead of a page of computation following your rules, have students develop their own method of multiplying two-digit numbers. For every skill there are underlying concepts and relationships. Identify these concepts at this step of your planning. The best tasks will get at skills through concepts.

Step 2: **Think About Your Students.** What do your students know or understand about this topic? Are they ready to tackle this bit of mathematics or are there some background ideas that they have not yet developed?

Be sure that the mathematics you identified in step 1 includes something new or at least slightly unfamiliar to your students. At the same time, be certain that your objectives are not out of reach. For real learning to take place, there must be some challenge, some new ideas—even if it is simply see-

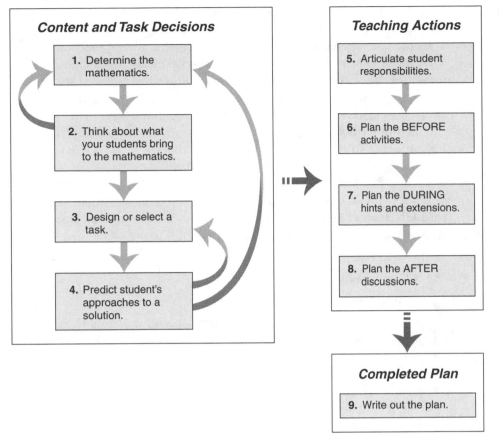

FIGURE 1.10 • • • • • • • • •

Planning steps for thinking
through a problem-based lesson.

Content and Task Decisions

1. Determine the mathematics.

2. Think about what your students bring to the mathematics.

3. Design or select a task.

4. Predict student's approaches to a solution.

Teaching Actions

5. Articulate student responsibilities.

6. Plan the BEFORE activities.

7. Plan the DURING hints and extensions.

8. Plan the AFTER discussions.

Completed Plan

9. Write out the plan.

ing an old idea in a new format or with a different model. If necessary, now is the time to revisit step 1 and make adjustments in your goals.

Step 3: **_Decide on a Task._** Keep it simple! Good tasks need not be elaborate. Often a simple story problem is all that is necessary as long as the solution involves students in the intended mathematics. Do not feel compelled to search through books for clever or elaborate tasks.

Keep the content foremost in mind. Frantically searching through books for a problem can be a waste of time due to the difficulty of finding a task that meets your needs. Teachers frequently realize the task that looked so good in the resource did not exactly get at the intended mathematics.

Good tasks can often come directly from your text. A direct-instruction lesson can be modified to allow students to wrestle with the main idea. This book is full of tasks and is intended as a resource for you. NCTM has numerous publications with excellent ideas. Children's literature can often inspire great tasks. There are many excellent resource books but stick with those that allow the mathematics to be problem based. The longer you have had to build a repertoire of task ideas from journals, resource books, conferences, and in-service, the easier this important step in planning will become.

Step 4: **_Predict What Will Happen._** You have made hypotheses about what your students know and have selected a task. Now use that information and think about all of the things your students are likely to do with this task. If you catch yourself saying, "Well, I hope that they will . . . ," then *stop*. Predict! Don't hope!

Does every student in your class have a chance of engaging in this problem in some manner that is meaningful? Although students may each tackle the task differently, don't leave your struggling students to flounder. Perhaps you want to provide for modifications in the task for different students. (See the discussion of diversity later in this chapter.) This is also a good time to think about whether your students will work alone, in pairs, or in groups. Group work may assist students in need of some extra help.

If your predictions are beginning to make you uneasy about your task, this is the time to revisit the task. Maybe it needs to be modified, or perhaps it is simply too easy or too difficult.

These first four decisions define the heart of your lesson. The next four decisions define how you will carry out the plan in your classroom.

Step 5: ***Articulate Student Responsibilities.*** You always want more than answers. For nearly every task, you want students to be able to tell you

- What they did to get the answer
- Why they did it that way
- Why they think the solution is correct

Decide how you want students to supply this information. If responding in writing, will students write individually or prepare a group presentation? Will they write in their journals, on paper to be turned in, on a page you prepare that includes the problem, or perhaps on acetate that can be used for sharing with the class?

You may choose to have students simply report or discuss their ideas without writing. Although this option may occasionally be adequate, it should not be used often. The reflective value of written work is too great to ignore. Students are less likely to be prepared for discussion if they have not written out their ideas. Writing is a form of rehearsal for discussion.

Step 6: ***Plan the Before Portion of the Lesson.*** Sometimes you can simply begin a lesson with the task and articulation of students' responsibilities. In many instances, however, you will want to orient students' thinking with a related task or warm-up exercise. After presenting the task, will you "let go" or do you want students to brainstorm solutions or estimate answers? (See the earlier discussion of the "before phase" of a lesson on pp. 16–19.)

Consider how you will present the task. Options include having it written on paper, taken from their texts, shown on the overhead, or written on the board or overhead projector.

Step 7: ***Think About the During Portion of the Lesson.*** Look back at your predictions. What hints or assists can you plan in advance for students who may be stuck? Are there particular groups or individual students you wish to specially observe or assess in this lesson? Make a note to do so. Think of extensions or challenges you can pose to students who finish quickly.

Estimate how much time you think students should be given for the task. It is useful to tell students in advance. Some teachers set a timer that all students can see. Plan to be flexible but do not use up your discussion period.

Step 8: ***Think About the After Portion of the Lesson.*** How will you begin your discussion? One option is to simply list all of the different answers from groups or individuals, doing so without comment, and then returning to students or groups to explain their solutions and justify their answers. You may also begin with full explanations from each group or student before you get all the answers. Will you record on the board what is being said or have students write on the board or show their work in other ways?

Plan an adequate amount of time for your discussion. A good average is about 15 to 20 minutes.

Step 9: ***Write Your Lesson Plan.*** If you have thought through these steps, a plan is simply a listing of the critical decisions you have already made. The outline shown here is a possible format:

- The mathematics or goals
- The task and expectations
- The *before* activities
- The *during* hints and extensions for early finishers
- The *after*-lesson discussion format
- Assessment notes (what to be looking for, students to watch)

Note that at the end of each of the remaining chapters of this book, we have selected an activity from the chapter and expanded it into a complete lesson plan utilizing this structure.

Variations of the Three-Part Lesson

Certainly, not every lesson is developed around a task given to a full class. This is especially true in kindergarten and first grade. However, the basic concept of tasks and discussions can be adapted to most problem-based lessons.

Mini-Lessons

Many tasks do not require the full period. The three-part format can be compressed to as little as 10 minutes. You might plan two or three cycles in a single lesson. For example, consider these tasks:

- "Make up two questions that we can answer using the information in our graphs."
- Pose a simple story problem structured to evoke possible strategies for basic facts. For example: *Molly's mother bought 8 cartons of soft drinks for the picnic. Each carton had six cans. How many cans did she bring in all?* (Possible strategies: 4 sixes doubled OR 5 eights and 8 more.) "Solve this problem in your head. Discuss your method with your partner and then we'll listen to your ideas."

These are worthwhile tasks that do not require a full period to do and discuss. A think-pair-share strategy is useful for these shorter tasks.

Computer Activities and Games

There is no reason in a problem-based classroom to abandon the use of the many interactive computer activities (applets) that focus on a small conceptual area of content. Nor are games or station activities necessarily inappropriate.

The before portion of a lesson adapted for computer tasks, games, or stations generally happens with the whole class when you explain the activity or show briefly how the applet works.

A game or other repeatable activity may not look like a problem, but it can nonetheless be problem based. The determining factor is whether the activity causes students to be reflective about new or developing mathematical relationships. If the activity merely has students repeating a procedure without wrestling with an emerging idea, then it is not a problem-based experience. For example, the electronic activities in the NCTM *e-Standards* or the Illuminations website can often be used more than once and still maintain a problematic spirit for students who have not yet mastered the ideas. When selecting games, look for those that cause students to reflect on ideas rather than simply provide drill.

The time during which students are working on the computer or playing games is analogous to the during phase of a lesson. A discussion with students who have been working on a task, the after phase, is just as important for computer tasks and games. Generally you can wait until all in the class have worked at the same game or activity and have a full group discussion. Computer tasks should always involve a problem that can be discussed as would any other problem. For games, ask about strategies that were helpful or ideas that were discovered.

Just as with any task, some form of recording or writing should be included with computer tasks. Students solving a problem on a computer can write up what they did and explain what they learned. Students playing a game can keep records and then tell about how they played the game—what thinking or strategies they used.

Diversity in the Classroom

Perhaps one of the most difficult challenges for teachers today is to reach all of the students in their increasingly diverse classrooms. Every teacher faces this dilemma because every classroom contains a range of student abilities and backgrounds.

Interestingly, a problem-based approach can be the best way to attend to the range of students. In the problem-based classroom, children make sense of the mathematics in their own way, bringing to the problems only the skills and ideas that they own. The sophistication of the methods and approaches used will vary according to the range of ideas found within the class. In contrast, in a traditional, highly directed lesson, it is assumed that all students will understand and use the same approach and the same ideas. Students not ready to understand the ideas presented by the teacher must focus their attention on following the rules or directions in a mindless manner. This, of course, leads to endless difficulties and leaves many students behind or in need of serious remediation and reteaching.

In addition to using a problem-based approach, specific things you can do to help attend to the diversity of learners in your classroom include:

- Making sure that problems have multiple entry points.
- Planning differentiated tasks.
- Using heterogeneous groupings.

Plan for Multiple Entry Points

Step 4 in the planning guidelines suggests that you predict how all of the students in the class are likely to approach the task you've selected. Many tasks can be solved with a range of strategies. This is especially true of computational tasks in classes in which student-invented methods are encouraged and valued. For many tasks, the use or nonuse of manipulative models is all that is necessary to vary the entry point. Other students can be challenged to devise rules or to use methods that are less dependent on manipulatives or drawings. When considering a task, think of the least sophisticated method of solution you can imagine. Will this method provide an entry for struggling students? Is there a clever method or extension you can imagine that will challenge more able students?

Plan Differentiated Tasks

The idea here is to plan a task with multiple versions; some less difficult, others more so.

For many problems involving computations, you can insert multiple sets of numbers. In the following problem students are permitted to select the first, second, or third number in each bracket. These choices create progressively harder tasks, an idea students quickly learn.

Michelle has a new after-school job. She makes {$5.50, $5.15, $5.59} for each hour she works. Last week Michelle worked {6, 9, 7} hours. How much money did she earn?

Students tend to select the numbers that provide them with the greatest challenge without being too difficult. For this example, consider the products in the three problems: 5.50×6, 5.15×9, and 5.59×7. In the discussions, all students benefit and feel as though they worked on the same task. More importantly, by selecting the numbers carefully, strategies that may arise in one problem may help students with the others. Here the easier problems may influence a round-and-adjust strategy for 5.59×7. Students selecting the easier tasks may not be ready for that, but they can begin to see how easier computations help with harder ones.

As another example, here are three related tasks for area and perimeter. Each addresses the same general concepts but with differing degrees of difficulty.

- One side of the rectangle is 6 cm. The area is 48 square centimeters. How long is the other side? Make a drawing and use words and numbers to explain your answer.
- On centimeter grid paper, draw two different rectangles with a perimeter of 24. What is the area of each?
- Find at least three rectangles with an area of 36 square centimeters. What can you find out about the perimeters of these rectangles? Is there a pattern?

Again, these problems are progressively more difficult. Students can pick any problem to solve. If they finish with one task, they can try another.

Use Heterogeneous Groupings

Avoid ability grouping! Trying to split a class into ability groups is futile; every group still has diversity. It is demeaning to those students not in the top group. Students in the lower group will not experience the thinking and language of the top group, and top students will not hear the often unconventional but interesting approaches to tasks in the lower group. Furthermore, having two or more groups means that you must diminish the time you can spend with each group.

It is much more profitable to capitalize on the diversity in your room by using pairs or cooperative groups that are heterogeneous. Try to pair students in need of help with not only capable students but also students who will be compatible and willing to assist. Students will find that everyone has ideas to contribute. This does not mean that every cooperative group must be of mixed ability. Some teachers find it useful to vary this approach, sometimes grouping students homogeneously and other times heterogeneously.

ASSESSMENT IN A PROBLEM-BASED CLASSROOM

In a problem-based approach, teachers often ask, "How do I assess?" The question stems from the realization and acceptance of the fact that the traditional skill-oriented testing fails to adequately tell what students know.

Both the *Assessment Standards for School Mathematics* (1995) and *Principles and Standards for School Mathematics* (2000) stress that the line between assessment and instruction should be blurred. Teaching with problems allows us to blur that line. Assessment need not look different from instruction. The typical approach of an end-of-chapter test of skills may have some value but it is not appropriate as the main method of assessment. Assessment can and should happen every day as an integral part of instruction. If you restrict your view of assessment to tests and quizzes, you will miss seeing how assessment can help students grow and inform instruction. "Assessment should focus on what students *do know* instead of what they *do not know*" (NCTM, 1989).

Appropriate Assessment

An *appropriate assessment task* refers to a task or problem that allows students to demonstrate what they know. Both you and your students must see it as an integral part of the learning process.

If you take a problem-based approach to instruction but most of your assessments focus on recall and closed response items, you are sending mixed messages to your students. Recall and skill assessments tell students that what is valued is getting answers. Soon they will not be willing to solve problems or engage in class discussions but rather will insist that you simply "show them how to get the answers."

Assessment Tasks

Recall that a problem was any task or activity for which the students have no pre-scribed or memorized rules or specific correct solution method. The same definition should be used for assessment tasks. Perhaps you have heard about *performance assess-ment tasks* or *alternative assessments*. These terms seem to refer to tasks that are in some way different from those used in instruction. They should not be different! An assess-ment task should be a performance task as should problem-based tasks for learning.

STOP Do you think that you can or should use problem-based tasks such as those that have been described to assess your students? What are the pros and cons of such an approach?

Good tasks—for either instruction and/or assessment purposes—should permit every student in the class, regardless of mathematical prowess, to demonstrate his or her knowledge, skill, or understanding. Lower-ability students should be encouraged to use the best ideas they possess to work on a problem, even if these are not the same skills or strategies used by others in the room. When problem-based tasks are used for assessment and evaluation, then rather than finding out what students *do not know* (e.g., He can't add mixed numbers), you will have a broad description of the ideas and skills that students possess—what they *do know* (e.g., He understands simple fractions, is not clear about mixed numbers, does not estimate answers).

Tasks used in this way focus attention on the thinking and processes that stu-dents use in solving tasks. The percentage of correct responses is a very incomplete pic-ture of what a student knows. However, the potential data about your students can and should come daily as you "listen" in as many ways as possible to the methods that your students use to grapple with the tasks you give them.

Collecting Assessment Data

In some instances, the real value of a task or what can be learned about students will come primarily during the discussion in the after phase of your lesson. At other times the best assessment data will be in the written work that students do. To consis-tently receive valid data, it is important that you develop in your students the habit of adding justifications to their answers and listening to and evaluating the explanations of others.

The amount of information available from students, both from their written work and their discussions, is voluminous. However, you must find ways to record the infor-mation so that you have the data when you need it. Your memory of what transpired today may be sufficient for planning tomorrow's lesson. However, to help with grades and parent conferences, you need records. Here are some ideas:

- Make a habit of recording quick observational data. There are lots of options. A full-class checklist with space for comments is one method. Another is to write anecdotal notes on address labels and stick them into binders.
- Focus on big ideas rather than small skills. For example, "is beginning to see how multiplication facts can be related" is more helpful than "knows the easy multiplication facts but not the hard ones."

- You need not assess every child on every task. By focusing on big ideas, you will not feel required to check on every student on any given day. Make a habit of selecting a small number of students to focus on during a lesson. Gather data on a big idea over a week or so.

- Save or make copies of student work that accurately indicates the thinking of a child. There may be days when you announce to students that you are going to keep their written work in their folders. However, some students may produce better work the next day or will have done better thinking the day before. Use written work to show what students know.

- Use traditional tests for skills that you feel are essential. Use this technique sparingly.

Rubrics and Their Uses

Appropriate assessment tasks yield an enormous amount of information that cannot be evaluated by simply counting correct answers. We need to find ways to manage this information and make it useful. One important tool is a rubric.

A *rubric* consists of a scale of three to six points that is used as a rating of performance rather than a count of how many items are correct or incorrect. The rating is applied by examining total performance on a single task as opposed to counting the number of correct items.

Simple Rubrics

The following simple four-point rubric was developed by the New Standards Project and is used by many teachers and some school districts:

4   Excellent: Full Accomplishment

3   Proficient: Substantial Accomplishment

2   Marginal: Partial Accomplishment

1   Unsatisfactory: Little Accomplishment

This four-point rubric allows a teacher to rate performances using a double-sort technique as illustrated in Figure 1.11. The broad categories of the first sort (*Got It* or *Not Yet*) are relatively easy to discern. The scale then allows you to separate each category into two levels as shown. Some teachers use a 4 rating to note truly exceptional performance. A rating of 0 can be given for no response or effort, or for responses that are completely off-task.

The advantage of the four-point scale is the relatively easy double sort that can be made. The first sort, between those who have basically developed the idea from those students who need further experiences or instruction, is most important for judging how to pace your lessons and identifying students in need of additional instruction.

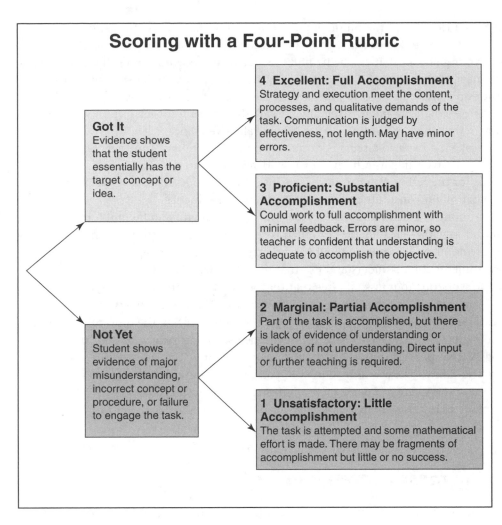

Scoring with a Four-Point Rubric

Got It
Evidence shows that the student essentially has the target concept or idea.

4 Excellent: Full Accomplishment
Strategy and execution meet the content, processes, and qualitative demands of the task. Communication is judged by effectiveness, not length. May have minor errors.

3 Proficient: Substantial Accomplishment
Could work to full accomplishment with minimal feedback. Errors are minor, so teacher is confident that understanding is adequate to accomplish the objective.

Not Yet
Student shows evidence of major misunderstanding, incorrect concept or procedure, or failure to engage the task.

2 Marginal: Partial Accomplishment
Part of the task is accomplished, but there is lack of evidence of understanding or evidence of not understanding. Direct input or further teaching is required.

1 Unsatisfactory: Little Accomplishment
The task is attempted and some mathematical effort is made. There may be fragments of accomplishment but little or no success.

FIGURE 1.11 ● ● ● ● ● ● ● ● ●
With a four-point rubric, performances are first sorted into two categories. Each performance is then considered again and assigned to a point on the scale.

Other teachers prefer a three-point rubric such as the following example:

3   Above and beyond—uses exemplary methods, shows creativity, goes beyond the requirements of the problem

2   On target—completes the task with no more than minor errors, uses expected approaches

1   Not there yet—makes significant errors or omissions, uses inappropriate approaches

The exact rubric you use is less important than having a well-understood method of communicating with your students and parents and for making recording assessment data easier for you.

Involve Students with Rubrics

In the beginning of the year, discuss your general rubric with the class. You may find that your students respond more to words such as "Wow," "Got It," "Not Quite," and "Need Help." Post the rubric prominently. It is possible to use the same rubric for all subjects. If you do not teach your students all day, discuss this with the other teachers in your grade level. It can be helpful to students if the words for evaluation that students hear are the same throughout the day. In your discussion, let students know that as they do activities and solve problems in class, you will look at their work and listen to their explanations and occasionally provide them with feedback in terms of the rubric, rather than as a letter grade or other evaluative mark.

Make it a habit to discuss performance on tasks in terms of the general rubric. You might have students rate their own work according to the rubric and explain their reasons for the rating. You can have class discussions about a task that has been done and what might constitute good and exceptional performance.

A rubric is much more than a grade. It is a meaningful and helpful form of communication with your students (and their parents). It should let students know how well they are doing and encourage them to work harder. When their performance is less than okay, students should understand not that they have failed but that there are ideas they need to work on. Your task is to see that they get that opportunity and your help.

You do not need to use rubrics with every task. Nor is it necessary to reserve rubrics for assessments that you want to grade. If you are using the four-point rubric just described, the language of the rubric can be used informally with your students. "Maggie, that paper is only a 2. I know you can do better."

The rubric scale can also be used in your observation recordings. If you describe the task at the top of a class roster, then it is easier and faster to record a 2, 3, or 4 next to a name than it is to write out a detailed comment.

Diagnostic Interviews

An interview is simply a one-on-one discussion with a student to help you see how she is thinking about a particular subject, what processes she uses in solving problems, or what attitudes and beliefs she may have. It may be as short as 5 to 10 minutes.

Many teachers avoid interviews because of time constraints. This is unfortunate because interviews have the potential to give you information that you simply cannot get in any other way. Think of interviews as a method to be used for only a few students at a time—not for every student in the class. You can interview a single student while the rest of the class is working on a task.

The most obvious reason to consider an interview is that you need more information concerning a particular student and how he or she is constructing concepts or using a procedure. Remediation will almost always be more successful if you can pinpoint *why* a student is having difficulty before you try to fix the problem.

A second reason is to get information either to plan your instruction or to assess the effectiveness of your instruction. For example, are you sure that your students have a good understanding of equivalent fractions or are they just doing the exercises according to rote rules?

Planning an Interview

There is no magic right way to plan or structure an interview. In fact, flexibility is a key ingredient. You should, however, have some overall game plan before you begin and be prepared with key questions and materials. Begin an interview with questions that are easy or closest to what the child is likely to be able to do, usually some form of procedural exercise. For numeration or computation topics, for example, begin with a pencil-and-paper task such as a computation, writing or comparing numerals. When the opening task has been completed, ask the child to explain what was done. "How would you explain this to a second grader (or your younger sister)?" "What does this (point to something on the paper) stand for?" "Tell me about why you do it that way." At this point, you may try a similar task but with a different feature; for example, after doing 372 – 54, try 403 – 37. The second problem has a zero in the tens place, a possible source of difficulty.

The next phase of the interview might involve models or drawings that the student can use to demonstrate understanding of the earlier procedural task. Decimal numeration or computation can be explored with base-ten materials or 10 × 10 grids. There are numerous models for fractions, and it may be useful to see if one model is more meaningful than another. Be careful not to interject or teach. The temptation to do so is sometimes overwhelming. Watch and listen. Next, explore connections between what was done with models and what was done with pencil and paper. Many students will do the very same task and get two different answers. Does it matter to the student? How is the discrepancy explained? Can the student connect actions using models to what he or she wrote or explained earlier?

Alternative beginnings to an interview include making an estimate of the answer to either a computation or a word problem, doing a computation mentally, or trying to predict the solution to a given task. Your goal is not to use the interview to teach but to find out where the child is in terms of concepts and procedures at this time.

Suggestions for Effective Interviews

The following suggestions have been adapted from excellent discussions of interviewing children by Labinowicz (1985, 1987), Liedtke (1988), and Scheer (1980).

- *Be accepting and neutral as you listen to the child.* Smiles, frowns, or other body language can make the child think that the answer he or she gave is right or wrong. Develop neutral responses such as "Uh-huh," "I see," or even a silent nod of the head.

- *Avoid cuing or leading the child.* "Are you sure about that?" "Now look again closely at what you just did." "Wait. Is that what you mean?" These responses will indicate to students that they have made some mistake and cause them to change their responses. This can mask what they really think and understand. A similar form of leading is a series of easily answered questions that directs the student to a correct response. That is teaching, not interviewing.

- *Wait silently.* Give the student plenty of time before you ask a different question or probe. After the student makes a response, wait again! This second wait time is even more important because it allows and encourages the student to elaborate on the initial thought and provide you with more information. Wait even when the response is correct. Waiting can also give you a bit more time to think about the direction you want the interview to take. Your wait time will almost never be as long as you imagine it is.

- *Do not interrupt.* Let students' thoughts flow freely. Encourage students to use their own words and ways of writing things down. Interjecting questions or correcting language can be distracting to the students' thinking.

- *Use imperatives rather than questions.* Say, "show me," "tell me," "do," or "try," rather than "can you?" or "will you?" In response to a question, the student can simply say no, leaving you without information.

- *Avoid confirming a request for validation.* Students frequently follow answers or actions with "Is that right?" This query can easily be answered with a neutral, "That's fine," or "You're doing okay," regardless of whether the answer is right or wrong.

Interviewing is not an easy thing to do well. Many teachers are timid about it and fail to take the time. But not much damage is possible, and the rewards of listening to children, both for you and your students, are so great that you really do not want to pass it up.

Grading

Myth: A grade is an average of a series of scores on tests and quizzes. The accuracy of the grade is dependent primarily on the accuracy of the computational technique used to calculate the final numeric grade.

Reality: A grade is a statistic that is used to communicate to others the achievement level that a student has attained in a particular area of study. The accuracy or validity of the grade is dependent on the information that is used in preparing the grade, the professional judgment of the teacher, and the alignment of the assessments with the true goals and objectives of the course.

Confronting the Myth

Most experienced teachers will say that they know a great deal about their students in terms of what the students know, how they perform in different situations, their attitudes and beliefs, and their various levels of skill attainment. Unfortunately, when it comes to grades, they often ignore this rich storehouse of information and rely on test scores and rigid averages that tell only a small fraction of the story.

The myth of grading by statistical number crunching is so firmly ingrained in schooling at all levels that you may find it hard to abandon. But it is unfair to students, to parents, and to you as the teacher to ignore all of the information you get almost daily from a problem-based approach in favor of a handful of numbers based on tests that usually focus on low-level skills.

Grading Issues

Some hard decisions are inevitable for effective use of the assessment information gathered from problems, tasks, and other appropriate methods to assign grades. Some decisions are philosophical, some require school or district agreements about grades, and all require us to examine what we value and the objectives we communicate to students and parents.

Using rubric scales to provide feedback and to encourage a pursuit of excellence must also relate to grades. However, "converting four out of five to 80 percent or three out of four to a grade of C can destroy the entire purpose of alternative assessment and the use of scoring rubrics" (Kulm, 1994, p. 99). Kulm explains that directly translating rubrics to grades focuses attention on grades and away from the purpose of every good problem-solving activity, which is to strive for an excellent performance. When papers are returned with less than top ratings, the purpose is to help students know what is necessary to achieve at a higher level. (This purpose must be explicitly communicated to students and parents.) Early on, there should be opportunities to improve based on feedback. When a grade of 75 percent or a C– is returned, all the student knows is that he or she did poorly. If, for example, a student's ability to justify his or her own answers and solutions has improved, should the student be penalized in the averaging of numbers that includes a weaker performance early in the marking period?

What this means is that grading must be based on the performance tasks and other activities for which you assigned rubric ratings; otherwise, students will soon realize that these are not important scores. At the same time, they need not be added or averaged in any numeric manner. The grade at the end of a unit or chapter should reflect a holistic view of where the student is now relative to your goals for that unit.

The grades you assign should reflect all of your objectives. Procedural skills remain important but should be weighted in proportion to other goals in keeping with your value system. If you are restricted to assigning a single grade for mathematics, different factors probably have different weights or values in making up the grade. There are no simple answers to how you balance all of your objectives—concepts, skills, problem solving, communication, and so on. However, these questions should be addressed at the beginning of the grading period and not the night you set out to assign grades.

A multidimensional reporting system is a big help. If you can assign several grades for mathematics and not just one, then your report to parents will be more meaningful. Even if the school's report card does not permit multiple grades, you can devise a supplement indicating several ratings for different objectives. A place for comments is also helpful. This form can be shared with students periodically during a grading period and can easily accompany a report card.

GET STARTED

In this chapter we have briefly touched on the foundational ideas of how students learn, teaching through problem solving, planning problem-based lessons, and assessment. It may take some time for you to completely adopt these ideas and approaches. Some things may make more sense to you than others. It may be discomforting to give up methods with which you've become familiar. It is hard to think of allowing—even planning for—the students in your room to struggle. Most people get into teaching because they want to help students learn. To not show them a solution when they are experiencing difficulty seems almost counterintuitive.

It is unrealistic to think you could simply read this chapter and then turn around and become a problem-based teacher. However, if you give this approach a fair chance and try to apply your understanding of how children learn to your daily teaching, your students will reward you with their performance, enthusiasm, and understanding. No, it will not happen overnight. But now is the time to begin—so get started!

As reflective thinking is the key ingredient in student learning, so also is reflection necessary to improve as a teacher. Do not be discouraged by lessons that did not go as you planned. Rather, ask yourself what happened and why. How could you have changed the lesson to make it better? How will you apply what you learned to the next lesson?

Social learning is also an important tool for teachers. Get other teachers on your grade level or in your school to try new ideas together. Talk informally about what seems to make a good lesson and what gets in the way. Use the planning guide discussed in this chapter to create lessons together. Don't try to jointly plan every lesson—just one every two or three weeks. Then have everyone teach the same lesson and compare notes. Make revisions based on your experiences. File these "special" lessons away and use them next year.

In addition to simply getting started and trying these ideas, the most important ingredient is to *believe in your kids!* Your students can think and can make sense of mathematics—*all of your students*. Some may learn more slowly or create different approaches that have never occurred to you, but they all can think and they all can learn. By allowing the mathematics to be problematic for students every day, we demonstrate our belief every day in their abilities to do and learn mathematics. Just give them the chance and let them amaze you.

NUMBER AND OPERATION SENSE

Number is a complex and multifaceted concept. *Number sense,* a rich, relational understanding of number, involves many different ideas, relationships, and skills.

We can think of *number sense* as a "good intuition about numbers and their relationships . . . [that] develops gradually as a result of exploring numbers, visualizing them in a variety of contexts, and relating them in ways that are not limited by traditional algorithms" (Howden, 1989, p. 11).

In grades K–2, children should develop "good intuition" about numbers up to 20. However, flexible, intuitive thinking with numbers—number sense—does not end with these smaller whole numbers. Number sense should continue to be developed throughout the school years as other types of numbers—fractions, decimals, percents, and integers—are added to students' repertoire of number ideas. Thus, number sense includes flexible thinking about all kinds of numbers. This chapter focuses on number sense with respect to larger whole numbers. Chapter 5 focuses on fraction sense, whereas decimal and percent concepts are discussed in Chapter 7.

big ideas

1 Numbers are related to each other through a variety of number relationships. The number 67, for example, is more than 50, 3 less than 70, and composed of 60 and 7 as well as 50 and 17. Each of these forms of 67 may be useful in a variety of situations, from estimation to comparison to computation.

2 "Really big" numbers possess the same place-value structure as the smaller numbers that students have worked with in earlier grades. But quantities as large as 1000 or more can be difficult to conceptualize because of their size. "Really big" numbers are best understood in terms of familiar real-world contexts. For example, the number of people that will fill the local sports arena is a meaningful concept for those who have experienced that crowd.

3 Multiplication is related to addition and involves counting groups of like size and determining how many there are in all. Division can be interpreted as fair sharing or as repeated subtraction. Multiplication and division are also related. Division names a missing factor in terms of the known factor and the product.

4 Whole numbers can be described by different characteristics, such as even and odd, prime and composite, square and cube, and so on. Understanding these different characteristics of number increases flexibility in working with number.

It is difficult to separate number sense from operation sense—a complete and flexible understanding of the operations. Students in grades 3–5 should develop their operation sense for multiplication and division. In particular, students should focus on the meanings of and the relationships between multiplication and division as well as connections between these two operations and addition and subtraction.

Developing Number Relationships

After children learn to count meaningfully, number relationships must become the focal point to move students away from merely counting and toward developing number sense, a flexible concept of number not completely tied to counting. Figure 2.1 illustrates two types of relationships with numbers that students should develop in grades 1 and 2 that can and should be extended to work with multidigit numbers.

Anchoring Numbers to 5 and 10

We want to help children relate a given number to other numbers, specifically 5 and 10. These relationships are especially useful in thinking about various combinations of numbers. For example, in each of the following, consider how the knowledge of 8 as "5 and 3 more" and as "2 away from 10" can play a role: 5 + 3, 8 + 6, 8 + 2, 8 – 3, 8 – 4, 13 – 8. (It may be worth stopping here to consider the role of 5 and 10 in each of these examples.) Similar relationships can be used in the development of mental computation skills on larger numbers such as 68 + 7.

The most common and perhaps most important model for this relationship is the ten-frame. The ten-frame is simply a 2 × 5 array in which counters or dots are placed to illustrate numbers (see Figure 2.2). Ten-frames can be simply drawn on a full sheet of construction paper (or use the Blackline Master). Nothing fancy is required, and each student can have one.

BLMs 1, 2

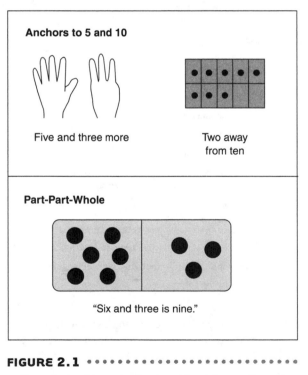

FIGURE 2.1 •

Two relationships to be developed involving small numbers that can be extended to larger numbers.

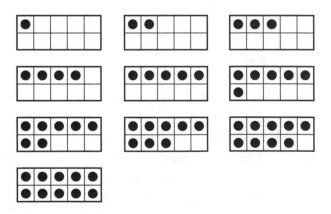

FIGURE 2.2 •

Ten-frames.

The following activity can be used to introduce students to the ten-frame. Provide students with about 20 counters that will fit in the ten-frame sections and conduct the next activity.

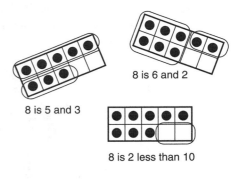

FIGURE 2.3 • • • • • • • • • • • • • • •

A ten-frame focuses on the anchors of 5 (each row) and 10 (the entire frame). Counters are placed one to a section, and students tell how they see their number in the frame.

ACTIVITY 2.1

Ten-Frame Tell-About

Explain that only one counter is permitted in each section of the ten-frame. No other counters are allowed on the ten-frame mat. Have students show 8 on their ten-frame mat. "What can you tell us about 8 from looking at your mat?" After hearing from several students, try other numbers from 0 to 10. Students may place their counters on the ten-frame in any manner. What they observe will differ a great deal from student to student. For example, with eight counters, a student with 5 in the top row and 3 in the bottom row may say, "It's 5 and 3," or "It's 6 and 2," or "It's 2 less than 10" (see Figure 2.3). There are no wrong answers. For numbers less than 5, focus attention on how many more counters are needed to make 5. For numbers greater than 5, focus attention on how many more counters are needed to make 10 or how many more markers over 5 are needed to make the target number.

Soon after this introduction to the ten-frame, introduce the following rule for showing numbers on the ten-frame: *Always fill the top row first, starting from the left, the same way you read. When the top row is full, counters can be placed in the bottom row, also from the left.* This will produce the "standard" way to show numbers on the ten-frame as in Figure 2.2. The ten-frame helps students visualize number relationships, such as how far away a number is from 10 or how the number can be decomposed into different parts. Again, such number relationships are key to developing efficient computational strategies with larger numbers.

Ten-frame flash cards are an important variation of ten-frames. Make cards from poster board about the size of a small index card, with a ten-frame on each and dots drawn in the frames. A set of 20 cards consists of a 0 card, a 10 card, and two each of the numbers 1 to 9. The cards allow for simple drill activities to reinforce the 5 and 10 anchors.

ACTIVITY 2.2

Ten-Frame Flash

Flash ten-frame cards to the class or group and see how fast the children can tell how many dots are shown. This activity is fast-paced, takes only a few minutes, can be done at any time, and is a lot of fun if you encourage speed.

Important variations of "Ten-Frame Flash" include

- Saying the number of spaces on the card instead of the number of dots
- Saying one more than the number of dots (or two more, and also less than)
- Saying the "ten fact"—for example, "six and four make ten"

Ten-frame tasks can be surprisingly problematic for some students. Students must reflect on the two rows of five, the spaces remaining, and how a particular number is more or less than 5 and how far away from 10. The discussions of how numbers are seen on the ten-frames are examples of brief "after" activities in which students learn from one another. Although these ten-frame activities are most appropriate for grades K–2, they have proven quite beneficial to older students who have yet to develop 5 and 10 benchmark relationships.

Part-Part-Whole Relationships

 Before reading on, get some counters or coins. Count out a set of eight counters in front of you as if you were a first- or second-grade child counting them.

Any child who has learned how to count meaningfully can count out eight objects as you just did. What is significant about the experience is what it did *not* cause you to think about. Nothing in counting a set of eight objects will cause a child to focus on the fact that it could be made of two parts. For example, separate the counters you just set out into two piles and reflect on the combination. It might be 2 and 6 or 7 and 1 or 4 and 4. Make a change in your two piles of counters and say the new combination to yourself. Focusing on a quantity in terms of its parts has important implications for developing number sense. A noted researcher in children's number concepts, Lauren Resnick (1983) states:

> *Probably the major conceptual achievement of the early school years is the interpretation of numbers in terms of part and whole relationships. With the application of a Part-Whole schema to quantity, it becomes possible for children to think about numbers as compositions of other numbers. This enrichment of number understanding permits forms of mathematical problem solving and interpretation that are not available to younger children. (p. 114)*

If your students have not experienced interpreting numbers in terms of parts and wholes, it is very important to provide opportunities to develop this foundation. Before moving to multidigit numbers, consider the following activity, which includes a design component that can make the activity a bit more interesting for students in grades 3–5.

ACTIVITY 2.3

Build It in Parts

Provide students with one type of material, such as multilink cubes, pattern blocks, toothpicks, or squares of colored paper. The task is to see how many different combinations for a particular number they can make using two parts. (If you wish, you can allow for more than two parts.) For each combination, they create a design with the assigned number of elements. For each design, students are challenged to see and read the design in two parts. Each different combination can be displayed on a small mat, such as a quarter-sheet of construction paper. Here are some ideas, each of which is illustrated in Figure 2.4.

Chapter 2 NUMBER AND OPERATION SENSE

- Make arrangements of wooden cubes.
- Make designs with pattern blocks. It is a good idea to use only one or two shapes at a time.
- Make designs with flat toothpicks. These can be dipped in white glue and placed on small squares of construction paper to create a permanent record.
- Make designs with touching squares or triangles. Cut a large supply of small squares or triangles out of construction paper. These can also be pasted down.

For each design, have students write an addition equation that matches the way they see the parts within the design.

Writing the combinations encourages reflective thought focused on the part-whole relationship. It also helps make apparent the clear connection between part-whole concepts and addition concepts.

It is both fun and useful to challenge children to see their designs in different ways, producing different number combinations. In Figure 2.4, decide how children look at the designs to get the combinations listed under each.

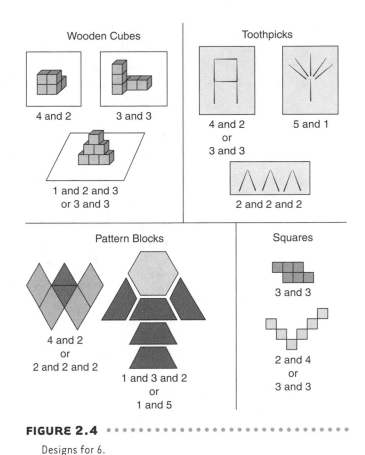

FIGURE 2.4

Designs for 6.

Extending Number Relationships to Larger Numbers

Teachers can capitalize on some of the early number relationships on smaller numbers and extend them to numbers up to 100. A useful set of materials to help with these relationships is the little ten-frames found in the Blackline Masters. Each student should have a set of 10 tens and a set of frames for each number 1 to 9 with an extra 5.

The following three ideas are illustrated with the little ten-frames in Figure 2.5. First are the relationships of one more than and one less than. If you understand that one more than 6 is 7, then in a similar manner, ten more than 60 is 70 (that is, one more ten). The second idea is connected to fact strategies. If a student has learned to think about adding on to 8 or 9 by first adding up to 10 and then adding the rest, the extension to similar two-digit numbers is quite simple; see Figure 2.5(b). Finally, the most powerful idea for small numbers is thinking of them in parts. It is a very useful idea (though not one found in textbooks) to take apart larger numbers to begin to develop some flexibility in the same way. Students can begin by thinking of ways to take apart a multiple of 10 such as 80. Once they do it with tens, the challenge can be to think of ways to take apart 80 when one part has a 5 in it, such as 25 or 35.

Being able to recognize and generate equivalent representations of the same number is the part of number sense that will serve students well during tasks that require estimation, comparison, or computation. This ability increases students' flexibility in dealing with numbers because they can easily generate equivalent representations

BLMs 3, 4

DEVELOPING NUMBER RELATIONSHIPS

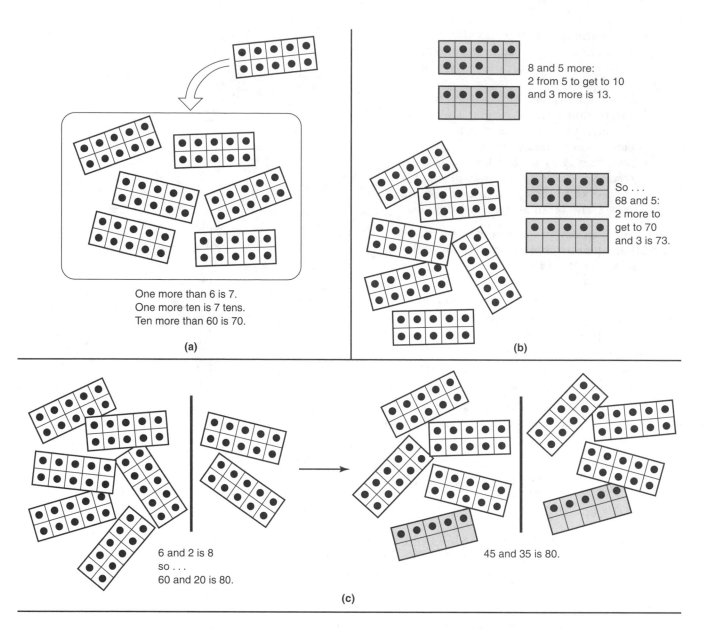

One more than 6 is 7.
One more ten is 7 tens.
Ten more than 60 is 70.

(a)

8 and 5 more:
2 from 5 to get to 10
and 3 more is 13.

So . . .
68 and 5:
2 more to
get to 70
and 3 is 73.

(b)

6 and 2 is 8
so . . .
60 and 20 is 80.

45 and 35 is 80.

(c)

FIGURE 2.5 • • • • • • • •

Extending early number
relationships to mental
computation activities.

that will make their work in a given task easier. Challenge students to find as many
different ways to represent a given number as possible. The number 67, for example,
is 65 and 2 more, 3 less than 70, and composed of 60 and 7 as well as 50 and 17
or 40 and 27. Each of these forms of 67 may be useful in a variety of situations. For
instance, if you are adding 67 and 56, thinking of 67 as 50 and 17 allows you to add
50 and 50 (from the 56) to get 100. Now add the 17 and 6 to get 23. Combine the
100 and 23 to get 123. Once students are able to think flexibly like this, they will be
able to do additions such as 67 and 56 mentally much faster than using a pencil-and-
paper procedure.

More will be said about mental computation in Chapter 4. The important point
here is that number relationships have a great impact on students' capability to develop
flexible strategies. The end result is a more meaningful as well as a more efficient
means of working with number.

Relative Magnitude

Number sense also includes having a grasp on the size of numbers. Relative magnitude refers to the size relationship one number has with another—is it much larger, much smaller, close, or about the same? There are several quick activities that can be done with a number line sketched on the board. The number line can help students see how one number is related to another.

ACTIVITY 2.4

Who Am I?

Sketch a line labeled 0 and 100 at opposite ends. Mark a point with a ? that corresponds to your secret number. (Estimate the position the best you can.) Students try to guess your secret number. For each guess, place and label a mark on the line.

Continue marking each guess until your secret number is discovered. As a variation, the endpoints can be other than 0 and 100. For example, try 0 and 1000, 200 and 300, or 500 and 800.

ACTIVITY 2.5

Who Could They Be?

Label two points on a number line with numbers (not necessarily the ends).

Ask students what numbers they think different points labeled with letters might be and why they think that. In the example shown here, B and C are less than 100 but probably more than 60. E could be about 180. You can also ask where 75 might be or where 400 is. About how far apart are A and D? Why do you think D is more than 100?

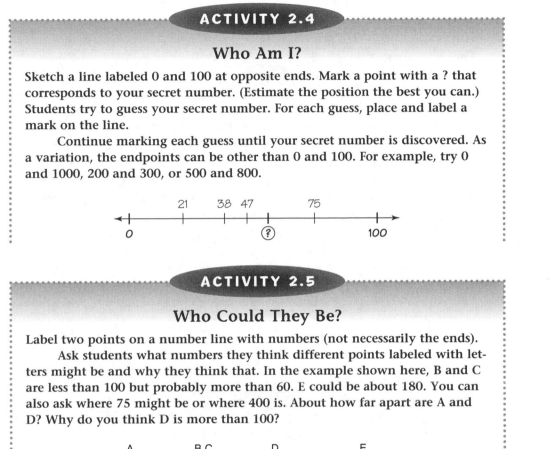

In the next activity, some of the same ideas are discussed without benefit of a number line.

ACTIVITY 2.6

Close, Far, and in Between

Put any three numbers on the board. If appropriate, use larger numbers.

With these three numbers as referents, ask questions such as the following, and encourage discussion of all responses:

Which two are closest? Why?
Which is closest to 300? To 250?

EXPANDED LESSON

(pages 72–73)
A complete lesson plan based on "Close, Far, and in Between" can be found at the end of this chapter.

(continued)

DEVELOPING NUMBER RELATIONSHIPS

Name a number between 457 and 364.
Name a multiple of 25 between 219 and 364.
Name a number that is more than all of
    these.
About how far apart are 219 and 500? 219
    and 5000?
If these are "big numbers," what are some small numbers? Numbers about
    the same? Numbers that make these seem small?

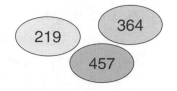

Connections to Real-World Ideas

Encourage students to see number in the world about them. You do not need a prescribed activity to bring real numbers into the classroom.

Look for numbers around your school: the number of students in each grade level, the numbers on the school buses, the number of minutes devoted to mathematics each day throughout the school and then each week, the number of cartons of chocolate and plain milk served in the cafeteria each day, the number of hours (or minutes!) school has been in session since the beginning of the year. And then there are measurements, numbers at home, numbers on a field trip, and so on.

What do you do with these numbers? Turn them into interesting graphs, write stories using them, make up problems, devise contests.

The interest in numbers can expand beyond the school and classroom. All sorts of things can and should be measured to create graphs, draw inferences, and make comparisons. For example, what numbers are associated with the "average" fifth grader? Height, weight, arm span, age in months, number of siblings, number of grandparents, distance from home to school, length of standing broad jump, number of pets, hours spent watching TV in a week. How can you find the average for these or other numbers that may be of interest to the students in your room? Is anyone really average?

The next activity is another way to help students connect numbers to real situations.

ACTIVITY 2.7

Is It Reasonable?

Select a number and a unit—for example, 15 feet. Could the teacher be 15 feet tall? Could your living room be 15 feet wide? Can a man jump 15 feet high? Could the school building be 15 feet tall? Could three students stretch out their arms 15 feet? Pick any number, large or small, and a unit with which students are familiar. Then make up a series of these questions.

Once students are familiar with Activity 2.7, have them select the number and the unit of things (10 kids, 20 bananas, etc.), and see what kinds of questions students can make up. When a difference of opinion arises, capitalize on the opportunity to explore and find out. Resist the temptation to supply your adult-level knowledge. Instead, say, "Well, how can we find out if it is or is not reasonable? Who has an idea about what we could do?" Students can easily begin to pose their own questions and explore number in the part of the environment most interesting to them.

The particular way you bring number and the real world together in your class is up to you. But do not underestimate the value of connecting the real world to the classroom.

Approximate Numbers and Rounding

In our number system, some numbers are "nice" or easy to think about and work with. What makes a nice number is sort of fuzzy. However, numbers such as 100, 500, and 750 are easier to use than 94, 517, and 762. Multiples of 100 are very nice, and multiples of 10 are not bad either. Multiples of 25 (50, 75, 425, 675, etc.) are nice because they combine into 100s and 50s rather easily, and we can mentally place those between multiples of 100s. Multiples of 5 are a little easier to work with than other numbers.

Flexible thought with numbers and many estimation skills are related to the ability to substitute a nice number for one that is not so nice. The substitution may be to make a mental computation easier, to compare it to a familiar reference, or simply to store the number in memory more easily.

In the past, students were taught rules for rounding numbers to the nearest 10 or nearest 100. Unfortunately, the emphasis was placed on applying the rule correctly. (If the next digit is 5 or more, round up; otherwise, leave the number alone.) A context to suggest why they may want to round numbers was usually a lesser consideration.

To round a number simply means to substitute a nice number that is close so that some computation can be done more easily. The close number can be any nice number and need not be a multiple of 10 or 100, as has been traditional. It should be whatever makes the computation or estimation easier or simplifies numbers sufficiently in a story, chart, or conversation. You might say, "Last night it took me 57 minutes to do my homework" or "Last night it took me about one hour to do my homework." The first expression is more precise; the second substitutes a rounded number for better communication.

A number line with nice numbers highlighted can be useful in helping children select near nice numbers. An unlabeled number line like the one shown in Figure 2.6 can be made using three strips of poster board taped end to end. Labels are written above the line on the chalkboard. The ends can be labeled 0 and 100, 100 and 200, . . . , 900 and 1000. The other markings then show multiples of 25, 10, and 5. Indicate a number above the line that you want to round. Discuss the marks (nice numbers) that are close.

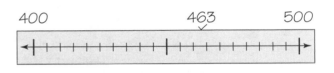

FIGURE 2.6

A blank number line can be labeled in different ways to help students with near and nice numbers.

Numbers Beyond 1000

Extending students' conceptual understanding of numbers beyond 1000 is sometimes difficult to do because physical models for thousands are not commonly available. Encouraging students to extend the patterns in the place-value system and to create familiar real-world referents helps students develop a fuller sense of these larger numbers.

Extending the Place-Value System

Two important ideas typically developed for three-digit numbers should be carefully extended to larger numbers. First, the grouping of ten idea should be generalized.

That is, 10 in any position makes a single thing (group) in the next position, and vice versa. Second, the oral and written patterns for numbers in three digits are duplicated in a clever way for every three digits to the left. These two related ideas are not as easy for children to understand as adults seem to believe. Because models for large numbers are so difficult to have or picture, textbooks must deal with these ideas in a predominantly symbolic manner. That is not sufficient!

ACTIVITY 2.8

What Comes Next?

Have a "What Comes Next?" discussion with the use of base-ten strips and squares. The unit or ones piece is a 1-centimeter (cm) square. The tens piece is a 10 × 1 strip. The hundreds piece is a square, 10 cm × 10 cm. What is next? Ten hundreds is called a thousand. What shape? It could be a strip made of 10 hundreds squares. Tape 10 hundreds together. What is next? (Reinforce the idea of "ten makes one" that has progressed to this point.) Ten one-thousand strips would make a square measuring 1 meter (m) on a side. Once the class has figured out the shape of the thousand piece, the problem-based task is "What comes next?" Let small groups work on the dimensions of a ten-thousand piece.

If your students become interested in seeing the big pieces from "What Comes Next?" engage them in measuring them out on paper. Ten ten-thousand squares (100,000) go together to make a huge strip. Draw this strip on a long sheet of butcher paper, and mark off the 10 squares that make it up. You will have to go out in the hall.

How far you want to extend this square, strip, square, strip sequence depends on your class. The idea that 10 in one place makes 1 in the next can be brought home dramatically. You can make the next 10 m × 10 m square using chalk lines on the playground. The next strip is 100 m × 10 m. This can be measured out on a large playground with kids marking the corners. By this point, the payoff includes an appreciation of the increase in size of each successive amount as well as the ten-makes-one progression.

The 100 m × 10 m strip is the model for 10 million, and the 10 m × 10 m square models 1 million. The difference between 1 million and 10 million is dramatic. Even the concept of 1 million tiny centimeter squares is dramatic.

The three-dimensional wooden or plastic base-ten materials are all available with a model for thousands, which is a 10-cm cube. These models are expensive, but having at least one large cube to show and talk about is a good idea.

Try the "What Comes Next?" discussion in the context of these three-dimensional models. The first three shapes are distinct: a *cube*, a *long*, and a *flat*. What comes next? Stack 10 flats and they make a cube, the same shape as the first one only 1000 times larger. What comes next? (See Figure 2.7.) Ten *cubes* make another *long*. What comes next? Ten big *longs*

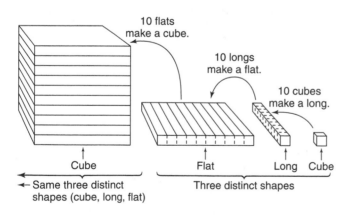

10 flats make a cube.

10 longs make a flat.

10 cubes make a long.

Cube | Flat | Long | Cube

← Same three distinct shapes (cube, long, flat) | Three distinct shapes

FIGURE 2.7 •

With every three places, the shapes repeat. Each cube represents a 1, each long represents a 10, and each flat represents a 100.

FIGURE 2.8 • • • • • • • • • • • •

The triples system for naming large numbers.

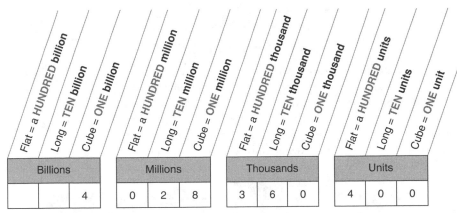

"Four billion, twenty-eight million, three hundred sixty thousand, four hundred."

make a big *flat*. The first three shapes have now repeated! Ten big flats will make an even bigger cube, and the triplet of shapes begins again.

Each cube has a name. The first one is the *unit* cube, the next is a *thousand*, the next a *million*, then a *billion*, and so on. Each long is 10 cubes: 10 units, 10 thousands, 10 millions. Similarly, each flat shape is 100 cubes.

To read a number, first mark it off in triples from the right. The triples are then read, stopping at the end of each to name the unit (or cube shape) for that triple (see Figure 2.8). Leading zeros in each triple are ignored. If students can learn to read numbers like 059 (fifty-nine) or 009 (nine), they should be able to read any number. To write a number, use the same scheme. If first mastered orally, the system is quite easy.

It is important for students to realize that the system does have a logical structure, is not totally arbitrary, and can be understood.

Conceptualizing Large Numbers

The ideas just discussed are only partially helpful in thinking about the actual quantities involved in very large numbers. For example, in extending the square, strip, square, strip sequence, some appreciation for the quantities of 1000 or of 100,000 is included. But it is hard for anyone to translate quantities of small squares into quantities of other items, distances, or time.

 How do you think about 1000 or 100,000? Do you have any real concept of a million?

Creating References for Special Big Numbers

In these activities, numbers like 1000, 10,000, or even 1 million are translated literally or imaginatively into something that is easy or fun to think about. Interesting quantities become lasting reference points or benchmarks for large numbers and thereby add meaning to numbers encountered in real life.

ACTIVITY 2.9

Collecting 10,000

Collections. As a class or grade-level project, collect some type of object with the objective of reaching some specific quantity—for example, 1000 or 10,000 buttons, walnuts, old pencils, jar lids, pieces of junk mail, soup labels, or cereal box tops. If you begin aiming for 100,000 or 1 million, be sure to think it through. One teacher spent nearly 10 years with her classes before amassing a million bottle caps. It takes a small dump truck to hold that many!

ACTIVITY 2.10

Showing 10,000

Illustrations. Sometimes it is easier to create large amounts. For example, start a project where students draw 100 or 200 or even 500 dots on a sheet of paper. Each week, different students contribute a specified number. Another idea is to cut up newspaper into pieces the same size as dollar bills to see what a large quantity would look like. Paper chain links can be constructed over time and hung down the hallways with special numbers marked. Let the school be aware of the ultimate goal.

ACTIVITY 2.11

How Long?/How Far?

Real and imagined distances. How long is a million baby steps? Other ideas that address length: toothpicks, dollar bills, or candy bars end to end; children holding hands in a line; blocks or bricks stacked up; children lying down head to toe. Real measures can also be used: feet, centimeters, meters.

ACTIVITY 2.12

A Long Time

Time. How long is 1000 seconds? How long is a million seconds? A billion? How long would it take to count to 10,000 or 1 million? (To make the counts all the same, use your calculator to do the counting. Just press the $=$.) How long would it take to do some task like buttoning a button 1000 times?

Estimating Large Quantities

Activities 2.9 through 2.12 focus on a specific number. The reverse idea is to select a large quantity and find some way to measure, count, or estimate how many.

ACTIVITY 2.13

Really Large Quantities

Ask how many

Candy bars would cover the floor of your room
Steps an ant would take to walk around the school building

Grains of rice would fill a cup or a gallon jug
Quarters could be stacked in one stack floor to ceiling
Pennies can be laid side by side down an entire block
Pieces of notebook paper would cover the gym floor
Seconds you have lived

Big-number projects need not take up large amounts of class time. They can be explored over several weeks as take-home projects or group projects or, perhaps best of all, be translated into great schoolwide estimation contests.

Literature Connections

Many books have wonderful explorations of large quantities and how they can be combined and separated. One example is *A Million Fish . . . More or Less* by McKissack (1992).

The story is full of exaggerations such as a turkey that weighs 500 pounds and a jump-rope contest (using a snake) where the story's hero wins with 5553 jumps. "Could these things really be? How long would it take to jump 5553 times? Could Hugh put a million fish in his wagon? How do you write half of a million?" Rusty Bresser (1995) suggests a number of excellent ways this tale can be used to investigate large numbers and how they are written. The connection to real things and real ideas is just the ticket to add number sense to an upper-grade unit on place value.

Many other excellent books investigate very large numbers in interesting contexts. *How Much Is a Million?* (1985) and *If You Made a Million* (1989), both by David Schwartz, have become very popular. Wanda Gag's *Millions of Cats* (1928) is a classic that is still worth the time to investigate. The imagination that these books inspire can lead children into fascinating investigations of large numbers, and with a bit of guidance, good place-value concepts can be visited along the way.

Activities for Flexible Thinking with Whole Numbers

Many of the ideas discussed in the previous section involve an understanding of place value. In grades 3–5, place-value concepts are best expanded beyond those learned in earlier grades by incorporating them into activities that use these concepts. That is, rather than conduct lessons focused exclusively on place value, create tasks that require the use of place-value ideas and place-value models. The goal is to promote what is sometimes called "ten-structured thinking," that is, flexibility in using the structure of tens and hundreds in the number system. This section offers additional ideas.

The Hundreds Chart

The hundreds chart (see the Blackline Masters) is an important tool for developing ten-structured thinking. The hundreds chart should not be abandoned after grade 2 as is often the case. When students are exploring invented strategies for addition and subtraction, the hundreds chart is often a used as a model. The rows of ten encourage students to think about working with multiples of ten. For example, in adding 47 + 25,

BLM 6

students might locate the number 47 on the chart and see that three more counts get them to 50 and then 22 more is easy to compute. Similarly, students might begin with 47 and go down two rows—adding 20—and then count on two more. What is important is not the particular methods that are used but rather the use of multiples of ten that is encouraged by the chart.

In the earlier grades, students look for patterns on the hundreds chart, especially those found in rows and columns. The hundreds chart is especially useful for skip counting. Patterns in skip counts can be observed both in the numbers and in the way that the numbers appear on the chart. For example, skip counts by 3 will form diagonal patterns. You may want to see how familiar your students are with hundreds-chart patterns. In Chapter 10 you will find additional explorations with the hundreds chart that will challenge your students in their search for patterns.

In the following activity, number relationships on the hundreds chart are made more explicit by connecting the chart numbers to representations using base-ten models.

ACTIVITY 2.14

Models with the Hundreds Chart

This activity has several variations that can be conducted with the full class or can be made into an activity in which two students work together to explore an idea and write about what they have discovered. Use any physical model for two-digit numbers with which the students are familiar. The little ten-frames are a good suggestion.

- Give children one or more numbers to first make with the models and then find on the chart. Use groups of two or three numbers either in the same row or the same column.
- Have students make all of the numbers in a row or in a column. How are the numbers in the row (or column) alike? How are they different? What happens at the end of the row?
- Indicate a number on the chart. What would you have to change to make each of its neighbors (the numbers to the left, right, above, and below)?

It is becoming more and more popular to have a chart that extends to 200. Perhaps a more powerful idea is to extend the hundreds chart to 1000, even at the second or third grade.

ACTIVITY 2.15

The Thousands Chart

Provide students with several sheets of the blank hundreds charts from the Blackline Masters. Assign groups of three or four students the task of creating a 1-to-1000 chart. The chart is to be made by taping ten charts together in a long strip. Students should decide how they are going to divide up the task with different students taking different parts of the chart.

BLM 5

The thousands chart should be discussed as a class to examine how numbers change as you count from one hundred to the next, what the patterns are, and so on. In fact, the earlier hundreds chart activities can all be extended to a thousands chart.

You may want to make a blank thousands chart (clearly indicating each 100-square). Use the students' charts for other discussions.

Working with Tens and Hundreds

Many of the skills related to invented strategies for addition and subtraction computation appear in the next activity, which combines symbolism with base-ten representations. When you have students do this activity and those in the following section, remember that your objective is to improve students' number sense and prepare them for flexible methods of computation. These activities should not be viewed as tasks to be mastered.

ACTIVITY 2.16

Numbers, Squares, Sticks, and Dots

As illustrated in Figure 2.9, prepare a worksheet or overhead transparency on which a numeral and some base-ten pieces are shown. Use small squares, sticks, and dots for base-ten pieces to keep the drawing simple. Students write the totals that they compute mentally.

Figure 2.10 is a take-away version of the same activity. As shown, the amount removed can be either the numeral or the squares and sticks. Try it both ways.

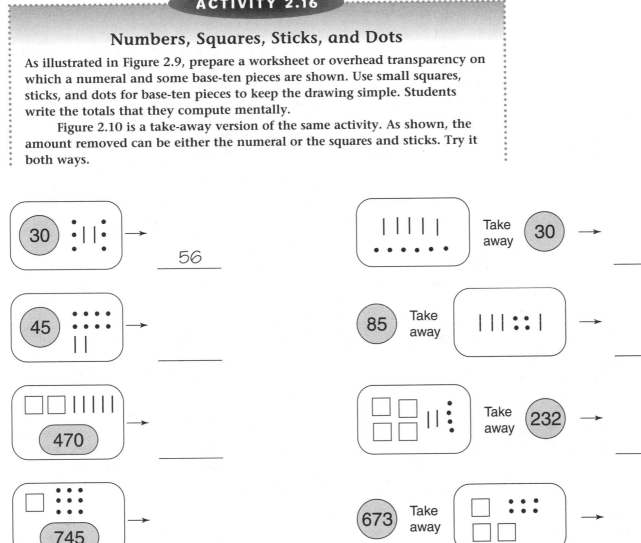

FIGURE 2.9 • • • • • • • • • • • •
Flexible counting on or addition using both models and numerals.

FIGURE 2.10 •
Counting back or subtraction using both models and numerals.

ACTIVITIES FOR FLEXIBLE THINKING WITH WHOLE NUMBERS

Thinking About Parts of Numbers

Another important focus involves further extending part-part-whole ideas, especially thinking about a missing part, which is the agenda of the next several activities.

Often in computations it is useful to recognize that a number can be made up of a "nice" number and some more. The nice part (maybe a multiple of 50 or 100) is dealt with first and then the smaller leftover piece can be considered.

ACTIVITY 2.17

50 and Some More

Say a number between 50 and 100. Students respond with "50 and ____." For 63, the response is "50 and 13." Use other numbers that end in 50 such as "450 and some more."

Nice numbers also are often broken apart in computations. The next two activities are extremely useful for developing the thinking required for counting-up approaches to subtraction. Introduce these activities to the full class using the overhead projector. Have students share their thinking strategies.

ACTIVITY 2.18

The Other Part of 100

Two students work together with a set of little ten-frame cards. One student makes a two-digit number. Then both students work mentally to determine what goes with the ten-frame amount to make 100. They write their solutions on paper and then check by making the other part with the cards to see if the total is 100. Students take turns making the original number. Figure 2.11 shows three different thought processes that students might use.

Being able to give the other part of 100 is so useful in invented strategies that students should get quite good at it.

If your students are adept at parts of 100, you can change the whole from 100 to another number. At first try other multiples of 10 such as 70 or 80. Then extend the whole to any number less than 100.

 Suppose that the whole is 83. Sketch four little ten-frame cards showing 36. Looking at your "cards," what goes with 36 to make 83? How did you think about it?

What you just did in finding the other part of 83 was subtract 36 from 83. You did not borrow or regroup. Most likely you did it in your head. With more practice you (and students as early as the third grade) can do this without the aid of the cards. These ideas are discussed further in Chapter 4.

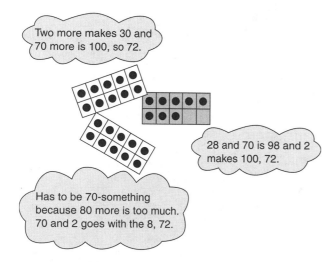

FIGURE 2.11 ● ● ● ● ● ● ● ● ● ● ● ● ● ● ●

Using little ten-frames to help think about the "other part of 100."

Compatible numbers for addition and subtraction are numbers that go together easily to make nice numbers. Numbers that make tens or hundreds are the most common examples. Compatible sums also include numbers that end in 5, 25, 50, or 75, since these numbers are easy to work with as well. The teaching task is to get students accustomed to looking for combinations that work together and then looking for these combinations in computational situations.

ACTIVITY 2.19

Compatible Pairs

Searching for compatible pairs can be done as a worksheet activity or with the full class using the overhead projector. Prepare a transparency, or duplicate a page with a search task. Five possibilities of different difficulty levels are shown in Figure 2.12. Students call out or connect the compatible pairs as they see them.

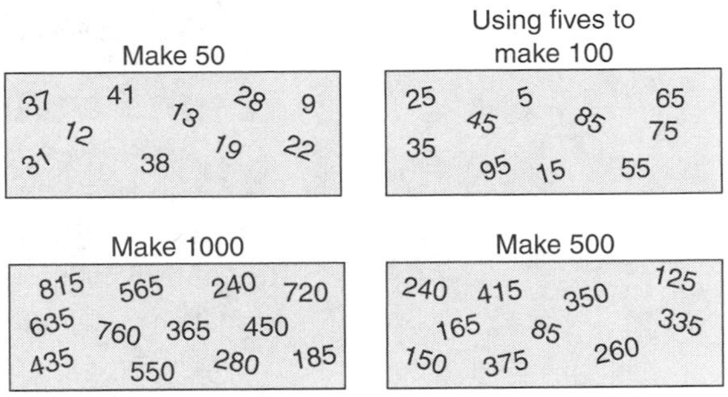

FIGURE 2.12 • • • • • • • • • • • • • • • •

Compatible-pair searches.

Here are two more activities that combine some of the ideas we have been exploring.

ACTIVITY 2.20

Calculator Challenge Counting

Students press any number on the calculator (e.g., 17), then ➕ 8. They say the sum before they press ✹. Then they continue to add 8 mentally, challenging themselves to say the number before they press ✹. They should see how far they can go before making a mistake.

The constant addend in "Challenge Counting" can be any number, even a two- or three-digit number. Try 20 or 25. Try 40 and then 48. As an added challenge, after a student has progressed eight or ten counts, have the student reverse the process by pressing ➖ followed by the same number and then ✹, ✹, ... Discuss patterns that appear.

ACTIVITY 2.21

Little Ten-Frame Addition and Subtraction

Provide a set of little ten-frame cards for each of two students. Each student makes a number with his or her cards. When both have their number ready, they place it out so both can see. Then they try to be the first to tell the total. For the subtraction version, one student makes a number greater than 50 and the other writes a number on paper that is less than 50. The written number is to be subtracted from the modeled number. Students should be encouraged to share strategies to see how fast they can get.

Although activities like those in this section can be done independently or in pairs, it is good to occasionally do them with the full class so that strategies can be discussed.

ACTIVITIES FOR FLEXIBLE THINKING WITH WHOLE NUMBERS

Will these activities develop place-value concepts, number sense, or flexible strategies for computation? The answer is "all three." By grade 3, there is little reason to separate whole-number place-value development from whole-number computation.

Developing Multiplication and Division Operation Sense

This section of the chapter is about helping students develop *operation sense* with respect to multiplication and division, that is, helping students connect different meanings of multiplication and division to each other as well as to addition and subtraction so that they can effectively use these operations in real-world settings.

Using Contextual Problems

A significant method of developing meanings for operations is to have students solve contextual problems or story problems. However, there is more to think about than simply giving students word problems to solve. Consider the following problems.

· ·

George bought 12 packs of game cards with 15 cards each. How many cards did George buy?

· ·

· ·

Yesterday as we planned for the school's Fall Festival, we discovered that it took 7 yards of paper to cover the bulletin board in the front lobby of the school. There are 25 more bulletin boards in the hallways and classrooms around the school. How many yards of paper will we need if we help to cover all the bulletin boards in the school?

· ·

The first problem is similar to a typical problem that you could find in a textbook and is rather sterile. The second problem is based on students' recent experience in the classroom and builds on that earlier work. Fosnot and Dolk (2001) point out that in story problems students tend to focus on getting the answer, probably in the way that the teacher wants. "Context problems, on the other hand, are connected as closely as possible to children's lives, rather than to 'school mathematics.' They are designed to anticipate and to develop children's mathematical modeling of the real world" (p. 24). Contextual problems might derive from recent experiences in the classroom, as in the bulletin board problem, or from a field trip, a discussion you have been having in art or social studies, or from children's literature. Students are more likely to exhibit their most spontaneous and meaningful approaches when solving contextual problems because they have some connection to it.

So, what might a good lesson look like for a third-, fourth-, or fifth-grade class that is built around word problems? The tendency in the United States is to have students solve several problems in a single class period, where the focus of the lesson is getting answers. If the focus of the lesson is sense making, solving several problems in one class period might not be the best approach. The answer comes more naturally if you think about students not just solving the problems but also using words, pictures, and numbers to explain how they went about solving the problem and why they think they are correct. Students should be allowed to use whatever physical materials they feel they need to help them, or they can simply draw pictures. Whatever they put on their paper should explain what they did well enough to allow someone else to understand it (allow at least a half page of space for a problem). A complete lesson will often revolve around one or two problems and the related discussion.

Problem Structures for Multiplication and Division

Two types of multiplicative structures involve groups of equal size. These are described in Figure 2.13, *equal groups (repeated addition, rates)* and *multiplicative comparison*. Problems matching these structures can be modeled with sets of counters, number lines, or arrays. They represent a large percentage of the multiplicative problems in the real world. (The term *multiplicative* is used here to describe all problems that involve multiplication and division structure.)

FIGURE 2.13 • • • • • • • • • • • • • •

Two of the four basic structures for multiplication and division story problems. Each structure has three numbers. Any one of the three numbers can be the unknown in a story problem.

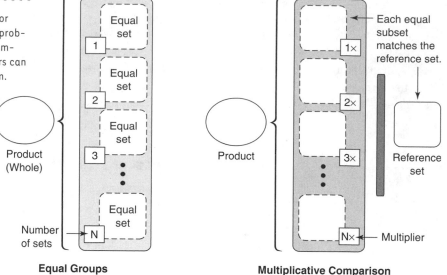

Equal Groups   **Multiplicative Comparison**

These problem structures are not intended for students but will help you as the teacher in formulating and assigning multiplication and division tasks.

Examples of Problems for Each Structure

In multiplicative problems one number or *factor* counts how many sets, groups, or parts of equal size are involved. The other factor tells the size of each set or part. These two factors have traditionally been referred to as the *multiplier* (number of parts) and the *multiplicand* (size of each part). These terms are not particularly useful to students and will not be used here unless needed for clarity. The third number in each of these two structures is the *whole* or *product* and is the total of all of the parts. The parts and wholes terminology is useful in making the connection to addition.

Equal-Group Problems

When the number and size of groups are known, the problem is a multiplication situation. When either the number of sets or the size of sets is unknown, division results. But note that these latter two situations are not alike. Problems in which the size of the sets is unknown are called *fair-sharing* or *partition* problems. The whole is shared or distributed among a known number of sets to determine the size of each. If the number of sets is unknown but the size of the equal sets is known, the problems are called *measurement* or sometimes *repeated-subtraction* problems. The whole is "measured off" in sets of the given size. These terms are used with the examples to follow. Keep in mind the structure in Figure 2.13 to see which numbers are given and which is unknown.

There is also a subtle difference between problems that might be termed *repeated-addition* problems (If 3 children have 4 apples each, how many apples are there?) and those that might be termed *rate* problems (If there are 4 apples per child, how many apples would 3 children have?). For each category, two examples of rate problems are provided.

Equal Groups: Whole Unknown
(Multiplication)

Mark has 4 bags of apples. There are 6 apples in each bag. How many apples does Mark have altogether?

If apples cost 7 cents each, how much did Jill have to pay for 5 apples? (*rate*)

Peter walked for 3 hours at 4 miles per hour. How far did he walk? (*rate*)

Equal Groups: Size of Groups Unknown
(Partition Division)

Mark has 24 apples. He wants to share them equally among his 4 friends. How many apples will each friend receive?

Jill paid 35 cents for 5 apples. What was the cost of 1 apple? (*rate*)

Peter walked 12 miles in 3 hours. How many miles per hour (how fast) did he walk? (*rate*)

Equal Groups: Number of Groups Unknown
(Measurement Division)

Mark has 24 apples. He put them into bags containing 6 apples each. How many bags did Mark use?

Jill bought apples at 7 cents apiece. The total cost of her apples was 35 cents. How many apples did Jill buy? (*rate*)

Peter walked 12 miles at a rate of 4 miles per hour. How many hours did it take Peter to walk the 12 miles? (*rate*)

Multiplicative Comparison Problems

In multiplicative comparison problems, there are really two different sets, as there were with comparison situations for addition and subtraction. One set consists of multiple copies of the other. Two examples of each possibility are provided here. In the former, the comparison is an amount or quantity difference. In multiplicative situations, the comparison is based on one set's being a particular multiple of the other.

Comparison: Product Unknown
(Multiplication)

Jill picked 6 apples. Mark picked 4 times as many apples as Jill. How many apples did Mark pick?

This month Mark saved 5 times as much money as last month. Last month he saved $7. How much money did Mark save this month?

Comparison: Set Size Unknown
(Partition Division)

Mark picked 24 apples. He picked 4 times as many apples as Jill. How many apples did Jill pick?

This month Mark saved 5 times as much money as he did last month. If he saved $35 this month, how much did he save last month?

Comparison: Multiplier Unknown
(Measurement Division)

Mark picked 24 apples, and Jill picked only 6. How many times as many apples did Mark pick as Jill did?

This month Mark saved $35. Last month he saved $7. How many times as much money did he save this month as last?

> **STOP**
>
> What you just read is a lot to take in without reflection. Stop now and get a collection of counters—at least 35. Use the counters to solve each of the problems. In the equal-group problems, do the "Mark problems" or the first problem in each set. Match the numbers with the structure model in Figure 2.13. How are these problems alike and how are they different, especially the two division problems? Repeat the exercise with the "Jill problems" and then the "Peter problems." Can you see how the problems in each group are alike and how the problems across groups are related?
>
> When you are comfortable with the equal-group problems, repeat the same process with the multiplicative comparison problems. Again, start with the first problem in all three sets and then the second problem in all three sets. Reflect on the same questions posed earlier.

Teaching Multiplication and Division

Multiplication and division are taught separately in most traditional programs, with multiplication preceding division. It is important, however, to combine multiplication and division soon after multiplication has been introduced in order to help students see how they are related. In most curricula, these topics are a main focus of the third grade with continued development in the fourth and fifth grades.

One of the major conceptual hurdles of working with multiplicative structures is that of understanding groups of things as single entities while also understanding that a group contains a given number of objects. Students can solve the problem *How many apples in 4 baskets of 8 apples each?* by counting out 4 sets of 8 counters and then counting them all. To think multiplicatively about this problem as 4 *sets of eight* requires students to conceptualize each group of eight as a single item to be counted. Experiences with making and counting groups, especially in contextual situations, are extremely useful.

Symbolism for Multiplication and Division

The usual convention is that 4 × 8 refers to four sets of eight, not eight sets of four. There is absolutely no reason to be rigid about this convention. The important thing is that the students can tell you what each factor in *their* equations represents. In vertical form, it is usually the bottom factor that indicates the number of sets. Again, this distinction is not terribly important.

The quotient 24 divided by 6 is represented in three different ways: 24 ÷ 6, $6\overline{)24}$, and $\frac{24}{6}$. The computational form $6\overline{)24}$ would probably not exist if it were not for the standard pencil-and-paper procedure that utilizes it. Students have a tendency to read this as "6 divided by 24" due to the left-right order of the numerals. Generally this error does not match what they are thinking.

Compounding the difficulty of division notation is the unfortunate phrase, "six goes into twenty-four." This phrase carries little meaning about division, especially in connection with a fair-sharing or partitioning context. The "goes into" (or "guzinta") terminology is simply engrained in adult parlance and has not been in textbooks for years. If you tend to use that phrase, it is probably a good time to consciously abandon it.

Choosing Numbers for Problems

When selecting numbers for multiplicative story problems or activities, there is a tendency to think that large numbers pose a burden to students or that 3 × 4 is somehow easier to understand than 4 × 17. Conceptually, products or quotients are not affected by the size of numbers as long as the numbers are within the grasp of the students. Little is gained by restricting early explorations of multiplication to small numbers. Even in early third grade, students can work with larger numbers using whatever counting strategies they have at their disposal. A contextual problem involving 14 × 8 is not at all too large for third graders even before they have learned a computation technique. When given these challenges, students are likely to invent computational strategies.

Remainders

More often than not, division does not result in a simple whole number. For example, problems with 6 as a divisor will "come out even" only one time out of six. In the absence of a context, a remainder can be dealt with in only two ways: It can either remain a quantity left over or be partitioned into fractions. In Figure 2.14, the problem 11 ÷ 4 is modeled to show fractions.

In real contexts, remainders sometimes have three additional effects on answers:

The remainder is discarded, leaving a smaller whole-number answer.

The remainder can "force" the answer to the next highest whole number.

The answer is rounded to the nearest whole number for an approximate result.

The following problems illustrate all five possibilities.

Partition $11 \div 4 = 2\frac{3}{4}$
$2\frac{3}{4}$ in each of the 4 sets
(each leftover divided in fourths)

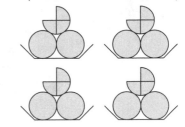

Measurement $11 \div 4 = 2\frac{3}{4}$
$2\frac{3}{4}$ sets of 4
(2 full sets and $\frac{3}{4}$ of a set)

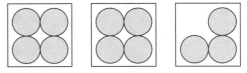

FIGURE 2.14 • • • • • • • • • • • • • • •

Remainders expressed as fractions.

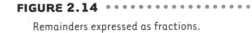

DEVELOPING MULTIPLICATION AND DIVISION OPERATION SENSE

You have 30 pieces of candy to share fairly with 7 children. How many pieces of candy will each child receive?

Answer: 4 pieces of candy and 2 left over. (*left over*)

Each jar holds 8 ounces of liquid. If there are 46 ounces in the pitcher, how many jars will that be?

Answer: 5 and $\frac{6}{8}$ jars. (*partitioned as a fraction*)

The rope is 25 feet long. How many 7-foot jump ropes can be made?

Answer: 3 jump ropes. (*discarded*)

The ferry can hold 8 cars. How many trips will it have to make to carry 25 cars across the river?

Answer: 4 trips. (*forced to next whole number*)

Six children are planning to share a bag of 50 pieces of bubble gum. About how many pieces will each child get?

Answer: About 8 pieces for each child. (*rounded, approximate result*)

Students should not just think of remainders as "R 3" or "left over." Remainders should be put in context and dealt with accordingly.

It is useful for you to make up problems in different contexts. Include continuous quantities such as length, time, and volume. See if you can come up with problems in each division category for equal-group and comparison problems that would have remainders dealt with as fractions or as rounded-up or rounded-down results.

Using Models-Based Problems

In the beginning, students will be able to use the same models—sets and number lines—for all four operations. A model not generally used for addition but extremely important and widely used for multiplication and division is the array. An *array* is any arrangement of things in rows and columns, such as a rectangle of square tiles or blocks.

To make clear the connection to addition, early multiplication activities should also include writing an addition sentence for the same model. A variety of models are shown in Figure 2.15. Notice that the products are not included—only addition and multiplication "names" are written. This is another way to avoid the tedious counting of large sets. A similar approach is to write one sentence that expresses both concepts at once, for example, $9 + 9 + 9 + 9 = 4 \times 9$.

Multiplication and Division Activities

Students can benefit from a few activities with models and no context. The purpose of such activities is to focus on the meaning of the operation and the associated symbolism. Activities 2.22 and 2.23 have a good problem-solving spirit. The language you use depends on what you have used with your students in the past.

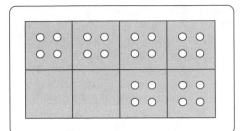

$6 \times 4 = 4 + 4 + 4 + 4 + 4 + 4$

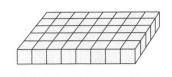

FIGURE 2.15 • • • • • • • • • • • • • • •

Models for equal-group multiplication.

$5 \times 3 = 3 + 3 + 3 + 3 + 3$

$5 \times 8 = 8 + 8 + 8 + 8 + 8$

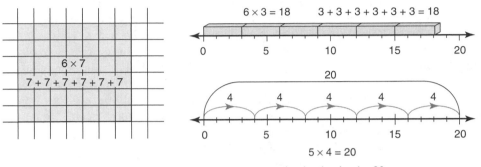

6×7

$7 + 7 + 7 + 7 + 7 + 7$

$6 \times 3 = 18 \qquad 3 + 3 + 3 + 3 + 3 + 3 = 18$

20

$5 \times 4 = 20$

$4 + 4 + 4 + 4 + 4 = 20$

ACTIVITY 2.22

Finding Factors

Start by assigning a number that has several factors—for example, 12, 18, 24, 30, or 36. Have students find multiplication expressions for their assigned number. With counters, students attempt to find a way to separate the counters into equal subsets. With arrays (perhaps made from square tiles or cubes or drawn on grid paper), students try to build rectangles that have the given number of squares. For each such arrangement of sets or appropriate rectangles, a multiplication equation should be written.

Make sure to draw students' attention to the dimensions of the rectangles (length and width). You want students to make the connection that the factors in the multiplication expression they have written indicate the number of rows and columns (the dimensions) in a rectangle that consist of the given number of squares. Your class will undoubtedly want to decide if a rectangle that is 3 by 8 should be counted differently from one that is 8 by 3. Leave the decision to the class but take advantage of the opportunity to discuss how 3 rows of 8 are the same as 8 rows of 3. Note that if sets rather than arrays are made, 3 sets of 8 look very different from 8 sets of 3.

The next activity is an extension of "Finding Factors" in that students look for patterns in the factors they find for numbers, such as the number of factors, the type of factors, the shape of the resulting array, and so on. Rather than always assigning numbers that have several factors, this activity suggests including numbers that have only a few factors so that differences between numbers become more distinct.

DEVELOPING MULTIPLICATION AND DIVISION OPERATION SENSE

BLMs 8, 9

Factor Patterns

Tell students that they are going to look for multiplication expressions and the corresponding rectangular array for several numbers (e.g., 1 through 16 or 10 through 25). Their task includes trying to find *all* the multiplication expressions and rectangular arrays for each number. Have square tiles available that students can use to explore possible arrays. They are to record their rectangles on grid paper (see the Blackline Masters) and label each rectangle with the number of squares and a multiplication equation. Students should group together all arrays with the same number of squares. This organization helps when students are comparing arrays across different numbers. After identifying the multiplication expressions and the rectangular arrays, students are to look for patterns in the factors and rectangular arrays. For example, which numbers have the least number of arrays and, therefore, the least number of factors? Which numbers have a factor of 2? Which numbers have arrays that form a square? What can you say about the factors for even numbers? Do even numbers always have 2 even factors? What about odd numbers? Encourage students to think about why different patterns occur.

Activities 2.22 and 2.23 can also include division concepts. When students have learned that 3 and 6 are factors of 18, they can write the equations $18 \div 3 = 6$ and $18 \div 6 = 3$ along with $3 \times 6 = 18$ and $6 + 6 + 6 = 18$ (assuming that three sets of six were modeled). The following variation of these activities focuses on division. Having students create word problems is another excellent elaboration of this activity. Require students to explain how their story problems fit with what they did with the counters.

Learning About Division

Provide students with an ample supply of counters and some way to place them into small groups. Small paper cups work well. Have students count out a number of counters to be the whole or total set. They record this number: "Start with 31." Next specify either the number of equal sets to be made or the size of the sets to be made: "Separate your counters into four equal-sized sets," or "Make as many sets of four as is possible." Next, have the students write the corresponding multiplication equation for what their materials show; under that, have them write the division equation.

Be sure to include both types of exercises: number of equal sets and size of sets. Discuss with the class how these two are different, yet each is related to multiplication and each is written as a division equation. You can show both ways to write division equations at this time. Do Activity 2.24 several times. Start with whole quantities that are multiples of the divisor (no remainders) but soon include situations with remainders. (Note that it is technically incorrect to write $31 \div 4 = 7$ R 3. However, in the beginning, that form may be the most appropriate to use.)

The activity can be varied by changing the model. Have students build arrays using square tiles or blocks or by having them draw arrays on grid paper. Present the exercises by specifying how many squares are to be in the array. You can then specify the number of rows that should be made (partition) or the length of each row (measurement). How could students model fractional answers using drawings of arrays on grid paper?

ACTIVITY 2.25

The Broken Multiplication Key

The calculator is a good way to relate multiplication to addition. Students can be told to find various products on the calculator without using the ⊠ key. For example, 6 × 4 can be found by pressing ⊞ 4 ⊟ ⊟ ⊟ ⊟ ⊟ ⊟. (Successive presses of ⊟ add 4 to the display each time. You began with zero and added 4 six times.) Students can be challenged to demonstrate their result with sets of counters. But note that this same technique can be used to determine products such as 23 × 459 (⊞ 459 and then 23 presses of ⊟). Students will want to compare to the same product using the ⊠ key.

"The Broken Multiplication Key" can profitably be followed by "The Broken Division Key."

ACTIVITY 2.26

The Broken Division Key

Have students work in groups to find methods of using the calculator to solve division exercises without using the divide key. The problems can be posed without a story context. "Find at least two ways to figure out 61 ÷ 14 without pressing the divide key." If the problem is put in a story context, one method may actually match the problem better than another. Good discussions may follow different solutions with the same answers. Are they both correct? Why or why not?

STOP There is no reason ever to show students how to do Activity 2.26. However, it would be a good idea for *you* to see if you can find *three* ways to solve 61 ÷ 14 on a calculator without using the divide key. For a hint, see the footnote.*

Assessment Note

A good way to check on students' understanding of the operations is to provide several story problems with different operations. It is not necessary to do this all on one day. Have students work on two or three problems a day over the course of a week. If your objective is to find out about their understanding of the operations, you can focus on this by not having them actually do the computations. Rather, have them indicate what operations they would use and with what numbers. To avoid guessing, have students draw a picture to explain why they chose the operations that they did.

---

*There are two measurement approaches or two ways to find out how many 14s are in 61. A third way is essentially related to partitioning or finding 14 times what number is close to 61.

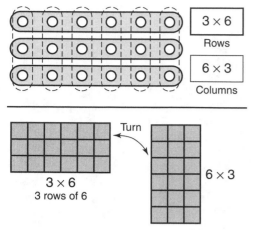

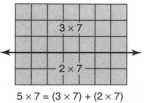

FIGURE 2.16 • • • • • • • • • • • • • • • • • •

Two ways an array can be used to illustrate the order (commutative) property of multiplication.

Useful Multiplication and Division Properties

There are some multiplicative properties that are useful and, thus, worthy of attention. The emphasis should be on the ideas and not terminology or definitions.

The Order Property in Multiplication

It is not intuitively obvious that 3 × 8 is the same as 8 × 3 or that, in general, the order of the numbers makes no difference (the *order* or *commutative* property). A picture of 3 sets of 8 objects cannot immediately be seen as 8 piles of 3 objects. Eight hops of 3 land at 24, but it is not clear that 3 hops of 8 will land at the same point.

The array, by contrast, is quite powerful in illustrating the order property, as is shown in Figure 2.16. Students should draw or build arrays and use them to demonstrate why each array represents two different multiplications with the same product.

The Role of Zero and One in Multiplication

Zero and, to a lesser extent, 1 as factors often cause difficulty for students. In a third-grade text (Charles et al., 1998), a lesson on factors of 0 and 1 has children use a calculator to examine a wide range of products involving 0 or 1 (423 × 0, 0 × 28, 1536 × 1, etc.) and look for patterns. The pattern suggests the rules for factors of 0 and 1 but not a reason. In the same lesson, a word problem asks how many grams of fat there are in 7 servings of celery with 0 grams of fat in each serving. This approach is far preferable to an arbitrary rule, since it asks students to reason. Make up interesting word problems involving 0 or 1, and discuss the results. Problems with 0 as a first factor are really strange. Note that on a number line, 5 hops of 0 land at 0 (5 × 0). What would 0 hops of 5 be? Another fun activity is to try to model 6 × 0 or 0 × 8 with an array. (Try it!) Arrays for factors of 1 are also worth investigating.

The Distributive Property

The *distributive* property is very useful in relating one basic fact to another, and it is also involved in the development of two-digit computation. Figure 2.17 illustrates how the array model can be used to illustrate that a product can be broken up into two parts.

The next activity is designed to help students discover how to partition factors or, in other words, learn about the distributive property.

$4 \times 9 = (4 \times 6) + (4 \times 3)$

$5 \times 7 = (3 \times 7) + (2 \times 7)$

FIGURE 2.17 • • • • • • • •

Models for the distributive property.

ACTIVITY 2.27

Slice It Up

Supply students with several sheets of centimeter grid paper (see Blackline Master 6). Assign each pair of students a product such as 6 × 8. (Products can vary across the class or all be the same.) The task is to find all of the different ways to make a single slice through the rectangle. For each slice students write an equation. For a slice of one row of 8, students would write 6 × 8 = 5 × 8 + 1 × 8. The individual products can be written in the arrays as was done in Figure 2.17.

Why Not Division by Zero?

Students are often simply told "Division by zero is not allowed." To avoid an arbitrary rule, pose problems to be modeled that involve zero: "Take thirty counters. How many sets of zero can be made?" or "Put twelve blocks in zero equal groups. How many in each group?"

Solving Contextual Problems

We have suggested the use of contextual problems or story problems to help students develop meanings for multiplication and division. However, in the upper grades (although not exclusively so) students see context or story problems and are often at a loss for what to do.

Assessment Note

What do you do if a student is having difficulty solving word problems? The first thing is to find out what is causing the difficulty. If you can't tell from the student's written efforts or from observation, a short interview is highly recommended. Prepare some problems written out on paper, one problem to the page. Provide appropriate physical materials (e.g., counters, square tiles, grid paper, etc.), but encourage the student to use whatever she wishes in order to solve the problem. Explain that you want to hear what she is thinking so that you will know how to help her. Do not make the session too long. Remember that the purpose of your interview is to gain insight into the student's difficulties. Use this information to prepare problems or other tasks for a later lesson. Do not use the interview as a time to intervene or teach!

When a student does not seem to know what to do with a problem, a simple yet effective suggestion is to have him work through the story problem sentence by sentence. With each sentence, have him describe how the information provided impacts the situation. If appropriate, have him use physical materials or models to act out the problem. Have him describe what the physical materials or models stand for and explain with them what is happening in the problem. This can help the student with similar analyses when you are not there to make these suggestions.

There are many reasons why students may have difficulties with number or computation that have nothing to do with understanding the problem. Many students simply do not have the computational skills but try to use techniques for which they are not ready. If you suspect this, have the student work on similar computations without story problems. Make the use of models completely optional. Be sure to have her explain what she did and to use drawings to support her explanation. Most importantly, help the student to focus on number relationships to improve computational skill.

The student's difficulty may arise from the size of the numbers used in the problem. If you suspect this is the difficulty, adjust the numbers in the problems so that the numbers are within her comfort range. However, avoid making the numbers so easy that they are insulting.

Following are some additional ideas for helping students approach word problems.

Analyzing Context Problems

Consider the following problem:

> **In building the road through the subdivision, a low section in the land was filled in with dirt that was hauled in by trucks. The complete fill required 638 truckloads of dirt. The average truck carried $6\frac{1}{4}$ cubic yards of dirt, which weighed 17.3 tons. How many tons of dirt were used in the fill?**

Typically, in fifth-grade books, problems of this type are found as part of a series of problems revolving around a single context or theme. Data may be found in a graph or chart or perhaps a short news item or story. Most likely the problems will include all four of the operations. Students have difficulty deciding on the correct operation and even finding the appropriate data for the problem. Many students will find two numbers in the problem and guess at the correct operation. These students simply do not have any tools for analyzing problems. At least two strategies can be taught that are very helpful: Think about the answer before solving the problem, or solve a simpler problem that is just like this one.

Think About the Answer Before Solving the Problem

Poor problem solvers fail to spend adequate time thinking about the problem and what it is about. They rush in and begin doing calculations, believing that "number crunching" is what solves problems. That is simply not the case. Rather, students should spend time talking about (later, thinking about) what the answer might look like. For our sample problem, it might go as follows:

What is happening in this problem? Some trucks were bringing dirt in to fill up a hole.

What will the answer tell us? How many tons of dirt were needed in the fill.

Will that be a small number of tons or a large number of tons? Well, there were 17.3 tons on a truck, but there were a lot of trucks, not just one. It's probably going to be a whole lot of tons.

About how many do you think it will be? It's going to be really big. If there were just 100 trucks, it would be 1730 tons. It might be close to 10,000 tons. That's a lot of tons!

In this type of discussion, three things are happening. First, the students are asked to focus on the problem and the meaning of the answer instead of on numbers. The numbers are not important in thinking about the structure of the problem. Second, with a focus on the structure of the problem, students can identify the numbers that are important or data that they must look up in a table or graph as well as numbers that are not important to the problem. Third, the thinking leads to a rough estimate of the answer. Sometimes, for everyday things, this can simply be based on common sense. In any event, thinking about what the answer tells and about how large it might be is a useful first step.

Work a Simpler Problem

The reason that models are rarely used with problems such as the dirt problem is that the numbers are impossible to model easily. Dollars and cents, distances in thousands of miles, and time in minutes and seconds are all examples of data likely to be found in the upper grades, and all are difficult to model. The general problem-solving strategy of "try a simpler problem" can almost always be applied to problems with unwieldy numbers.

A simple strategy has the following steps:

1. Substitute small whole numbers for all relevant numbers in the problem.
2. Model the problem using the new numbers (counters, drawing, number line, array).
3. Write an equation that solves the small-number version of the problem.
4. Write the corresponding equation with the original numbers used where the small-number substitutes were.
5. Use a calculator to do the computation.
6. Write the answer in a complete sentence, and decide if it makes sense.

Figure 2.18 shows what might be done for the dirt problem. It also shows an alternative in which only one of the numbers is made smaller and the other number is illustrated symbolically. Both methods are effective.

The idea is to provide a tool students can use to analyze a problem and not just guess at what computation to do. It is much more useful to have students do a few problems where they must use a model of a drawing to justify their solution than to give them a lot of problems where they guess at a solution but don't know if their guess is correct.

Caution: Avoid the Key Word Strategy!

It is often suggested that students should be taught to find "key words" in story problems. Some teachers even post lists of key words with their corresponding meanings. For example, "altogether" and "in all" mean you should add and "left"

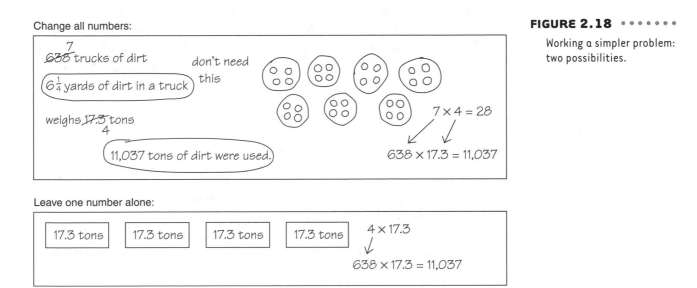

FIGURE 2.18 • • • • • • •

Working a simpler problem: two possibilities.

and "fewer" indicate you should subtract. The word "each" suggests multiplication. To some extent, teachers have been reinforced by the overly simple and formulaic story problems often found in textbooks. When problems are written in this way, it may appear that the key word strategy is effective.

In contrast with this belief, researchers and mathematics educators have long cautioned against the strategy of key words. Here are three arguments against the key word approach.

1. Key words are misleading. Often the key word or phrase in a problem suggests an operation that is incorrect. For example:

Maxine took the 28 stickers she no longer wanted and gave them to Zandra. Now Maxine has 73 stickers *left*. How many stickers did Maxine have to begin with?

2. Many problems have no key words. Especially when you get away from the overly simple problems found in primary textbooks, you will find that a large percentage of problems have no key words. A student who has been taught to rely on key words is left with no strategy. In the multiplicative problems in this chapter, you will find numerous examples of problems with no key words. And this is from a collection of overly simple problems designed to help you with structure.
3. The key word strategy sends a terribly wrong message about doing mathematics. The most important approach to solving any contextual problem is to analyze its structure—to make sense of it. The key word approach encourages students to ignore the meaning and structure of the problem and look for an easy way out. Mathematics is about reasoning and making sense of situations. A sense-making strategy will *always* work.

Two-Step Problems

Students often have difficulty with multistep problems. If your students are going to work with multistep problems, be sure they can analyze one-step problems in the way that we have discussed. The following ideas, adapted from suggestions by Huinker (1994), are designed to help children see how two problems can be chained together.

1. Give students a one-step problem and have them solve it. Before discussing the answer, have each student or group make up a second problem that uses the answer to the first problem. The rest of the class can then be asked to use the answer to the first problem to solve the second problem. Here is an example:

Given problem: It took $3\frac{1}{3}$ hours for the Joneses to drive the 195 miles to Washington. What was their average speed?

Second problem: The Jones children remember crossing the river at about 10:30, or 2 hours after they left home. About how far from home is the river?

2. Make a "hidden question." Repeat the first exercise by beginning with a one-step problem. You might give different problems to different groups. This time, have students write out both problems as before. Then write a single related problem that leaves out the question from the first problem. That question from the first problem is the "hidden question." Here is a simple example:

Given problem: Tony bought three dozen eggs for 89 cents a dozen. How much was the bill?

Second problem: How much change did Tony get back from $5?

Hidden-question problem: Tony bought three dozen eggs for 89 cents a dozen. How much change did Tony get back from $5?

Have other students identify the hidden question. Since all students are working on a similar task but with different problems (be sure to mix the operations), they will be more likely to understand what is meant by a hidden question.

3. Pose standard two-step problems, and have the students identify and answer the hidden question. Consider the following problem:

Willard Sales decides to add widgets to its line of sale items. To begin with, Willard bought 275 widgets wholesale for $3.69 each. In the first month, the company sold 205 widgets at $4.99 each. How much did Willard make or lose on the widgets? Do you think Willard Sales should continue to sell widgets?

Begin by considering the questions that were suggested earlier: "What's happening in this problem?" (Something is being bought and sold at two different prices.) "What will the answer tell us?" (How much profit or loss there was.) These questions will get you started. If students are stuck, you can ask, "Is there a hidden question in this problem?"

EXPANDED LESSON

Close, Far, and in Between

Based on: Activity 2.6, p. 45

GRADE LEVEL: Third or fourth grade.

MATHEMATICS GOALS

- To develop number sense through thinking about relative magnitude of numbers.
- To develop strategies for mental mathematics.

THINKING ABOUT THE STUDENTS

Students should have had experience pulling smaller numbers apart to do addition and subtraction (e.g., to add 18 and 25, they can think, "Take two away from 25 and add that to 18 to get 20. 20 + 23 is 43"). That is, students are familiar with using 5 and 10 as benchmarks. Students are also familiar with using a number line.

MATERIALS AND PREPARATION:

- There are no materials to prepare for this lesson.
- You will need to think ahead of time about the numbers that you will use. (See "The Task.")

lesson

BEFORE

Begin with a simpler version of the task:

- On the chalkboard or overhead, write the numbers 27, 83, and 62.
- Draw a number line on the chalkboard or overhead and label the points for 0 and 100. Ask a student to come forward and place one of the numbers on the number line and explain why he or she placed the number in that location. Ask the class if they agree or disagree with the placement and the reasoning. Discuss as needed. Repeat this process for the other two numbers.
- Ask questions such as these: *Which number is closest to 50? Which two numbers are closest? How far apart are 27 and 100, 62 and 100, and 83 and 100?* With each question, give students time to think individually. Then ask students to share their ideas and strategies for doing these comparisons. The methods that they use will be quite varied. Therefore, do not stop with the ideas from just a single student. Look for students who are breaking numbers apart and using tens rather than simply subtracting numbers to find the difference.

The Task

You will need to decide on three numbers for students to compare. The numbers can be chosen purposefully to either assess the understanding of a particular idea or to increase the likelihood that students will grapple with a particular idea or strategy. For example, if students have not yet explicitly used the notion of using hundreds as a benchmark, the numbers chosen might be 298, 402, and 318. Because 298 is so close to 300 and 402 is so close to 400, at least some students will use this idea to compare 298 and 402 to each other and the third number. For this lesson, we will use 219, 457, and 364.

Write the numbers 219, 457, and 364 on the board along with the following:

The task is to answer these questions:

- Which two are closest? Why?
- Which is closest to 300? To 250?
- About how far apart are 219 and 500? 219 and 5000?

Establish Expectations

Students are to explain how they answered the questions using words, numbers, and/or a number line, so that they can remember what they did and be ready to discuss their ideas with the class.

DURING

- For students who are having difficulty getting started, suggest that they use the number line as an aid to identify benchmarks such as 200 or 450. Once the students have identified possible benchmarks, ask them how they might use a benchmark to get closer to one of the numbers. Give no more assistance than is absolutely necessary to get students started.
- Look for different strategies students are using so that you can highlight the variety of ways to think about comparing numbers.
- For students who finish quickly, ask them questions about finding particular multiples between given numbers (e.g., *Name a multiple of 25 between 219 and 364*).

AFTER

- Ask students to share their strategies for responding to each question. Record ideas on the board in a manner that illustrates students' thinking.
- As students share, you might have to ask questions to either slow down a student's explanation so that classmates have a chance to process the ideas or to make explicit a subtle idea that you want students to think about.
- Do not evaluate the strategy but ask students if they agree and understand the strategy and if they have questions. Allow other students to offer ideas for the same question.
- As new strategies emerge, ask students to compare and contrast them to strategies already shared. The discussion might pertain to which strategies seem quicker or more efficient and why or how various strategies use the notion of place value and/or benchmarks.

ASSESSMENT NOTES

- Look for students who are simply counting up or down by ones to determine how far away numbers are from each other. They likely need more work with using 5 and 10 (which includes multiples of 5 and 10) as benchmarks to move between numbers.
- Are students using a variety of strategies depending on the numbers or do they always use the same strategy? Being able to develop and use different strategies is evidence of number sense as well as the ability to think flexibly.
- Many students will simply subtract numbers with pencil and paper. Encourage them to find methods that do not involve subtraction.

* * *

next steps

- If students are having difficulty with three-digit numbers, use either two-digit numbers or three-digit numbers that are exact multiples of 50 (e.g., 250, 400, 550). Continue to offer the number line as one tool to use in comparing numbers. Another tool that might be useful when comparing two-digit numbers is a hundreds chart (see Blackline Master 6).
- For related work on number sense, try Activities 2.4 and 2.5, "Who Am I?" and "Who Could They Be?"

- For students who relied heavily on the number line to reason about the comparisons, encourage them to move toward more mental approaches. In these approaches, the students may still talk about "seeing" the number line, but they are not using a physical number line to make the comparisons.
- For students who are ready for a challenge, begin comparisons of numbers in the thousands.

EXPANDED LESSON

HELPING CHILDREN MASTER THE BASIC FACTS

Basic facts for addition and multiplication refer to combinations in which both addends or both factors are less than 10. Subtraction facts can and should be related to the corresponding addition facts, although this is not always done well in traditional curricula. Division facts are likewise closely related to multiplication facts. In contrast with subtraction facts, the multiplication–division connection is generally made quite well. Fluency with the basic facts is developed through a strong understanding of the four operations and an emphasis on conceptual strategies for retrieving the facts.

Mastery of a basic fact means that a child can give a quick response (in about 3 seconds) without resorting to nonefficient means, such as counting. All children are able to master the basic facts—including children with learning disabilities. They simply need to construct efficient mental tools that will help them, which is what this chapter is about.

big ideas

1 Number relationships provide the foundation for strategies that help students remember basic facts. For example, knowing how numbers are related to 5 and 10 helps students master facts such as 3 + 5 (think of a ten-frame) and 8 + 6 (since 8 is 2 away from 10, take 2 from 6 to make 10 + 4 = 14).

2 "Think addition" is the most powerful way to think of subtraction facts. Rather than 13 "take away 6," which requires a lot of counting, students can think 6 and what makes 13. They might add up to 10 or they may think double 6 is 12 so it must be 13.

3 All of the facts are conceptually related. You can figure out new or unknown facts from those you already know. For example, 6 × 8 can be thought of as five 8s (40) and one more 8. It might also be three 8s doubled.

From Concepts and Strategies to Fact Mastery

Every teacher of grades 4 to 10 knows students who are still counting on their fingers, making marks in the margins to count on, or simply guessing at answers. These students have certainly been given more than adequate opportunity to drill their facts in years past. They have not mastered their facts because they have not developed efficient methods of producing a fact answer. Drill of inefficient methods does not produce mastery!

Fortunately, we know quite a bit about helping children develop fact mastery, and it has little to do with quantity of drill or drill techniques. Three components or steps to this end can be identified:

1. Help children develop a strong understanding of number relationships of the operations.
2. Develop efficient strategies for fact retrieval through practice.
3. Then provide drill in the use and selection of those strategies once they have been developed.

The Role of Number and Operation Concepts

Number relationships play a significant role in fact mastery. The 8 + 6 example in the first big idea requires the relationship between 8 and 10 (8 is 2 away from 10), the part-part-whole knowledge of 6 (2 and 4 more makes 6), and the fact that 10 and 4 is 14. For 6 × 7, it is efficient to think "5 times 7 and 7 more." For many children, the efficiency of this approach is lost because they need to count on 7 to get from 35 to 42. With an extension of the number relationships just noted, it is possible to think "35 and 5 more is 40, and 2 more is 42." Every relationship discussed in Chapter 2 can contribute to fact mastery.

The meanings of the operations also play a role in the construction of efficient strategies. The ability to relate 6 × 7 to "5 times 7 and 7 more" is based on an understanding of the meanings of the first and second factors. To relate 13 − 7 to "7 and what makes 13" requires an understanding of how addition and subtraction are related. The commutative or "turnaround" properties for addition and multiplication reduce the number of addition and multiplication facts from 100 each to 55 each.

Teachers in the upper grades with students who have not mastered basic facts will do well to investigate what command of number relationships and operations the students have. Without these relationships and concepts, the strategies discussed throughout this chapter will be difficult.

Development of Efficient Strategies

An efficient strategy is one that can be done mentally and quickly. The emphasis is on *efficient*. Counting is not efficient. If drill is undertaken when counting is the only strategy available, all you get is faster counting.

What Is a Strategy?

We have already seen some efficient strategies: the use of building up through 10 in adding 8 + 6 and the use of the related fact 5 × 7 to help with 6 × 7.

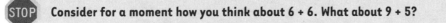 **STOP**   **Consider for a moment how you think about 6 + 6. What about 9 + 5?**

You may think that you just "know" these. What is more likely is that you used some ideas similar to double six (for 6 + 6) and 10 and 4 more (for 9 + 5). Your response may be so automatic by now that you are not reflecting on the use of these

FROM CONCEPTS AND STRATEGIES TO FACT MASTERY

relationships or ideas. That is one of the features of efficient mental processes—they become automatic with use.

Many students have learned basic facts without being taught efficient strategies. They develop or learn many of these methods in spite of the drill they may have endured. The trouble is that far too many students do not develop strategies without instruction and far too many students in middle school continue to count on their fingers. The challenge for teachers is to devise lessons in which all students will develop strategies that are useful. A strategy is most useful to students when it is theirs, built on and connected to concepts and relationships they already own.

For your students to develop effective strategies, you yourself need to have a command of as many good strategies as possible, even if you have never used them. This will help you recognize your students' invented strategies and capitalize on those ideas.

Two Approaches to Fact Strategies

You need to plan lessons or short activities in which specific strategies are likely to be developed. There are two basic types of lessons suggested for this purpose. The first is to use simple story problems designed in such a manner that students are most likely to develop a strategy as they solve it. In the discussion of these solution methods, you can focus attention on the methods that are most useful. You can have all students try the methods others have developed.

A second possible approach is a bit more direct. A lesson may revolve around a special collection of facts for which a particular type of strategy is appropriate. You can discuss how these facts might all be alike in some way, or you might suggest an approach and see if students are able to use it on similar facts.

There is a huge temptation simply to tell students about a strategy and then have them practice it. Though this can be effective for some students, many others will not personally relate to your ideas or may not be ready for them. Continue to discuss strategies invented in your class and plan lessons that encourage strategies.

Drill of Efficient Methods and Strategy Selection

It is appropriate here to make a distinction between drill and practice. Practice refers to problem-based activities in which students are encouraged to develop (invent, consider, try—but not master) flexible and useful strategies that are meaningful. The types of lessons just described can be thought of as practice lessons. Whether from story problems or from consideration of a collection of similar facts, students are wrestling with the development of strategies that they can use themselves.

Drill refers to repetitive non-problem-based activity. Drill activity is appropriate for students who have a strategy that they understand, like, and know how to use but have not yet become facile with it. Drill with an in-place strategy focuses students' attention on that strategy and helps to make it more automatic.

Drill plays a significant role in fact mastery, and the use of old-fashioned methods such as flash cards and fact games can be effective if used wisely.

Avoid Premature Drill

It is critical that you do not introduce drill too soon. Suppose that a student does not know the 4 × 6 fact and has no way to deal with it other than to begin to skip count, 6, 12, and then continue to count fingers by ones to get to 24. This is an inefficient method. Premature drill introduces no new information and encourages no new connections. It is both a waste of time and a frustration to the child.

As you read through this chapter, you may feel that the strategies for some facts, especially the harder multiplication facts, do not seem to be efficient at all. However, as long as the strategy is completely mental and does not rely on a model, picture, or tedious counting, repeated use of the strategy will almost certainly render it automatic. The strategy provides a mental path from fact to answer. Soon the fact and answer are "connected" as the strategy becomes almost unconscious.

The discussion in this chapter focuses on one strategy at a time. It is not at all unreasonable for students to be engaged in drill activities with one strategy before they have developed (via practice or problem-based activity) strategies for other facts.

Many of the activities suggested in the chapter are simple drills—flash cards, matching games, dice, or spinner activities—in which the objective is quick response. Do not misinterpret these activities that are clearly drills as the way to introduce or develop strategies. Drill should only be used when an efficient strategy is in place.

Practice Strategy Selection or Strategy Retrieval

Strategy selection or *strategy retrieval* is the process of deciding what strategy is appropriate for a particular fact. If you don't think to use a strategy, you probably won't. Many teachers who have tried teaching fact strategies report that the method works well while the students are focused on whatever strategy they are working on. They acknowledge that students can learn and use strategies. But, they continue, when the facts are all mixed up or the student is not in "fact practice" mode, old counting habits return.

For example, suppose that your students have been practicing the near-doubles facts for addition: Use the better-known double, 7 + 7, to derive the unknown 8 + 7. Students become quite skilled at doubling the smaller number and adding 1. All of the facts they are practicing are selected to fit this model. On other days, they have learned and practiced other strategies. Later, on a worksheet or in a mental math exercise, the children are presented with a mixture of facts. In a single exercise, a child might see

$$
\begin{array}{cccc}
7 & 4 & 2 & 8 \\
+\,6 & +\,9 & +\,6 & +\,5 \\
\end{array}
$$

There is no mind-set or reminder to use different processes for each. Especially if the children have previously been habituated to counting to get answers, they will very likely revert to counting and ignore the efficient methods that were the focus of recent drills. When they were drilling the strategy, there was no need to decide what strategy might be useful. All of the facts in the near-doubles practice were near-doubles, and the strategy worked. Later, however, there is no one to suggest the strategy.

A simple activity that is useful is to prepare a list of facts selected from two or more strategies and then, one fact at a time, ask students to name a strategy that would work for that fact. They should explain why they picked the strategy and demonstrate its use. This type of activity turns the attention to the features of a fact that lend it to this or that strategy.

Overview of the Approach

For each particular strategy, from development to eventual drill when the strategy is well understood, the general approach for instruction is very similar.

Make Strategies Explicit in the Classroom

As has been discussed, your students will develop strategies as they solve word problems or as they investigate a category of facts you present. When a student suggests a new strategy, be certain that everyone else in the room understands how it is used. Suppose that Helen explains how she figured out 3 × 7 by starting with double 7 (14) and then adding 7 more. She knew that 6 more onto 14 is 20 and one more is 21. You can ask another student to explain what Helen just shared. This requires students to attend to ideas that come from their classmates. Now explore with the class to see what other facts would work with Helen's strategy. This discussion may go in a variety of directions. Some may notice that all of the facts with a 3 in them will work. Others may say that you can always add one more set on if you know the smaller fact. For example, for 6 × 8 you can start with 5 × 8 and add 8.

Don't expect to have a strategy introduced and understood with just one word problem or one exposure such as this. Try on several successive days problems in which the same type of strategy might be used. Students need lots of opportunities to make a strategy their own. Many students will simply not be ready to use an idea the first few days, and then all of a sudden something will click and a useful idea will be theirs.

It is a good idea to write new strategies on the board or make a poster of strategies students develop. Give the strategies names that make sense. (*Double and add one more set. Helen's idea. Use with 3s.* Include an example.)

No student should be forced to adopt someone else's strategy, but every student should be required to understand strategies that are brought to the discussion.

Drill Established Strategies

When you are comfortable that children are able to use a strategy without recourse to skip counting and that they are beginning to use it mentally, it is time to drill it. You might have as many as ten different activities for each strategy or group of facts. File folder or boxed activities can be used by students individually, in pairs, or even in small groups. With a large number of activities, students can work on strategies they understand and on the facts that they need the most.

Flash cards are among the most useful approaches to fact strategy practice. For each strategy, make several sets of flash cards using all of the facts that fit that strategy. On the cards, you can label the strategy or use drawings or cues to remind the children of the strategy. Examples appear throughout the chapter.

Other activities involve the use of special dice made from wooden cubes or foam rubber, teacher-made spinners, matching activities in which a helping fact or a relationship is matched with the new fact being learned, and games of all sorts. A game or drill suggested for one strategy can usually be adapted to another.

Individualize

To some extent, you want to individualize drills in such a way that students are using their preferred strategy in the drills. This is not as difficult as it may seem at first.

Different students will likely invent or adopt different strategies for the same collection of facts. For example, there are several methods or strategies that use 10 when adding 8 or 9. Therefore, a drill that includes all of the addition facts with an 8 or a 9 can accommodate any child who has a strategy for that collection. Two children can be playing a spinner drill game, each using different strategies.

It is imperative that you listen to your students. Keep track of what strategies different students are using. This will help you occasionally create groups of students that can all benefit from the same drills. This will also help you know which students have yet to develop an efficient strategy for one or more collection of facts. If you are not sure who knows what facts, gather small groups of students to take a diagnostic test, a simple fact test with facts mixed randomly. Explain that you want them to first answer only those facts that they "know" without any counting. Then they should go back and attempt the unknown facts. Listen to find out how they approach these strategies.

Practice Strategy Selection

After students have worked on two or three strategies, strategy selection drills are very important. These can be conducted quickly with the full class or a group, or independent games and activities can be prepared. Examples are described toward the end of the chapter.

Strategies for Addition Facts

Addition facts—the sums through 18—are generally considered mastery items in the second-grade curriculum. However, very few third-grade teachers will ever see a new class that has mastered all of these facts, and many teachers of fifth grade and higher have students who have not mastered these facts.

For teachers in grades 3–5, the following ideas are important:

- All of the addition facts can be connected to a handful of very important number relationships. For students who have not mastered addition facts, more time will be saved by some attention to those relationships than with more drill.

- It is almost never the case that a student will know a subtraction fact without also knowing the corresponding addition fact. That is, if a student knows 12 – 8, it is almost certain that he or she also knows 8 + 4. Therefore, mastery of addition facts should be seen as a prerequisite to subtraction facts.

- Diagnosis of what facts individual students have mastered will help you plan a method of helping your students. Time spent in this manner will save time in the long run.

The following sections are intended only to provide a brief look at the possibilities of strategies for addition facts. With this information you can plan efficient activities to help students master these facts quickly.

Facts with a Zero, One, or Two

As shown in the following table, 51 of the 100 addition facts involve a 0, 1, or a 2.

Students who are missing facts with a zero are likely responding based on a faulty notion that "addition makes bigger." Therefore, they might answer "8" to 7 + 0. These facts do not require any strategy but rather a good understanding of the meaning of zero and addition.

+	0	1	2	3	4	5	6	7	8	9
0	0	1	2	3	4	5	6	7	8	9
1	1	2	3	4	5	6	7	8	9	10
2	2	3	4	5	6	7	8	9	10	11
3	3	4	5							
4	4	5	6							
5	5	6	7							
6	6	7	8							
7	7	8	9							
8	8	9	10							
9	9	10	11							

Many students in grades 1 and 2 have been taught to use a "count-on" strategy for facts with addends of 1 or 2 as well as those involving a 3. This is a common strategy found in traditional textbooks. If students are using a counting-on strategy efficiently—and using it *only* for these small addends—do not try to stop it. However, we strongly suggest that you not encourage the use of counting on for *any* facts. It is difficult for students to separate counting on for some facts and not for others. Intermediate-grade students who have not yet mastered addition facts are probably counting on for 8 + 5 and other facts for which counting is certainly not efficient.

Rather than counting on, consider focusing on the relationships of one-more-than and two-more-than: 8 is 2 more than 6; one more than 5 is 6. Try simple drills in which a die is thrown, a numeral card is turned up, or a ten-frame card is shown and students respond with the number that is one-more-than (or two-more-than) the given number. Students who become proficient with this relationship can then be helped to connect it to the corresponding addition facts. Two drill ideas are shown in Figure 3.1.

It is helpful to point out to students that with only an understanding of 0 and the one- and two-more-than ideas, they know 51 addition facts. This is especially powerful for a fourth or fifth grader who is struggling to learn the facts.

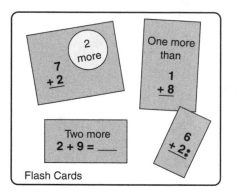

Flash Cards

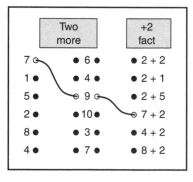

FIGURE 3.1 • • • • • • • • • • • • • • • • •

One-more and two-more facts.

Doubles and Near-Doubles Facts

It is well documented that children and adults alike seem to know the doubles facts (both addends alike) better than most other combinations. There are only 10 doubles facts and only seven of these have addends of 3 or greater. However, these seven facts provide a useful anchor for those facts often referred to as the near-doubles: facts such as 6 + 7 or 5 + 4 in which the addends are only one apart. The strategy for the near-doubles is to double the smaller addend and add 1. The doubles and near-doubles facts are shown in the table to the right.

When the doubles and near-doubles are added on to the 0, 1, and 2 facts, a total of 70 facts are accounted for. To help students with these facts, first check to see if they know the doubles facts. If not, here are two suggestions.

+	0	1	2	3	4	5	6	7	8	9
0	0	1								
1	1	2	3							
2		3	4	5						
3			5	6	7					
4				7	8	9				
5					9	10	11			
6						11	12	13		
7							13	14	15	
8								15	16	17
9									17	18

Have students solve simple word problems that focus on a pair of like addends. *Alex and Zack each found 7 seashells at the beach. How many did they find all together?* Students should solve the problem mentally. Then have several students share their solutions.

The following activity is a useful drill that is easily individualized and requires no preparation on your part.

Calculator Doubles

Students first make their calculator into a "double maker" by pressing
2 ⊠ =. Working in pairs, one student says a double fact, for example
"double seven." The student with the calculator first presses a 7 and then
tries to give the sum (without counting). He or she then presses = to see
the correct double on the display.

To make a double maker with some calculators may require pressing
⊠ 2 = or using an operation key. (Note that the calculator is also a good tool
for practicing the +1 and +2 facts.)

When students know the doubles, they can quickly connect these to the near-
doubles. Simple story problems are again a good method for getting the double-plus-
one strategy into the classroom. For a story problem involving a near-double, it is
highly probable that some students will use the double-plus-one approach. Note that
some students may double the larger addend and subtract one. Encourage any strategy
that seems helpful to the individual student. However, students with weak number
concepts sometimes apply double-plus-one incorrectly by beginning with the larger
addend rather than the smaller. For example, they may use double 7 plus 1 for 7 + 6.
Therefore, it is a good idea to focus especially on the doubling of the smaller addend.

If you want to discuss this (or any strategy) with the full class, you can use the
following approach. Write approximately ten near-doubles facts on the board. Vary
which addend is smaller. Have students work independently to write the answers. Then
discuss their ideas for "good" (i.e., efficient) methods of answering these facts. As with
the use of a story problem, it is almost certain that some students will use a double-
plus-one approach. When this happens, focus on that
method by having all students try the strategy with
other near-doubles facts.

When the strategy is clear to students, drill activities similar to those shown in Figure 3.2 are appropriate.

Make-Ten Facts

These facts all have at least one addend of 8 or 9.
One strategy for these facts is to build onto the 8 or 9
up to 10 and then add on the rest. For 6 + 8, start with
8, then 2 more makes 10, and that leaves 4 more for 14.

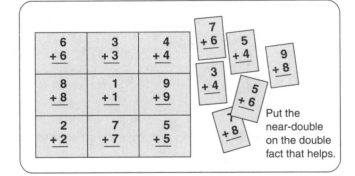

Put the near-double on the double fact that helps.

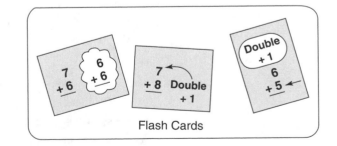

Flash Cards

+	0	1	2	3	4	5	6	7	8	9
0										
1										10
2									10	11
3									11	12
4									12	13
5									13	14
6									14	15
7									15	16
8			10	11	12	13	14	15	16	17
9		10	11	12	13	14	15	16	17	18

FIGURE 3.2 •

Near-doubles facts.

Before using this strategy, be sure that students have learned to think of the numbers 11 to 18 as 10 and some more. Many second- and third-grade children have not constructed this relationship.

The next activity is a good way to introduce the make-ten strategy.

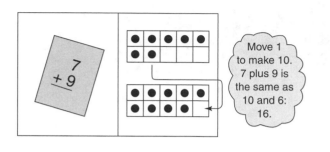

FIGURE 3.3 •

Make-ten with two ten-frames.

ACTIVITY 3.2

Make 10 on the Ten-Frame

Give students a mat with two ten-frames (see Figure 3.3). Flash cards are placed next to the ten-frames or a fact can be given orally. The students should first model each number in the two ten-frames and then decide on the easiest way to show (without counting) what the total is. The obvious (but not the only) choice is to move counters into the frame showing either 8 or 9. Get students to explain what they did. Focus especially on the idea that 1 (or 2) can be taken from the other number and put with the 9 (or 8) to make 10. Then you have 10 and whatever is left.

Provide a lot of time with the make-ten activity. Encourage discussion and exploration of "easy ways" to think about adding two numbers when one of them is 8 or 9. Perhaps discuss why this is not a useful idea for a fact such as 6 + 5 where neither number is near 10.

Note that children will have many other ways of using 10 to add with 8 or 9. For example, with the fact 9 + 5, some will add 10 + 5 and subtract 1. This is a perfectly good strategy, and it uses 10. You may want to give efficient strategies unique names determined by the students and discuss which ones seem especially useful.

With two ten-frames showing, another common strategy is to use a row of 5 from each frame to make ten. For the 7 + 9 fact in Figure 3.2, this strategy would first take the two rows of 5 (10) and then add 2 + 4, the leftover parts of each number. Interestingly, this is a popular strategy in Japan. Perhaps more importantly, this idea can be used with any fact in which each addend is 5 or more. There are 25 such facts and they include those typically thought of as difficult to learn.

BLMs 3, 4

When children seem to have the make-ten idea or a similar strategy, try the same activity without counters. Use the little ten-frame cards found in the Blackline Masters. Students can set out an 8 (or 9) card on their desk and place other cards beneath it one at a time. Suggest *mentally* "moving" two dots into the 8 ten-frame. Have students say orally what they are doing. For 8 + 4, they might say, "Take 2 from the 4 and put it with 8 to make 10. Then 10 and 2 left over is 12." The activity can be done independently with the little ten-frame cards.

> As has been noted, there is more than one way to efficiently use 10 in a strategy for facts involving 8 or 9. Imagine two or three children who have on the table a small ten-frame card for 9 so that all can see. One at a time, other cards are turned up and the students are to name the total of the two cards. How many different efficient methods involving 10 can you think of that can be accommodated by this simple activity?

Other Strategies and the Last Six Facts

To appreciate the power of strategies for fact learning, consider the following. We have discussed only five ideas or strategies (one- or two-more than, zeros, doubles, near-doubles, and make-ten), yet these ideas have covered 88 of the 100 addition facts! Furthermore, these ideas are not really new but rather the application of important relationships. The 12 remaining facts are really only six facts and their respective turnarounds as shown on the chart.

+	0	1	2	3	4	5	6	7	8	9
0										
1										
2										
3						8	9	10		
4							10	11		
5				8				12		
6				9	10					
7				10	11	12				
8										
9										

Before trying to develop any particular strategies for these facts, spend several days with word problems in which these facts are the addends. Listen carefully to the ideas that students use in figuring out the answers.

Doubles Plus Two, or Two-Apart Facts

Of the six remaining facts, three have addends that differ by 2: 3 + 5, 4 + 6, and 5 + 7. There are two possible relationships that might be useful here, each depending on knowledge of doubles. Some children find it easy to extend the idea of the near-doubles to double plus 2. For example, 4 + 6 is double 4 and 2 more. A different idea is to take 1 from the larger addend and give it to the smaller. Using this idea, the 5 + 3 fact is transformed into the double 4 fact—*double the number in between*.

Make-Ten Extended

Three of the six facts have 7 as one of the addends. The make-ten strategy is frequently extended to these facts as well. For 7 + 4, the idea is *7 and 3 more makes 10 and 1 left is 11*. You may decide to suggest this idea at the same time that you initially introduce the make-ten strategy.

Ten-Frame Facts

If you have been keeping track, five of the remaining six facts have been covered by the discussion so far, with a few being touched by two different thought patterns. Only 6 + 3 has been neglected. The ten-frame model is so valuable in seeing certain number relationships that these ideas cannot be passed by in thinking about facts. The ten-frame helps children learn the combinations that make 10. Ten-frames immediately model all of the facts from 5 + 1 to 5 + 5 and the respective turnarounds. Even 5 + 6, 5 + 7, and

+	0	1	2	3	4	5	6	7	8	9
0						5				
1						6				10
2						7		10		
3						8	10			
4						9	10			
5	5	6	7	8	9	10	11	12	13	14
6					10	11				
7				10		12				
8			10			13				
9		10				14				

5 + 8 are quickly seen as two fives and some more when depicted with these powerful models (see Figure 3.4).

A good idea might be to group the facts shown in the chart here and practice them using one or two ten-frames as a cue to the thought process.

The next two activities are suggestive of the type of relationships that can be developed.

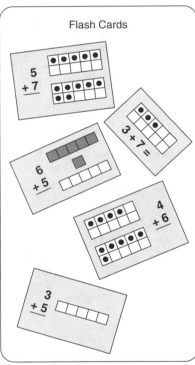

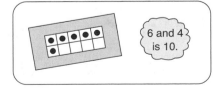

FIGURE 3.4 • • • • • • • • • • • • •

Ten-frame facts.

A Plus-Five Machine

Use the calculator to practice adding five. Enter ⊞ 5 ⊟. Next enter any number and say the sum of that number plus 5 before pressing ⊟. Continue with other numbers. (The ⊞ 5 ⊟ need not be repeated.) If a ten-frame is present, the potential for strengthening the 5 and 10 relationships is heightened.

Obviously, the calculator can be made into a machine for adding any number and is a powerful drill device.

Say the Ten Fact

Hold up a ten-frame card, and have students say the "ten fact." For a card with 7 dots, the response is "seven and three is ten." Later, with a blank ten-frame drawn on the board, say a number less than 10. Students start with that number and complete the "ten fact." If you say, "four," they say, "four plus six is ten." Use the same activities in independent or small group modes.

Strategies for Subtraction Facts

Subtraction facts prove to be more difficult than addition. This is especially true when children have been taught subtraction through a "count-count-count" approach; for 13 – 5, *count* 13, *count* off 5, *count* what's left. There is little evidence that anyone who has mastered subtraction facts has found this approach helpful. Unfortunately, many sixth, seventh, and eighth graders are still counting.

Subtraction as Think-Addition

In Figure 3.5 subtraction is modeled in such a way that students are encouraged to think, "What goes with this part to make the total?" When done in this *think-addition* manner, the child uses known addition facts to produce the unknown quantity or part. If this important relationship between parts and wholes—between addition and subtraction—can be made, subtraction facts will be much easier. When children see 9 – 4, you want them to think spontaneously, "Four and *what* makes nine?" By contrast, observe a third-grade child who struggles with this fact. The idea of thinking addition never occurs. Instead, the child will begin to count either back from 9 or up from 4. The value of think-addition cannot be overstated.

Word problems that promote think-addition are those that sound like addition but have a missing addend. Consider this problem: *Janice had 5 fish in her aquarium. Grandma gave her some more fish. Then she had 12 fish. How many fish did Grandma give Janice?* Notice that the action is

Connecting Subtraction to Addition Knowledge

1. Count out 13 <u>and</u> <u>cover.</u>

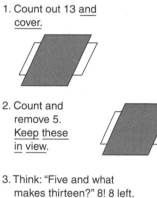

2. Count and remove 5. <u>Keep these</u> <u>in view.</u>

3. Think: "Five and what makes thirteen?" 8! 8 left. 13 minus 5 is 8.

4. Uncover.

8 and 5 is 13.

FIGURE 3.5

Using a think-addition model for subtraction.

join and, thus, suggests addition. There is a high probability that students will think 5 *and how many more makes 12.* In the discussion in which you use problems such as this, your task is to connect this thought process with the subtraction fact, 12 – 5.

Subtraction Facts with Sums to 10

Think-addition is most immediately applicable to subtraction facts with sums of 10 or less. Sixty-four of the 100 subtraction facts fall into this category.

Assessment Note

For think-addition to be used effectively, addition facts must be mastered first. If you suspect students have not yet mastered their subtraction facts, prepare a page of them and a different page of addition facts. To make the correlation between the addition and subtraction facts easier for you to see, match the facts on the two pages. That is, put the addition fact 5 + 4 in the same row and column on the addition page as 9 – 4 on the subtraction page.

Ask students to respond only to those facts that they know quickly without having to resort to counting. Explain that you only want to find out what they know so that you can help them with those facts they have yet to master.

If you find that they have not mastered all or nearly all of their addition facts, then that is the place to begin. The paired addition and subtraction facts may give you a clue whether students are using addition facts to respond to subtraction facts. If addition facts are known but subtraction facts are not known, then your task is to help students develop a think-addition approach.

The 36 "Hard" Subtraction Facts: Sums Greater Than 10

STOP Before reading further, look at the three subtraction facts shown here and try to reflect on what thought process you use to get the answers. Even if you "just know them," think about what a likely process might be.

$$
\begin{array}{ccc}
14 & 12 & 15 \\
-\,9 & -\,6 & -\,6 \\
\end{array}
$$

Many people will use a different strategy for each of these facts. For 14 – 9, it is easy to start with 9 and work up through 10: *9 and 1 more is 10, and 4 more makes 5.* For the 12 – 6 fact, it is quite common to hear "double 6," a think-addition approach. For the last fact, 15 – 6, 10 is used again but probably by working backward from 15—a take-away process: *Take away 5 to get 10, and 1 more leaves 9.* We could call these three approaches, respectively, build up through 10, think-addition, and back down through 10. Each of the remaining 36 facts with sums of 11 or more can be learned using one or more of these strategies. Figure 3.6 shows how these facts, in three overlapping groups, correspond to these three strategies. Keep in mind that these are not required strategies. Some students may use a think-addition method for all. Others may have a completely different strategy for some or all of these. The three approaches suggested here are

STRATEGIES FOR SUBTRACTION FACTS

FIGURE 3.6 • • • • • • • • • • • •

The 36 "hard" subtraction facts.

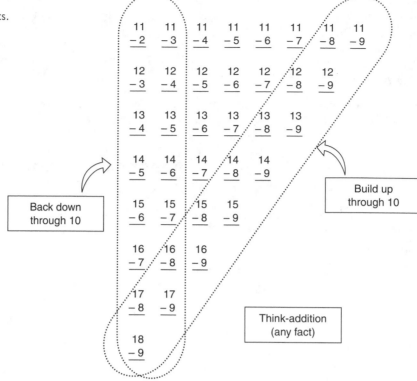

based on ideas already developed: the relationship between addition and subtraction and the power of 10 as a reference point.

Note that the build-up group includes all facts in which the part or subtracted number is either 8 or 9. Examples are 13 – 9 and 15 – 8. In contrast, the back-down-through-ten facts are really take-away and not think-addition. It is useful for facts where the ones digit of the whole is close to the number being subtracted. For example, with 15 – 6, you start with the total of 15 and take off 5. That gets you down to 10. Then take off 1 more to get 9. For 14 – 6, just take off 4 and then take off 2 more to get 8. Here we are working backward with 10 as a "bridge."

Extend Think-Addition

Think-addition remains one of the most powerful ways to think about subtraction facts. When the think-addition concept of subtraction is well developed, many children will use that approach for all subtraction facts. (Notice that virtually everyone uses a think-multiplication approach for division. Why?)

What may be most important is to listen to children's thinking as they attempt to answer subtraction facts that they have not yet mastered. If they are not using one of the three ideas suggested here, it is a good bet that they are counting—an inefficient method.

The activities that follow are all of the think-addition variety. There is, of course, no reason why these activities could not be used for all of the subtraction facts. They need not be limited to the "hard facts."

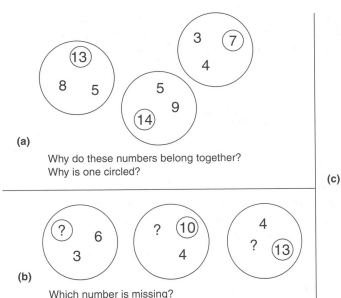

(a)

Why do these numbers belong together?
Why is one circled?

(b)

Which number is missing?
How can you tell what it is?

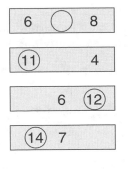

(c)

These missing-number
cards are just like the
number families. Say
the missing number.

FIGURE 3.7 ··········

Introducing missing-
number cards.

ACTIVITY 3.5

Missing-Number Cards

Show children, without explanation, families of numbers with
the sum circled as in Figure 3.7(a). Ask why they think the
numbers go together and why one number is circled. When
this number family idea is fairly well understood, show some
families with one number replaced by a question mark, as in
Figure 3.7(b), and ask what number is missing. When students
understand this activity, explain that you have made some
missing-number cards based on this idea. Each card has two
of three numbers that go together in the same way. Sometimes
the circled number is missing (the sum), and sometimes one
of the other numbers is missing (a part). The object is to name
the missing number.

ACTIVITY 3.6

Missing-Number Worksheets

Make copies of the blank form found in the Blackline Masters
to make a wide variety of drill exercises. In a row of 13
"cards," put all of the combinations from two families with
different numbers missing, some parts and some wholes. Put
blanks in different positions. An example is shown in Figure 3.8. After filling in numbers, run the sheet off, and have
students fill in the missing numbers. Another idea is to group
facts from one strategy or number relation or perhaps mix
facts from two strategies on one page. Have students write an

(continued)

Make-ten facts	Near-doubles	Two fact families (7, 8, 15) (4, 8, 12)
4 ◯ 8	5 6 ◯	4 ⑫
◯ 9 6	⑬ 7	⑮ 8
8 7 ◯	⑮ 8	⑫ 4
⑮ 6	5 ⑪	7 8 ◯
5 ⑬	7 ⑮	⑫ 8
8 ⑰	⑨ 4	⑫ 8
6 ◯ 8	⑰ 8	4 ⑫
3 9 ◯	⑪ 6	8 ⑮
9 ⑯	5 ◯ 4	⑮ 7
◯ 6 8	3 ⑦	7 ◯ 8
7 ⑯	⑨ 5	4 ⑫
3 ◯ 9	6 ⑬	◯ 4 8
8 ◯ 8	⑰ 9	8 ⑮

FIGURE 3.8 ···················

Missing-part worksheets. The blank version
can be used to fill in any sets of facts you
wish to emphasize (see Blackline Masters).

BLM 14

STRATEGIES FOR SUBTRACTION FACTS

addition fact and a subtraction fact to go with each missing-number card. This is an important step because many children are able to give the missing part in a family but do not connect this knowledge with subtraction.

Strategies for Multiplication Facts

Multiplication facts can and should be mastered by relating new facts to existing knowledge.

It is imperative that students completely understand the commutative property (go back and review Figure 2.16, p. 66). For example, 2 × 8 is related to the addition fact double 8. But the same relationship also applies to 8 × 2 that many students think about as 2 + 2 + 2 + 2 + 2 + 2 + 2 + 2. Most of the fact strategies are more obvious with the factors in one order than in the other, but turnaround facts should always be learned together.

Of the five groups or strategies discussed next, the first four strategies are generally easier and cover 75 of the 100 multiplication facts. You are continually reminded that these strategies are suggestions, not rules, and that the most general approach with children is to have them discuss ways that *they* can use to think of facts easily.

Doubles

Facts that have 2 as a factor are equivalent to the addition doubles (e.g., 7 + 7) and should already be known by students who know their addition facts. The major problem is to realize that not only is 2 × 7 double 7, but so is 7 × 2. Try word problems where 2 is the number of sets. Later use problems where 2 is the size of the sets.

Make and use flash cards with the related addition fact or word *double* as a cue (see Figure 3.9).

×	0	1	2	3	4	5	6	7	8	9
0			0							
1			2							
2	0	2	4	6	8	10	12	14	16	18
3			6							
4			8							
5			10							
6			12							
7			14							
8			16							
9			18							

Fives Facts

This group consists of all facts with 5 as the first or second factor, as shown here.

Practice counting by fives to at least 45. Connect counting by fives with rows of 5 dots (see Figure 3.10). Point out that six rows is a model for 6 × 5, eight rows is 8 × 5, and so on.

×	0	1	2	3	4	5	6	7	8	9
0						0				
1						5				
2						10				
3						15				
4						20				
5	0	5	10	15	20	25	30	35	40	45
6						30				
7						35				
8						40				
9						45				

ACTIVITY 3.7

Clock Facts

Focus on the minute hand of the clock. When it points to a number, how many minutes after the hour is it? Draw a large clock face, and point to numbers 1 to 9 in random order. Students respond with the minutes after. Now connect this idea to the multiplication facts with 5. Hold up a flash

FIGURE 3.9 ●

Multiplication doubles.

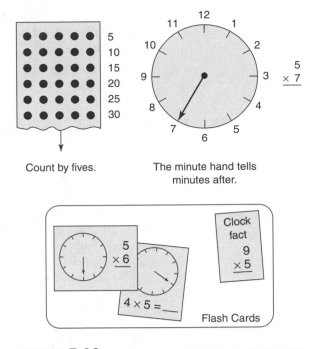

FIGURE 3.10 ●

Fives facts.

card and then point to the number on the clock corresponding to the other factor. In this way, the fives facts become the "clock facts."

Include the clock idea on flash cards or to make matching activities (see Figure 3.10).

×	0	1	2	3	4	5	6	7	8	9
0	0	0	0	0	0	0	0	0	0	0
1	0	1	2	3	4	5	6	7	8	9
2	0	2								
3	0	3								
4	0	4								
5	0	5								
6	0	6								
7	0	7								
8	0	8								
9	0	9								

×	0	1	2	3	4	5	6	7	8	9
0										0
1										9
2										18
3										27
4										36
5										45
6										54
7										63
8										72
9	0	9	18	27	36	45	54	63	72	81

Zeros and Ones

Thirty-six facts have at least one factor that is either 0 or 1. These facts, though apparently easy, sometimes confuse students with "rules" they may have learned for addition. The fact 6 + 0 stays the same, but 6 × 0 is always zero. The 1 + 4 fact is a one-more idea, but 1 × 4 stays the same. The concepts behind these facts can be developed best through story problems. Above all else, avoid rules that sound arbitrary and without reason such as "Any number multiplied by zero is zero."

Nifty Nines

Facts with a factor of 9 include the largest products but can be among the easiest to learn. The table of nines facts includes some nice patterns that are fun to discover. Two of these patterns are useful for mastering the nines: (1) The tens digit of the product is always

89

STRATEGIES FOR MULTIPLICATION FACTS

one less than the "other" factor (the one other than 9), and (2) the sum of the two digits in the product is always 9. These two ideas can be used together to get any nine fact quickly. For 7 × 9, *1 less than 7 is 6, 6 and 3 make 9, so the answer is 63.*

Students are not likely to invent this strategy simply by solving word problems involving a factor of 9. Therefore, consider building a lesson around the following task.

ACTIVITY 3.8

Patterns in the Nines Facts

In column form, write the nines table on the board (9 × 1 = 9, 9 × 2 = 18, . . . , 9 × 9 = 81). The task is to find as many patterns as possible in the table. (Do not ask students to think of a strategy.) As you listen to the students work on this task, be sure that somewhere in the class the two patterns necessary for the strategy have been found. After discussing all the patterns, a follow-up task is to use the patterns to think of a clever way to figure out a nine fact if you didn't know it. (Note that even for students who know their nines facts, this remains a valid task.)

Once students have invented a strategy for the nines, practice activities such as those shown in Figure 3.11 are appropriate. Also consider word problems with a factor of 9 and check to see if the strategy is in use.

Warning: Although the nines strategy can be quite successful, it also can cause confusion. Because two separate rules are involved and a conceptual basis is not apparent, students may confuse the two rules or attempt to apply the idea to other facts. It is not, however, a "rule without reason." It is an idea based on a very interesting pattern that exists in the base-ten numeration system. One of the values of patterns in mathematics is that they help us do seemingly difficult things quite easily. The nifty-nine pattern illustrates clearly one of the values of pattern and regularity in mathematics.

An alternative strategy for the nines is almost as easy to use. Notice that 7 × 9 is the same as 7 × 10 less one set of 7, or 70 − 7. This can easily be modeled by displaying rows of 10 cubes, with the last one a different color, as in Figure 3.12. For students who can easily subtract 4 from 40, 5 from 50, and so on, this strategy may be preferable.

You might introduce this idea by showing a set of bars such as those in the figure with only the end cube a different color. After explaining that every bar has ten cubes, ask students if they can think of a good way to figure out how many are yellow.

Helping Facts

The following chart shows the remaining 25 multiplication facts. It is worth pointing out to students that there are actually only 15 facts remaining to master because 20 of them consist of 10 pairs of turnarounds.

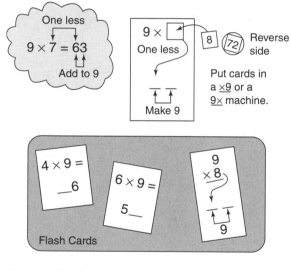

FIGURE 3.11 •

"Nifty nines" rule.

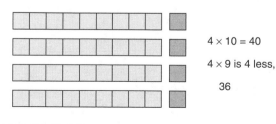

4 × 10 = 40

4 × 9 is 4 less,

36

FIGURE 3.12 •

Another way to think of the nines.

×	0	1	2	3	4	5	6	7	8	9
0										
1										
2										
3				9	12		18	21	24	
4				12	16		24	28	32	
5										
6				18	24		36	42	48	
7				21	28		42	49	56	
8				24	32		48	56	64	
9										

These 25 facts can be learned by relating each to an already known fact or *helping* fact. For example, 3 × 8 is connected to 2 × 8 (double 8 and 8 more). The 6 × 7 fact can be related to either 5 × 7 (5 sevens and 7 more) or to 3 × 7 (double 3 × 7). The helping fact must be known, and the ability to do the mental addition must also be there. For example, to go from 5 × 7 is 35 and then add 7 for 6 × 7, a student must be able to efficiently add 35 and 7.

Assessment Note

How to find a helping fact that is useful varies with different facts and sometimes depends on which factor you focus on. Figure 3.13 illustrates models for four overlapping groups of facts and the thought process associated with each.

The *double and double again* approach is applicable to all facts with 4 as one of the factors. Remind students that the idea works when 4 is the second factor as well as when it is the first. For 4 × 8, double 16 is also a difficult fact. Help children with this by noting, for example, that 15 + 15 is 30, 16 + 16 is two more, or 32. Adding 16 + 16 on paper defeats the purpose.

Double and one more set is a way to think of facts with one factor of 3. With an array or a set picture, the double part can be circled, and it is clear that there is one more set. Two facts in this group involve difficult mental additions.

If either factor is even, a *half then double* approach can be used. Select the even factor, and cut it in half. If the smaller fact is known, that product is doubled to get the new fact. For 6 × 7, half of 6 is 3. Three times 7 is 21. Double 21 is 42. For 8 × 7, the double of 28 may be hard, but it remains an effective approach to that traditionally hard fact. (Double 25 is 50 + 2 times 3 is 56 or double 30 is 60, 60 subtract 4 is 56.)

Many children prefer to go to a fact that is "close" and then *add one more set* to this known fact. For example, think of 6 × 7 as 6 sevens. Five sevens is close: That's 35. Six sevens is one more seven, or 42. When using 5 × 8 to help with 6 × 8, the set language "6 eights" is very helpful in remembering to add 8 more and not 6 more. Admittedly difficult, this approach is used by many children, and it

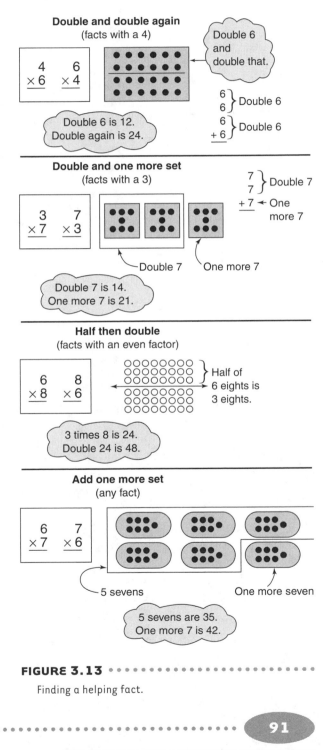

FIGURE 3.13

Finding a helping fact.

STRATEGIES FOR MULTIPLICATION FACTS

becomes the best way to think of one or two particularly difficult facts. "What is seven times eight? Oh, that's 8 sevens or 49 and 7 more—56." The process can become almost automatic.

The relationships between easy and hard facts are fertile ground for good problem-solving tasks. Rather than tell students what helping facts to use and how to use them, select a hard multiplication fact and challenge students to find interesting and useful ways to answer it. This approach is described in the next activity.

EXPANDED LESSON

(pages 98–99)
A complete lesson plan based on "If You Didn't Know" can be found at the end of this chapter.

BLM 15

ACTIVITY 3.9

If You Didn't Know

Pose the following task to the class: **If you didn't know the answer to 6 × 8 (or any fact that you want students to think about), how could you figure it out by using something that you do know?** Explain to students that their method should be something that they can do in their head and should not rely on counting. Encourage students to come up with more than one way. Use a think-pair-share approach in which students discuss their ideas with a partner before they share them with the class.

STOP Go through each of the 20 "hard facts" and see how many of the strategies in Figure 3.13 you can use for each one. Many students will not think in terms of the arrays shown but rather will use a symbolic representation. For example, for 6 × 8 they might think of a vertical sum of six 8s or eight 6s. Try to see how this type of representation works for the ideas in Figure 3.13.

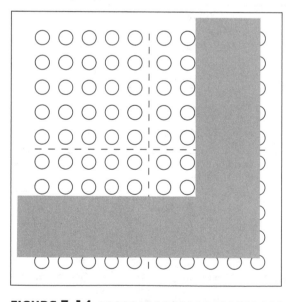

FIGURE 3.14 • • • • • • • • • • • • • • • •

An array is a useful model for developing strategies for the hard multiplication facts. An array like this can be found in the Blackline Masters.

Since arrays are a powerful thinking tool for these strategies, provide students with copies of the ten-by-ten dot array found in the Blackline Masters. A tagboard *L* is used to outline specific product arrays as shown in Figure 3.14. The lines in the array make counting the dots easier and often suggest the use of the easier fives facts as helpers. For example, 7 × 7 is 5 × 7 plus double 7 $\longrightarrow$ 35 + 14.

Don't forget to use word problems as a vehicle for developing these harder facts. Consider this problem: *Connie bundled up all of her old crayons into bags of 7 crayons each. She was able to make 8 bags with 3 crayons left over. How many crayons did she have?* As students work to get an answer, many of the strategies just discussed are possible. Plus there is the added benefit of the assessment value gained by listening to the methods different students bring to a situation that does not look like a fact drill.

Word problems can also be structured to prompt a strategy. *Carlos and Jose kept their baseball cards in albums with 6 cards on each page. Carlos had 4 pages filled, and Jose had 8 pages filled. How many cards did each boy have?* (Do you see the half-then-double strategy?)

It should be clear that arrays and set pictures play a large part in helping students establish multiplication facts and relationships. They can be used to help with multiplication facts, the relationship between multiplication and division, and in the development of computational procedures for multiplication. They provide students with a visual image of strategies. After they understand the strategy, move away from these visuals in an effort to build efficiency.

Division Facts and "Near Facts"

STOP **What thought process do you use to recall facts such as 48 ÷ 6 or 36 ÷ 9?**

If we are trying to think of 36 ÷ 9, we tend to think, "Nine times what is thirty-six?" For most, 42 ÷ 6 is not a separate fact but is closely tied to 6 × 7. (Would it not be wonderful if subtraction were so closely related to addition? It can be!)

An interesting question to ask is, "When children are working on a page of division facts, are they practicing division or multiplication?" There is undoubtedly some value in limited practice of division facts. However, mastery of multiplication facts and connections between multiplication and division are the key elements of division fact mastery. Word problems continue to be a key vehicle to create this connection.

Exercises such as 50 ÷ 6 might be called "near facts." Divisions that do not come out evenly are much more prevalent in computations and in real situations than division facts or division without remainders. To determine the answer to 50 ÷ 6, most people run through a short sequence of the multiplication facts, comparing each product to 50: "6 times 7 (low), 6 times 8 (close), 6 times 9 (high). Must be 8. That's 48 and 2 left over." This process can and should be drilled. That is, children should be able to do problems with one-digit divisors and one-digit answers plus remainders mentally and with reasonable speed.

ACTIVITY 3.10

How Close Can You Get?

To practice "near facts," try this exercise. As illustrated, the idea is to find the one-digit factor that makes the product as close as possible to the target without going over. Help children develop the process of going through the multiplication facts that were just described. This can be a drill with the full class by preparing a list for the overhead, or it can be a worksheet activity.

Find the largest factor without going over the target number.

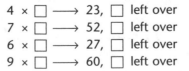

4 × ☐ ⟶ 23, ☐ left over
7 × ☐ ⟶ 52, ☐ left over
6 × ☐ ⟶ 27, ☐ left over
9 × ☐ ⟶ 60, ☐ left over

Effective Drill

There is little doubt that strategy development and general number sense (number relationships and operation meanings) are the best contributors to fact mastery. Drill in the absence of these factors has repeatedly been demonstrated as ineffective. However, the positive value of drill should not be completely ignored. Drill of nearly any mental activity strengthens memory and retrieval capabilities.

When and How to Drill

Teachers and parents hold tenaciously to their belief in drill. Undoubtedly, far too much time is devoted to inefficient drill of basic facts, often with a negative impact on students' attitudes toward mathematics and beliefs in their abilities.

Avoid Inefficient Drill

Adopt this simple rule and stick with it: *Do not subject any student to fact drills unless the student has developed an efficient strategy for the facts included in the drill.* Drill can strengthen strategies with which students feel comfortable—ones they "own"—and will help to make these strategies increasingly automatic. Therefore, drill of strategies such as those discussed in this chapter will allow students to use them with increased efficiency, even to the point of recalling the fact without being conscious of using a strategy. Counting on fingers and making marks on paper can never result in automatic fact recall regardless of the amount of drill. Drill without an efficient strategy present offers no assistance.

The preceding statement even applies to students in the upper elementary grades who have not yet mastered facts. Because the curriculum at these levels typically does not include strategy development, drill is often the only approach offered. Alternatives to this serious error are discussed later in the chapter.

Individualize Drill

It is unreasonable to expect every student in your class to develop and be comfortable with the same strategies. As you have seen, there are multiple paths to most facts. Different students will bring different number tools to the task and will develop strategies at different rates. This means that there are few drills that are likely to be efficient for a full class at any given time. That is why so many of the suggested activities are designed as flash cards, games, or simple repeatable worksheets. By creating a large number of drill activities promoting different strategies and addressing different collections of facts, it is not at all unreasonable to direct students to activities that are most useful for them.

It is important to listen carefully to the strategies different students are using. For example, if a student tends to solve multiplication facts with a 9 by multiplying by 10 and subtracting, it is not profitable to push the "nifty nine" strategy. A student who has not mastered addition facts is not ready for subtraction practice.

Drill for Strategy Retrieval

When a fact is presented without a reminder of a strategy, students need to select from their memory the mental method that works best for that fact. Drills can be devised that help students look at a fact and recall a strategy that works. The next activity suggests how this might be done.

ACTIVITY 3.11

Sort Them as You Do Them

Mix ordinary flash cards from two or more strategies into a single packet. Prepare simple pictures or labels for the strategies in the packet. Students first match a card with a strategy and then use the strategy to answer that fact.

"Sort Them as You Do Them" can be tailored to match the strategies that an individual student is using and working on. Talk with the students, and have them help you put the activity together.

Technology Note

There are literally hundreds of software programs that offer drill of basic facts. Nearly all fact programs offer games or exercises at various difficulty levels. Unfortunately, there do not seem to be any programs that organize facts based on strategies. It should be clear that computerized fact practice should be used only after students have developed some strategies.

Many commercial programs automatically keep performance records of individual students. Plus, there are numerous sites on the Internet that offer fact practice with immediate feedback, and many provide options for the number of problems, the size of the numbers, and whether or not to time the student.

What About Timed Tests?

Consider the following:

Teachers who use timed tests believe that the tests help children learn basic facts. This makes no instructional sense. Children who perform well under time pressure display their skills. Children who have difficulty with skills, or who work more slowly, run the risk of reinforcing wrong learning under pressure. In addition, children can become fearful and negative toward their math learning. (Burns, 2000, p. 157)

Think about this quotation whenever you are tempted to give a timed test. Reasoning and pattern searching are never facilitated by restricting time. Some children simply cannot work well under pressure or in situations that provoke stress.

Although speed may encourage children to memorize facts, it is effective only for students who are goal oriented and who can perform in pressure situations. The pressure of speed can be debilitating and provides no positive benefits.

The value of speed drills or timed tests as a learning tool can be summed up as follows:

Timed tests

- Cannot promote reasoned approaches to fact mastery
- Will produce few long-lasting results
- Reward few
- Punish many
- Should generally be avoided

Assessment Note

If there is any defensible purpose for a timed test of basic facts it may be for diagnosis—to determine which combinations are mastered and which remain to be learned. Even for diagnostic purposes there is little reason for a timed test more than once every couple of months.

Fact Remediation with Upper-Grade Students

Students who have not mastered their basic facts by the fifth grade are in need of something other than more drill. They have certainly seen and practiced facts countless times in previous grades. There is no reason to believe that the drills *you* provide will somehow be more effective than last year's. These students need something better. The following key ideas can guide your efforts to help these older students.

1. *Recognize that more drill will not work.* Students' fact difficulties are due to a failure to develop or to connect concepts and relationships such as those that have been discussed in this chapter, not a lack of drill. At best, more drill will provide temporary results. At worst, it will cause negative attitudes about mathematics.

2. *Inventory the known and unknown facts for each student in need.* Find out from each student what facts are known quickly and comfortably and which are not. Fifth- and sixth-grade students can do this diagnosis for you. Provide sheets of all facts for one operation in random order and have the students circle the facts they are hesitant about and answer all others. Suggest that finger counting or making marks in the margin is not permitted.

3. *Diagnose strengths and weaknesses.* Find out what students do when they encounter one of their unknown facts. Do they count on their fingers? Add up numbers in the margins? Guess? Try to use a related fact? Write down times tables? Are they able to use any of the relationships that might be helpful as suggested in this chapter? Some of this you may be able to accomplish by having students write about how they approach two or three specific facts. More efficiently, you should conduct a 15-minute diagnostic interview with each student in need. Simply pose unknown facts and ask the student how he or she approaches them. Try an idea from this chapter and see what connections are already there. Don't try to teach; just find out.

4. *Provide hope.* Children who have experienced difficulty with fact mastery often believe that they cannot learn facts or that they are doomed to finger counting forever. Let these children know that you will help them and that you will provide some new ideas that will help them as well. Take that burden on yourself and spare them the prospect of more defeat.

5. *Build in success.* As you begin a well-designed fact program for a child who has experienced failure, be sure that successes come quickly and easily. Begin with easy strategies, and introduce only a few new facts at a time. Even with pure rote drill, repetitive exposure to five facts in three days will provide more success than introducing 15 facts in a week. Success builds success! With strategies as an added assist, success comes even more quickly. Point out to children how one idea, one strategy, is all that is required to learn many facts. Use fact charts to show what set of facts you are working on. It is surprising how the chart quickly fills up with mastered facts. Keep reviewing newly learned facts and those that were already known. This is success. It feels good and failures are not as apparent. Short practice exercises can be designed as homework. Explain strategies and build them into the exercises. At the end of the exercises, have students write about which ideas are helpful and which are not. Use this information to design the next exercise.

Your extra effort beyond class time can be a motivation to a student to make some personal effort on his or her own time. During class, these students should continue to work with all students on the regular curriculum. You must believe and communicate to these students that the reason they have not mastered basic facts is not a reflection of their ability. With efficient strategies and individual effort, success will come. Believe!

Facts: No Barrier to Good Mathematics

Students who have total command of basic facts do not necessarily *reason better* than those who, for whatever reason, have not yet mastered facts. Today, mathematics is not about computation, especially pencil-and-paper computation. Mathematics is about reasoning and patterns and making sense of things. Mathematics is problem solving. There is no reason that a student who has not yet mastered all basic facts should be excluded from real mathematical experiences.

The most obvious alternative is the calculator. It should be on the desk every day for all students. There is absolutely no evidence that the presence of a calculator will impede basic fact mastery. On the contrary, the more students use the calculator, the more proficient they will be with it. This will make many of the calculator fact drills more effective and provide students with ready access to electronic flash cards. In a classroom climate where most students do know their facts and where students help one another and share thinking strategies as has been suggested, very few students will rely on the calculator for any prolonged period. In fact, when equipped with effective strategies many students see using the calculator to complete basic facts as slowing them down.

Students who are relegated to drill of facts when the rest of the class is engaged in meaningful experiences will soon feel stupid and incapable of doing "real" mathematics. By contrast, when students who have not mastered facts are engaged in exciting and meaningful experiences, they have real motivation to learn facts and real opportunities to develop relationships that can aid in that endeavor. Do not allow students who are behind in fact mastery to fall behind in mathematics.

EXPANDED LESSON

If You Didn't Know

Based on: Activity 3.9, p. 92

GRADE LEVEL: Third or fourth grade.

MATHEMATICS GOALS
- To develop student-invented strategies for basic multiplication facts.
- To develop problem-solving skills in the context of basic multiplication facts.

THINKING ABOUT THE STUDENTS

Students understand that multiplication is the same thing as repeated addition. They are proficient with their addition facts and have mastered the easier multiplication facts but still struggle with some of the more difficult multiplication facts.

MATERIALS AND PREPARATION
- Identify multiplication facts that most students are having difficulty mastering.
- Provide each student with a copy of a ten-by-ten multiplication array (see Blackline Master 15) and a tagboard L (as shown in Figure 3.14) to outline specific product arrays.
- Make a transparency of the ten-by-ten dot array for the "After" portion of the lesson. You will also need a tagboard L to outline specific product arrays on the overhead.

lesson

BEFORE

Begin with a simpler version of the task:
- Ask students to remember when they were learning addition facts and how knowing 6 + 6 could help them figure out 6 + 7. Elicit student ideas. The point to emphasize is what is meant by a fact that they know (e.g., a fact that they have already mastered and know without counting).
- Ask students to pretend that they do not know 6 × 5 but that they do know 5 × 5. Use the transparency of the ten-by-ten dot array and the tagboard L to illustrate a 6 × 5 array on the overhead. How could they use 5 × 5 to help them determine 6 × 5? Elicit student ideas. For example, 5 × 5 is 25 and one more 5 is 30.
- Without using the dot array, ask students to suppose they know 3 × 5 but not 6 × 5. How could they use 3 × 5 to determine 6 × 5? Again elicit student ideas. For example, 3 × 5 is 15 and means 3 groups of 5; 6 × 5 means 6 groups of 5, so just double the 15 to get 30.

The Task

If you did not know the answer to 6 × 8, how could you figure it out by using something that you do know?

Establish Expectations
- Explain to students that their methods should be something that they can do in their heads and should not rely on counting. In other words, they should use a fact that they know—a fact that they have already mastered and know without counting.
- Encourage students to come up with more than one way.
- Explain that the ten-by-ten array is only one tool to help them think about different strategies. They do not have to use this tool.

DURING
- If students have difficulty getting started, first ask them what 6 × 8 means in terms of addition (e.g., 6 groups of 8). Suggest they write the 6 eights either vertically or horizontally and look for different ways to group the numbers so that they can determine the answer more quickly. Do not press for a particular approach. Alter-

natively, suggest that they use the ten-by-ten dot array. Is there a part of the array that they can use easily?

- Encourage students to come up with more than one way to find 6 × 8. You might have to suggest ideas to try.
- As students work, ask them to explain their strategies. You may need to provide guidance in how they can better explain or illustrate their approach to their classmates.

AFTER

- Use a think-pair-share approach in which students discuss their ideas with a partner before they share them with the class.
- As students share their ways of thinking about how to determine 6 × 8 mentally, they may need to accompany their explanations with drawings or equations so that classmates can follow along. You may need to step in to help students make explicit the particular strategy they are using, such as half then double, add one more set, and so on.
- Help students make connections between symbolic approaches such as a listing of 6 eights and a portion of the ten-by-ten array.
- Ideas students may use include 3 × 8 and then double, 4 × 6 and then double, 5 × 8 and one more 8, and double-double-double (12, 24, 48). Each of these ideas can be used with other hard multiplication facts as well. For a given strategy, challenge students to find other facts with which they can use the same approach.

ASSESSMENT NOTES

- Look for students who only use repeated addition to determine the answer to the multiplication fact. Have these students mastered the easier multiplication facts?
- Some students may need skills with mental addition to make a strategy useful. For example, to use 3 × 8 and then double, a student must be able to double 24 mentally.

- Use word problems as a vehicle for prompting and developing different strategies. For example, to prompt the *double and double again* approach, pose a word problem such as the following: *Mike and Sarah were making goody bags for the end-of-the-year party. They wanted to put 6 pieces of candy in each student's bag. Mark made 2 bags while Sarah made 4 bags. How many pieces of candy did each person use?*

next steps

- For students having difficulty with easier facts, provide meaningful practice with strategies for groups of facts (double, fives, threes, nines) as described in this chapter.

STRATEGIES FOR WHOLE-NUMBER COMPUTATION

Much of the public sees computational skill as the hallmark of what it means to know mathematics at the elementary school level. Although this is far from the truth, the issue of computational skills with whole numbers is, in fact, a very important part of the elementary curriculum, especially in grades 2 to 6.

Rather than constant reliance on a single method of subtracting (or any operation), computational methods can and should change flexibly as the numbers and the context change. In the spirit of the *Standards,* the issue is no longer a matter of "knows how to subtract three-digit numbers"; rather it is the development over time of an assortment of flexible skills that will best serve students in the real world.

It is quite possible that you do not have these skills, but you can acquire them. Work at them as you learn about them. Equip yourself with a flexible array of computational strategies.

Toward Computational Fluency

With today's technology the need for doing tedious computations by hand has essentially disappeared. At the same time,

big ideas

1 Flexible methods of computation involve taking apart and combining numbers in a wide variety of ways. Most of the partitions of numbers are based on place value or "compatible" numbers—number pairs that work easily together, such as 25 and 75.

2 Invented strategies are flexible methods of computing that vary with the numbers and the situation. Successful use of the strategies requires that they be understood by the one who is using them—hence, the term *invented.* Strategies may be invented by a peer or the class as a whole; they may even be suggested by the teacher. However, they must be constructed by the student.

3 Flexible methods for computation require a good understanding of the operations and properties of the operations, especially the turnaround property and the distributive property for multiplication. How the operations are related—addition to subtraction, addition to multiplication, and multiplication to division—is also an important ingredient.

4 The traditional algorithms are clever strategies for computing that have been developed over time. Each is based on performing the operation on one place value at a time with transitions to an adjacent position (trades, regrouping, "borrows," or "carries"). These algorithms work for all numbers but are often far from the most efficient or useful methods of computing.

we now know that there are numerous methods of computing that can be handled either mentally or with pencil-and-paper support. In most everyday instances, these alternative strategies for computing are easier and faster, can often be done mentally, and contribute to our overall number sense. The traditional algorithms (procedures for computing) do not have these benefits.

Consider the following problem.

....

Mary has 114 spaces in her photo album. So far she has 89 photos in the album. How many more photos can she put in before the album is full?

....

 Try solving the photo album problem using some method other than the one you were taught in school. If you want to begin with the 9 and the 4, try a different approach. Can you do it mentally? Can you do it in more than one way? Work on this before reading further.

Here are just four of many methods that have been used by students in the primary grades to solve the computation in the photo album problem:

- 89 + 11 is 100. 11 + 14 is 25.
- 90 + 10 is 100 and 14 more is 24 plus 1 (for 89, not 90) is 25.
- Take away 14 and then take away 11 more or 25 in all.
- 89, 99, 109 (that's 20). 110, 111, 112, 113, 114 (keeping track on fingers) is 25.

Strategies such as these can be done mentally, are generally faster than the traditional algorithms, and make sense to the person using them. Every day, students and adults resort to error-prone, traditional strategies when other, more meaningful methods would be faster and less susceptible to error. Flexibility with a variety of computational strategies is an important tool for successful daily living. It is time to broaden our perspective of what it means to compute.

Figure 4.1 lists three general types of computing. The initial, inefficient direct modeling methods can, with guidance, develop into an assortment of invented strategies that are flexible and useful. As noted in the diagram, many of these methods can be handled mentally, although no special methods are designed specifically for mental computation. The traditional pencil-and-paper algorithms remain in the mainstream curricula. However, the attention given to them should, at the very least, be debated.

Direct Modeling

The developmental step that usually precedes invented strategies is called *direct modeling:* the use of manipulatives or drawings along with counting to represent directly the meaning of an operation or story problem. Figure 4.2 provides an example using base-ten materials, but often students use simple counters and count by ones.

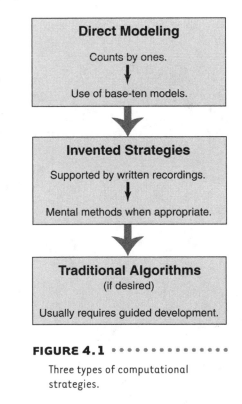

FIGURE 4.1 ....

Three types of computational strategies.

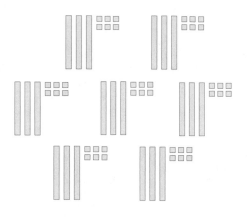

FIGURE 4.2 •

A possible direct modeling of 36 × 7 using base-ten models.

Students who consistently count by ones most likely have not developed base-ten grouping concepts. That does not mean that they should not continue to solve problems involving two-digit numbers. As you work with these children, suggest (don't force) that they group counters by tens as they count. Perhaps instead of making large piles, they might make bars of ten from connecting cubes or organize counters in cups of ten. Some students will use the ten-stick as a counting device to keep track of counts of ten, even though they are counting each segment of the stick by ones.

When children have plenty of experience with base-ten concepts and models, they begin to use these ideas in the direct modeling of the problems. Even when students use base-ten materials, they will find many different ways to solve problems.

Invented Strategies

We will refer to any strategy other than the traditional algorithm and that does not involve the use of physical materials or counting by ones as an *invented strategy*. These invented strategies might also be called *personal and flexible strategies*. At times, invented strategies are done mentally. For example, 75 + 19 can be done mentally (75 + 20 is 95, less 1 is 94). For 847 + 256, some students may write down intermediate steps to aid in memory as they work through the problem. (Try that one yourself.) In the classroom, some written support is often encouraged as strategies develop. Written records of thinking are more easily shared and help students focus on the ideas. The distinction between written, partially written, and mental is not important, especially in the development period.

Over the past two decades, a number of research projects have focused attention on how children handle computational situations when they have not been taught a specific algorithm or strategy. Three elementary curricula each base the development of computational methods on student-invented strategies. These are often referred to as "reform curricula" *(Investigations in Number, Data, and Space; Trailblazers; and Everyday Mathematics)*. "There is mounting evidence that children both in and out of school can construct methods for adding and subtracting multi-digit numbers without explicit instruction" (Carpenter et al., 1998, p. 4). Data supporting students' construction of useful methods for multiplication and division have also been gathered (Baek, 1998; Fosnot & Dolk, 2001; Kamii & Dominick, 1997; Schifter, Bastable, & Russell, 1999b).

Not all students invent their own strategies. Strategies invented by class members are shared, explored, and tried out by others. However, no student should be permitted to use any strategy without understanding it.

Contrasts with Traditional Algorithms

There are significant differences between invented strategies and the traditional algorithms.

1. *Invented strategies are number oriented rather than digit oriented.* For example, one invented strategy for 68 × 7 begins 7 × 60 is 420 and 56 more is 476. The first product is 7 times *sixty,* not the digit 6, as would be the case in the traditional algorithm. Using the traditional algorithm for 45 + 32, children never think of 40

and 30 but rather 4 + 3. Kamii, long a crusader against standard algorithms, claims that they "unteach" place value (Kamii & Dominick, 1998).

2. *Invented strategies are left-handed rather than right-handed.* Invented strategies begin with the largest parts of numbers, those represented by the leftmost digits. For 26 × 47, many invented strategies begin with 20 × 40 is 800, providing some sense of the size of the eventual answer in just one step. The traditional algorithm begins with 7 × 6 is 42. By beginning on the right with a digit orientation, traditional methods hide the result until the end. Long division is an exception.

3. *Invented strategies are flexible rather than rigid.* Invented strategies tend to change with the numbers involved in order to make the computation easier. Try each of these mentally: 465 + 230 and 526 + 98. Did you use the same method? The traditional algorithm suggests using the same tool on all problems. The traditional algorithm for 7000 – 25 typically leads to student errors, yet a mental strategy is relatively simple.

Benefits of Invented Strategies

The development of invented strategies delivers more than computational facility. Both the development of these strategies and their regular use have positive benefits that are difficult to ignore.

- *Base-ten concepts are enhanced.* There is a definite interaction between the development of base-ten concepts and the process of inventing computational strategies (Carpenter et al., 1998). "Invented strategies demonstrate a hallmark characteristic of understanding" (p. 16). The development of invented strategies should be integrated with the development of base-ten concepts, even as early as first grade.

- *Invented strategies are built on student understanding.* Students rarely use an invented strategy they do not understand. In contrast, students are frequently seen to use traditional algorithms without being able to explain why they work (Carroll & Porter, 1997).

- *Students make fewer errors with invented strategies.* Data collected by Kamii and Dominick (1997) provide some hard evidence for this claim. With traditional algorithms, students tend to develop systematic errors or "buggy algorithms" that they use again and again. Careless errors often result from confusion with carried digits or column alignment. Systematic errors are not typical of invented strategies.

- *Invented strategies serve students at least as well on standard tests.* Evidence suggests that students not taught traditional algorithms fare about as well in computation on standardized tests as students in traditional programs (Campbell, 1996; Carroll, 1996, 1997; Chambers, 1996). As an added bonus, students tend to do quite well with word problems, since they are the principal vehicle for developing invented strategies. The pressures of external testing do not dictate a focus on the traditional algorithms.

Mental Computation

A mental computation strategy is simply any invented strategy that is done mentally. What may be a mental strategy for one student may require written support by

TOWARD COMPUTATIONAL FLUENCY

another. Initially, students should not be asked to do computations mentally, as this may threaten those who have not yet developed a reasonable invented strategy or who are still at the direct modeling stage. At the same time, you may be quite amazed at the ability of students (and at your own ability) to do computations mentally.

Try your own hand with this example:

$$342 + 153 + 481$$

 For the addition task just shown, try this method: Begin by adding the hundreds, saying the totals as you go—*3 hundred, 4 hundred, 8 hundred.* Then add on to this the tens in a successive manner and finally the ones. Do it now.

When the computations are a bit more complicated, the challenge is more interesting and generally there are more alternatives. Here is an example taken from the grades 3–5 chapter of the *NCTM Standards* (p. 152).

$$7 \times 28$$

The *Standards* lists three paths to a solution but there are at least two more (NCTM, 2000, p. 152). How many ways can you find to do this one?

As your students become more adept, they can and should be challenged from time to time to do appropriate computations mentally. Do not expect the same skills of all students.

Traditional Algorithms

Teachers often ask, "How long should I wait until I show them the 'regular' way?" The question is based on a fear that without learning the same methods that all of us grew up with, students will somehow be disadvantaged. For addition and subtraction this is simply not the case. The primary goal for all computation should be students' ability to compute in some efficient manner—not what algorithms are used. That is, the *method* of computing is not the objective; the ability to compute is the goal. For multiplication and division, many teachers will see a greater need for traditional approaches, especially with three or more digits involved.

Abandon or Delay Traditional Algorithms

Flexible left-handed methods done mentally with written support are absolutely all that are necessary for addition and subtraction. Developed with adequate practice, these flexible approaches will become mental and very efficient for most students by fifth grade and will serve them more than adequately throughout life. You may find this difficult to accept for two reasons: first, because the traditional algorithms have been a significant part of your mathematical experiences and, second, because you may not have learned these skills. These are not reasons to teach the traditional algorithms for addition and subtraction.

For multiplication and division, the argument requires some discussion, especially as the number of digits involved increases. In the third grade, when students need only multiply or divide by a single digit, invented strategies are not only adequate but also will provide the benefits of understanding and flexibility mentioned earlier. The same types of skills used for two-digit numbers will be carried over to more complex computations as long as the focus remains on invented strategies and does not shift to the traditional algorithms. It is worth noting again that there is evidence that students do quite well on the computation portions of standardized tests even if they are never taught the traditional methods.

If, for whatever reason, you feel you must teach the traditional algorithms, consider the following:

- Students will not invent the traditional methods because right-handed methods are simply not natural. This means that you will have to introduce and explain each algorithm.

- No matter how carefully you suggest that these right-handed, borrow-and-carry, digit-oriented methods are simply another alternative, students will sense that these are the "right ways" or the "real ways" to compute. *This is how Mom and Dad do it. This is what the teacher taught us.* As a result, most students will abandon any flexible left-handed methods they may have been developing.

It is not that the traditional algorithms cannot be taught with a strong conceptual basis. Textbooks have been doing an excellent job of explaining these methods for years. The problem is that the traditional algorithms, especially for addition and subtraction, are not natural methods for students. As a result, the explanations generally fall on deaf ears. Far too many students learn them as meaningless procedures, develop error patterns, and require an excessive amount of reteaching or remediation. If you are going to teach the traditional algorithms, you are well advised to spend a significant amount of time—months, not weeks—with invented methods. Delay! The understanding that children gain from working with invented strategies will make it much easier for you to teach the traditional methods.

Traditional Algorithms Will Happen

You probably cannot keep the traditional algorithms out of your classroom. Children pick them up from older siblings, last year's teacher, or well-meaning parents. Traditional algorithms are in no way evil, and so to forbid their use is somewhat arbitrary. However, students who latch on to a traditional method often resist the invention of more flexible strategies. What do you do then?

First and foremost, apply the same rule to traditional algorithms as to all strategies: *If you use it, you must understand why it works and be able to explain it.* In an atmosphere that says, "Let's figure out why this works," students can profit from making sense of these algorithms just like any other. But the responsibility should be theirs, not yours.

Accept a traditional algorithm (once it is understood) as one more strategy to put in the class "tool box" of methods. But reinforce the idea that like the other strategies, it may be more useful in some instances than in others. Pose problems in which a mental strategy is much more useful, such as 504 − 498 or 75 × 4. Discuss which method seemed better. Point out that for a problem such as 4568 + 12,813, the traditional algorithm has some advantages. But in the real world, most people do those computations on a calculator.

Development of Invented Strategies: A General Approach

Students do not spontaneously invent wonderful computational methods while the teacher sits back and watches. Among different reform or progressive programs, students tended to develop or gravitate toward different strategies suggesting that teachers and the programs do have an effect on what methods students develop. This section discusses general pedagogical methods for helping children develop invented strategies.

Use Story Problems Frequently

When computational tasks are embedded in simple contexts, students seem to be more engaged than they are with bare computations. Furthermore, the choice of story problems influences the strategies students use to solve them. Consider these problems:

> **Max had already saved 68 cents when Mom gave him some money for running an errand. Now Max has 93 cents. How much did Max earn for his errand?**

> **George took 93 cents to the store. He spent 68 cents. How much does he have left?**

The computation 93 – 68 solves both problems, but the first is more likely than the second to be solved by an add-on method. In a similar manner, fair-share division problems are more likely to encourage a share strategy than a measurement or repeated subtraction problem.

Not every task need be a story problem. Especially when students are engaged in figuring out a new strategy, bare arithmetic problems are quite adequate.

Use the Three-Part Lesson Format

The three-part lesson format described in Chapter 1 is a good structure for an invented-strategy lesson. The task can be one or two story problems or even a bare computation but always with the expectation that the method of solution will be discussed.

Allow plenty of time to solve a problem. Listen to the different strategies students are using but do not interject your own. Challenge able students to find a second method, solve a problem without models, or improve on a written explanation. Allow children who are not ready for thinking with tens to use simple counting methods. Students who finish quickly may share their methods with others before sharing with the class.

The most important portion of the lesson comes when students explain their solution methods. Help students write their explanations on the board or overhead. Encourage students to ask questions of their classmates. Occasionally have the class try a particular method with different numbers to see how it works.

Remember, not every student will invent strategies. However, students can and will try strategies that they have seen and that make sense to them.

Select Numbers with Care

With traditional algorithms you are used to distinguishing between problems that require regrouping and those that do not. The number of digits involved is another common method of judging problem difficulty. When encouraging students to develop their own methods, there are more factors to consider. For addition, 35 + 42 is generally easier than 35 + 47. However, 30 + 20 is easier than both and can help students begin to think in terms of tens. A next step might be 46 + 10 or 20 + 63.

For subtraction, being able to give the other part of 100 is especially useful. Therefore, tasks such as *Thirty-five and how much more make 100?* can provide important readiness for later problems. Tasks such as 417 – 103 or 417 – 98 may each encourage students to subtract 100 and then adjust.

For multiplication, multiples of 5, 10, and 25 are good starting points. Even 325 × 4 may be easier than 86 × 7 even though there are three digits in the former example. For division, it is the divisor that requires attention. And, because most invented strategies for division rely on multiplication, the same comment applies. For example, 483 ÷ 75 is easier than 483 ÷ 67 and not much harder than 327 ÷ 6.

Integrate Computation with Place-Value Development

In Chapter 2 we made the point that as students develop computational strategies, they are enhancing their understanding of place value. Notice how the examples in the preceding section on number selection can help reinforce the way that our number system is built on a structure of groups of tens. In Chapter 2 there is a section entitled "Activities for Flexible Thinking with Whole Numbers" (pp. 51–56). The activities in that section are appropriate for grades 3 or 4 and complement the development of invented strategies, especially for addition and subtraction.

Progression from Direct Modeling

Direct modeling involving tens and ones can and will lead eventually to invented strategies. However, students may need to be encouraged to move away from the direct modeling process. Here are some ideas:

- Record students' verbal explanations on the board in ways that they and others can model. Have the class follow the recorded method using different numbers.
- Ask students who have just solved a problem with models to see if they can do it in their heads.
- Pose a problem to the class and ask students to solve it mentally if they are able.
- Ask children to make a written numeric record of what they did when they solved the problem with models. Explain that they are then going to try to use the same method on a new problem.

DEVELOPMENT OF INVENTED STRATEGIES: A GENERAL APPROACH

Invented Strategies for Addition and Subtraction

Research has demonstrated that children will invent a lot of different strategies for addition and subtraction. Your goal might be that each of your students has at least one or two methods that are reasonably efficient, mathematically correct, and useful with lots of different numbers. Expect different children to settle on different strategies.

It is not at all unreasonable for students to be able to add and subtract two-digit numbers mentally in the third grade. However, even in fourth grade, do not push all students to pure mental computation. By recording on the board the ideas that students use, you help all students develop new approaches. Those who need short-term memory assistance can see ways to support their strategies by jotting down intermediate results on paper. The goal should be flexible, meaningful computation. These methods tend to become mental with frequent use.

Most of the ideas suggested here for addition and subtraction can be taught and even mastered by the end of second grade. However, most third-grade students and even fifth- and sixth-grade students have not developed invented strategies. The sequence of ideas proposed is appropriate at any grade.

Adding and Subtracting Single Digits

Children can easily extend addition and subtraction facts to higher decades.

- -

Tommy was on page 47 of his book. Then he read 8 more pages. How many pages did Tommy read in all?

- -

If students are simply counting on by ones, the following activity may be useful. It is an extension of the make-ten strategy for addition facts.

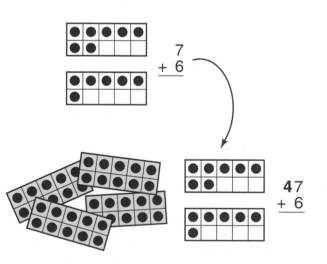

FIGURE 4.3 • • • • • • • • • • • • • • • • • •

Little ten-frame cards can help students extend the make-ten idea to larger numbers.

Notice how building up through ten (as in 47 + 6) or down through ten (as in 53 – 7) is different from carrying and borrowing. No ones are exchanged for a ten nor a ten for ones. The ten-frame cards encourage students to work with multiples of ten without regrouping.

Another important model to use is the hundreds chart. The hundreds chart has the same tens structure as the little ten-frame cards. For 47 + 6 you count 3 to get out to 50 at the end of the row and then 3 more in the next row.

Adding Two-Digit Numbers

For each of the examples that follow, a possible recording method is offered. These are intended to be suggestions, not prescriptions. Students have difficulty inventing recording techniques. If you record their ideas on the board as they explain their ideas, you are helping them develop written techniques. You may even discuss recording methods with individuals or with the class to decide on a form that seems to work well. Horizontal formats encourage students to think in terms of numbers instead of digits. A horizontal format is also less likely to encourage use of the traditional algorithms.

Students will often use a counting-by-tens-and-ones technique for some of these methods. That is, instead of "46 + 30 is 76," they may count "46 ⟶ 56, 66, 76." These counts can be written down as they are said to help students keep track.

Figure 4.4 illustrates four different strategies for addition of two two-digit numbers. The following story problem is a suggestion.

· ·

The two Scout troops went on a field trip. There were 46 Girl Scouts and 38 Boy Scouts. How many Scouts went on the trip?

· ·

The *move to make-ten* and *compensation* strategies are useful when one of the numbers ends in 8 or 9. To promote that strategy, present problems with addends like 39 or 58. Note that it is only necessary to adjust one of the two numbers.

 Try adding 367 + 155 in as many different ways as you can. How many of your ways are like those in Figure 4.4?

Invented Strategies for Addition with Two-Digit Numbers	
Add Tens, Add Ones, Then Combine 46 + 38 40 and 30 is 70. 6 and 8 is 14. 70 and 14 is 84. $\begin{array}{r} 46 \\ +38 \\ \hline 70 \\ 14 \\ \hline 84 \end{array}$	**Move Some to Make Tens** 46 + 38 Take 2 from the 46 and put it with the 38 to make 40. Now you have 44 and 40 more is 84. $\overset{2}{\overbrace{46 + 38}}$ $44 + 40$ 84
Add On Tens, Then Add Ones 46 + 38 46 and 30 more is 76. Then I added on the other 8. 76 and 4 is 80 and 4 is 84. $46 + 38 \rightarrow$ $76 + 8 \rightarrow 80, 84$	**Use a Nice Number and Compensate** 46 + 38 46 and 40 is 86. That's 2 extra, so it's 84. $46 + 38$ $46 + 40 \rightarrow$ $86 - 2 \rightarrow 84$

FIGURE 4.4 · · · · · · · ·

Four different invented strategies for adding two two-digit numbers.

Subtracting by Counting Up

This is an amazingly powerful way to subtract. Students working on the *think-addition* strategy for their basic facts can also be solving problems with larger numbers. The concept is the same. It is important to use *join with change unknown* problems or *missing-part* problems to encourage the counting-up strategy. Here is an example of each.

. . . .

Sam had 46 baseball cards. He went to a card show and got some more cards for his collection. Now he has 73 cards. How many cards did Sam buy at the card show?

. . . .

. . . .

Juanita counted all of her crayons. Some were broken and some not. She had 73 crayons in all. 46 crayons were not broken. How many were broken?

. . . .

The numbers in these problems are used in the strategies illustrated in Figure 4.5.

Emphasize the value of using tens by posing problems involving multiples of 10. In 50 – 17, the use of ten can happen by adding up from 17 to 20, or by adding 30 to 17. Some students may reason that it must be 30-something because 30 and 17 is less than 50, and 40 and 17 is more than 50. Because it takes 3 to go with 7 to make 10, the answer must be 33. Work on naming the missing part of 50 or 100 is also valuable. (See Activity 2.18, "The Other Part of 100," p. 54.)

Take-Away Subtraction

Take-away methods are more difficult to do mentally or even with the help of paper and pencil. This is especially true when problems involve three digits. Exceptions involve problems such as 423 – 8 or 576 – 300 (subtracting a number less than 10 or a multiple of 10 or 100). However, take-away strategies are bound to occur, probably because traditional textbooks emphasize take-away as the meaning of subtraction. Take-

FIGURE 4.5 · · · · · · · ·

Subtraction by counting up is a powerful method.

Invented Strategies for Subtraction by Counting Up	
Add Tens to Get Close, Then Ones	**Add Ones to Make a Ten, Then Tens and Ones**
73 – 46 $\quad$ $46 > 20$ $\quad$ $66 > 4$ $\quad$ $70 > 3$ $\quad$ $73 \underline{\quad} 27$ 46 and 20 is 66. $\quad$ (30 more is too much.) Then 4 more is 70 and 3 is 73. That's 20 and 7 or 27.	73 – 46 $\quad$ $73 - 46$ 46 and 4 is 50. $\quad$ $46 + 4 \rightarrow 50$ 50 and 20 is 70 and 3 $\quad$ $+\ 20 \rightarrow 70$ more is 73. The 4 and 3 $\quad$ $+\ 3 \rightarrow 73$ is 7 and 20 is 27. $\quad\quad\quad$ $\overline{27}$
Add Tens to Overshoot, Then Come Back	
73 – 46 $\quad$ $73 - 46$ 46 and 30 is 76. $\quad$ $46 + 30 \rightarrow 76 - 3 \rightarrow 73$ That's 3 too $\quad$ $30 - 3 = 27$ much, so it's 27.	Similarly, 46 and 4 is 50. $\quad$ $46 + 4 \rightarrow 50$ 50 and 23 is 73. $\quad$ $50 + 23 \rightarrow 73$ 23 and 4 is 27. $\quad$ $23 + 4 = 27$

away is very likely the strategy that will come to mind first for students who have previously been taught the traditional algorithm.

Four take-away strategies are shown in Figure 4.6, and these should not be discouraged. We suggest, however, that you emphasize adding-on methods whenever possible.

. . . .

There were 73 children on the playground. The 46 third-grade students came in first. How many children were still outside?

. . . .

The two methods that begin by taking tens from tens are reflective of what most students do with base-ten pieces. The other two methods leave one of the numbers intact and subtract from it. Try 83 – 29 in your head by first taking away 30 and adding 1 back. This is a good mental method when subtracting a number that is close to a multiple of ten.

 Try computing 82 – 57. Use both take-away and counting up methods. Can you use all of the strategies in Figures 4.5 and 4.6 without looking?

Extensions and Challenges

Each of the examples in the preceding sections involved sums less than 100 and all involved *bridging a ten;* that is, if done with a traditional algorithm, they require carrying or borrowing. Bridging, the size of the numbers, and the potential for doing problems mentally are all issues to consider.

Invented Strategies for Take-Away Subtraction	
Take Tens from the Tens, Then Subtract Ones	**Take Away Tens, Then Ones**
73 – 46	73 – 46
70 minus 40 is 30. Take away 6 more is 24. Now add in the 3 ones → 27. $73 - 46$ $70 - 40 \rightarrow 30 - 6 \rightarrow$ $24 + 3 \rightarrow 27$	73 minus 40 is 33. $73 - 40 \rightarrow 33 - 3$ Then take away 6: 3 makes 30 and $30 - 3 \rightarrow 27$ 3 more is 27.
	Take Extra Tens, Then Add Back
Or	73 – 46
70 minus 40 is 30. I can take those 3 away, but I need 3 more from the 30 to make 27. $\begin{array}{r} 7\cancel{3} \\ -46 \\ \hline 30 \\ -3 \\ \hline 27 \end{array}$	73 take away 50 is 23. $73 - 50 \rightarrow 23 + 4$ That's 4 too many. 23 and 4 is 27. 27
	Add to the Whole If Necessary
	73 – 46 $+3$
	Give 3 to 73 to make 76. $73 - 46$ 76 take away 46 is 30. $76 - 46 \rightarrow 30$ Now give 3 back → 27. $-3 \rightarrow 27$

FIGURE 4.6 . . . .

Take-away strategies work reasonably well for two-digit problems. They are a bit more difficult with three digits.

Bridging

For most of the strategies, it is easier to add or subtract when bridging is not required. Try each strategy with 34 + 52 or 68 – 24 to see how it works. Easier problems instill confidence. They also permit you to challenge your students with a "harder one." There is also the issue of bridging 100 or 1000. Try 58 + 67 with different strategies. Bridging across 100 is also an issue for subtraction. Problems such as 128 – 50 or 128 – 45 are more difficult than ones that do not bridge 100.

Larger Numbers

Most curricula will expect third graders to add and subtract three-digit numbers. Your state standards may even require work with four-digit numbers. Try seeing how *you* would do these without using the traditional algorithms: 487 + 235 and 623 – 247. For subtraction, a counting-up strategy is usually the easiest. Occasionally, other strategies appear with larger numbers. For example, "chunking off" multiples of 50 or 25 is often a useful method. For 462 + 257, pull out 450 and 250 to make 700. That leaves 12 and 7 more ⟶ 719.

Traditional Algorithms for Addition and Subtraction

The traditional computational methods for addition and subtraction are significantly different from nearly every invented method. In addition to starting with the rightmost digits and being digit oriented (as already noted), the traditional approaches involve the concept generally referred to as *regrouping,* exchanging 10 in one place-value position for 1 in the position to the left ("carrying"), or the reverse, exchanging 1 for 10 in the position to the right ("borrowing"). The terms *borrowing* and *carrying* are obsolete and conceptually misleading. The word *regroup* also offers no conceptual help to students. A preferable term is *trade.* Ten ones are *traded* for a ten. A hundred is *traded* for 10 tens. Trading makes sense with the use of base-ten pieces when, in fact, pieces must be traded; for example, a ten piece is traded in for 10 ones pieces.

Terminology aside, the trading process is quite different from the bridging process used in all invented and mental strategies. Consider the task of adding 28 + 65. Using the traditional method, we first add 8 and 5. The resulting 13 ones are separated into 3 ones and 1 ten. The newly formed ten is then combined with the other tens. This process of "carrying a ten" is conceptually difficult and is different from the bridging process that occurs in invented strategies. In fact, nearly all major textbooks now teach this process of regrouping prior to and separate from direct instruction with the addition and subtraction algorithm, an indication of the difficulties involved. The process is even more difficult for subtraction, especially across a zero in the tens place where two successive trades are required.

Compounding all of this is the issue of recording each step. The traditional algorithms do not lend themselves to mental computation, so students must learn to record. The literature of the past 50 years is replete with the errors that students make with these recording methods.

All of these observations are offered to encourage you to abandon the traditional algorithms for addition and subtraction and, failing that, to alert you to the difficulties your students will likely have. Having said that, we offer some guidance for you if you must teach the standard procedures.

- Because it will never occur to students to add or subtract beginning in the ones place, you will have to use a more direct approach to instruction rather than a strictly problem-oriented approach.

- Use base-ten models and no recording at all until students seem to understand the process.

- For subtraction, model only the whole or top number. For the bottom number, have students write the digits on small slips of paper as shown in Figure 4.7.

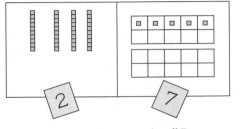

Not enough ones to take off 7.
Trade a ten for 10 ones.

FIGURE 4.7 •

Setting up the subtraction algorithm.

- Develop the written method in a do-then-record approach. Whenever any change is made with the base-ten models, students record the action in the standard manner. Most traditional textbook explanations generally offer good guidance. However, they move to pure drill far too quickly with the result often being rules without reasons.

- Pay special attention to difficulties involving zero, especially in problems such as 504 – 347 where students must "borrow across zero." These problems should be solved with models and discussed as a class.

Invented Strategies for Multiplication

Computation strategies for multiplication are considerably more complex than for addition and subtraction. Often, but by no means always, the strategies that students invent are very similar to the traditional algorithm. The big difference is that students think about numbers, not digits. They always begin with the large or left-hand numbers.

For multiplication, the ability to break numbers apart in flexible ways is even more important than in addition or subtraction. The distributive property is another concept that is important in multiplication computation. For example, to multiply 43 × 5, one might think about breaking 43 into 40 and 3, multiplying each by 5, and then adding the results. Children require ample opportunities to develop these concepts by making sense of their own ideas and those of their classmates.

Useful Representations

The problem 34 × 6 may be represented in a number of ways, as illustrated in Figure 4.8. Often the choice of a model is influenced by a story problem. To determine how many Easter eggs 34 children need if each colors 6 eggs, children may model 6 sets of 34 (or possibly 34 sets of 6). If the problem is about the area of a rectangle that is 34 cm by 6 cm, then some form of an array is likely. But each representation is appropriate for thinking about 34 × 6 regardless of the context, and students should get to a point where they select ways to think about multiplication that are meaningful to them.

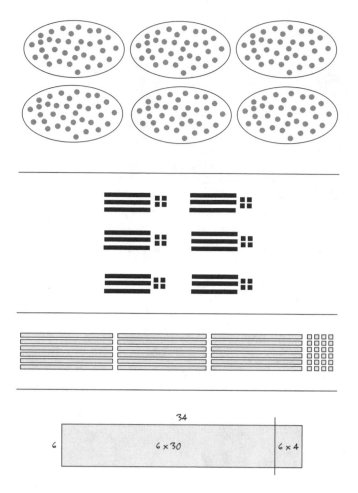

FIGURE 4.8 •••••••••••••••••••••••••••••••••••••

Different ways to model 34 × 6 may support different computational strategies.

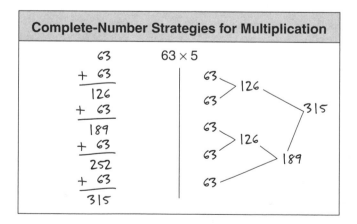

FIGURE 4.9 •••••••••••••••••••••••••••••••••••••

Children who use a complete-number strategy do not break numbers apart into decades or tens and ones.

How students represent a product interacts with their methods for determining answers. The groups of 34 might suggest repeated additions—perhaps taking the sets two at a time. Double 34 is 68 and there are three of those, so 68 + 68 + 68. From there a variety of methods are possible.

The six sets of base-ten pieces might suggest breaking the numbers into tens and ones: 6 times 3 tens or 6 × 30 and 6 × 4. Some children use the tens individually: 6 tens make 60. So that's 60 and 60 and 60 (180). Then add on the 24 to make 204.

It is not uncommon to arrange the base-ten pieces in a nice array, even if the story problem does not suggest it. The area model is very much like an arrangement of the base-ten pieces.

All of these ideas should be part of students' repertoire of models for multidigit multiplication. Introduce different representations (one at a time) as ways to explore multiplication until you are comfortable that the class has a collection of useful ideas. At the same time, do not force students who reason very well without drawings to use models when they are not needed.

Multiplication by a Single-Digit Multiplier

As with addition and subtraction, it is helpful to place multiplication tasks in contextual story problems. Let students model the problems in ways that make sense to them. Do not be concerned about mixing of factors (6 sets of 34 or 34 sets of 6). Nor should you be timid about the numbers you use. The problem 3 × 24 may be easier than 7 × 65, but the latter provides challenge. The types of strategies that students use for multiplication are much more varied than for addition and subtraction. However, the following three categories can be identified from the research to date.

Complete-Number Strategies

Students who are not yet comfortable breaking numbers into parts using tens and ones will approach the numbers in the sets as single groups. For students who think this way, Figure 4.9 illustrates two methods they may use. These children will benefit from listening to students who use base-ten models. They may also need more work with base-ten grouping activities where they take numbers apart in different ways.

Chapter 4 STRATEGIES FOR WHOLE-NUMBER COMPUTATION

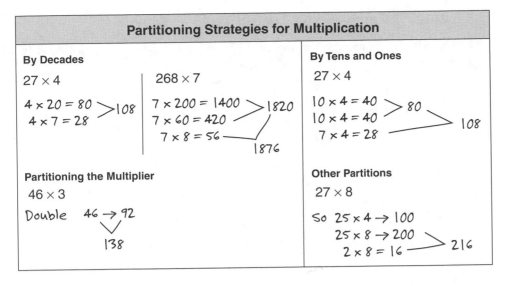

FIGURE 4.10 ········

Numbers can be broken apart in different ways to make easier partial products, which are then combined. Partitioning by decades is useful for mental computation and is very close to the standard algorithm.

Partitioning Strategies

Students break numbers up in a variety of ways that reflect an understanding of base-ten concepts, at least four of which are illustrated in Figure 4.10. The "By Decades" approach is the same as the standard algorithm except that students always begin with the large values. It extends easily to three digits and is very powerful as a mental math strategy. Another valuable strategy for mental methods is found in the "Other Partitions" example. It is easy to compute mentally with multiples of 25 and 50 and then add or subtract a small adjustment. All partition strategies rely on the distributive property.

Compensation Strategies

Students look for ways to manipulate numbers so that the calculations are easy. In Figure 4.11, the problem 27 × 4 is changed to an easier one, and then an adjustment or compensation is made. In the second example, one factor is cut in half and the other doubled. This is often used when a 5 or a 50 is involved. Because these strategies are so dependent on the numbers involved, they can't be used for all computations. However, they are powerful strategies, especially for mental math and estimation.

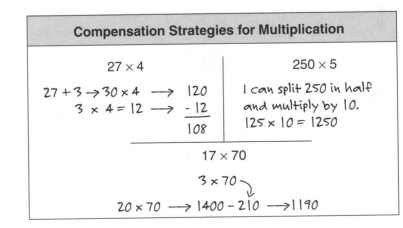

FIGURE 4.11 ········

Compensation methods use a product related to the original. A compensation is made in the answer, or one factor is changed to compensate for a change in the other factor.

INVENTED STRATEGIES FOR MULTIPLICATION

Using Multiples of 10 and 100

There is a value in exposing students early to products involving multiples of 10 and 100.

....

The Scout troop wanted to package up 400 fire starter kits as a fund-raising project. If each pack will have 12 fire starters, how many fire starters are the Scouts going to need?

....

Students will use 4 × 12 = 48 to figure out that 400 × 12 is 4800. There will be discussion around how to say and write "forty-eight hundred." Be aware of students who simply tack on zeros without understanding why. Try problems such as 30 × 60 or 210 × 40 where tens are multiplied by tens.

Two-Digit Multipliers

A problem such as this one can be solved in many different ways:

....

The parade had 23 clowns. Each clown carried 18 balloons. How many balloons were there altogether?

....

Some children look for smaller products such as 6 × 23 and then add that result three times. Another method is to do 20 × 23 and then subtract 2 × 23. Others will calculate four separate partial products: 10 × 20 = 200, 8 × 20 = 160, 10 × 3 = 30, and 8 × 3 = 24. And still others may add up a string of 23s. Two-digit multiplication is both complex and challenging. But students can solve these problems in a variety of interesting ways, many of which will contribute to the development of the traditional algorithm or one that is just as efficient. Time devoted to working on these tasks in the fourth and fifth grades is well spent.

Area Models

When working on multiplication strategies, a key idea is finding ways to break one or both of the numbers into smaller numbers. For 34 × 6, if 34 is broken into 30 and 4, both the 30 and the 4 must be multiplied by 6. Models are an enormous help in developing this idea. Refer again to Figure 4.8 (p. 114) to see models of 34 × 6. An area model can expand this idea to two-digit multipliers.

A valuable exploration is to prepare large rectangles for each group of two or three students. The rectangles should be measured carefully, with dimensions between 25 cm and 60 cm, and drawn accurately with square corners. (Use the corner of a piece of poster board for a guide.) The students' task is to determine how many small ones pieces (base-ten materials) will fit inside. Wooden or plastic base-ten pieces are best, but cardboard strips and squares are adequate. Alternatively, rectangles can be drawn on base-ten grid paper (see Blackline Masters).

Most students will fill the rectangle first with as many hundreds pieces as possible. One obvious approach is to put the 12 hundreds in one corner. This will leave narrow regions on two sides that can be filled with tens pieces and a final small rectangle

BLM 16

that will hold ones. Especially if students have had earlier experiences with finding products in arrays, figuring out the size of each subrectangle is not terribly difficult. The sketch in Figure 4.12 shows the four regions.

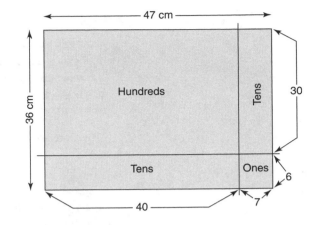

If you did not already know the algorithm, how would you determine the size of the rectangle? Use your method (not the standard algorithm) on a rectangle that measures 68 cm × 24 cm. Make a sketch to show and explain your work.

FIGURE 4.12 •

Ones, tens, and hundreds pieces fit exactly into the four sections of this 47 x 36 rectangle. Figure the size of each section to determine the size of the whole rectangle.

As you will see in the discussion of the traditional algorithm, the area model leads to a fairly reasonable approach to multiplying numbers, even if you never have students "carry," which is a source of many errors.

Cluster Problems

In the fourth and fifth grades of *Investigations in Number, Data, and Space* (one of the NSF-supported reform curricula), one approach to multidigit multiplication is called "cluster problems." This rather unique approach to the topic encourages students to use facts and combinations that they know or can easily figure out in order to find the answers to more complex computations. For example, the following cluster is used in an introductory lesson in the fourth-grade unit: 3 × 7, 5 × 7, 10 × 7, 50 × 7, and 53 × 7. The goal is to figure out the last product. Students solve all of the problems and explain what problems were helpful in solving the last problem. Not every problem in the cluster needs to be used to solve the final problem. If students wish to add other problems to the cluster to aid in finding their solution to the final problem, they are encouraged to do so.

Here are two cluster problems taken from a fourth-grade worksheet.

EXPANDED LESSON

(pages 129–130)

The expanded lesson for this chapter has students work with the area model for two-digit multiplication.

2 × 50	60 × 20
10 × 50	62 × 10
34 × 25	62 × 3
30 × 50	**62 × 23**
34 × 50	

It is useful to have students make an estimate of the final product before doing any of the problems in the cluster. In the first example cluster, 2 × 50 may be helpful in thinking about 10 × 50, which in turn is useful in knowing 30 × 50. Also 2 × 50 can be used to get 4 × 50. The results of 30 × 50 and 4 × 50 combine to give you 34 × 50. It may seem that 34 × 25 is harder than 34 × 50. However, if you know 34 × 25, it need only be doubled to get the desired product. Students should be encouraged to add problems to the cluster if they need them. Here is a good example: Think how you could use 10 × 34 (and some other related problems) to find 34 × 25.

The cluster-problem approach begins with students being provided with the cluster of problems. After they have become familiar with the approach, students should make up their own cluster of problems for a given product. At first, have students brainstorm clusters together as a class.

INVENTED STRATEGIES FOR MULTIPLICATION

First, solve the two preceding clusters each in at least two ways. Now, try your hand at making up a cluster of problems for 86 × 42. Include all possible problems that you think might possibly be helpful, even if they are not all related to one approach to finding the product. Then use your cluster to find the product. Is there more than one way?

Here are some problems that might be in your cluster.

2 × 80   4 × 80   2 × 86   40 × 80   6 × 40   10 × 86   40 × 86

Of course, your cluster may have included products not shown here. All that is required to begin the cluster-problem approach is that your cluster eventually leads to a solution. Besides your own cluster, see if you can use the problems in this cluster to find 86 × 42.

Cluster problems help students think about ways that they can break numbers apart into easier parts. The strategy of breaking the numbers apart and multiplying the parts—the distributive property—is an extremely valuable technique for flexible computation. It is also fun to find different clever paths to the solution. For many problems, finding a workable cluster is actually faster than using an algorithm.

The Traditional Algorithm for Multiplication

The traditional multiplication algorithm is probably the most difficult of the four algorithms if students have not had plenty of opportunities to explore their own strategies. Time spent allowing your students to develop a range of invented strategies will pay off in their understanding of the traditional algorithm. While your students are working on multiplication using their invented strategies, be sure to emphasize partitioning techniques, especially those that are similar to the "By Decades" approach shown in Figure 4.10 (p. 115). These strategies tend to be the most efficient and are very close to the traditional algorithm. In fact, students who are using one or more partitioning strategies with a one-digit multiplier have no real need to learn any other approach.

The multiplication algorithm can be meaningfully developed using either a repeated addition model or an area model. For single-digit multipliers, the difference is minimal. When you move to two-digit multipliers, the area model has some advantages. For that reason, the discussion here will use the area model.

One-Digit Multipliers

As with the other algorithms, as much time as possible should be devoted to the conceptual development of the algorithm with the recording or written part coming later.

Begin with Models

Give students a drawing of a rectangle 47 cm by 6 cm. *How many small square centimeter pieces will fit in the rectangle?* (What is the area of the rectangle in square centimeters?) Let students solve the problem in groups before discussing it as a class.

FIGURE 4.13 • • • • • • • •

A rectangle filled with base-ten pieces is a useful model for two-digit-by-one-digit multiplication.

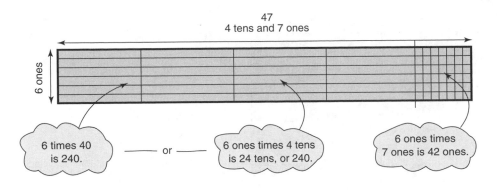

47

4 tens and 7 ones

6 ones

6 times 40 is 240. — or — 6 ones times 4 tens is 24 tens, or 240. 6 ones times 7 ones is 42 ones.

As shown in Figure 4.13, the rectangle can be "sliced" or separated into two parts so that one part will be 6 ones by 7 ones, or 42 ones, and the other will be 6 ones by 4 tens, or 24 tens. Notice that the base-ten language "6 ones times 4 tens is 24 tens" tells how many *pieces* (sticks of ten) are in the big section. To say "6 times 40 is 240" is also correct and tells how many units or square centimeters are in the section. Each section is referred to as a *partial product*. By adding the two partial products, you get the total product or area of the rectangle.

To avoid the tedium of drawing large rectangles and arranging base-ten pieces, use the base-ten grid paper found in the Blackline Masters. On the grid paper, students can easily draw accurate rectangles showing all of the pieces. Check to be sure students understand that for a product such as 74 × 8, there are two partial products, 70 × 8 = 560 and 4 × 8 = 32, and the sum of these is the product. Do not force any recording technique on students until they understand how to use the two dimensions of a rectangle to get a product.

Develop the Written Record

When the two partial products are written separately as in Figure 4.14(a), there is little new to learn. Students simply record the products and add them together. As illustrated, it is possible to teach students how to write the first product with a carried digit so that the combined product is written on one line. This traditional recording scheme is known to be problematic. The little carried digit is often the source of difficulty—it gets added in before the second multiplication or is forgotten.

There is absolutely no practical reason why students can't be allowed to record both partial products and avoid the errors related to the carried digit. When you accept that, it makes no difference in which order the products are written. Why not simply permit students to do written multiplication as shown in Figure 4.14 without carrying? Furthermore, that is precisely how this is done mentally.

Most standard curricula progress from two digits to three digits with a single-digit multiplier. Students can make this progression easily. They still should be permitted to write all three partial products separately and not have to bother with carrying.

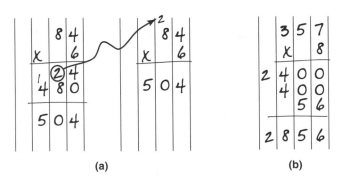

(a) (b)

FIGURE 4.14 • • • • • • • • • • • • • •

(a) In the standard form, the product of ones is recorded first. The tens digit of this first product can be written as a "carried" digit above the tens column. (b) It is quite reasonable to abandon the carried digit and permit the partial products to be recorded in any order.

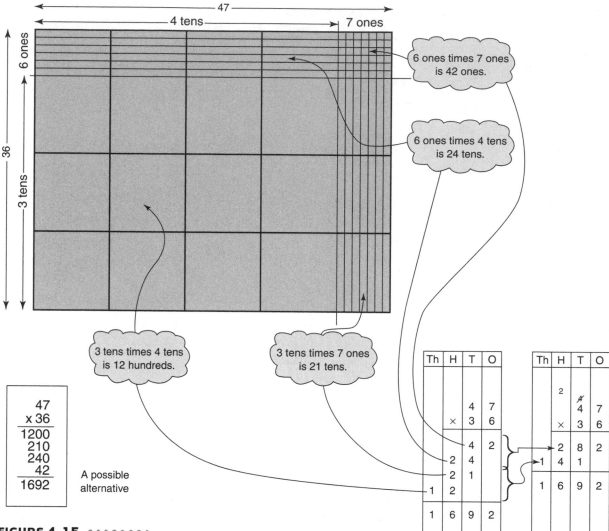

FIGURE 4.15 · · · · · · · · ·

47 × 36 rectangle filled with base-ten pieces. Base-ten language connects the four partial products to the traditional written format. Note the possibility of recording the products in some other order.

Two-Digit Multipliers

With the area model, the progression to a two-digit multiplier is relatively straightforward. Rectangles can be drawn on base-ten grid paper, or full-sized rectangles can be filled in with base-ten pieces. There will be four partial products, corresponding to four different sections of the rectangle.

Figure 4.15 also shows the recording of four partial products in the traditional order and how these can be collapsed to two lines if carried digits are used. Here the second "carry" technically belongs in the hundreds column but it rarely is written there. Often it gets confused with the first and is thus an additional source of errors. The lower left of the figure shows the same computation with all four products written in a different order. This is quite an acceptable algorithm. In the rare instance when someone multiplies numbers such as 538 × 29 with pencil and paper, there would be six partial products. But far fewer errors would occur, requiring less instructional time and much less remediation.

Invented Strategies for Division

In our discussion of division facts (Chapter 3), we included something we called "near facts." In a near fact, the divisor and quotient are both less than ten but there is a remainder, as in 44 ÷ 8. Third- and fourth-grade students should have ample experiences with near facts. When these problems are expanded to those in which the quotients are more than 9 (e.g., 73 ÷ 6), the process evolves into invented strategies for division.

Sharing and Measurement Problems

Recall that there are two concepts of division. First there is the partition or fair-sharing idea, illustrated by this story problem:

> **The bag has 783 jelly beans, and Aidan and her four friends want to share them equally. How many jelly beans will Aidan and each of her friends get?**

Then there is the measurement or repeated subtraction concept:

> **Jumbo the elephant loves peanuts. His trainer has 625 peanuts. If he gives Jumbo 20 peanuts each day, how many days will the peanuts last?**

Students should be challenged to solve both types of problems. However, the fair-share problems are often easier to solve with base-ten pieces. Furthermore, the traditional algorithm is built on this idea. Eventually, students will develop strategies that they will apply to both types of problem, even when the process does not match the action of the story.

Figure 4.16 shows some strategies that fourth-grade students have used to solve division problems. The first example illustrates 92 ÷ 4 using base-ten pieces and a sharing process. A ten is traded when no more tens can be passed out. Then the 12 ones are distributed, resulting in 23 in each set. This direct modeling approach with base-ten pieces is quite easy even for third-grade students to understand and use.

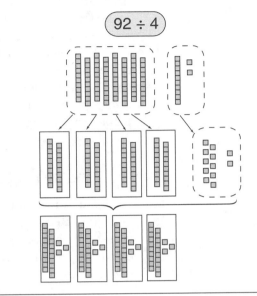

(a) 92 ÷ 4

(b) 453 ÷ 6
(share with 6 kids)

(c) 143 jelly beans shared with 8 kids

Try 14 × 8 → 112
12 groups of 8 is 96.
12 groups in 100 leaves 4.
5 groups of 8 is 40.
And 3 more left over.
12 + 5 is 17 with 7 left.

FIGURE 4.16 •

Students use both models and symbols to solve division tasks.

Source: From *Developing Mathematical Ideas: Numbers and Operations, Part I: Building a System of Tens Casebook,* by D. Schifter, V. Bastable, & S. J. Russell. Copyright © 1999 by Education Development Center, Inc. Published by Dale Seymour Publications, an imprint of Pearson Learning. Used by permission.

In the second example, the student sets out the base-ten pieces and draws a "bar graph" with six columns. After noting that there are not enough hundreds for each kid, he mentally splits the 3 hundreds in half, putting 50 in each column. That leaves him with 1 hundred, 5 tens, and 3 ones. After trading the hundred for tens (now 15 tens), he gives 20 to each, recording 2 tens in each bar. Now he is left with 3 tens and 3 ones, or 33. He knows that 5×6 is 30, so he gives each kid 5, leaving him with 3. These he splits in half and writes $\frac{1}{2}$ in each column.

The student in the third example is solving a sharing problem but tries to do it as a measurement process. She wants to find out how many 8s are in 143. Initially she guesses. By multiplying 8 first by 10, then by 20, and then by 14, she knows the answer is more than 14 and less than 20. After some more work (not shown), she rethinks the problem as how many 8s in 100 and how many in 40.

Missing Factor Strategies

You can see in Figure 4.16 how the use of base-ten pieces tends to lead to a digit-by-digit strategy—share the hundreds first, then the tens, then the ones. Although this is precisely the conceptual background behind the traditional algorithm, it is digit oriented as opposed to an approach that helps students think of the whole value of the dividend. In Figure 4.16(c), the student is using a multiplicative approach. She is trying to find out, "What number times 8 will be close to 143 with less than 8 left over?" This is a good method to suggest to students in grades 3–5. It will build on their multiplication skills, it is a method that lends itself to mental estimation, and it can work quite well for most purposes.

 Before reading further, consider the task of determining the quotient of 318 ÷ 7 by trying to figure out *what number times 7 (or 7 times what number)* is close to 318 without going over. Do not use the standard algorithm.

There are several places to begin solving this problem. For instance, since 10×7 is 70 and 100×7 is 700, it has to be between 10 and 100, probably closer to 10. You might start adding up 70s:

$$
\begin{aligned}
&70 \\
+\ &70 \text{ is } 140 \\
+\ &70 \text{ is } 210 \\
+\ &70 \text{ is } 280 \\
+\ &70 \text{ is } 350
\end{aligned}
$$

So four 70s is not enough and five is too much. It has to be forty-something. At this point you could guess at numbers between 40 and 50. Or you might add on 7s. Or you could notice that forty 7s (280) leaves you with 20 plus 18 or 38. Or five 7s will be 35 of the 38 with 3 left over. In all, that's $40 + 5$ or 45 with a remainder of 3.

Another starting point might be 50×7. This beginning likely indicates that 40×7 will be the largest multiple of ten.

This missing-factor approach is likely to be invented by some students if they are solving measurement problems such as the following:

Grace can put 6 pictures on one page of her photo album. If she has 82 pictures, how many pages will she need?

Alternatively, you can simply pose a task such as 82 ÷ 6 and ask students, "What number times 6 would be close to 82?" and continue from there.

Another approach to developing missing-factor strategies is to use cluster problems as discussed for multiplication. (See p. 117.) Here are two examples:

$$
\begin{array}{ll}
100 \times 4 & 10 \times 72 \\
500 \div 4 & 5 \times 70 \\
4 \times 25 & 2 \times 72 \\
6 \times 4 & 4 \times 72 \\
\mathbf{527 \div 4} & 5 \times 72 \\
& \mathbf{381 \div 72}
\end{array}
$$

Notice that the missing-factor strategy is equally as good for one-digit divisors as for two-digit divisors. Also notice that it is okay to include division problems in the cluster. In the preceding example, 125 × 4 could easily have replaced 500 ÷ 4, and 400 ÷ 4 could replace 100 × 4. The idea is to keep multiplication and division as closely connected as possible.

Cluster problems accentuate a flexible approach to computation, helping students realize that there are many different good ways to compute. Another way to develop flexibility is to pose a division problem (or a multiplication problem) and have students solve the problem using two different approaches. Of course, neither of the methods should be the traditional algorithm or a calculator.

STOP **Solve 514 ÷ 8 in two different, nontraditional ways. Your ways may converge in similar places but begin with different first steps, or they may be completely different.**

Here are four possible starting points and there are certainly others:

$$10 \times 8 \qquad 400 \div 8 \qquad 60 \times 8 \qquad 80 \div 8$$

Try to solve 514 ÷ 8 beginning with each of these starting points.

When students are first asked to solve problems using two methods, they often use a primitive or completely inefficient method for their second approach. For example, to solve 514 ÷ 8, a student might perform a very long string of subtractions (514 − 8 = 506, 506 − 8 = 498, 498 − 8 = 490, and so on) and count how many times he or she subtracted 8. Others will actually draw 514 tally marks and loop groups of 8. These students have not developed sufficient flexibility to think of other efficient

INVENTED STRATEGIES FOR DIVISION

methods. To help with this, pose problems along with two or three starting points and have students use each of the starting points to solve the problem. Your class discussions will help students begin to see more flexible approaches.

The Traditional Algorithm for Division

If you have been working along with the examples and approaches in this section, we hope you are convinced that students can use invented strategies for both one-digit divisors and two-digit divisors as long as the dividends are less than 1000 and a whole-number quotient with a remainder is all that is required. That is, it is not significantly faster to do 738 ÷ 43 by the traditional algorithm than to use a missing-factor approach. (Try it!) Notice that while doing the traditional algorithm you also have to do 308 ÷ 43, another problem as hard as the original. That is, the task often does not get easier as you go along. Compound this with the abundant difficulties of the traditional algorithm and the concomitant reteaching that inevitably takes place.

However, many will argue that students simply must have a more efficient method of dividing than those suggested here. Furthermore, if the curriculum requires division with decimal divisors or quotients to be carried out to get decimal results (in contrast to whole-number remainders), an argument can possibly be made for teaching a traditional algorithm. We, therefore, share with you one approach to the traditional long-division algorithm. Because the algorithm most often taught in textbooks is based on the partition or fair-sharing concept of division, that is the method described here. (Some teachers may want to explore a repeated subtraction algorithm that is very much like a missing-factor approach with partial products recorded in a column to the right of the division computation. See Figure 4.17 for an example.)

One-Digit Divisors

Typically, the division algorithm with one-digit divisors is introduced in the third grade. If done well, it should not have to be retaught, and it should provide the basis for two-digit divisors.

Begin with Models

Traditionally, for a problem such as 4)583, we might say "4 goes into 5 one time." This is quite mysterious to students. How can you just ignore the "83" and keep changing the problem? Preferably, you want students to think of the 583 as 5 hundreds, 8 tens, and 3 ones, not as the independent digits 5, 8, and 3. One idea is to use a context such as candy bundled in boxes of ten with 10 boxes to a carton. Then the problem becomes *We have 5 boxes, 8 cartons, and 3 pieces of candy to share between 4 schools evenly.* In this context, it is reasonable to share the cartons first until no more can be shared. Those remaining are "unpacked," and the boxes shared, and so on. Money ($100, $10, and $1) can be used in a similar manner.

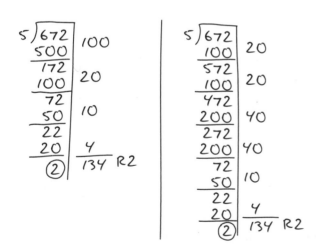

FIGURE 4.17

In the division algorithm shown, the numbers on the side indicate the quantity of the divisor being subtracted from the dividend. As the two examples indicate, the divisor can be subtracted from the dividend in any amount desired.

STOP Try the distributing or sharing process yourself using base-ten pieces (or draw squares, sticks, and dots). Use the problem 524 ÷ 3. Try to talk through the process without using "goes into." Think sharing.

Language plays an enormous role in thinking about the algorithm conceptually. Most adults are so accustomed to the "goes into" language that it is hard to let it go. For the problem 583 ÷ 4, here is some suggested language as you work through the task:

> *I want to share 5 hundreds, 8 tens, and 3 ones among these four sets. There are enough hundreds for each set to get 1 hundred. That leaves 1 hundred that I can't share.*
>
> *I'll trade the hundred for 10 tens. That gives me a total of 18 tens. I can give each set 4 tens and have 2 tens left over. Two tens is not enough to go around the four sets.*
>
> *I can trade the 2 tens for 20 ones and put those with the 3 ones I already had. That makes a total of 23 ones. I can give 5 ones in each of the four sets. That leaves me with 3 ones as a remainder. In all I gave out 1 hundred, 4 tens, and 5 ones with 3 left over.*

Develop the Written Record

The recording scheme for the long-division algorithm is not completely intuitive. You will need to be quite directive in helping children learn to record the fair sharing with models. There are essentially four steps:

1. *Share* and record the number of pieces put in each group.
2. *Record* the number of pieces shared in all. Multiply to find this number.
3. *Record* the number of pieces remaining. Subtract to find this number.
4. *Trade* (if necessary) for smaller pieces and combine with any that are there already. Record the new total number in the next column.

When students model problems with a one-digit divisor, steps 2 and 3 seem unnecessary. Explain that these steps really help when you don't have the pieces there to count.

Record Explicit Trades

Figure 4.18 details each step of the recording process just described. On the left, you see the traditional algorithm. To the right is a suggestion that matches the actual action with the models by explicitly recording the trades. Instead of the somewhat mysterious "bring-down" procedure, the traded pieces are crossed out, as is the number of existing pieces in the next column. The combined number of pieces is written in this column using a two-digit number. In the example, 2 hundreds are traded for 20 tens, combined with the 6 that were there for a total of 26 tens. The 26 is therefore written in the tens column.

Students who are required to make sense of the long-division procedure find the explicit-trade method easier to follow. It is important to spread out the digits in the dividend when writing down the problem. (The explicit-trade method is a Van de Walle invention. It has been used successfully in grades 3 to 8. You will not find it in textbooks.)

FIGURE 4.18 •••••••••••

The traditional and explicit-trade methods are connected to each step of the division process. Every step can and should make sense.

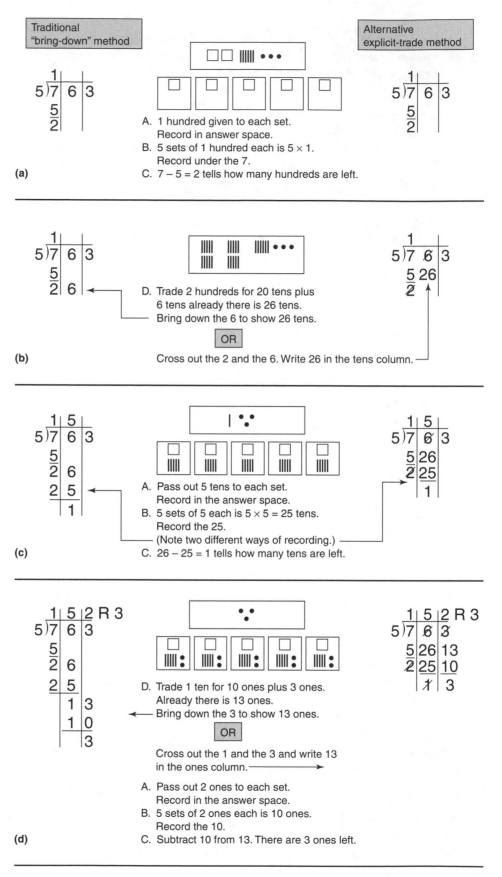

A. 1 hundred given to each set.
   Record in answer space.
B. 5 sets of 1 hundred each is 5×1.
   Record under the 7.
C. $7 - 5 = 2$ tells how many hundreds are left.

(a)

D. Trade 2 hundreds for 20 tens plus 6 tens already there is 26 tens.
   Bring down the 6 to show 26 tens.

   OR

   Cross out the 2 and the 6. Write 26 in the tens column.

(b)

A. Pass out 5 tens to each set.
   Record in the answer space.
B. 5 sets of 5 each is $5 \times 5 = 25$ tens.
   Record the 25.
   (Note two different ways of recording.)
C. $26 - 25 = 1$ tells how many tens are left.

(c)

D. Trade 1 ten for 10 ones plus 3 ones.
   Already there is 13 ones.
   Bring down the 3 to show 13 ones.

   OR

   Cross out the 1 and the 3 and write 13 in the ones column.

A. Pass out 2 ones to each set.
   Record in the answer space.
B. 5 sets of 2 ones each is 10 ones.
   Record the 10.
C. Subtract 10 from 13. There are 3 ones left.

(d)

Traditional "bring-down" method

Alternative explicit-trade method

Both the explicit-trade method and the use of place-value columns will help with the problem of leaving out a middle zero in a problem (see Figure 4.19).

Two-Digit Divisors

There is almost no justification for having students master the division algorithm with two-digit divisors. A large chunk of the fourth, fifth, and sometimes sixth grade is frequently spent on this outdated skill. The cost in terms of time and students' attitudes toward mathematics is enormous. Only a few times in any adult's life will an exact result to such a computation be required and a calculator not be available. If you can possibly influence the removal of this outdated skill from your school's curriculum, you are encouraged to speak up.

With a two-digit divisor, it is hard to come up with the right amount to share at each step. A guess too high or too low means you have to erase and start all over.

An Intuitive Idea

Suppose that you were sharing a large pile of candy with 36 friends. Instead of passing them out one at a time, you conservatively estimate that each person could get at least 6 pieces. So you give 6 to each of your friends. Now you find there are more than 36 pieces left. Do you have everyone give back the 6 pieces so you can then give them 7 or 8? That would be silly! You simply pass out more.

The candy example gives us two good ideas for sharing in long division. First, always underestimate how much can be shared. You can always pass out some more. Second, if there is enough left to share some more, just do it! To avoid ever overestimating, always pretend there are more sets among which to share than there really are. For example, if you are dividing 312 by 43 (sharing among 43 sets or "friends"), pretend you have 50 sets instead. Round *up* to the next multiple of 10. You can easily determine that 6 pieces can be shared among 50 sets because 6 × 50 is an easy product. Therefore, since there are really only 43 sets, clearly you can give *at least* 6 to each. Always consider a larger divisor; *always round up*. If your underestimate leaves you with more to share, simply pass out some more.

Using the Idea Symbolically

These ideas are used in Figure 4.20. Both the traditional method and the explicit-trade method of recording are illustrated. The rounded-up divisor, 70, is written in a little "think bubble" above the real divisor. Rounding up has another advantage: It is easy to run through the multiples of 70 and compare them to 374.

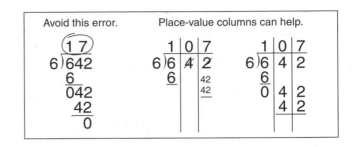

FIGURE 4.19 •

Using lines to mark place-value columns can help avoid forgetting to record zeros.

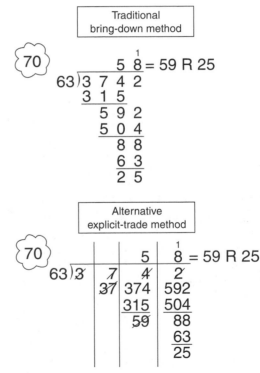

FIGURE 4.20 •

Round the divisor up to 70 to think with, but multiply what you share by 63. In the ones column, share 8 with each set. Oops! 88 left over, just give 1 more to each set.

THE TRADITIONAL ALGORITHM FOR DIVISION

Work through the problem one step at a time, saying exactly what each recorded step stands for.

Always rounding the divisor up has two advantages. It reduces the mental strain of making choices and essentially eliminates the need to erase. If an estimate is too low, that's okay. And if you always round up, the estimate will never be too high. Nor is there any reason ever to change to the more familiar approach. It is just as good for adults as for children. The same is true of the explicit-trade notation. It is certainly an idea to consider.

Assessment Note

Parents are perhaps more interested in their children's computational skills than in any other area. When students do well on computation tests, parents are pleased. But what do you know when students do not do well? At best you can make inferences based on the papers turned in. You can look for basic-fact errors and carelessness or perhaps find a systematic error in an algorithm. What you do not know is how students are solving these problems and what ideas and strategies they have developed that are useful or need further development.

When computational strategies and algorithms are developed in the manner suggested in this chapter, every day you are presented with a wealth of assessment data. The important thing is to gather, record, and use these data for individual children the same as you would for tests and quizzes. A simple chart something like the one in Figure 4.21 may be all you need. Note that the third column includes a minirubric or a three-point scale. Students' names can be arranged in groups, by how they sit in the room, or alphabetically—any way that makes them easy to find.

As you walk around in the during portion of your lessons, and also in the after portion when students explain their computation strategies and reasoning, you can make notes on the chart. Make a new chart each week, but keep the old ones to provide evidence of growth over time. These charts can be useful for grading and for parent conferences. There is no harm in giving an occasional quiz or test of computational skills. But avoid giving more value to tests simply because they are objective.

FIGURE 4.21 • • • • • • •

A checklist with space for comments or notes lets you record daily observations of students' direct modeling and invented strategies.

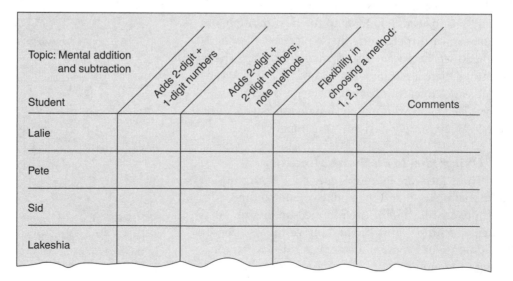

Chapter 4 STRATEGIES FOR WHOLE-NUMBER COMPUTATION

EXPANDED LESSON

Area Model for Multiplication

GRADE LEVEL: Fourth or fifth grade.

MATHEMATICS GOALS

To develop strategies for two-digit multiplication using the area model.

THINKING ABOUT THE STUDENTS

Students have mastered most of their basic multiplication facts and understand that multiplication can be thought of as repeated addition. They have multiplied numbers by multiples of 10. They understand that length times width gives the area of a rectangle.

MATERIALS AND PREPARATION

- Accurately cut from poster board a rectangle that is 47 cm by 36 cm. Use this to trace rectangles on large sheets of paper, one for each group of two or three students.
- Provide each group of students with base-ten materials, enough to fill the rectangle.
- Draw a 23 cm x 4 cm rectangle on a transparency.
- Overhead base-ten materials or regular base-ten materials.
- *Note:* If your base-ten models are not based on centimeters, adjust all rectangles to match the size of your materials.

lesson

BEFORE

- Show the transparency of the 23 cm × 4 cm rectangle and write the dimensions of all four sides. Explain that you want to find out how many unit squares (show some) will fit in the rectangle, but you don't have that many unit pieces. *How else could we fill the rectangle?* When students suggest the use of tens pieces, have them work quickly in pairs to decide how many tens pieces and how many ones will fit in the rectangle.
- Position 8 tens and 12 ones inside the rectangle. Ask: *Now can we tell how many small squares are in the rectangle?* Again, have students solve this quickly and share their solutions (80 and 12, or 92 units in all).

The Task

- Determine the area of a 47 cm × 36 cm rectangle.

Establish Expectations

- Recognize counting the squares one by one as a legitimate way to determine the area of the rectangle, but explain to students that they need to find a quicker way to determine the number of squares inside the rectangle.
- Solutions must include a drawing, numbers, and explanation of how students determined the total.

DURING

- Most students will first fill the rectangle with as many hundreds pieces as possible. If some students use only the small ones pieces, suggest that they might try using large pieces.
- Once students have filled their rectangle, they should work to add up the total number of ones. Observe the way students count the pieces. Expect that students will count the individual pieces rather than use the dimensions of the rectangle in a multiplication.
- For students who have solved the problem and completed their written explanation, see if they can connect what they have done to the numbers in the rectangle dimensions.

AFTER

- Begin by recording (without comment) all answers to the task. It is quite possible that not all groups will have gotten 1692.
- Have students share strategies. Begin with students who may have used less than efficient methods. Try to include students who wrote down and added the four partial products (1200, 210, 240, and 42). These four partial products most directly relate to the standard algorithm and are useful for invented strategies as well.
- As new strategies emerge, ask students to compare and contrast the new strategies to ones already shared. Do not evaluate any approach or answer.

ASSESSMENT NOTES

- Do students see the efficiency of using the larger hundreds pieces? Do they see and use four separate sections to the filled-in rectangle?
- Do students make connections between the dimensions of the rectangle and its area? Do they seem aware of the connection between multiplication and area?
- Can students use multiples of ten to determine the smaller regions?

- This task is profitably repeated using rectangles drawn on base-ten grid paper (see Blackline Master 16).
- For students who have difficulty with this task, use cm-grid paper (see Blackline Master 8) to draw a 15 x 30 rectangle. Have students use base-ten materials to fill inside the rectangle to determine the area. Hundreds pieces fit into this region so that students have to deal with only one narrow region left uncovered.

next steps

- When students are clearly using four partial products in their solutions, challenge them to connect their strategies to the dimensions of the rectangle and then see if they can determine the area of a 64 x 73 rectangle without using a drawing.

DEVELOPING FRACTION CONCEPTS

For students in the upper elementary grades and even middle school, fractions present a considerable challenge. The area of fractions is where students often give up trying to understand and resort instead to rules. This lack of understanding is then translated into untold difficulties with fraction computation, decimal and percent concepts, the use of fractions in measurement, and ratio and proportion concepts.

Traditional programs for primary grades typically offer students limited exposure to fractions, with most of the work on fraction development occurring in the third grade. Few if any programs provide students with adequate time or experiences to help them with this complex area of the curriculum. This chapter will explore a conceptual development of fraction concepts that can help students construct a firm foundation, preparing them for the skills that are later built on these ideas.

Sharing and the Concept of Fractional Parts

The first goal in the development of fractions should be to help children construct the idea of *fractional parts of the*

big ideas

1 Fractional parts are equal shares or equal-sized portions of a whole or unit. A unit can be an object or a collection of things. More abstractly, the unit is counted as 1. On the number line, the distance from 0 to 1 is the unit.

2 Fractional parts have special names that tell how many parts of that size are needed to make the whole. For example, *thirds* require three parts to make a whole.

3 The more fractional parts used to make a whole, the smaller the parts. For example, eighths are smaller than fifths.

4 The denominator of a fraction indicates by what number the whole has been divided in order to produce the type of part under consideration. Thus, the denominator is a divisor. In practical terms, the denominator names the kind of fractional part that is under consideration. The numerator of a fraction counts or tells how many of the fractional parts (of the type indicated by the denominator) are under consideration. Therefore, the numerator is a multiplier—it indicates a multiple of the given fractional part.

5 Two equivalent fractions are two ways of describing the same amount by using different-sized fractional parts. For example, in the fraction $\frac{6}{8}$, if the eighths are taken in twos, then each pair of eighths is a fourth. The six-eighths then can be seen to be three-fourths.

whole—the parts that result when the whole or unit has been partitioned into *equal-sized portions* or *fair shares*.

Children seem to understand the idea of separating a quantity into two or more parts to be shared fairly among friends. They eventually make connections between the idea of fair shares and fractional parts. Sharing tasks are, therefore, good places to begin the development of fractions.

Sharing Tasks

Considerable research has been done with children from first through eighth grades to determine how they go about the process of forming fair shares and how the tasks posed to students influence their responses (e.g., Empson, 2002; Lamon, 1996; Mack, 2001; Pothier & Sawada, 1983).

Sharing tasks are generally posed in the form of a simple story problem. *Suppose there are four square brownies to be shared among three children so that each child gets the same amount. How much (or show how much) will each child get?* Task difficulty changes with the numbers involved, the types of things to be shared (regions such as brownies, discrete objects such as pieces of chewing gum), and the presence or use of a model.

Students initially perform sharing tasks (division) by distributing items one at a time. When this process leaves leftover pieces, it is much easier to think of sharing them fairly if the items can be subdivided. Typical "regions" to share are brownies (rectangles), sandwiches, pizzas, crackers, cake, candy bars, and so on. The problems and variations that follow are adapted from Empson (2002).

· ·

Four children are sharing 10 brownies so that each one will get the same amount. How much can each child have?

· ·

Problem difficulty is determined by the relationship between the number of things to be shared and the number of sharers. Because students' initial strategies for sharing involve halving, a good place to begin is with two, four, or even eight sharers. For ten brownies and four sharers, many children will deal out two to each child and then halve each of the remaining brownies. (See Figure 5.1.)

Consider these variations in numbers:

5 brownies shared with 2 children   4 brownies shared with 8 children

2 brownies shared with 4 children   3 brownies shared with 4 children

5 brownies shared with 4 children

FIGURE 5.1 · · · · · · · · ·

Ten brownies shared with four students.

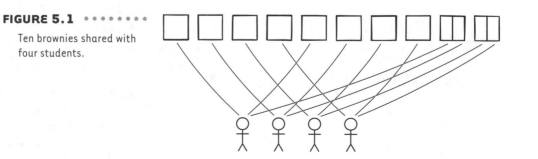

Chapter 5 **DEVELOPING FRACTION CONCEPTS**

> **STOP** Try drawing pictures for each of the preceding sharing tasks. Which do you think is most difficult? Which of these represents essentially the same degree of difficulty? What other tasks involving two, four, or eight sharers would you consider as similar, easier, or more difficult than these?

When the numbers allow for some items to be distributed whole (five shared with two), some students will first share whole items and then cut up the leftovers. Others will slice every piece in half and then distribute the halves. When there are more sharers than items, some partitioning must happen at the beginning of the solution process.

When students who are still using a halving strategy try to share five things among four children, they will eventually get down to two halves to give to four children. For some, the solution is to cut each half in half; that is, "each child gets a whole (or two halves) and a half of a half."

It is a progression to move to three or six sharers because this will force students to confront their halving strategies.

> **STOP** Try solving the following variations using drawings. Can you do them in different ways?

4 pizzas shared with 6 children

7 pizzas shared with 6 children

5 pizzas shared with 3 children

To subdivide a region into a number of parts other than a power of two (four, eight, etc.) requires an odd subdivision at some point. Several types of sharing solutions might be observed. Figure 5.2 shows some different approaches.

Use a variety of representations for these problems. The items to be shared can be drawn on worksheets as rectangles or circles along with a statement of the problem. Another possibility is to cut out construction paper circles or squares. Some students may need to cut and physically distribute the pieces. Students can use connecting cubes to make bars that they can separate into pieces. Or they can use more traditional fraction models such as circular "pie" pieces.

Models for Fractions

There is substantial evidence to suggest that the use of models in fraction tasks is important. Unfortunately, many teachers in the upper grades, where manipulative materials are not as common, fail to use models for fraction development. Models can help

(a) Four candy bars shared with six children:

Cut all the bars in half.
Cut the last two halves into three parts.
Each child gets a half and sixth.

(b) Four pizzas shared with three children:

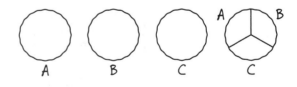

Pass out whole pizzas.
Cut the last pizza in three parts.
Each child gets 1 whole and one-third.

(c) Five sandwiches shared with three children:

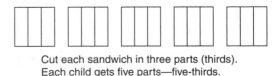

Cut each sandwich in three parts (thirds).
Each child gets five parts—five-thirds.

FIGURE 5.2 •

Three different sharing processes.

students clarify ideas that are often confused in a purely symbolic mode. Sometimes it is useful to do the same activity with two quite different models; from the viewpoint of the students, the activity is quite different. In this chapter we will distinguish among three types of models: area or region models, length models, and set models.

Region or Area Models

In the discussion of sharing, all of the tasks involved sharing something that could be cut into smaller parts. The fractions are based on parts of an area or region. This is a good place to begin and is almost essential when doing sharing tasks. There are many good region models, as shown in Figure 5.3.

Circular "pie" piece models are by far the most commonly used area model. (See the Blackline Masters for masters of pie models.) The main advantage of the circular region is that it emphasizes the amount that is remaining to make up a whole. The other models in Figure 5.3 are more flexible and allow for different-sized units or wholes. Paper grids, several of which can be found in the Blackline Masters, are especially flexible and do not require management of materials.

Length or Measurement Models

With measurement models, lengths are compared instead of areas. Either lines are drawn and subdivided or physical materials are compared on the basis of length, as shown in Figure 5.4. Manipulative versions provide more opportunity for trial and error and for exploration.

FIGURE 5.3 • • • • • • • •

Area or region models for fractions.

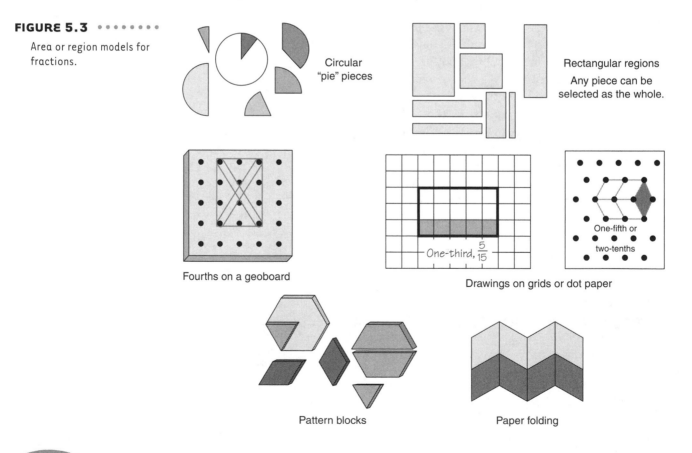

Circular "pie" pieces

Rectangular regions
Any piece can be selected as the whole.

Fourths on a geoboard

One-third, $\frac{5}{15}$

One-fifth or two-tenths

Drawings on grids or dot paper

Pattern blocks

Paper folding

Fraction strips are a teacher-made version of Cuisenaire rods. Both the strips and the rods have pieces that are in lengths of 1 to 10 measured in terms of the smallest strip or rod. Each length is a different color for ease of identification. Strips of construction paper or adding-machine tape can be folded to produce equal-sized subparts.

The rod or strip model provides the most flexibility while still having separate pieces for comparisons. To make fraction strips, cut 11 different colors of poster board into strips 2 cm wide. Cut the smallest strips into 2-cm squares. Other strips are then 4, 6, 8, . . . , 20 cm, producing lengths 1 to 10 in terms of the smallest strip. Cut the last color into strips 24 cm long to produce a 12 strip. If you are using Cuisenaire rods, tape a red 2 rod to an orange 10 rod to make a 12 rod. In this chapter's illustrations, the colors of the strips will be the same as the corresponding lengths of the Cuisenaire rods:

1 White	7 Black
2 Red	8 Brown
3 Light green	9 Blue
4 Purple	10 Orange
5 Yellow	12 Pink or red-orange
6 Dark green	

The number line is a significantly more sophisticated measurement model. From a student's vantage point, there is a real difference between putting a number on a number line and comparing one length to another. Each number on a line denotes the distance of the labeled point from zero, not the point itself. This distinction is often difficult for students.

Set Models

In set models, the whole is understood to be a set of objects, and subsets of the whole make up fractional parts. For example, three objects are one-fourth of a set of 12 objects. The set of 12, in this example, represents the whole or 1. It is the idea of referring to a collection of counters as a single entity that makes set models difficult for some students. However, the set model helps establish important connections with many real-world uses of fractions and with ratio concepts. Figure 5.5 illustrates several set models for fractions.

Counters in two colors on opposite sides are frequently used. They can easily be flipped to change their color to model various fractional parts of a whole set.

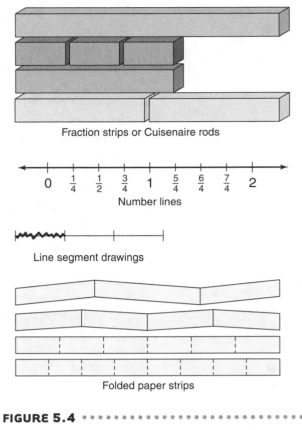

FIGURE 5.4 •

Length or measurement models for fractions.

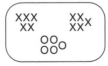

Two-color counters in arrays. Rows and columns help show parts. Each array makes a whole. Here $\frac{3}{5} = \frac{9}{15}$.

Sets of 6

Two-color counters in loops drawn on paper. Shows $1\frac{2}{6}$.

Drawings using Xs and Os. Shows $\frac{2}{3} = \frac{10}{15}$.

FIGURE 5.5 •

Set models for fractions.

From Fractional Parts to Fraction Symbols

During the discussions of students' solutions (and discussions are essential!) is a good time to emphasize the vocabulary of fractional parts. Students need to be aware of two aspects or components of fractional parts: (1) the number of parts and (2) the equality of the parts (in size, not necessarily in shape). Emphasize that the number of equal parts or fair shares that make up a whole determines the name of the fractional parts or shares. One of the best ways to introduce the concept of fractional parts is through sharing tasks. However, the idea of fractional parts is so fundamental to a strong development of fraction concepts that it should be explored further with additional tasks.

Fractional Parts and Words

In addition to helping students use the words *halves, thirds, fourths, fifths,* and so on, be sure to make regular comparison of fractional parts to the whole. Make it a point to use the terms *whole,* or *one whole,* or simply *one* so that students have a language that they can use regardless of the model involved.

The following activity is a simple extension of the sharing tasks. It is important that students can tell when a region has been separated into a particular type of fractional part.

ACTIVITY 5.1

Correct Shares

As in Figure 5.6, show examples and nonexamples of specified fractional parts. Have students identify the wholes that are correctly divided into requested fractional parts and those that are not. For each response, have students explain their reasoning. The activity should be done with a variety of models, including length and set models.

In the "Correct Shares" activity, the most important part is the discussion of the nonexamples. The wholes are already partitioned either correctly or incorrectly, and the students were not involved in the partitioning. It is also useful for students to create designated equal shares given a whole, as they are asked to do in the next activity.

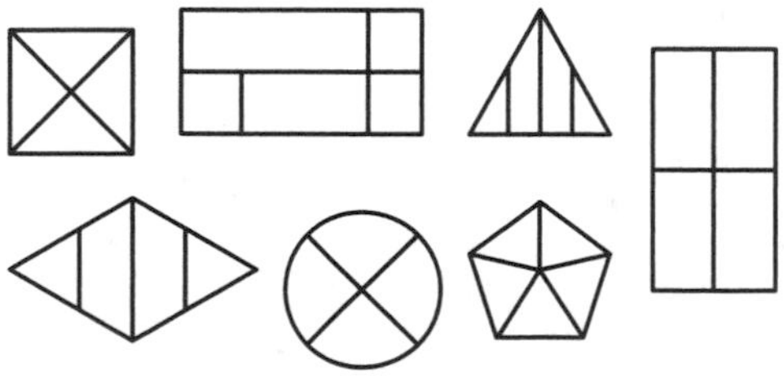

FIGURE 5.6 • • • • • • • • • • • • • • • • • • •

Students learning about fractional parts should be able to tell which of these figures are correctly partitioned in fourths. They should also be able to explain why the other figures are not showing fourths.

ACTIVITY 5.2

Finding Fair Shares

Give students models, and have them find fifths or eighths or other fractional parts using the models. (The models should never have fractions written on them.) The activity is especially interesting when different wholes can be designated in the same model. That way, a given fractional part does not get identified with a special shape or color but with the relationship of the part to the designated whole. Some ideas are suggested in Figure 5.7.

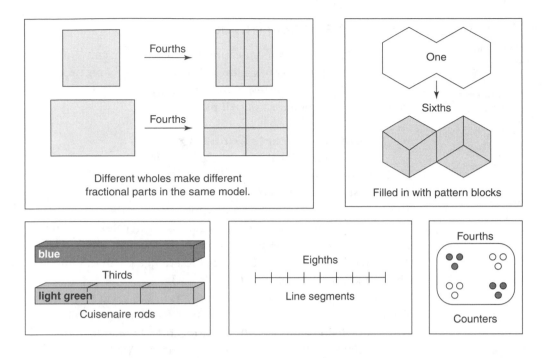

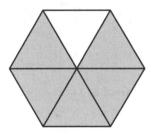

FIGURE 5.7 • • • • • • • • •

Given a whole, find fractional parts.

Notice when partitioning sets that children frequently confuse the number of counters in a share with the name of the share. In the example in Figure 5.7, the 12 counters are partitioned into four sets—*fourths*. Each share or part has three counters, but it is the number of shares that makes the partition show *fourths*.

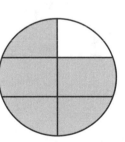

FIGURE 5.8 • • • • • • • •

A student represents $\frac{5}{6}$ using pattern blocks.

Assessment Note

Many of the activities in this chapter suggest the use of various models such as fraction strips, pie pieces, and pattern blocks. Suppose that a student represents $\frac{5}{6}$ using pattern blocks as in Figure 5.8. Based on this representation, you might be inclined to think that this student has a good grasp of the two components of fractional parts (number of parts and equality of parts). Now consider this same student's work in which he was asked to draw a picture of $\frac{5}{6}$ and $\frac{5}{9}$. (See Figure 5.9.) Now what are you inclined to think? The student appears to understand the component about the number of parts; however, he does not seem to understand the necessity for the parts to be equal. With the pattern blocks, the idea of equal parts is never an issue. It's not until the student is asked to *draw* a fraction representation that it becomes apparent that the notion of equal parts has not been incorporated into his emerging understanding of fractions.

Although their own drawings can sometimes mislead students, drawings provide opportunities for you to assess students' understanding. At the very least, drawings provide opportunities for you to ask students questions about their ideas to gain insight into how they are making sense of fractions. Be careful to distinguish between incorrect drawings that are due to weak drawing skills and those that are the result of mistaken ideas. Help make students' ideas public by encouraging the use of a variety of models—various physical materials as well as student-made drawings.

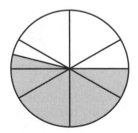

FIGURE 5.9 • • • • • • • •

A student represents $\frac{5}{6}$ and $\frac{5}{9}$ by partitioning circles.

FROM FRACTIONAL PARTS TO FRACTION SYMBOLS

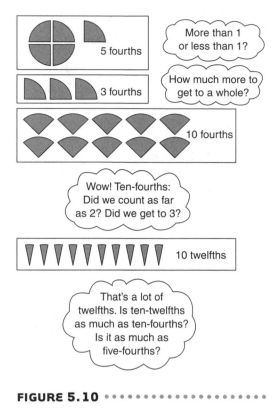

FIGURE 5.10 ● ● ● ● ● ● ● ● ● ● ● ● ● ●

Counting fractional parts.

Understanding Fraction Symbols

Fraction symbolism represents a fairly complex convention that is often misleading to children. It is well worth your time to help students develop a strong understanding of what the top and bottom numbers of a fraction tell us.

Fractional-Parts Counting

Counting fractional parts to see how multiple parts compare to the whole creates a foundation for the two parts of a fraction. Students should come to think of counting fractional parts in much the same way as they might count apples or any other objects. If you know the kind of part you are counting, you can tell when you get to one, when you get to two, and so on. Students who under-stand factional parts should not need to arrange pie pieces into a circle to know that four-fourths make a whole.

Display some pie-piece fraction parts in groups as shown in Figure 5.10. For each collection, tell students what type of piece is being shown and simply count them together: "*one*-fourth, *two*-fourths, *three*-fourths, *four*-fourths, *five*-fourths." Ask, "If we have five-fourths, is that more than one whole, less than one whole, or the same as one whole?"

As students count each collection of parts, discuss the relation-ship to one whole. Make informal comparisons between different collections. "Why did we get almost two wholes with seven-fourths, and yet we don't even have one whole with ten-twelfths?"

Also take this opportunity to lay verbal groundwork for mixed fractions. "What is another way that we could say seven-thirds?" (Two wholes and one more third or one whole and four-thirds.)

With this introduction, students are ready for the following task.

ACTIVITY 5.3

More, Less, or Equal to One Whole

Give students a collection of fractional parts (all the same type) and indicate the kind of fractional part they have. Parts can be drawn on a worksheet or physical models can be placed in plastic baggies with an identifying card. For example, if done with Cuisenaire rods or fraction strips, the collection might have seven light green rods/strips with a caption or note indicating "these are eighths." The task is to decide if the collection is less than one whole, equal to one whole, or more than one whole. Students must draw pictures and/or use numbers to explain their answer. They can also tell how close the set is to a complete whole. Several collections constitute a reasonable task.

Try Activity 5.3 with several different fraction models (although pie pieces are too much of a giveaway). Pattern blocks make a good manipulative format and are also eas-ily drawn with a template. The same is true of Cuisenaire rods. A set model may cause students some initial difficulty but it is especially important, even if they have been successful with region or length models. For example, show a collection of 15 counters

Chapter **5** DEVELOPING FRACTION CONCEPTS

(dots or actual counters) and indicate that a set of 5 counters is one-fourth. How much is the set of 15 counters?

Top and Bottom Numbers

The way that we write fractions with a top and a bottom number and a bar between is a convention—an arbitrary agreement for how to represent fractions. (By the way, always write fractions with a horizontal bar, not a slanted one. Write $\frac{3}{4}$, not 3/4.) As a convention, it falls in the category of things that you simply tell students. However, a good idea is to make the convention so clear by way of demonstration that students will tell *you* what the top and bottom numbers stand for. The following procedure is recommended even if your students have been "using" symbolic fractions for several years.

Display several collections of fractional parts in a manner similar to those in Figure 5.10. Have students count the parts together. After each count, write the correct fraction, indicating that this is how it is written as a symbol. Include sets that are more than one but write them as simple or "improper" fractions and not as mixed numbers. Include at least two pairs of sets with the same top numbers such as $\frac{4}{8}$ and $\frac{4}{3}$. Likewise, include sets with the same bottom numbers. After the class has counted and you have written the fraction for at least six sets of fractional parts, pose the following questions:

- What does the bottom number in a fraction tell us?
- What does the top number in a fraction tell us?

STOP Before reading further, answer these two questions in your own words. Don't rely on formulations you've heard before. Think in terms of what we have been talking about—namely, fractional parts and counting fractional parts. Imagine counting a set of 5 eighths and a set of 5 fourths and writing the fractions for these sets. Use children's language in your formulations and try to come up with a way to explain these meanings that has nothing to do with the type of model involved.

Here are some reasonable explanations for the top and bottom numbers.

- *Top number:* This is the counting number. It tells how many shares or parts we have. It tells how many have been counted. It tells how many parts we are talking about. It counts the parts or shares.
- *Bottom number:* This tells what is being counted. It tells what fractional part is being counted. If it is a 4, it means we are counting *fourths;* if it is a 6, we are counting *sixths;* and so on.

This formulation of the meanings of the top and bottom numbers may seem unusual to you. It is often said that the top number tells "how many." (This phrase seems unfinished. How many *what?*) And the bottom tells "how many parts it takes to make a whole." This may be correct but can be misleading. For example, a $\frac{1}{6}$ piece is often cut from a cake without making any slices in the remaining $\frac{5}{6}$ of the cake. That the cake is only in two pieces does not change the fact that the piece taken is $\frac{1}{6}$. Or if a pizza is cut in 12 pieces, two pieces still make $\frac{1}{6}$ of the pizza. In neither of these instances does the bottom number tell how many pieces make a whole.

FROM FRACTIONAL PARTS TO FRACTION SYMBOLS

There is evidence that an iterative notion of fractions, one that views a fraction such as $\frac{3}{4}$ as a count of three things called *fourths,* is an important idea for children to develop. The iterative concept is most clear when focusing on these two ideas about fraction symbols:

- The top number *counts.*
- The bottom number tells *what is being counted.*

The *what* of fractions are the fractional parts. They can be counted. Fraction symbols are just a shorthand for saying *how many* and *what.*

Smith (2002) points out a slightly more "mathematical" definition of the top and bottom numbers that is completely in accord with the one we've just discussed. For Smith, it is important to see the bottom number as the divisor and the top as the multiplier. That is, $\frac{3}{4}$ is three *times* what you get when you *divide* a whole into four parts. This multiplier and divisor idea is especially useful when students are asked later to think of fractions as an indicated division; that is, $\frac{3}{4}$ also means $3 \div 4$.

Numerator and Denominator

To count a set is to *enumerate* it. The common name for the top number in a fraction is the *numerator.*

A denomination is the name of a class or type of thing. A \$1 bill, a \$5 bill, and a \$10 bill are said to be bills of different *denominations.* The common name for the bottom number in a fraction is the *denominator.*

The words *numerator* and *denominator* have no common reference for children. Whether these words are used or not, the words themselves will not help young students understand the meanings.

Mixed Numbers and Improper Fractions

If you have counted fractional parts beyond a whole, your students already know how to write $\frac{13}{16}$ or $\frac{13}{3}$. Ask, "What is another way that you could say 13 *sixths?*" Students may suggest "two wholes and one-sixth more," or "two plus one-sixth." Explain that these are correct and that $2 + \frac{1}{6}$ is usually written as $2\frac{1}{6}$ and is called a *mixed number.* Note that this is a symbolism convention and must be explained to students. What is not at all necessary is to teach a rule for converting mixed numbers to common fractions and the reverse. Rather, consider the following task.

ACTIVITY 5.4

Mixed-Number Names

Give students a mixed number such as $3\frac{2}{5}$. Their task is to find a single fraction that names the same amount. They may use any familiar materials or make drawings, but they must be able to give an explanation for their result. Similarly, have students start with a fraction greater than 1, such as $\frac{17}{4}$, and have them determine the mixed number and provide a justification for their result.

Repeat the "Mixed-Number Names" task several times with different fractions. After a while, challenge students to figure out the new fraction name without the use of models. A good explanation for $3\frac{1}{4}$ might be that there are 4 fourths in one whole, so there are 8 fourths in two wholes and 12 fourths in three wholes. The extra fourth makes 13 fourths in all, or $\frac{13}{4}$. (Note the iteration concept playing a role.)

There is absolutely no reason ever to provide a rule about multiplying the whole number by the bottom number and adding the top number. Nor should students need a rule about dividing the bottom number into the top to convert fractions to mixed numbers. These rules will readily be developed by the students but in their own words and with complete understanding.

ACTIVITY 5.5

Calculator Fraction Counting

Calculators that permit fraction entries and displays are now quite common in schools. Many, like the TI-15, now display fractions in correct fraction format and offer a choice of showing results as mixed numbers or simple fractions. Counting by fourths with the TI-15 is done by first storing $\frac{1}{4}$ in one of the two operation keys: [Opl] [+] 1 [n] 4 [d] [Opl]. To count, press 0 [Opl] [Opl] [Opl] . . . . The display will show the counts by fourths and also the number of times that the [Opl] key has been pressed. Students should coordinate their counts with fraction models, adding a new fourths piece to the pile with each count. At any time the display can be shifted from mixed form to simple fractions with a press of a key. The TI-15 can be set so that it will not simplify fractions automatically, the appropriate setting prior to the introduction of equivalent fractions.

Fraction calculators provide a powerful way to help children develop fractional symbolism. A variation on Activity 5.5 is to show students a mixed number such as $3\frac{1}{8}$ and ask how many counts of $\frac{1}{8}$ on the calculator it will take to count that high. The students should try to stop at the correct number $\frac{25}{8}$ before pressing the mixed number key.

Parts-and-Whole Tasks

The exercises presented here can help students develop their understanding of fractional parts as well as the meanings of the top and bottom numbers in a fraction. Models are used to represent wholes and parts of wholes. Written or oral fraction names represent the relationship between the parts and wholes. Given any two of these—whole, part, and fraction—the students can use their models to determine the third.

Any type of model can be used as long as different sizes can represent the whole. Traditional pie pieces do not work because the whole is always the circle, and all the pieces are *unit fractions*. (A *unit fraction* is a single fractional part. The fractions $\frac{1}{3}$ and $\frac{1}{8}$ are unit fractions.)

Examples of each type of exercise are provided in Figure 5.11, Figure 5.12, and Figure 5.13. Each figure

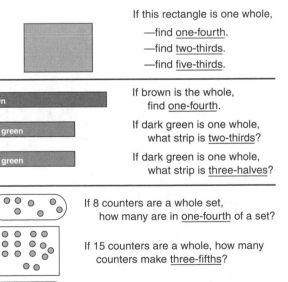

If this rectangle is one whole,
—find <u>one-fourth</u>.
—find <u>two-thirds</u>.
—find <u>five-thirds</u>.

If brown is the whole,
find <u>one-fourth</u>.

If dark green is one whole,
what strip is <u>two-thirds</u>?

If dark green is one whole,
what strip is <u>three-halves</u>?

If 8 counters are a whole set,
how many are in <u>one-fourth</u> of a set?

If 15 counters are a whole, how many
counters make <u>three-fifths</u>?

If 9 counters are a whole, how many
are in <u>five-thirds</u> of a set?

FIGURE 5.11 •

Given the whole and the fraction, find the part.

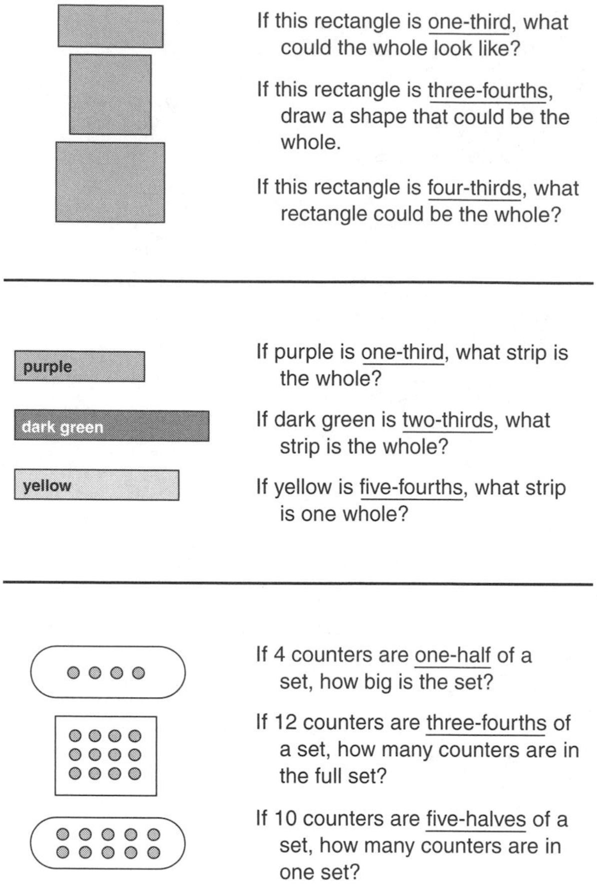

If this rectangle is one-third, what could the whole look like?

If this rectangle is three-fourths, draw a shape that could be the whole.

If this rectangle is four-thirds, what rectangle could be the whole?

---

purple

dark green

yellow

If purple is one-third, what strip is the whole?

If dark green is two-thirds, what strip is the whole?

If yellow is five-fourths, what strip is one whole?

If 4 counters are one-half of a set, how big is the set?

If 12 counters are three-fourths of a set, how many counters are in the full set?

If 10 counters are five-halves of a set, how many counters are in one set?

FIGURE 5.12 •

Given the part and the fraction, find the whole.

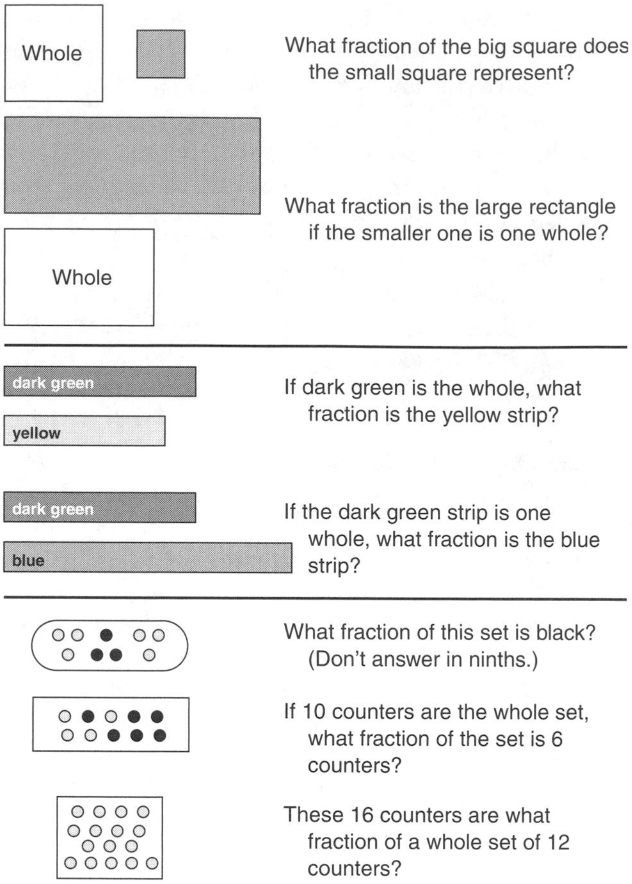

Whole

What fraction of the big square does the small square represent?

What fraction is the large rectangle if the smaller one is one whole?

Whole

---

dark green

yellow

If dark green is the whole, what fraction is the yellow strip?

dark green

blue

If the dark green strip is one whole, what fraction is the blue strip?

What fraction of this set is black? (Don't answer in ninths.)

If 10 counters are the whole set, what fraction of the set is 6 counters?

These 16 counters are what fraction of a whole set of 12 counters?

FIGURE 5.13 •

Given the whole and the part, find the fraction.

---

includes examples with a region model (freely drawn rectangles), a length model (Cuisenaire rods or fraction strips), and set models.

> **It would be a good idea to work through these exercises before reading on. For the rectangle models, simply sketch a similar rectangle on paper. For the rod or strip models, use Cuisenaire rods or make fraction strips. The colors used correspond to the actual rod colors. Lengths are not given in the figures so that you will not be tempted to use an adult-type numeric approach. If you do not have access to rods or strips, just draw lines on paper. The process you use with lines will correspond to what is done with rods.**

These three types of problems vary in difficulty as well as in what they can help students learn. The first type, in which students find the part given the whole and fraction (Figure 5.11), is commonly encountered in textbooks. What may make it different is that the given whole is not partitioned at all. Students must know that the denominator will tell them how to partition the whole—it is the divisor. The numerator counts. Therefore, once partitioned, they count the necessary number of fractional parts. Notice that you can ask for students to show a fraction that is more than a whole even though only one whole is provided. Usually students will create a second whole and partition that as well.

In the second type of task, students are asked to find or create the whole given a part of the whole. (See Figure 5.12.) Students will find this task a bit more difficult than the first. The struggle and discussion among students will be worth the effort. This exercise emphasizes that a fraction is not an absolute quantity; rather it is a relationship between the part and the whole. If the white strip is given as $\frac{1}{4}$, then the purple strip is the whole (see the lengths of the Cuisenaire rods on p. 135). However, if the red strip is given as $\frac{1}{4}$, then the brown strip is the whole. Furthermore, if the white strip is given as $\frac{1}{5}$, then the yellow is the whole. When the given part is not a unit fraction, the task is considerably more difficult. For the second example in Figure 5.12, students first must realize that the given rectangle is three of something called *fourths*. Therefore, if that given piece is subdivided into three parts, then one of those parts will be a fourth. From the unit fraction, counting produces the whole—four of the one-fourth pieces make a whole. Notice again how the task forces students to think of counting unit fractional parts.

The third type of exercise will likely involve some estimation, especially if drawings are used. Different estimates can prompt excellent discussion. With Cuisenaire rods or sets, one specific answer is always correct.

Two or three challenging parts-and-whole questions can make an excellent lesson. The tasks should be presented to the class in just the same form as in the figures. Physical models are often the best way to present the tasks so that students can use a trial-and-error approach to determine their results. As with all tasks, it should be clear that an explanation is required to justify each answer. For each task, let several students supply answers and explanations.

Sometimes it is a good idea to create simple story problems that ask the same questions.

· ·

Mr. Samuels has finished $\frac{2}{5}$ of his patio. It looks like this:

Draw a picture that might be the shape of the finished patio.

· ·

The problems can also involve numbers instead of models:

· ·

If the swim team sold 400 raffle tickets, it would have enough money to pay for new team shirts. So far the swimmers have $\frac{5}{8}$ of the necessary raffle tickets sold. How many more tickets do they need to sell?

· ·

With some models, it is necessary to be certain that the answer exists within the model. For example, if you were using fraction strips, you could ask, "If the blue strip (9) is the whole, what strip is two-thirds?" The answer is the 6 strip, or dark green. You could not ask students to find "three-fourths of the blue strip" because each fourth of 9 would be $2\frac{1}{4}$ units, and no strip has that length. Similar caution must be taken with rectangular pieces.

Questions involving unit fractions are generally the easiest. The hardest questions usually involve fractions greater than 1. For example, *If 15 chips are five-thirds of one whole set, how many chips are in a whole?* However, in every question, the unit fraction plays a significant role. If you have $\frac{5}{3}$ and want the whole, you first need to find $\frac{1}{3}$.

Avoid being the answer book for your students. Make students responsible for determining the validity of their own answers. In these exercises, the results can always be confirmed in terms of what is given.

It is good to periodically place fraction activities into a context. Context encourages students to explore ideas in a more open and informal manner and not to overly depend on rules. The way that children approach fraction concepts in these contexts may surprise you. The following activity uses literature to provide an excellent context for discussing fractional parts of sets and how fractional parts change as the whole changes.

ACTIVITY 5.6

Sharing Camels

As a class, read the story "Beasts of Burden" in the book *The Man Who Counted: A Collection of Mathematical Adventures* (Tahan, 1993). This story is about a wise mathematician, Beremiz, and the narrator, who are traveling together on one camel. They are asked by three brothers to solve an argument. Their father has left them 35 camels to divide among them in this way: one-half to one brother, one-third to another, and one-ninth to the third. Have students grapple with this situation to try to come up with a solution. Make sure to discuss students' approaches and their conjectures before changing the number of camels. Try to choose the number of camels based on students' conjectures so they have an opportunity to test their hunches. For example, if students claim that they cannot divide an odd number of camels (e.g., 35) in half, they may state that the starting number has to be even. So start with an even number of camels, say 34 or 36. Or students may claim that the starting number must be divisible by three because there are three brothers. In this case, start with a number such as 33. Students should share what they think they have discovered as each number is tested. No matter how many camels are involved, the problem of the indicated shares cannot be resolved. (Why does this happen?)

 STOP Before going further, try the preceding activity. What do you discover as you test various numbers? Why can you not find a number that will work?

The problem of the indicated shares cannot be resolved because the sum of $\frac{1}{2}$, $\frac{1}{3}$, and $\frac{1}{9}$ will never be one whole. No matter how many camels are involved, there will always be some "left over." Bresser (1995) describes three full days of wonderful discussions with his fifth graders, who proposed a wide range of solutions. Bresser's suggestions are worth considering.

Fraction Number Sense

The focus on fractional parts is an important beginning. But number sense with fractions demands more—it requires that students have some intuitive feel for fractions. They should know "about" how big a particular fraction is and be able to tell easily which of two fractions is larger.

Benchmarks of Zero, One-Half, and One

The most important reference points or benchmarks for fractions are 0, $\frac{1}{2}$, and 1. For fractions less than 1, simply comparing them to these three numbers gives quite a lot of information. For example, $\frac{3}{20}$ is small, close to 0, whereas $\frac{3}{4}$ is between $\frac{1}{2}$ and 1. The fraction $\frac{9}{10}$ is quite close to 1. Since any fraction greater than 1 is a whole number plus an amount less than 1, the same reference points are just as helpful: $3\frac{3}{7}$ is almost $3\frac{1}{2}$.

ACTIVITY 5.7

Zero, One-Half, or One

On the board or overhead, write a collection of 10 to 15 fractions. A few should be greater than 1 ($\frac{9}{8}$ or $\frac{11}{10}$), with the others ranging from 0 to 1. Let students sort the fractions into three groups: those close to 0, close to $\frac{1}{2}$, and close to 1. For those close to $\frac{1}{2}$, have them decide if the fraction is more or less than $\frac{1}{2}$. The difficulty of this task largely depends on the fractions. The first time you try this, use fractions such as $\frac{1}{20}$, $\frac{53}{100}$, or $\frac{9}{10}$ that are very close to the three benchmarks. On subsequent days, use fractions with most of the denominators less than 20. You might include one or two fractions such as $\frac{2}{8}$ or $\frac{3}{4}$ that are exactly in between the benchmarks. As usual, require explanations for each fraction.

The next activity is also aimed at developing the same three reference points for fractions. In "Close Fractions," however, the students must come up with the fractions rather than sort them.

ACTIVITY 5.8

Close Fractions

Have your students name a fraction that is close to 1 but not more than 1. Next have them name another fraction that is even closer to 1 than that. For the second response, they have to explain why they believe the fraction is closer to 1 than the previous fraction. Continue for several fractions in the same manner, each one being closer to 1 than the previous fraction. Similarly, try close to 0 or close to $\frac{1}{2}$ (either under or over). The first several times you try this activity, let the students use models to help with their thinking. Later, see how well their explanations work when they cannot use models or drawings. Focus discussions on the relative size of fractional parts.

Understanding why a fraction is close to 0, $\frac{1}{2}$, or 1 is a good beginning for fraction number sense. It begins to focus on the size of fractions in an important yet simple manner. The next activity also helps students reflect on fraction size.

ACTIVITY 5.9

About How Much?

Draw a picture like one of those in Figure 5.14 (or prepare some ahead of time for the overhead). Have each student write down a fraction that he or

(continued)

EXPANDED LESSON

(pages 158–159)
A complete lesson plan
based on "About How Much?"
can be found at the end
of this chapter.

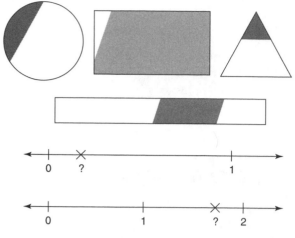

FIGURE 5.14 •

About how much? Name a fraction for each drawing and explain why you chose that fraction.

she thinks is a good estimate of the amount shown (or the indicated mark on the number line). Listen without judgment to the ideas of several students and discuss with them why any particular estimate might be a good one. There is no single correct answer, but estimates should be "in the ballpark." If students have difficulty coming up with an estimate, ask if they think the amount is closer to 0, $\frac{1}{2}$, or 1.

Thinking About Which Is More

The ability to tell which of two fractions is greater is another aspect of number sense with fractions. That ability is built around concepts of fractions, not on an algorithmic skill or symbolic tricks.

Concepts, Not Rules

Students have a tremendously strong mind-set about numbers that causes them difficulties with the relative size of fractions. In their experience, larger numbers mean "more." The tendency is to transfer this whole-number concept to fractions: Seven is more than four, so sevenths should be bigger than fourths. The inverse relationship between number of parts and size of parts cannot be told but must be a creation of each student's own thought process.

ACTIVITY 5.10

Ordering Unit Fractions

List a set of unit fractions such as $\frac{1}{3}$, $\frac{1}{8}$, $\frac{1}{5}$, and $\frac{1}{10}$. Ask students to put the fractions in order from least to most. Challenge students to defend the way they ordered the fractions. The first few times you do this activity, have them explain their ideas by using models.

This idea is so basic to the understanding of fractions that arbitrary rules ("larger bottom numbers mean smaller fractions") are not only inappropriate but also dangerous. Come back to this basic idea periodically. Students will seem to understand one day and revert to their more comfortable ideas about big numbers a day or two later. Repeat Activity 5.10 with all numerators equal to 4. See how students' ideas change.

You have probably learned rules or algorithms for comparing two fractions. The usual approach is to find a common denominator. This rule can be effective in getting correct answers but requires no thought about the size of the fractions. If students are taught the common denominator rule before they have had the opportunity to think about the relative size of various fractions, there is little chance that they will develop any familiarity with or number sense about fraction size. Comparison activities (which fraction is more?) can play a significant role in helping students develop concepts of relative fraction sizes. But keep in mind that reflective thought is the goal, not an algorithmic method of choosing the correct answer.

Before reading further, try the following exercise. Assume for a moment that you know nothing about equivalent fractions or common denominators or cross-multiplication. Assume that you are a fourth- or fifth-grade student who was never taught these procedures. Now examine the pairs of fractions in Figure 5.15 and select the larger of each pair. Write down or explain one or more reasons for your choice in each case.

Which fraction in each pair is greater? Give one or more reasons. Try not to use drawings or models. <u>Do</u> not <u>use</u> common denominators or cross-multiplication. Rely on concepts.

A. $\frac{4}{5}$ or $\frac{4}{9}$ G. $\frac{7}{12}$ or $\frac{5}{12}$

B. $\frac{4}{7}$ or $\frac{5}{7}$ H. $\frac{3}{5}$ or $\frac{3}{7}$

C. $\frac{3}{8}$ or $\frac{4}{10}$ I. $\frac{5}{8}$ or $\frac{6}{10}$

D. $\frac{5}{3}$ or $\frac{5}{8}$ J. $\frac{9}{8}$ or $\frac{4}{3}$

E. $\frac{3}{4}$ or $\frac{9}{10}$ K. $\frac{4}{6}$ or $\frac{7}{12}$

F. $\frac{3}{8}$ or $\frac{4}{7}$ L. $\frac{8}{9}$ or $\frac{7}{8}$

FIGURE 5.15 •

Comparing fractions using concepts.

Conceptual Thought Patterns for Comparison

The first two comparison schemes listed here rely on the meanings of the top and bottom numbers in fractions and on the relative sizes of unit fractional parts. The third and fourth ideas use the additional ideas of $0, \frac{1}{2}$, and 1 as convenient anchors or benchmarks for thinking about the size of fractions.

1. *More of the same-size parts.* To compare $\frac{3}{8}$ and $\frac{5}{8}$, it is easy to think about having 3 of something and also 5 of the same thing. It is common for children to choose $\frac{5}{8}$ as larger simply because 5 is more than 3 and the other numbers are the same. Right choice, wrong reason. Comparing $\frac{3}{8}$ and $\frac{5}{8}$ should be like comparing 3 apples and 5 apples.

2. *Same number of parts but parts of different sizes.* Consider the case of $\frac{3}{4}$ and $\frac{3}{7}$. If a whole is divided into 7 parts, the parts will certainly be smaller than if divided into only 4 parts. Many children will select $\frac{3}{7}$ as larger because 7 is more than 4 and the top numbers are the same. That approach yields correct choices when the parts are the same size, but it causes problems in this case. This is like comparing 3 apples with 3 melons. You have the same number of things, but melons are larger.

3. *More and less than one-half or one whole.* The fraction pairs $\frac{3}{7}$ versus $\frac{5}{8}$ and $\frac{5}{8}$ versus $\frac{7}{8}$ do not lend themselves to either of the previous thought processes. In the first pair, $\frac{3}{7}$ is less than half of the number of sevenths needed to make a whole, and so $\frac{3}{7}$ is less than a half. Similarly, $\frac{5}{8}$ is more than a half. Therefore, $\frac{5}{8}$ is the larger fraction. The second pair is determined by noting that one fraction is less than 1 and the other is greater than 1.

4. *Distance from one-half or one whole.* Why is $\frac{9}{10}$ greater than $\frac{3}{4}$? Not because the 9 and 10 are big numbers, although you will find that to be a common student response. Each is one fractional part away from one whole, and tenths are smaller than fourths. Similarly, notice that $\frac{5}{8}$ is smaller than $\frac{4}{6}$ because it is only one-eighth more than a half, while $\frac{4}{6}$ is a sixth more than a half. Can you use this basic idea to compare $\frac{3}{5}$ and $\frac{5}{9}$? (*Hint:* Each is half of a fractional part more than $\frac{1}{2}$.) Also try $\frac{5}{7}$ and $\frac{7}{9}$.

How did your reasons for choosing fractions in Figure 5.15 compare to these ideas? It is important that you are comfortable with these informal comparison strategies as a major component of your own number sense as well as for helping students develop theirs.

Tasks you design for your students should assist them in developing these and possibly other methods of comparing two fractions. It is important that the ideas come from your students and their discussions. To teach "the four ways to compare fractions" would be adding four more mysterious rules and would be defeating for many students.

ACTIVITY 5.11

Choose, Explain, Test

Present two or three pairs of fractions to students. The students' task is to decide which fraction is greater (choose), to explain why they think this is so (explain), and then to test their choice using any model that they wish to use. They should write a description of how they made their test and whether or not it agreed with their choice. If their choice was incorrect, they should try to say what they would change in their thinking. In the student explanations, rule out drawing as an option. Explain that it is difficult to draw fraction pictures accurately and for this activity, pictures may cause them to make mistakes.

Rather than directly teach the different possible methods for comparing fractions, select pairs that will likely elicit desired comparison strategies. On one day, for example, you might have two pairs with the same denominators and one with the same numerators. On another day, you might pick fraction pairs in which each fraction is exactly one part away from a whole. Try to build strategies over several days by the appropriate choice of fraction pairs.

The use of a model in Activity 5.11 is an important part of students' development of strategies as long as the model is helping students create the strategy. However, after several experiences, change the activity so that the testing portion with a model is omitted. Place greater emphasis on students' reasoning. If class discussions yield different choices, allow students to use their own arguments for their choices in order to make a decision about which fraction is greater.

The next activity extends the comparison task a bit more.

ACTIVITY 5.12

Line 'Em Up

Select four or five fractions for students to put in order from least to most. Have them indicate approximately where each fraction belongs on a number line labeled only with the points 0, $\frac{1}{2}$, and 1. Students should include a description of how they decided on the order for the fractions. To place the fractions on the number line, students must also make estimates of fraction size in addition to simply ordering the fractions.

Including Equivalent Fractions

The discussion to this point has somewhat artificially ignored the idea that students might use equivalent fraction concepts in making comparisons. Equivalent fraction concepts are such an important idea that we have devoted a separate section to the development of that idea. However, equivalent fraction concepts need not be put off until last and certainly should be allowed in the discussions of which fraction is more.

Smith (2002) thinks that it is essential that the comparison question is asked as follows: "Which of the following two (or more) fractions is greater, or *are they equal?*" (p. 9, emphasis added). He points out that this question leaves open the possibility that two fractions that may look different can, in fact, be equal.

In addition to this point, with equivalent fraction concepts, students can adjust how a fraction looks so that they can use ideas that make sense to them. Burns (1999) told of fifth graders who were comparing $\frac{6}{8}$ to $\frac{4}{5}$. (You might want to stop for a moment and think how you would compare these two.) One child changed the $\frac{4}{5}$ to $\frac{8}{10}$ so that both fractions would be two parts away from the whole and he reasoned from there. Another changed both fractions to a common *numerator* of 12.

Be absolutely certain to revisit the comparison activities and include pairs such as $\frac{8}{12}$ and $\frac{2}{3}$ in which the fractions are equal but do not appear to be. Also include fractions that are not in lowest terms.

Only One Size for the Whole

A key idea about fractions that students must come to understand is that a fraction does not say anything about the size of the whole or the size of the parts. A fraction tells us only about the *relationship between* the part and the whole. Consider the following situation.

Mark is offered the choice of a third of a pizza or a half of a pizza. Since he is hungry and likes pizza, he chooses the half. His friend Jane gets a third of a pizza but ends up with more than Mark. How can that be? Figure 5.16 illustrates how Mark got misdirected in his choice. The point of the "pizza fallacy" is that whenever two or more fractions are discussed in the same context, the correct assumption (the one Mark made in choosing a half of the pizza) is that the fractions are all parts of the same size whole.

Comparisons with any model can be made only if both fractions are parts of the same whole. For example, $\frac{2}{3}$ of a light green strip cannot be compared to $\frac{2}{5}$ of an orange strip.

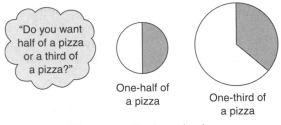

"Do you want half of a pizza or a third of a pizza?"

One-half of a pizza

One-third of a pizza

What assumption is made when answering this question?

FIGURE 5.16 • • • • • • • • • • • • • • • • • •

The "pizza fallacy."

Assessment Note

It is a good idea to periodically pose tasks in which students are required to draw representations of the fractions they are comparing. Consider the drawing in Figure 5.17, in which a student is comparing $\frac{4}{5}$ to $\frac{2}{3}$. What insights into his understanding does this student's work provide?

This student came to the correct conclusion but in an erroneous way. It appears that the student used the same size "fractional piece" to build his representations, resulting in inequivalent wholes. His representations suggest that he may not realize that the wholes should be the same size when comparing fractions.

Physical models, such as pie pieces and fraction bars, can mask this misconception because the size of the whole circle or whole rectangle is fixed. This eliminates the need for the student to think about the relative sizes of the associated wholes. Providing outlines of the wholes for students also diverts the focus from the size of the wholes. In short, if the representations are always provided for the students, a teacher may not realize a student has this misconception.

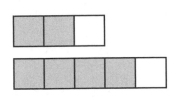

Since it has more, four-fifths is bigger than two-thirds.

FIGURE 5.17 • • • • • • • •

A student compares $\frac{2}{3}$ and $\frac{4}{5}$.

It is probably best to postpone fraction computation until at least fourth grade so that students can have an adequate amount of time to develop a firm foundation of fraction concepts. Having said that, consider the following: For addition and subtraction of fractions, a surprising number of problems found on standardized tests can be solved with simple number sense without knowledge of an algorithm. For example, $\frac{3}{4} + \frac{1}{2}$ requires only that students can think of $\frac{3}{4}$ as $\frac{1}{2}$ and $\frac{1}{4}$ more, or alternatively, think of $\frac{1}{2}$ as $\frac{1}{4}$ and $\frac{1}{4}$. This sort of thinking is a result of a focus on fraction meanings, not on algorithms.

The development of fraction number sense, even at grade 3, should certainly involve estimation of sums and differences of fractions. Estimation focuses on the size of the fractions and encourages students to use a variety of strategies.

The following activity can be used as a regular short warm-up for any fraction lesson.

ACTIVITY 5.13

First Estimates

Tell students that they are going to estimate a sum or difference of two fractions. They are to decide only if the exact answer is more or less than one. On the overhead projector show, for no more than about 10 seconds, a fraction addition or subtraction problem involving two proper fractions. Keep all denominators to 12 or less. Students write down on paper their choice of more or less than one. Do several problems in a row. Then return to each problem and discuss how students decided on their estimate.

Restricting Activity 5.13 to proper fractions keeps the difficulty to a minimum. When students are ready for a tougher challenge, choose from the following variations:

- Use fractions that are less than one. Estimate to the nearest half (0, $\frac{1}{2}$, 1, $1\frac{1}{2}$, 2).
- Use both proper and mixed fractions. Estimate to the nearest half.
- Use proper and mixed fractions. Estimate the best answer you can.

In the discussions following these estimation exercises, ask students if they think that the exact answer is more or less than the estimate that they gave. What is their reasoning?

Figure 5.18 shows six sample sums and differences that might be used in a "First Estimates" activity.

Test your own estimation skills with the sample problems in Figure 5.18. Look at each computation for only about 10 seconds and write down an estimate. After writing down all six of your estimates, look at the problems and decide if your estimate is higher or lower than the actual computation. Don't guess! Have a good reason.

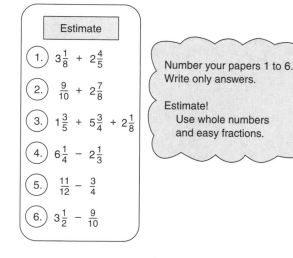

FIGURE 5.18

Fraction estimation drill.

In most cases students' estimates should not be much more than $\frac{1}{2}$ away from the exact sum or difference.

Equivalent-Fraction Concepts

STOP **How do you know that $\frac{4}{6} = \frac{2}{3}$? Before reading further, think of at least two different explanations.**

Concepts Versus Rules

Here are some possible answers to the question just posed:

1. They are the same because you can reduce $\frac{4}{6}$ and get $\frac{2}{3}$.
2. If you have a set of 6 things and you take 4 of them, that would be $\frac{4}{6}$. But you can make the 6 into groups of 2. So then there would be 3 groups, and the 4 would be 2 groups out of the 3 groups. That means it's $\frac{2}{3}$.

3. If you start with $\frac{2}{3}$, you can multiply the top and the bottom numbers by 2, and that will give you $\frac{4}{6}$, so they are equal.
4. If you had a square cut into 3 parts and you shaded 2, that would be $\frac{2}{3}$ shaded. If you cut all 3 of these parts in half, that would be 4 parts shaded and 6 parts in all. That's $\frac{4}{6}$, and it would be the same amount.

All of these answers are correct. But let's think about what they tell us. Responses 2 and 4 are very conceptual, although not very efficient. The procedural responses, 1 and 3, are quite efficient but indicate no conceptual knowledge. All students should eventually be able to write an equivalent fraction for a given fraction. At the same time, the rules should never be taught or used until the students understand what the result means. Consider how different the algorithm and the concept appear to be.

> *Concept:* Two fractions are equivalent if they are representations for the same amount or quantity—if they are the same number.
>
> *Algorithm:* To get an equivalent fraction, multiply (or divide) the top and bottom numbers by the same nonzero number.

In a problem-based classroom, students can develop an understanding of equivalent fractions and also develop from that understanding a conceptually based algorithm. As with most algorithms, a serious instructional error is to rush too quickly to the rule. Be patient! Intuitive methods are always best at first.

Equivalent-Fraction Concepts

The general approach to helping students create an understanding of equivalent fractions is to have them use models to find different names for a fraction. Consider that this is the first time in their experience that a fixed quantity can have multiple names (actually an infinite number of names). The following activities are possible starting places.

Different Fillers

Using an area model for fractions that is familiar to your students, prepare a worksheet with two or at most three outlines of different fractions. Do not limit yourself to unit fractions. For example, if the model is circular pie pieces, you might draw an outline for $\frac{2}{3}$, $\frac{1}{2}$, and $\frac{3}{4}$. The students' task is to use their own fraction pieces to find as many single-fraction names for the region as possible. After completing the three examples, have students write about the ideas or patterns they may have noticed in finding the names. Follow the activity with a class discussion.

In the class discussion following the "Different Fillers" activity, a good question to ask involves what names could be found if students had any size pieces that they wanted. For example, ask students, "What names could you find if we had sixteenths in our fraction kit? What names could you find if you could have any piece at all?" The idea is to push beyond filling in the region in a pure trial-and-error approach.

The following activity is just a variation of "Different Fillers." Instead of a manipulative model, the task is constructed on dot paper.

BLMs 10–13

Dot Paper Equivalencies

Create a worksheet using a portion of either isometric or rectangular dot grid paper. (These can be found in the Blackline Masters.) On the grid, draw the outline of a region and designate it as one whole. Draw and lightly shade a part of the region within the whole. The task is to use different parts of the whole determined by the grid to find names for the part. Figure 5.19 includes an example drawn on an isometric grid. Students should draw a picture of the unit fractional part that they use for each fraction name. The larger the size of the whole, the more names the activity will generate.

FIGURE 5.19 • • • • • • •

Area models for equivalent fractions.

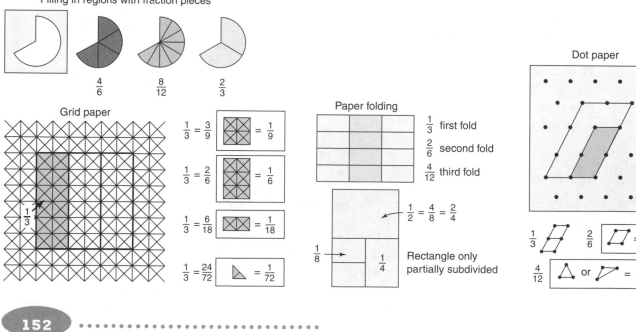

Chapter 5 DEVELOPING FRACTION CONCEPTS

The "Dot Paper Equivalencies" activity is a form of what Lamon (2002) calls "unitizing," that is, given a quantity, finding different ways to chunk the quantity into parts in order to name it.

Length models can be used to create activities similar to the "Different Fillers" task. For example, as shown in Figure 5.20, rods or strips can be used to designate both a whole and a part. Students use smaller rods to find fraction names for the given part. To have larger wholes and, thus, more possible parts, use a train of two or three rods for the whole and the part. Folding paper strips is another method of creating fraction names. In the example shown in Figure 5.20, one-half is subdivided by successive folding in half. Other folds would produce other names and these possibilities should be discussed if no one tries to fold the strip in an odd number of parts.

The following activity is also a unitizing activity in which students look for different units or chunks of the whole in order to name a part of the whole in different ways. This activity is significant because it utilizes a set model.

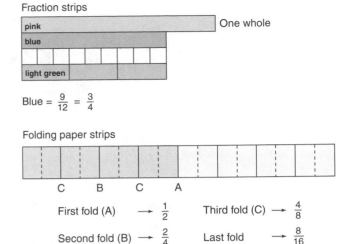

Fraction strips

pink

blue

light green

One whole

Blue = $\frac{9}{12}$ = $\frac{3}{4}$

Folding paper strips

C   B   C   A

First fold (A) → $\frac{1}{2}$ Third fold (C) → $\frac{4}{8}$

Second fold (B) → $\frac{2}{4}$ Last fold → $\frac{8}{16}$

FIGURE 5.20 •

Length models for equivalent fractions.

ACTIVITY 5.16

Group the Counters, Find the Names

Have students set out a specific number of counters in two colors—for example, 24 counters, 16 of them black and 8 white. The 24 make up the whole. The task is to group the counters into different fractional parts of the whole and use the parts to create fraction names for the black and the white counters. In Figure 5.21, 24 counters are arranged in different array patterns. You might want to suggest arrays or allow students to arrange them in any way they wish. Students should record their different groupings and explain how they found the fraction names. They can simply use Xs and Os for the counters.

In Lamon's version of the last activity, she prompts students with questions such as, "If we make groups of four, what part of the set is black?" With these prompts you can suggest fraction names that students are unlikely to think of. For our example in Figure 5.21, if we make groups of one-half counters, what would the white set be called? Suppose we made groups of six? (Groups of six result in a fractional numerator. Why not?)

A challenging exploration of finding equivalent fractions is presented in *Gator Pie* (Mathews, 1979), a delightful book about Alice, Alvin, and other alligators sharing a pie they found in the woods. At first glance this book seems too juvenile for students in the upper grades. However, students can enjoy this story when it is a springboard into an interesting problem-solving situation.

FIGURE 5.21 ●●●●●●●

Set models for equivalent
fractions.

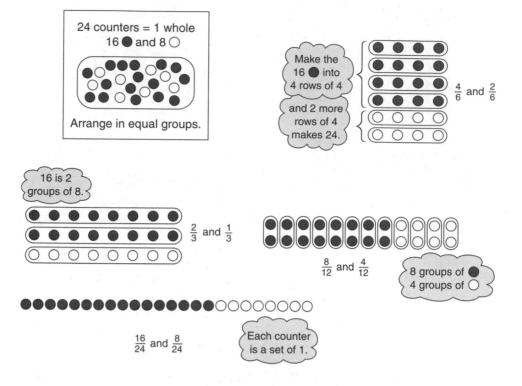

ACTIVITY 5.17

Divide and Divide Again

In the book *Gator Pie*, Alvin and Alice find a pie in the woods. However, before they can cut it, another gator appears and demands a share of the pie. As the story continues, more and more gators arrive until there are 100 gators who want a piece of the pie. Finally, Alice painstakingly cuts the pie into hundredths. In the story, Alvin and Alice are prevented from cutting the pie each time because more gators show up. An interesting twist is to change the story so that the pie is cut before more gators appear. The problem is how to share it among a larger number once it is already cut. To illustrate, cut a circle (or rectangle) into halves or thirds, and then ask students to decide how to share it among a larger number once it is already cut. You may want to start going from halves to sixths. This is reasonably easy but may surprise you. After students have shared their approaches, progress into more difficult divisions. For example, what if the pie is cut in thirds and we want to share it in tenths? Students should be expected to identify the fractional parts they used and explain how and why they used those particular fractional parts.

As students work through "Divide and Divide Again," they have to think about the part-whole meaning of fractions: how to divide an amount into equal-sized portions or fair shares. What is challenging is that oftentimes the equal-sized portions may not be the same shape or may be pieced together from smaller pieces. Placing a challenging task in the familiar context of fair sharing makes the task seem possible to students.

In the activities so far, there has only been a hint of a rule for finding equivalent fractions. The following activity moves a bit closer but should still be done before development of a rule.

Missing-Number Equivalencies

Give students an equation expressing an equivalence between two fractions but with one of the numbers missing. Here are four different examples:

$$\frac{5}{3} = \frac{\square}{6} \qquad \frac{2}{3} = \frac{6}{\square} \qquad \frac{8}{12} = \frac{\square}{3} \qquad \frac{9}{12} = \frac{3}{\square}$$

The missing number can be either a numerator or a denominator. Furthermore, the missing number can either be larger or smaller than the corresponding part of the equivalent fraction. (All four of these possibilities are represented in the examples.) The task is to find the missing number and to explain your solution.

When doing "Missing-Number Equivalencies" you may want to specify a particular model, such as sets or pie pieces. Alternatively, you can allow students to select whatever methods they wish to solve these problems. One or two equivalencies followed by a discussion is sufficient for a good lesson. This activity is surprisingly challenging, especially if students are required to use a set model.

Before continuing with development of an algorithm for equivalent fractions with your class, you should revisit the comparison tasks as students begin to realize that they can change the names of fractions in order to help reason about which fraction is greater.

Developing an Equivalent-Fraction Algorithm

Kamii and Clark (1995) argue that undue reliance on physical models does not help students construct equivalence schemes. When students understand that fractions can have different names, they should be challenged to develop a method for finding equivalent names. It might also be argued that students who are experienced at looking for patterns and developing schemes for doing things can invent an algorithm for equivalent fractions without further assistance. However, the following approach will certainly improve the chances of that happening.

An Area Model Approach

Your goal is to help students see that if they multiply both the top and bottom numbers by the same number, they will always get an equivalent fraction. The approach suggested here is to look for a pattern in the way that the fractional parts in both the part as well as the whole are counted. Activity 5.19 is a good beginning, but a good class discussion following the activity will also be required.

Slicing Squares

Give students a worksheet with four squares in a row, each approximately 3 cm on a side. Have them shade in the same fraction in each square using vertical dividing lines. For example, slice each square in fourths and shade three-fourths as in Figure 5.22. Next, tell students to slice each square into an

(continued)

Start with each square showing $\frac{3}{4}$.

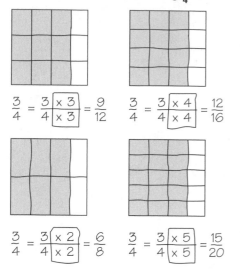

$$\frac{3}{4} = \frac{3\boxed{\times 3}}{4\boxed{\times 3}} = \frac{9}{12} \qquad \frac{3}{4} = \frac{3\boxed{\times 4}}{4\boxed{\times 4}} = \frac{12}{16}$$

$$\frac{3}{4} = \frac{3\boxed{\times 2}}{4\boxed{\times 2}} = \frac{6}{8} \qquad \frac{3}{4} = \frac{3\boxed{\times 5}}{4\boxed{\times 5}} = \frac{15}{20}$$

What <u>product</u> tells how many parts are shaded?

What <u>product</u> tells how many parts in the whole?

Notice that the same factor is used for both part and whole.

FIGURE 5.22 •

A model for the equivalent-fraction algorithm.

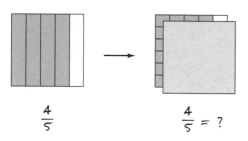

$$\frac{4}{5} \qquad\qquad \frac{4}{5} = ?$$

FIGURE 5.23 •

How can you count the fractional parts if you cannot see them all?

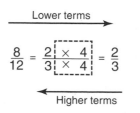

Lower terms →

$$\frac{8}{12} = \frac{2\ \vdots\ \times\ 4\ \vdots}{3\ \vdots\ \times\ 4\ \vdots} = \frac{2}{3}$$

← Higher terms

FIGURE 5.24 •

Using the equivalent-fraction algorithm to write fractions in simplest terms.

equal number of horizontal slices. Each square is sliced with a different number of slices, using anywhere from one to eight slices. For each sliced square, they should write an equation showing the equivalent fraction. Have them examine their four equations and the drawings and challenge them to discover any patterns in what they have done. You may want them to repeat this with four more squares and a different fraction.

Following this activity, write on the board the equations for four or five different fraction names found by the students. Discuss any patterns they found. To focus the discussion, show on the overhead a square illustrating $\frac{4}{5}$ made with vertical slices as in Figure 5.23. Turn off the overhead and slice the square into six parts in the opposite direction. Cover all but two edges of the square as shown in the figure. Ask, "What is the new name for my $\frac{4}{5}$?"

The reason for this exercise is that many students simply count the small regions and never think to use multiplication. With the covered square, students can see that there are four columns and six rows to the shaded part, so there must be 4×6 parts shaded. Similarly, there must be 5×6 parts in the whole. Therefore, the new name for $\frac{4}{5}$ is $\frac{4 \times 6}{5 \times 6}$.

Using this idea, have students return to the fractions on their worksheet to see if the pattern works for other fractions.

Examine examples of equivalent fractions that have been generated with other models, and see if the rule of multiplying top and bottom numbers by the same number holds there also. If the rule is correct, how can $\frac{6}{8}$ and $\frac{9}{12}$ be equivalent? What about fractions like $2\frac{1}{4}$? How could it be demonstrated that $\frac{9}{4}$ is the same as $2\frac{1}{12}$?

Writing Fractions in Simplest Terms

The multiplication scheme for equivalent fractions produces fractions with larger denominators. To write a fraction in *simplest terms* means to write it so that numerator and denominator have no common whole number factors. (Some texts use the name *lowest terms* instead of *simplest terms*.) One meaningful approach to this task of finding simplest terms is to reverse the earlier process, as illustrated in Figure 5.24. Try to devise a problem-based task that will help students develop this reverse idea.

Of course, finding and eliminating a common factor is the same as dividing both top and bottom by the same number. The search for a common factor keeps the process of writing an equivalent fraction to one rule: Top and bottom numbers of a fraction can be multiplied by the same nonzero number. There is no need for a different rule for rewriting fractions in lowest terms.

Two additional notes:

1. Notice that the phrase *reducing fractions* was not used. This unfortunate terminology implies making a fraction smaller and is rarely used anymore in textbooks.
2. Many teachers seem to believe that fraction answers are incorrect if not in simplest or lowest terms. This is also unfortunate. When students add $\frac{1}{6} + \frac{1}{2}$ and get $\frac{4}{6}$, they have added correctly and have found the answer. Rewriting $\frac{4}{6}$ as $\frac{2}{3}$ is a separate issue.

Multiplying by One

A strictly symbolic approach to equivalent fractions is based on the multiplicative property that says that any number multiplied by 1 remains unchanged. Any fraction of the form $\frac{n}{n}$ can be used as the identity element. Therefore, $\frac{3}{4} = \frac{3}{4} \times 1 = \frac{3}{4} \times \frac{2}{2} = \frac{6}{8}$. Furthermore, the numerator and denominator of the identity element can also be fractions. In this way, $\frac{6}{12} = \frac{6}{12} \times \left(\frac{1/6}{1/6}\right) = \frac{1}{2}$.

This explanation relies on an understanding of the multiplicative identity property, which most students in grades 4 to 6 do not fully appreciate. It also relies on the procedure for multiplying two fractions. Finally, the argument uses solely deductive reasoning based on an axiom of the rational number system. It does not lend itself to intuitive modeling. A reasonable conclusion is to delay this important explanation until at least seventh or eighth grade in an appropriate prealgebra context and not as a method or a rationale for producing equivalent fractions.

Technology Note

In the NCTM e-examples (www.nctm.org), there is a very nice fraction game for two players (*Applet 5.1, Communicating About Mathematics Using Games*). The game uses a number-line model, and knowledge of equivalent fractions plays a significant role.

The NLVM website (http://matti.usu.edu/nlvm/nav/vlibrary.html) has a limited applet tool for exploring equivalent fractions, *Fractions—Equivalent*. Proper fractions are presented randomly in either square or circular formats. Students can slice the model in as many parts as they wish to see which slicings create equivalent fractions. For squares, the new slices go in the same direction as the original slices. For circles, it is a bit hard to distinguish new slices from old. Students enter an equivalent fraction and then click a button to check their response.

EQUIVALENT-FRACTION CONCEPTS

EXPANDED LESSON

About How Much

Based on: Activity 5.9, p. 145

GRADE LEVEL: Third or fourth grade.

MATHEMATICS GOALS
- To develop a concept of the size of fractions.
- To develop the reference points or benchmarks of 0, $\frac{1}{2}$, and 1 for fractions.

THINKING ABOUT THE STUDENTS
Students understand that in the context of part-whole fractions, the whole is divided into equivalent parts. They also understand the symbolic notation of fractions; that is, they know what the top number in the fraction means (the number of parts) and what the bottom number in the fraction means (the kind of parts we are counting). Equivalent fractions have not been explored fully.

MATERIALS AND PREPARATION
- Make copies of Blackline Master L-1 for each student and also a transparency of L-1.
- Prepare a transparency with a rectangle divided into 6 equal pieces as shown here.
- A colored overhead pen.

- -

lesson

BLM L-1

BEFORE

Begin with a simpler version of the task:
- Show the transparency with the rectangle divided into six equal pieces. Shade in three of the six sections. Ask students to tell how much of the rectangle is shaded. Be sure that answers include $\frac{1}{2}$ as well as $\frac{3}{6}$.
- Now shade in just a bit more of the rectangle as shown here. Ask students what an estimate is. Negotiate an appropriate definition of an estimate. Ask students what a good estimate might be for the shaded amount. Most students will say $\frac{3}{6}$ or $\frac{1}{2}$. Discuss why they think their answer is a good estimate.
- Add to the shaded portion so that half of the fourth piece in the rectangle is now shaded. Ask whether their estimate would change if this is the amount that they want to estimate. If students still want to use $\frac{3}{6}$ as an estimate, ask what they could do if they wanted a closer estimate (e.g., divide the pieces in half to form twelfths).

Brainstorm
- Now draw a rectangle on the transparency with no partitions. Shade in about $\frac{1}{3}$ of the rectangle.
- Ask students to determine how they would get an estimate for the shaded amount. Give them a minute to think about it individually and then share their ideas with a partner. Come together as a class to hear different strategies. Two possible strategies: (1) Divide the rectangle into equal parts and use those parts to determine the estimate; and (2) decide whether the amount is closer to 0, $\frac{1}{2}$, or 1. Then you might divide the parts further to decide if the amount is closer to 0, $\frac{1}{4}$, $\frac{1}{2}$, $\frac{3}{4}$, or 1. It is a good idea to list these ideas on the board for students to refer to when doing the task.

The Task
Each student is to determine a fraction that he or she thinks is a good estimate of the amount shown in each picture.

Establish Expectations
Students should be ready to share their estimates and the ways that they determined the estimates for each picture. They should use the handout to draw on the pictures and write words and numbers to explain their thinking.

DURING

- Without evaluating the ideas of several students, listen to why any particular estimate might be a good one.
- If students have difficulty coming up with an estimate, ask if they think the amount is closer to 0, $\frac{1}{2}$, or 1.

AFTER

- Ask various students to come forward to share their estimates and their ways of determining the estimates. Ask the class to comment or ask questions about the estimate and/or the strategy.
- If there are students who divided shapes into unequal parts, have them share their approaches. Do not evaluate but instead encourage the class to discuss their approaches.
- When discussing the pictures with number lines, focus on the interval between 0 and 1 as the whole, not the point where the number 1 is.

ASSESSMENT NOTES

- How are students finding equivalent pieces, in particular for circles and triangles? Are they dividing the shapes into equivalent pieces? How do they know they are equivalent?
- Are estimates "in the ballpark"?
- When working with number lines, are students counting intervals between numbers or are they counting the numbers?

- If students have difficulty with this task, continue helping them develop the reference points of 0, $\frac{1}{2}$, and 1 for fractions by doing activities such as "Zero, One-Half, or One" (Activity 5.7) and "Close Fractions" (Activity 5.8).
- If students have difficulty understanding the problem with unequal parts in circles and triangles, provide them with circles and triangles from which they can cut various pieces to lay over each other to show that they are not the same area.
- Ordering unit fractions and making comparisons are appropriate next activities. (See Activities 5.10 and 5.11.) It is also reasonable to begin exploring equivalent fractions.

next steps

FRACTION COMPUTATION

A fifth-grade student asks, "Why is it when we times 29 times two-ninths that the answer goes down?" (Taber, 2002, p. 67). Although generalizations from whole numbers can confuse students, you should realize that their ideas about the operations were developed with whole numbers. Students need to build on their ideas of whole-number operations. This is where students are. We can use their understanding of what the operations mean to give meaning to fraction computation.

However, as you will discover in this chapter, a firm understanding of fractions is the most critical foundation for fraction computation. Without this foundation, your students will almost certainly be learning rules without reasons, an unacceptable goal.

Number Sense and Fraction Algorithms

Today it is important to be able to compute with fractions, primarily for the purpose of making estimates, for understanding computations done with technology, and for relatively simple calculations. Even standardized testing reflects an emphasis on less-tedious computations with fractions.

big ideas

1 The meanings of each operation on fractions are the same as the meanings for the operations on whole numbers. Operations with fractions should begin by applying these same meanings to fractional parts.

- For addition and subtraction, it is critical to understand that the numerator tells the number of parts and the denominator the type of part.

- For multiplication by a fraction, it is useful to recall that the denominator is a divisor. This idea allows us to find parts of the other factor.

- For division by a fraction, the two ways of thinking about the operation—partition and measurement—are extremely important. The partition or fair-sharing concept of division will lead to a very different division procedure than will the measurement or repeated subtraction concept.

2 Estimation of fraction computations is tied almost entirely to concepts of the operations and of fractions. A computation algorithm is not required for making estimates. Estimation should be an integral part of computation development to keep students' attention on the meanings of the operations and the expected size of the results.

The Dangerous Rush to Rules

It is important to give students ample opportunity to develop fraction number sense as described in the previous chapter and not immediately to start talking about common denominators and other rules of computation.

Premature attention to rules for fraction computation has a number of serious drawbacks. None of the rules helps students think about the operations and what they mean. Armed only with rules, students have no means of assessing their results to see if they make sense. Surface mastery of rules in the short term is quickly lost. When mixed together, the myriad rules of fraction computation soon become a meaningless jumble. Students ask, "Do I need a common denominator, or do you just add the bottom numbers like in multiplication?" "Which one do you invert, the first or the second number?" The algorithm rules do not immediately apply to mixed numbers. More rules! And perhaps most important is that this approach to mathematics is immensely defeating to the child.

A Problem-Based, Number Sense Approach

Even if your curriculum guidelines call for teaching all four of the operations with fractions in the fifth grade, you are still advised to delay a rush to algorithmic procedures until it becomes clear that students are ready. (Very few states call for multiplication and division of fractions before the fifth grade.) Students can become adequately proficient using informal, student-invented methods that they understand.

The following guidelines should be kept in mind when developing computational strategies for fractions:

1. *Begin with simple contextual tasks.* Huinker (1998) makes an excellent case for the use of contextual problems and for letting students develop their own methods of computation with fractions. Problems or contexts need not be elaborate. What you want is a context for both the meaning of the operation and the fractions involved.

2. *Connect the meaning of fraction computation with whole-number computation.* To consider what $2\frac{1}{2} \times \frac{3}{4}$ might mean, we should ask, "What does 2 × 3 mean?" The concepts of each operation are the same, and benefits can be had by connecting these ideas.

3. *Let estimation and informal methods play a big role in the development of strategies.* "Should $2\frac{1}{2} \times \frac{3}{4}$ be more or less than 1? More or less than 3?" Estimation keeps the focus on the meanings of the numbers and the operations, encourages reflective thinking, and helps build informal number sense with fractions.

4. *Explore each of the operations using models.* Use a variety of models. Have students defend their solutions using the models. You will find that sometimes it is possible to get answers with models that do not seem to help with pencil-and-paper approaches. That's fine! The ideas will help children learn to think about the fractions and the operations, contribute to mental methods, and provide a useful background when you eventually do get to the standard algorithms.

In the discussions that follow, informal exploration is encouraged for each operation. There is also a guided development of each traditional algorithm.

Addition and Subtraction

The idea of developing invented strategies for fractions beginning with contextual problems is similar to the approach described in Chapter 4 for whole-number computation. As with whole numbers, expect that students will use a variety of methods and that the methods will vary widely with the fractions encountered in the problems.

No attempt is made in this chapter to describe all of the solution strategies that students might develop. Students will continue to find ways to solve problems with fractions, and their informal approaches will contribute to the development of more standard methods (Huinker, 1998; Lappan & Mouck, 1998; Schifter, Bastable, & Russell, 1999c).

Informal Exploration

Consider the following simple context:

> Paul and his brother were each eating the same kind of candy bar. Paul had $\frac{3}{4}$ of his candy bar. His brother still had $\frac{7}{8}$ of a candy bar. How much candy did the two boys have together?

This is an example of the type of task you can pose to students from the very beginning of their exploration with fraction computation.

STOP **Using nothing other than simple drawings, how would you solve this problem without setting it up in the usual manner and finding common denominators? Can you think of two different methods?**

3/4   7/8

FIGURE 6.1

How could you combine these two quantities to determine the sum?

Many students will draw a simple rectangle for the two candy bars as in Figure 6.1. The drawing of $\frac{7}{8}$ suggests that if you had one more eighth it would be a whole. So it is the same as $1\frac{3}{4}$ with $\frac{1}{8}$ taken off. Or the drawing might suggest taking a fourth from the $\frac{7}{8}$ and putting it with the $\frac{3}{4}$ to make a whole. That would leave $\frac{5}{8}$.

Drawings are not always as helpful as physical models because students draw conclusions based on inaccurate drawings. Sometimes there is value in specifying that a particular model be used. Suppose that you ask students to solve the following problem by using fraction strips.

> Jack and Jill ordered two identical-sized pizzas, one cheese and one pepperoni. Jack ate $\frac{5}{6}$ of a pizza and Jill ate $\frac{1}{2}$ of a pizza. How much pizza did they eat together?

The first decision that must be made is what strip to use as the whole. That decision is not required with a circular model. The whole must be the same for both fractions although there is a tendency to use the easiest whole for each fraction. Again, this

Find a strip for a whole that allows both fractions to be modeled.

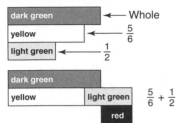

The sum is 1 whole and a red rod more than a whole. A red is $\frac{1}{3}$ of a dark green.

So $\frac{5}{6} + \frac{1}{2} = 1\frac{1}{3}$.

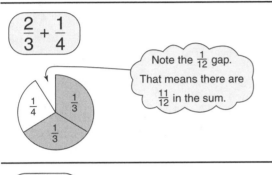

Note the $\frac{1}{12}$ gap. That means there are $\frac{11}{12}$ in the sum.

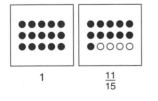

What set size can be used for the whole? The smallest is a set of 15.

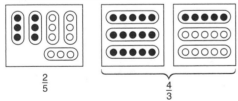

Combine (add) the fractions. $\frac{2}{5}$ is 6 counters, and $\frac{4}{3}$ is 20 counters. In sets of 15, that is $\frac{26}{15}$, or $1\frac{11}{15}$.

FIGURE 6.2 •

Using models to add fractions.

issue does not arise with circles. In this case, the smallest strip that will work is the 6 strip or the dark green strip. Figure 6.2 illustrates a solution. The thinking required in this task helps pave the way for a common denominator

Subtraction of two fractions with models is a similar process, as shown in Figure 6.3. Notice that it is sometimes possible to find the sum or difference of two fractions without splitting pieces into smaller parts. Often the answer is determined by looking at the part left over.

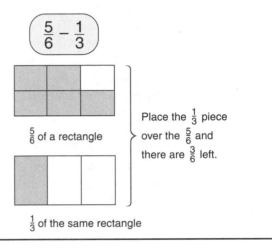

$\frac{5}{6}$ of a rectangle

Place the $\frac{1}{3}$ piece over the $\frac{5}{6}$ and there are $\frac{3}{6}$ left.

$\frac{1}{3}$ of the same rectangle

Find a rod that can be broken into eighths and halves: brown.

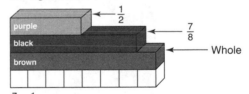

$\frac{7}{8} - \frac{1}{2}$ is the difference between a magenta and a black rod. That is three whites, or $\frac{3}{8}$. So $\frac{7}{8} - \frac{1}{2} = \frac{3}{8}$.

Get a set that can be divided into both halves and thirds. Use sets of 6.

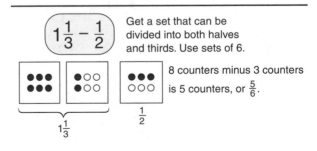

8 counters minus 3 counters is 5 counters, or $\frac{5}{6}$.

FIGURE 6.3 •

Using models to subtract fractions.

ADDITION AND SUBTRACTION

Most of your problems should involve simple fractions with "friendly" denominators no greater than 12. There is no need to add fifths and sevenths or even fifths and twelfths. The results involve numbers that cannot be handled with any model or drawing. Those numbers are rarely found in real problems. At the same time, do not be afraid of including mixed numbers and unlike denominators.

The Myth of Common Denominators

Teachers commonly tell students, "In order to add or subtract fractions, you must first get common denominators." The explanation usually goes something like, "After all, you can't add apples and oranges." This well-intentioned statement is essentially false. A correct statement might be, "In order *to use the standard algorithm* to add or subtract fractions, you must first get common denominators." And the explanation is then, "The algorithm is designed to work only with common denominators."

Using their own invented strategies, students will see that many correct solutions are found without ever getting a common denominator. Consider these sums and differences:

$$\tfrac{3}{4} + \tfrac{1}{8} \qquad \tfrac{1}{2} - \tfrac{1}{8} \qquad \tfrac{2}{3} + \tfrac{1}{2} \qquad 1\tfrac{1}{2} - \tfrac{3}{4} \qquad 1\tfrac{2}{3} + \tfrac{3}{4}$$

Working with the ways different fractional parts are related one to another often provides solutions without common denominators. For example, halves, fourths, and eighths are easily related. Also, picture three-thirds making up a whole in a circle. Have you ever noticed that one-half of the whole is a third and a half of a third or a sixth? Similarly, the difference between a third and a fourth is a twelfth. With relationships such as these, many fraction computations can be solved without first getting common denominators.

Assessment Note

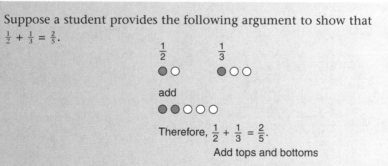

Suppose a student provides the following argument to show that $\tfrac{1}{2} + \tfrac{1}{3} = \tfrac{2}{5}$.

$\tfrac{1}{2}$ $\tfrac{1}{3}$

● ○   ● ○ ○

add

● ● ○ ○ ○

Therefore, $\tfrac{1}{2} + \tfrac{1}{3} = \tfrac{2}{5}$.

Add tops and bottoms

From the student's work we can see that he has used a common misconception to combine the fractions: simply adding the numerators and the denominators. And he has provided a picture that seems to support his answer. Why is this student's argument flawed? Consider how the whole changes with each fraction ($\tfrac{1}{2}$, $\tfrac{1}{3}$, $\tfrac{2}{5}$). When adding or subtracting fractions, the associated wholes must be alike.

A tenuous understanding of fraction concepts coupled with a picture that appears to support this flawed approach can cause students to resist examining the approach. Placing the fractions into a context can help students begin to critically examine the approach. For example, suppose you had $\tfrac{1}{2}$ of a small pizza and $\tfrac{1}{3}$ of a large pizza. When you put the two amounts together, you will have part of a pizza. But what is the size of that pizza?

By this time, students have likely worked with comparing fractions and grappled with the notion that to compare fractions, they must be associated with like-size wholes (see Chapter 5, p. 149). Another way to encourage students to examine the flawed approach is by asking them to compare their answer ($\frac{2}{5}$) to the first fraction ($\frac{1}{2}$). Comparing the fractions draws students' attention to the fact that the wholes for $\frac{1}{2}$ and $\frac{2}{5}$ are not alike. Plus, students are faced with the dilemma that the sum ($\frac{2}{5}$) is smaller than one of the addends ($\frac{1}{2}$).

Developing the Algorithm

The foregoing notwithstanding, it is important to develop an algorithm for addition and subtraction, and students will likely need some guidance in doing so. At the same time, they can easily build on their informal explorations and see that the common-denominator approach is meaningful.

Like Denominators

Most lists of objectives first specify addition and subtraction with like denominators. This is both unfortunate and unnecessary! If students have a good foundation with fraction concepts, they should be able to add or subtract like fractions immediately. Students who are not confident solving problems such as $\frac{3}{4} + \frac{2}{4}$ or $3\frac{7}{8} - 1\frac{3}{8}$ almost certainly do not have good fraction concepts and will be lost in any further development. The idea that the top number counts and the bottom number tells what is counted makes addition and subtraction of like fractions the same as adding and subtracting whole numbers.

Unlike Denominators

To get students to move to common denominators, consider a task such as $\frac{5}{8} + \frac{2}{4}$. Let students use pie pieces to get the result of $1\frac{1}{8}$ using any approach. Many will note that the models for the two fractions make one whole and there is $\frac{1}{8}$ extra. The key question to ask at this point is, "How can we change this problem into one that is just like the easy ones where the parts are the same?" For this example, it is relatively easy to see that fourths could be changed into eighths. Have students use models to show the original problem and also the converted problem. The main idea is to see that $\frac{5}{8} + \frac{2}{4}$ is exactly the same problem as $\frac{5}{8} + \frac{4}{8}$.

Next try some examples where both fractions need to be changed—for example, $\frac{2}{3} + \frac{1}{4}$. Again, focus attention on *rewriting the problem* in a form that is like "adding apples and apples," where the parts of both fractions are the same. As students discuss solutions, be sure they understand clearly that the new form of the problem is the same problem. This can and should be demonstrated with models.

Assessment Note

Suppose that you showed $\frac{2}{3} + \frac{1}{2}$ with pie pieces. By some informal means your students are now convinced that the sum is $1\frac{1}{6}$. Substitute $\frac{16}{24}$ for the $\frac{2}{3}$ and $\frac{7}{14}$ for the $\frac{1}{2}$ and ask students, "What is this sum ($\frac{16}{24} + \frac{7}{14}$)?" Students who understand that the two problems are equivalent should not hesitate and state that the answer remains the same—$1\frac{1}{6}$. If your students express any doubt about the equivalence of the two problems, that should be a clue that the concept of equivalent fractions is not well understood.

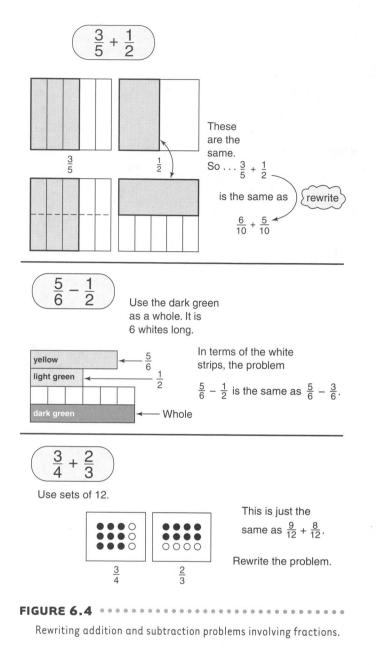

These are the same. So... $\frac{3}{5} + \frac{1}{2}$

is the same as

$\frac{6}{10} + \frac{5}{10}$

rewrite

Use the dark green as a whole. It is 6 whites long.

yellow $\frac{5}{6}$

light green $\frac{1}{2}$

dark green ← Whole

In terms of the white strips, the problem

$\frac{5}{6} - \frac{1}{2}$ is the same as $\frac{5}{6} - \frac{3}{6}$.

Use sets of 12.

This is just the same as $\frac{9}{12} + \frac{8}{12}$.

Rewrite the problem.

$\frac{3}{4}$ $\frac{2}{3}$

FIGURE 6.4 •

Rewriting addition and subtraction problems involving fractions.

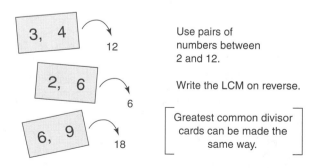

3, 4 → 12

2, 6 → 6

6, 9 → 18

Use pairs of numbers between 2 and 12.

Write the LCM on reverse.

Greatest common divisor cards can be made the same way.

FIGURE 6.5 •

Least common multiple (LCM) flash cards.

As a result of modeling and rewriting fractions to make the problems easy, students will come to understand that the process of getting a common denominator is really one of looking for a way to change the *statement* of the problem without changing the problem itself. These ideas are illustrated in Figure 6.4.

Subtraction of two simple fractions follows exactly the same approach.

Common Multiples

Many students have trouble with finding common denominators because they are not able to come up with common multiples of the denominators quickly. This skill depends on having a good command of the basic facts for multiplication. For students who have mastered their multiplication facts, this is a skill that can be drilled. Here is an activity aimed at the skill of finding least common multiples or common denominators.

ACTIVITY 6.1

LCM Flash Cards

Make flash cards with pairs of numbers that are potential denominators. Most should be less than 16. For each card, students try to give the least common multiple (LCM; see Figure 6.5). Be sure to include pairs that are prime, such as 9 and 5; pairs in which one is a multiple of the other, such as 2 and 8; and pairs that have a common divisor, such as 8 and 12.

Mixed Numbers

A separate algorithm for mixed numbers in addition and subtraction is not necessary even though mixed numbers are often treated as separate topics in traditional textbooks and in some lists of objectives. Avoid layering fractions with yet another rule. Include mixed numbers in all of your activities with addition and subtraction, and let students solve these problems in ways that make sense to them. Furthermore, it is almost certain that students will add the whole numbers first and then deal with the fractions using the algorithm or whatever method makes sense.

For subtraction, dealing with the whole numbers first still makes sense. Consider this problem: $5\frac{1}{8} - 3\frac{5}{8}$. After subtracting 3 from 5, students will need to deal

Chapter 6 **FRACTION COMPUTATION**

with the $\frac{5}{8}$. Some will take $\frac{5}{8}$ from the whole part, 2, leaving $1\frac{3}{8}$, and then $\frac{1}{8}$ more is $1\frac{4}{8}$. Others may take away the $\frac{1}{8}$ that is there and then $\frac{4}{8}$ from the remaining 2. A third but unlikely method is to trade one of the wholes for $\frac{8}{8}$, add it to the $\frac{1}{8}$, and then take $\frac{5}{8}$ from the resulting $\frac{9}{8}$. This last method is the same as the traditional algorithm.

Estimation and Simple Methods

With denominators of 16 or less, estimation using "nice" fractions like halves and fourths is usually possible and should be encouraged. Estimation also leads to informal methods that are often easier than traditional algorithms for getting exact answers.

Consider $7\frac{1}{8} - 2\frac{3}{4}$. A first estimate might be 5, ignoring the fractions. Will it be more or less than 5? Others may begin by thinking $7\frac{1}{8}$ is close to 7 and $2\frac{3}{4}$ is close to 3 $\longrightarrow$ about 4, maybe a little more. Once students begin to think in these terms, a meaningful method for an exact answer is often possible without using an algorithm.

Examine the fraction exercises for addition and subtraction in a middle grades textbook. See how many of them you can do without pencil and paper. Challenge students to do the same.

Multiplication

When working with whole numbers, we would say that 3 × 5 means "3 sets of 5." The first factor tells how much of the second factor you have or want. This is a good place to begin. Simple story problems are a significant help in this development.

Informal Exploration

The story problems that you use to pose multiplication tasks to children need not be elaborate, but it is important to think about the numbers that you use in the problems. A possible progression of problem difficulty is developed in the sections that follow.

Beginning Concepts

Consider these two problems as good starting tasks:

> There are 15 cars in Michael's toy car collection. Two-thirds of the cars are red. How many red cars does Michael have?

> Suzanne has 11 cookies. She wants to share them with her three friends. How many cookies will Suzanne and each of her friends get?

Finding the fractional part of a whole number, which is the task in both problems, is not unlike the task of finding a fractional part of a whole. In Michael's car problem, think of the 15 cars as the whole and you want $\frac{2}{3}$ of the whole. First, find thirds by dividing 15 by 3. Multiplying by thirds, regardless of how many thirds, involves dividing by 3. The denominator is a divisor.

Suzanne's cookie problem is the same as the sharing problems discussed in the last chapter. Dividing by 4 is the same as multiplication by $\frac{1}{4}$. Or think of the 11 cookies as the whole. How many in one-fourth? Cookies are used so that the items can be subdivided.

Problems in which the first factor or multiplier is a whole number are also important.

· ·

Wayne filled 5 glasses with $\frac{2}{3}$ liter of soda in each glass. How much soda did Wayne use?

· ·

This problem may be solved in different ways. Some children will put the thirds together, making wholes as they go. Others will count all of the thirds and then find out how many whole liters are in 10 thirds.

Unit Parts Without Subdivisions

To expand on the ideas just presented, consider these three problems:

· ·

You have $\frac{3}{4}$ of a pizza left. If you give $\frac{1}{3}$ of the leftover pizza to your brother, how much of a whole pizza will your brother get?

· ·

· ·

Someone ate $\frac{1}{10}$ of the cake, leaving only $\frac{9}{10}$. If you eat $\frac{2}{3}$ of the cake that is left, how much of a whole cake will you have eaten?

· ·

· ·

Gloria used $2\frac{1}{2}$ tubes of blue paint to paint the sky in her picture. Each tube holds $\frac{4}{5}$ ounce of paint. How many ounces of blue paint did Gloria use?

· ·

Notice that the units or fractional parts in these problems do not need to be subdivided further. The first problem is $\frac{1}{3}$ of three things, the second is $\frac{2}{3}$ of nine things, and the last is $2\frac{1}{2}$ of four things. The focus remains on the number of unit parts in all, and then the size of the parts determines the number of wholes. Figure 6.6 shows how problems of this type might be modeled. However, it is very important to let students model and solve these problems in their own way, using whatever models or drawings they choose. Require only that they be able to explain their reasoning.

Subdividing the Unit Parts

When the pieces must be subdivided into smaller unit parts, the problems become more challenging.

· ·

Zack had $\frac{2}{3}$ of the lawn left to cut. After lunch, he cut $\frac{3}{4}$ of the grass he had left. How much of the whole lawn did Zack cut after lunch?

· ·

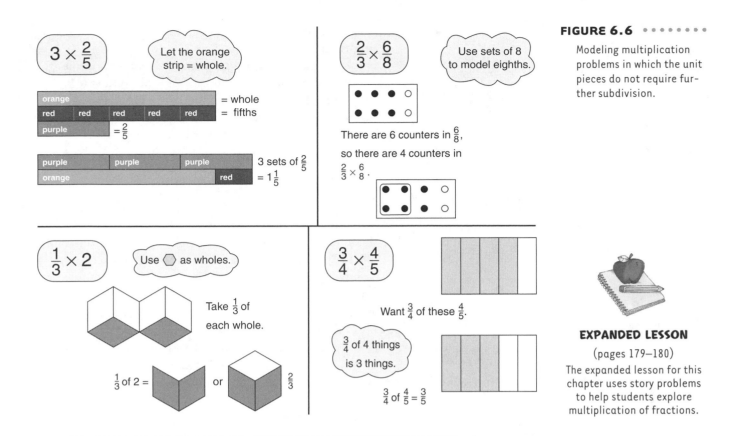

FIGURE 6.6 ● ● ● ● ● ● ● ● ●

Modeling multiplication problems in which the unit pieces do not require further subdivision.

EXPANDED LESSON

(pages 179–180)

The expanded lesson for this chapter uses story problems to help students explore multiplication of fractions.

The zookeeper had a huge bottle of the animals' favorite liquid treat, Zoo Cola. The monkey drank $\frac{1}{5}$ of the bottle. The zebra drank $\frac{2}{3}$ of what was left. How much of the bottle of Zoo Cola did the zebra drink?

> **STOP** **Stop for a moment and figure out how you would solve each of these problems. Draw pictures to help you, but do not use a computational algorithm.**

In Zack's lawn problem, it is necessary to find fourths of two things, the 2 *thirds* of the grass left to cut. In the Zoo Cola problem, you need thirds of four things, the 4 *fifths* of the cola that remain. Again, the concepts of the top number counting and the bottom number naming what is counted play an important role. Figure 6.7 shows two possible solutions for Zack's lawn problem. Similar approaches can be used for the Zoo Cola problem. You may have used different drawings, but the ideas should be the same.

If students use counters to model problems where the units require subdivision, an added difficulty arises. Figure 6.8 illustrates what might happen solving the problem $\frac{3}{5} \times \frac{2}{3}$. (*Three-fifths of $\frac{2}{3}$ of a whole is how much of a whole?*) Here the representation of a whole must be changed so that the thirds can be subdivided. Do not discourage students from using

How much is $\frac{3}{4}$ of $\frac{2}{3}$?

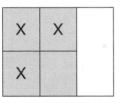

Cut each third in half, and take 3 parts. Half of a third is a sixth, so it's $\frac{3}{6}$.

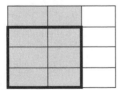

Cut all 3 thirds into 4 parts. Each part is $\frac{1}{12}$. Three-fourths of the 8 twelfths of the grass left to cut is $\frac{6}{12}$.

FIGURE 6.7 ● ● ● ● ● ● ● ● ● ● ● ●

Solutions to fraction products when the unit parts must be subdivided.

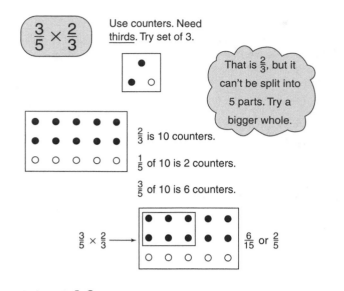

FIGURE 6.8 •

Modeling multiplication of fractions with counters.

Speech bubble text in figure 4: "That is $\frac{2}{3}$, but it can't be split into 5 parts. Try a bigger whole."

$\frac{3}{5} \times \frac{2}{3}$ — Use counters. Need <u>thirds</u>. Try set of 3.

$\frac{2}{3}$ is 10 counters.

$\frac{1}{5}$ of 10 is 2 counters.

$\frac{3}{5}$ of 10 is 6 counters.

$\frac{3}{5} \times \frac{2}{3} \longrightarrow \frac{6}{15}$ or $\frac{2}{5}$

counters, but be prepared to help them find ways to show thirds using larger sets.

The problem in Figure 6.8 offers another possible twist worth mentioning. Since there is no context to the problem, why not use the commutative property—turn the factors around and consider $\frac{2}{3}$ of $\frac{3}{5}$. Wow! Do you see that the answer is $\frac{2}{5}$ almost immediately?

Developing the Algorithm

If you have spent adequate time with your students exploring multiplication of fractions as just described, the traditional multiplication algorithm will be relatively simple to develop. Shift from contextual problems to a straight computation. Have students use a square or a rectangle as the model.

A Beginning Task

To make the development problem based for students, provide them with a drawing of $\frac{3}{4}$ of a square as shown in Figure 6.9. The task is to use the drawing to determine the product $\frac{3}{5} \times \frac{3}{4}$ (three-fifths of three-fourths of a whole) and explain the result. Remember, you want to find a fractional part of the shaded part. The *unit,* however, the way the parts are measured, must remain the whole.

Drawn as shown, the easiest way to get $\frac{3}{5}$ of the shaded region is to divide it into fifths using lines in the opposite direction. Then the problem is to determine what types of unit pieces these are. Although students may not think of it, an easy method

FIGURE 6.9 • • • • • • • • •

Development of the algorithm for multiplication of fractions.

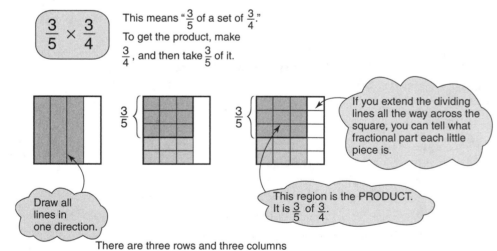

$\frac{3}{5} \times \frac{3}{4}$

This means "$\frac{3}{5}$ of a set of $\frac{3}{4}$."
To get the product, make $\frac{3}{4}$, and then take $\frac{3}{5}$ of it.

Speech bubbles in figure: "Draw all lines in one direction." "If you extend the dividing lines all the way across the square, you can tell what fractional part each little piece is." "This region is the PRODUCT. It is $\frac{3}{5}$ of $\frac{3}{4}$."

There are three rows and three columns in the PRODUCT, or 3 × 3 parts.

The WHOLE is now five rows and four columns, so there are 5 × 4 parts in the whole.

PRODUCT $= \frac{3}{5} \times \frac{3}{4} = \frac{\boxed{\text{Number}} \text{ of parts in product}}{\boxed{\text{Kind}} \text{ of parts}} = \frac{3 \times 3}{5 \times 4} = \frac{9}{20}$

of doing this is to extend the lines, subdividing the entire whole into fifths. Then the product of the denominators tells how many pieces are in the whole (the kind of unit), and the product of the numerators tells the number of pieces in the product.

 Why is it reasonable to extend the lines to subdivide the entire whole into fifths when we are looking for three-fifths of three-fourths, not three-fifths of a whole?

Keep in mind that we are finding three-fifths of three-fourths *of a whole* or $\frac{3}{5}$ of $\frac{3}{4}$ of 1. Extending the lines to subdivide the entire whole is maintaining the relationship between the fractional parts and their associated whole.

Avoid pushing students to formalize the rule or algorithm of multiplying tops and bottoms. Many students will simply count each small part in the drawings and not notice that the numbers of rows and columns are actually the two numerators and the two denominators, respectively. You might steer students in this direction by posing a problem with the initial sketch but asking them to determine the product without additional drawing. Try this with $\frac{7}{8} \times \frac{4}{5}$, where the numbers make it almost mandatory that you multiply.

A cautionary note: Many texts make this sliced-square approach so mechanical that it actually becomes a meaningless algorithm in itself. Students are told to shade a square one way for the first factor and the opposite way for the second factor. Without rationale, they are told that the product is the region that is double-shaded. You might as well give students the rule and forget about explanations.

Factors Greater Than One

Once students have explored products with both factors less than 1, it may be challenging to have them see if they can use a similar type of drawing to explain products with either or both factors greater than 1. Figure 6.10 shows how this might look when both factors are mixed numbers. Keep the task problem based. This can be a significant and worthwhile challenge. There is no need to explain how to do this.

Mental Techniques and Estimation

In the real world, there are many instances when the product of a whole number times a fraction occurs, and a mental estimate or even an exact answer is quite useful. For example, sale items are frequently listed as "$\frac{1}{4}$ off," or we read of a "$\frac{1}{3}$ increase" in the number of registered voters. Fractions are excellent substitutes for percents. To get an estimate of 60 percent of $36.69, it is useful to think of 60 percent as $\frac{3}{5}$ or as a little less than $\frac{2}{3}$.

These products of fractions with large whole numbers can be calculated mentally by thinking of the meanings of the top and bottom numbers. For example, $\frac{3}{5}$ is 3 *one*-fifths. So if you want $\frac{3}{5}$ of 350, for example, first think about *one*-fifth of 350, or 70. If *one*-fifth is 70, then *three*-fifths is 3×70, or 210. Although this example

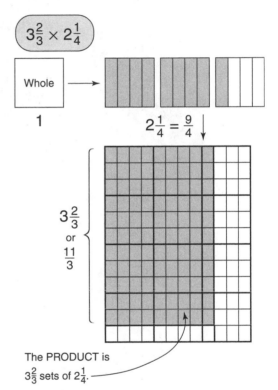

The PRODUCT is $3\frac{2}{3}$ sets of $2\frac{1}{4}$.

There are 11 rows and 9 columns, or 11×9 parts, in the PRODUCT.

The WHOLE now has three rows and four columns, or 3×4 parts.

$3\frac{2}{3} \times 2\frac{1}{4} = \frac{11}{3} \times \frac{9}{4} = \text{PRODUCT} =$

$$\frac{\boxed{\text{Number}} \text{ of parts}}{\boxed{\text{Kind}} \text{ of parts}} = \frac{11 \times 9}{3 \times 4} = \frac{99}{12} = 8\frac{1}{4}$$

FIGURE 6.10 • • • • • • • • • • • • • • • •

The same approach used to develop the algorithm for fractions less than 1 can be expanded to mixed numbers.

has very accommodating numbers, it illustrates a process for mentally multiplying a large number by a fraction: First determine the unit fractional part, and then multiply by the number of parts you want.

When numbers are not so nice, encourage students to use compatible numbers. To estimate $\frac{3}{5}$ of $36.69, a useful compatible is $35. One-fifth of 35 is 7, so three-fifths is 3 × 7, or 21. Now adjust a bit—perhaps add an additional 50 cents, for an estimate of $21.50.

Students should practice estimating fractions times whole numbers in lots of real contexts: $3\frac{1}{4}$ gallons of paint at $14.95 per gallon or $\frac{7}{8}$ of the 476 students who attended Friday's football game. When working with decimals and percents, these skills will be revisited, and once again mathematics will seem more connected than disconnected.

Division

Invert the divisor and multiply is probably one of the most mysterious rules in elementary mathematics. We want to avoid this mystery at all costs. However, first it makes sense to examine division with fractions from a more familiar perspective.

As with the other operations, go back to the meaning of division with whole numbers. Recall that there are two meanings of division: partition and measurement. We will review each briefly and look at some story problems that involve fractions. (Can you make up a word problem right now that would go with the computation $2\frac{1}{2} \div \frac{1}{4}$?)

You should have students explore both measurement and partition problems. Here we will discuss each type of problem separately for the purpose of clarity. In the classroom, the types of problems should probably be mixed. As with multiplication, how the numbers relate to each other in the problems tends to affect the difficulty.

Informal Exploration: Partition Concept

Too often we think of the partition problems strictly as sharing problems: 24 apples to be shared with 4 friends. How many will each friend get? However, this same sharing structure applies to rate problems: If you walk 12 miles in 3 hours, how many miles do you walk per hour? Both of these problems, in fact, all partition problems, ask the questions, "How much is one?" "How much is the amount for one friend?" "How many miles are walked in one hour?" The 24 is the amount for the 4 friends. The 12 miles is the amount for the 3 hours.

Whole-Number Divisors

Having the total amount be a fraction with the divisor a whole number is not really a big leap. These problems still are easy to think of as sharing situations. However, as you work through these questions, notice that you are answering the question, "How much is the whole?" or "How much for one?"

....

Cassie has $5\frac{1}{4}$ yards of ribbon to make three bows for birthday packages. How much ribbon should she use for each bow if she wants to use the same length of ribbon for each?

....

When the $5\frac{1}{4}$ is thought of as fractional parts, there are 21 fourths to share, or 7 fourths for each ribbon. Alternatively, one might think of first allotting 1 yard per bow, leaving $2\frac{1}{4}$ yards, or 9 fourths. These 9 fourths are then shared, 3 fourths per bow, for a total of $1\frac{3}{4}$ yards for each bow. Regardless of the particular process, the unit parts required no further subdivision in order to do the division. In the following problem, the parts must be split into smaller parts.

Mark has $1\frac{1}{4}$ hours to finish his three household chores. If he divides his time evenly, how many hours can he give to each?

Note that the question is, "How much for one chore?" The 5 fourths of an hour that Mark has do not split neatly into three parts. So some or all of the parts must be subdivided. Figure 6.11 shows three different models for figuring this out. In each case, all of the fourths are subdivided into three equal parts, producing twelfths. There are a total of 15 twelfths, or $\frac{5}{12}$ hour for each chore. (Test this answer against the solution in minutes: $1\frac{1}{4}$ hours is 75 minutes, which divided among 3 chores is 25 minutes per chore.)

Fractional Divisors

The sharing concept appears to break down when the divisor is a fraction. However, it is enormously helpful to keep in mind that for partition and rate problems the fundamental question is, "How much is one?" Interestingly, this is exactly the second type of question in the parts-and-whole tasks from Chapter 5: Given the part, find the whole—how much is one? For example, if a set of 18 counters is $2\frac{1}{4}$, how much is a whole set? In solving these problems, the first task is to find the number in *one*-fourth

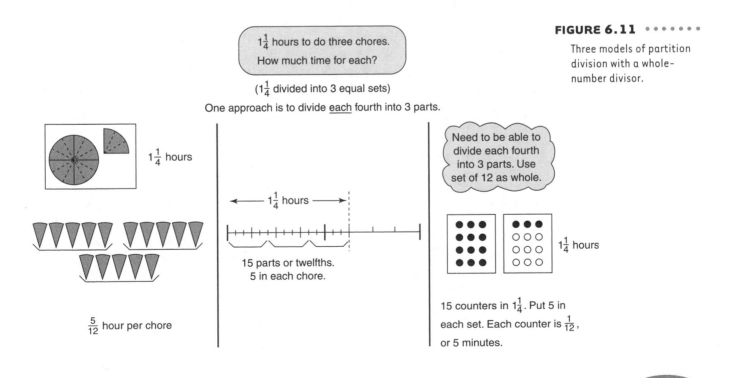

FIGURE 6.11 • • • • • • •

Three models of partition division with a whole-number divisor.

$1\frac{1}{4}$ hours to do three chores. How much time for each?

($1\frac{1}{4}$ divided into 3 equal sets)

One approach is to divide <u>each</u> fourth into 3 parts.

$1\frac{1}{4}$ hours

15 parts or twelfths. 5 in each chore.

$\frac{5}{12}$ hour per chore

Need to be able to divide each fourth into 3 parts. Use set of 12 as whole.

$1\frac{1}{4}$ hours

15 counters in $1\frac{1}{4}$. Put 5 in each set. Each counter is $\frac{1}{12}$, or 5 minutes.

and then multiply by 4 to get four-fourths or one. Let's see if we can see the same process in the following problem:

Elizabeth bought $3\frac{1}{3}$ pounds of tomatoes for $2.50. How much did she pay per pound?

 The given amount of $2.50 is (distributed across) $3\frac{1}{3}$ pounds. How much is (distributed across) 1 pound? Solve the problem the same way as you would a parts-and-whole problem. Try it now before reading on.

In $3\frac{1}{3}$ there are 10 thirds. Since the $2.50 covers (or is distributed across) ten-thirds, one third is covered by one-tenth of the $2.50 or 25 cents. There are three-thirds in one. Therefore, 75 cents must cover 1 pound, or 75 cents per pound.

Try the following problems using a similar strategy.

Dan paid $2.40 for a $\frac{3}{4}$-pound box of candy. How much is that per pound?

Aidan found out that if she walks really fast during her morning exercise, she can cover $2\frac{1}{2}$ miles in $\frac{3}{4}$ of an hour. She wonders how fast she is walking in miles per hour.

In these two problems, what is known is the amount of *part* of a whole. You want to find out how much is in one whole. With both problems, first find the amount of one-fourth (there are three of these, so divide by three) and then the value of one whole (there are 4 fourths in a whole, so multiply by 4).

Aidan's walking problem is a bit harder because the $2\frac{1}{2}$ miles, or 5 half-miles, do not neatly divide into three parts. If this was difficult for you, try dividing each half into three parts. Draw pictures or use models if that will help.

Informal Exploration: Measurement Concept

Almost all division explorations with fractions found in the U.S. elementary and middle school curriculum involve the measurement concept. To review, 13 ÷ 3 with this concept means "How many sets of 3 are in 13?" Here is a contextual setting: *If you have 13 quarts of lemonade, how many canteens holding 3 quarts each can you fill?* A key idea to get from this example involves how to deal with that last quart after filling the first four canteens. If you continue to fill a fifth canteen, it will get only one quart. It will be only one-third full. So one answer is $4\frac{1}{3}$ *canteens.*

Since this is the concept of division that is almost always seen in textbooks and will be used to develop an algorithm for dividing fractions, it is important for students to explore this idea in contextual situations.

Whole-Number Results

Students readily understand problems such as the following:

> You are going to a birthday party. From Ben and Jerry's ice cream factory, you order 6 pints of ice cream. If you serve $\frac{3}{4}$ of a pint of ice cream to each guest, how many guests can be served? (Schifter, Bastable, & Russell, 1999 b, p. 120)

Students typically draw pictures of six things divided into fourths and count out how many sets of $\frac{3}{4}$ can be found. The difficulty is in seeing this as $6 \div \frac{3}{4}$, and that part will require some direct guidance on your part. One idea is to compare the problem to one involving whole numbers (6 pints, 2 per guest) and make a comparison.

Here is a slightly more complex problem:

> Farmer Brown found that he had $2\frac{1}{4}$ gallons of liquid fertilizer concentrate. It takes $\frac{3}{4}$ gallon to make a tank of mixed fertilizer. How many tankfuls can he mix?

Try solving this problem yourself. Use any model or drawing you wish to help explain what you are doing. Notice that you are trying to find out *How many sets of 3 fourths are in a set of 9 fourths?* Your answer should be 3 tankfuls (not 3 fourths). Here is another problem to try:

> Linda has $4\frac{2}{3}$ yards of material. She is making baby clothes for the bazaar. Each dress pattern requires $1\frac{1}{6}$ yards of material. How many dresses will she be able to make from the material she has?

What makes this problem a bit different is that the given quantity is in thirds and the divisor is in sixths. Since you want to measure off "sets" of $1\frac{1}{6}$, someplace in the solution, sixths will need to be used. Two ideas are shown in Figure 6.12.

Answers That Are Not Whole Numbers

If Linda had 5 yards of material, she could still make only four dresses because a part of a dress does not make sense. But suppose that Farmer Brown began with 4 gallons of concentrate. After making five tanks of mix, he would have used $\frac{15}{4}$, or $3\frac{3}{4}$ gallons, of the concentrate. With the $\frac{1}{4}$ gallon remaining he could

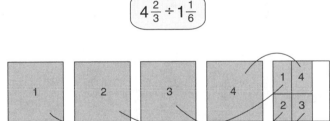

I broke the 2 thirds into 4 sixths. Then I used 1 whole and 1 sixth for each piece. There were four pieces.

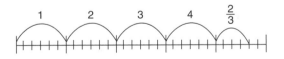

I broke it all up into sixths. That made 24 (from the 4) and 4 more from the $\frac{2}{3}$. That's 28 in all. Then $1\frac{1}{6}$ is $\frac{7}{6}$, so I divided the 28 by 7 and got 4.

FIGURE 6.12 • • • • • • • • • • • • • • • • • •

Two solutions to the problem: *How many lengths of $1\frac{1}{6}$ yards can be cut from $4\frac{2}{3}$ yards of cloth?*

make a *partial* tank of mix. He could make $\frac{1}{3}$ of a tank of mix, since it takes *3* fourths to make a whole, and he has *1* fourth of a gallon.

Here is another problem to try:

· ·

John is building a patio. Each section requires $\frac{2}{3}$ of a cubic yard of concrete. The concrete truck holds $2\frac{1}{4}$ cubic yards of concrete. If there is not enough for a full section at the end, John can put in a divider and make a partial section. How many sections can John make with the concrete in the truck?

· ·

 You should first try to solve this problem in some way that makes sense to *you*. Stop and do this now.

After you have solved it your way, try this method. Change all of the numbers to the same unit (twelfths). Then the problem becomes: *How many sets of 8 twelfths are in a set of 27 twelfths?* Figure 6.13 shows two noncontextual problems solved in this same way, each with a different model. That is, both the dividend or given quantity and the divisor are expressed in the same type of fractional parts. This results in a whole-number division problem. (In the concrete problem, the answer is the same as $27 \div 8$.) In the classroom, after students have solved problems such as this using their own methods, suggest this common-unit approach.

Developing the Algorithms

There are two different algorithms for division of fractions. Methods of teaching both algorithms are discussed here.

FIGURE 6.13 · · · · · · ·

Models for the measurement concept of fraction division.

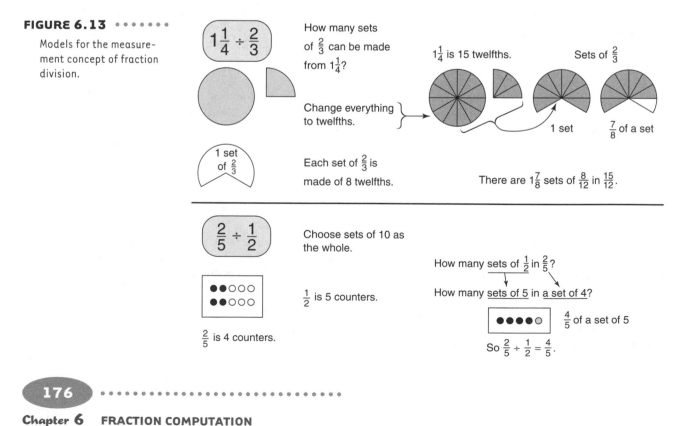

The Common-Denominator Algorithm

The common-denominator algorithm relies on the measurement or repeated subtraction concept of division. Consider the problem $\frac{3}{5} \div \frac{1}{2}$. As shown in Figure 6.14, once each number is expressed in terms of the same fractional part, the answer is exactly the same as the whole-number problem $10 \div 3$. The name of the fractional part (the denominator) is no longer important, and the problem is one of dividing the numerators. The resulting rule or algorithm, therefore, is as follows: *To divide fractions, first get common denominators, and then divide numerators.* For example, $\frac{5}{3} \div \frac{1}{4} = \frac{20}{12} \div \frac{3}{12} = 20 \div 3 = \frac{20}{3} = 6\frac{2}{3}$.

Try using pie pieces, fraction strips, and then sets of counters to model $1\frac{2}{3} \div \frac{3}{4}$ and $\frac{5}{8} \div \frac{1}{2}$ to help yourself develop this algorithm.

The Invert-and-Multiply Algorithm

To invert the divisor and multiply may be one of the most poorly understood procedures in the K–8 curriculum. (Do you know why invert-and-multiply works?) Interestingly, in a much discussed study of Chinese and U.S. teachers, Liping Ma (1999) found that most Chinese teachers not only use and teach this algorithm, but they also understand why it works. U.S. teachers were found to be sadly lacking in their understanding of fraction division.

If you return to the few partition problems that were discussed, you will find that solving these problems almost immediately gives rise to the invert-and-multiply algorithm. Let's look at one more example in which both the dividend and the divisor are proper fractions.

A small pail can be filled to $\frac{7}{8}$ full using $\frac{2}{3}$ of a gallon of water. How much will the pail hold if filled completely?

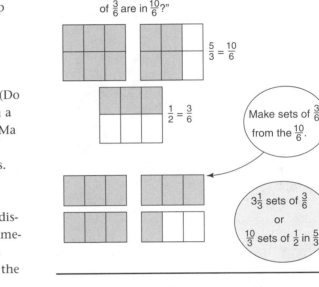

$$\frac{5}{3} \div \frac{1}{2} = \frac{10}{6} \div \frac{3}{6} = 10 \div 3 \text{ or } \frac{10}{3}$$

FIGURE 6.14 • • • • • • • • • • • • • • •

Models for the common-denominator method for fraction division.

Ignore temporarily that the amount is $\frac{2}{3}$ of a gallon of water. Draw a simple picture like the one in Figure 6.15. Again, recall the parts-and-whole problems in which the task was to find the whole. That is what is done here—find the *whole* pail if the given water is $\frac{7}{8}$ of the whole. A full pail is $\frac{8}{8}$. Because the water in the pail is seven of the eight parts needed to fill the pail, dividing the water by 7 and multiplying that amount by 8 solves the problem. Therefore, take the $\frac{2}{3}$, divide by 7, and multiply by 8.

Now recall the meanings of the denominator and numerator. The denominator in a fraction divides the whole into parts, thus indicating the type of part. The denominator is a divisor. The numerator tells us the number of those parts. The numerator is a multiplier. In the problem we divided the $\frac{2}{3}$ by 7 and multiplied by 8. Therefore, we multiplied the $\frac{2}{3}$ by $\frac{8}{7}$.

In many middle school textbooks, a more symbolic justification for the invert-and-multiply procedure is offered. That explanation goes something like the one shown in Figure 6.16.

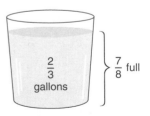

FIGURE 6.15 • • • • • • • •

The pail is $\frac{7}{8}$ full. One-eighth of the water times 8 will be how much it takes to fill the entire pail.

FIGURE 6.16 • • • • • • • • • • • • •

To divide, invert the divisor
and multiply.

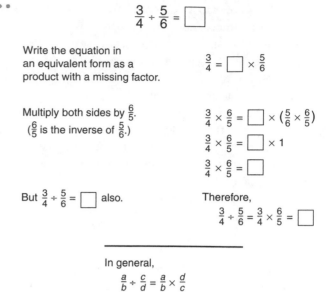

Read through the explanation in Figure 6.16. Is that rationale more or less
meaningful to you than the one based on the problem with the pail of water?
Given your choice, which algorithm—common denominator or invert-and-
multiply—would you select to teach to your students?

Curricular Decisions

Your answers to the questions just posed may have an influence on how you
teach division of fractions. It matters very little *how* students do operations, only that
they can do them meaningfully and accurately in a reasonably efficient manner. Each
of the algorithms has value. Regardless of which algorithm is your goal, you are
strongly advised to build on informal work with story problems. Most textbook story
problems for fraction division seem to be measurement problems. This is not the case
in China. In the United States, very little research has been done to explore the partition approach to invert-and-multiply.

EXPANDED LESSON

Multiplication of Fractions

GRADE LEVEL: Fourth grade.

MATHEMATICS GOALS

*   To develop the meaning of multiplication of fractions through informal explorations.
*   To emphasize that a fraction is connected to a particular whole and that the whole can change in a context.

THINKING ABOUT THE STUDENTS

Students understand that multiplication can be thought of as repeated addition; that is, 3 × 6 means 3 sets of 6. They understand that in the context of part-whole fractions, the whole is divided into equivalent parts. They also understand the symbolic notation of fractions; that is, they know what the top number in the fraction means (the number of parts) and what the bottom number in the fraction means (the kind of parts we are counting).

MATERIALS AND PREPARATION

Make copies of Blackline Master L-2 for each student and also a transparency of L-2.

- -

lesson

BLM L-2

BEFORE

Begin with a simpler version of the task:

*   Ask students what 3 × 4 means. Have them either draw a picture or give a word problem to show what 3 × 4 means. Listen to students' ideas. Capitalize on ideas that emphasize that 3 × 4 means 3 groups of 4.
*   Pose the following word problem to students: *There are 15 cars in Michael's toy car collection. Two-thirds of the cars are red. How many red cars does Michael have?*
*   Encourage students to draw pictures not only to help them think about how to do the problem but also as a way to explain how they did the problem. Have students share their work with the class. Many students will draw 15 rectangles (cars) and then divide the 15 into three equal parts. At this point, make sure to have the students explain why they divided the 15 into three equal parts (e.g., looking for thirds because $\frac{2}{3}$ are red). Once they have three equal parts or thirds, they count two of those sets because they need $\frac{2}{3}$.
*   Help students connect this situation with multiplication with whole numbers. Just as 3 × 4 means 3 groups of 4, $\frac{2}{3}$ × 15 means $\frac{2}{3}$ of a group of 15.

The Task

Students are to solve the problems on the worksheet and be ready to explain their thinking.

>   *You have $\frac{3}{4}$ of a pizza left. If you give $\frac{1}{3}$ of the leftover pizza to your brother, how much of a whole pizza will your brother get?*
>   *Someone ate $\frac{1}{10}$ of the cake, leaving only $\frac{9}{10}$. If you eat $\frac{2}{3}$ of the cake that is left, how much of a whole cake will you have eaten?*
>   *Gloria used $2\frac{1}{2}$ tubes of blue paint to paint the sky in her picture. Each tube holds $\frac{4}{5}$ ounce of paint. How many ounces of blue paint did Gloria use?*

Establish Expectations

Students should use both words and pictures to help them think through the problems and to show how they solved them. They should be prepared to explain their thinking.

DURING

*   Look for students who use different representations to think about the problems. Highlight those different ways in the "After" portion of the lesson.

- 179

- If students have difficulty getting started, have them represent the information in the first sentence of the task. Have them explain why their picture represents this information. Then have them read the first part of the "if" statement in the second sentence and identify what part of their original picture this statement refers to. Have them color the part they just identified with a different color to make it stand out. Now have them read the question at the end of the task and think about how the part they just colored can help them answer this question.
- For students ready for a challenge, pose the following task in which the pieces must be subdivided into smaller unit parts: *Zack had $\frac{2}{3}$ of the lawn to cut. After lunch, he cut $\frac{3}{4}$ of the grass he had left. How much of the whole lawn did Zack cut after lunch?*

AFTER

- Starting with the first problem, ask a student to come to the board to explain his or her strategy for thinking about the problem. Ask questions about why the student drew what he or she did to make sure everyone in the class follows the rationale. Encourage the class to comment or ask questions about the student's representation or thinking.
- Help students make explicit what the whole is at each stage of the problem.
- Ask if others solved the problem in a different way. If so, have the students come forward to share their solutions.
- As students share their solutions, it is important to have them compare and contrast the different solutions. Some solutions that at first appear to be different are actually equivalent in many ways. Through questioning, help students make these connections.
- Help students connect fraction multiplication with the meaning of multiplication: $\frac{1}{3} \times \frac{3}{4}$ means $\frac{1}{3}$ of a group of $\frac{3}{4}$.

ASSESSMENT NOTES

- Look for students who struggle when the whole changes in the problem. They need more experience working with parts-and-whole tasks as described in Chapter 5 (see Figures 5.11 and 5.12).
- Are students correctly using the meaning of the numerator and denominator? These problems are easily solved by thinking of the fractional parts as discrete units. For example, $\frac{2}{3}$ of $\frac{3}{4}$ is $\frac{2}{3}$ of three things called fourths.
- Are students answering the question that is being asked?

- -

- For students who are ready, pose tasks in which the pieces must be subdivided into smaller unit parts. For example, $\frac{2}{3} \times \frac{1}{2}$ or $\frac{3}{4}$ of $\frac{2}{3}$.
- Eventually you will want to connect the algorithm for multiplying fractions to these informal explorations.

Resist moving to the algorithm too quickly. One idea is to see if students can develop an algorithm for multiplying fractions based on their informal explorations.

 next steps

DECIMAL AND PERCENT CONCEPTS AND DECIMAL COMPUTATION

In the U.S. curriculum, decimals are typically introduced in the fourth grade and most of the computation work with decimals occurs in the fifth grade and is repeated later in grades 6 and 7. This fractions-first, decimals-later sequence is arguably the best approach. However, the unfortunate fact is that the topics of fractions and decimals are too often developed separately. Linking the ideas of fractions to decimals can be extremely useful, both from a pedagogical view as well as a practical, social view. Most of this chapter focuses on that connection.

big ideas

1 Decimal numbers are simply another way of writing fractions. Both notations have value. Maximum flexibility is gained by understanding how the two symbol systems are related.

2 The base-ten place-value system extends infinitely in two directions: to tiny values as well as to large values. Between any two place values, the ten-to-one ratio remains the same.

3 The decimal point is a convention that has been developed to indicate the units position. The position to the left of the decimal point is the unit that is being counted as singles or ones.

4 Percents are simply hundredths and as such are a third way of writing both fractions and decimals.

5 Addition and subtraction with decimals are based on the fundamental concept of adding and subtracting the numbers in like position values—a simple extension from whole numbers.

6 Multiplication and division of two numbers will produce the same digits, regardless of the positions of the decimal point. As a result, for most practical purposes, there is no reason to develop new rules for decimal multiplication and division. Rather, the computations can be performed as whole numbers with the decimal placed by way of estimation.

Connecting Two Different Representational Systems

The symbols 3.75 and $3\frac{3}{4}$ represent the same quantity, yet on the surface the two appear quite different. For children especially, the world of fractions and the world of decimals are very distinct. Even adults tend to think of fractions as sets or regions (three-fourths *of* something), whereas we think of decimals as being more like numbers. When we tell children that 0.75 is the same as $\frac{3}{4}$, this can be especially confusing. Even though different ways of writing the numbers have been invented, the numbers themselves are not different. A significant goal of instruction in decimal and fraction numeration should be to help students see that both systems represent the same concepts.

To help students see the connection between fractions and decimals, we can do three things. First, we can use familiar fraction concepts and models to explore rational numbers that are easily represented by decimals: tenths, hundredths, and thousandths. Second, we can help them see how the base-ten system can be extended to include numbers less than 1 as well as large numbers. Third, we can help children use models to make meaningful translations between fractions and decimals. These three components are discussed in turn.

Base-Ten Fractions

Fractions that have denominators of 10, 100, 1000, and so on will be referred to in this chapter as *base-ten fractions*. This is simply a convenient label and is not one commonly found in the literature. Fractions such as $\frac{7}{10}$ or $\frac{63}{100}$ are examples of base-ten fractions.

BLMs 17–19

Base-Ten Fraction Models

Most of the common models for fractions are somewhat limited for the purpose of depicting base-ten fractions. Generally, the familiar fraction models cannot show hundredths or thousandths. It is important to provide models for these fractions using the same conceptual approaches that were used for fractions such as thirds and fourths.

Two very important region models can be used to model base-ten fractions. First, to model tenths and hundredths, circular disks such as the one shown in Figure 7.1 can be printed on tagboard (see Blackline Masters). Each disk is marked with 100 equal intervals around the edge and is cut along one radius. Two disks of different colors, slipped together as shown, can be used to model any fraction less than 1. Fractions modeled on this hundredths disk can be read as base-ten fractions by noting the spaces around the edge but are still reminiscent of the traditional pie model.

The most common model for base-ten fractions is a 10 × 10 square. These squares can be run off on paper for students to shade in various fractions (see Figure 7.2 and Blackline Masters). Another important variation is to use base-ten place-value strips and squares. As a fraction model, the 10-cm square that is used as the hundreds model for whole numbers is taken as the whole or 1. Each strip is then 1 tenth, and each small square is 1 hundredth. In the Blackline Masters you will find a large square that is subdi-

FIGURE 7.1 • • • • • • • • •

A hundredths disk for modeling base-ten fractions.

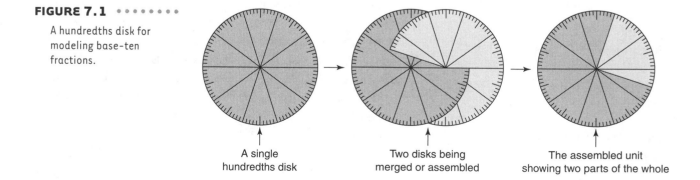

A single hundredths disk   Two disks being merged or assembled   The assembled unit showing two parts of the whole

vided into 10,000 tiny squares. When shown on an overhead projector, individual squares or ten-thousandths can easily be identified and shaded in with a pen on the transparency.

One of the best length models is a meter stick. Each decimeter is one-tenth of the whole stick, each centimeter is one-hundredth, and each millimeter is one-thousandth. Any number-line model broken into 100 subparts is likewise a useful model for hundredths.

Many teachers use money as a model for decimals, and to some extent this is helpful. However, for children, money is almost exclusively a two-place system: Numbers like 3.2 or 12.1389 do not relate to money. Students' initial contact with decimals should be more flexible, and so money is not recommended as a decimal model. However, money is certainly an important *application* of decimal numeration.

Multiple Names and Formats

Early work with base-ten fractions is designed primarily to acquaint students with the models, to help them begin to think of quantities in terms of tenths and hundredths, and to learn to read and write base-ten fractions in different ways.

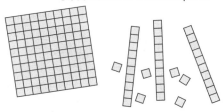

10 × 10 squares on paper. Each square is one whole. Students shade fractional parts.

Base-ten strips and squares can be used to model base-ten fractions. Instead of shading in the large square, strips and small squares are placed on it to show a fractional part.

FIGURE 7.2 •

10 × 10 squares model base-ten fractions.

Have students show a base-ten fraction using any base-ten fraction model. Once a fraction, say, $\frac{65}{100}$, is modeled, the following things can be explored:

- Is this fraction more or less than $\frac{1}{2}$? Than $\frac{2}{3}$? Than $\frac{3}{4}$? Some familiarity with these fractions can be developed by comparison with fractions that are easy to think about.

- What are some different ways to say this fraction using tenths and hundredths? ("6 tenths and 5 hundredths," "65 hundredths") Include thousandths when appropriate.

- Show two ways to write this fraction ($\frac{65}{100}$ or $\frac{6}{10} + \frac{5}{100}$).

The last two questions are very important. When base-ten fractions are later written as decimals, they are usually read as a single fraction. That is, 0.65 is read "sixty-five hundredths." But to understand them in terms of place value, the same number must be thought of as 6 tenths and 5 hundredths. A mixed number such as $5\frac{13}{100}$ is usually read the same way as a decimal: 5.13 is "five and thirteen-hundredths." For purposes of place value, it should also be understood as $5 + \frac{1}{10} + \frac{3}{100}$.

The expanded forms will be helpful in translating these fractions to decimals. Exercises at this introductory level should include all possible connections between models, various oral forms, and various written forms. Given a model or a written or oral fraction, students should be able to give the other two forms of the fraction, including equivalent forms when appropriate.

Extending the Place-Value System

Before considering decimal numerals with students, it is advisable to review some ideas of whole-number place value. One of the most basic of these ideas is the 10-to-1 relationship between the value of any two adjacent positions. In terms of a base-ten

CONNECTING TWO DIFFERENT REPRESENTATIONAL SYSTEMS

model such as strips and squares, 10 of any one piece will make 1 of the next larger, and vice versa.

A Two-Way Relationship

The 10-makes-1 rule continues indefinitely to larger and larger pieces or positional values. This concept is fun to explore in terms of how large the strips and squares will actually be if you move six or eight places out.

If you are using the strip-and-square model, for example, the strip and square shapes alternate in an infinite progression as they get larger and larger. Having established the progression to larger pieces, focus on the idea that each piece to the right in this string gets smaller by one-tenth. The critical question becomes "Is there ever a smallest piece?" In the students' experience, the smallest piece is the centimeter square or unit piece. But couldn't even that piece be divided into 10 small strips? And couldn't these small strips be divided into 10 very small squares, and so on? In the mind's eye, there is no smallest strip or smallest square.

The goal of this discussion is to help students see that a 10-to-1 relationship can extend *infinitely in two directions*. There is no smallest piece and no largest piece. The relationship between adjacent pieces is the same regardless of which two adjacent pieces are being considered. Figure 7.3 illustrates this idea.

The Role of the Decimal Point

An important idea to be realized in this discussion is that there is no built-in reason why any one piece should naturally be chosen to be the unit or ones position. In

FIGURE 7.3 • • • • • • • • • •

Theoretically, the strips and squares extend infinitely in both directions.

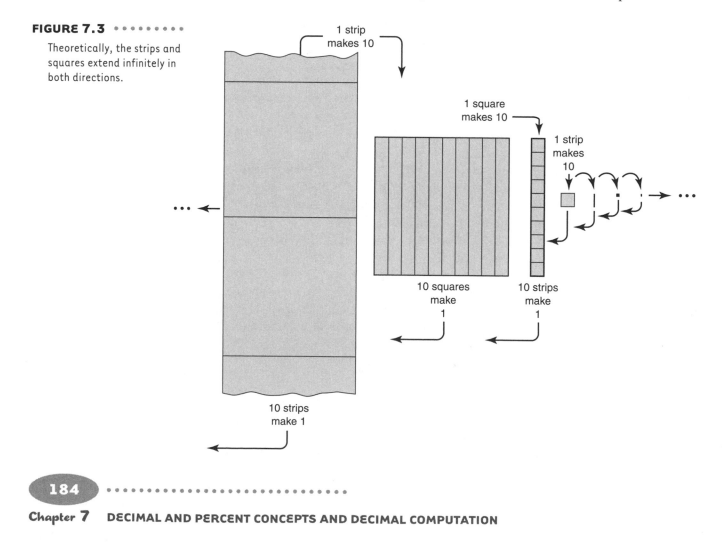

Chapter **7** DECIMAL AND PERCENT CONCEPTS AND DECIMAL COMPUTATION

terms of strips and squares, for example, which piece is the ones piece? The small centimeter square? Why? Why not a larger or a smaller square? Why not a strip? *Any piece could effectively be chosen as the ones piece.*

As shown in Figure 7.4, a given quantity can be written in different ways, depending on the choice of the unit or what piece is used to count the entire collection. The decimal point is placed between two positions with the convention that the position to the left of the decimal point is the units or ones position. Thus, the role of the decimal point is *to designate the units position,* and it does so by sitting just to the right of that position.

A fitting caricature of the decimal point is shown in Figure 7.5. The "eyes" of the decimal point always focus up toward the name of the units or ones. A tagboard disk of this decimal-point face can be used between adjacent base-ten models or on a place-value chart (found with the hundredths disk in the Blackline Masters). If such a decimal point were placed between the squares and strips in Figure 7.4, the squares would then be designated as the units, and 16.24 would be the correct written form for the model.

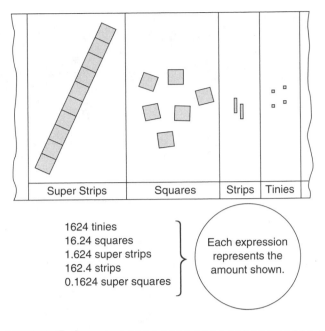

1624 tinies
16.24 squares
1.624 super strips
162.4 strips
0.1624 super squares

Each expression represents the amount shown.

FIGURE 7.4 •
The decimal point indicates which position is the units.

ACTIVITY 7.1

The Decimal Names the Unit

Have students display a certain number of base-ten pieces on their desks. For example, put out 3 squares, 7 strips, and 4 tinies. Refer to the pieces as "squares," "strips," and "tinies," and reach an agreement on names for the theoretical pieces both smaller and larger. To the right of tinies can be "tiny strips" and "tiny squares." To the left of squares can be "super strips" and "super squares." Each student should also have a tagboard smiley decimal point. Now ask students to write and say how many squares they have, how many super strips, and so on, as in Figure 7.4. The students position their decimal point accordingly and both write and say the amounts.

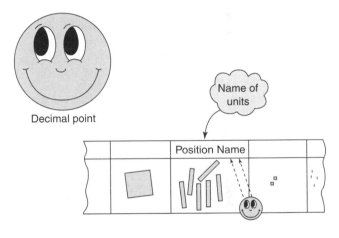

FIGURE 7.5 •
The decimal point always "looks up at" the name of the units position.

Activity 7.1 illustrates vividly that the decimal point indicates the named unit and that the unit can change without changing the quantity.

The Decimal Point with Measurement and Monetary Units

The notion that the decimal point "looks at the units place" is useful in a variety of contexts. For example, in the metric system, seven place values have names. As shown in Figure 7.6, the decimal point can be used to designate any of these places as

CONNECTING TWO DIFFERENT REPRESENTATIONAL SYSTEMS

FIGURE 7.6 • • • • • • • •

In the metric system, each
place-value position has a
name. The decimal point
can be placed to designate
which length is the unit
length.

kilometer	hectometer	dekameter	meter	decimeter	centimeter	millimeter	
		4	**3**	**8**	**5**		

4 dekameters, 3 meters, 8 decimeters, and 5 centimeters =

43.85	meters
43850	millimeters
0.04385	kilometers
4385	centimeters

Unit names

the unit without changing the actual measure. Our monetary system is also a decimal system. In the amount $172.95, the decimal point designates the dollars position as the unit. There are 1 hundred (of dollars), 7 tens, 2 singles, 9 dimes, and 5 pennies or cents in this amount of money regardless of how it is written. If pennies were the designated unit, the same amount would be written as 17,295 cents or 17,295.0 cents. It could just as correctly be 0.17295 thousands of dollars or 1729.5 dimes.

In the case of actual measures such as metric lengths or weights or the U.S. monetary system, the name of the unit is written after the number rather than above the digit as on a place-value chart. You may be 1.62 meters tall, but it does not make sense to say you are "1.62 tall." In the paper, we may read about Congress spending $7.3 billion. Here the units are billions of dollars, not dollars. A city may have a population of 2.4 million people. That is the same as 2,400,000 individuals.

Making the Fraction–Decimal Connection

To connect the two numeration systems, fractions and decimals, students should make concept-oriented translations. The purpose of such activities has less to do with the skill of converting a fraction to a decimal than with construction of the concept that both systems express the same ideas.

ACTIVITY 7.2

Base-Ten Fractions to Decimals

For this activity, have students use their place-value strips and squares. Agree that the large square represents one. Have students cover a base-ten fractional amount of the square using their strips and tinies. For example, have them cover $2\frac{35}{100}$ of the square. Whole numbers require additional squares. The task is to decide how to write this fraction as a decimal and demonstrate the connection using their physical models.

For the last activity, a typical (and correct) reason why $2\frac{35}{100}$ is the same as 2.35 is that there are 2 wholes, 3 tenths, and 5 hundredths. It is important to see this physically. The exact same materials that are used to represent $2\frac{35}{100}$ of the square can be rearranged or placed on an imaginary place-value chart with a paper decimal point used to designate the units position as shown in Figure 7.7.

The reverse of this activity is also worthwhile. Give students a decimal number such as 1.68 and have them show it with base-ten pieces. Their task is to write it as a fraction and show it as a fractional part of a square.

Although these translations between decimals and base-ten fractions are rather simple, the main agenda is for students to learn from the beginning that decimals are simply fractions.

The calculator can also play a significant role in decimal concept development.

ACTIVITY 7.3

Calculator Decimal Counting

Recall how to make the calculator "count" by pressing $+$ 1 $=$ $=$. . . . Now have students press $+$ 0.1 $=$ $=$. . . . When the display shows 0.9, stop and discuss what this means and what the display will look like with the next press. Many students will predict 0.10 (thinking that 10 comes after 9). This prediction is even more interesting if, with each press, the students have been accumulating base-ten strips as models for tenths. One more press would mean one more strip, or 10 strips. Why should the calculator not show 0.10? When the tenth press produces a display of 1 (calculators never display trailing zeros to the right of the decimal), the discussion should revolve around trading 10 strips for a square. Continue to count to 4 or 5 by tenths. How many presses to get from one whole number to the next? Try counting by 0.01 or by 0.001. These counts illustrate dramatically how small one-hundredth and one-thousandth really are. It requires 10 counts by 0.001 to get to 0.01 and 1000 counts to reach 1.

The fact that the calculator counts 0.8, 0.9, 1, 1.1 instead of 0.8, 0.9, 0.10, 0.11 should give rise to the question "Does this make sense? If so, why?"

Calculators that permit entry of fractions also have a fraction–decimal conversion key. On some calculators a decimal such as 0.25 will convert to the base-ten fraction $\frac{25}{100}$ and allow for either manual or automatic simplification. Graphing calculators can be set so that the conversion is either with or without simplification. The ability of fraction calculators to go back and forth between fractions and decimals makes them a valuable tool as students begin to connect fraction and decimal symbolism.

Developing Decimal Number Sense

So far, the discussion has revolved around the connection of decimals with base-ten fractions. Number sense implies more. It means having intuition about or a flexible understanding of numbers. To this end, it is useful to connect decimals to the fractions with which students are familiar, to be able to compare and order decimals readily, and to approximate decimals with useful familiar numbers.

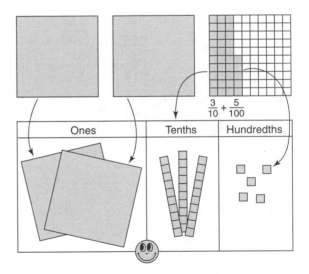

$2\frac{35}{100} = 2.35 =$ "two and thirty-five hundredths"

FIGURE 7.7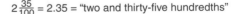

Translation of a base-ten fraction to a decimal.

Familiar Fractions Connected to Decimals

Chapter 5 showed how to help students develop a conceptual familiarity with simple fractions, especially halves, thirds, fourths, fifths, and eighths. We should extend this familiarity to the same concepts expressed as decimals. One way to do this is to have students translate familiar fractions to decimals by means of a base-ten model.

The following two activities have the same purpose—to help students think of decimals in terms of familiar fraction equivalents and to make this connection in a conceptual manner.

EXPANDED LESSON

(pages 202–203)

A complete lesson plan based on "Friendly Fractions to Decimals" can be found at the end of this chapter.

ACTIVITY 7.4

Friendly Fractions to Decimals

Students are given a "friendly" fraction to convert to a decimal. They first model the fraction using either a 10 × 10 grid or the base-ten strips and squares. With the model as a guide, they then write and draw an explanation for the decimal equivalent. If strips and squares are used, be sure that students draw pictures as part of their explanations.

A good sequence is to start with halves and fifths, then fourths, and possibly eighths. Thirds are best done as a special activity.

Figure 7.8 shows how translations in the last activity might go with a 10 × 10 grid. For fourths, students will often shade a 5 × 5 section (half of a half). The question then becomes how to translate this to decimals. Ask these students how they would cover $\frac{1}{4}$ with strips and squares if they were only permitted to use nine or fewer tinies. The fraction $\frac{3}{8}$ represents a wonderful challenge. A hint might be to find $\frac{1}{4}$ first and then notice that $\frac{1}{8}$ is half of a fourth. Remember that the next smaller pieces are tenths of the little squares. Therefore, a half of a square is $\frac{5}{1000}$.

Because the circular model carries such a strong mental link to fractions, it is well worth the time to do some fraction-to-decimal conversions with the hundredths disk.

ACTIVITY 7.5

Estimate, Then Verify

With the blank side of the disk facing them, have students adjust the disk to show a particular friendly fraction, for example, $\frac{3}{4}$. Next they turn the disk over and record how many hundredths were in the section they estimated (note that the color reverses when the disk is turned over). Finally, they should make an argument for the correct number of hundredths and the corresponding decimal equivalent.

The estimation component of the last activity adds interest, and the visual "feeling" for fractions is greater than with strips and squares. In one fifth-grade class that was having difficulty finding a decimal equivalent for their hundredths disk fraction, the teacher

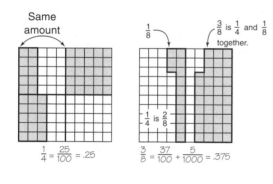

Same amount

$\frac{1}{4} = \frac{25}{100} = .25$

$\frac{1}{8}$

$\frac{3}{8}$ is $\frac{1}{4}$ and $\frac{1}{8}$ together.

$\frac{1}{4}$ is $\frac{2}{8}$

$\frac{3}{8} = \frac{37}{100} + \frac{5}{1000} = .375$

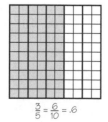

$\frac{3}{5} = \frac{6}{10} = .6$

FIGURE 7.8 • • • • • • • • • • • • • • • •

Familiar fractions converted to decimals using a 10 × 10 square.

cut up some extra disks into tenths and hundredths so that these parts of the fraction could be placed on a chart. (See Figure 7.9.)

The exploration of modeling $\frac{1}{3}$ as a decimal is a good introduction to the concept of an infinitely repeating decimal. Try to partition the whole square into 3 parts using strips and squares.

 STOP **Before reading further, try this with the square, strips, and smaller squares.**

Each part receives 3 strips with 1 left over. To divide the leftover strip, each part gets 3 small squares with 1 left over. To divide the small square, each part gets 3 tiny strips with 1 left over. (Recall that with base-ten pieces, each smaller piece must be $\frac{1}{10}$ of the preceding size piece.) Each of the 3 parts will get 3 tiny strips with 1 left over. It becomes obvious that this process is never-ending. As a result, $\frac{1}{3}$ is the same as 0.333333 . . . or $0.\overline{3}$. For practical purposes, $\frac{1}{3}$ is about 0.333. Similarly, $\frac{2}{3}$ is a repeating string of sixes, or about 0.667. Later, students will discover that many fractions cannot be represented by a finite decimal.

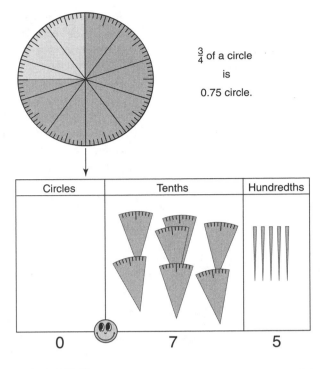

$\frac{3}{4}$ of a circle is 0.75 circle.

Circles	Tenths	Hundredths
0	7	5

FIGURE 7.9

Fraction models could be decimal models.

Assessment Note

Observe how students deal with the 1 left over. Do they readily divide it into 10 equal parts? Or do they divide it into 3 equal parts since we are looking for a third? Either approach tells you something about how students are connecting decimals and fractions. A student who divides the leftover piece into thirds may not understand how the place-value system extends continually with each succeeding place representing a tenth smaller piece. An interesting question to pose is this: "In the number $4.26\frac{1}{3}$, in what position is the fraction $\frac{1}{3}$?" The $\frac{1}{3}$ is in the hundredths position. That is, the hundredths position is $6\frac{1}{3}$. When students divide the leftover piece into thirds, they are not looking at smaller pieces in the next position, but rather, fractional parts of pieces in the current position.

The number line is another good connecting model. Students are more apt to think of decimals as numbers that appear on the number line than they are to think of fractions in that way. The following activity continues the development of fraction–decimal equivalences.

ACTIVITY 7.6

Decimals on a Friendly Fraction Line

Give students five decimal numbers that have friendly fraction equivalents. Keep the numbers between two consecutive whole numbers. For example, use 3.5, 3.125, 3.4, 3.75, and 3.66. On a worksheet, show a number line

(continued)

encompassing the same whole numbers. The subdivisions on the number line should be only fourths, only thirds, or only fifths but without labels. The students' task is to locate each of the decimal numbers on the number line and to provide the fraction equivalent for each.

Results of National Assessment of Educational Progress (NAEP) examinations consistently reveal that students have difficulties with the fraction–decimal relationship. Among the difficulties noted are providing a decimal equivalent for a mixed number, placing decimals on a number line where the subdivisions were fractions, and placing decimals on a number line where the subdivisions were multiples of 0.1. Division of the numerator by the denominator may be a means for converting fractions to decimals, but it contributes nothing to understanding the resulting equivalence. For this reason, this method has not been and will not be suggested in this chapter.

Approximation with a Nice Fraction

In the real world, decimal numbers are rarely those with exact equivalents to nice fractions. What fraction would you say approximates the decimal 0.52? In the sixth NAEP exam, only 51 percent of eighth graders selected $\frac{1}{2}$. The other choices were $\frac{1}{50}$ (29 percent), $\frac{1}{5}$ (11 percent), $\frac{1}{4}$ (6 percent), and $\frac{1}{3}$ (4 percent) (Kouba et al., 1997). Again, the most plausible explanation for this performance is a reliance on rules. Students need to wrestle with the size of decimal numbers and begin to develop a sense of familiarity with them in grades 3–5 to prevent a reliance on rules.

As with fractions, the first benchmarks that should be developed are 0, $\frac{1}{2}$, and 1. For example, is 7.3962 closer to 7 or 8? Why? (Should you accept this response: "Closer to 7 because 3 is less than 5"?) Is it closer to 7 or $7\frac{1}{2}$? Often the 0, $\frac{1}{2}$, or 1 benchmarks are good enough to make sense of a situation. If a closer approximation is required, students should be encouraged to consider the other friendly fractions (thirds, fourths, fifths, and eighths). In this example, 7.3962 is close to 7.4, which is $7\frac{2}{5}$. A good number sense with decimals would imply the ability to think quickly of a meaningful fraction that is a close substitute for almost any number.

To develop this type of familiarity with decimals, students do not need new concepts or skills. They do need the opportunity to apply and discuss the related concepts of fractions, place value, and decimals in activities such as the following.

ACTIVITY 7.7

Close to a Friendly Fraction

Make a list of about five decimals that are close to but not exactly equal to a nice or friendly fraction equivalent. For example, use 24.8025, 6.59, 0.9003, 124.356, and 7.7.

The students' task is to decide on a decimal number that is close to each of these decimals and that also has a friendly fraction equivalent that they know. For example, 6.59 is close to 6.6, which is $6\frac{3}{5}$. They should write an explanation for their choices. Different students may select different equivalent fractions providing for a discussion of which is closer.

Best Match

On the board, list a scattered arrangement of five familiar fractions and at least five decimals that are close to the fractions but not exact. Students are to pair each fraction with the decimal that best matches it. Figure 7.10 is an example. The difficulty is determined by how close the various fractions are to one another.

In Activities 7.7 and 7.8, students will have a variety of reasons for their answers. Sharing their thinking with the class provides a valuable opportunity for all to learn. Do not focus on the answers but instead on the rationales.

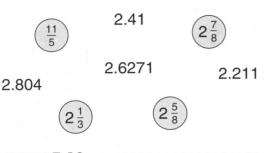

FIGURE 7.10

Match the decimal numbers with the closest fraction expression.

Ordering Decimal Numbers

Putting a list of decimal numbers in order from least to most is a skill closely related to the one just discussed. When identifying the largest decimal number from a given list, the most common error is to select the number with more digits, which is an incorrect application of whole-number ideas. Some students pick up the idea that digits far to the right represent very small numbers. They then incorrectly identify numbers with more digits as smaller. Both errors reflect a lack of conceptual understanding of how decimal numbers are constructed. The following activities can help promote discussion about the relative size of decimal numbers.

Line 'Em Up

Prepare a list of four or five decimal numbers that students might have difficulty putting in order. They should all be between the same two consecutive whole numbers. Have students first predict the order of the numbers, from least to most. Next have them place each number on a number line with 100 subdivisions, as in Figure 7.11. As an alternative, have students shade in the fractional part of each number on a separate 10 × 10 grid using estimates for the thousandths and ten-thousandths. In either case, it quickly becomes obvious which digits contribute the most to the size of a decimal.

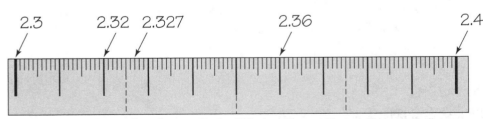

FIGURE 7.11

A decimal number line.

Cut four strips of poster board measuring 6 × 28 inches. Tape end to end. Place on chalk tray.

Write on board above. Endpoints can be any interval of 1, $\frac{1}{10}$, $\frac{1}{100}$.

Close "Nice" Numbers

Write a four-digit decimal on the board—3.0917, for example. Start with the whole numbers: "Is it closer to 3 or 4?" Then go to the tenths: "Is it closer to 3.0 or 3.1?" Repeat with hundredths and thousandths. At each answer, challenge students to defend their choices with the use of a model or other conceptual explanation. A large number line without numerals, shown in Figure 7.11, is useful.

Too often, the process of rounding numbers is taught as an algorithm without any reflection on why the algorithm makes sense. Students come to believe that to "round" a number means to do something to it or change it in some way. In reality, to *round* a number means that you *substitute* a "nice" number as an approximation for the cumbersome original number. In this sense, we can also round decimal numbers to "nice fractions" and not just to tenths and hundredths. For example, instead of rounding 6.73 to the nearest tenth, a number sense perspective might suggest rounding it to the nearest quarter (6.75 or $6\frac{3}{4}$) or to the nearest third (6.67 or $6\frac{2}{3}$).

Other Fraction–Decimal Equivalents

Recall that the denominator is a divisor and the numerator is a multiplier. For example, $\frac{3}{4}$, therefore, means the same as $3 \times (1 \div 4) = 3 \div 4$. So how would you express $\frac{3}{4}$ on a simple four-function calculator? Simply enter $3 \div 4$. The display will read 0.75.

Too often students think that dividing the denominator into the numerator is simply an algorithm for converting fractions to decimals, and they have no understanding of why this might work. Use the opportunity to help students develop the idea that in general $\frac{a}{b} = a \div b$. (See Chapter 5, p. 140.)

Finding the decimal equivalents with a calculator can produce some interesting patterns and observations. For example, here are some questions to explore:

- Which fractions have decimal equivalents that terminate? Is the answer based on the numerator, the denominator, or both?

- For a given fraction, how can you tell the maximum length of the repeating part of the decimal? Try dividing by 7 and 11 and 13 to reach an answer.

- Explore all of the ninths—$\frac{1}{9}, \frac{2}{9}, \frac{3}{9}, \ldots, \frac{8}{9}$. Remember that $\frac{1}{3}$ is $\frac{3}{9}$ and $\frac{2}{3}$ is $\frac{6}{9}$. Use only the pattern you discover to predict what $\frac{9}{9}$ should be. But doesn't $\frac{9}{9} = 1$?

- How can you find what fraction produced this repeating decimal: 3.454545 . . . ?

The final task in this list can be generalized for any repeating decimal, illustrating that every repeating decimal is a rational number. It is not at all useful for students to become skillful at this.

Introducing Percents

Percents do not appear in many state standards until after fifth grade. When percents do appear, textbooks have traditionally treated them as a separate topic from fractions and decimals or included them in a chapter on ratios in middle school. The connection of percents to fractions and decimal concepts is so strong that it makes sense to discuss percents as students begin to have a good grasp of the fraction–decimal relationships. Even if percents do not appear in your curriculum until later, do not miss the opportunity to help students make connections between these different representations.

A Third Operator System

Percents are correctly thought of as part of a whole, in particular *part of a whole divided into 100 parts*. In middle school texts, percents are typically found in a chapter entitled "Ratio, Proportion, and Percent." There the emphasis is on proportionate part-to-whole ratios. For example, $\frac{3}{4}$ is *proportional* to $\frac{75}{100}$ or 75 percent. For grades 3–5, it is appropriate to focus on connecting percents to the part-whole notion of fractions and decimals. Students' understanding of percent as a ratio will be further developed in middle school.

Another Name for Hundredths

The term *percent* is simply another name for *hundredths*. If students can express common fractions and simple decimals as hundredths, the term *percent* can be substituted for the term *hundredth*. Consider the fraction $\frac{3}{4}$. As a fraction expressed in hundredths, it is $\frac{75}{100}$. When $\frac{3}{4}$ is written in decimal form, it is 0.75. Both 0.75 and $\frac{75}{100}$ are read in exactly the same way, "seventy-five hundredths." When used as operators, $\frac{3}{4}$ of something is the same as 0.75 or 75 percent of that same thing. Thus, percent is merely a new notation and terminology, not a new concept.

Models provide the main link among fractions, decimals, and percents, as shown in Figure 7.12. Base-ten fraction models are suitable for fractions, decimals, and percents, since they all represent the same idea.

Another helpful approach to the terminology of percent is through the role of the decimal point. Recall that the decimal identifies the units. When the unit is ones, a number such as 0.659 means a little more than 6 tenths of 1. The word *ones* is understood (6 tenths of 1 *one*). But 0.659 is also 6.59 tenths and 65.9 hundredths and 659 thousandths. In each case, the name of the unit must be explicitly identified, or else the unit ones would be assumed. Since *percent* is another name for *hundredths,* when the decimal identifies the hundredths position as the units, the word *percent* can be specified as a synonym for *hundredths.* Thus, 0.659 (of some whole or 1) is 65.9 hundredths or 65.9 percent of that same whole. As illustrated in Figure 7.13, the notion of placing the decimal point to *identify the percent position* is conceptually more meaningful than the apparently arbitrary rule: "To change a decimal to a

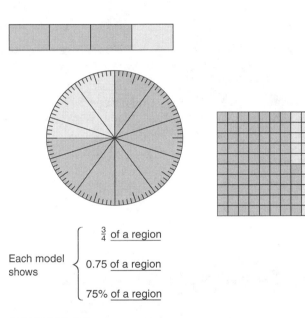

Each model shows
$$\begin{cases} \frac{3}{4} \text{ of a region} \\ 0.75 \text{ of a region} \\ 75\% \text{ of a region} \end{cases}$$

FIGURE 7.12 •

Models connect three different notations.

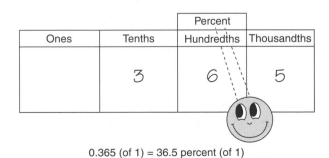

Ones	Tenths	Percent Hundredths	Thousandths
	3	6	5

0.365 (of 1) = 36.5 percent (of 1)

FIGURE 7.13 •

Hundredths are also known as percents.

percent, move the decimal point two places to the right." A better idea is to equate hundredths with percent both orally and in notation.

Using Percent with Familiar Fractions

Students should use base-ten models for percents in much the same way as for decimals. The disk with 100 markings around the edge is now a model for percents as well as a fraction model for hundredths. The same is true of a 10 × 10 square. Each tiny square inside is 1 percent of the square. Each row or strip of 10 squares is not only a tenth but also 10 percent of the square.

Similarly, the familiar fractions (halves, thirds, fourths, fifths, and eighths) should become familiar in terms of percents as well as decimals. Three-fifths, for example, is 60 percent as well as 0.6. One-third of an amount is frequently expressed as $33\frac{1}{3}$ percent instead of 33.3333 . . . percent. Likewise, $\frac{1}{8}$ of a quantity is $12\frac{1}{2}$ percent or 12.5 percent of the quantity. These ideas should be explored with base-ten models and not as rules about moving decimal points.

Realistic Percent Problems

The Three Percent Problems

Teachers talk about "the three percent problems." The sentence "____ is ____ percent of ____" has three spaces for numbers; for example, "20 is 25 percent of 80." The classic three percent problems come from this sterile expression; two of the numbers are given, and the students are asked to produce the third. Students learn very quickly that you either multiply or divide the two given numbers, and sometimes you have to move a decimal point. But they have no way of determining when to do what, which numbers to divide, or which way to shift the decimal point. As a result, performance on percentage problems is very poor. Furthermore, commonly encountered expressions using percent terminology, such as sales figures, taxes, census data, political information, and trends in economics, are almost never in the "____ is ____ percent of ____" format. So when asked to solve a realistic percent problem, students are frequently at a loss.

Chapter 5 explored three types of exercises with fractions, in which one element—part, whole, or fraction—was unknown. Students used models and simple fraction relationships in those exercises. Those three types of exercises are precisely the same as the three percent problems. Developmentally, then, it makes sense to help students make the connection between the exercises done with fractions and those done with percents. How? Use the same types of models and the same terminology of parts, wholes, and fractions. The only thing that is different is that the word *percent* is used instead of *fraction*. In Figure 7.14, three exercises from Chapter 5 have been changed to the corresponding percent terminology. A good idea for early work with percents would be to review (or explore for the first time) all three types of exercises in terms of percents. The same three types of models can be used (refer to Figures 5.11, 5.12, and 5.13 on pp. 141–142).

(From Figure 5.11)

100%
If this strip is one whole,
66⅔%
what strip is two-thirds?
150%
What strip is three-halves?

(From Figure 5.12)

75%
If this rectangle is three-fourths, draw a shape
100%
that could be the whole.

(From Figure 5.13)

percent
What fraction of this set is black?

FIGURE 7.14 •

Part-whole-fraction exercises can be translated into percent exercises.

Chapter **7** DECIMAL AND PERCENT CONCEPTS AND DECIMAL COMPUTATION

Realistic Percent Problems and Nice Numbers

Though students must have some experience with the noncontextual situations in Figure 7.14, it is important to have them explore these relationships in real contexts. Find or make up percent problems and present them in the same way that they appear in newspapers, on television, and in other real contexts. In addition to realistic problems and formats, follow these maxims for your unit on percents:

- Limit the percents to familiar fractions (halves, thirds, fourths, fifths, and eighths) or easy percents ($\frac{1}{10}$, $\frac{1}{100}$) and use numbers compatible with these fractions. The focus of these exercises is the relationships involved, not complex computational skills.

- Do not suggest any rules or procedures for different types of problems. Do not categorize or label problem types.

- Use the terms *part, whole,* and *percent* (or *fraction*). *Fraction* and *percent* are interchangeable. Help students see these percent exercises as the same types of exercises they did with simple fractions.

- Require students to use models or drawings to explain their solutions. It is better to assign three problems requiring a drawing and an explanation than to give 15 problems requiring only computation and answers. Remember that the purpose is the exploration of relationships, not computational skill.

- Encourage mental computation.

The following sample problems meet these criteria for easy fractions and numbers. Try working each problem, identifying each number as a part, a whole, or a fraction. Draw length or area models to explain or work through your thought process. Examples of this informal reasoning are illustrated with additional problems in Figure 7.15.

1. The PTA reported that 75 percent of the total number of families were represented at the meeting last night. If children from 320 families go to the school, how many were represented at the meeting?

2. The baseball team won 80 percent of the 25 games it played this year. How many games were lost?

3. In Mrs. Carter's class, 20 students, or $66\frac{2}{3}$ percent, were on the honor roll. How many students are in her class?

4. George bought his new computer at a $12\frac{1}{2}$ percent discount. He paid $700. How many dollars did he save by buying it at a discount?

5. If Joyce has read 60 of the 180 pages in her library book, what percent of the book has she read so far?

6. The hardware store bought widgets at 80 cents each and sold them for $1 each. What percent did the store mark up the price of each widget?

STOP Examine the examples in Figure 7.15. Notice how each problem is solved with simple fractions and mental math. Then try each of the six problems just listed. Each can be done easily and mentally using friendly fraction equivalents.

FIGURE 7.15 • • • • • • •

Real percent problems
with nice numbers.
Simple drawings help
with reasoning.

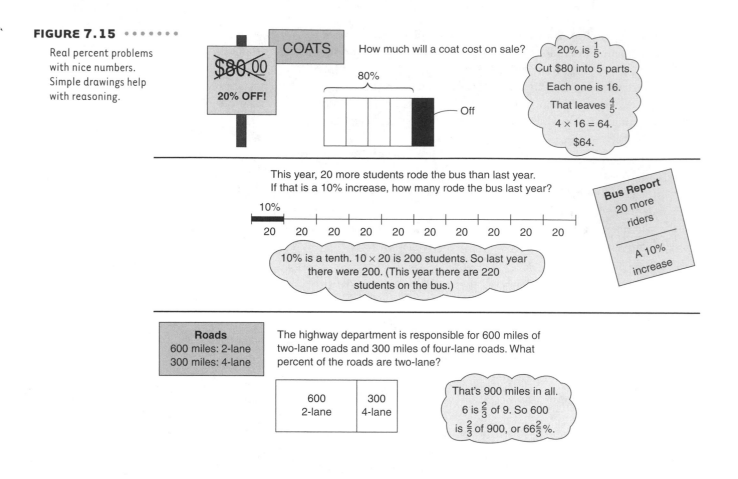

Assessment Note

Realistic percent problems are still the best way to assess a student's understanding of percent. Assign one or two, and have students explain why they think their answer makes sense. You might take a realistic percent problem and substitute fractions for percents (e.g., use $\frac{1}{8}$ instead of 12.5 percent) to see how students handle these problems with fractions compared to decimal numbers.

Computation with Decimals

Certainly, students should develop some computational fluency with decimal numbers. In the past, decimal computation was dominated by the following rules: Line up the decimal points (addition and subtraction), count the decimal places (multiplication), and shift the decimal point in the divisor and dividend so that the divisor is a whole number (division). Traditional textbooks continue to emphasize these rules. The position taken in this book is that specific rules for decimal computation are not really necessary, especially if computation is built on a firm understanding of place value and a connection between decimals and fractions.

The Role of Estimation

Contrary to the traditional curriculum, students should become adept at estimating decimal computations well before they learn to compute with pencil and paper. For many decimal computations, rough estimates can be made easily by rounding the numbers to nice whole numbers or simple base-ten fractions. A minimum goal for your students should be to have the estimate contain the correct number of digits to the left of the decimal—the whole-number part. Select problems for which estimates are not terribly difficult.

 Before going on, try making easy whole-number estimates of the following computations. Do not spend time with fine adjustments in your estimates.

1. 4.907 + 123.01 + 56.1234   3. 24.67 × 1.84
2. 459.8 – 12.345   4. 514.67 ÷ 3.59

Your estimates might be similar to the following:

1. Between 175 and 200
2. More than 400, or about 425 to 450
3. More than 25, closer to 50 (1.84 is more than 1 and close to 2)
4. More than 125, less than 200 (500 ÷ 4 = 125 and 600 ÷ 3 = 200)

In these examples, an understanding of decimal numeration and some simple whole-number estimation skills can produce rough estimates. When estimating, thinking focuses on the meaning of the numbers and the operations and not on counting decimal places. However, students who are taught to focus on the pencil-and-paper rules for decimal computation do not even consider the actual values of the number much less estimate.

Therefore, a good *place* to begin decimal computation is with estimation. Not only is it a highly practical skill, but it also helps students look at answers in ballpark terms and can form a check on calculator computation.

A good *time* to begin computation with decimals is as soon as a conceptual background in decimal numeration has been developed. Learning the rules for decimal computation will do little or nothing to help students understand decimal numeration and will interfere with a more robust development of number sense.

Addition and Subtraction

Consider this problem:

> Max and Moe each timed his own quarter-mile run with a stopwatch. Max says that he ran the quarter in 74.5 seconds. Moe was more accurate. He reported his run as 81.34 seconds. How many seconds faster did Max run than Moe?

COMPUTATION WITH DECIMALS

Students who understand decimal numeration should first of all be able to tell approximately what the difference is—close to 7 seconds. With an estimate as a beginning, students should then be challenged to figure out the exact difference. The estimate will help them avoid the typical error of lining up the 5 under the 4. A variety of student strategies are possible. For example, students might note that 74.5 and 7 is 81.5 and then figure out how much extra that is. Others may count on from 74.5 by adding 0.5 and then 6 more seconds to get to 81 seconds and then add on the remaining 0.34 second. These and other strategies will eventually confront the difference between the one-place decimal (.5) and the two-place decimal (.34). Students can resolve this issue by returning to their understanding of place value. Similar story problems for addition and subtraction, some involving different numbers of decimal places, will help develop students' understanding of these two operations. Always request an estimate prior to computation.

After students have had several opportunities to solve addition and subtraction story problems, the following activity is reasonable.

ACTIVITY 7.11

Exact Sums and Differences

Give students a sum involving different numbers of decimal places. For example: 73.46 + 6.2 + 0.582. The first task is to make an estimate and explain the way the estimate was made. The second task is to compute the exact answer and explain how that was done (no calculators). In the third and final task students devise a method for adding and subtracting decimal numbers that they can use with any two numbers.

When students have completed these three tasks, have students share their strategies for computation and test them on a new computation that you provide.

The same task can be repeated for subtraction.

The earlier estimation practice will focus students' attention on the meanings of the numbers. It is reasonable to expect that students will develop an algorithm that is essentially the same as aligning the decimal points.

Multiplication

Estimation should play a significant role in developing an algorithm for multiplication. As a beginning point, consider this problem:

The farmer fills each jug with 3.7 liters of cider. If you buy 4 jugs, how many liters of cider is that?

Begin with an estimate. It is more than 12 liters. What is the most it could be? Could it be 16 liters? Once an estimate of the result is decided on, let students use their own methods for determining an exact answer. Many will use repeated addition: 3.7 + 3.7 + 3.7 + 3.7. Others may begin by multiplying 3 × 4 and then adding up 0.7 four times. Eventually, students will agree on the exact result of 14.8 liters. Explore other problems involving whole-number multipliers. Multipliers such as 3.5 or 8.25 that involve nice fractional parts—here, one-half and one-fourth—are also reasonable.

As a next step, have students compare a decimal product with one involving the same digits but no decimal. For example, how are 23.4 × 6.5 and 234 × 65 alike? Interestingly, both products have exactly the same digits: 15210. (The zero may be missing from the decimal product.) Using a calculator, have students explore other products that are alike except for the decimals involved. The digits in the answer are always alike.

ACTIVITY 7.12

Where Does the Decimal Go? Multiplication

Have students compute the following product: 24 × 63. Using only the result of this computation and estimation, have them give the exact answer to each of the following:

$$0.24 \times 6.3 \qquad 24 \times 0.63 \qquad 2.4 \times 63 \qquad 0.24 \times 0.63$$

For each computation they should write a rationale for their answers. They can check their results with a calculator. Any errors must be acknowledged and the rationale that produced the error adjusted.

 The product of 24 × 63 is 1512. Use this information to give the answer to each of the products in the previous activity. Do *not* count decimal places. Remember your fractional equivalents.

The method of placing the decimal point in a product by way of estimation is more difficult as the product gets smaller. For example, knowing that 54 × 83 is 4482 does not make it easy to place the decimal in the product 0.0054 × 0.00083. Even the product 0.054 × 0.83 is hard. The practical question is this: Can you think of any situation outside of school in which someone might require an exact answer to a product such as one of these but would not have access to a calculator? When precision is important, technology makes sense and is always available. Yes, there is a conceptual rationale for counting the decimal places. Even if learned, it focuses attention on the smallest part of the product and provides absolutely no practice with estimation. It is a non-number-sense method that need not be used today.

Assessment Note

Questions such as the following keep the focus on number sense and provide useful information about your students' understanding.

1. Consider these two computations: $3\frac{1}{2} \times 2\frac{1}{4}$ and 2.276 × 3.18. Without doing the calculations, which do you think is larger? Provide a reason for your answer that can be understood by someone else in this class.

2. How much larger is 0.76 × 5 than 0.75 × 5? How can you tell without doing the computation (Kulm, 1994)?

(continued)

Listen to students' discussions and explanations as they work on these questions or questions like them. Examine pictures that students have drawn to support their explanations. How are they making these comparisons? Do they focus on the decimal representations of the numbers or do they convert everything to "nice" fractions and work from that representation? These observations can provide insights into your students' decimal and fraction number sense and the connections between the two representations.

Division

Division can be approached in a manner exactly parallel to multiplication. In fact, the best approach to a division estimate generally comes from thinking about multiplication rather than division. Consider the following problem:

The trip to Washington was 282.5 miles. It took exactly $4\frac{1}{2}$ hours or 4.5 hours to drive. What was the average miles per hour?

To make an estimate of this quotient, think about what times 4 or 5 is close to 280. You might think $60 \times 4.5 = 240 + 30 = 270$. So maybe about 61 or 62 miles per hour.

Here is a second example without context. Make an estimate of $45.7 \div 1.83$. Think only of what times $1\frac{8}{10}$ is close to 45.

 STOP Will the answer be more or less than 45? Why? Will it be more or less than 20? Now think about 1.8 being close to 2. What times 2 is close to 46? Use this to produce an estimate.

Since 1.83 is close to 2, the estimate is near 22. And since 1.83 is less than 2 the answer must be greater than 22—say 25 or 26. (The actual answer is 24.972677.)

Okay, so estimation can produce a reasonable result, but you may still require a pencil-and-paper algorithm to produce the digits the way it was done for multiplication. Figure 7.16 shows division by a whole number and how that can be carried out to as many places as you wish. (The explicit-trade method described in Chapter 4 is shown on the right.) It is not necessary to move the decimal point up into the quotient. Leave that to estimation.

ACTIVITY 7.13

Where Does the Decimal Go? Division

Provide a quotient such as $146 \div 7 = 20857$ correct to five digits but without the decimal point. The task is to use only this information and estimation to give a fairly precise answer to each of the following:

$146 \div 0.7$ $1.46 \div 7$ $14.6 \div 0.7$ $1460 \div 70$

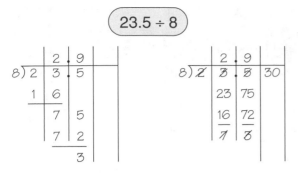

FIGURE 7.16 • • • • • • • • • • • •

Extension of the division algorithm.

Trade 2 tens for 20 ones, making 23 ones.
Put 2 ones in each group, or 16 in all.
That leaves 7 ones.

Trade 7 ones for 70 tenths, making 75 tenths.
Put 9 tenths in each group, or 72 in all.

Trade the 3 tenths for 30 hundredths.

(Continue trading for smaller pieces as long as you wish.)

For each computation students should write a rationale for their answers and then check their results with a calculator. Any errors should be acknowledged and the rationale that produced the error adjusted.

STOP Give the answer to each of the products in the previous activity.

A reasonable algorithm for division is parallel to that for multiplication: *Ignore the decimal points and do the computation as if all numbers were whole numbers. When finished, place the decimal point by estimation.* This is reasonable for divisors with no more than two significant digits. If students have a method for dividing by 45, they can divide by 0.45 and 4.5 and even 0.045.

Assessment Note

The real danger in teaching the topics discussed in this chapter is in emphasizing skills instead of the concepts and big ideas. Traditional tests will focus on students' ability to round numbers, order decimals, compute with pencil and paper, and solve sterile percent problems. These assessments are far too skill oriented. The activities described in this chapter will involve discussions and explanations, if you are not overly directive. From these discussions, you can gather data about your students' understanding of concepts and keep the focus on sense-making.

EXPANDED LESSON

Friendly Fractions to Decimals

Based on: Activity 7.4, p. 188

GRADE LEVEL: Fourth or fifth grade.

MATHEMATICS GOALS
- To help students connect decimals and familiar fraction equivalents in a conceptual manner.
- To reinforce the notion of the 10-to-1 relationship between adjacent digits in our numeration system.

THINKING ABOUT THE STUDENTS
Students are familiar with the 10-to-1 relationship between adjacent digits in our numeration system. They have worked with decimals and can add and subtract decimals somewhat successfully, but they appear to have at best a procedural understanding of the process. Students also understand the part-whole meaning of fractional parts and the meaning of the numerator and denominator in a fraction.

MATERIALS AND PREPARATION
- Provide each student with at least two sheets of 10 × 10 grids (see Blackline Master 18).
- Make a transparency of the 10 × 10 grid sheet to use in the before and after portions of the lesson.

---

lesson

BLM 18

BEFORE

Begin with a simpler version of the task:
- Write the number 34 on the board. Remind students that 34 is 3 tens and 4 ones. Ask students to describe 34 with tens and ones in other ways. As students suggest names such as 2 tens and 14 ones, focus on the 10-to-1 relationship between adjacent digits: A larger unit can be exchanged for 10 of the next smaller unit and vice versa.
- Ask students what it means to have $\frac{1}{10}$ of something. Highlight the idea that the whole is divided into 10 *equal* parts and $\frac{1}{10}$ means you have one of those parts. Showing students the 10 × 10 grid, ask them to shade $\frac{1}{10}$ of the grid. Ask students to share different ways to shade $\frac{1}{10}$ of the grid. It might be helpful to illustrate using base-ten materials as one way to think about this task (i.e., the flat hundreds piece is used as the whole and the long ten stick is then used as a tenth). Suggest to students how you could represent 1.3 with the base-ten materials (e.g., if the flat piece is the whole, one flat piece and three long pieces).

The Task
Using a 10 × 10 grid, for each of the following fractions determine the decimal equivalent and explain your reasoning.

$$\frac{3}{4} \qquad \frac{2}{5} \qquad \frac{3}{8}$$

Establish Expectations
Using the 10 × 10 grids, students should:
- Shade the fractional amount.
- Identify the decimal number that also represents this amount.
- Be prepared to explain their reasoning.

DURING

- Look for students who are shading their 10 × 10 grids differently. Highlight those different ways in the "After" portion of the lesson.
- If students have shaded their grid in a way that does not use long rows of ten, ask students how they would cover the area using strips and squares if they could use no more than nine tinies.
- The $\frac{3}{8}$ task is the most challenging. A useful hint is to ask students how they would find $\frac{1}{8}$ if they had $\frac{1}{4}$.

- You may need to remind students that as they need something smaller than the smallest square on the grid, that the next smaller pieces are tenths of the little squares. Since a small square is $\frac{1}{100}$, one-tenth of it would be $\frac{1}{1000}$ and half of it would be $\frac{5}{1000}$.

AFTER

- Students are likely to shade their grids differently. It is important to compare and contrast between different shadings so that students see that they have shaded an equivalent amount. For example, for fourths, students might shade a 5 × 5 section (half of a half). Others may shade two and a half rows of ten. Ask students to determine how these both show one-fourth.
- For some shadings, it may be difficult for students to see the decimal equivalent. For example, when students shade a 5 × 5 section to show a fourth, it can be difficult for them to translate that representation into a decimal. You might focus students' attention to finding tenths within the 10 × 10 grid by looking at rows of 10. One way to help them think about this is to ask students how they would cover the area using strips and squares if they could use no more than nine tinies.

ASSESSMENT NOTES

- Some students will be very successful with shading equal parts but have difficulty connecting this to the decimal representation. As you suggest to them to use strips and tinies, make sure they can explain why they are using these groupings rather than, say, strips of 5.
- Students who are able to move quickly between the equal parts for fractions and the decimal equivalents in this task are ready to think about the decimal equivalent for one-third.

- For students who have difficulty with these tasks, instead of providing them with a 10 × 10 grid, provide them with a comparable-sized square that is divided into tenths (10 long rectangles). Have them use this representation before moving back to the 10 × 10 grid.

- To continue to help students build connections between fractions and decimals, have them engage in tasks that use the hundredths disk (Blackline Master 17), such as Activity 7.5, "Estimate, Then Verify."

next steps

EXPANDED LESSON

GEOMETRIC THINKING AND GEOMETRIC CONCEPTS

Geometry in grades K–8 is finally being taken seriously. Geometry used to be the chapter that was skipped or put off until late in the year. Many teachers were not comfortable with geometry, associating it with high school and proofs. Nor was geometry seen as important because it was only minimally tested on standardized tests. Now geometry is a strand of the curriculum in nearly every state and district.

This change is due in large part to the influence of the NCTM standards movement beginning in 1989. A second significant influence is an attention to a theoretical perspective that has helped us understand how students reason about spatial concepts.

Geometry Goals for Your Students

It is useful to think about your geometry objectives in terms of two quite different yet related frameworks: spatial reasoning, or spatial sense, and the specific content such as that most likely found in your state or district objectives. The first of these frameworks has to do with the way students think and reason about shape and space. There is a well-researched theoretical basis for organizing the development of geometric thought that guides this framework. The second framework is content in the more traditional sense—knowing about symmetry, triangles, parallel lines, and so forth. The NCTM *Principles and Standards for*

big ideas

1. What makes shapes alike and different can be determined by an array of geometric properties. For example, shapes have sides that are parallel, perpendicular, or neither; they have line symmetry, rotational symmetry, or neither; they are similar, congruent, or neither.

2. Shapes can be moved in a plane or in space. These changes can be described in terms of translations (slides), reflections (flips), and rotations (turns).

3. Shapes can be described in terms of their location in a plane or in space. Coordinate systems can be used to describe these locations precisely. In turn, the coordinate view of shape offers another way to understand certain properties of shapes, changes in position (transformations), and how they appear or change size (visualization).

4. Shapes can be seen from different perspectives. The ability to perceive shapes from different viewpoints helps us understand relationships between two- and three-dimensional figures and mentally change the position and size of shapes.

School Mathematics authors have helped describe content goals across the grades. We need to understand both of these aspects of geometry—thought and content—so that we can best help students grow.

Spatial Sense

Spatial sense can be defined as an intuition about shapes and the relationships among shapes. Individuals with spatial sense have a feel for the geometric aspects of their surroundings and the shapes formed by objects in the environment.

Spatial sense includes the ability to visualize mentally objects and spatial relationships—to turn things around in your mind. It includes a comfort with geometric descriptions of objects and position. People with spatial sense appreciate geometric form in art, nature, and architecture. They are able to use geometric ideas to describe and analyze their world.

Many people say they aren't very good with shape or that they have poor spatial sense. The typical belief is that you are either born with spatial sense or not. This simply is not true! We now know that rich experiences with shape and spatial relationships, when provided consistently over time, can and do develop spatial sense. Without geometric experiences, most people do not grow in their spatial sense or spatial reasoning. Between 1990 and 1996, NAEP data indicated a steady, continuing improvement in students' geometric reasoning at all three grades tested, 4, 8, and 12 (Martin & Strutchens, 2000). Students did not just get smarter. More likely there has been an increasing emphasis on geometry at all grades. Still, much more needs to be done if U.S. children are to rise to the same level as their European and Asian counterparts.

Geometric Content

For too long, the geometry curriculum in the United States has been somewhat of an eclectic mix of activities and lists of "bold print words"—too much emphasis has been placed on learning terminology. At the same time, the growing emphasis placed on geometry has spawned a huge assortment of wonderful tasks for students. Fortunately, the authors of *Principles and Standards for School Mathematics* have provided a content framework for the pre-K–12 curriculum. As with each of the content standards, the geometry standard has a number of goals that apply to all grade levels. The four goals for geometry can be loosely summarized with these headings: *Shapes and Properties, Transformation, Location,* and *Visualization.* A very brief description of these headings is offered next.

- *Shapes and Properties* includes a study of the properties of shapes in both two and three dimensions, as well as a study of the relationships built on properties.

- *Transformation* includes a study of translations, reflections, and rotations (slides, flips, and turns) and the study of symmetries.

- *Location* refers primarily to coordinate geometry or other ways of specifying how objects are located in the plane or in space.

- *Visualization* includes the recognition of shapes in the environment, developing relationships between two- and three-dimensional objects, and the ability to draw and recognize objects from different perspectives.

GEOMETRY GOALS FOR YOUR STUDENTS

The value of these content goals is that a content framework finally exists that cuts across grades so that both teachers and curriculum planners can examine growth from year to year.

You are strongly encouraged to read the geometry goals for grades pre-K–2 and 3–5 in *Principles and Standards* (NCTM, 2000).

Geometric Thought: Reasoning About Shapes and Relationships

Not all people think about geometric ideas in the same manner. Certainly, we are not all alike, but we are all capable of growing and developing in our ability to think and reason in geometric contexts. The research of two Dutch educators, Pierre van Hiele and Dina van Hiele-Geldof, has provided insight into the differences in geometric thinking and how the differences come to be.

The van Hieles' work began in 1959 and immediately attracted a lot of attention in the Soviet Union but for nearly two decades received little notice in this country (Hoffer, 1983; Hoffer & Hoffer, 1992). But today the van Hiele theory has become the most influential factor in the American geometry curriculum.

The van Hiele Levels of Geometric Thought

The most prominent feature of the model is a five-level hierarchy of ways of understanding spatial ideas. Each of the five levels describes the thinking processes used in geometric contexts. The levels describe how we think and what types of geometric ideas we think about rather than how much knowledge we have. A significant difference from one level to the next is the objects of thought—what we are able to think about geometrically.

Level 0: Visualization

The objects of thought at level 0 are shapes and what they "look like."

Students recognize and name figures based on the global, visual characteristics of the figure—a gestaltlike approach to shape. Students operating at this level are able to make measurements and even talk about properties of shapes, but these properties are not abstracted from the shapes at hand. It is the appearance of the shape that defines it for the student. A square is a square "because it looks like a square." Because appearance is dominant at this level, appearances can overpower properties of a shape. For example, a square that has been rotated so that all sides are at a 45-degree angle to the vertical may now be a diamond and no longer a square. Students at this level will sort and classify shapes based on their appearances—"I put these together because they are all pointy" (or "fat," or "look like a house," or are "dented in sort of," and so on). With a focus on the appearances of shapes, students are able to see how shapes are alike and different. As a result, students at this level can create and begin to understand classifications of shapes.

The products of thought at level 0 are classes or groupings of shapes that seem to be "alike."

Level 1: Analysis

The objects of thought at level 1 are classes of shapes rather than individual shapes.

Students at the analysis level are able to consider all shapes within a class rather than a single shape. Instead of talking about *this* rectangle, it is possible to talk about *all* rectangles. By focusing on a class of shapes, students are able to think about what makes a rectangle a rectangle (four sides, opposite sides parallel, opposite sides same length, four right angles, congruent diagonals, etc.). The irrelevant features (e.g., size or orientation) fade into the background. At this level, students begin to appreciate that a collection of shapes goes together because of properties. Ideas about an individual shape can now be generalized to all shapes that fit that class. If a shape belongs to a particular class such as cubes, it has the corresponding properties of that class. "All cubes have six congruent faces, and each of those faces is a square." These properties were only implicit at level 0. Students operating at level 1 may be able to list all the properties of squares, rectangles, and parallelograms but not see that these are sub-classes of one another, that all squares are rectangles and all rectangles are parallelograms. In defining a shape, level 1 thinkers are likely to list as many properties of a shape as they know.

The products of thought at level 1 are the properties of shapes.

Level 2: Informal Deduction

The objects of thought at level 2 are the properties of shapes.

As students begin to be able to think about properties of geometric objects without the constraints of a particular object, they are able to develop relationships between and among these properties. "If all four angles are right angles, the shape must be a rectangle. If it is a square, all angles are right angles. If it is a square, it must be a rectangle." It is at this level that students can appreciate the nature of a definition. With greater ability to engage in "if–then" reasoning, shapes can be classified using only minimum characteristics. For example, four congruent sides and at least one right angle can be sufficient to define a square. Rectangles are parallelograms with a right angle. Observations go beyond properties themselves and begin to focus on logical arguments *about* the properties. Students at level 2 will be able to follow and appreciate an informal deductive argument about shapes and their properties. "Proofs" may be more intuitive than rigorously deductive. However, there is an appreciation that a logical argument is compelling. An appreciation of the axiomatic structure of a formal deductive system, however, remains under the surface.

The products of thought at level 2 are relationships among properties of geometric objects.

Level 3: Deduction

The objects of thought at level 3 are relationships among properties of geometric objects.

At level 3, students begin to appreciate the need for a system of logic that rests on a minimum set of assumptions and from which other truths can be derived. This is the level of the traditional high school geometry course.

The products of thought at level 3 are deductive axiomatic systems for geometry.

Level 4: Rigor

The objects of thought at level 4 are deductive axiomatic systems for geometry.

At the highest level of the van Hiele hierarchy, the objects of attention are axiomatic systems themselves, not just the deductions within a system. This is generally the level of a college mathematics major who is studying geometry as a branch of mathematical science.

The products of thought at level 4 are comparisons and contrasts among different axiomatic systems of geometry.

We have given brief descriptions of all five levels to illustrate the scope of the van Hiele theory. Most students in grades 3–5 will be at level 0 or 1.

Characteristics of the van Hiele Levels

You no doubt noticed that the products of thought at each level are the same as the objects of thought at the next. This object–product relationship between levels of the van Hiele theory is illustrated in Figure 8.1. The objects (ideas) must be created at one level so that relationships among these objects can become the focus of the next level. In addition to this key concept of the theory, four related characteristics of the levels of thought merit special attention.

1. The levels are sequential. To arrive at any level above level 0, students must move through all prior levels. To move through a level means that one has experienced geometric thinking appropriate for that level and has created in one's own mind the types of objects or relationships that are the focus of thought at the next level.

2. The levels are not age dependent in the sense of the developmental stages of Piaget. A third grader or a high school student could be at level 0. Indeed, some students and adults remain forever at level 0, and a significant number of adults never reach level 2. But age is certainly related to the amount and types of geometric experiences that we have. Therefore, it is reasonable to assume that many students in grades 3 and 4 will be at level 0.

3. Geometric experience is the greatest single factor influencing advancement through the levels. Activities that permit children to explore, talk about, and interact with content at the next level, while increasing their experiences at their current level, have the best chance of advancing the level of thought for those students. Some researchers believe that it is possible to be at one level with respect to a familiar area of content and at a lower level with less familiar ideas (Clements & Battista, 1992).

4. When instruction or language is at a level higher than that of the student, there will be a lack of communication. Students required to wrestle with objects of thought that have not been constructed at the earlier level may be forced into rote learning and achieve only temporary and superficial success. A student can, for example, memorize that all squares are rectangles without having constructed that relationship. A student may memorize a geometric proof but fail to create the steps or understand the rationale involved (Fuys, Geddes, & Tischler, 1988; Geddes & Fortunato, 1993).

The van Hiele Theory of Geometric Thought

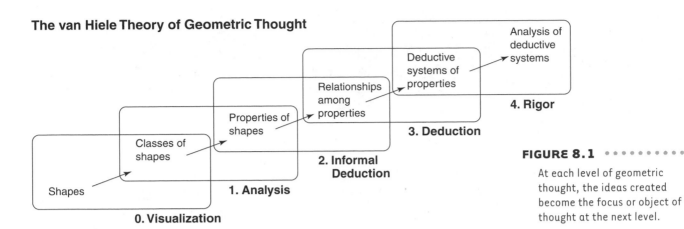

Implications for Instruction

If the van Hiele theory is correct—and there is much evidence to support it—then a major goal of the K–8 curriculum must be to advance students' level of geometric thought. If students are to be adequately prepared for the deductive geometry curriculum of high school, then it is important for their thinking to have grown to level 2 by the end of the eighth grade.

Not every child will be ready to move to the next level. However, all teachers should be aware that the experiences they provide are the single most important factor in moving children up this developmental ladder. Every teacher should be able to see some growth in geometric thinking over the course of the year.

The van Hiele theory and the developmental perspective of this book highlight the necessity of teaching at the child's level of thought. However, almost any activity can be modified to span two levels of thinking, even within the same classroom. For many activities, how we interact with individual children will adapt the activity to their levels and encourage them or challenge them to operate at the next higher level.

Explorations help develop relationships. The more students play around with the ideas in activities, the more relationships they will discover. However, students need to learn how to explore ideas in geometry and play around with the relationships in order for ideas to develop and become meaningful.

The following sections contain descriptions of the types of activity and questioning that are appropriate for the first two levels. Apply these descriptors to the tasks that you pose to students and use them to guide your interaction with students. The use of physical materials, drawings, and computer models is a must at every level.

Instruction at Level 0

Instructional activities in geometry appropriate for level 0 should:

- Involve lots of sorting and classifying. Seeing how shapes are alike and different is the primary focus of level 0. As students learn more content, the types of things that they notice will become more sophisticated. At an early stage they may talk about very non-geometric-sounding attributes of shape such as "fat" or even the color of the pieces. When properties such as symmetry and numbers of sides and corners are introduced, students should be challenged to use these features to classify shapes.

- Include a sufficient variety of examples of shapes so that irrelevant features do not become important. Students need ample opportunities to draw, build, make, put together, and take apart shapes in both two and three dimensions. These activities should be built around specific characteristics or properties so that students develop an understanding of geometric properties and begin to use them naturally.

To help students move from level 0 to level 1, students should be challenged to test ideas about shapes for a variety of examples from a particular category. Say to them, "Let's see if that is true for other rectangles," or "Can you draw a triangle that does *not* have a right angle?" In general, students should be challenged to see if observations made about a particular shape apply to other shapes of a similar kind.

Instruction at Level 1

Instructional activities in geometry appropriate for level 1 should:

- Focus more on the properties of figures rather than on simple identification. As new geometric concepts are learned, the number of properties that figures have can be expanded.

- Apply ideas to entire classes of figures (e.g., *all* rectangles, *all* prisms) rather than on individual models. Analyze classes of figures to determine new properties. For example, find ways to sort all possible triangles into groups. From these groups, define types of triangles. Dynamic geometry software such as *The Geometer's Sketchpad* (Key Curriculum Press, 2001) is especially useful for exploring many examples of a class of shapes and is appropriate for grade 4 and higher.

To assist students in moving from level 1 to level 2, challenge them with questions such as "Why?" and those that involve some reasoning. For example, ask "If the sides of a four-sided shape are all congruent, will you always have a square?" and "Can you find a counterexample?"

Instruction at Level 2

Instructional activities in geometry appropriate for level 2 should:

- Encourage the making and testing of hypotheses or conjectures. "Do you think that will work all the time?" "Is that true for all triangles or just equilateral ones?"

- Examine properties of shapes to determine necessary and sufficient conditions for different shapes or concepts. "What properties of diagonals do you think will guarantee that you will have a square?"

- Use the language of informal deduction: *all, some, none, if . . . then, what if,* and so on.

- Encourage students to attempt informal proofs. As an alternative, require them to make sense of informal proofs that other students or you have suggested.

By grade 3 you certainly want to begin to challenge students who seem able to begin to engage in level 1 thinking. In the upper grades you may have children at two or even all three levels within the same classroom.

How do you discover the level of each student? Once you know, how will you select the right activities to match your students' levels?

No simple test exists to pigeonhole students at a certain level. However, examine the descriptors for the first two levels. As you conduct an activity, listen to the types of observations that students make. Can they talk about shapes as classes? Do they refer, for example, to "rectangles" rather than basing discussion around a particular rectangle? Do they generalize that certain properties are attributable to a type of shape or simply the shape at hand? Do they understand that shapes do not change when the orientation changes? With simple observations such as these, you will soon be able to distinguish between levels 0 and 1.

By grade 5 you may want to attempt to push students from level 1 to level 2. If students are not able to follow or appreciate logical arguments and are not comfortable with conjectures and if–then reasoning, these students are likely still at level 1 or below.

Content and the Levels of Thinking

This chapter offers a sample of activities organized around the four content areas: Shapes and Properties, Transformations, Location, and Visualization. A section of the chapter is devoted to each of these areas. The van Hiele theory applies to all geometric activity, regardless of content. However, it is within the content area of shapes and properties that the theory is most clearly seen. For that reason the activities in that section are subdivided into those appropriate for level 0 and level 1 thinkers. You will find this subdivision helpful for matching activities to your students and encouraging student development of thinking to higher levels. The three remaining sections focus on activities for developing spatial sense through location, transformation, and visualization. Each of these sections is organized in a progression of difficulty and sophistication.

Understand that all of these subdivisions are quite fluid; that is, the content areas overlap and build on each other. Activities in one section may help develop geometric thinking in another area. For example, developing spatial sense through an investigation of symmetry can help students move from level 0 to level 1. A more sophisticated analysis of symmetry can continue to help students move to level 2. In most instances, an activity described for one level of thinking can easily be adapted to an adjacent level simply by the way it is presented to students.

Shapes and Properties Activities

Children need experiences with a rich variety of both two- and three-dimensional shapes. It is useful for students to be able to identify common shapes, notice likenesses and differences among shapes, become aware of the properties that different shapes have, and eventually use these properties to further define and understand their geometric world. As students find out more about shapes over time, they can begin to appreciate how definitions of special shapes come to be.

This gradual development of student understanding of shapes and their properties clearly reflects the van Hiele theory of geometric thought. Within this aspect of geometric content, an awareness and application of the theory to your instruction are most important.

Activities for Level 0 Thinkers

The emphasis at level 0 is on the shapes that students can observe, feel, build, take apart, and perceive in many ways. The general goal is to explore how shapes are alike and different and use these ideas to create classes of shapes (both physically and mentally). Some of these classes of shapes have names—rectangles, triangles, prisms, cylinders, and so on. Properties of shapes, such as parallel sides, symmetry, right angles, and so on, are included at this level but only in an informal, observational manner. Triangles should be more than just equilateral. Shapes should have curved sides, straight sides, and combinations of these. The names of shapes and their properties can be introduced casually but only after students have described the shape or property.

Remember that *level 0* is not a synonym for *primary*. If you teach in grade 4 or 5, you will almost certainly have students who need to begin with activities similar to these.

Sorting and Classifying

As young students work at classification of shapes, be prepared for some of them to notice features that you do not consider to be "real" geometric attributes, such as "curvy" or "looks like a rocket." Children at this level will also attribute to shapes ideas that are not part of the shape, such as "points up" or "has a side that is the same as the edge of the board."

For variety in two-dimensional shapes, create your own materials. A good set found in the Blackline Masters is called 2-D Shapes. Make multiple copies so that groups of children can all work with the same shapes. The shapes in Figure 8.2 are similar to those in the Blackline Masters, but you will want many more. Once you have your sets constructed, the following activities provide several ideas.

BLMs 20–26

FIGURE 8.2 • • • • • • • • • •

An assortment of shapes for sorting.

ACTIVITY 8.1

Shape Sorts

Have students work in groups of four with a set of 2-D Shapes similar to those in Figure 8.2. Here are several related activities that might be done in order:

- Each student randomly selects a shape. In turn, the students tell one or two things they find interesting about their shape. There are no right or wrong responses.
- Students each randomly select two shapes. The task is to find something that is alike about their two shapes and something that is different. (Have them select their shapes before they know the task.)
- The group selects one shape at random and places it in the center of the workspace. Their task is to find all other shapes that are like the target

shape but all according to the same rule. For example, if they say, "This one is like our shape because it has a curved side and a straight side," then all other shapes that they put in the collection must have these properties. Challenge them to do a second sort with the same target shape but using a different property.

- Have students share their sorting rules with the class and show examples. All students then draw a new shape that will also fit in the group according to the same rule. They should write about their new shape and why it fits the rule.

- Do a "secret sort." You or one of the students creates a small collection of about five shapes that fit a secret rule. Leave others that belong in your group in the pile. The other students try to find additional pieces that belong to the set and/or guess the secret rule.

STOP Why do you think that the teacher should not say things such as, "Find all the pieces with straight sides," or "Find the triangles," and instead have students choose how to sort?

In any sorting activity, the students should decide how to sort, not the teacher. This allows the students to do the activity using ideas *they* own and understand. By listening to the kinds of attributes that they use in their sorting, you will be able to tell what properties they know and use and how they think about shapes. Figure 8.3 illustrates a few of the many possible ways a set might be sorted.

The secret sorting activity is one option for introducing a new property. For example, sort the shapes so that all have at least one right angle or "square corner." When students discover your rule, you have an opportunity to talk more about that property.

The following activity is also done with the 2-D Shapes.

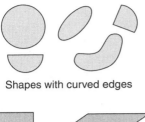
Shapes with curved edges

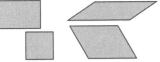
Opposite sides "go the same way"—parallelograms

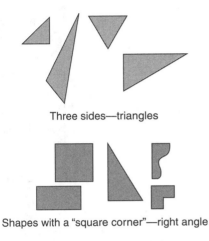
Three sides—triangles

Shapes with a "square corner"—right angle

These all "dent in"—concave

FIGURE 8.3
By sorting shapes, students begin to recognize properties.

ACTIVITY 8.2

What's My Shape?

From the Blackline Masters, make a set of 2-D Shapes on paper. Cut out about a third of the shapes and paste each inside a folded half-sheet of construction paper to make "secret shape" folders.

In a group, one student is designated the leader and given a secret-shape folder. The other students are to find the shape that matches the shape in the folder. To this end, they ask questions to which the leader can answer only "yes" or "no." The group can sort the shapes as they ask questions to help narrow down the possibilities. They are not allowed to point to a piece and ask, "Is it this one?" Rather, they must continue to ask questions that reduce the choices to one shape. The final piece is tested against the one in the leader's folder.

SHAPES AND PROPERTIES ACTIVITIES

The difficulty of Activity 8.2 largely depends on the shape in the folder. The more shapes in the collection that resemble the secret shape, the more difficult the task.

Most of the activities in "Shape Sorts" can and should be done with three-dimensional shapes as well. The difficulty is finding or making a collection that has sufficient variability. Geoblocks are a large set of wooden blocks available through various distributors. The variety is good, but no blocks have curved surfaces. Check catalogs for other collections. Consider combining several different sets to get variation.

Assessment Note

The ways in which children describe shapes in "Shape Sorts" and similar activities with three-dimensional shapes is a good clue to their level of thinking. The classifications made by level 0 thinkers will generally be restricted to the shapes that they can actually put into a group. As they begin to think in terms of the properties of shapes, they will create categories based on properties and their language will indicate that there are many more shapes in the group than those that are physically present. Students may comment, "These shapes have square corners sort of like rectangles," or "These look like boxes that all have square [rectangular] sides."

Constructing and Dissecting Shapes

BLM 27

Students need to freely explore how shapes fit together to form larger shapes and how larger shapes can be made of smaller shapes. Among two-dimensional shapes for these activities, pattern blocks and tangrams are the best known. In a 1999 article, Pierre van Hiele describes an interesting set of tiles he calls the mosaic puzzle (see Figure 8.4). Another excellent tile set for building is a set of triangles cut from squares (isosceles right triangles). Patterns for the mosaic puzzle and tangrams can be found in the Blackline Masters.

Although tangrams are extremely popular, their value begins to diminish in the intermediate grades. (An exception is their use in measuring area. See Chapter 9, p. 262.) Nonetheless, level 0 students do gain experiences with the way that shapes fit together when they solve tangram puzzles. A full-sized outline that will contain exactly all seven tangram pieces can be challenging. The most difficult tangram puzzle is a shape that can be made of all seven pieces but shown to the student in reduced form. (See Figure 8.5.) This latter puzzle format involves proportional reasoning as the student must mentally enlarge the shape in order to create it with the tangrams.

NCTM's *e-Standards* includes a tangram applet (Example 4.4). One form of the applet includes eight figures that can be made using all seven of the pieces. The e-version of tangrams has the advantage of motivation and the fact that you must be much more deliberate in arranging the shapes.

Van Hiele's mosaic puzzle is a bit more challenging than the tangram because six of the seven pieces are different shapes and there are many more different lengths on the various sides. As a result, the mosaic puzzle provides a good alternative at the third or fourth grade to step up the level of construction activities for children who are ready. (See Figure 8.6 on p. 217.) Also notice that there is more variety in the angles found in the mosaic puzzle compared to tangrams and pattern blocks. Angles can and should be classified in comparison to a *right angle* or "square corner." All angles are either right angles, less than right angles (*acute*), or larger than right angles (*obtuse*).

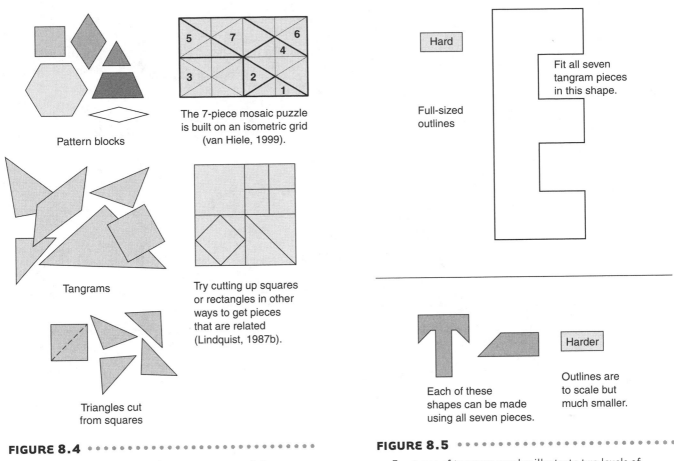

FIGURE 8.4 ●

Activities with tiles can involve an assortment of shapes or can be designed with just one shape.

FIGURE 8.5 ●

Two types of tangram puzzles illustrate two levels of difficulty.

Notice that students can and should make these geometric distinctions without measuring angles or even mentioning degrees. Remember that the names for these angles come after the ideas are developed.

The geoboard is one of the best devices for "drawing" two-dimensional shapes. Here are just a few of the many possible activities appropriate for level 0.

ACTIVITY 8.3

Geoboard Expansion

Prepare small cards on which you have drawn designs that can be made on a geoboard. (See Figure 8.7.) To make the designs, place a sheet of centimeter grid paper beneath the sketch and use the dots as a guide. Students expand the designs onto their geoboards and copy the result on dot paper.

"Geoboard Expansion" has an element of proportional thinking in it just as the tangram puzzles where students work from small designs (Figure 8.5). With the next activity, the concept of congruence can be introduced or reinforced. However, the real value of the activity is in the spatial reasoning with shapes that is developed.

SHAPES AND PROPERTIES ACTIVITIES

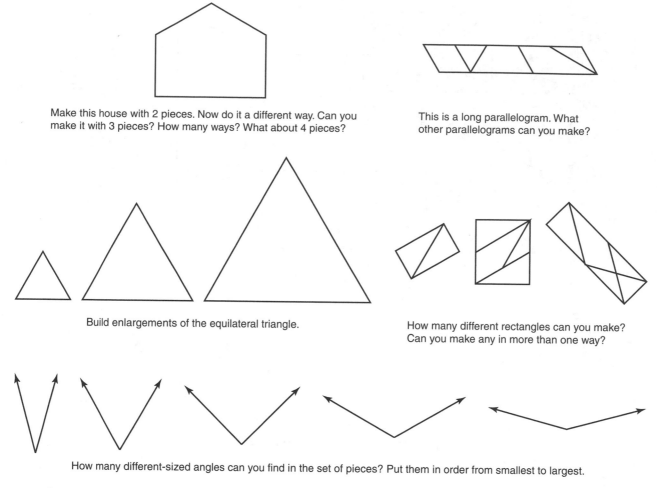

Make this house with 2 pieces. Now do it a different way. Can you make it with 3 pieces? How many ways? What about 4 pieces?

This is a long parallelogram. What other parallelograms can you make?

Build enlargements of the equilateral triangle.

How many different rectangles can you make? Can you make any in more than one way?

How many different-sized angles can you find in the set of pieces? Put them in order from smallest to largest.

FIGURE 8.6 •

A sample of activities with the mosaic puzzle.

Reprinted with permission from van Hiele, P. M. Developing geometric thinking through activities that begin with play. *Teaching Children Mathematics, 5,* 310–316. Copyright © 1999 by the National Council of Teachers of Mathematics. All rights reserved.

Besides pattern cards with and without dots, have children copy <u>real</u> shapes—tables, houses, letters of the alphabet, etc.

FIGURE 8.7 •

Make small cards that can be enlarged on geoboards.

ACTIVITY 8.4

Congruent Parts

Copy a shape from a card and have students subdivide or cut it into smaller shapes on their geoboards. Specify the number of smaller shapes. Also specify whether they are all to be congruent or simply of the same type as shown in Figure 8.8. Depending on the shapes involved, this activity can be made quite easy or relatively challenging.

In the next activity, students are challenged to create shapes that have specific properties. This is a good way to begin to focus on properties of shapes that have some geometric significance. Properties of symmetry are discussed later in this chapter in the section on transformations.

Can You Make It?

Create a collection of challenges. Each challenge describes one or more properties of a shape, and the student challenge is to create a shape with these properties on the geoboard. The list that follows is only a sample. Try combining properties to create new challenges. Also have students create challenges that can be posted for others to make.

- A shape with just one square corner and four sides.
- A shape with two square corners (or three, four, five, or six square corners).
- A shape with a line of symmetry (or two lines of symmetry).
- A shape with rotational symmetry of order 4.
- A shape with two pairs of parallel lines.
- A shape with two pairs of parallel lines and no right angles.

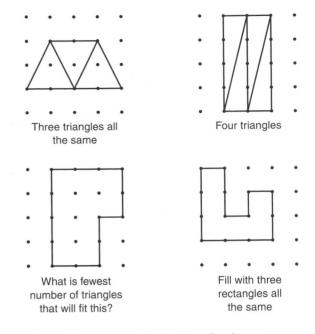

Three triangles all the same

Four triangles

What is fewest number of triangles that will fit this?

Fill with three rectangles all the same

Start with a shape and cut it into smaller shapes. Add special conditions to make the activity challenging.

FIGURE 8.8 •

Subdividing shapes.

If the class keeps track of solutions to the challenges in the last activity, there is an added possibility of creating classes of shapes with certain properties. These may result in definitions of new classes of shapes. The activity can also include impossible tasks. For example, a four-sided shape with exactly three right angles is an impossible shape to make. A triangle with three congruent sides (equilateral) is not possible on a geoboard. Finally, a connection to measurement can be included as well. Tasks can include the requirement of having a particular area or having a particular perimeter, or both. Measurement tasks can be joined with geometric tasks.

Have lots of geoboards available in the classroom. It is better for two or three children to have 10 or 12 boards at a station than for each to have only one. That way, a variety of shapes can be made and compared before they are changed.

You should nearly always have students copy their geoboard designs. Paper copies permit students to create complete sets of drawings that fulfill a particular task. Drawings can be placed on the bulletin board for classification and discussion and sent home to show parents what is happening in geometry. You can use small geoboard recording sheets or centimeter dot grids. Both are found in the Blackline Masters.

BLMs 10, 28

Technology Note

The *e-Standards* provides a very good electronic geoboard. Although found in the K–2 section and entitled "Investigating the Concept of a Triangle," this is actually a great geoboard applet for any grade. It allows you to select and delete bands, and select and delete vertices. The *Geoboard* applet from the National Library of Virtual Manipulatives (http://matti.usu.edu/nlvm/nav/vlibrary.html) is essentially the same but with instant calculation of area and perimeter.

Assorted dot and grid papers provide an alternative to geoboards. Virtually all of the activities suggested for tiles and geoboards can also be done on dot or grid paper. Changing the type of paper changes the activity and provides new opportunity for insight and discovery. The Blackline Masters have a variety of dot and grid paper.

Building three-dimensional shapes is a little more difficult compared with two-dimensional shapes. A variety of commercial materials permit fairly creative construction of geometric solids (for example, 3D Geoshapes, Polydron, and the Zome System). The 3D Geoshapes and Polydron are examples of materials consisting of plastic polygons that snap together to make three-dimensional models. The Zome System is a stick and connector set; skeletal models can be created with a great deal of variation. Zome is probably too difficult to use below the third grade. The following are three highly recommended homemade approaches to skeletal models.

- *Plastic coffee stirrers with pipe cleaners.* Plastic stirrers can be easily cut to different lengths. To connect the corners, cut the pipe cleaners into 2-inch lengths. These are inserted into the ends of the stirrers.

- *Plastic drinking straws with flexible joints.* Cut the straws lengthwise with scissors from the top down to the flexible joint. These slit ends can then be inserted into the uncut bottom ends of other straws, making a strong but flexible joint. Three or more straws are joined in this fashion to form two-dimensional polygons. To make skeletal solids, use tape or wire twist ties to join polygons side to side.

- *Rolled newspaper rods.* Fantastic superlarge skeletons can be built using newspaper and masking tape. Roll three large sheets of newspaper on the diagonal to form a rod. The more tightly the paper is rolled, the less likely the rod is to bend. Secure the roll at the center with a bit of masking tape. The ends of the rods are thin and flexible for about 6 inches where there is less paper. Connect rods by bunching this thin part together and fastening with tape. Use masking tape freely, wrapping it several times around each joint. Additional rods can be joined after two or three are already taped (see Figure 8.9).

With these homemade models, students should compare the rigidity of a triangle with the lack of rigidity of polygons with more than three sides. Point out that triangles

FIGURE 8.9

Large skeletal structures and special shapes can be built with tightly rolled newspaper. Young children can build free-form sculptures. Older children can be challenged to build shapes with specific properties. Overlap the ends about 6 inches to ensure strength.

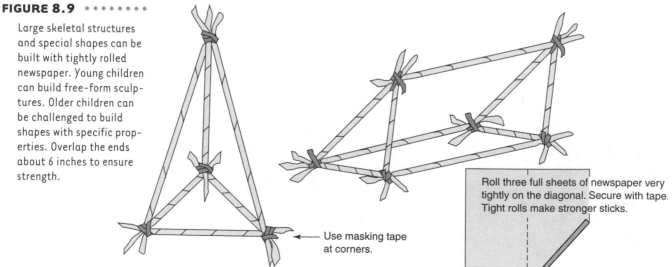

Use masking tape at corners.

Roll three full sheets of newspaper very tightly on the diagonal. Secure with tape. Tight rolls make stronger sticks.

are used in many bridges, in the long booms of construction cranes, in gates, and in the structural parts of buildings. Discuss why this may be so. As children build large skeletal structures, they will find that they need to add diagonal members to form triangles. The more triangles, the less likely their structure will collapse.

The newspaper rod method is exciting because the structures quickly become large. Let students work in groups of four or five. They will soon discover what makes a structure rigid and ideas of balance and form. Older students can be challenged to make more well-defined shapes. (See p. 246.)

Tessellations

A *tessellation* is a tiling of the plane using one or more shapes in a repeated pattern with no holes or gaps. Making tessellations is an artistic way for level 0 and level 1 students to explore patterns in shapes and to see how shapes combine to form other shapes. One-shape or two-shape tessellation activities can vary considerably in difficulty.

Some shapes are easier to tessellate than others (see Figure 8.10). When the shapes can be put together in more than one pattern, both the problem-solving level and the creativity increase. Literally hundreds of shapes can be used as tiles for tessellations.

For their first experience with tessellations, most students will benefit from using actual tiles to create patterns. Simple construction paper tiles can be cut quickly on a paper cutter. Other tiles can be traced onto construction paper and several thicknesses cut at once with scissors. When the tile shape fits on a grid, students will be able to use dot or line grids and plan their tessellations with pencil and paper. To plan a tessellation, use only one color so that the focus is on the spatial relationships. To complete an artistic-looking tessellation, add a color design. Use only two colors with younger children and never more than four. Color designs are also repeated regularly all over the tessellation.

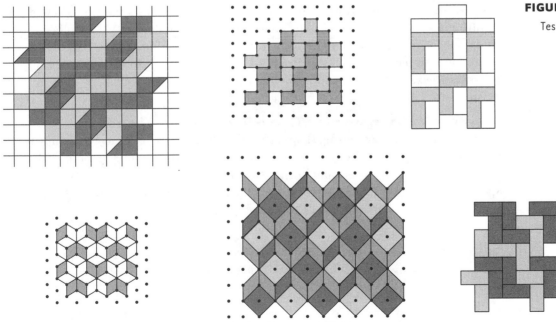

FIGURE 8.10 • • • • • • •

Tessellations.

Tessellations can be drawn on grids or made of construction paper tiles. They are challenging and provide an opportunity for both artistic creativity and spatial reasoning.

Tessellations can be made by gluing paper tiles to large sheets of paper, by drawing them on dot or line grids, or by tracing around a poster board tile. Work from the center out, leaving ragged edges to indicate that the pattern goes on and on.

 Look at the top-left tessellation in Figure 8.10. What single tile (a combination of squares and half squares) made this pattern?

Activities for Level 1 Thinkers

A significant difference between level 1 and level 0 is the object of students' thought. Although students will continue to use models and drawings of shapes, they begin to see these as representatives of classes of shapes. Their understanding of the properties of shapes—such as symmetry, perpendicular and parallel lines, and so on—continues to be refined.

For the sake of clarity, the important definitions of two- and three-dimensional shapes are provided here. You will notice that shape definitions include relationships between and among shapes.

Special Categories of Two-Dimensional Shapes

Table 8.1 lists some important categories of two-dimensional shapes. Examples of these shapes can be found in Figure 8.11 on p. 222.

In the classification of quadrilaterals and parallelograms, the subsets are not all disjoint. For example, a square is a rectangle and a rhombus. All parallelograms are trapezoids, but not all trapezoids are parallelograms.* Children at level 1 have difficulty seeing this type of subrelationship. They may quite correctly list all the properties of a square, a rhombus, and a rectangle and still identify a square as a "nonrhombus" or a "nonrectangle." Is it wrong for students to refer to subgroups as disjoint sets? By fourth or fifth grade, it is only wrong to encourage such thinking. Burger (1985) points out that upper elementary students correctly use such classification schemes in other contexts. For example, individual students in a class can belong to more than one club. A square is an example of a quadrilateral that belongs to two other clubs.

Special Categories of Three-Dimensional Shapes

Important and interesting shapes and relationships also exist in three dimensions. Table 8.2 on p. 223 describes classifications of solids. Figure 8.12 on p. 224 shows examples of cylinders and prisms. Note that prisms are defined here as a special category of cylinder—a cylinder with a polygon for a base. Figure 8.13 on p. 224 shows a similar grouping of cones and pyramids.

 Explain the following: Prisms are to cylinders as pyramids are to cones. How is this relationship helpful in learning volume formulas?

---

*Some definitions of trapezoid specify *only one* pair of parallel sides, in which case parallelograms would not be trapezoids. The University of Chicago School Mathematics Project (UCSMP) uses the "at least one pair" definition, meaning that parallelograms and rectangles are trapezoids.

Chapter 8   GEOMETRIC THINKING AND GEOMETRIC CONCEPTS

TABLE 8.1 •••

Categories of Two-Dimensional Shapes

Shape	Description
Simple Closed Curves	
Concave, convex	An intuitive definition of *concave* might be "having a dent in it." If a simple closed curve is not concave, it is *convex*. A more precise definition of *concave* may be interesting to explore with older students.
Symmetrical, nonsymmetrical	Shapes may have one or more lines of symmetry and may or may not have rotational symmetry. These concepts will require more detailed investigation.
Polygons	Simple closed curves with all straight sides.
Concave, convex	
Symmetrical, nonsymmetrical	
Regular	All sides and all angles are congruent.
Triangles	
Triangles	Polygons with exactly three sides.
Classified by sides	
Equilateral	All sides are congruent.
Isosceles	At least two sides are congruent.
Scalene	No two sides are congruent.
Classified by angles	
Right	Has a right angle.
Acute	All angles are smaller than a right angle.
Obtuse	One angle is larger than a right angle.
Convex Quadrilaterals	
Convex quadrilaterals	Convex polygons with exactly four sides.
Kite	Two opposing pairs of congruent adjacent sides.
Trapezoid	At least one pair of parallel sides.
Isosceles trapezoid	A pair of opposite sides is congruent.
Parallelogram	Two pairs of parallel sides.
Rectangle	Parallelogram with a right angle.
Rhombus	Parallelogram with all sides congruent.
Square	Parallelogram with a right angle and all sides congruent.

Many textbooks define cylinders strictly as circular cylinders. These books do not have special names for other cylinders. Under that definition, the prism is not a special case of a cylinder. This points to the fact that definitions are conventions, and not all conventions are universally agreed upon. If you look at the development of the volume formulas in Chapter 9, you will see that the more inclusive definition of cylinders and cones given here allows one formula for any type of cylinder—hence, prisms—with a similar statement that is true for cones and pyramids.

FIGURE 8.11 • • • • • • • •

Classification of two-dimensional shapes.

Simple Closed Curves

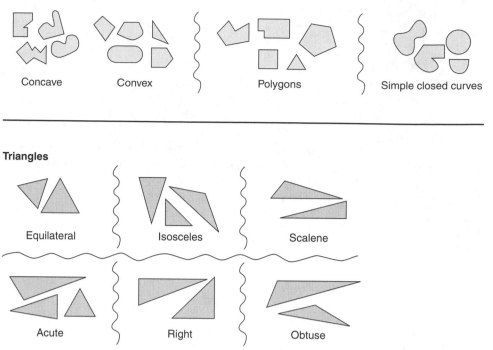

Triangles

Convex Quadrilaterals

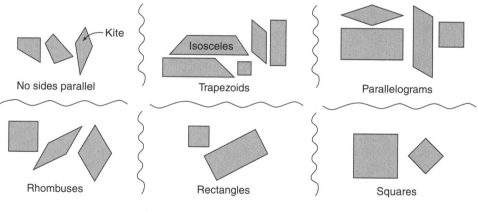

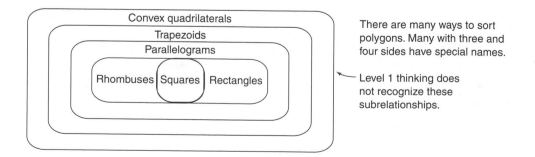

There are many ways to sort polygons. Many with three and four sides have special names.

Level 1 thinking does not recognize these subrelationships.

TABLE 8.2 •

Categories of Three-Dimensional Shapes

Shape	Description
Sorted by Edges and Vertices	
Sphere and "egglike" shapes	Shapes with no *edges* and no *vertices* (corners). Shapes with *edges* but no *vertices* (e.g., a flying saucer). Shapes with *vertices* but no *edges* (e.g., a football).
Sorted by Faces and Surfaces	
Polyhedron	Shapes made of all faces (a *face* is a flat surface of a solid). If all surfaces are faces, all the edges will be straight lines. Some combination of faces and rounded surfaces (cylinders are examples, but this is not a definition of a cylinder). Shapes with curved surfaces. Shapes with and without edges and with and without vertices. Faces can be parallel. Parallel faces lie in places that never intersect.
Cylinders	
Cylinder	Two congruent, parallel faces called *bases*. Lines joining corresponding points on the two bases are always parallel. These parallel lines are called *elements* of the cylinder.
Right cylinder	A cylinder with elements perpendicular to the bases. A cylinder that is not a right cylinder is an *oblique cylinder*.
Prism	A cylinder with polygons for bases. All prisms are special cases of cylinders.
Rectangular prism	A cylinder with rectangles for bases.
Cube	A square prism with square sides.
Cones	
Cone	A solid with exactly one face and a vertex that is not on the face. Straight lines (elements) can be drawn from any point on the edge of the base to the vertex. The base may be any shape at all. The vertex need not be directly over the base.
Circular cone	Cone with a circular base.
Pyramid	Cone with a polygon for a base. All faces joining the vertex are triangles. Pyramids are named by the shape of the base: *triangular* pyramid, *square* pyramid, *octagonal* pyramid, and so on. All pyramids are special cases of cones.

FIGURE 8.12 • • • • • • •
Cylinders and prisms.

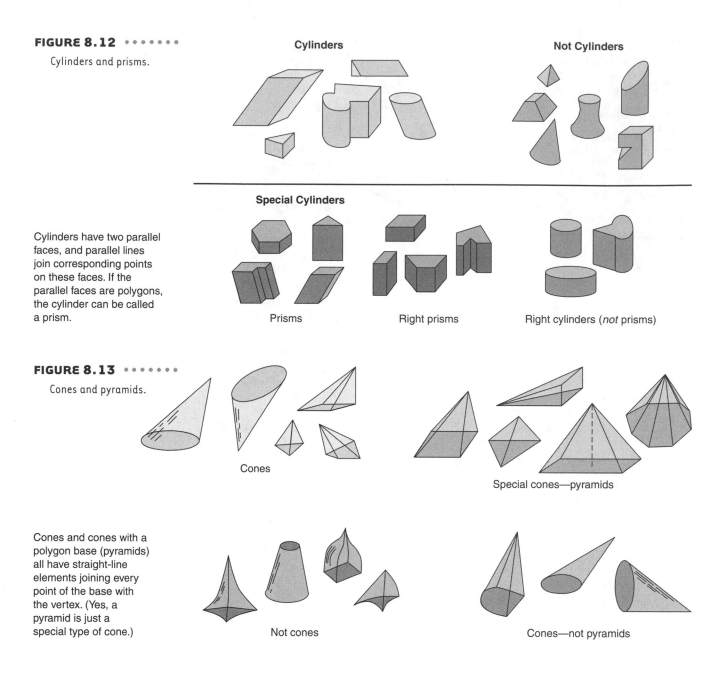

Cylinders have two parallel faces, and parallel lines join corresponding points on these faces. If the parallel faces are polygons, the cylinder can be called a prism.

Cylinders

Not Cylinders

Special Cylinders

Prisms   Right prisms   Right cylinders (*not* prisms)

FIGURE 8.13 • • • • • • •
Cones and pyramids.

Cones   Special cones—pyramids

Cones and cones with a polygon base (pyramids) all have straight-line elements joining every point of the base with the vertex. (Yes, a pyramid is just a special type of cone.)

Not cones   Cones—not pyramids

Sorting and Classifying Activities

The next activity provides a good method when you want to introduce a category of shapes.

ACTIVITY 8.6

Mystery Definition

Use the overhead or chalkboard to conduct activities such as the example in Figure 8.14. For your first collection be certain that you have allowed for all possible variables. In Figure 8.14, for example, a square is included in the set of rhombi. Similarly, choose nonexamples to be as close to the positive examples as is necessary to help with an accurate definition. The third or mixed set should also include those nonexamples with which students are most likely to be confused.

Rather than confirm the choice of shapes in the third set, students should write an explanation for their choice.

The value of the "Mystery Definition" approach is that students develop ideas and definitions based on their own concept development. After their definitions have been discussed and compared, you can offer the usual "book" definition for the sake of clarity.

For defining types or categories of triangles, the next activity is especially good and uses a different approach.

ACTIVITY 8.7

Triangle Sort

Make copies of the Assorted Triangles sheet found in the Blackline Masters. Note the examples of right, acute, and obtuse triangles; examples of equilateral, isosceles, and scalene triangles; and triangles that represent every possible combination of these categories. Have students cut them out. The task is to sort the entire collection into three groups so that no triangle belongs to two groups. When this is done and descriptions of the groupings have been written, students should then find a second criterion for creating three different groupings. Students may need a hint to look only at angle sizes or only at the issue of congruent sides, but hold these hints if you can.

"Triangle Sort" results in definitions of the six different types of triangles without having to list these definitions on the board and have students memorize them. As a follow-up activity, make a chart such as the one shown here. Challenge students to sketch a triangle in each of the nine cells.

All of these have something in common.

None of these has it.

Which of these have it?

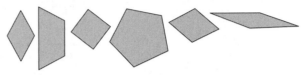

The name of a property is not necessary for it to be understood. It requires more careful observation of properties to discover what shapes have in common.

FIGURE 8.14 •

All of these, none of these: a mystery definition.

BLM 29

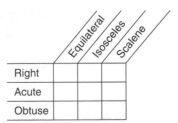

	Equilateral	Isosceles	Scalene
Right			
Acute			
Obtuse			

STOP Of the nine cells in the chart, two of them are impossible to fill. Can you tell which ones and why?

Quadrilaterals (polygons with four sides) are an especially rich source of investigations. For the following activity, students should be familiar with the concepts of right, obtuse, and acute angles, congruence of line segments, and symmetry (line and rotational).

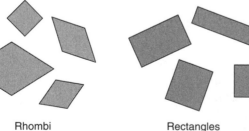

ACTIVITY 8.8

Property Lists for Quadrilaterals

Prepare worksheets for parallelograms, rhombi, rectangles, and squares. (See the Blackline Masters.) On each sheet are three or four examples of that category of shape. Examples are illustrated in Figure 8.15. Assign students working in groups of three or four to one type of quadrilateral. Their task is to list as many properties as they can. Each property listed must be applicable to all of the shapes on their sheet. They will need a simple index card to check right angles, to compare side lengths, and to draw straight lines. Mirrors (to check line symmetry) and tracing paper (for angle congruence and rotational symmetry) are also useful tools. Encourage students to use the words "at least" when describing how many of something: for example, "rectangles have at least two lines of symmetry," since squares—included in the rectangles—have four.

Have students prepare their property lists under these headings: Sides, Angles, Diagonals, and Symmetries. Groups then share their lists with the class and eventually a class list for each shape will be developed.

This last activity may take two or three days. Share lists beginning with parallelograms, then rhombi, then rectangles, and finally squares. Have one group present its list. Then others who worked on the same shape should add to or subtract from it. The class must agree with everything that is put on the list. As new relationships come up in this presentation-and-discussion period, you can introduce proper terminology. For example, if two diagonals intersect in a square corner, then they are *perpendicular*. Other terms such as *parallel, congruent, bisect, midpoint,* and so on can be clarified as you help students write their descriptions. This is also a good time to introduce symbols such as ≅ for "congruent" or ‖ for "parallel."

As an extension, repeat Activity 8.8 using kites and trapezoids. "Property Lists for Quadrilaterals" has some important follow-ups that are described in the section on level 2 activities (see Activities 8.11 and 8.12, pp. 230–231). Furthermore, similar activities can be used to introduce three-dimensional shape definitions.

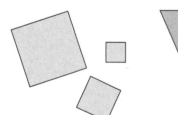

Squares   Parallelograms

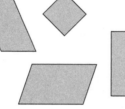

Rhombi   Rectangles

FIGURE 8.15 •

Shapes for "Property Lists for Quadrilaterals" worksheets can be found in the Blackline Masters.

Construction Activities

Students building or drawing shapes continues to be important at level 1. Dynamic geometry software (*Geometer's Sketchpad, The Geometry Inventor,* and *Cabri*) dramatically enhances the exploration of shapes at this level.

In the "Property Lists" activity (Activity 8.8), students examine the diagonals of various classes of quadrilaterals. If that activity has not been done already, the following exploration is very interesting. Rather than beginning with the shapes, it begins with the diagonals.

ACTIVITY 8.9

Diagonal Strips

For this activity, students need three strips of tagboard about 2 cm wide. Two should be the same length (about 30 cm) and the third somewhat shorter (about 20 cm). Punch nine holes equally spaced along the strip. (Punch a hole near each end. Divide the distance between the holes by 8. This will be the distance between the remaining holes.) Use a brass fastener to join two strips. A quadrilateral is formed by joining the four end holes as shown in Figure 8.16. Provide students with the list of possible relationships for angles, lengths, and ratios of parts. Their task is to use the strips to determine the properties of diagonals that will produce different quadrilaterals. The strips are there to help in the exploration. Students may want to make drawings on dot grids to test the various hypotheses.

EXPANDED LESSON

(pages 250–251)
A complete lesson plan based on "Diagonal Strips" can be found at the end of this chapter.

Every type of quadrilateral can be uniquely described in terms of its diagonals using only the conditions of length, ratio of parts, and whether or not they are perpendicular. Some students will work with the diagonal relationships to see what shapes can be made. Others will begin with examples of the shapes and observe the diagonal relationships. A dynamic geometry program such as *The Geometer's Sketchpad* is an excellent vehicle for this investigation.

Circles

Many interesting relationships can be observed between measures of different parts of the circle. Among the most astounding and important is the ratio between measures of the circumference and the diameter.

STOP **True or False: All circles are similar. Explain.**

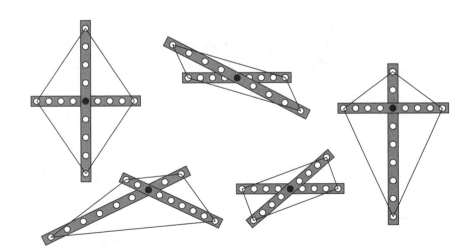

FIGURE 8.16 • • • • • • • • •

Diagonals of quadrilaterals.

Quadrilaterals can be determined by their diagonals. Consider the length of each, where they cross, and the angles between them. What conditions will produce parallelograms? Rectangles? Rhombi? Challenge: What properties will produce a nonisosceles trapezoid?

Discovering Pi

Have groups of students carefully measure the circumference and diameter of many different circles. Each group measures different circles.

Measure both the circumference and diameter of circular items such as jar lids, tubes, cans, and wastebaskets. To measure circumference, wrap string once around the object and then measure that length of string.

Also measure large circles marked on gym floors and playgrounds. Use a trundle wheel or rope to measure the circumference.

Collect measures of circumference and diameter from all groups and enter them in a table. Ratios of the circumference to the diameter should also be computed for each circle. A scatter plot of the data should be made with the horizontal axis representing diameters and the vertical axis circumferences.

Most ratios should be in the neighborhood of 3.1 or 3.2. The scatter plot should approximate a straight line through the origin. The exact ratio is an irrational number, about 3.14159, represented by the Greek letter π (pi).

What is most important in Activity 8.10 is that students develop a clear understanding of π as the ratio of circumference to diameter in any circle. The quantity π is not some strange number that appears in math formulas; it is a naturally occurring and universal ratio.

As students begin to do more than build with geometric "blocks" (tangrams, pattern blocks, grid drawing, etc.), the computer begins to offer powerful tools for explorations.

Dynamic Geometry Software

In a dynamic geometry program, points, lines, and geometric figures are easily constructed on the computer using only the mouse. Once drawn, the geometric objects can be moved about and manipulated in endless variety. Distances, lengths, areas, angles, slopes, and perimeters can be measured. As the figures are changed, the measurements update instantly.

Lines can be drawn perpendicular or parallel to other lines or segments. Angles and segments can be drawn congruent to other angles and segments. A point can be placed at the midpoint of a segment. A figure can be produced that is a reflection, rotation, or dilation of another figure. The most significant thing is that when a geometric object is created with a particular relationship to another, that relationship is maintained no matter how either object is moved or changed.

Three of the best-known dynamic geometry programs are *The Geometer's Sketchpad* (Key Curriculum Press, 2001), *Geometry Inventor* (Riverdeep, 1996), and *Cabri Geometry II* (Texas Instruments, 1998). Although each operates somewhat differently, they are sufficiently alike that separate descriptions are not required here. Originally designed for high school students, all can be used profitably and should be used starting about grade 4.

Dynamic Geometry Examples

To appreciate the potential (and the fun) of dynamic geometry software, you really need to experience it on a computer. In the meantime, an example is offered here in an attempt to illustrate how these programs work.

In Figure 8.17, the midpoints of a freely drawn quadrilateral ABCD have been joined. The diagonals of the resulting quadrilateral (EFGH) are also drawn and mea-

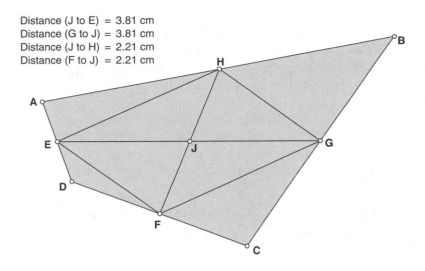

Distance (J to E) = 3.81 cm
Distance (G to J) = 3.81 cm
Distance (J to H) = 2.21 cm
Distance (F to J) = 2.21 cm

sured. No matter how the points A, B, C, and D are dragged around the screen, even inverting the quadrilateral, the other lines will maintain the same relationships (joining midpoints and diagonals), and the measurements will be instantly updated on the screen.

Remember that at level 1, the objects of thought are *classes* of shapes. In a dynamic geometry program, if a quadrilateral is drawn, only one shape is observed, as would be the case on paper or on a geoboard. But now that quadrilateral can be stretched and altered in endless ways. Students actually explore not one shape but an enormous number of examples from that class of shapes. If a property does not change when the figure changes, the property is attributable to the *class* of shapes rather than any particular shape.

Another example is shown in Figure 8.18 showing how *Sketchpad* can be used to investigate quadrilaterals starting with the diagonals. The directions for creating the

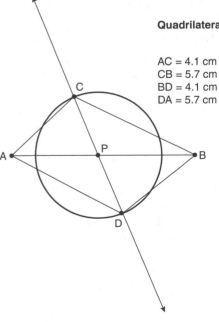

Quadrilaterals with diagonals that bisect each other.

AC = 4.1 cm
CB = 5.7 cm
BD = 4.1 cm
DA = 5.7 cm

Draw segment AB with midpoint P.

Construct circle with center P and control point C.

Construct line through C and P and then construct intersection point D.

Construct ABCD and measure each side.

Drag C. What different quadrilaterals can you make?

What is true about the diagonals of every shape you make?

What can you find out about the diagonals of the shapes you make?

FIGURE 8.18 • • • • • • • • • • • • • • • •

With *The Geometer's Sketchpad* students can construct two line segments that will always bisect each other. When the endpoints are joined, the resulting quadrilateral will always be of the same class, regardless of how points A, B, C, and D are moved around.

sketch are included and can be done quite simply with minimal experience with the software. By creating the drawing in this manner, the diagonals of ABCD will always bisect each other no matter how the drawing is altered. By dragging point C around, ABCD can be made into a parallelogram, rectangle, rhombus, and square. But for each of these figures, additional information about the diagonals can be determined by looking at the drawing.

Dynamic geometry programs are also powerful for investigating concepts of symmetry and transformations (slides, flips, and turns). The publishers of these programs provide excellent activities that are appropriate for level 1 investigations. Many activities are included with the software, and others are found in supplemental publications.

 Why can't the drawing in Figure 8.18 be transformed into a kite or a trapezoid that is not also a parallelogram?

Activities for Level 2 Thinkers

The hallmark of level 2 activities is the inclusion of informal logical reasoning. Most fourth- and fifth-grade students will still be at level 1 or even at level 0. However, as students develop an understanding of various geometric properties and attach these properties to important categories of shapes, it is time—even at this grade level—to begin to encourage conjecture and to explore informal deductive arguments. Do not be afraid to explore some of the activities at this level just because you are not teaching middle school.

Definitions and Proofs

To really understand the difference between levels 1 and 2 of the van Hiele theory, contrast the required thinking in the level 1 activity "Property Lists for Quadrilaterals" (Activity 8.8, p. 226) and the following activity that is designed as a follow-up to that one.

ACTIVITY 8.11

Minimal Defining Lists

(This activity must be done as a follow-up to the "Property Lists for Quadrilaterals" activity on p. 226.) Once property lists for the parallelogram, rhombus, rectangle, and square (and possibly the kite and trapezoid) have been agreed upon by the class, have these lists posted or type them up and duplicate them. In groups, the task is to find "minimal defining lists," or MDLs, for each shape. An MDL is a subset of the properties for a shape that is "defining" and "minimal." "Defining" here means that any shape that has all the properties on the MDL *must* be that shape. Thus, an MDL for a square will guarantee that you have a square. "Minimal" means that if any single property is removed from the list it is no longer defining. For example, one MDL for a square is a quadrilateral with four congruent sides and one right angle. Students should attempt to find at least two or three MDLs for their shape. A proposed list can be challenged as either not minimal or not defining. A list is not minimal if a property can be removed yet the list still defines the shape. A list is not defining if a counterexample—a shape other than one being described—can be produced using only the properties on the list.

The parallelogram, rhombus, rectangle, and square each have at least four MDLs. One of the most interesting MDLs for each shape consists only of the properties of its diagonals. For example, a quadrilateral with diagonals that bisect each other and are perpendicular (intersect at right angles) is a rhombus. Several MDLs have only one property. For example, a parallelogram is a quadrilateral with rotational symmetry of at least order 2.

The MDL activity is worth some further discussion. First, notice the logic component. "If a quadrilateral has these properties, *then* it must be a square." Logic is also involved in disproving a faulty list. A second feature is the opportunity to discuss what constitutes a definition. In fact, any MDL could be the definition of the shape. The definitions we usually use are MDLs that have been chosen probably due to the ease with which we can understand them. A quadrilateral with diagonals that bisect each other does not immediately call to mind a parallelogram. Recall that when students created their property lists, no definition was given, only a collection of shapes and a label. Theoretically, the lists could have been created without ever having heard of these shapes. Finally, notice that the object of students' thinking in this activity is clearly on properties, not on shapes. The products of the activity are relationships among the properties.

The next activity is also a good follow-up to the "Property Lists for Quadrilaterals" activity, although it is not restricted to quadrilaterals and can include three-dimensional shapes as well. Notice again the logic involved.

ACTIVITY 8.12

True or False?

Prepare statements of the following forms: "If it is a _____, then it is also a _____." "All are _____." "Some are _____." A few examples are suggested here but numerous possibilities exist.

- If it is a square, then it is a rhombus.
- All squares are rectangles.
- Some parallelograms are rectangles.
- All parallelograms have congruent diagonals.
- If it has exactly two lines of symmetry, it must be a quadrilateral.
- If it is a cylinder, then it is a prism.
- All prisms have a plane of symmetry.
- All pyramids have square bases.
- If a prism has a plane of symmetry, then it is a right prism.

The task is to decide if the statements are true or false and to present an argument to support the decision. Four or five true-or-false statements will make a good lesson. Once this format is understood, let students challenge their classmates by making their own lists of five statements. Each list should have at least one true statement and one false statement. Use the students' lists in subsequent lessons.

STOP **Use the property list for squares and rectangles to prove "All squares are rectangles." Notice that you must use logical reasoning to understand this statement. It does little good to simply force it on students who are not ready to develop the relationship.**

SHAPES AND PROPERTIES ACTIVITIES

If a student makes a statement about a geometric situation the class is exploring, it can be written on the board with a question mark as a *conjecture,* a statement whose truth has not yet been determined. You can ask, "Is it true? Always? Can we prove it? Can we find a counterexample?" Reasonable deductive arguments can be forged out of discussions.

The Pythagorean Relationship

The *Pythagorean relationship* is so important that it deserves some special attention, although it is generally not found in traditional curricula until middle school. In geometric terms, this relationship states that if a square is constructed on each side of a right triangle, the areas of the two smaller squares will together equal the area of the square on the longest side, the hypotenuse. To help students discover this relationship, consider the following activity.

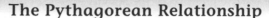

ACTIVITY 8.13

The Pythagorean Relationship

Have students draw a right triangle on centimeter grid paper. Assign each student a different triangle by specifying the lengths of the two legs. Students are to draw a square on each leg and the hypotenuse and find the area of all three squares. (For the square on the hypotenuse, the exact area can be found by making each of the sides the diagonal of a rectangle. See Figure 8.19.) Make a table of the area data (Sq. on leg 1, Sq. on leg 2, Sq. on hyp.), and ask students to look for a relationship between the squares.

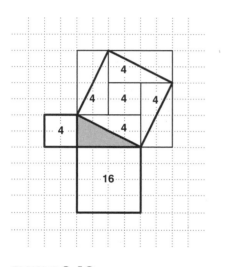

FIGURE 8.19 • • • • • • • • • • • •

The Pythagorean relationship. Note that if drawn on a grid, the area of all squares is easily determined. Here 4 + 16 = area of the square on the hypotenuse.

Activity 8.13 establishes the Pythagorean relationship. What about a proof? Although there are over 100 proofs of the Pythagorean relationship, most fifth-grade students will probably not be able to appreciate most of them. The two drawings in Figure 8.20 are taken from the book *Proofs without Words* (Nelson, 1993). The shapes in the drawing on the left can be arranged to fit the drawing on the right. No algebra or formulas are required to show that the area of the two squares on the left must be the same as the large square on the right.

 Use the two drawings in Figure 8.20 to create a proof of the Pythagorean relationship.

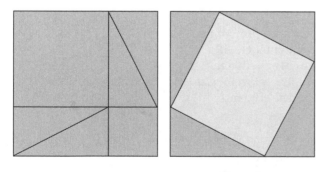

FIGURE 8.20 •

A proof of the Pythagorean relationship. The two drawings are a "proof without words." Can you supply the words?

Technology Note ———

The NCTM *e-Standards* includes a dynamic proof without words that is worth sharing with your students (Applet 6.5). Because it requires knowing that parallelograms and rectangles with the same base and height have the same area (see Chapter 9), it is also a good review.

Transformation Activities

Transformations are also called "rigid motions"—movements that do not change the size or shape of the object moved. Usually, three transformations are discussed: *translations* or slides, *reflections* or flips, and *rotations* or turns. Interestingly, the study of symmetry is also included under the study of transformations. Do you know why?

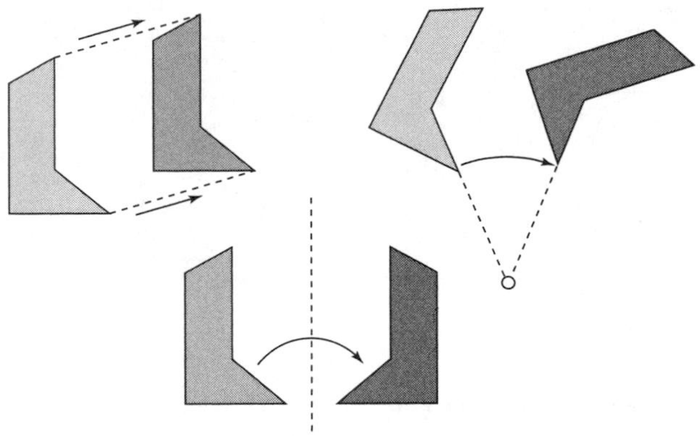

Slides, Flips, and Turns

At the beginning level, the terms *slide, flip,* and *turn* are adequate. The goal is to help students recognize and apply these transformations. You can use a nonsymmetric shape on the overhead to introduce these terms (see Figure 8.21). Most textbooks use the center of a shape as the point of rotation and restrict reflections to those through horizontal and vertical lines through the center. These restrictions are not necessary and may even be misleading.

The Motion Man described in the next activity can also be used as a way of introducing the meanings of slides, flips, and turns to your class. In the activity, rotations are restricted to $\frac{1}{4}$, $\frac{1}{2}$, and $\frac{3}{4}$ turns in a clockwise direction. The center of the turn will be the center of the figure. Reflections will be flips over vertical or horizontal lines. These restrictions are for simplicity. In the general case, the center of rotation can be anywhere on or off of the figure. Lines of reflection can also be anywhere.

FIGURE 8.21 •

Translation (slide), reflection (flip), rotation (turn).

ACTIVITY 8.14

Motion Man

Using the Motion Man Blackline Masters, make copies of the first Motion Man and then copy the mirror image on the backs of these copies. Experiment first. You want the back image to match the front image when held to the light. Cut off the excess paper to leave a square. Give each student a Motion Man.

Demonstrate each of the possible motions. A slide is simply that. The figure does not rotate or turn over. Demonstrate $\frac{1}{4}$, $\frac{1}{2}$, and $\frac{3}{4}$ turns. Emphasize that only clockwise turns will be used for this activity. Similarly, demonstrate a horizontal flip (top goes to bottom) and a vertical flip (left goes to right). Practice by having everyone start with his or her Motion Man in the same orientation. As you announce one of the moves, students slide, flip, or turn Motion Man accordingly.

Then display two Motion Men side by side in any orientation. The task is to decide what motion or combination of motions will get the man on the left to match the man on the right. Students use their own man to work out a solution. Test the solutions that students offer. If both men are in the same position, call that a slide. (If you allow for each of the two diagonal flips as well, the Motion Man can assume any new position in one move.)

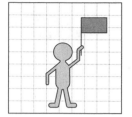
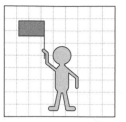

FIGURE 8.22 •

The Motion Man is printed back to back. Use to show slides, flips, and turns. (See Blackline Masters.)

BLMs 34, 35

Begin with the Motion Man in the left position shown in Figure 8.22. Now place a second Motion Man next to the first in any position at all. Will it take one or more than one move (transformation) to get from the first to the second Motion Man? Can you describe all of the positions that require more than one move? Are there any positions that require more than two moves?

At first, students will be confused when they can't get their Motion Man into the new position with one move. This causes an excellent problem. Don't be too quick to suggest that it may take two moves. If you allow for flips across each of the two diagonals as well as vertical and horizontal flips, Motion Man can assume any position in exactly one move. This provides a challenge for students. Two students begin with their Motion Man figures in the same position. One student then changes his or her Motion Man and challenges the other student to say what motion is required to make the two Motion Men match. The solution is then tested and the roles reversed.

Line and Rotational Symmetry

If a shape can be folded on a line so that the two halves match, then it is said to have *line symmetry* (or mirror symmetry). Notice that the fold line is actually a line of reflection—the portion of the shape on one side of the line is reflected onto the other side. That is the connection between line symmetry and transformations.

Most of your students will have experienced line symmetry. One way to review this concept is to show examples and nonexamples using an all-of-these/none-of-these approach as in Figure 8.14 on p. 225. Another approach that may be novel for them is to use mirrors. When you place a mirror on a picture or design so that the mirror is perpendicular to the table, you see a shape with symmetry when you look in the mirror.

Here is an activity with line symmetry.

ACTIVITY 8.15

Pattern Block Mirror Symmetry

Students need a plain sheet of paper with a straight line through the middle. Using about six to eight pattern blocks, students make a design completely on one side of the line that touches the line in some way. The task is to make the mirror image of their design on the other side of the line. When finished, they use a mirror to check their work. They place the mirror on the line and look into it from the side of the original design. With the mirror in place they should see exactly the same image as they see when they lift the mirror. You can also challenge them to make designs with more than one line of symmetry.

Building symmetrical designs with pattern blocks tends to be easier if the line is "pointing" at the student, that is, with a left and a right side. With the line oriented horizontally or diagonally, the task is harder.

The same task can be done with a geoboard. First, stretch a band down the center or from corner to corner. Make a design on one side of the line and its mirror image on the other. Check with a mirror. This can also be done on either isometric or rectangular dot grids as described in the following activity.

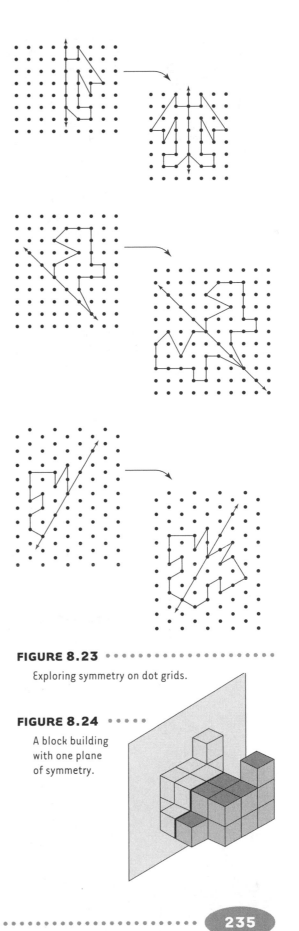

FIGURE 8.23 • • • • • • • • • • • • • • • •

Exploring symmetry on dot grids.

ACTIVITY 8.16

Dot Grid Line Symmetry

For this activity, students need to use either isometric or rectangular dot grid paper. Students should draw a line through several dots. This line can be horizontal, vertical, or skewed. Students should make a design completely on one side of the drawn line that touches the line in some way (see the left-hand drawings in Figure 8.23). Now the task is to make the mirror image of their design on the other side of the line. (Students can exchange designs and make the mirror image of each other's design.) When finished, they can use a mirror to check their work. They place the mirror on the line and look into it from the side of the original design. With the mirror in place, they should see exactly the same image as they see when they lift the mirror. You can also challenge them to make designs with more than one line of symmetry.

A plane of symmetry in three dimensions is analogous to a line of symmetry in two dimensions. Figure 8.24 illustrates a shape built with cubes that has a plane of symmetry.

 A cube has nine different planes of symmetry. Get a cube and try to find them all.

ACTIVITY 8.17

Plane Symmetry Buildings

With cubes, build a building that has a plane of symmetry. If the plane of symmetry goes between cubes, slice the shape by separating the building into two symmetrical parts. Try making buildings with two or three planes of symmetry. Build various prisms. Do not forget that a plane can slice diagonally through the blocks.

A shape has *rotational symmetry* if it can be rotated about a point and land in a position exactly matching the one in which it began. A square has rotational symmetry as does an equilateral triangle.

FIGURE 8.24 • • • • • •

A block building with one plane of symmetry.

FIGURE 8.25 •

This parallelogram fits in its box two ways without flipping it over. Therefore, it has rotational symmetry of order 2.

A good way to understand rotational symmetry is to take a shape with rotational symmetry, such as a square, and trace around it on a piece of paper. Call this tracing the shape's "box." The order of rotational symmetry will be the number of ways that the shape can fit into its box without flipping it over. A square has rotational symmetry of *order* 4, whereas an equilateral triangle has rotational symmetry of *order* 3. The parallelogram in Figure 8.25 has rotational symmetry of order 2. Some books would call order 2 symmetry "180-degree symmetry." The degrees refer to the smallest angle of rotation required before the shape matches itself or fits into its box. A square has 90-degree rotational symmetry.

ACTIVITY 8.18

Pattern Block Rotational Symmetry

Have students construct designs with pattern blocks with different rotational symmetries. They should be able to make designs with order 2, 3, 4, 6, or 12 rotational symmetry. Which of the designs have mirror symmetry as well?

Rotational symmetry in the plane (also referred to as *point symmetry*) has an analogous counterpart in three dimensions. Whereas a figure in a plane is rotated about a point, a three-dimensional figure is rotated about a line. This line is called an *axis of symmetry*. As a solid with rotational symmetry revolves around an axis of symmetry, it will occupy the same position in space (its "box") but in different orientations. A solid can have more than one axis of rotation. For each axis of symmetry, there is a corresponding order of rotational symmetry. A regular square pyramid has only one axis of symmetry that runs through the tip of the pyramid and the center of the square. A cube, by contrast, has a total of 13 axes of symmetry: three (through opposite faces) of order 4, four (through diagonally opposite vertices) of order 3, and six (through midpoints of diagonally opposite edges) of order 2.

ACTIVITY 8.19

Find the Spin Lines

Give students a solid shape that has one or more axes of rotational symmetry. Color or label each face of the solid to help keep track. The task is to find all axes of rotational symmetry (spin lines) and determine the order of rotational symmetry for each. Suggest that students use one finger of each hand to hold the solid at the two points where the axis of symmetry emerges. A partner can then slowly turn the solid, and both can decide when the solid is again "in its box"—that is, in the same space it was in originally (see Figure 8.26).

Composition of Transformations

One transformation can be followed by another. For example, a figure can be reflected over a line, and then that figure can be rotated about a point. A combination of two or more transformations is called a *composition*.

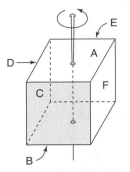

With A on top, the cube fits in its "box" four ways. Through this axis, the order of rotational symmetry is order 4.

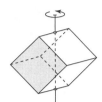

These two axes also have rotational symmetry of order 4.

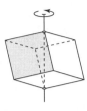

FIGURE 8.26 • • • • • • • • • • • • •

Rotations of a cube.

Edge-to-edge axes each have symmetry of order 2. How many are there?

If the axis is corner to opposite corner, what is the order of symmetry? How many of these axes are there?

The idea of a one transformation followed by another is not a difficult concept. Trying to keep track of the individual transformations can be a bit challenging. As we will see later in this chapter, the use of a coordinate grid is a good approach.

Technology Note

In NCTM's *e-Standards*, "Using Congruence, Similarity, and Symmetry" (Applet 6.4) is one of the best examples of a simple yet valuable interactive applet. In the first part of the applet, students explore all three rigid transformations. In the second part, a transformation is shown as completed and the student uses a guess-and-check procedure to determine what transformation was done. When the original shape is either moved or changed on the screen, the image moves accordingly providing hints to the transformation (slide, flip, or turn) that was used. In the last two parts of this applet, students can explore compositions of reflections and then other compositions up to three transformations. This applet is strongly recommended.

Another vivid illustration of slides, flips, and turns is found in the dynamic geometry programs such as *The Geometer's Sketchpad*. These programs will also allow you to create compositions of transformations. At this level, however, students will need considerable guidance to create the compositions.

Tessellations Revisited

Either by using transformations or by combining compatible polygons, students can create tessellations that are artistic and quite complex.

The Dutch artist M. C. Escher is well known for his tessellations, where the tiles are very intricate and often take the shape of things like birds, horses, angels, or lizards.

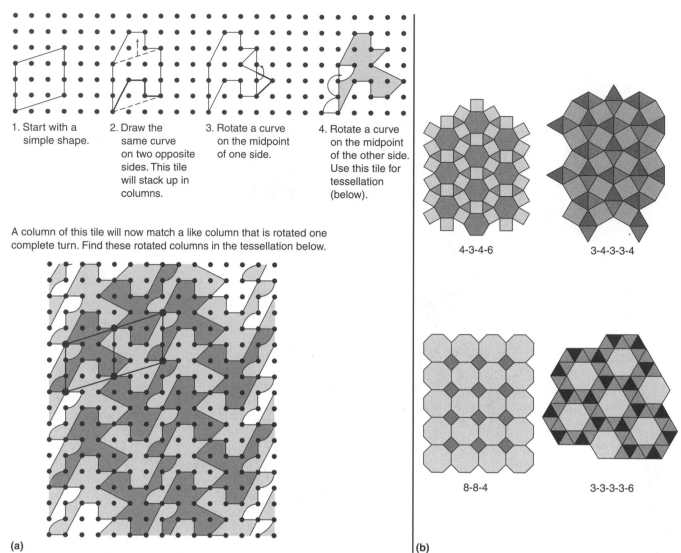

1. Start with a simple shape.

2. Draw the same curve on two opposite sides. This tile will stack up in columns.

3. Rotate a curve on the midpoint of one side.

4. Rotate a curve on the midpoint of the other side. Use this tile for tessellation (below).

A column of this tile will now match a like column that is rotated one complete turn. Find these rotated columns in the tessellation below.

4-3-4-6

3-4-3-3-4

8-8-4

3-3-3-3-6

(a)

(b)

FIGURE 8.27 ● ● ● ● ● ● ●

(a) One of many ways to create an Escher-type tessellation. (b) Examples of semiregular tessellations.

Escher took a simple shape such as a triangle, parallelogram, or hexagon and performed transformations on the sides. For example, a curve drawn along one side might be translated (slid) to the opposite side. Another idea was to draw a curve from the midpoint of a side to the adjoining vertex. This curve was then rotated about the midpoint to form a totally new side of the tile. These two ideas are illustrated in part (a) of Figure 8.27. Dot paper is used to help draw the lines. *Escher-type tessellations,* as these have come to be called, are quite popular projects for students in grades 4 or 5 and up. Once a tile has been designed, it can be cut from two different colors of construction paper instead of drawing the tessellation on a dot grid.

A *regular tessellation* is made of a single tile that is a regular polygon (all sides and angles congruent). Each vertex of a regular tessellation has the same number of tiles meeting at that point. A checkerboard is a simple example of a regular tessellation. A *semiregular tessellation* is made of two or more tiles, each of which is a regular polygon. At each vertex of a semiregular tessellation, the same collection of regular polygons come together in the same order. A vertex (and, therefore, the complete semiregular tessellation) can be described by the series of shapes meeting at a vertex. Under each example of these tessellations in part (b) of Figure 8.27, the vertex numbers are given. Students can figure out what polygons are possible at a vertex and design their own semiregular tessellations.

Tessellations like these are very popular with teachers in grades 3 and above. A number of excellent resource books can be found in catalogs such as ETA/Cuisenaire.

Technology Note

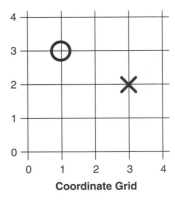

Several computer programs make it easy to create Escher-type tessellations. One example is *TesselMania!* (Learning Company, 1994). Although exciting to use, these programs should be used with care. It is so easy to create intricate results with almost no understanding of the transformations being used. Planning on paper before using the computer is strongly recommended. Then the computer can be used to do the tedious work of creating a finished product complete with color and embellishments.

Location Activities

In kindergarten children learn about everyday positional descriptions—*over, under, near, far, between, left,* and *right.* These are the beginnings of the *Standards'* goal of specifying locations. Eventually, a need for a coordinate system will develop and can easily be introduced at grade 3.

To introduce a coordinate system, draw a grid with coordinates on the board or on the overhead projector. (See Figure 8.28.) Explain how to use two numbers to designate an intersection point on the grid. The first number tells how far to move to the right. The second number tells how far to move up. In the beginning use the words along with the numbers: 3 right and 0 up. Be sure to include 0 in your introduction. Select a point on the grid and have students decide what two numbers name that point. If your point is at (2, 4) and students incorrectly say "four, two," then simply indicate where the point is that they named. Emphasize that when they say or write the two numbers, the first number is the number of steps to the right and the second is the number of steps up.

Once a coordinate system has been introduced, students may want to use it in a simple game similar to the commercial game called "Battleship." Each player has a grid similar to the one in Figure 8.28. Players secretly put their initials on five intersections of their own grid. Then, with the grids kept hidden from each other, the players take turns trying to "hit" the other player's targets by naming a point on the grid using coordinates. The other player indicates if the "shot" was a hit or a miss. When a player scores a hit, he or she gets another turn. Each player keeps track of where he or she has taken shots, recording an "X" for a hit and an "0" for a miss. The game ends when one player has hit all of the other player's targets.

At this level, students are simply using coordinates to describe positions. Although important, this is not very challenging or exciting. By grade 5, students will be able to use coordinates to describe transformations on a coordinate grid. This can be done as an alternative method of introducing slides, flips, and turns, or as a follow-up to that discussion.

Coordinate Grid

FIGURE 8.28 • • • • • • • • •

A simple coordinate grid. The X is at (3,2) and the 0 is at (1,3). Use the grid to play Three in a Row (like Tic-Tac-Toe). Put marks on intersections, not spaces.

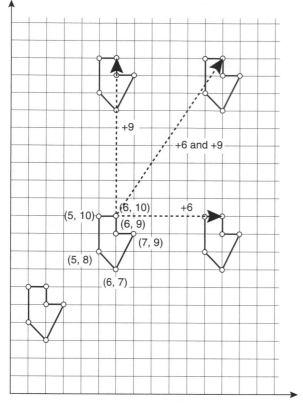

FIGURE 8.29 •

Begin with a simple shape and record the coordinates. By adding or subtracting from the coordinates, new shapes are found that are translations (slides) of the original.

ACTIVITY 8.20

Coordinate Slides

Students will need a sheet of centimeter grid paper on which to draw two coordinate axes near the left and bottom edges. Have them plot and connect about five or six points on the grid to form a small shape. (See Figure 8.29.) If you direct them to use only coordinates between 5 and 12, the figure will be reasonably small and near the center of the paper. Next, students make a new shape by adding 6 to each of the first coordinates (typically called the *x*-coordinates) of their shape, leaving the second coordinates the same. That is, for the point (5, 10) a new point, (11, 10) is plotted. When new points for each point in the figure have been plotted, these are connected as before. Students then create a second figure by adding 9 to each second coordinate. A third figure is formed by adding 6 to the first coordinate and adding 9 to the second coordinate. Finally, a figure is drawn by subtracting 4 from both the first and second coordinates. Students' papers should show their original shape and four copies, each in a different location on the grid. What does adding (or subtracting) a number from the first coordinate cause? What if the number is added or subtracted from the second coordinate? From both coordinates? Have students draw lines connecting corresponding points in the original figure with one of those where both coordinates were changed. What do they notice? (The lines are parallel and the same length.) Pick any two of the five shapes in the final drawing. How can you begin with one of the shapes and change the coordinates to get to the other?

In the last activity students caused a translation of a shape by either adding or subtracting from the coordinates. The shape "slid" along a path that matched the lines between the corresponding points. Reflections can be explored on a coordinate grid just as easily as translations. At the elementary level, however, you will want to restrict the lines of reflection to the *x*- or *y*-axis as in the following activity.

ACTIVITY 8.21

Coordinate Reflections

Have students draw a five-sided shape in the first quadrant on coordinate grid paper using grid points for vertices. Label the Figure ABCDE and call it Figure 1. Use the *y*-axis as a line of symmetry and draw the reflection of the shape in the second quadrant. Call it Figure 2 (for second quadrant) and label the reflected points A'B'C'D'E'. Now use the *x*-axis as the line of symmetry.

Reflect both Figure 2 and Figure 1 into the third and fourth quadrants, respectively, and call these Figures 3 and 4. Label the points of these figures with double and triple primes (A" and A''', and so on). Write in the coordinates for each vertex of all four figures.

- How is Figure 3 related to Figure 4? How else could you have gotten Figure 3? How else could you have found Figure 4?
- How are the coordinates of Figure 1 related to its image in the *y*-axis, Figure 2? What can you say about the coordinates of Figure 4?
- Make a conjecture about the coordinates of a shape reflected in the *y*-axis and a different conjecture about the coordinates of a shape reflected in the *x*-axis.
- Draw lines from the vertices of Figure 1 to the corresponding vertices of Figure 2. What can you say about these lines? How is the *y*-axis related to each of these lines?

STOP **Use Figure 8.30 or a drawing of your own to answer the questions in the last activity.**

Rotations can be explored in a similar manner to Activity 8.21 although the process is a bit more difficult to keep track of. Should you want to try this, use $\frac{1}{4}$ turns with the origin as the point of rotation.

Students who have done the two preceding activities should have a general way to describe translations and reflections across an axis in terms of coordinates. In the following activity, multiplying each coordinate makes a different type of change.

ACTIVITY 8.22

Coordinate Dilations

Students begin with a four-sided shape in the first quadrant. They then make a list of the coordinates and make a new set of coordinates by multiplying each of the original coordinates by 2. They plot the resulting shape. What is the result? Now have students multiply each of the original coordinates by $\frac{1}{2}$ and plot that shape. What is the result? Next, students draw a line from the origin to a vertex of the largest shape on their paper. Repeat for one or two additional vertices and ask for observations. (An example is shown in Figure 8.31.)

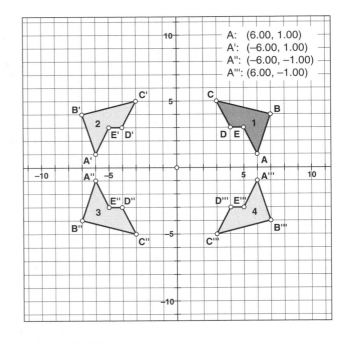

FIGURE 8.30 •

Figure 1 (ABCDE) is reflected across the *y*-axis. Then both Figures 1 and 2 are reflected across the *x*-axis.

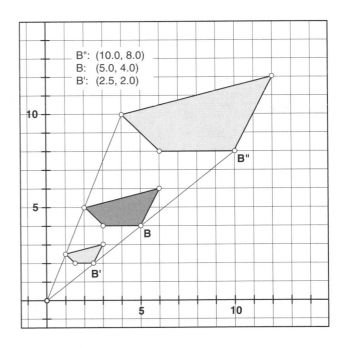

FIGURE 8.31 •

Dilations with coordinates. Coordinates of the center figure were multiplied by 2 and also by 0.5 to create the other two figures.

LOCATION ACTIVITIES

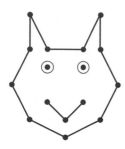

When the coordinates of a shape are multiplied as in the last activity, each by the same factor, the shape either gets larger or smaller. The size is changed but not the shape. The new shape is similar to the old shape. This is called a *dilation,* a transformation that is *not* rigid because the shape changes.

Your students may enjoy exploring this phenomenon a bit further because they can get some quite interesting effects. If they start with a line drawing of a simple face, boat, or some other shape drawn with straight lines connecting vertices, they see an interesting effect by multiplying just the first coordinates, just the second coordinates, or using a different factor for each. For example, students could sketch the cat shown here on a coordinate grid. Then suggest that they add 10 to each first coordinate and multiply each second coordinate by 3.

STOP **Before reading on, predict what you think will happen to the cat if you add 10 to the first coordinates and multiply the second coordinates by 3. What will happen if you do the reverse—multiply the first coordinates by 3 and add 10 to the second coordinates?**

FIGURE 8.32 •

Using multiplication of coordinates to cause a distortion. The coordinates for the larger cat are based on those of the smaller: (*x* + 10, 3*y*).

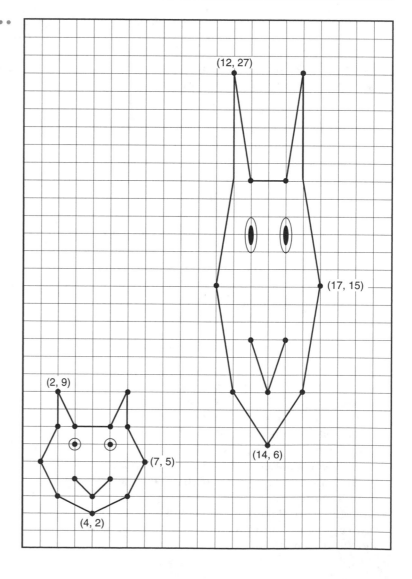

Multiplication of both coordinates by a factor greater than one dilates the figure to a similar but larger shape. When only one coordinate is multiplied, the vertical dimensions alone are dilated, so the figure is proportionately stretched in a vertical manner as in Figure 8.32. By adding 10 units to the first coordinates the new stretched figure is moved to the right so as not to interfere with the original. Students will enjoy exploring with variations of stretching and dilating shapes in various ways.

Visualization Activities

Visualization activities involve seeing and understanding shapes from different perspectives.

Finding out how many different shapes can be made with a given number of simple tiles demands that students mentally flip and turn shapes in their minds and find ways to decide if they have found them all. Although pentominoes have been around for decades, as a visualization activity they remain superb. If your students are not familiar with pentominoes, the following activity is strongly recommended.

ACTIVITY 8.23

Pentominoes

A pentomino is a shape formed by joining five squares as if cut from a square grid. Each square must have at least one side in common with another. Provide students with five square tiles and a sheet of square grid paper for recording. Challenge them to see how many different pentomino shapes they can find. Shapes that are flips or turns of other shapes are not considered different. Do not tell students how many pentomino shapes there are. Good discussions will come from deciding if some shapes are really different and if all shapes have been found.

Once students have decided that there are just 12 pentominoes (see Figure 8.33), the 12 pieces can then be used in a variety of activities. Paste the grids with the children's pentominoes onto tagboard and let them cut out the 12 shapes. These can be used in the next two activities.

It is also fun to explore the number of shapes that can be made from six equilateral triangles or from four 45-degree right triangles (halves of squares). With the right triangles, sides that touch must be the same length. How many of each of these "ominoes" do you think there are? These variations of pentominoes are excellent for a class that has worked previously with pentominoes and still is in need of an early visualization experience.

Lots of activities can be done with pentominoes. For example, try to fit all 12 pieces into a 6 × 10 or 5 × 12 rectangle. Also, each of the 12 shapes can be used as a tessellation tile. Another task is to

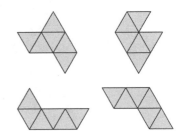

There are 12 pentominoes.

Finding all possible shapes made with five squares—or six squares (called "hexominoes") or six equilateral triangles and so on—is a good exercise in spatial problem solving.

Four of the different shapes that six equilateral triangles will make.

Four of the different shapes that four "half-square" triangles will make.

FIGURE 8.33 • • • • • • • • • • • • • • •

Pentominoes and related shape challenges.

examine each of the 12 pentominoes and decide which will fold up to make an open box. For those that are "box makers," which square is the bottom? Once a "box maker" has been identified, challenge students to write the letters M–A–T–H on the four sides so that the box will spell "MATH" around the sides.

As students work at mentally folding a "box maker" pentomino and attempting to correctly orient the letters of "MATH" on the sides, they are making connections between the two-dimensional world and the three-dimensional world. If a "box maker" had one more square attached at an appropriate place, you could fold it up to make a cube. A flat shape that will fold up to make a solid figure is called a *net* of that solid. The following activity suggests several challenges involving nets.

ACTIVITY 8.24

Net Challenges

The following tasks are only related because each involves nets of solids.

- For each of the pentomino "box makers," see how many different places a sixth square can be attached to create a net for a cube. Are there other nets for a cube that do not begin with a pentomino?
- Begin with a solid, such as a rectangular prism or square pyramid. Sketch as many nets as possible for this shape. Add to the collection some arrangements of the sides of the solid that are not nets. Challenge a friend to decide which are nets of the shape and which are not.
- Use Polydrons or 3D Geoshapes to create a flat figure that you think will fold up into a solid. Test the result. If the number and/or the type of flat shapes is specified, the task can be made more or less difficult. Can you make a net of a solid with 12 regular pentagons or 8 equilateral triangles? (These can be made into a *dodecahedron* and an *octahedron* respectively, two of the five completely regular polyhedra, also known as the five *Platonic solids*.

The following activity also provides students with experiences in the three-dimensional world but in a rather different manner. Here students also must mentally move shapes and predict the results. The activity combines ideas of line symmetry (reflections) as well as visualization and spatial reasoning.

ACTIVITY 8.25

Notches and Holes

Use a half-sheet of paper that will easily fit on the overhead. Fold it in half and then half again, making the second fold in the opposite direction from the first. Students make a sketch of the paper when it is opened, showing a line for each fold. With the paper folded, cut notches in one or two sides and/or cut off one or two corners. You can also use a paper punch to make a hole or two. While still folded, place the paper on the overhead showing the notches and holes. The folded edges should be to the left and at the bottom. (See Figure 8.34.) The task is for students to draw the notches and holes that they think will appear when you open the paper.

To introduce this activity, begin with only one fold and only two cuts. Stay with one fold until students are ready for a more difficult challenge.

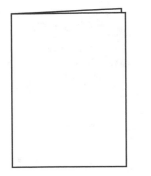

Step 1:
Fold paper twice

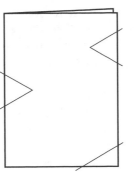

Step 2:
Cut notches

FIGURE 8.34 ● ● ● ● ● ● ● ● ● ● ● ● ● ● ●

An example showing how the "Notches and Holes" activity is done. Students make two folds and cut notches and/or punch holes in the folded paper. Before unfolding, they draw a sketch predicting the result when the paper is unfolded.

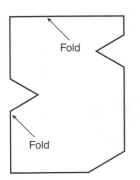

Fold

Fold

Step 3:
Show on overhead projector

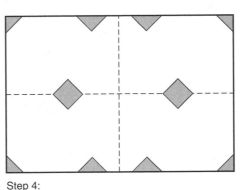

Step 4:
Students draw their predictions

In "Notches and Holes" students will eventually learn which cuts create holes and how many and which cuts make notches in the edges or on the corners. Notice how line symmetry, or reflection, plays a major role in the activity. Symmetry determines the position, the shape, and the number of holes created by each cut.

 Stop now and try the "Notches and Holes" activity yourself. Try cuts in various places on the folded paper and see what is involved in this well-known activity.

One of the main goals of the visualization strand of the Geometry standard is to be able to identify and draw two-dimensional images of three-dimensional figures and to build three-dimensional figures from two-dimensional images. Activities aimed at this goal often involve drawings of small "buildings" made of 1-inch cubes.

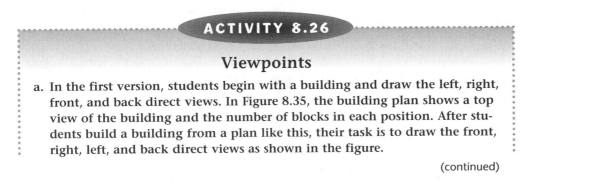

ACTIVITY 8.26

Viewpoints

a. In the first version, students begin with a building and draw the left, right, front, and back direct views. In Figure 8.35, the building plan shows a top view of the building and the number of blocks in each position. After students build a building from a plan like this, their task is to draw the front, right, left, and back direct views as shown in the figure.

(continued)

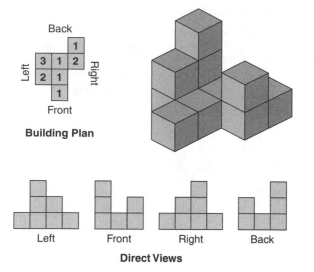

Building Plan

Direct Views

Left Front Right Back

FIGURE 8.35 •

Tasks can begin with the Building Plan, or with the
Direct View, or even with the building. Students give the
other representations.

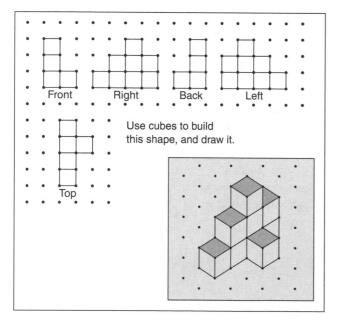

Front Right Back Left

Top

Use cubes to build
this shape, and draw it.

FIGURE 8.36 •

Develop perspective and visual perception with cubes and
plain views. Draw block "buildings" on isometric grids.

b. In the reverse version of the task, students
are given a right and front view. The task is
to build the building that has those views. To
record their solution, they draw a building
plan (top view with numbers).

Notice that front and back direct views are sym-
metric, as are the left and right views. That is why only
one of each is given in part (b) of the activity.

In "Viewpoints," students made "buildings" out of
1-inch cubes and coordinated these with direct views
of the sides and top. A significantly more challenging
activity is to draw perspective views of these block
buildings or to match perspective drawings with a building. Isometric dot grids are used for the drawings. The
next activity provides a glimpse at this form of visualization activity.

ACTIVITY 8.27

Perspective Drawings

a. In the first version, students begin with a
perspective drawing of a building. The
assumption is that there are no hidden
blocks. From the drawing the students build
the actual building with their blocks. To
record the result, they draw a building plan
indicating the number of blocks in each
position.

b. In the second version, students are given
either a block plan or the five direct views.
They build the building accordingly and
draw two or more of the perspective views.
There are four possible perspectives from
above the table: the front left and right, and
the back left and right. It is useful to build
the building on a sheet of paper with the
words "front," "back," "left," and "right"
written on the edges to keep from getting
different viewpoints confused.

Figure 8.36 shows an example of this last activity.
Some excellent resource books exist for this type of
activity. It is not necessary to prepare these tasks yourself. Perhaps the best-known book is *Middle Grades Mathematics Project: Spatial Visualization* (Winter, Lappan,
Phillips, & Fitzgerald, 1986). NCTM's *Navigating Through
Geometry* books have similar activities in both the 3–5
and 6–8 grade books.

FIGURE 8.37 •••••••••••••••••••••

Predict the slice face before you cut a clay model with a potter's wire.

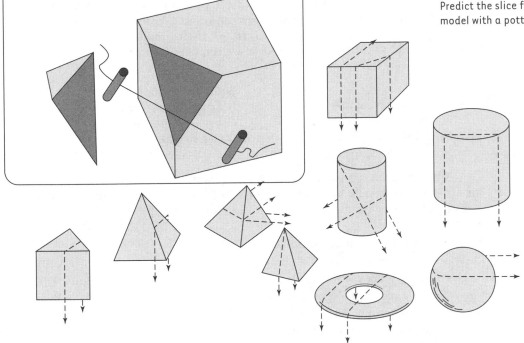

Technology Note

An amazing computer tool for drawing perspective views of block buildings such as in Activity 8.27 is available on the NCTM/*Illuminations* website (http://illuminations.nctm.org/tools/index.aspx). This applet, the Isometric Drawing Tool, requires only mouse clicks to draw either whole cubes, any single face of a cube, or just lines. The drawings, however, are actually "buildings" and can be viewed as three-dimensional objects. They can be rotated in space so that they can be seen from any vantage. Prepared investigations are informative and also lead students through the features of the tool.

Another interesting connection between two and three dimensions is found in slicing solids in different ways. When a solid is sliced into two parts, a two-dimensional figure is formed on the slice faces. Figure 8.37 shows a cube being sliced off at the corner, leaving a triangular face. Slices can be explored with clay sliced with a potter's wire as shown in the figure. A niftier method is to partially fill a plastic solid with water. The surface of the water is the same as the face of a slice coinciding with the surface of the water. By tilting the shape in different ways, every possible "slice" can be observed. Small plastic solids such as *Power Solids* are excellent for this.

ACTIVITY 8.28

Water Slices

Students are given a solid and challenged to find out how to slice it to make a designated slice face. The list of challenges should include some that are

(continued)

impossible. Before water is poured into the solids, students must commit themselves on paper as to whether or not the slice is possible. If they think it is possible, they write and/or draw a description of where the slice must be made. Then water is put into the shape to test their predictions. If there are no plastic shapes available, clay models are the next best option. Here is a list of potential slice faces for a cube:

Square	Equilateral triangle
Nonsquare rectangle	Isosceles right triangle
Nonrectangular parallelogram	Other isosceles triangle
Isosceles trapezoid	Scalene right triangle
Nonisosceles trapezoid	Other scalene triangle

A tetrahedron, a square pyramid, and prisms offer similar challenges. For other solids, it may be more interesting to find out how many different types of slice faces can be found and to describe each.

A *polyhedron* is a three-dimensional shape with polygons for all faces. Among the various polyhedra, the Platonic solids are especially interesting. *Platonic solids* is the name given to the set of completely regular polyhedrons. "Completely regular" means that each face is a regular polygon and every vertex has exactly the same number of faces joining at that point. An interesting visualization task appropriate for this level is to find and describe all of the Platonic solids.

ACTIVITY 8.29

Search for the Platonic Solids

Provide students with a supply of equilateral triangles, squares, regular pentagons, and regular hexagons from one of the plastic sets for building solids (e.g., *Polydron* or *Geofix*). Explain what a completely regular solid is. The task is to find as many different completely regular solids as possible.

One approach to conducting this activity is to leave it as stated and allow students to work with no additional guidance. Success will depend on their problem-solving skills. Alternatively, you might suggest a systematic approach as follows. Because the smallest number of sides a face can have is three, begin with triangles, then squares, then pentagons, and so on. Furthermore, because every vertex must have the same number of faces, try three faces at a point, then four, and so on. (It is clearly impossible to have only two faces at a point.)

With this plan, students will find that for triangles they can have three, four, or five triangles coming to a point. For each of these, they can begin with a "tent" of triangles and then add more triangles so that each vertex has the same number. With three at a point you get a four-sided solid called a *tetrahedron* (*tetra* = four). With four at each point you get an eight-sided solid called an *octahedron* (*octa* = eight). It is really exciting to build the shape with five triangles at each point. It will have 20 sides and is called an *icosahedron* (*icosa* = twenty).

In a similar manner, students will find that there is only one solid made of squares—three at each point and six in all—a *hexahedron* (*hex* = six), also called a cube. And there is only one solid with pentagons, three at each point, 12 in all. This is called a *dodecahedron* (*dodeca* = twelve).

> **STOP** Why are there no regular polyhedra with six or more triangles or four or more squares? Why are there no regular polyhedra made with hexagons or with polygons with more than six sides? The best way to answer these questions is to experiment with the polygons and explain the answers in your own words. Students should do the same.

A fantastic skeletal icosahedron can be built out of the newspaper rods described earlier in the chapter. (See Figure 8.9, p. 218.) Because five triangles converge at each point, there are also five edges at each point. Simply work at bringing five rods to each vertex and remember that each face is a triangle. This icosahedron will be about 4 feet across and will be amazingly sturdy.

Assessment Note

Principles and Standards is extremely helpful for articulating growth in geometric content across the grades. For each of the four goals articulated by the standards (shape and properties, location, transformations, and visualization) examine the grade-level expectations at least for the 3–5 grade band. It is also helpful to look at the expectations for the grades above or below the one you teach.

Try to include a sense of growth over time in your assessment of content. If you limit your assessment to a mastery of skills or definitions, the spirit of exploration that you want in your geometry program will be lost. We most often teach in a manner that reflects our assessment plans. Although mastery of some ideas is perhaps important, conceptual development is rarely reflected in memorizing definitions.

In deciding what to assess and how, it is best to take a long-term view of geometry rather than a more traditional mastery-oriented approach.

EXPANDED LESSON

Diagonal Strips
Based on Activity 8.9, p. 227

GRADE LEVEL: Fifth grade.

MATHEMATICS GOALS
- To investigate the properties of the diagonals of quadrilaterals.
- To provide opportunities to clarify the meaning of the terms *quadrilateral, diagonal, perpendicular,* and *bisect,* as well as the names of specific types of quadrilaterals.

THINKING ABOUT THE STUDENTS
Students should be able to identify different types of quadrilaterals (rectangle, parallelogram, trapezoid, kite, rhombus) and talk about their properties in terms of the length of sides and angles formed by the sides. They should also understand the terms *quadrilateral, diagonal, congruent, perpendicular,* and *bisect.*

MATERIALS AND PREPARATION
- For each pair of students, prepare three strips of tagboard about 2 cm wide. Two strips should be about 30 cm and the third about 20 cm. Punch a hole near each end. Divide the distance between the holes by 8 and use this distance to space 7 holes between the ends. (See Figure 8.16, p. 227.) Each student also needs a brass fastener to join two diagonal strips.
- Make copies of Blackline Master L-3 and the 1-cm square dot grid paper (Blackline Master 10) for each student.
- Make a transparency of Blackline Master L-3 and at least two transparencies of Blackline Master 10.

lesson

Properties of Quadrilateral Diagonals

Name

Name of Quadrilateral	Congruent Diagonals		Diagonals Bisected			Intersection of Diagonals	
	Yes	No	Both	One	Neither	Perpendicular	Not

BLM L-3

BEFORE

Begin with a simpler version of the task:
- On the board write the terms *congruent, bisect,* and *perpendicular.*
- Using the two diagonal strips that are equal in length, show students how to join them with the brass fastener. Join the diagonals so that they bisect each other at a right angle. Lay the diagonals on the overhead and ask students to tell what they can about how the two are related. Refer to the terms on the board. As students share their observations, record the properties on the first line of the L-3 transparency by putting Xs under *congruent, bisect each other,* and *perpendicular.* Clarify the meaning of terminology as necessary. Now ask students to think about what quadrilateral would be formed if the ends of the diagonals were connected. On the overhead, mark the vertices through the holes at the end of each diagonal. Use a straightedge to connect the vertices and, thus, form a square.
- On the dot-grid transparency, show students how they can draw two intersecting lines with the same properties (congruent, bisecting each other, and perpendicular). Then connect the endpoints of these lines to form the quadrilateral. Have students draw a pair of intersecting lines on their own paper. Have them use lines that are either shorter or longer than the two on the transparency. When they connect the endpoints, all students should get squares regardless of the lengths of their diagonals.

Brainstorm
Together generate a list of possible types of quadrilaterals that might be formed. You may wish to put this list on the board.

The Task
Students are to use the three strips of tagboard to determine the properties of diagonals that will produce different types of quadrilaterals.

Establish Expectations

- Before giving students the task, remind them that they can use the third shorter diagonal with one of the longer diagonals to form a quadrilateral with noncongruent diagonals.
- Make clear to students that they are to work in pairs to identify the properties of the diagonals and the quadrilateral formed by the diagonals. They are to record their findings on the worksheet and also draw a corresponding pair of diagonals and the quadrilateral on their dot grid. They should put the name of the quadrilateral on each drawing.

DURING

- Observe how students are determining the properties of diagonals that produce different quadrilaterals. Do they start with the diagonal relationships to see what shapes can be made? Or do they start with examples of the shapes and determine the diagonal relationships? Either approach is fine.
- If students are having difficulty getting started, suggest that they try creating diagonals with one set of properties from the worksheet.
- Do they have a systematic way of generating different quadrilaterals? For example, do they use the same two diagonals, keep one property constant (e.g., diagonals are perpendicular), and then look for ways to vary the other property (e.g., diagonals bisect or do not bisect each other)?
- For students who are ready for a challenge, have them determine the properties that will produce a nonisosceles trapezoid.

AFTER

- As students share their findings, have them draw the diagonals and quadrilateral on your transparency of Blackline Master 10.
- Referring to the descriptions (properties) of the diagonals, ask students if *all* quadrilaterals of a given type have the same diagonal properties. For example, will all rhombuses have these same diagonal properties? Use the transparency of the dot-grid paper to have students make drawings to test various hypotheses regarding the quadrilateral type and their diagonals.
- Ask students to look at the quadrilaterals that have a diagonal property in common (e.g., all quadrilaterals whose diagonals bisect each other) and to make conjectures about other properties in the quadrilaterals that happen as a result of the common diagonal property.

ASSESSMENT NOTES

Are they testing their hypotheses with different sizes of quadrilaterals using the grid paper? Or are they convinced without using the grid paper? If so, how are they convinced? Are they even questioning what might happen with different examples of the same quadrilateral? The answers to these questions will provide evidence that students are or are not beginning to think at van Hiele level 2.

- If students need more exploration to convince themselves that *all* quadrilaterals of a given type have the same diagonal properties, using a dynamic geometry program such as *Sketchpad* is an excellent way to continue this investigation. Students can also continue to explore and build relationships between different shapes that have common diagonal properties (e.g., rectangles and squares).
- If not done already, have students continue to explore the properties of quadrilaterals by doing Activity 8.8, "Property Lists for Quadrilaterals."

next steps

EXPANDED LESSON

DEVELOPING MEASUREMENT CONCEPTS

easurement is a complex area of the curriculum. Unfortunately, the measurement curriculum in most states asks that students learn something about nearly every type of measurement almost every year, even in the primary grades. Traditional textbooks, in an attempt to respond to state mandates, pack all of this information into the books in what often becomes a superficial "covering of the material." As a result, students in the intermediate grades often have a meager understanding of measurement with lots of gaps in their development.

A goal for the primary teacher is to help students understand what it means to measure length, volume, weight, and area, and to help students understand the most important measuring instrument for young children, the ruler. Familiarity with a few standard units is another goal, although most curricula are too ambitious in this regard. For some attributes, if not all, the intermediate-grade teacher must review or reteach many of these basic ideas.

The Meaning and Process of Measuring

Suppose that you asked your students to measure an empty bucket. The first thing they would need to know is *what* about the

big ideas

1 Measurement involves a comparison of an attribute of an item or situation with a unit that has the same attribute. Lengths are compared to units of length, areas to units of area, time to units of time, and so on. Before anything can be measured meaningfully, it is necessary to understand the attribute to be measured.

2 Meaningful measurement and estimation of measurements depend on a personal familiarity with the unit of measure being used.

3 Estimation of measures and the development of personal benchmarks for frequently used units of measure help students increase their familiarity with units, prevent errors in measurements, and aid in the meaningful use of measurement.

4 Measurement instruments are devices that replace the need for actual measurement units. It is important to understand how measurement instruments work so that they can be used correctly and meaningfully.

5 Area and volume formulas provide a method of measuring these attributes by using only measures of length.

6 Area, perimeter, and volume are related to each other, although not precisely or by formula. For example, as the shapes of regions or three-dimensional objects change but maintain the same areas or volumes, there is a predictable effect on the perimeters and surface areas.

bucket is to be measured. They might measure the height or depth, diameter (distance across), or circumference (distance around). All of these are length measures. The surface area of the side could be determined. A bucket also has capacity and weight. Each of these *aspects that can be measured* is an *attribute* of the bucket.

Once they determine the attribute to be measured, they need to choose a unit of measure. The unit must have the attribute that is being measured. Length is measured with units that have length, volume with units that have volume, and so on.

Technically, a *measurement* is a number that indicates a comparison between the attribute of the object (or situation, or event) being measured and the same attribute of a given unit of measure. We commonly use small units of measure to determine in some way a numeric relationship (the measurement) between what is measured and the unit. For example, to measure a length, the comparison can be done by lining up copies of the unit directly against the length being measured. To measure weight, which is a pull of gravity or a force, the weight of the object might first be applied to a spring. Then the comparison is made by finding out how many units of weight produce the same effect on the spring. In either case, the number of units is the measure of the object.

For most of the attributes that are measured in schools, we can say that *to measure* means that the attribute being measured is "filled" or "covered" or "matched" with a unit of measure with the same attribute (as illustrated in Figure 9.1). This concept of filling or covering is a good way to talk with students about measurement. It is appropriate with this understanding, then, to say that the measure of an attribute is a count of how many units are needed to fill, cover, or match the attribute of the object being measured.

In summary, to measure something, one must perform three steps:

1. Decide on the attribute to be measured.
2. Select a unit that has that attribute.
3. Compare the units, by filling, covering, matching, or some other method, with the attribute of the object being measured.

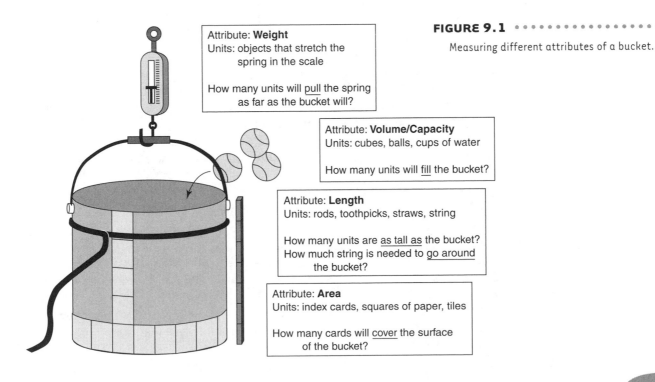

FIGURE 9.1 • • • • • • • • • • • • • • • • • •

Measuring different attributes of a bucket.

Attribute: **Weight**
Units: objects that stretch the spring in the scale

How many units will <u>pull</u> the spring as far as the bucket will?

Attribute: **Volume/Capacity**
Units: cubes, balls, cups of water

How many units will <u>fill</u> the bucket?

Attribute: **Length**
Units: rods, toothpicks, straws, string

How many units are <u>as tall as</u> the bucket?
How much string is needed to <u>go around</u> the bucket?

Attribute: **Area**
Units: index cards, squares of paper, tiles

How many cards will <u>cover</u> the surface of the bucket?

Measuring instruments such as rulers, scales, protractors, and clocks are devices that make the filling, covering, or matching process easier. A ruler lines up the units of length and numbers them. A protractor lines up the unit angles and numbers them. A clock lines up units of time and marks them off.

Developing Measurement Concepts and Skills

When teaching measurement, it is important to distinguish between students going about a measurement process and students conceptually understanding what they are doing as they measure. The use of protractors to measure angles is a good example; students are often found to be following directions about how to line up the little marks on the edge of the protractor with little understanding of what the marks represent or even what a degree is. Many protractors have two sets of numbers around the edge—one reading clockwise, the other counterclockwise. Would students get these confused if they understood where the numbers came from and what they were really measuring?

Unfortunately, protractors are simply one area of confusion. National test data suggest that students have a poor understanding of rulers and other measurement processes.

A General Plan of Instruction

A basic understanding of measurement suggests how to help children develop a conceptual knowledge of measuring, as summarized in Table 9.1. Let's briefly discuss each of these three instructional components described in the table.

Making Comparisons

The first and most critical goal is for students to understand the attribute they are going to measure. For students in grades 3–5, we might assume that they know what length is and probably weight and volume. However, area continues to be a difficult concept (perhaps due to formulas based on lengths), and angles are certainly not part of their knowledge base.

When students compare objects on the basis of some measurable attribute, that attribute becomes the focus of the activity. For example, is the size of one angle more than, less than, or about the same as the size of another? No measurement is required, but some manner of comparing one angle to the other must be devised. The attribute of "angular spread" (the spread of the rays of the angle) is inescapable.

Using Models of Units

The second goal is for students to understand what a unit of measure is and how it is used to produce a measurement. Here you should make no assumptions about what students may have learned in the primary grades.

For most attributes that are measured in elementary schools, it is possible to have physical models of the units of measure. Time and temperature are exceptions. (Many other attributes not commonly measured in school also do not have physical units of measure. Light intensity, speed, loudness, viscosity, and radioactivity are just a few examples.) Unit models can usually be found for both informal units and standard

TABLE 9.1 ●
Plan for Measurement Instruction

Step One

Goal: Students will understand the attribute to be measured.
Type of Activity: Make comparisons based on the attribute. For example, longer/shorter, heavier/lighter. Use direct comparisons whenever possible.
Notes: When it is clear that the attribute is understood, there is no further need for comparison activities.

Step Two

Goal: Students will understand how filling, covering, matching, or making other comparisons of an attribute with measuring units produces a number called a measure.
Type of Activity: Use physical models of measuring units to fill, cover, match, or make the desired comparison of the attribute with the unit.
Notes: In most instances it is appropriate to begin with informal units. Progress to the direct use of standard units when appropriate and certainly before using formulas or measuring tools.

Step Three

Goal: Students will use common measuring tools with understanding and flexibility.
Type of Activity: Make measuring instruments and use them in comparison with the actual unit models to see how the measurement tool is performing the same function as the individual units. Be certain to make direct comparisons between the student-made tools and the standard tools.
Notes: Student-made tools are usually best made with informal units. Without a careful comparison with the standard tools, much of the value in making the tools can be lost.

units. For angles a thin wedge of tagboard is a good informal unit but a degree is so small that a physical model is not possible.

The most easily understood use of unit models is actually to use as many copies of the unit as are needed to fill or match the attribute measured. To measure the area of the desktop with an index card unit, you can literally cover the entire desk with index cards. The same desktop area can be measured with a single index card by moving it from position to position and keeping track of which areas the card has covered, although this iteration process may not adequately portray the measurement concept for some students.

Making and Using Measuring Instruments

An understanding of the devices we use to measure is the third goal. In the sixth National Assessment of Educational Progress (Kenney & Kouba, 1997), only 24 percent of fourth-grade students and 62 percent of eighth-grade students could give the correct measure of an object not aligned with the end of a ruler, as in Figure 9.2. These results point to the difference between using a measuring device and understanding how it works. Students also experienced difficulty when the increments on a measuring device were other than one unit.

If students actually make simple measuring instruments using unit models with which they are familiar, it is

FIGURE 9.2 ● ● ● ● ● ● ● ● ● ● ● ● ● ● ● ● ● ●

"How long is this crayon?"

more likely that they will understand how an instrument measures. As we will see later in the chapter, a protractor based on informal units will make it clear how protractors are designed and how to use them. It is essential that the informal instrument be compared with the standard instrument. Without this comparison, students may not understand that these two instruments are really two means to the same end. A discussion of student-made measuring instruments for each attribute is provided in the text that follows.

Informal Units and Standard Units: Reasons for Using Each

Although common in primary grades to use nonstandard or informal units, measurement activities in the upper grades often do not begin with informal units. This is unfortunate because the use of informal units for beginning measurement activities is beneficial at all grade levels. It is useful to understand the reasons for using informal units so that we can do so wisely.

- Informal units make it easier to focus directly on the attribute being measured. For example, in a discussion of how to measure the area of an irregular shape, units such as lima beans, square tiles, or circular counters may be suggested. Each unit covers area and each will give a different result. The discussion focuses on what it means to measure area.

- The use of informal units can avoid conflicting objectives in the same beginning lesson. Is your lesson about what it means to measure area or about understanding square centimeters?

- Informal units provide a good rationale for standard units. A discussion of the need for a standard unit can have more meaning after groups in your class have measured the same objects with their own units and arrived at different answers.

- Using informal units can be fun.

The use of standard units is also important in your measurement program at any grade level.

- Knowledge of standard units is a valid objective of a measurement program and must be addressed. Students must not only develop a familiarity with standard units but must also learn appropriate relationships between them.

- Once a measuring concept is fairly well developed, it is frequently just as easy to use standard units. If there is no good instructional reason for using informal units, why not use standard units and provide the exposure?

There is no simple rule for when to use standard or informal units. Students' initial measurement of any attribute should probably begin with informal units and progress over time to the use of standard units and standard measuring tools.

If there is an error in the use of informal units, it may be in not progressing to standard units soon enough. In grades 3–5, when the measured attribute and the way that it is measured with units are clear to students, it is probably time to move to standard units. Just be sure that a shift to standard units is not premature.

The Role of Estimation in Learning Measurement

It is very important to have students estimate a measurement before they make it. This is true with both informal and standard units. There are at least four good reasons for including estimation in measurement activities:

- Estimation helps students focus on the attribute being measured and the measuring process. Think how you would estimate the area of the front of this book with standard playing cards as the unit. To do so, you have to think about what area is and how the units might be fitted into the book cover.
- Estimation provides intrinsic motivation to measurement activities. It is fun to see how close you can come in your estimate or if your team can make a better estimate than the other teams in the room.
- When standard units are used, estimation helps develop familiarity with the unit. If you estimate the height of the door in meters before measuring, you have to devise some way to think about the size of a meter.
- The use of a benchmark to make an estimate promotes multiplicative reasoning. The width of the building is about one-fourth of the length of a football field—perhaps 25 yards.

The Approximate Nature of Measurement

In all measuring activities, emphasize the use of approximate language. The desk is *about* 4 feet long. The chair is *a little less than* 16 inches high. Many measurements do not come out even. Older children will begin to search for smaller units or will use fractional units to try to measure exactly. Here is an opportunity to develop the idea that all measurements include some error. Each smaller unit or subdivision does produce a greater degree of *precision*. For example, a length measure can never be more than one-half unit in error. And yet, since there is mathematically no "smallest unit," there is always some error involved.

Measuring Length

By third grade the attribute of length is generally understood. That is, most students can correctly identify the longer or shorter of two objects that are easily compared. Therefore, length comparison activities are not necessary.

Using Units of Length

Although the attribute of length may be understood by most students by third grade, a full understanding of how units are used to measure length may be incomplete or even misunderstood.

Assessment Note

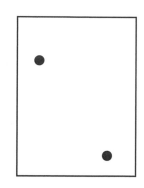

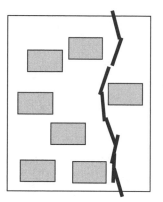

When considering length instruction in the third or fourth grade, a quick assessment may be in order to be sure that students have gained the ideas that are often taken for granted at this level. Here are two ideas that will not take too much time.

- Provide students with a supply of small paper clips or another suitable informal unit of length. Prepare a paper with two dots as shown to the left. Have students determine how far apart the dots are in terms of paper clips.
- If students know to line up the paper clips in a straight line between the dots without any significant gaps or overlapping units, then it may be assumed that they understand the process of using units to measure.
- On the board make a sketch similar to the one shown at the bottom left. Explain that a second grader used strips of cardboard to measure the length of the room and did it as shown. The students' task is to explain to the second grader why her measurement may be inaccurate.

   In their explanations you are looking for the same issues as stated earlier: straight alignment of units without overlap or gaps.

   If your assessment of students indicates that there is some confusion about how length is measured, then the results of the assessment will undoubtedly produce different ideas and answers among the students. Rather than correcting inappropriate ideas or techniques, utilize the class discussion of these results so that students will themselves come to the conclusion that units must be aligned end to end in a straight path. This will avoid making measurement seem like another rule to follow.

In addition to the basic question of how units of length are used to measure lengths, the issue of how measures change when the size of the unit changes is also important. The following activity addresses this concept.

ACTIVITY 9.1

Changing Units

Have students measure a length with one unit, or simply tell them what the measurement is. Then provide them with a different unit and see if they can predict the measure of the same length with the new unit. Students should write down their predictions and explanations of how they were made. Then have them make the actual measurement. In the class discussions that follow, the predictions and explanations will be the most educational part of the activity. The first few times you do this activity, the larger unit should be a simple multiple of the smaller unit. Cuisenaire rods are excellent for this activity.

   The first thing that you want to look for in the "Changing Units" activity is that students realize that smaller units produce larger measures and vice versa. Even when this is understood, the actual prediction of the second measure provides a good opportunity for students to reason with multiples and factors. For example, if a measurement made with yellow Cuisenaire rods was 12 rods, what will the measurement be if the orange rod is used as the unit? (The orange rod is twice as long as the yellow, so the measurement will be half, or 6 rods.) What if the white rod is used? (It takes 5 whites to make 1 yellow rod, so the new measure will be 5 times as big.) Do not explain these solutions to the students. Rather, allow students to struggle with and discuss their reasoning. Conjectures can be tested by actually measuring.

"Changing Units" is also a good activity to do just before any discussion of unit conversion with standard units. For example, if the doorway is 80 inches high, how many feet is that? This typical conversion task is exactly the same as the one in "Changing Units."

Making and Using Rulers

We often assume that students in the intermediate grades understand how rulers are used to measure. Evidence suggests otherwise, even for students in the fifth grade. Rather than trying to explain how to use a standard ruler, your time may well be better spent with at least one lesson in which students actually make and use their own rulers and compare them to standard rulers. When a measurement instrument is understood, it is more likely to be used correctly.

Rulers can be made on long strips of tagboard about 5 cm wide. As a unit you can use a nonstandard unit such as a paper clip or a standard unit, perhaps 1 inch or 5 centimeters. (One centimeter is too small for this purpose.)

If you precut narrow strips of construction paper, students can cut these into shorter pieces using their unit model as a guide. Discuss how the paper strips could be used for measuring just as well as the actual units. Next, students can paste the paper units along the edge of the tagboard. Use two contrasting colors, and alternate them as shown in Figure 9.3.

Pasting down copies of the units on a ruler maximizes the connection between the spaces on a ruler and the actual units. Older students can make rulers by using a real unit to make marks along the tagboard strip and then coloring in the spaces. Students should not be encouraged to use the end of a ruler as a starting point; many real rulers are not made that way. If the first unit on a ruler does not coincide with the end of the ruler, the student is forced to attend to aligning the units on the ruler with the object measured.

Before students put numbers on their rulers, have them measure with them. Have them measure a length once with their ruler and once using the actual units. Although the results should be the same, inaccuracies or incorrect use of the ruler may produce differences that are important to discuss. Also use the ruler to measure lengths that are longer than the ruler.

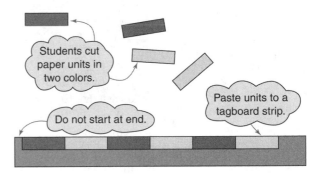

Students cut paper units in two colors.

Do not start at end.

Paste units to a tagboard strip.

FIGURE 9.3 •
Making a simple ruler.

ACTIVITY 9.2

More Than One Way

Challenge students to find different ways to measure the same length with one ruler. (Start from either end; start at a point not at the end; measure different parts of the object and add the results.)

Next have students put numbers on their rulers. Discuss why numbers might be helpful on a ruler (e.g., so that you do not need to count all of the units). Allow students to number their rulers in a way that makes sense to them rather than tell them how they must do it.

Assessment Note

By having students make and number their own rulers, you receive an enormous amount of assessment data about how well your students understand the measurement process. By contrast, if you carefully direct how to use the unmarked ruler and then how to number it, students' attention is now focused on following directions.

Research indicates that when students see standard rulers with the numbers on the hash marks, they often believe that the numbers are counting the marks rather than indicating the units or spaces between the marks. Not only is this an incorrect understanding of rulers, it can lead to wrong answers when using rulers. As an assessment, provide students with a ruler as shown in Figure 9.4, with hash marks but no numbers. Have students use the ruler to measure an item that is shorter than the ruler. A correct understanding of rulers is indicated if students count the spaces between the hash marks.

Another good assessment of ruler understanding is to have students measure with a "broken" ruler, one with the first two units broken off. Some students will say that it is impossible to measure with such a ruler because there is no starting point. Those who understand rulers will be able to match and count the units meaningfully in their measures. (See Barrett, Jones, Thornton, & Dickson, 2003, for a complete discussion of students' development of length measurement including the use of rulers.)

Observing how children use a ruler to measure an object that is longer than the ruler is also informative. Children who are simply reading the last mark on the ruler may not be able to do this task because they do not understand how a ruler is a representation of a row of units.

Much of the value of student-made rulers can be lost if you do not transfer this knowledge to standard rulers. Give children a standard ruler and discuss how it is like and how it differs from the ones they have made. What are the units? Could you make a ruler with paper units the same as this? Could you make some cardboard units and measure the same way as with the ruler? What do the numbers mean? What are the other marks for? Where do the units begin?

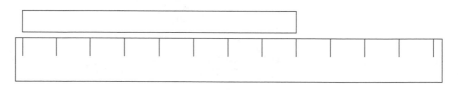

FIGURE 9.4 •

Use an unmarked ruler and ask students to measure an object. Do the students count spaces or hash marks? In the example shown, the correct length is 8 units. Students counting hash marks would respond 9 units.

Measuring Area

Area is a measure of the space inside a region or how much it takes to cover a region. As with other attributes, students must first understand the attribute of area before measuring. Data from the seventh National Assessment of Educational Progress suggest that fourth- and eighth-grade students have an incomplete understanding of area (Martin & Strutchens, 2000).

Comparison Activities

One of the purposes of comparison activities with areas is to help students distinguish between size (or area) and shape, length, and other dimensions. A long, skinny rectangle may have less area than a triangle with shorter sides. This is an especially difficult concept for young children to understand. Piagetian experiments indicate that many 8- or 9-year-olds do not understand that rearranging areas into different shapes does not affect the amount of area.

Direct comparison of two areas is nearly always impossible except when the shapes involved have some common dimension or property. For example, two rectangles with the same width can be compared directly, as can any two circles. Comparison of these special shapes, however, fails to deal with the attribute of area. Instead, activities in which one area is rearranged are suggested. In the following activity, students confront the issue of size as an attribute different from length or width.

ACTIVITY 9.3

Rectangle Comparison—No Units

Provide students with pairs of rectangles as follows.

Pair A:	2 × 9 and 3 × 6
Pair B:	1 × 10 and 3 × 5
Pair C:	3 × 8 and 4 × 5

(These three rectangles can be found in the Blackline Masters.)

The rectangles should be blank except for the labels. The students' task is to decide for each pair which rectangle has the greater area or if the two are the same size. They are allowed to cut or fold the rectangles in any way they wish, but they must include an explanation for their decision in each pair. Pair C will cause the most difficulty, and you may wish to reserve it as a challenge.

BLM 36

STOP **Consider how you would compare each pair of rectangles in the preceding activity without relying on a formula or drawing squares.**

In the first two pairs, the skinny rectangle can be folded and cut to either match (pair A) or be easily compared (pair B) to the second rectangle. For pair C, one rectangle can be placed on the other and then the extended pieces compared.

Tangrams can be used for the same purpose. The standard set of seven tangram pieces is cut from a square, as shown in Figure 9.5. The two small triangles can be used

BLM 27

to make the parallelogram, the square, and the medium triangle. Four small triangles will make the large triangle. This permits a similar discussion about the pieces having the same size (area) but different shapes. (Tangram pieces can be found in the Blackline Masters.)

The following activities suggest methods for comparing areas without measuring.

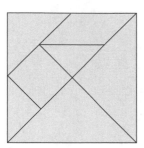

7 tangram shapes

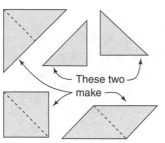

The two small triangles make each of the medium shapes.

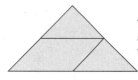

Two small triangles with any of the medium pieces will make the large triangle.

FIGURE 9.5 •

Tangrams provide a nice opportunity to investigate size and shape concepts.

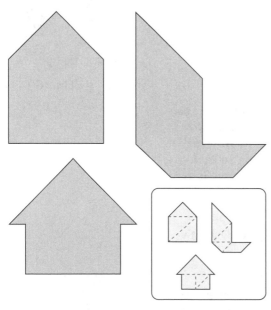

One solution

FIGURE 9.6 •

Compare shapes made of tangram pieces.

ACTIVITY 9.4

Tangram Areas

Draw the outline of several shapes made with tangram pieces, as in Figure 9.6. Let students use tangrams to decide which shapes are the same size, which are larger, and which are smaller. Let students explain how they came to their conclusions. There are several different approaches to this task, and it is best if students determine their own solutions rather than blindly follow your directions.

Using Units of Area

Although squares are very nice units of area (and the most commonly used), any tile that conveniently fills up a plane region can be used. Even filling a region with uniform circles or lima beans provides a useful idea of what it means to measure areas. Here are a few suggestions for area units that are easy to gather or make in the large quantities you will need.

- Round plastic chips, pennies, or lima beans can be used. It is not necessary at a beginning stage that the area units fit with no gaps.

- Color Tiles (1-inch squares) are an excellent square unit. Squares can be cut from cardboard. Large squares (about 20 cm on a side) work well for large areas.

- Pattern blocks provide six different units. The hexagon, trapezoid, blue rhombus, and triangle can be related to each other in a manner similar to the tangrams.

- A square grid or triangular grid is a good way to cover a region with squares. Trace the region on the grid. See the Blackline Masters for grids.

BLMs 7–9, 11, 13

Students can use units to measure surfaces in the room such as desktops, bulletin boards, or books. Large regions can be outlined with masking tape on the floor. Small regions can be duplicated on paper so that students

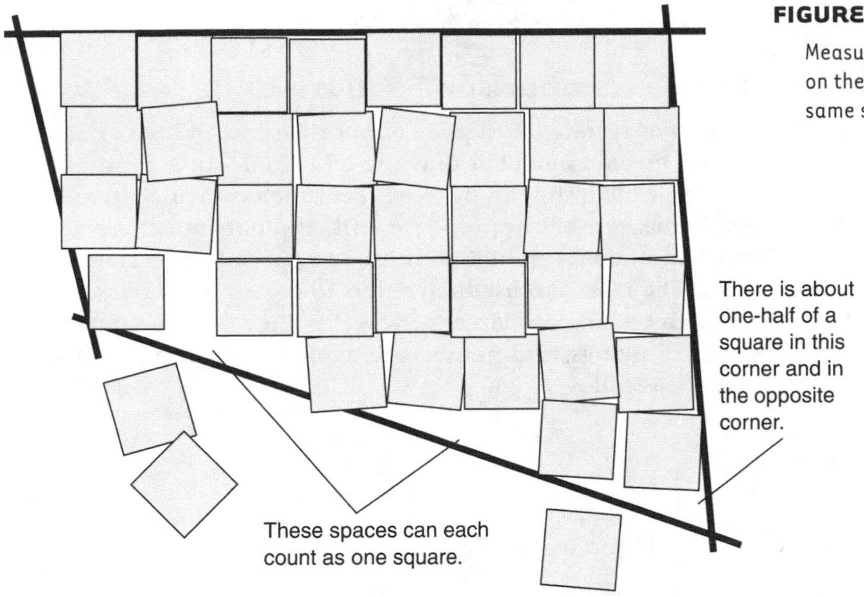

FIGURE 9.7 •

Measuring the area of a large shape drawn with tape on the floor. Units are pieces of tagboard all cut to the same shape.

There is about one-half of a square in this corner and in the opposite corner.

These spaces can each count as one square.

can work at their desks. Odd shapes and curved surfaces provide more challenge and interest.

In area measurements, there may be lots of units that only partially fit. By third or fourth grade, students should begin to wrestle with partial units and mentally put together two or more partial units to count as one (see Figure 9.7).

The following activity is a good starting point to see what ideas your students bring to their understanding of area measurement.

ACTIVITY 9.5

Fill and Compare

Draw two rectangles and a blob shape on a sheet of paper. Make it so that the three areas are not the same but with no clearly obvious largest or smallest. The students' task is to first make a guess about which are the smallest and the largest of the three shapes. After recording their guess, they should use a filler of their choice to decide. Provide small units such as circular disks, Color Tiles, or lima beans. They should explain in writing what they found.

Your objective in the beginning is to develop the idea that area is a *measure of covering*. Do not introduce formulas. Simply have the students fill the shapes and count the units. Be sure to include estimation before measuring (this is significantly more difficult than for length), use approximate language, and relate precision to the size of the units in the same manner as with length.

It is important to stress that filling areas with units to determine a measure has almost no impact on students' understanding of formulas such as $L \times W$ for determining area. The filling process does not help them focus on the dimensions or on multiplying as a means of counting units. The only goal of these activities is to understand the meaning of measurement. When you feel that goal has been met, it is time to move forward. The following activity encourages students to connect multiplication in an array format (rows and columns) to determine the area of rectangles.

BLM 37

ACTIVITY 9.6

Rectangle Comparison—Square Units

Students are given a pair of rectangles that are either the same in area or are very close. They are also given a model or drawing of a single square unit and an appropriate ruler. (The units can be either centimeters or inches, and the ruler should clearly measure the appropriate unit. Students must be familiar with rulers.) The students are not permitted to cut out the rectangles or even draw on them. The task is to use their rulers to determine, in any way that they can, which rectangle is larger or whether they are the same. They should use words, drawings, and numbers to explain their conclusions. Some suggested pairs are as follows:

4×10 and 5×8
5×10 and 7×7
4×6 and 5×5

The first two pairs can be found in the Blackline Masters.

The preceding activity is good for pairs or groups of three to work on together. The goal is not necessarily to develop an area formula but to apply students' developing concepts of multiplication to the area of rectangles. Not all students will use a multiplicative approach. Many will draw copies of the rectangles and attempt to draw in all the squares. However, it is likely that some will use their rulers to determine the number of squares that will fit along each side and, from that, use multiplication to determine the total area. (See Figure 9.8.) By having students share their strategies, more students can be exposed to the use of multiplication.

Aside from computer tools, there are really no commonly used instruments for measuring area.

Area and Perimeter

Area and perimeter (the distance around a region) are continually a source of confusion for students. Perhaps it is because both involve measuring length or because students are taught formulas for both concepts and tend to get formulas confused. Whatever the reason, expect that students even in the fifth and sixth grades will confuse these two ideas.

An interesting approach to alleviating this confusion is to contrast the two ideas as in the next activities.

FIGURE 9.8 • • • • • • • •

Some students will be able to figure out how many squares fit along each side and know that multiplication will tell the total number.

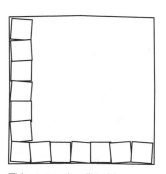

This rectangle will hold 49 squares: 7×7 is 49.

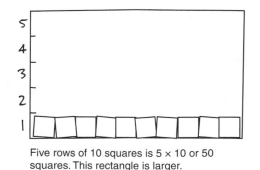

Five rows of 10 squares is 5×10 or 50 squares. This rectangle is larger.

ACTIVITY 9.7

Fixed Perimeters

Give students a loop of string that is exactly 24 units long. (Use a non-stretchy string. Double the string and make a mark 1 foot from the loop. Tie a knot just beyond the marks so that the resulting loop is 24 inches.) The task is to decide what different-sized rectangles can be made with a perimeter of 24 inches. Students may want to use a 1-inch grid to place their strings on. Each different rectangle can be recorded on grid paper with the area noted.

An alternative to the string loop is to simply use centimeter grid paper and ask students to find rectangles with a perimeter of 24.

ACTIVITY 9.8

Fixed Areas

Provide students with 36 square tiles such as Color Tiles. The task is to see how many rectangles can be made with an area of 36—that is, using all 36 tiles to make filled-in rectangles, not just borders. Each new rectangle should be recorded by sketching the outline and the dimensions on grid paper. Centimeter or half-centimeter grids are good for recording. For each rectangle, students should determine and record the perimeter.

EXPANDED LESSON

(pages 288–289)

A complete lesson plan based on "Fixed Areas" can be found at the end of this chapter.

STOP Before reading further, think about the two previous activities. For "Fixed Areas," will all of the perimeters be the same? If not, what can you say about the shapes with longer or shorter perimeters? For "Fixed Perimeters," will the areas remain the same? Why or why not?

You may have been surprised to find out that two rectangles having the same area do not necessarily have the same perimeter. Similarly, two shapes with the same perimeter do not always have the same area. And, of course, this fact is not restricted to rectangles.

There is a relationship of sorts that is fairly interesting. If you have explored the last two activities, you may have noticed that, when the area is fixed, the shape with the smallest perimeter is a square. For a fixed perimeter, the rectangle with the largest area is also a square. If you allow for any shapes whatsoever, the shape with the smallest perimeter and a fixed area is a circle. That is, the "fatter" a shape, the smaller its perimeter and the skinnier a shape, the larger its perimeter, assuming the areas are the same. (A corresponding result is true in three dimensions. Replace perimeter with surface area and area with volume. With a fixed volume, the shape with the least surface area is a sphere.)

Measuring Volume and Capacity

Volume and *capacity* are both terms for measures of the "size" of three-dimensional regions. *Volume* typically refers to the amount of space that an object takes up. Volume is measured with units such as cubic inches or cubic centimeters—units that are based on linear measures. The term *capacity* is generally used to refer to the amount that a container will hold. Standard units of capacity include quarts and gallons, liters and milliliters—units used for liquids as well as the containers that hold them. Having made these distinctions, they are not ones to worry about. The term *volume* can also be used to refer to the capacity of a container.

Comparison Activities

By third grade most students will understand the concept of "holds more" with reference to containers. That is, there is no need to develop a concept of that attribute. The concept of volume for solid objects may not be as readily understood. Even if these ideas are understood, one or two comparison activities can be fun.

ACTIVITY 9.9

Capacity Lineup

Given a series of five or six labeled containers of different sizes and shapes, the task is to order them from least capacity to most. This can be quite challenging. Do not provide answers. Let students work in groups to come up with a solution and also explain how they arrived at it.

> **Even adults have difficulty judging which of two containers will hold more. Try the following task yourself as well as with students. Take two sheets of construction paper. Make a tube shape (cylinder) of one by taping the two long edges together. Make a shorter, fatter tube from the other sheet by taping the short edges together. When placed upright, which cylinder holds the most, or do they have the same capacity?**

This task is a good exploration for older students, and the results may be surprising. Before doing this with your class, survey them to see how many select which option. Most groups split roughly in thirds: short and fat, tall and skinny, same. Without using formulas, try using a filler such as Styrofoam packing peanuts or lima beans. Place the skinny cylinder inside the fat one. Fill the inside tube and then lift it up, allowing the filler to empty into the fat cylinder.

The apparent volumes of solid objects are sometimes misleading, and a method of comparison is also difficult. To compare volumes of solids such as a ball and an apple, some method of displacement must be used. Provide students with two or three containers that will each hold the objects to be compared and a filler such as rice or beans. With this equipment some students may be able to devise their own comparison method. One approach is to first fill a container completely and then pour it into an empty holding container. Next, place an object in the first container and fill it again to the top, using filler from the holding container. The volume of filler remaining is equal to the volume of the object. Mark the level of the leftover filler in the holding container before repeating the experiment with other objects. By comparing the level of the leftover filler for two or more objects, the volumes of the objects can be compared.

Using Units of Volume and Capacity

Two types of units can be used to measure volume and capacity: solid units and containers. Solid units are things like wooden cubes or old tennis balls that can be used to fill the container being measured. The other type of unit model is a small container that is filled and poured repeatedly into the container being measured. The following are a few examples of units that you might want to collect.

- Plastic caps and liquid medicine cups are all good for very small units.

- Plastic jars and containers of almost any size can serve as a unit.

- Wooden cubic blocks or blocks of any shape can be units as long as you have a lot of the same size.

- Styrofoam packing peanuts can be used. Even though they do not pack perfectly, they still produce conceptual measures of volume.

Measuring activities for capacity are similar to those for length and area. Estimation of capacity is a lot more fun because it is much more difficult. Finding ways to measure containers such as a large cardboard carton in terms of a relatively small container-type unit can be an excellent challenge for groups of fourth or fifth graders. This can be done long before volume formulas are developed.

Volumes of rectangular boxes such as a shoebox can be determined by filling with any of the units mentioned earlier. However, here is an opportunity to prepare students for volume formulas in a manner similar to what was discussed for the area of rectangles. If students are given a box and sufficient cubes to fill it, they will most likely count the cubes rather than use any multiplicative structure. The following activity is similar to "Rectangle Comparison—Square Units" (Activity 9.6).

ACTIVITY 9.10

Box Comparison—Cubic Units

Provide students with a pair of small boxes that you have folded up from poster board. (See Figure 9.9.) Use unit dimensions that match the blocks that you have. Students are given two boxes, exactly one block, and an appropriate ruler. (If you use 2-cm cubes, make a ruler with the unit equal to 2 centimeters.) The students' task is to decide which box has the greater volume or if they have the same volume.

Here are some suggested box dimensions ($L \times W \times H$):

$6 \times 3 \times 4$ $5 \times 4 \times 4$ $3 \times 9 \times 3$ $6 \times 6 \times 2$ $5 \times 5 \times 5$

Students should use words, drawings, and numbers to explain their conclusions.

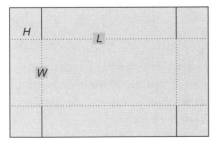

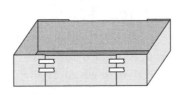

FIGURE 9.9

Make small boxes by starting with a rectangle and drawing a square on each corner as shown. Cut on the solid lines and fold the box up, wrapping the corner squares to the outside and tape or glue them to the sides as shown.

A useful hint in the last activity is to first figure out how many cubes will fit on the bottom of the box. Some, although certainly not all, third-grade students will discover a multiplicative rule for the volume. The boxes can be filled with cubes to confirm conclusions. No formulas should be used unless students can explain them. The development of a formula is not necessarily the goal of this activity.

Making and Using Measuring Cups

Instruments for measuring capacity are generally used for small amounts of liquids or pourable materials such as rice or water. These tools are commonly found in kitchens and laboratories. As with other instruments, if children make their own, they are likely to develop a better understanding of the units and the approach to the measuring process.

A measuring cup can be made by using a small container as a unit. Select a large, transparent container for the cup and a small container for a unit. Fill the unit with beans or rice, empty it into the large container, and make a mark indicating the level. Repeat until the cup is nearly full. If the unit is small, marks may only be necessary after every 5 units. Numbers need not be written on the container for every marking. Students frequently have difficulty reading scales in which not every mark is labeled or where each mark represents more than one unit. This is an opportunity to help them understand how to interpret lines on a real measuring cup.

Students should use their measuring cups and compare the measures with those made by directly filling the container from the unit. The cup is likely to produce errors due to inaccurate markings. This is an opportunity to point out that measuring instruments themselves can be a source of error in measurement. The more accurately made the instrument, and the finer the calibration, the less the error from that source.

Measuring Weight and Mass

Weight is a measure of the pull or force of gravity on an object. *Mass* is the amount of matter in an object and a measure of the force needed to accelerate it. On the moon, where gravity is much less than on Earth, an object has a smaller weight but the identical mass as on Earth. For practical purposes, on Earth, the measures of mass and weight will be about the same. In this discussion, the terms *weight* and *mass* will be used interchangeably.

By third grade students usually understand what it means for one object to be heavier or to weigh more than a second object. Therefore, comparison activities are not necessary.

Using Units of Weight or Mass

Any collection of uniform objects with the same mass can serve as weight units. For very light objects, wooden or plastic cubes work well. Large metal washers found in hardware stores are effective for weighing slightly heavier objects. You will need to rely on standard weights to weigh things as heavy as a kilogram or more.

Weight cannot be measured directly. Either a two-pan balance or a spring scale must be used. Figure 9.10 shows a homemade version of each. In a balance scale, place an object in one pan and weights in the other until the two pans balance. In a spring scale, first place the object in and mark the position of the pan on a piece of paper taped behind the pan. Remove the object and place just enough weights in the pan to pull it down to the same level. Discuss how equal weights will pull the spring or rubber band with the same force.

At any grade level, even a brief experience with informal unit weights is good preparation for standard units and scales.

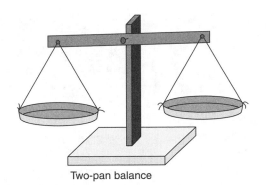

Two-pan balance

Making and Using a Scale

Most scales that we use in our daily lives produce a number when an object is placed on or in it. There are no visible unit weights. How does the scale produce the right number? By making a scale that gives a numeric result without recourse to units, students can see how scales work in principle.

Students can use informal weight units and calibrate a simple rubber-band scale like the one in Figure 9.10. Mount the scale with a piece of paper behind it, and place weights in the pan. After every five weights, make a mark on the paper. The resulting marks correspond to the markings around the dial of a standard scale. The pan serves as the pointer. In the dial scale, the downward movement of the pan mechanically causes the dial to turn. The value of this activity is seeing how scales are made. Even digital readout scales are based on the same principle.

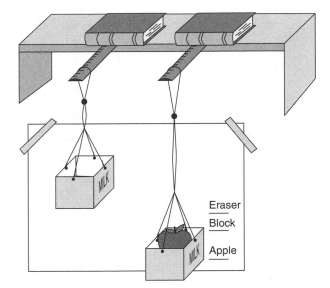

Eraser
Block
Apple

Rubber-band (spring) scales
Marks show where different objects pulled the scale.

FIGURE 9.10 •

Two simple scales.

Measuring Time

Time is measured in the same way that other attributes are measured: A unit of time is selected and used to "fill" the time to be measured. *Time* can be thought of as the duration of an event from its beginning to its end. An informal unit of time might be the duration of a pendulum swing, the steady drip of a water faucet, or the movement of the sun's shadow between two fixed points (as on a sundial). To measure time, the units of time are started at the same time as the activity being measured ("timed") and counted until the activity is finished. Thus the pendulum swings, for example, are "fitted into" the duration of time that it takes the child to print his or her name. By third grade, the concept of duration is generally understood. The related skills of reading a clock and computing elapsed time are another matter.

"About 7 o'clock"

"A little bit
past 9 o'clock"

"Halfway between
2 o'clock and 3 o'clock"

FIGURE 9.11 •••••••

Approximate time with
one-handed clocks.

BLM 38

Clock Reading

Telling time has little to do conceptually with the measurement of time. The skills of clock reading are related to the skills of reading any meter that uses pointers on a numbered scale. Clock reading is a difficult skill to teach yet nearly everyone learns to tell time by middle school.

By third grade, clock reading is generally a review. Some students continue to experience difficulty with reading clocks to the minute, distinguishing between minutes before and minutes after the hour, and understanding the designations of A.M. and P.M.

For students experiencing real difficulties with clock reading, a one-handed clock is a good suggestion. As shown in Figure 9.11, a one-handed clock—a clock with only an hour hand—can be read with reasonable accuracy. Practice this idea of reading approximate times using a one-handed clock before trying the following activity.

ACTIVITY 9.11

One-Handed Clocks

Prepare a page of clock faces (see the Blackline Masters). On each clock draw an hour hand. Include placements that are approximately a quarter past the hour, a quarter until the hour, half past the hour, and some that are close to but not on the hour. For each clock face, the students' task is to write the digital time and draw a minute hand on the clock where they think it would be.

Assessment Note

The "One-Handed Clocks" activity is also a good assessment of students' clock reading. If students are having difficulty with this activity, one-on-one work with a one-handed clock paired with both a digital clock and a regular two-handed clock is suggested. Students should first learn to say the approximate time with a one-handed clock. Next they should be able to place the minute hand, as was done in the activity. Then, given a digital time, discuss first where the hour hand should go and then the minute hand. On an ongoing basis, help students by having them focus first on the hour hand and making an estimate of the time. Then they use the minute hand for precision.

Elapsed Time

Determining elapsed time is a skill required by most state curricula. It is also a skill that can be difficult for students, especially when the period of time includes noon. Consider the concepts and skills involved.

First, do students know how many minutes are in an hour, and, if given the digital time or the time after the hour, can they tell how many minutes to the next hour? This should certainly be a mental process for multiples of five minutes. Avoid having students use pencil and paper to subtract 25 from 60.

Figuring the time from, say, 8:15 A.M. to 11:45 A.M. is a multistep task regardless of how it is done. It involves understanding about minutes before and after the hour, as just discussed. Keeping track of the intermediate steps is difficult, as is deciding what to do first. In this case you could count hours from 8:15 to 11:15 and add on 30 minutes. But then what do you do if the endpoints are 8:45 and 11:15? To propose a singular method or algorithm is not helpful.

Next is the issue of A.M. and P.M. It is less the fact that students don't understand what happens on the clock at noon and midnight as it is that they now have trouble counting the intervals.

When we consider all of these potential difficulties, it is no small wonder that elapsed time is such a dilemma. In the discussion so far, we have only addressed one form of the problem. There is also the task of finding the end time given the start time and elapsed time, or finding the start time given the end time and the elapsed time. In keeping with the spirit of problem solving and the use of models, consider the following.

As a general model for all of these elapsed time problems, suggest that students sketch a time line. When the end times are both known, the time line should stretch from one to the other. When the elapsed time and one end time are known, sketch only the one given time and a line in the direction of the other end time. Examples are shown in Figure 9.12. It is important not to be overly prescriptive in telling students how to use the time line. As with mental computation, there are various alternatives. For example, in Figure 9.12(a), a student might count by full hours from 10:45 (11:45, 12:45, 1:45, 2:45, 3:45) and then subtract 15 minutes.

(a) School began late today at 10:45 a.m. If you get out at 3:30, how much time will you be in school today?

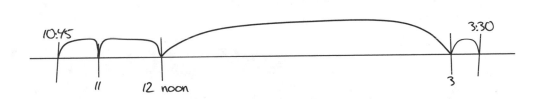

Four hours from 11 to 3 (1 and 3). Then 15 minutes in front and 30 minutes at the end – 45 minutes. Three hours 45 minutes in all.

(b) The game begins at 11:30 a.m. If it lasts 2 hours and 15 minutes, when will it be over?

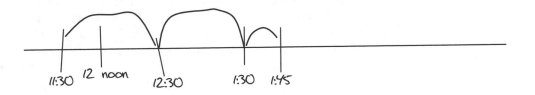

One hour after 11:30 is 12:30 and a second hour gets you to 1:30 and then 15 minutes more is 1:45. It's p.m. because it is after noon.

FIGURE 9.12 • • • • • • •

A simple sketch of a line can be useful in solving elapsed time problems. Students should not be told how to use the time line. For each of the examples here, the problem can be solved in a different manner. The value of the time line is in seeing where noon is and keeping track of the different parts of the interval.

MEASURING TIME

Measuring Angles

Angle measurement causes difficulty for two reasons: The attribute of angle size is often misunderstood, and protractors are introduced and used without understanding how they work.

Comparing Angles

The attribute of angle size might be called the "spread of the angle's rays." Angles are composed of two rays that are infinite in length with a common vertex. The only difference in their size is how widely or narrowly the two rays are spread apart.

Some authors have students think of how much one ray has rotated away from the other. Two rulers held together near the ends can be used to demonstrate this idea. As one ruler is rotated, the size of the angle is seen to get larger. However, when we see angles, the rays have already been spread—there is no rotation. Do you think of the angles in a triangle as one side being rotated away from the other?

To help students conceptualize the attribute of the spread of the rays, two angles can be directly compared by tracing one and placing it over the other. Be sure to have students compare angles with sides of different lengths. A wide angle with short sides may seem smaller than a narrow angle with long sides. This is a common misconception among students. As soon as students can tell the difference between a large angle and a small one, regardless of the length of the sides, you can move on to measuring angles.

Using Units of Angular Measure

A unit for measuring an angle must be an angle. Nothing else has the same attribute of spread that we want to measure. (Contrary to popular opinion, you do not need to use degrees to measure angles.)

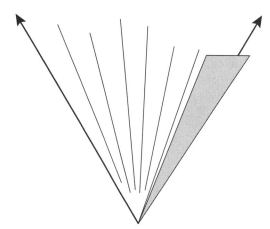

FIGURE 9.13 • • • • • • • • • • • • • • • • • •

Using a small wedge cut from an index card as a unit angle, this angle measures about $7\frac{1}{2}$ wedges. Accuracy of measurement with those nonstandard angles is less important than the idea of how an angle is used to measure the size of another angle.

ACTIVITY 9.12

A Unit Angle

Give each student an index card or a small piece of tagboard. Have students draw a narrow angle on the tagboard using a straightedge and then cut it out. The resulting wedge can then be used as a unit of angular measure by counting the number that will fit in a given angle. See Figure 9.13. Pass out a worksheet with assorted angles on it, and have students use their unit to measure them. Because students made their own unit angles, the results will differ and can be discussed in terms of unit size. For a uniform unit angle, use the tan rhombus pattern block.

Activity 9.12 illustrates that measuring an angle is the same as measuring length or area. Unit angles are used to fill or cover the spread of an angle just as unit lengths fill or cover a length. Once this concept is well understood, you can move on to the use of measuring instruments.

Making a Protractor

The protractor is one of the most poorly understood measuring instruments found in schools. Part of the difficulty arises because the units (degrees) are so very small. It would be physically impossible to cut out a single degree and use it in, say, Activity 9.12. Another problem is that there are no visible angles showing; there are only little marks around the outside edge of the protractor. Finally, the numbering that appears on most protractors runs both clockwise and counterclockwise along the marked edges. "Which numbers do I use?" By making a protractor with a large unit angle, all of these mysterious features can be understood. A careful comparison with a standard protractor will then permit that instrument to be used with understanding.

Tear off about a foot of ordinary waxed paper for each student. Have the students fold the paper in half and crease the fold tightly. Fold in half again so that the folded edges match. Repeat this two more times, each time bringing the folded edges together and creasing tightly. Cut or tear off the resulting wedge shape about 4 or 5 inches from the vertex and unfold. If done correctly, there will be 16 angles surrounding the center, as in Figure 9.14. This serves as an excellent protractor with a unit angle that is one-eighth of a straight angle. It is sufficiently transparent that it can be placed over an angle on paper, on the blackboard, or on the overhead projector to measure angles, as shown in Figure 9.15. Reasonable estimates of angle measures can be made with a waxed-paper protractor as small as the one in Figure 9.15. In that figure, one angle of a free-form polygon is measured for you. Use a waxed-paper protractor to measure the other four angles in this polygon as carefully as possible. Use fractional estimates. Your sum for all five interior angles should be very close to 24 wedges. There are two possible ways to get the measure of the angle indicated with the arrow. How would you measure that angle if your protractor was only a half circle instead of a full circle?

The waxed-paper protractor makes it quite clear how a protractor fits unit angles into an angle for measurement. When measuring angles, students can easily estimate halves, thirds, or fourths of a "wedge," a possible name for this informal unit angle. This is sufficiently accurate to measure, for example, the interior angles of a polygon and discover the usual relationship between number of sides and sum of the interior angles. For a triangle, the sum is 8 wedges, recorded as 8^w. For a quadrilateral, the sum is 16^w. And in general, the sum for an n-sided polygon is $(n - 2) \times 8^w$. The superscript w is a forerunner of the degree symbol (°).

Figure 9.16 illustrates how a tagboard semicircle can be made into a protractor to measure angles in wedges. This tagboard version is a bit closer to a standard protractor, since the rays do not extend down to the vertex and the markings are numbered in two directions. The only difference between this protractor and a standard one is the size of the unit angle. The standard unit angle is the *degree*,

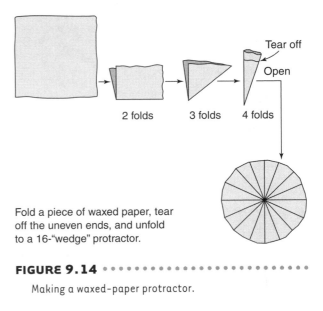

Fold a piece of waxed paper, tear off the uneven ends, and unfold to a 16-"wedge" protractor.

FIGURE 9.14 •

Making a waxed-paper protractor.

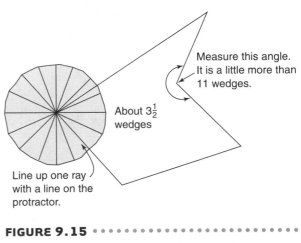

Measure this angle. It is a little more than 11 wedges.

About $3\frac{1}{2}$ wedges

Line up one ray with a line on the protractor.

FIGURE 9.15 •

Measuring angles in a polygon using a waxed-paper protractor.

FIGURE 9.16 • • • • • • •

Comparisons of protrac-
tors and unit angles.

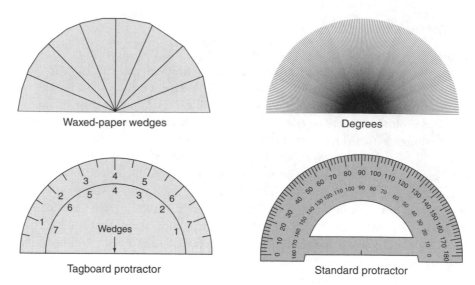

Waxed-paper wedges

Degrees

Tagboard protractor

Standard protractor

The marks on the tagboard wedge protractor are the rays on the waxed-paper version.
The marks on a plastic protractor are the rays of <u>degrees</u>. A degree is just a very small angle.
A large picture of 180 degrees can be found in Blackline Masters.

BLM 39

which is simply a very small angle. A standard protractor is not very helpful in teaching the meaning of a degree. But an analogy between wedges and degrees and between
these two protractors is a very effective approach. (See the Blackline Masters.)

Introducing Standard Units

As pointed out earlier, there are a number of reasons for teaching measurement
using nonstandard units. However, measurement sense demands that students be familiar with the common measurement units and that they be able to make estimates in
terms of these units and meaningfully interpret measures depicted with standard units.

Perhaps the biggest error in measurement instruction is the failure to recognize
and separate two types of objectives: first, understanding the meaning and technique of
measuring a particular attribute and, second, learning about the standard units commonly used to measure that attribute. These two objectives can be developed separately; when both objectives are attempted together, confusion is likely.

 **How many of the four reasons why you might use informal units can you recall?
Which of these seem most important to you and why?**

Reread the list of reasons for using informal units on p. 256. Not all reasons apply
to every situation you may face. To avoid wasting time in your measurement program
it is important to know why you are or are not using informal or nonstandard units. It
is only when students are comfortable with measurement of an attribute that they can
focus on things like cups and quarts or the number of inches in a foot or feet in a yard
or have a feel for grams and kilograms.

Instructional Goals

Three broad goals relative to standard units of measure can be identified:

1. *Familiarity with the unit.* Familiarity means that students should have a basic idea of the size of commonly used units and what they measure. Without this familiarity, measurement sense is impossible. It is more important to know about how much 1 liter of water is or to be able to estimate a shelf as 5 feet long than to have the ability to measure either of these accurately.
2. *Ability to select an appropriate unit.* Related to unit familiarity is knowing what is a reasonable unit of measure in a given situation. The choice of an appropriate unit is also a matter of required precision. (Would you measure your lawn to purchase grass seed with the same precision as you would use in measuring a window to buy a pane of glass?) Students need practice in using common sense in the selection of appropriate standard units.
3. *Knowledge of a few important relationships between units.* The emphasis should be kept to those relationships that are commonly used, such as inches, feet, and yards or milliliters and liters. Tedious conversion exercises do little to enhance measurement sense. The goal of unit relationships is the least important of all measurement objectives.

Developing Unit Familiarity

Two types of activities can help develop familiarity with standard units: (1) comparisons that focus on a single unit and (2) activities that develop personal referents or benchmarks for single units or easy multiples of units.

ACTIVITY 9.13

About One Unit

Give students a model of a standard unit and have them search for things that measure about the same as that one unit. For example, to develop familiarity with the meter, give students a piece of rope 1 meter long. Have them make lists of things that are about 1 meter. Keep separate lists for things that are a little less (or more) or twice as long (or half as long). Encourage students to find familiar items in their daily lives. In the case of lengths, be sure to include circular lengths. Later, students can try to predict if a given object is more than, less than, or close to 1 meter.

The same activity can be done with other unit lengths. Parents can be enlisted to help students find familiar distances that are about 1 mile or about 1 kilometer. Suggest in a letter that they check the distances around the neighborhood, to the school or shopping center, or along other frequently traveled paths.

For capacity units such as cup, quart, and liter, students need a container that holds or has a marking for a single unit. They should then find other containers at home and at school that hold about as much, more, and less. Remember that the shapes of containers can be very deceptive when estimating their capacity.

For the standard weights of gram, kilogram, ounce, and pound, students can compare objects on a two-pan balance with single copies of these units. It may be more effective to work with 10 grams or 5 ounces. Students can be encouraged to bring in familiar objects from home to compare on the classroom scale.

Standard area units are in terms of lengths such as square inches or square feet, so familiarity with lengths is important. Familiarity with a single degree is not as important as some idea of 30, 45, 60, and 90 degrees.

The second approach to unit familiarity is to begin with very familiar items and use their measures as references or benchmarks. A doorway is a bit more than 2 meters. A bag of flour is a good reference for 5 pounds. A bedroom may be about 10 feet long. A paper clip weighs about a gram and is about 1 centimeter wide. A gallon of milk weighs a little less than 4 kilograms.

ACTIVITY 9.14

Familiar References

For each unit of measure you wish to focus on, have students make a list of at least five familiar things and measure those things using that unit. For lengths, encourage them to include long and short things; for weight, to find both light and heavy things; and so on. The measures should be rounded off to nice whole numbers. Discuss lists in class so that different ideas are shared.

Of special interest for length are benchmarks found on our bodies. These become quite familiar over time and can be used as approximate rulers in many situations. Even though young children grow quite rapidly, it is useful for them to know the approximate lengths that they carry around with them.

ACTIVITY 9.15

Personal Benchmarks

Measure your body. About how long is your foot, your stride, your hand span (stretched and with fingers together), the width of your finger, your arm span (finger to finger and finger to nose), the distance around your wrist and around your waist, and your height to waist, to shoulder, and to head? Perhaps you cannot remember all of these, but some may prove to be useful benchmarks, and some may be excellent models for single units. (The average child's fingernail width is about 1 cm, and most people can find a 10-cm length somewhere on their hands.)

To help remember these references, they must be used in activities in which lengths, volumes, and so on are compared to the benchmarks to estimate measurements.

Choosing Appropriate Units

Should the room be measured in feet or inches? Should the concrete blocks be weighed in grams or kilograms? The answers to questions such as these involve more than simply knowing how big the units are, although that is certainly required. Another consideration involves the need for precision. If you were measuring your wall in order to cut a piece of molding or woodwork to fit, you would need to measure it very precisely. The smallest unit would be an inch or a centimeter, and you would also use small fractional parts. But if you were determining how many 8-foot molding strips to buy, the nearest foot would probably be sufficient.

Guess the Unit

Find examples of measurements of all types in newspapers, on signs, or in other everyday situations. Present the context and measures but without units. The task is to predict what units of measure were used. Have students discuss their choices.

Important Standard Units and Relationships

Both the customary and metric systems include many units that are rarely if ever used in everyday life. Table 9.2 lists the units that are most common in each system. Your state or local curriculum is the best guide to help you decide which units your students should be learning. Remember that textbooks are written to satisfy the needs of many states and so they may touch on units not in your curriculum. This excess of tedious information can be boring. Unit familiarity with the most popularly used units should be the principal focus of almost all instruction with standard units. (See Activities 9.14, 9.15, and 9.16.)

The relationships between units within either the metric or customary systems are conventions. As such, students must simply be told what the relationships are, and exercises must be devised to reinforce them. It can be argued that knowing about how much liquid makes a cup or a quart, or being able to pace off 3 yards—unit familiarity—is more important than knowing how many cups in a quart or inches in a yard. However, in the intermediate grades, knowing basic relationships becomes more important for testing purposes. Your curriculum should be your guide.

In the customary system there are very few patterns or rules to guide students in converting units. Liquid or capacity units involve mostly multiples of 2, 4, and 8, but there is no real pattern. The relationships between inches, feet, and yards are quite common and can be the source of good word problems involving multiplication and division.

On the other hand, the metric system was designed systematically around powers of ten. An understanding of the role of the decimal point as indicating the units position is a powerful concept for making metric conversions. (See Chapter 7, Figure 7.6.) As students begin to appreciate the structure of decimal notation, the metric system can and should be developed with all seven places: three prefixes for smaller units (*deci-*, *centi-*, *milli-*) and three for larger units (*deka-*, *hecto-*, *kilo-*). Avoid mechanical rules such as "To change centimeters to meters, move the decimal point two places to the left." When the students themselves do not create conceptual, meaningful methods for conversions, arbitrary-sounding rules are bound to be misused and forgotten.

TABLE 9.2
Commonly Encountered Units of Measure

	Metric System	*Customary System*
Length	millimeter centimeter meter kilometer	inch foot yard mile
Area	square centimeter square meter	square inch square foot square yard
Volume	cubic centimeter cubic meter	cubic inch cubic foot cubic yard
Capacity	millimeter liter	ounce* teaspoon tablespoon cup quart gallon
Weight	gram kilogram metric ton	ounce* pound ton

*In the U.S. customary system, the term *ounce* refers to a weight or *avoirdupois* unit, 16 of which make a pound, and also a volume or capacity unit, 8 of which make a cup. Though the two units have the same name, they are not related.

Exact conversions between the metric and the customary system should never be done. As long as we live in a country that uses two systems of measurement, "soft" or "friendly" conversions are useful. For example, a liter is a "gulp more" than a quart, and a meter is a bit longer than a yard. The same is true of familiar references. One hundred meters is about one football field plus one end zone, or about 110 yards.

Assessment Note

In assessing students' understanding and familiarity with standard units, there is a danger of focusing on the traditional conversion tasks. Consider these two tasks:

1. 4 feet = _____ inches
2. Estimate the length of this rope in feet and then in inches. How did you decide on your estimate?

Both tasks relate feet and inches. However, the second task requires students to have a familiarity with the units as well. With the estimation task we can observe whether the student uses the first estimate to make the second (understanding and *using* the feet–inches relationship) or rather makes two separate estimates. This task also allows us to see how an estimate is made. This information is unavailable in the narrower, traditional task.

The point is to ask questions that require more than recall and ask students to *use* the information that you helped them to develop.

Estimating Measures

Measurement estimation is the process of using mental and visual information to measure or make comparisons without the use of measuring instruments. It is a practical skill. Almost every day, we make estimates of measures. Do I have enough sugar to make the cookies? Can you throw the ball 50 feet? Is this suitcase over the weight limit? About how long is the fence?

Besides its value outside the classroom, estimation in measurement activities helps students focus on the attribute being measured, adds intrinsic motivation, and helps develop familiarity with standard units. Therefore, measurement estimation both improves measurement instruction and develops a valuable life skill.

Techniques of Measurement Estimation

Just as for computational estimation, specific strategies exist for estimating measures. Four strategies can be taught specifically:

1. *Develop and use benchmarks or referents for important units.* (This strategy was also mentioned as a way to develop familiarity with units.) Students should have a good referent for single units and also useful multiples of standard units. Referents or benchmarks for 1, 5, 10, and perhaps 100 pounds might be useful. A referent for 500 milliliters is very useful. These benchmarks can then be compared mentally to objects being estimated: "That tree is about as tall as four doorways, or between 8 and 9 meters tall."

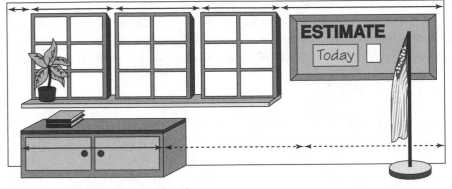

FIGURE 9.17 • • • • • • • • • • • • •

Estimating measures by chunking.

Estimate the room length.
Use: windows, bulletin board, and spaces between as "chunks."
Use: cabinet length—looks like about three cabinets will fit into
    the room—plus a little bit.

2. *Use "chunking" when appropriate.* Figure 9.17 is an example. It may be easier to estimate the shorter chunks along the wall than to estimate the whole length as one. The weight of a stack of books is easier if some estimate is given to an "average" book.

3. *Use subdivisions.* This is a similar strategy to chunking, with the chunks imposed on the object by the estimator. For example, if the wall length to be estimated has no useful chunks, it can be mentally divided in half and then in fourths or even eighths by repeated halving until a more manageable length is arrived at. Length, volume, and area measurements all lend themselves to this technique.

4. *Iterate a unit mentally or physically.* For length, area, and volume, it is sometimes easy to mark off single units visually. You might use your hands or make marks or folds to keep track as you go. For length, it is especially useful to use a body measure as a unit and iterate with that. If you know, for example, that your stride is about $\frac{3}{4}$ meter, you can walk off a length and then multiply to get an estimate. Hand and finger widths are useful for shorter measures.

Tips for Teaching Estimation

Each of the four strategies just listed should be taught directly and discussed with students. But the best approach to improving estimation skills is to have students do a lot of estimating. Keep the following tips in mind:

1. Help students learn strategies by having them use a specified approach. Later activities should permit students to choose whatever techniques they wish.
2. Periodically discuss how different students made their estimates. This will help students understand that there is no single right way to estimate and also remind them of different approaches that are useful.
3. Accept a range of estimates. Think in relative terms about what is a good estimate. Within 10 percent for length is quite good. Even 30 percent off may be reasonable for weights or volumes.
4. Sometimes have students give a range of measures that they believe includes the actual measure. This not only is a practical approach in real life but also helps focus on the approximate nature of estimation.

5. Make measurement estimation an ongoing activity. A daily measurement to estimate can be posted on the bulletin board. Students can turn in their estimates on paper and discuss them in a 5-minute period. Older students can even be given the task of making up the things to estimate, with a team assigned this task each week.

Measurement Estimation Activities

Estimation activities need not be elaborate. Any measurement activity can have an "estimate first" component. For more emphasis on the process of estimation itself, simply think of things that can be estimated and have students estimate. Here are a few suggestions.

ACTIVITY 9.17

Estimation Quickie

Select a single object such as a box, a watermelon, a jar, or even the principal. Each day select a different attribute or dimension to estimate. For a watermelon, for example, students can estimate its length, girth, weight, volume, and surface area.

ACTIVITY 9.18

Estimation Scavenger Hunt

Conduct measurement scavenger hunts. Give teams a list of measurements and have them find things that are close to having those measurements. Permit no measuring instruments. A list might include the following items:

- A length of 3.5 m
- Something that weighs more than 1 kg but less than 2 kg
- A container that holds about 200 ml

Let students suggest how to judge results in terms of accuracy.

ACTIVITY 9.19

E-M-E Sequences

Use estimate-measure-estimate sequences (Lindquist, 1987a). Select pairs of objects to estimate that are somehow related or close in measure but not the same. Have students estimate the measure of the first and check by measuring. Then have them estimate the second. Here are some examples of pairs:

- Width of a window, width of a wall
- Volume of a coffee mug, volume of a pitcher
- Distance between the eyes, width of the head
- Weight of a handful of marbles, weight of a bag of marbles

Activity 9.19 can help students understand how benchmarks are used in estimation.

Developing Formulas for Area and Volume

The relationship between measurement and geometry is most evident in the development of area and volume formulas for measures of geometric figures.

Some state and local testing programs allow students access to formulas during the test. Apparently, the idea is that use of a formula is more important than having memorized it. One can always look up a needed formula. If this is the practice where you teach, do not make the mistake of bypassing formula development with your students. A conceptual development of formulas does much more than provide formulas for students. As students develop formulas, they gain conceptual understanding of the ideas and relationships involved. There is less likelihood, for example, that students will confuse area and perimeter or that they will select the incorrect formula on the test. General relationships are developed. For example, students can see how all area formulas are related to one idea: length of the base times the height. And students who understand where formulas come from do not see them as mysterious, tend to remember them, and are reinforced in the idea that mathematics makes sense. Rote use of formulas from a book offers none of these advantages.

Common Difficulties

The results of National Assessment of Educational Progress (NAEP) testing indicate clearly that students do not have a very good understanding of formulas. For example, in the sixth NAEP, only 19 percent of fourth-grade students and 65 percent of eighth-grade students were able to give the area of a carpet 9 feet long and 6 feet wide (Kenney & Kouba, 1997). A common error is to confuse formulas for area and perimeter. Performances such as this are largely due to an overemphasis on formulas with little or no conceptual background. Simply telling students how a formula was derived does not work.

The tasks in Figure 9.18 cannot be solved with simple formulas; they require an understanding of concepts and how formulas work. "Length times width" is not a definition of area.

Another common error when students use formulas comes from failure to conceptualize the meaning of height and base in geometric figures, both two- and three-dimensional. The shapes in Figure 9.19 each have a slanted side and a height given. Students tend to confuse these two. Any side or flat surface of a figure can be called a *base* of the figure. For each base that a figure has, there is a corresponding height. If the figure were to slide into a room on a selected base, the *height* would be the height of the shortest door it could pass through without bending over—that is, the perpendicular distance to the base. Students have a lot of early experiences with the length-times-width formula

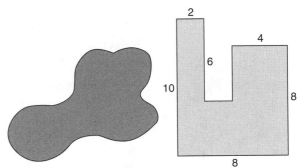

"How would you determine the areas of these shapes?"

Note: Many children believe that such shapes do not have areas or that the areas are impossible to determine because there are no formulas.

FIGURE 9.18 •

Understanding the attribute of area.

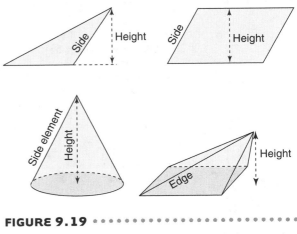

FIGURE 9.19 •

Heights of figures are not always measured along an edge or a surface.

for rectangles, in which the height is exactly the same as the length of a side. Perhaps this is the source of the confusion.

Before formulas involving heights are discussed, students should be able to identify where a height could be measured for any base that a figure has.

The Area of Rectangles, Parallelograms, Triangles, and Trapezoids

The formula for the area of a rectangle is one of the first that is developed and is usually given as $A = L \times W$, "area equals length times width." Looking forward to other area formulas, an equivalent but more unifying idea might be $A = b \times h$, "area equals *base* times *height.*" The base-times-height formulation can be generalized to all parallelograms (not just rectangles) and is useful in developing the area formulas for triangles and trapezoids. Furthermore, the same approach can be extended to three dimensions, where volumes of cylinders are given in terms of the *area of the base* times the height. Base times height, then, helps connect a large family of formulas that otherwise must be mastered independently.

Rectangles

The following sequence of activities to develop the area formula for a rectangle is illustrated in Figure 9.20. Approach each step of this sequence with a problem-solving spirit: How can we figure this out?

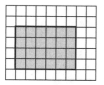

Area can be determined by counting the squares.

5 unit squares fit on the <u>base</u>. Since the height is 6, it looks as though 6 rows will fit.

6

5 ⌐Base

6

3

Explain how to determine the number of 1 × 1 squares that will fit in this rectangle. Can you do it two ways?

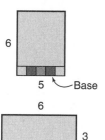

$2\frac{1}{3}$

$4\frac{1}{2}$

Select one side as a base. How many unit squares will fit on that base? How many rows will fill the rectangle?

1. Have students determine the areas of rectangles drawn on square grids or geoboards. Or have students draw rectangles that have specified areas (but do not give the dimensions). Some may count every square; others may multiply to find the total number of squares.

2. Examine rectangles not on a grid but with whole-number dimensions. Provide students with a single square and a ruler. Challenge students to find a way to determine the area with just these two tools but without drawing in all of the squares or moving the square from place to place. Require justifications and share different ideas.

3. Give students rectangles with only the dimensions provided, and have them determine the area. Require them to justify their results.

4. Examine rectangles with dimensions that are not whole numbers. If the base is $4\frac{1}{2}$ units, then $4\frac{1}{2}$ unit squares will fit along the base. If the height is $2\frac{1}{3}$ units, then there are $2\frac{1}{3}$ rows with $4\frac{1}{2}$ squares in each, or $2\frac{1}{3}$ sets of $4\frac{1}{2}$.

STOP

Before reading further, return to step 2 in the preceding sequence. How would you solve this task, assuming that you did not know a formula for the area of a rectangle?

FIGURE 9.20

Determining the area of a rectangle.

Step 2 in the preceding sequence is the critical point in the development. As students discuss their various approaches, focus on those ideas that are closest to this idea: *The length of a side will determine the number of squares that can be fit on the side. The length of the other side will determine how many rows of these squares will fit in the rectangle all together. Multiply the length of a row by the number of rows.* When this concept is well understood, introduce the vocabulary of *base* and *height*. Students should be able to explain why any side of the rectangle can be called the base and the length of the adjoining side can be called the height.

From Rectangles to Other Parallelograms

Once students understand the base-times-height formula for rectangles, the next challenge is to determine the areas of parallelograms. Do not provide a formula or other explanation. Rather, give students several parallelograms drawn on a grid or on a plain sheet of paper. Their task is to develop a method for finding the area of a parallelogram that they can use with any parallelogram, not just those they are working with. If students are stuck, ask them to examine ways that the parallelogram is like a rectangle or how it can be changed into a rectangle. As shown in Figure 9.21, a parallelogram can always be transformed into a rectangle with the same base, the same height, and the same area. Thus, the formula for the area of a parallelogram is exactly the same as for a rectangle: base times height.

From Parallelograms to Triangles

It is very important for students to understand the parallelogram formula before exploring triangle area. With that background, the area of a triangle is relatively simple.

As with parallelograms, students should be challenged to figure the area of a triangle in such a manner that the method applies to all triangles. If students require a hint, suggest that they try putting together two identical triangles to make a different shape for which they have an area formula.

As shown in Figure 9.22, two congruent triangles can always be arranged to form a parallelogram with the same base and the same height as the triangle. The area of the triangle will, therefore, be one-half as much as the parallelogram. Have students further explore all three possible parallelograms, one for each triangle side serving as base. Will the computed areas always be the same?

From Parallelograms to Trapezoids

After developing formulas for parallelograms and triangles, your students may be interested in tackling trapezoids without any further assistance. There are at least ten different methods of arriving at a formula for trapezoids, each related to the area of parallelograms or triangles. One of the nicest methods uses the same general approach that was used for triangles. Suggest that students try working with two trapezoids that are identical, just as they did with triangles. Figure 9.23 shows how this method results in the formula. Now, not only are all of these formulas connected, but similar methods were used to develop them.

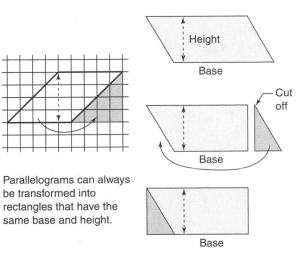

Parallelograms can always be transformed into rectangles that have the same base and height.

FIGURE 9.21 •

Area of a parallelogram.

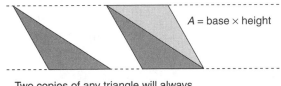

$A = \text{base} \times \text{height}$

Two copies of any triangle will always form a parallelogram with the same base and height; therefore, the triangle has an area of half of the parallelogram, $A = \frac{1}{2} (\text{base} \times \text{height})$.

FIGURE 9.22 •

Two triangles always make a parallelogram.

DEVELOPING FORMULAS FOR AREA AND VOLUME

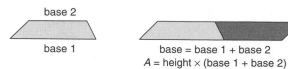

base = base 1 + base 2
A = height × (base 1 + base 2)

Two trapezoids always make a parallelogram with the same height and a base equal to the sum of the bases in the trapezoid. Therefore,

$$A = \tfrac{1}{2} \times \text{height} \times (\text{base 1} + \text{base 2})$$

FIGURE 9.23 •

Two trapezoids always form a parallelogram.

Here are a few hints, each leading to a different approach to finding the area of a trapezoid.

- Make a parallelogram inside the given trapezoid using three of the sides.
- Make a parallelogram using three sides that surround the trapezoid.
- Draw a diagonal forming two triangles.
- Draw a line through the midpoints of the nonparallel sides. The length of that line is the average of the lengths of the two parallel sides.
- Draw a rectangle inside the trapezoid leaving two triangles and then put those two triangles together.

> **STOP** Do you think that students should learn special formulas for the area of a square? Why or why not? Do you think students need formulas for the perimeters of squares and rectangles?

Circle Formulas

The relationship between the *circumference* of a circle (the distance around or the perimeter) and the length of the *diameter* (a line through the center joining two points on the circle) is one of the most interesting that children can discover. The circumference of every circle is about 3.14 times as long as the diameter. The exact ratio is an irrational number close to 3.14 and is represented by the Greek letter π. So $\pi = C/D$, the circumference divided by the diameter. In a slightly different form, $C = \pi D$. Half the diameter is the radius (r), so the same equation can be written $C = 2\pi r$. (In Chapter 8, Activity 8.10 describes how students can discover this important ratio.)

Figure 9.24 presents an argument for the area formula $A = \pi r^2$. This development is one commonly found in textbooks.

Regardless of the approach you use to develop the area formula, students should be challenged to figure it out on their own. For example, show students how to arrange 8 or 12 sectors of a circle into an approximate parallelogram. Their task should be to use this as a hint toward development of an area formula for the circle. You may need to help them notice that the arrangement of sectors is an approximate parallelogram and that the smaller the sectors, the closer the arrangement gets to a rectangle. But the complete argument for the formula should come from your students.

Volumes of Common Solid Shapes

The relationships between the formulas for volume are completely analogous to those for area. As you read, notice the similarities between rectangles and prisms, between parallelograms and "sheered" (oblique) prisms, and between triangles and pyramids. Not only are the formulas related, but the process for development of the formulas is similar.

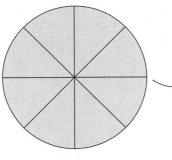

8 sectors can be arranged in a "near parallelogram."

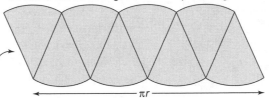

$C = 2\pi r$

The circle and each shape made from sectors all have the same area.

24 sectors is even closer to a parallelogram.

As the number of sectors gets larger, the figure becomes closer and closer to a rectangle (a special parallelogram).

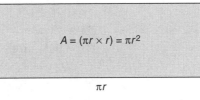

r

$A = (\pi r \times r) = \pi r^2$

πr

FIGURE 9.24 • • • • • • • • • • • • •

Development of the circle area formula.

Students can cut a circle into eight sectors or perhaps even more and rearrange them to form a near rectangle with dimensions of half the circumference by the radius.

Volumes of Cylinders

A *cylinder* is a solid with two congruent parallel bases and sides with parallel elements that join corresponding points on the bases. There are several special classes of cylinders, including *prisms* (with polygons for bases), *right prisms, rectangular prisms,* and *cubes* (see Chapter 8). Interestingly, all of these solids have the same volume formula, and that one formula is analogous to the area formula for parallelograms.

Provide students with some cardboard shoe boxes or similar cardboard boxes, a few cubes, and a ruler. As was done with rectangles, the task is to determine how many cubes will fit inside the box. Most likely your boxes will not have whole-number dimensions, so tell students to ignore any fractional parts of cubes. Although they may have seen or used a volume formula before, for this task they may not rely on a formula. Rather, they must come up with a method or formula that they can explain or justify. If a hint is required, suggest that they begin by finding out how many cubes will fit on the bottom of the box. (See also Activity 9.10, "Box Comparison—Cubic Units.")

The development of the volume formula from this box exploration is exactly parallel to the development of the formula for the area of a rectangle. Figure 9.25 shows the development as if the grid paper were on the bottom of the box.

Base is 3×5. Area of base is 15 squares.

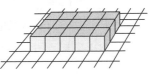

Base "holds" 15 cubes. A $3 \times 5 \times 1$ box has a volume of 15 cubic units.

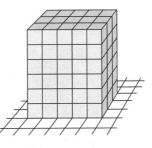

Six layers of cubic units make a box with a height of 6.
Volume = (area of base) × (height) = 15×6

FIGURE 9.25 •

Volume of a prism.

DEVELOPING FORMULAS FOR AREA AND VOLUME

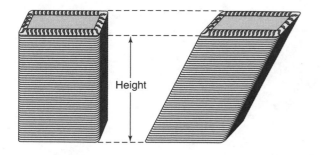

FIGURE 9.26 •••••••••••••••••••••••••••

Two cylinders with the same base and height have the same volume.

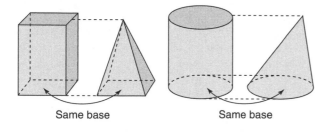

The volume of a pyramid or cone is one-third the volume of a prism or cylinder with the same base and same height.

FIGURE 9.27 •••••••••••••••••••••••••••

Comparing volumes of prisms to pyramids and cones to cylinders.

Recall how the area formula for rectangles was developed (see Figure 9.20, p. 282) and notice how that development is like the one for volume. Instead of *length* of the base × height (for *area* of rectangles), in three dimensions, the *volume* formula for the corresponding figure is *area* of the base × height.

Recall that a parallelogram can be thought of as a "sheered" rectangle. Show students a stack of three or four decks of playing cards (or a stack of books or paper). When stacked straight, they form a rectangular solid. The volume, as just discussed, is $V = A \times h$, with A equal to the area of one card. Now if the stack is sheered or slanted to one side as shown in Figure 9.26, what will the volume of this new figure be? Students should be able to argue that this figure has the same volume (and same volume formula) as the original stack.

What if the cards in this activity were some other shape? If they were circular, the volume would still be the area of the base times the height; if they were triangular, still the same. The conclusion is that the volume of *any* cylinder is equal to the *area of the base* times the *height*.

Volumes of Cones and Pyramids

Recall that when parallelograms and triangles have the same height and base, the areas are in a 2-to-1 relationship. Interestingly, the relationship between the volumes of cylinders and cones with the same height and base is 3 to 1.

To investigate this relationship use plastic models of these related shapes such as Power Solids. Have students estimate the number of times the pyramid will fit into the prism. Then have them test their prediction by filling the pyramid with water or rice and emptying it into the prism. They will discover that exactly three pyramids will fill a prism with the same base and height. (See Figure 9.27.)

The 3-to-1 ratio of volumes is true of all cylinders and cones with the same base and height regardless of the shape of the base or the position of the vertex. That is, for any cone or pyramid, $V = \frac{1}{3}(A \times h)$.

Assessment Note ——————

Gathering useful assessment data in the area of measurement requires open-ended activities that permit students to show how they understand measurement concepts. Traditional textbook tests tend to focus on prescriptive, procedural skills such as conversion of units from feet to inches or the use of a formula. Examine these test items and ask yourself if they really tell you what you want to know about your students and measurement.

Focus on Ideas

As you progress through your measurement unit, think about what students really need to know to develop an understanding of measurement of any given attribute.

How well do students understand the attribute being measured? Observing how students do comparison activities ("Which of these regions is the largest? How can you tell?") will tell you what you need to know. Be wary of overly directing students; make sure that the ideas you observe are theirs, not yours. Rather than direct students to measure something the way you prescribe, have students select their own methods and explain what they did and why they made the choices they made. If reasonable, ask them to find more than one way to measure the same object.

Do students use measuring tools meaningfully? Rulers and protractors are often poorly understood. Ask students to find two different ways to measure with a ruler, or have them react to the technique used by another student. ("Monique measured the width of her locker. She lined up the 10 cm mark on one side. The other side of the locker was lined up between the 42 and 43 cm marks. Monique was confused. Without measuring the locker again, how would you help Monique?") Another technique is to have students explain how a ruler or protractor works to make a measurement. To help with their explanations, have them compare a student-made device, such as the waxed-paper protractor, with the standard device.

EXPANDED LESSON

Fixed Areas

Based on: Activity 9.7, p. 265

GRADE LEVEL: Fourth or fifth grade.

MATHEMATICS GOALS
- To help contrast the concepts of area and perimeter.
- To develop the relationship between area and perimeter of different shapes when the area is fixed.
- To compare and contrast the units used to measure perimeter and those used to measure area.

THINKING ABOUT THE STUDENTS

Students have worked with the ideas of area and perimeter. Some if not the majority of students can find the area and perimeter of given figures and may even be able to state the formulas for finding the perimeter and area of a rectangle. However, they often become confused as to which formula to use.

MATERIALS AND PREPARATION
- Each student will need 36 square tiles such as Color Tiles, at least 2 sheets of centimeter or half-centimeter grid paper (see Blackline Masters 8 and 9), and a recording sheet (Blackline Master L-4). Have extra sheets of grid paper on hand.
- This activity can be done in pairs. If students are paired, still provide each student with 36 square tiles, as each student needs to explore how the rectangles can be constructed.
- Overhead tiles and a transparency of the grid paper and recording chart will be helpful to introduce the activity as well as to share students' ideas afterward. If overhead tiles are not available, the Color Tiles will suffice, although they will be opaque and it will be more difficult for students to see the individual tiles.

- -

lesson

Name _____
Rectangles made with 36 tiles

Rectangle Dimensions	Area	Perimeter

BLM L-4

BEFORE

Begin with a simpler version of the task:

- Have students build a rectangle using 12 tiles at their desk. Explain that the rectangle should be filled in, not just borders. After eliciting some ideas, ask a student to come to the overhead and make a rectangle that has been described.
- Model sketching the rectangle on the grid transparency. Record the dimensions of the rectangle in the recording chart, for example, "2 by 6."
- Ask: *What do we mean by perimeter? How do we measure perimeter?* After helping students define perimeter and describe how it is measured, ask students for the perimeter of this rectangle. Ask a student to come to the overhead to measure the perimeter of the rectangle. (Use either the rectangle made from tiles or the one sketched on grid paper.) Emphasize that the units used to measure perimeter are one-dimensional, or linear, and that perimeter is just the distance around an object. Record the perimeter in the chart.
- Ask: *What do we mean by area? How do we measure area?* After helping students define area and describe how it is measured, ask for the area of this rectangle. Here you want to make explicit that the units used to measure area are two-dimensional and, therefore, cover a region. After counting the tiles, record the area in the chart.
- Have students make a different rectangle using 12 tiles at their desks and record the perimeter and area as before. Students will need to decide what "different" means. Is a 2 by 6 rectangle different than a 6 by 2 rectangle? Although these are congruent, students may wish to consider these different. That is okay for this activity.

The Task

See how many different rectangles can be made with 36 tiles. Determine and record the perimeter and area for each rectangle.

Establish Expectations

Write the directions on the board:

- Find a rectangle using *all* 36 tiles.
- Sketch the rectangle on the grid paper.
- Measure and record the perimeter and area of the rectangle on the recording chart.
- Find a new rectangle using *all* 36 tiles and repeat steps 2–4.

DURING

- Observe how students are generating new rectangles. Are they using some systematic way (e.g., changing the length of the rectangle by one each time) to ensure they have found all the rectangles? Are they haphazardly finding rectangles with no apparent strategy?
- How do they measure the perimeters? Do they count or measure all four sides, or do they double the sum of length and width? Are they aware that the perimeters change?
- Do students realize that the areas must remain the same since all rectangles use 36 tiles?

AFTER

- Ask students what they have found out about perimeter and area. Ask: *Did the perimeter stay the same? Is that what you expected? When is the perimeter big and when is it small?*
- Ask students how they can be sure they have all of the possible rectangles. As a class, decide on a systematic method of recording rectangles on the recording chart. For example, start with a side of 1, then 2, and so on. After everyone has had time to consider the information in the chart, have students describe what happens to the perimeter as the length and width change. (The perimeter gets shorter as the rectangle gets fatter. The square has the shortest perimeter.)

ASSESSMENT NOTES

- Are students confusing perimeter and area?
- As students form new rectangles, are they aware that the area is not changing because they are using the same number of tiles each time? These students may not know what area is, or they may be confusing it with perimeter.
- Are students looking for patterns in how the perimeter changes before you guide them toward that idea?

· ·

- Students who continue to confuse perimeter and area should engage in tasks that ask them to use various informal units of area to fill and compare regions. They can also use string to provide a concrete representation of perimeter of various shapes. The string can be stretched into a straight line and can be measured with a ruler to reinforce that perimeter is a linear measure.

- Activity 9.7, "Fixed Perimeters," is a good activity to pair with this one if you have not already done so.
- If both activities (9.7 and 9.8) are successful, it is appropriate to move to formulas.

next steps

ALGEBRAIC REASONING

Chapter

10

*P*rinciples and Standards for School Mathematics (NCTM, 2000) lists algebra as one of the five content strands for pre-K–12 mathematics. Today, most states also have an algebra component to their curricula. Rather than the algebra you may remember from your high school days, the algebra intended for K–8 focuses on patterns, relationships and functions, and the use of various representations—symbolic, numeric, and graphic—to help make sense of all sorts of mathematical situations. As students become comfortable with these ideas and methods of representation, they will begin to utilize them in nearly all of mathematics, not just in a study of algebraic ideas.

It is common today to hear or read about *algebraic reasoning* or *algebraic thinking.* This involves the way a student uses the content of algebra—patterns, representations, and functions—in generalizing and formalizing regularity in all aspects of mathematics. Activities aimed at the goal of algebraic thinking should

big ideas

1 Logical patterns exist and are a regular occurrence in mathematics. They can be recognized, extended, and generalized with both words and symbols. The same pattern can be found in many different forms. Patterns are found in physical and geometric situations as well as in numbers.

2 A variety of representations such as diagrams, number lines, charts, and graphs can be used to illustrate mathematical situations and relationships. These representations help in conceptualizing ideas and in solving problems.

3 Symbolism, especially involving equations and variables, is used to express generalizations of patterns and relationships.

4 Variables are symbols that take the place of numbers or ranges of numbers. They have different meanings depending on whether they are being used as representations of quantities that vary or change, representations of specific unknown values, or placeholders in a generalized expression or formula.

5 Equations and inequalities are used to express relationships between two quantities. Symbolism on either side of an equation or inequality represents a quantity. Thus, 3 + 8 and 5n + 2 are both expressions for numbers, not something "to do."

6 Functions are a special type of relationship or rule that uniquely associates members of one set with members of another set. For example, *double* or *two times* is a functional relationship on the set of all numbers. It associates the number 3 with 6 and the number 2386 with 4772. Another example of a function is the rule that associates any polygon with the number of vertices of that polygon.

begin in kindergarten and continue to develop across the years, and not just in algebra lessons but, to some extent, in all other strands of mathematics.

This chapter focuses on the content of algebra: pattern and regularity, representation and symbolism, and relationships and functions.

Repeating Patterns

Identifying and extending patterns is an important process in algebraic thinking. The development of this process usually begins in kindergarten. Children typically use materials such as Color Tiles, pattern blocks, toothpicks, or simply drawings to both copy and extend patterns that repeat. A few examples of repeating patterns are shown in Figure 10.1.

The *core* of a repeating pattern is the shortest string of elements that repeats. Notice in Figure 10.1 that the core is always fully repeated and never only partially shown. If the core of a pattern is –oo, a card might have –oo–oo (two repetitions of the core), but it would be ambiguous if the card showed –oo–oo– or –oo–.

By third grade, students will have had numerous experiences with repeating patterns. Besides simply extending the patterns using materials or drawings, they should also have translated patterns from one medium to another. For example, a pattern made with triangles and circles can be translated to one involving red and yellow tiles. The essence of both patterns remains the same. It is common in the early grades for students to "read" a repeating pattern using letters of the alphabet. For example, the second pattern in Figure 10.1 can be read "A-B-C-C-A-B-C-C . . . ." When two patterns made with very different materials are each read in the same manner, how they are mathematically alike becomes obvious—they have the same pattern structure.

If you find that your students have not had experiences with repeating patterns, it may be worthwhile to spend a few days exploring them. After even a brief exposure, the next activity will be a useful challenge. It is a forerunner to looking at the function aspect of patterns.

Bread tags

Paper shapes

Pattern blocks

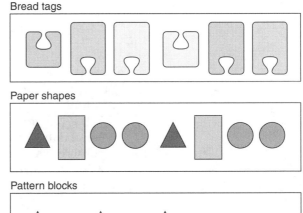

Toothpicks

FIGURE 10.1

Examples of repeating pattern cards drawn on tagboard. Each pattern repeats completely and does not split in the middle of a core.

ACTIVITY 10.1

Predict Down the Line

For most repeating patterns, the elements of the pattern can be numbered 1, 2, 3, and so on. Provide students with a pattern to extend. Before students begin to extend the pattern, have them predict exactly what element will be in, say, the fifteenth position. Students should be required to provide a reason for their prediction, preferably in writing. Students should then extend the pattern as before and check their prediction. If their prediction is incorrect, have them examine their reasoning and try to figure out why the prediction was off.

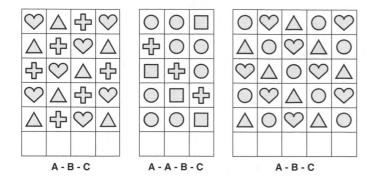

A - B - C   A - A - B - C   A - B - C

FIGURE 10.2 •

Repeating patterns can be transferred or built on a grid. In the examples shown, the patterns begin in the upper left corners and go left to right, beginning each new line on the left.

Eventually, students will figure out that the length of the core of the pattern plays a significant role. If you ask for a prediction of the hundredth element or even the three-hundredth element, students will not be able to check the prediction by extending the pattern. Verification focuses on the rationale for the prediction. Students may need to use a calculator to skip-count or multiply. But it is always the reasoning that is most important.

A variation of the prediction activity adds yet another challenge. Suppose that you are working with a red-blue-blue-red-blue-blue pattern made of blocks. Instead of asking what will be in position 38, ask in what position will the thirty-eighth blue block be? What color will come after it? Notice that it is more difficult to locate the position of an element that repeats in the pattern. The same question is more difficult for this pattern: blue-blue-blue-red.

Typically, we think of repeating patterns extending in a line. Figure 10.2 illustrates how repeat patterns can be positioned on a grid. Notice that the size of the grid affects how the pattern appears. It is interesting to observe how the pattern elements tend to make diagonal or column patterns. As illustrated with the following activity, patterns on a grid give rise to new and challenging questions.

ACTIVITY 10.2

Grid Patterns

Provide students with centimeter grid paper. On the paper they can mark off grids that are the width that they want to use: 3, 4, 5, or 6 squares wide. As an initial introduction to patterns on these grids, have them record an A-B-B-C pattern on a 3-square wide grid. They can use crayons and make colored dots or circles to record the patterns. Discuss what they see after recording five or six rows in the grid. Next have them record the same pattern on a 4-square wide grid. They will notice that the colors all line up in columns. What would happen with an A-B-C pattern? Suggest five or six different patterns for students to explore on the grid paper in any way that they wish. Have them write about what they have discovered.

As described, "Grid Patterns" is only the introduction to patterns on a grid. Once students are familiar with the results of placing patterns on a grid, try some of the following challenges. Begin by giving them a pattern to use, such as A-A-B-C.

- What grid sizes will result in columns of colors?
- In a 3-grid, what rows will be the same as the first row? How did you decide? Answer the same question for a 5-grid.
- On what size grids will the B color make a diagonal from left to right? Right to left?

- What will be in the fifteenth row of a 3-grid? What will be in the fifteenth row of a 5-grid? The hundredth row?
- What patterns happen in the columns? How will the column patterns change if you change the grid size?

You may find additional challenges to pose. The interesting feature is the interaction between the length of the core of the pattern and the width of the grids. All students will be able to answer most of these questions by simply making the grids and filling them in. Some may be able to use the numbers involved to offer a more sophisticated explanation.

Assessment Note

Students in the third grade should be able to translate patterns using letters and should be able to match one pattern with an equivalent one. They should also be able to identify the core of a pattern. Assessing these skills is simply a matter of observation while students are doing the related tasks.

Tasks that require numeric reasoning are considerably more difficult. "Predict Down the Line" and "Grid Patterns" offer the opportunity for third- and fourth-grade students to apply newly learned ideas about multiplication and division. These challenges allow you to extend pattern activities for all of your students before going to the next step of growing patterns.

Growing Patterns

Beginning at about the third grade and extending through the middle school years, students can explore patterns that involve a progression from step to step. In technical terms, these are called *sequences*; we will simply call them *growing patterns*. With these patterns, students not only extend patterns but also look for a generalization or an algebraic relationship that will tell them what the pattern will be at any point along the way. Growing patterns also demonstrate the concept of function and can be used as an entry point to this important mathematical idea.

Figure 10.3 illustrates some growing patterns that are built with various materials or drawings. The patterns consist of a series of separate steps, with each new step related to the previous one according to the pattern.

The first thing to do with growing patterns is to get students comfortable building them and talking about how they can be extended in a logical manner. Building the patterns with physical materials such as tiles, counters, or flat toothpicks allows students to make changes if necessary and to build onto one step to make a new step. It is also more fun! Some growing patterns quickly get quite large and can require more materials than you have. One solution to this dilemma is to have students make a step with materials and then draw it on grid paper. In this way, they will only need enough materials to make one step at a time. The following activity will introduce growing patterns to your students.

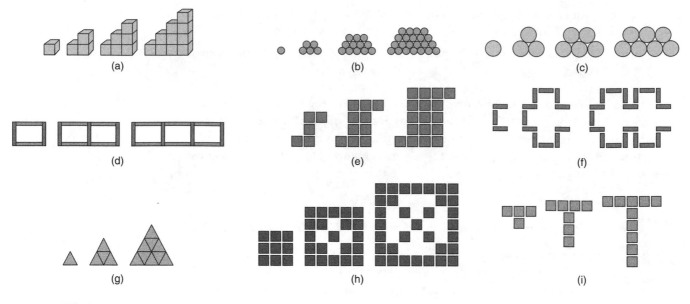

FIGURE 10.3 ● ● ● ● ● ● ●

Growing patterns with materials or drawings.

ACTIVITY 10.3

Extend and Explain

Show students the first three or four steps of a pattern. Provide them with appropriate materials and grid paper, have them extend the patterns recording each step, and explain why their extension indeed follows the pattern.

When discussing a pattern, students should try to determine how each step in the pattern differs from the preceding step. If each new step can be built by adding on to or changing the previous step, the discussion should include how this can be done. For example, each stairstep in Figure 10.3(a) can be made by adding a column of blocks to the preceding stairsteps. In contrast, the square pattern (Figure 10.3(h)) involves a form of expansion rather than adding on.

Growing patterns also have a numeric component, the number of objects in each step. As shown in Figure 10.4, a table can be made for any growing pattern. One row of the table or chart is always the number of steps, and the other is for recording how many objects are in that step. Frequently, a pattern grows so quickly and requires so many blocks or spaces to draw it that it is only reasonable to build or draw the first five or six steps. This leads to the following activity.

EXPANDED LESSON

(pages 318–319)

A complete lesson plan based on "Predict How Many" can be found at the end of this chapter.

ACTIVITY 10.4

Predict How Many

Have students begin to extend a growing pattern you provide. They should also make a table showing how many items are needed to make each step of the pattern. The task is to predict the number of items in the tenth or twentieth step of the pattern. The challenge is to see if there is a way to do this without filling in the first 19 entries of the table. Predictions should also be accompanied by an explanation.

Activity 10.4 is a natural progression from the earlier prediction activity with repeating patterns. Finding a way to determine the twentieth or even the hundredth entry in the table gets at the heart of finding a relationship that later students will understand is an example of a function. We next look at how to help students find these relationships.

Searching for Relationships

Once a table or chart is developed, students have two representations of the pattern: the one created with the drawing or materials and the numeric version that is in the table. When looking for relationships, some students will focus on the table and others will focus on the physical pattern. It is important for students to see that whatever relationships they discover, they exist in both forms. So if a relationship is found in a table, challenge students to see how that plays out in the physical version.

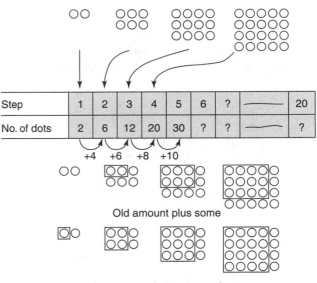

FIGURE 10.4 •

It is useful to try to see how each new step is built on the preceding step. Other similarities from step to step are also helpful.

Patterns from Step to Step: Recursive Relationships

For most students, it is easier to see the patterns from one step to the next. When you have a chart constructed, the differences from one step to the next can be written next to or below it, as in Figure 10.4. In that example, the number in each step can be determined from the previous step by adding successive even numbers. The description that tells how a pattern changes from step to step is known as a *recursive relationship.*

Whenever there is a pattern in the table, see if students can find that same pattern in the physical version. In Figure 10.4, notice that in each step the previous step has been outlined. That lets you examine the amount added and see how it creates the pattern of adding on even numbers. The picture or physical pattern and the table should be as closely connected as possible.

Patterns from Step Number to Step: Functional Relationships

The recursive step-to-step pattern is almost certainly the first that your students will observe. However, to find the table entry for the hundredth step, the only way a recursive pattern can help is to find all of the prior 99 entries in the table. If a rule or relationship can be discovered that connects the number of objects in a step to the number of the step, any table entry can be determined without building or calculating all of the intermediate entries. A rule that determines the number of elements in a step from the step number is an example of a *functional relationship.* Fourth grade is not too early to challenge students to find functional relationships.

There is no single best method for finding this relationship between step number and step. Some students may get insight by simply "playing around" with the numbers and asking, "How can I operate on the number of the step to get the corresponding number in the table?" Most will benefit from examining the physical pattern for regularities. For example, at the bottom of Figure 10.4, a square array is outlined for each step. Each successive square is one larger on a side. What relationship might exist between this subset of the pattern and the step numbers? In this example, the side of each square is the same as the step number. The row to the right of each square is also the step number.

 With that information, how would you describe the twentieth step? Can you determine how many elements will be in it without drawing the picture?

At this point, a significant activity is to write a numeric expression for each step number using the same pattern. For example, the first four steps in Figure 10.4 are $1^2 + 1$, $2^2 + 2$, $3^2 + 3$, and $4^2 + 4$.

It may take much searching and experimenting for students in groups or as a class to come up with an expression that is similar for each step. Do not get frustrated if students have difficulty. Encourage the search for relationships to continue, even if it takes more than one day. The search for relationships is the most significant portion of these activities.

Moving from Patterns to Function and Variable

When students have discovered numeric expressions for each step using step numbers, write them with brackets around the step numbers as shown in Figure 10.5. If this results in a pattern, the bracketed numbers will change from step to step, while the other numbers in the expressions remain the same. Now the bracketed numbers can be replaced by a letter or variable, resulting in a general formula. The formula defines the functional relationship between step numbers and step values.

Before reading on, explore some of the patterns in Figure 10.3 to see if you can find formulas (functional relationships) for each. You should be able to "plug in" the step numbers in your formulas and get the value for that step. Some are a bit harder than others.

FIGURE 10.5 • • • • • • •

Finding functional relationships in patterns.

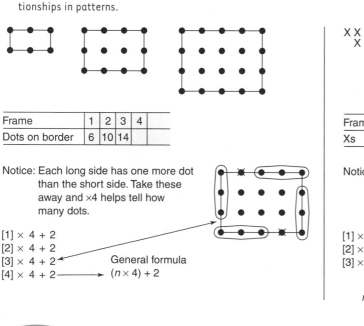

Frame	1	2	3	4
Dots on border	6	10	14	

Notice: Each long side has one more dot than the short side. Take these away and ×4 helps tell how many dots.

[1] × 4 + 2
[2] × 4 + 2
[3] × 4 + 2
[4] × 4 + 2 ⟶

General formula
$(n \times 4) + 2$

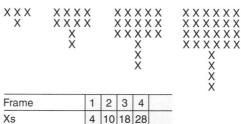

Frame	1	2	3	4
Xs	4	10	18	28

Notice: If the tail part is added to the side of the top part, there is always a square and three more columns.

[1] × [1] + (3 × [1])
[2] × [2] + (3 × [2])
[3] × [3] + (3 × [3])

⋮ General formula
$n \times n + 3n = n^2 + 3n$

Chapter **10** ALGEBRAIC REASONING

The discussion to this point is summarized in the following activity, an elaboration of "Predict How Many." It is best to do this in groups so that ideas can be generated more freely.

ACTIVITY 10.5

Find the Function in the Pattern

Give students the first three or four steps of a pattern. Their tasks are as follows:

1. Extend the pattern several more steps until students are sure they understand the pattern. They should always look backward to the beginning of the pattern to see that their idea works for all steps. Record this in a drawing.
2. Make a table that shows the number of elements in each step they have constructed.
3. Find and describe in writing as many patterns as possible, both from the table and from the physical pattern. For each pattern found in the table, they should see how that idea can be found in the physical pattern. The most important pattern to look for is the one from steps to number of elements, the functional relationship.
4. Write the functional relationship as a formula in terms of the step number. Show how the formula works for each part of the table already constructed. Use the formula to predict the next entry in the table, and check this with an actual construction of the pattern, if possible. Use the formula to predict the twentieth entry in the table.

Graphing the Patterns

So far, growing patterns have been represented by the physical materials or drawings and by a chart. Students may also have found a symbolic rule or functional representation. A graph adds a fourth representation. The individual points in a pattern can be plotted even if the physical pattern has not been discovered.

Before making a graph, students should extend a growing pattern and make a table of values, as discussed previously. Even if the physical pattern could not be created for more than five or six steps, students should use the recursive pattern to find at least the first ten entries. It is not the procedure for making graphs that is important but seeing the result and understanding what it represents. In fact, you may have a simple graphing program on your computer that will plot the points for the students. Figure 10.6 shows a growing pattern of dots forming rectangles. The table and graph were made with a simple spreadsheet.

Perhaps the easiest way for students to make a graph without use of technology is to use centimeter grid paper. Numbering along the bottom of the graph should correspond to the step numbers. If the numbers in the table are greater than 20, suggest a multiple of 2 or 5 for each square along the vertical axis. After showing students how to plot a few pairs from the table, they should be able to finish the graph.

Returning for a moment to the recursive relationships for growing patterns, notice that when the recursive pattern is constant, as it is for the "Dots in the Rectangle" pattern (Figure 10.6), the graph is a straight line or is *linear*. If the recursive pattern

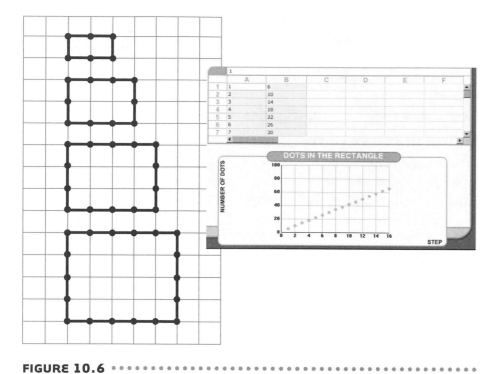

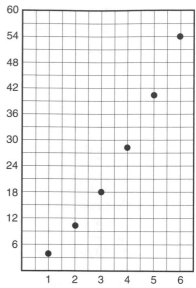

FIGURE 10.6 •

A growing figure, a table, and a graph: three representations of the same relationship. The table and graph were created in a simple spreadsheet designed for young students (E-Tools, Scott Foresman, 2004).

FIGURE 10.7 • • • • • • • • • • • •

Graph of the "Ts of Xs" pattern from Figure 10.5. This is an example of a nonlinear pattern. Note that the dots are not in a straight line.

is not constant, the graph is a curve. For the "Ts of Xs" pattern (Figure 10.5) the recursive pattern is + 6, + 8, + 10, ... The amount of change from step to step is increasing. The graph in Figure 10.7 reflects this as it curves upward in a steeper and steeper manner.

With all four representations—pattern, chart, rule or function, and graph—it is important for students to understand that each of these is a representation of the same relationship. The pattern is shown physically, numerically, symbolically, and graphically. However, it remains only one relationship.

Assessment Note ——————————————

It is important to connect the numbers in the tables or charts that students build with the actual patterns and with the graphs. After students have constructed a chart for their pattern, select different numbers in the chart and ask them to explain where these numbers came from in the pattern. Include the step number in this discussion as well. Students should be able to make similar connections between points on their graphs and the physical pattern.

If your students have been able to find a general rule or function related to the pattern, they should be able to use the rule to determine the number associated with any step and with any point in the graph.

Patterns with Numbers

The patterns discussed so far, repeating and growing patterns, are far from the only patterns in mathematics. Our number system is full of wonderful patterns. Numbers not only offer children an opportunity to explore patterns but also to learn to expect, see, and use patterns in all of mathematics.

Number Patterns

The simplest form of a number pattern is a string of numbers that follows some rule for determining how the string continues. The next activity is a good beginning.

ACTIVITY 10.6

What's Next and Why?

Show students five or six numbers from a number pattern. The task for students is to extend the pattern for several more numbers and to explain the rule for generating the pattern. The difficulty of the task depends on the number pattern and the familiarity of students with searching for patterns. Here is a short list of patterns to try with students.

1, 2, 2, 3, 3, 3, . . .	each digit repeats according to its value
2, 4, 6, 8, 10, . . .	even numbers—skip counting by 2
1, 2, 4, 8, 16, . . .	double the previous number
2, 5, 11, 23, . . .	double the previous number and add 1
1, 2, 4, 7, 11, 16, . . .	successively add 1, then 2, then 3, and so on
1, 4, 9, 16, 25, . . .	squares: $1^2, 2^2, 3^2, . . .$
0, 1, 5, 14, 30, . . .	add the next square number
2, 2, 4, 6, 10, 16, . . .	add the preceding two numbers

Most of these examples also have variations you can try. Make up your own or challenge students to make up their own number pattern rules.

The next activity encourages students to be more analytical about number patterns. Although it involves simple skip counting, the search for patterns is challenging. Students are asked to find patterns within a particular skip count and also compare that pattern with those found in other skip counts.

ACTIVITY 10.7

Start and Jump Numbers

To begin this activity, have students make a list of numbers beginning with 3 and skip count by 5. The 3 is called the "start number" and 5 is the "jump number." It is helpful to make the list in a vertical column as in Figure 10.8. The task is to examine the list of numbers and find as many patterns as possible. Ideas should be shared with others in the class. Students should be sure that all suggested patterns really exist.

(continued)

FIGURE 10.8 ● ● ● ● ● ●

Start with a number and list the numbers that occur by skip counting according to the "jump" number. How are the patterns for the same jump numbers alike? How are they different?

Start with 3 Jump by 5s	Start with 6 Jump by 5s	Start with 5 Jump by 4s	Start with 3 Jump by 4s	Start with 2 Jump by 3s
3	6	5	3	2
8	11	9	7	5
13	16	13	11	8
18	21	17	15	11
23	26	21	19	14
28	31	25	23	17
33	36	29	27	20
38	41	33	31	23
43	46	37	35	26
48	51	41	39	29
53	56	45	43	32
. . .	. . .	. . .	. . .	. . .

When students have found patterns for this first list, suggest that they change the start number and see how the patterns change. Different groups can explore different start numbers.

Next, make changes in the jump numbers. Jump-number changes will cause the patterns to change much more radically than a change in the start numbers.

STOP It would be a good idea to explore the patterns in "Start and Jump Numbers" before reading on and certainly before assigning it to your students. Extend the patterns in Figure 10.8 beyond 100 to see how the pattern works in three digits.

With a jump number of 5, you should see the following:

- There is at least one alternating pattern.
- There is an odd/even pattern.
- There is a pattern in the tens place as well as in the ones place. When the list goes over 100, you can think of each digit separately (1 hundred, 1 ten, 3 ones), in which case the pattern is starting over. However, you can also think of 113 as eleven tens ("eleventy-three"), in which case the pattern is continuing. Both interpretations are correct.
- Try adding the digits. For a start of 3 and a jump of 5, the numbers are 3, 8, 4, 9, 5, 10, 6, 11, 7, 12, 8, ... Examine every other number in this list. What is the sum for 113? It can either be 5 or 14 (thinking of 113 as 11 tens and 3 ones).

With a jump number of 5, the ones-place pattern repeats every two jumps—the core has a length of 2. When you change the jump numbers, you will probably change the length of this core. The core for jumps of 4, 6, and 8 all have a length of 5. Explore how these patterns are alike and different when each starts with the same number. What happens if you change the start number from one even number to another even number? Is there still a pattern when you add the digits? With a jump number of 3, the core length is 10. If you put the ten numbers in a circle as in Figure 10.9, students can see how the order for these ten digits is the same regardless of the starting number. Try putting the ending digits in order for the shorter patterns or for other jump numbers.

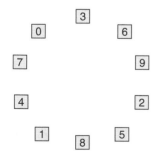

FIGURE 10.9 ● ● ● ● ● ● ●

For jumps of 3, this cycle of digits will occur in the ones place. The start number determines where the cycle begins.

Some students will want to explore these patterns even further. For example, there is no reason that jump numbers must be restricted to single digits. To explore jumps by larger numbers, use calculators so that tedious adding is not required.

Assessment Note

As your students work on the number patterns and other activities discussed in this chapter, try not to think about the activities in terms of mastery. It is not reasonable at any grade level to say that students have mastered number patterns. There are number patterns appropriate for kindergarten and others that will challenge capable high school students. (Those included are about right for students in grade 3 or 4.) Instead, look for how individual students are able to reason with the patterns you explore. Ideas about place value are included in many of the pattern ideas we've just discussed. If a student is having difficulty with skip counts beyond 20, you may want to examine his or her understanding of place-value concepts. Skip counting into the higher decades is closely related to mental computation skills. It is important to help students develop these skills.

Patterns with Operations

Interesting and useful patterns can be found in the operations on numbers as well as patterns made with numbers. The following tasks are each in the form of explorations. That is, students are asked to explore a situation and see what they can find out about that situation. What is alike? What is different? How do things change?

For example, in the first or second grade, students may find it interesting that if you start with a sum such as $7 + 7$, then increase one addend and decrease the other by the same amount, the results all remain the same. That is, $7 + 7 = 8 + 6$, and $458 + 276 = 459 + 275$. Furthermore, the result holds for an increase or decrease by any amount. By third or fourth grade, this result may seem obvious. A good question to ask is: Does this work for subtraction? The subtraction pattern, although different, is not much more difficult to understand than the addition pattern. Both of these patterns are useful in mental computation. For example, if faced with $346 - 198$, you can instead compute $348 - 200$ (both numbers increased by 2).

The next activity is an interesting exploration for intermediate-level students and extends the one-up/one-down idea to multiplication.

ACTIVITY 10.8

One Up and One Down: Multiplication

Show students that when you begin with $7 \times 7 = 49$ and then raise one factor and lower the other, each by one, the product is one less than the original: $8 \times 6 = 48$. Their task is to explore this for other numbers multiplied by themselves (squares). To help with their exploration, suggest that they cut out a square array from grid paper. How can they change the square array into the new rectangle using scissors and tape? Students should use words, pictures, and numbers to tell what they have found. Encourage students to explore similar situations and see what patterns they can discover.

FIGURE 10.10 • • • • • •

What happens when you begin with a number times itself and then make one factor one greater and the other one less?

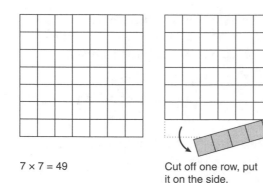

7 × 7 = 49

Cut off one row, put it on the side.

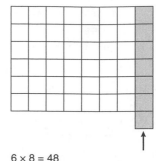

6 × 8 = 48
There will always be one unused square.

You might want to play around with the last activity yourself. The results are quite interesting and not nearly as obvious as those for addition. In the multiplication version, the new product will be one less if the original product is a square—a number multiplied by itself. Figure 10.10 illustrates how an array changes in the case of a square. When the original factors are not alike (increase the larger number and decrease the smaller), the difference can be related to the difference in the original factors.

Even in grades 3–5, the hundreds chart remains a valuable way for students to think about numbers. It helps reinforce the ten-structure of our number system and, as seen in Chapter 4, can help students develop invented computation strategies. There are many interesting patterns hiding in the hundreds chart that can be discovered with operations.

ACTIVITY 10.9

Diagonal Sums

Have students select any four numbers in the hundreds chart that form a square. Add the two numbers on each diagonal as in the example shown here.

47	48	49	50
57	58	59	60
67	68	69	70
77	78	79	80

Have students explore other diagonal sums on the chart. Expand their search to diagonals of any rectangle. For example, the numbers 15, 19, 75, and 79 form four corners of a rectangle. The sums 15 + 79 and 19 + 75 are equal. Challenge students to figure out why this is so. (See Figure 10.11.)

After finding that the diagonal sums are alike, a natural question to ask is: What about the differences in diagonal corners?

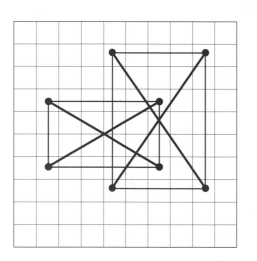

FIGURE 10.11 • • • • • • • • • • • • • • •

Diagonals on a hundreds chart. For any four numbers forming a rectangle arrangement on the hundreds chart, the sum of the corner numbers on one diagonal equals the sum of the corner numbers on the other diagonal. There is also a pattern for the differences of these same numbers and for the products.

STOP

Students will find that when exploring differences on the hundreds chart, the generalizations are not as obvious as they were with addition. The two diagonal differences will always differ by some amount. How much they differ can be predicted by knowing only the top two numbers in the rectangle, regardless of the choice of the two bottom numbers.

Stop and figure this out yourself.

If you explore the diagonal differences, you will find that they differ by twice the distance between the top two numbers. If the top numbers are 16 and 19 (three apart), the diagonal differences will differ by 2 × 3, or 6. To confirm this try 56 and 59 as the bottom numbers: 59 − 16 = 43; 56 − 19 = 37. The difference between 43 and 37 is 6.

Interested students may also want to examine multiplication patterns using a calculator. Again, there are patterns to be found, but they are perhaps more obscure. The difference between the larger and smaller diagonal products will be the same for all rectangles on the chart that have the same dimensions, regardless of orientations. Check these two rectangles as an example: 23, 27, 43, 47 and 56, 58, 96, 98. The first is a 4 by 2 rectangle and the second a 2 by 4 rectangle. The diagonal products in each differ by 80.

Finally, all of the patterns found through addition, subtraction, or multiplication remain even if the rectangles are "tilted," with sides not parallel to the chart. (The numbers 33, 15, 77, and 59 form a rectangle that is "tilted.")

Representing Ideas

Representation is one of the five process standards in the NCTM *Principles and Standards* document. When we talk of representing ideas, we refer to external things that we can see, such as drawings, graphs, numbers and equations, and manipulative models. If these things are to be representative of students' ideas, students must have those ideas before a representation will have any meaning for them. Meanings do not *come from* the representations. You cannot represent an idea you have not yet formed.

Students can learn to use symbolic representations and drawings to help them solve problems and communicate their ideas. However, as the *Standards* authors caution, we must not make these or other representations become an end in themselves.

> *Representations should be treated as essential elements in supporting students' understanding of mathematical concepts and relationships: in communicating mathematical approaches, arguments, and understandings to one's self and to others; in recognizing connections among related mathematical concepts; and in applying mathematics to realistic problem situations through modeling. (NCTM, 2000, p. 67)*

Chapter 1 described models for mathematical ideas as tools for learning. The reference was primarily to manipulative materials, representations such as base-ten blocks or counters. However, the term *model* was used to expand the notion of representation beyond physical materials to include any external representation onto which a concept can be imposed. This includes student drawings and symbolism. (See Figure 1.5, p. 10.)

The algebra standard in *Principles and Standards* also calls for students to "represent mathematical situations" and to use representations to "understand quantitative relationships." For example, in the area of data analysis, students are taught different graphing techniques to represent collected data. In probability, students are taught to use a tree diagram to help construct the set of all possible outcomes for an experiment. And so, once again, we see that algebra is not always a separate strand of the curriculum but is found whenever students are trying to represent quantitative relationships throughout the curriculum.

Drawings and Diagrams for Story Problems

In February, a class of third-grade students was asked to solve the following problem:

The circus came to town with 23 elephants. How many legs is that in all?

The students had received no instruction concerning the use of drawings. They were using a traditional curriculum. They were, however, told for this problem to use "words, numbers, and perhaps drawings" to show how they solved the problem and why the answer makes sense. Figure 10.12 shows the work of three students.

Jamie solves the problem twice, each time using a fairly symbolic drawing. His statement, "I counted every leg," indicates that he used no computation, but rather used the picture as a method of solution. In his second solution, he shows that he has thought of a better way to count, using groups of four elephants. It is not clear if he actually used these groups to solve the problem more easily.

Brenda's drawing is symbolic. She uses a numeral 4 instead of drawing legs. Like Jamie, she does rely on the drawing to help her solve the problem. It is very clear that she skip counted by 4s, using the drawing to keep track.

Beto begins with a "realistic" drawing of an elephant and apparently tires of the required tedium. It is unlikely that Beto used the drawing at all unless it helped him decide to add 23 four times. (Interestingly, most of the students added four 23s and no student, except Brenda, added twenty-three 4s.)

Beto's initial drawing of a realistic elephant is typical of young students who are told to use a drawing in this manner. He believes that if the problem is about elephants, he needs to draw elephants. Brenda's drawing could be used as an example for the class of how to draw a picture that is helpful but essentially symbolic.

Diezmann and English (2001) found that students need to be taught how to draw different types of diagrams and how to use them. Like Beto, many students interpret the instruction to draw a picture to mean "draw a realistic picture." For students in grades 3–5, who are usually dealing with fairly large numbers, this often poses an insurmountable task. This is one explanation for why students in these grades rarely draw pictures as a form of problem solving. Another reason is that most students have not been helped to know what it means to draw a picture to solve or help with a mathematics problem. One method of doing this is to model a variety of techniques or make useful suggestions to students.

In Figure 10.12, some of the students used their drawing to figure out the answer. In the intermediate grades, a drawing is perhaps most often useful in helping to decide what operation is appropriate. Students can use a box (☐), a question mark, or even a letter to represent a quantity that is unknown in the problem. The idea is to first represent the problem and then use the drawing to help find a solution.

Allen has a new book with 54 pages in it. He wants to finish the book in three days. If he wants to read the same number of pages each day, how many pages should he read on the first day?

Chapter 10 ALGEBRAIC REASONING

The circus came to town with 23 elephants. How many legs is that in all?

FIGURE 10.12 ‥‥‥

In February of the third grade, students used drawings as well as words and numbers to show their solutions to this problem of 23 elephants, how many legs. These students had no previous experiences with using drawings in the solutions of problems.

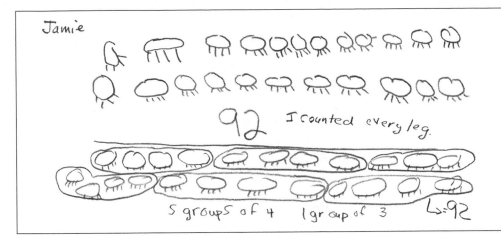

Jamie

92   I counted every leg.

5 groups of 4   1 group of 3   L=92

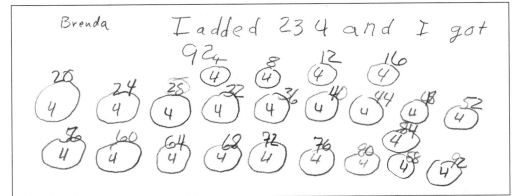

Brenda

I added 23 4 and I got 92

Beto

4 × 23 = 92

23
23
23
+ 23
92

I added 23 for times because the elephot has four legs.
I added 23 four times and it equal 92.

> **STOP** Sketch one or two drawings that you think might be helpful to students in representing this problem. Remember, you do not want them to draw details, just the essential features of the problem. After drawing your picture, write an equation that matches your picture. Use a letter to represent the unknown quantity in the problem.

FIGURE 10.13 • • • • • •

Drawings can also incorporate unknown amounts. Then the drawing doesn't solve the problem but instead helps students understand what operation to use.

Allen has a 54-page book. He wants to read the book in three days. If he wants to read the same number of pages each day, how many pages should he read on the first day?

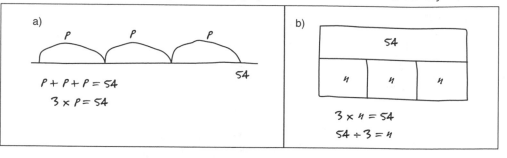

Figure 10.13 shows two possible drawings for solving the problem.

Remember not to make the drawing the focus of your lesson; rather, use drawings to solve problems. Casually model very simple drawings but do not require that students follow your examples. Your intent should be to move students toward the use of more abstract diagrams that get at the numbers and relationships involved. Talk with your students about drawing diagrams or pictures and listen to their ideas about what that means. When you ask students to draw a picture or diagram, be sure the task is worthy of the effort. Students should not be asked to draw pictures just to draw pictures or when they know how to solve a problem by other means.

Assessment Note

Students who typically have difficulty solving verbal problems can benefit most from learning to draw pictures to represent their ideas. In a one-on-one setting, ask the student if he or she could draw a diagram of the problem you have presented. First, you want to know if the student has any idea what you mean by "diagram" or picture of the problem. If the student tries to draw a realistic picture, you know that some instruction in the meaning of a diagram or a drawing is needed.

Some students will be able to make a drawing but fail to capture the correct or complete mathematics in their drawing. They may draw errors or leave out information. These students require time to explain how their diagram shows what the problem is about. They have probably rushed to make a drawing and have lost sight of the details. Relating the diagram to the problem can help.

Variables and Equations

Variables constitute an extremely powerful method of expressing the regularities found in mathematics. Variables enable us to use mathematical symbolism as a tool to think and help better understand mathematical ideas in the same way physical objects and drawings are used.

Variables

A *variable* is a symbol that can stand for any one of a set of numbers or other objects. Although correct, this simple-sounding definition has a variety of interpretations, depending on how the variables are used. Three uses of variables are commonly encountered in school mathematics:

1. *As a specific unknown.* In the early grades, this is the use found in equations such as $8 + \square = 12$. Later, we see exercises such as this: If $3x + 2 = 4x - 1$, solve for x.
2. *As a pattern generalizer.* Variables are used in statements that are true for all numbers. For example, $a \times b = b \times a$ for all real numbers.
3. *As quantities that vary in joint variation. Joint variation* occurs when change in one variable determines a change in another. In $y = 3x + 5$, as x changes or varies, so does y. Formulas are also an example of joint variation. In $A = L \times W$, as L and W change, so does A, the area.

There certainly is no need for elementary students to know or recognize the distinctions among these three uses of variables in algebraic reasoning. As noted, young students will most likely experience variables as specific unknowns more than other uses. It is useful for them to think of variables as numbers that can be operated on and manipulated like other numbers.

Variables as Unknowns

The following activity is a reasonable way for students to experience the meaning of a variable as a placeholder for a specific unknown.

ACTIVITY 10.10

Story Translations

Read a simple story problem to students but omit the question. Their task is to write an equation that means the same thing. For example: *There are 3 full boxes of pencils and 5 extra pencils. There are 41 pencils in all.* $(3 \times \square + 5 = 41)$ Be sure to include stories for all four operations. The activity can be reversed by providing an equation with an unknown and letting students make up a story to go with it. Once equations are agreed on, students should use whatever means they wish to find values that make the sentences true. Trial and error is a reasonable first strategy.

Sometimes students will write what may look like different equations. Consider this situation: *Al has 3 times as many baseball cards as Mark. If Mark has 75 cards, how many does Al have?* Some students may write $A = 3 \times 75$ while others may write $A \div 3 = 75$. Students can then discuss how these equations are alike and different. The result will be a better understanding of the relationship between multiplication and division.

The following activity illustrates how an unknown can be manipulated or treated just like a number.

Number Tricks

Have students do the following sequence of operations:

- *Write down any number.*
- *Add to it the number that comes after it.*
- *Add 9.*
- *Divide by 2.*
- *Subtract the number you began with.*

Now you can "magically" read their minds. Everyone ended up with 5!

The task is to see if students can discover how the trick works. If students need a hint, suggest that instead of using an actual number, they use a box or a letter to begin with. The box or letter represents a number, but even they do not need to know what the number is. Start with *N*. Add the next number: $N + (N + 1) = 2N + 1$. Adding 9 gives $2N + 10$. Dividing by 2 leaves $N + 5$. Now subtract the number you began with, leaving 5.

There are endless trick sequences like the one in this activity. Here are two more:

- Pick a number between 1 and 9, multiply by 5, add 3, multiply by 2, add another number between 1 and 9, subtract 6. What do you see?

- Pick a number, multiply by 6, add 12, take half of the result, subtract 6, divide by 3. What happens?

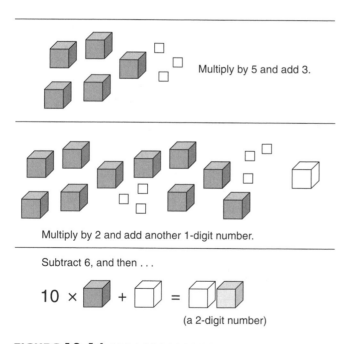

Pick a number between 1 and 9.

Multiply by 5 and add 3.

Multiply by 2 and add another 1-digit number.

Subtract 6, and then . . .

$10 \times \square + \square = \square\square$

(a 2-digit number)

FIGURE 10.14

Number tricks can be modeled using a block or a box for the unknown. Additional numbers are shown with counters or base-ten pieces.

These tricks can also be explored with models by using a small box or a cube for the unknown. Figure 10.14 shows how the first of the two preceding tricks might be modeled. Notice the place-value component required to understand the result.

Variables as Pattern Generators

Variables are often used to illustrate rules or regularities that exist in our number system. We often write down these rules using variables without giving much thought to the fact that students may not understand the variables involved.

What's True for All Numbers?

Ask students how they know that $465 + 137 = 137 + 465$ without doing the computation. Students' explanations should show evidence of understanding the commutative property for addition, although the name of the property is not important. How can this be written to show that it's a rule that is true for every number, even fractions and decimals? If students do not suggest it, offer the idea that letters or shapes could be used like this:

$$\Delta + \square = \square + \Delta \qquad \text{or} \qquad n + m = m + n$$

Be sure students understand that the choice of letter or shape is totally arbitrary as long as it is understood that each stands for any number and that when the same letter or shape appears in the same equation, it must represent the same value.

With this introduction, challenge students to find other statements that are true for all numbers.

Students may need some prodding to think about things that are always true, but it is best that they come up with the ideas themselves. One way to provide hints is to explore some specific examples. For example, draw a divided rectangle as shown in Figure 10.15. What are two ways to calculate the area? This can lead to the generalized version of the distributive property: $a(b + c) = (a \times b) + (a \times c)$. In addition to properties of the number system, also think about definitions of exponents or rules for negative numbers, all of which can be expressed in a general form using variables.

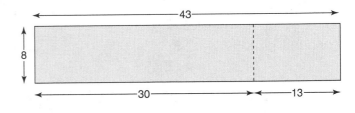

FIGURE 10.15 •

The distributive property is just one of many ideas that can be generalized using variables.

ACTIVITY 10.13

Special Quantities

What numeric expression would tell the number of chair legs on 376 chairs? (376 × 4) What about 195 chairs? (195 × 4) How would you write the number of legs on any number of chairs? (N × 4) Using this as an example, challenge students to write expressions for other types of quantities: fingers on students, eggs in cartons, crayons in boxes, wheels on tractor trailers, hours in days, inches in feet, quarts in gallons, and so on. Similarly, use variables to express these special numbers: any odd number, any even number, any multiple of 7, a multiple of 3 plus a different multiple of 5, any two-digit number, any power of 2. Once students get the idea, have them make up their own special quantities and see if others can describe them verbally.

The way that variables are used in the "Special Quantities" activity is essentially the way variables are used in spreadsheets. In Figure 10.16, odd and even numbers are generated from the numbers in column A. These values are then used in the sums and products columns.

Variables as Quantities That Vary

Whenever students develop charts that list the corresponding values of two related quantities, they are exploring the idea of *joint variation;* the value in one row varies according to the value in the other row. Students make charts relating cost to the number of units purchased or relating miles driven to gallons of gasoline used. In measurement, charts are made that relate circumference to diameter or perimeter of a square to the length of a side. In this chapter, we have seen that the study of growing

FIGURE 10.16

A spreadsheet formula uses variables to represent values in other cells. The expression in a cell is a pattern generalizer for that cell. The same spreadsheet is shown twice here, once with the formula in each cell and once with the cell values calculated. Note that any change in column A will produce changes in the entire row.

	A	B	C	D	E	F	G	H	I
1	Exploring Odd and Even Numbers								
2									
3	N	Even	Odd	E + E	E + O	O + O	E × E	E × O	O × O
4	1	2	3	4	5	6	4	6	9
5	2	4	5	8	9	10	16	20	25
6	7	14	15	28	29	30	196	210	225
7	10	20	21	40	41	42	400	420	441
8	15	30	31	60	61	62	900	930	961

	A	B	C	D	E	F	G	H	I
1	Exploring Odd and Even Numbers								
2									
3	N	Even	Odd	E + E	E + O	O + O	E × E	E × O	O × O
4	1	=2*A4	=2*A4+1	=B4+B4	=B4+C4	=C4+C4	=B4*B4	=B4*C4	=C4*C4
5	2	=2*A5	=2*A5+1	=B5+B5	=B5+C5	=C5+C5	=B5*B5	=B5*C5	=C5*C5
6	7	=2*A6	=2*A6+1	=B6+B6	=B6+C6	=C6+C6	=B6*B6	=B6*C6	=C6*C6
7	10	=2*A7	=2*A7+1	=B7+B7	=B7+C7	=C7+C7	=B7*B7	=B7*C7	=C7*C7
8	15	=2*A8	=2*A8+1	=B8+B8	=B8+C8	=C8+C8	=B8*B8	=B8*C8	=C8*C8

patterns results in formulas that connect the step number to the number of elements in that step of the pattern.

All of these are examples of joint variation—one value changing in relation to another. They are also examples of functions.

Equations and Inequalities

In the expression $3B + 7 = B - C$, the equal sign means that the quantity on the left *is the same as* the quantity on the right. To understand expressions in this way, students must interpret simple arithmetic expressions such as $3 + 5$ or 4×87 as *single quantities*.

Unfortunately, students tend to look on expressions such as $3 + 5$ and 4×87 as commands or things to do. The = tells you to add, and students think of *add* as a verb or an operator button, like pressing ⊟ on a calculator. As students read left to right in an equation, the = tells them, "Now give the answer." Because of this "get an answer" view of operations and equal signs, students fail to think of $5 + 2$ as another way to write 7.

A Balance-Pan Approach to Equality

The following activities are ways to help students with the basic concepts needed to understand equations.

ACTIVITY 10.14

Names for Numbers

Challenge students to find different ways to express a particular number, say, 10. Give a few simple examples, such as $5 + 5$ or $12 - 2$. Encourage the use of

Chapter 10 ALGEBRAIC REASONING

two or more different operations. "How many names for 8 can you find using only numbers less than 10 and at least three operations?" In your discussion, emphasize that each expression is a way of representing or writing a number.

Notice that there are no equal signs used in Activity 10.14. The next activity develops the concept of the equal sign. It begins with numbers only but can be quickly extended to include variables.

ACTIVITY 10.15

Tilt or Balance

On the board, draw a simple two-pan balance. In each pan, write a numeric expression, and ask which pan will go down or whether the two will balance (see Figure 10.17). Challenge students to write expressions for each side of the scale to make it balance. For each, write a corresponding equation to illustrate the meaning of =. Note that when the scale "tilts," either a "greater than" or "less than" symbol (> or <) is used.

After a short time, add variables to the two-pan balance activity as shown in Figure 10.17(b).

In Figure 10.18, a series of examples shows scale problems. Each shape on the scales represents a different value. Two or more scales for a single problem provide different information about the shapes or variables. Problems of this type can be adjusted in difficulty for students throughout first to eighth grades. (Books of worksheets with similar tasks are available. For example, see Greenes & Findell, 1999.)

When no numbers are involved, as in the top two examples of Figure 10.18, students can find combinations of numbers for the shapes that make all of the balances balance. If an arbitrary value is given to one of the shapes, then values for the other shapes can be found accordingly. In the second example, if the sphere = 2, then the cylinder must be 4 and the cube = 8. If a different value is given to the sphere, the other shapes will change accordingly.

The scale problems (with a number for each scale) are to be solved for a unique value for each shape. There are often several paths to finding a solution.

 How would you solve the last problem in Figure 10.18? Can you solve it in two ways?

You (and students) can tell if you are correct by checking your solutions with the original scale positions. Believe it or not, you have just solved a series of simultaneous equations, a skill generally left to a formal algebra class. Try making up your own scale problems. It is easier than you think. Start by giving values to two or three shapes. Place shapes in groups and add the values. These are the numbers on the scales. (Be sure your problems can be solved.)

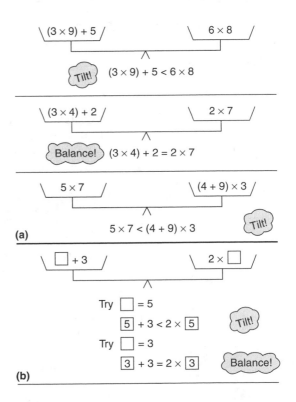

FIGURE 10.17 • • • • • • • • • • • • • • • • •

Using expressions and variables in equations and inequalities. The two-pan balance helps develop the meaning of =, <, and >.

VARIABLES AND EQUATIONS

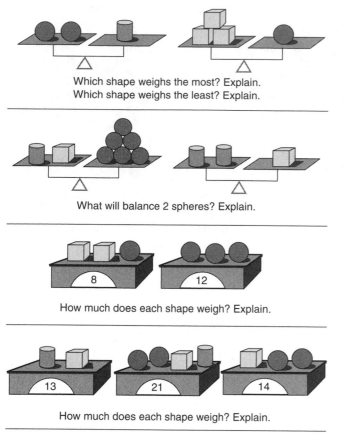

Which shape weighs the most? Explain.
Which shape weighs the least? Explain.

What will balance 2 spheres? Explain.

How much does each shape weigh? Explain.

How much does each shape weigh? Explain.

FIGURE 10.18 •

Examples of problems with multiple scales (equations).

Assessment Note ——————

You may be surprised at how common it is for students to interpret the equal sign as a symbol separating the problem from the answer. Ask students to write down (or tell you in an interview) what the equal sign means in an equation such as $5 \times 8 = 40$. Then ask the same question for $8 \times 2 = 15 + 1$ (an equation with an expression on each side.) Students often believe that there must be an "answer" or single number on one side of the equal sign. Finally, ask if it is okay to write something such as this: $5 = 5$. Here students sometimes believe that there must be an operation involved if there is an equal sign. The ways in which students answer these questions will depend a lot on how well you have taught the *balance* meaning of equality. Traditional textbooks do not spend a great deal of time on this issue. After early introductions to the equal sign in first grade, the assumption is that students understand what you mean by "equals."

Solving Equations

To *solve an equation* means to find values of the variable that make the equation true. To help students develop skills of solving equations in one variable, it is advisable to maintain the image of the balance pans. The balance makes it reasonably clear to students that if you add or subtract value from one side, you must add or subtract like values from the other side to keep the scales balanced.

ACTIVITY 10.16

Adjust the Balance

Show a balance with variable expressions in each side. Use only one variable. Try to make the tasks such that a solution by trial and error is not immediately obvious; for example, $3n + 2 = 14 - n$. Suggest that adjustments can be made to the quantities in each pan as long as the balance is maintained. If you begin with simple equations such as $n - 17 = 31 - n$, students should be able to develop skills and explain their rationale. Students should also be challenged to devise a method of proving that their solutions are correct. (Solutions can be tested by substitution in the original equation.)

Figure 10.19 shows a solution process for two equations, one in a balance and the other without. Even after you have stopped using the balance, it is a good idea to refer to the scale or balance-pan concept of equality and the idea of keeping the scales balanced.

The examples in Figure 10.19 are a bit more difficult than are typically seen in grade 4 or 5. The main difference is that the solutions involve more than one step. However, if equation tasks are made up carefully, there is no reason that fifth- or even fourth-grade students cannot work on them. Begin by giving a value to your variable and create an expression for one side of the equation. The other side can simply be the value of the first side or it can include a variable such as in these examples. You also need to be careful to avoid negative values. Students trying to subtract 5 from the expression $N - 3$ will likely be confused.

Functions

An important part of algebraic thinking involves recognizing and describing relations and functions. A *relation* is simply a correspondence between the elements of two sets of things. The correspondence can be between all sorts of things. The time of day can be related to what usually happens at that time, the height of a bean plant can be related to the number of days since planting or to the height of a different bean plant, and numbers can be related to other numbers in all sorts of ways.

A *function* is a special type of relation in which each element in one set is *uniquely* associated with another element, either in the same set or a different set. For example, in the relationship "is-more-than," the number 10 is associated with *all* numbers less than 10, not just one particular number. The rule does not define a unique relationship and, therefore, is not a function. On the other hand, the relation "ten-more-than" is a function. For any number there is a unique number associated with it; 10 is related to 20, 7 to 17, and so on. It is not at all necessary for elementary students to distinguish between functions and nonfunction relationships, but it is useful for you to be aware of the distinction.

Algebraic thinking also involves learning different ways to represent functions. As we saw with growing patterns, functional relationships can be represented in a real context, in a chart or table, with a graph, with an equation, and with words. Each different representation offers a different way to think about relationships and, thus, helps us to better understand them.

Functions arise in all sorts of ways. In addition to the growing patterns already discussed, students in the intermediate grades might explore a real-world situation such as the following.

. . . .

Brian is starting a summer lawn-mowing business to earn money to buy a new bike. He borrowed $225 from his Dad to buy a lawn mower. He charges $35 to mow the average lawn. It costs about 75¢ for gasoline for each lawn. That means that his profit from each lawn is $34.25. How many lawns must Brian mow to pay his father back? If he wants to buy a bike for $500, how many lawns must he mow?

. . . .

Add 6 to both sides and multiply right-hand expression.

Subtract $4 \times n$ from both sides.

Divide both sides by 2.

Check:

(a)   Both sides = 36 .

$4 \times N + 3 = N + 30$

Subtract 3

$4 \times N = N + 27$

Subtract N

$3 \times N = 27$

Divide by 3

$N = 9$

(b)

FIGURE 10.19 . . . .

Using a balance scale to think about solving equations.

This is just one example of the many situations that students could explore that involve functional relationships. Brian's lawn mowing is the context that defines the function: The number of lawns Brian mows is uniquely related to his profit. Students might begin to solve this problem by making a chart. By simply trying out some values for number of lawns mowed, students can begin to think about this relationship in a more systematic way. For example, if Brian doesn't mow any lawns, he will be $225 in debt to his Dad. If he mows 5 lawns, he would make 5 × $34.25 or $171.25. However, he will still owe his Dad $53.75 ($225.00 – $171.25). Students can try other values in a similar manner. Their initial table might look like this:

Lawns	Profit
0	–$ 225.00
5	–$ 53.75
10	+$ 117.50
30	+$ 802.50

Soon students will repeatedly use the same calculations, probably on their calculator: number of lawns × 34.25 – 225. This pattern of their calculations can now be expressed with a formula or an equation. Using P for Brian's profit and n for the number of lawns mowed, the equation is $P = n \times 34.25 - 225$.

Here, P and n are variables that *jointly vary*; as n changes so does the value of P. If students want to use their equation to find out how many lawns Brian needs to mow to buy the bike, they can enter 500 for P and try to find a value for n.

In words, students can now say with understanding, "Brian's profit is a function of the number of lawns he mows." They are verbally stating the relationship in a way that indicates the variable that, when it varies, causes a change in the other variable.

As we saw with growing patterns, functional relationships can be graphed. The two variables in the equation are represented on the two axes of the graph. Students could plot the graph on centimeter graph paper or they could use a simple spreadsheet program, as shown in Figure 10.20.

Note that if a spreadsheet is used, students can enter the expression for Brian's profit in column B in terms of the value for the number of lawns in column A. In Figure 10.20, the formula in cell B4 is "=A4*34.25 – 225." The spreadsheet will use whatever value is in cell A4, enter it into the formula, and print the result in B4. The formula is easily copied down the column, each time with reference to the cell to the left in column A. Students can experiment by entering values in column A and seeing the value for profit computed immediately. Even if you create the spreadsheet for stu-

FIGURE 10.20 • • • • • • • •

A spreadsheet can be used to graph the information in a table. Here the formula in cell B4 is =A4*34.25 − 225. This is copied down the column and students can enter any number they wish into column A. It appears that Brian will need to mow 22 lawns to buy his $500 bike.

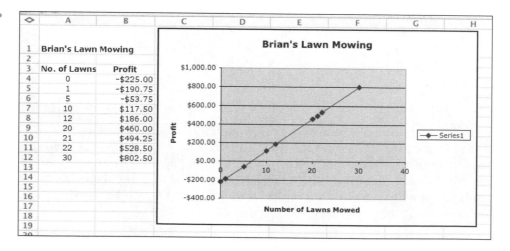

dents, the value of seeing how one variable immediately changes another is a dramatic example of joint variation and the use of variables. With the graph, students have five representations of a functional relationship—context, chart, graph, equation, and language. Note that we saw these same representations in the context of growing patterns, which were also examples of functions.

Real-World Functions

The idea of function is so important because the real world is full of related factors. The case of Brian's lawn mowing is just one example. After exploring a functional relationship with the class and discussing all of the different representations, students are ready to explore functions on their own, as described in the next activity.

ACTIVITY 10.17

Real-World Functions

Discuss with your class a real situation in which the value of one measure or count will be related to another measure or count. A list of examples follows this activity. Suppose the situation is the total sales of tickets to the class play. Tickets cost 75¢ each. If 20 tickets are sold, the income will be $15.00, for 21 tickets, $15.75, and so on. The task is to create a chart and a graph based on at least seven different values for the number of tickets. Students should also find an equation that relates income (I) to number of tickets (N). Once the graph is completed, they should use it to determine the income for values they did not have on their chart. In a similar manner, they should use their equation to find values and check to see if these values agree with the graphical representation.

For the example in "Real-World Functions," the graph will be a straight line and, if done correctly, can be used to predict other values not in the chart. The equation would be $I = N \times 75$¢. (To use 75¢, $0.75, or simply 75 in the equation is of minimal importance.)

Here are some other examples of real-world situations that give rise to functions appropriate for intermediate-grade students.

- The length of a row of students holding arms outstretched. *Row length is a function of the number of students.*

- Weight of jellybeans in increments of 10 jellybeans. *The weight of jelly beans is a function of the number of jelly beans.*

- Height of liquid in a bottle determined by the number of units poured in. Liquid is measured into the bottle using a small container, such as a medicine cup, or use milliliters or ounces. The experiment is most interesting if the bottle has an irregular shape that will cause the graph to curve. *The height of the liquid in the bottle is a function of the quantity of liquid poured in.*

- Height of bean plants compared to the days since they sprouted. *The height of the bean plant is a function of the number of days since it was planted.*

- The number of pendulum swings in 15 seconds depends on the length of the pendulum. Suspend a tennis ball or other suitable weight from a string. Start with a length of 2 feet measured to the bottom of the ball. Change the string in 6-inch increments and repeat the experiment. The graph for this experiment will be a curve. *The number of times a pendulum will swing in 15 seconds is a function of the length of the pendulum.*

- Distance a toy car will roll down a ramp depending on the height of the ramp. Use a board about 3 feet long. Raise one end 5 cm. Place a toy car at the top and let it roll. Measure the distance from the bottom of the ramp to the place where it started. You may want to repeat each trial several times to get a good reading. Raise the ramp in 5-cm increments. *The distance a toy car will roll down the ramp is a function of the height of the ramp.*

- Distance a wad of paper can be thrown. Start with a 2-square-inch piece of plain paper (not heavy). Have five students throw the paper from behind a line and measure the distance it can be thrown. Use the median distance in the chart. Repeat with larger pieces of paper in increments of 2 square inches. The distance will increase for a while and then eventually level off. *The distance that a wad of paper can be thrown is a function of the area of the paper.*

Clearly some of these real-world experiments will not produce perfectly straight lines or even smooth curves. For example, the paper-throwing task will have quite erratic data, but there will be a trend. For these situations, an equation is not at all possible. When the numbers come from computation rather than from an experiment, an equation is more likely. For example, in most any cost-versus-quantity situation, students should be able to see how an equation could work. Consider the task of creating a tower of 1-inch cubes. The tower is made on a 2- by 3-inch base of 6 cubes. As the height of the tower changes from 1 inch to 10 inches, the volume of the tower will increase in 6-cubic-inch increments. The equation would be $V = H \times 6$ and the graph will be a straight line.

When the points on the graph form an approximate straight line, discuss with your students how a straight line that comes close to the dots may be a good approximation of the real situation. The line can be used to predict the outcomes of trials not yet conducted.

Function Machines

When students examine real-world functions or explore growing patterns, the functional relationship is found in the context. The students' task is to represent that relationship in other ways—charts, graphs, and equations. Another important type of activity is to determine the functional relationship by simply seeing the numbers that are paired up, that is, without a context involved. This could be done by giving students a chart for a function and asking them to determine the function rule. A completely equivalent format that is generally more fun is a function "machine" as described in the next activity.

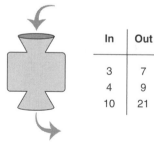

In	Out
3	7
4	9
10	21

FIGURE 10.21 ••••••

A simple function machine is used to play "Guess My Rule." Students suggest input numbers and the operator records the output value.

guess the rule by putting numbers into the machine and observing what comes out. A list of in–out pairs is kept on the board. Students who think they have guessed the rule raise their hands. As more numbers are put into the machine, those students who think they know the rule tell what comes out. Continue until most have guessed the rule.

"Guess My Rule" can be played with the whole class, or students can play in small groups, perhaps as a station activity. Provide a collection of rules on cards. Include at least two examples so that the machine operator is sure to understand the rule. The guesses can be kept in a chart on paper where all players can see. Eventually students can make up their own rules to try to stump their classmates.

Assessment Note

The main content of this chapter involves the ideas related to patterns (repeating, number, and growing) and the related ideas of variables, equations, and functions. At any particular grade level, your curriculum will likely specify particular skills in these areas. To assess this knowledge is straightforward. Can your students recognize and extend patterns of the appropriate type for their grade level? Do they use variables in ways that suggest an understanding of the various uses and meanings of *variable*—again, commensurate with their grade level? And do they solve equations appropriate for their grade level? Answers to these questions should be found in the way students respond to the activities you conduct in class or in end-of-unit tests that assess these ideas directly.

More pervasive than these specific ideas, however, is the general notion of algebraic reasoning. It is appropriate to gather data that indicate the degree to which students make generalizations based on their mathematical experiences and use appropriate language and symbolism to represent these generalizations. Since pattern and regularity can be found in nearly all areas of mathematics, algebraic reasoning should be developed and assessed throughout the curriculum. Students who ask questions like "Will that work for any numbers?" or who observe similarities from one area of mathematics to another are using algebraic reasoning. Students who have difficulty seeing and expressing relationships such as the way two patterns are alike or who have difficulty expressing rules and formulas are not as strong in their algebraic reasoning.

Make a conscious effort to observe and keep anecdotal records of behaviors that are indicative of algebraic reasoning. It is quite likely that such records over time will give you useful insights into the mathematical talents of your students.

EXPANDED LESSON

Predict How Many
Based on: Activity 10.4, p. 294

GRADE LEVEL: Fifth grade.

MATHEMATICS GOALS
- To explore growing patterns using three representations: pictures or drawings, table of values, and a rule.
- To practice searching for relationships between the step number and the step in a growing pattern as a foundation for the concept of function.

THINKING ABOUT THE STUDENTS
Students have had some experience with growing patterns. They have extended growing patterns with appropriate materials and explained why their extensions followed the patterns. Students have created tables to record the numeric component of patterns (the number of objects at each step). They have found and described recursive relationships (i.e., how the pattern changes from one step to the next). They have not begun to use variables in their explanations.

MATERIALS AND PREPARATION
- Make transparencies of the Windows and the Predict How Many worksheets (Blackline Masters L-5 and L-6).
- Make a copy of both worksheets for each student.

lesson

BLM L-5

BLM L-6

BEFORE

Brainstorm

- Distribute the Windows pattern worksheet and display it on the overhead. Explain that the table shows how many bars or sticks are needed to make all of the windows for that step. Have students draw the next two steps and fill in the next two entries of the table.
- Ask: *If we wanted to find how many sticks it would take to have 20 windows—the twentieth step—what patterns can we use to help us so that we would not have to draw all of the steps?* Suggest that students look for ways to count the sticks in groupings and try to connect the groupings to the step numbers. Have students work for a while in pairs and then solicit ideas from the class. Here are some possible ideas that students may suggest:

  1. *The tops and bottoms have the same number of sticks as the step number. There is one more vertical stick than the step number.* [Step + Step + Step + 1]
  2. *There is a square of four sticks, then each new step adds three more. That is, four plus three times one less than the step number.* [4 + 3 × (Step − 1)]
  3. *One stick (at either end), then there are as many sets of three as the step number.* [1 + 3 × Step]
  4. Looking only at the table and not the drawing: *Start with 4 then add 3, one less time than the step number.* This gives the same result as idea number 2. Help students make the connection to the drawing.

- For each suggestion that you get, write the idea in a manner similar to the expressions shown here. Notice in these expressions that "Step" is actually a variable and could be replaced by *n* or *S* or any other letter. It is not necessary that students come up with all of these ideas. Erase the ideas that have been suggested.
- Have students use an idea that they like and explain their rule on the Windows worksheet. Then have them use the rule to finish the table.
- Pass out the second worksheet, Predict How Many.

The Task
Determine the number of items in the twentieth step of the pattern on the Predict How Many worksheet without filling in the first 19 entries.

Establish Expectations

- Students should extend the pattern for two more steps, making table entries accordingly.
- Students should describe in words the pattern they see in the picture. They should use the picture and/or the table to determine the number of dots in the twentieth step.

DURING

- Be sure students understand what they did with the Windows worksheet before they continue with Predict How Many.
- If students are having difficulty finding a relationship, suggest that they look for ways to count the dots without having to count each one. If they use the same method of counting for each step, they should begin to see how their counting method relates to the step numbers. Have them write a numeric expression for each step that matches their counting procedure. For example, step two is 2×3, step four is 3×4, and so on.
- Once students think they have identified a relationship, make sure they test their conjecture with other parts of the table and picture.

AFTER

- Ask what entry students found for step 20. List all results on the board without comment. The correct result is 420, but do not evaluate any responses.
- Ask students to come to the board to explain their strategies for identifying and extending the pattern. Encourage the class to comment or ask questions about methods of counting the dots or thinking about the rule for step 20.
- For students who use only the table to find a pattern, have the class see how their idea can be related to the drawings of the dots.

ASSESSMENT NOTES

- Are students able to see the connections between the pictorial representation of the pattern and the table of values?
- Look for students who are simply generating all the entries in the table to determine the twentieth entry. These students need to be encouraged to look for patterns in the manner that they count the dots.

- For students who are having difficulty, continue having them work to see the connections between the pictorial or physical representation of the pattern and the table of values.
- If students are ready, you may want to begin to use a letter or variable in the rules that students describe. You may also want to begin to introduce variable notation into their written descriptions (e.g., using *n* for the step number).

next steps

EXPLORING DATA ANALYSIS

Data, especially in the form of various types of graphs, play a significant role in the information we receive every day in newspapers, magazines, and on television. It is certainly reasonable to expect students to develop an understanding of graphs and how graphs depict information. All states include some form of graphing and data analysis in their standards for nearly every grade.

A focus in grades 3–5 should be to add to and refine the various forms of data representations that students have likely been exposed to in the early grades. Students should see that the primary purpose of data, either in graphical form or in numeric form, is to answer questions about the population from which the data are drawn. That means that a good data analysis program will emphasize the selection of graphs and statistics that best answers realistic questions.

big ideas

1 A collection of objects with various attributes can be classified or sorted in different ways. A single object can belong to more than one class. Classification is the first step in the organization of data.

2 Data are gathered and organized in order to answer questions about the populations from which the data come. With data from only a sample of the population, inferences are made about the population—the larger the sample, the greater the confidence in inferences made.

3 Data sets can be analyzed in various ways to provide a sense of the shape of the data, including how spread out they are (range, variance) and how they are centered (mean, median, mode).

4 Measures that describe data with numbers are called statistics. Data can be organized in various graphical forms to visually convey information. The use of a particular graph or statistic can mediate what the data tell about the population.

Gathering Data to Answer Questions

Data analysis is about more than calculating statistics. It includes both asking and answering questions about our world. To answer the questions, data must be gathered and organized and then analyzed. The first goal in the Data Analysis and Probability standard of *Principles and Standards* says that students should "formulate questions that can be addressed with data and collect, organize, and display relevant data to answer them" (NCTM, 2000, p. 48). Notice that data collection should be for a purpose, to answer a question, just as in the real world. The analysis of data should have the agenda of adding information about some aspect of our world. This is what political pollsters, advertising agencies, market researchers, census takers, wildlife managers, and hosts of others do: gather data to answer questions. Textbooks often provide students with questions to answer and also the data with which to answer them. Although these may be interesting contexts for data analysis, the questions are not necessarily of interest to your students. Students should be given opportunities to generate their own questions, decide on appropriate data to help answer these questions, and determine methods of collecting the data. Avoid gathering data simply to make a graph.

When students formulate the questions they want to ask, the data they gather become more and more meaningful. How they organize the data and the techniques for analyzing them have a purpose. For example, one class of students gathered data concerning which cafeteria foods were most often thrown in the garbage. As a result of these efforts, certain items were removed from the regular menu. The activity illustrated to students the power of organized data, and it helped them get food that they liked better.

Ideas for Questions and Data

Often the need to gather data will come from the class naturally in the course of discussion or from questions arising in other content areas. Science, of course, is full of measurements and, thus, abounds in data requiring analysis. Social studies is also full of opportunities to pose questions requiring data analysis. The next few sections suggest some additional ideas.

Classroom Questions

Students often want to learn about themselves, their families and pets, measures such as arm span or time to get to school, their likes and dislikes, and so on. The easiest questions to deal with are those that can be answered by each class member's contributing one piece of data. When there are lots of possibilities, suggest that students restrict the number of choices. Here are a few ideas:

- *Favorites:* TV shows, games, movies, ice cream, video game platforms, sports teams.
- *Numbers:* Number of pets, sisters, or brothers; hours watching TV or hours of sleep; birthdays (month or day of month); bedtime; time spent on the computer.
- *Measures:* Height, arm span, area of foot, long-jump distance, shadow length, seconds to run around the track, minutes spent on the bus.

Beyond the Classroom

The questions in the previous section are designed for students to contribute data about themselves. This is appropriate for younger students who are interested in learning who they are as a class and how each fits into the class as an individual. Eventually, you will sense that your students are ready to gather data for which they need to go outside the class or at least ask questions about things beyond the classroom.

GATHERING DATA TO ANSWER QUESTIONS

Discussions about communities provide a good way to integrate social studies and mathematics. As you study the neighborhood in which students live, many questions arise:

- Counts of restaurants or stores (number of various burger franchises or convenience stores).
- Number of police officers, fire fighters, nurses, doctors, elected officials, and other similar data can most likely be found on websites of local institutions. If the information is not immediately available, this is a good chance to write a letter of request, even if it is just an e-mail.
- Types of businesses that are in your community. Students can solicit information from their parents, or a survey of the newspaper may be of use.

The newspaper itself suggests all sorts of data-related questions. For example, how many full-page ads occur on different days of the week? What types of stories are on the front page? Which comics are really for kids and which are not?

Science is another area where questions can be asked and data gathered. Students might collect leaves, rocks, or even insects from their own backyards. These objects can then be classified in various ways, creating categories for graphing. Experiments provide another type of question. How many times do different types of balls bounce when each is dropped from the same height? How many days does it take for different types of bean, squash, and pea seeds to germinate when kept in moist paper towels?

Comparisons

Another type of progression from the questions students ask about themselves is to consider if they as a class are like or different from other groups. Do the fifth-grade students spend the same amount of time watching TV or like the same foods as we do? How much taller are students in the next grade or two grades ahead of us? Comparisons can also be made between your own class and selected groups of adults to which the students have access, such as parents or faculty.

To expand your students' perspective, you might explore ways in which your class can compare themselves or their data with similar classes in your school district, other places in the state, other states, or perhaps even in a foreign country. With the Internet making communication so quick and easy, any connection you may have with teachers in other cities, states, or countries can open up not just a source of interesting data but also a way for your children to see beyond their own localities.

To describe a group usually involves asking a variety of questions, and deciding on which questions to ask is not nearly as easy as it may sound. How many questions should be asked? Should they be multiple choice? If not, how will the answers be handled? To describe a large group (say, the school), how many people should be surveyed? How should they be selected? Students should be involved in making these decisions as they formulate their questions and design surveys.

Other Sources of Information

Gathering data can mean using data that have been collected by others. For example, newspapers, almanacs, sports record books, maps, and various government publications are sources of data that may be used to answer student questions. Students may be interested in facts about another country as a result of a social studies unit. Olympic records in various events over the years or data related to space flight are other examples of topics around which student questions may be formulated. For these and hundreds of other questions, data can be found on the World Wide Web. Here are three websites with a lot of interesting data.

- U.S. Census Bureau (www.census.gov): This website contains copious statistical information by state, county, or voting district.
- The World Fact Book (www.odci.gov/cia/publications/factbook/index.html): This website provides demographic information for every nation in the world, including population, age distributions, death and birth rates, and information on the economy, government, transportation, and geography. Maps are included as well.
- Internet Movie Database (www.imdb.com): This website offers information about movies of all genres.

Classification of Data

After the information has been collected, we need to decide how to classify or categorize it to make sense of it. This basic activity is fundamental to data analysis. Data must be grouped into categories in order to begin to answer questions and to formulate and answer further questions. Vehicles might be categorized based on manufacturer, gas mileage, year, or type (e.g., truck, car, minivan, sports-utility vehicle). Possible groupings for favorite cold beverages are caffeinated and noncaffeinated. Other possibilities are soda, water, juice, tea, and other. Each of these groupings is based on a different attribute of the data.

Students need experiences with categorizing data in numerous ways so that they begin to understand that different classifications can provide different and sometimes more meaningful information about the data. Suppose from a survey about students' favorite games 25 different games are named. A bar graph with 25 categories is not particularly helpful. However, categorizing the games as board games, electronic games, or sports games provides more meaningful information about the data collected, such as which type of game is most liked.

The Shape of Data

A big conceptual idea in data analysis can be referred to as the *shape of data:* a sense of how data are spread or grouped, what characteristics they have, and what they tell us in a global way about the population from which they are taken.

Each of the graphical techniques we will discuss gives a visual picture of the shape of data. Students should learn that different graphs provide different snapshots of the data. For the particular question being answered, the choice of graphs is made around the notion of the shape of the data.

Statistical techniques provide a numeric picture of the shape of the data. The numbers can be thought of as measures of the shape. For example, the median tells us where the center is. The range tells about the spread of the data.

Descriptive Statistics

Although graphs provide visual images of data, measures of the data are a different and important way to describe data. Numbers that describe data are *statistics,* measures of the data that quantify some attribute of them. The things that are most often described numerically about a set of data are the distance between the highest and lowest data values (the *range*), some measure of where the center of the data is (an *average*), and how dispersed the data are within the range (the *variance* or *dispersion*). Students can get an idea of the importance of these statistics by exploring the ideas informally.

Averages

The term *average* is heard quite frequently in everyday usage. Sometimes it refers to an exact arithmetic average, as in "the average daily rainfall." Sometimes it is used quite loosely, as in "She is about average height." In either situation, an average is a single number or measure that is descriptive of a larger collection of numbers. If your test average is 92, it is assumed that somehow all of your test scores are reflected by this number.

The *mean, median,* and *mode* are specific types of averages or *measures of central tendency.* The *mode* is the value that occurs most frequently in the data set. Of these three statistics, the mode is the least useful as a descriptor of a data set as a whole. Consider the following set of numbers:

$$1, 1, 3, 5, 6, 7, 8, 9$$

The mode of this set is 1 and not a very good description of this set. If the 8 in this string of numbers were a 9, there would be two modes. If one of the ones were changed to a 2, there would be no mode at all. In short, the mode is a statistic that does not always exist, does not necessarily reflect the center of the data, and can be highly unstable, changeable with very small changes in the data.

The *mean* is computed by adding all of the numbers in the set and dividing the sum by the number of elements added. This is the statistic that is sometimes referred to as the *average,* although the terms are not synonymous. The mean of our sample set is 5 (40 ÷ 8). The mean is discussed in more detail in the next section.

The *median* is the middle value in an ordered set of data. Half of all values lie at or above the median and half below. For the eight numbers in our sample set, the median is between 5 and 6, or 5.5. The median is easier to understand and to compute and is not affected, as the mean is, by one or two extremely large or extremely small values outside the range of the rest of the data.

In the following activity students begin to develop definitions for mean, median, mode, and range by examining sets of data and their corresponding statistics.

ACTIVITY 11.1

What's the Meaning of This?

Provide groups of students with several data sets and the corresponding mean, median, mode, and range. Four data sets with corresponding statistics are provided for this purpose in Table 11.1. The task is for students to examine the data sets and their corresponding statistics to make conjectures about the meaning of mean, median, mode, and range. You may need to suggest to students to start with Data Set A and make a conjecture about the meanings of these terms. Then as they move to the next data set, they can revise their conjectures. Discuss as a class the meanings they have developed and how those meanings evolved as they examined each new data set.

	Data Set A	Data Set B	Data Set C	Data Set D
	1, 1, 3, 4, 5, 5, 7, 9, 9, 10	10, 12, 17, 24, 25, 32, 34, 34, 42, 47, 54, 68, 71, 79, 80, 85, 86, 87, 98, 99	8, 9, 11, 14, 32	0, 2, 2, 3, 3, 3.5, 3.75, 4, 4.25, 4.5
Mean	5.4	54.2	14.8	3
Median	5	50.5	11	3.25
Mode	1, 5, 9	34	None	2, 3
Range	9	89	24	4.5

Having students examine these statistics over several data sets and create their own definitions is a much more powerful and meaningful way to help them understand what these statistics are about than simply providing the definitions to them. You may need to help them tweak their definitions to better reflect the conventional definitions; however, the conventional definitions will make much more sense to students after attempting to generate their own.

Understanding the Mean: Two Concepts

Due to ease of computation and stability, the median when compared to the mean has some advantages as a practical average. However, the mean will continue to be used in popular media and in books. For smaller sets of data such as your test scores, the mean is perhaps a more meaningful statistic. Finally, the mean is used in the computation of other statistics such as the standard deviation. Therefore, it remains important that students have a good concept of what the mean tells them about a set of numbers.

There are actually two different ways to think about the mean. First, it is a number that represents what all of the data items would be if they were leveled out. In this sense, the mean represents all of the data items. Statisticians prefer to think of the mean as a central balance point. This concept of the mean is more in keeping with the notion of a measure of the "center" of the data or a measure of central tendency. Both concepts are discussed in the following sections.

A Leveling Concept of the Mean

Suppose that the average number of family members for the students in your class is 5. One way to interpret this is to think about distributing the entire collection of moms, dads, sisters, and brothers to each of the students so that each would have a "family" of the same size. To say that you have an average of 93 for the four tests in your class is like spreading the total of all of your points evenly across the four tests. It is as if each student had the same family size and each test score were the same, but the totals matched the actual distributions. This concept of the mean is easy to understand

and explain and has the added benefit that it leads directly to the algorithm for computing the mean.

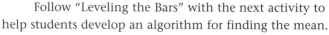

ACTIVITY 11.2

Leveling the Bars

Have students make a bar graph of some data using plastic connecting cubes such as Unifix. Choose a situation with 5 or 6 bars with no more than 10 or 12 cubes in each. For example, the graph in Figure 11.1 shows prices for six toys. The task for students is to use the graph itself to determine what the price would be if all of the toys were the same price, assuming that the total for all the toys remained the same. Students will use various techniques to rearrange the cubes in the graph but will eventually create six equal bars, possibly with some leftovers that could mentally be distributed in fractional amounts. (In the example, the total number of cubes is a multiple of six.) Do not tell students they are finding the average or mean, only that they are to find equal-length bars.

Explain to students that the size of the leveled bars is the *mean* of the data—the amount that each item would cost if all items cost the same amount but the total of the prices remained fixed.

Follow "Leveling the Bars" with the next activity to help students develop an algorithm for finding the mean.

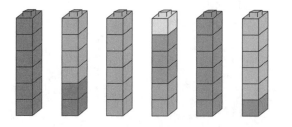

Bar graph made with plastic snap cubes

The same cubes rearranged into equal stacks.
Their height is the <u>mean</u> value of the bars above.

FIGURE 11.1 •

Understanding the mean as a leveling of the data.

ACTIVITY 11.3

The Mean Foot

Pose the following question: What is the mean length of our feet in inches? Have each student cut a strip of adding machine tape that matches the length of his or her foot. Students record their names and the length of their feet in inches on the strips. Suggest that before finding a mean for the class, you will first get means for smaller groups. Put students into groups of four, six, or eight students. (Groups of five or seven will prove to be problematic.) In each group, have the students tape their foot strips end to end. The task for each group is to come up with a method of finding the mean without using any of the lengths written on the strips. They can only use the combined strip. Each group will share their method with the class. From this work, they will devise a method for determining the mean for the whole class.

 Before reading on, what is a method that the students could use in "The Mean Foot"?

To evenly distribute the inches for each student's foot among the members of the group, they can fold the strip into equal parts so that there are as many sections as students in the group. Then they can measure the length of any one part.

How can you find the mean for the whole class? Suppose there are 23 students in the class. Using the strips already taped together, make one very long strip for the whole class. It is not reasonable to fold this long strip into 23 equal sections. But if you wanted to know how long the resulting strip would be, how could that be done? The total length of the strip is the sum of the lengths of the 23 individual foot strips. To find the length of one section if the strip were actually folded in 23 equal parts, simply divide the entire length by 23. In fact, students can mark off "mean feet" along the strip. There should be very close to 23 equal-length "feet." This dramatically illustrates the usual add-up-and-divide algorithm for finding the mean.

A Balance Point Concept of the Mean

Statisticians think about the mean as a point on a number line where the data on either side of the point are balanced. This balance-point interpretation of the mean has only recently found its way into school textbooks, and even then it is generally not discussed until about the fifth or sixth grade. You may wish to explore this idea with fifth-grade students so that their understanding of mean is more in keeping with ideas they may experience later. Therefore, we are offering some ideas you can try.

To help think about the mean as a balance point, it is useful to think about the data placed on a line plot rather than as bar graphs. What is important is not how many pieces of data are on either side of the mean or balance point but the distances of data from the mean that must balance.

To illustrate, draw a number line on the board, and arrange eight sticky notes above the number 3 as shown in Figure 11.2(a). Each sticky note represents one family. The notes are positioned on the line to indicate how many pets are owned by the family. Stacked up like this would indicate that all families have the same number of pets. The mean is three pets. But different families are likely to have different numbers of pets. So we could think of eight families with a range of numbers of pets. Some may have zero pets, and some may have as many as ten or even more. How could you change the number of pets for these eight families so that the mean remains at 3? Students will suggest moving the sticky notes in opposite directions, probably in pairs. This will result in a symmetrical arrangement. But what if one of the families has eight pets, a move of five spaces from the 3? This might be balanced by moving two families

FIGURE 11.2 • • • • • • •

(a) If all data points are the same, the mean is that value. (b) By moving data points away from the mean in a balanced manner, different distributions can be found that have the same mean.

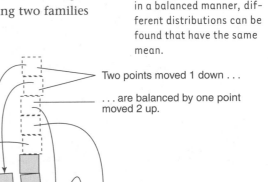

Two points moved 1 down . . .

. . . are balanced by one point moved 2 up.

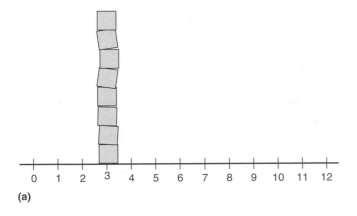

(a)

(b)

to the left, one three spaces to the 0 and one two spaces to the 1. Figure 11.2(b) shows one way the families could be rearranged to maintain a mean of 3. You should stop here and find at least two other distributions of the families, each having a mean of 3.

Use the next activity to find the mean or balance point given the data.

ACTIVITY 11.4

Finding the Balance Point

Have students draw a number line from 0 to 12 with about an inch between the numbers. Use six small sticky notes to represent the prices of six toys as shown in Figure 11.3. Have them place a light pencil mark on the line where they think the mean might be. For the moment, avoid the add-up-and-divide computation. The task is to determine the actual mean by moving the sticky notes in toward the "center." That is, the students are finding out what price or point on the number line balances out the six prices on the line. For each move of a sticky one space to the left (a toy with a lower price), a different sticky must be moved one space to the right (a toy with a higher price). Eventually, all stickies should be stacked above the same number, the balance point or mean.

Stop now and try this exercise yourself. Notice that after any pair of moves that keep the distribution balanced, you actually have a new distribution of prices with the same mean. The same was true when you moved the stickies out from the mean when they were all stacked on the same point.

The balance concept does not lead to the add-up-and-divide algorithm for computing the mean. However, it is useful to do the following side-by-side approach. Make bars of cubes for the original data in Figure 11.3. Level the bars by moving only one cube at a time from a longer bar to a shorter bar. Each time you move a cube off of a bar, the sticky note for that bar must be moved one space to the left. At the same time, the sticky note for the bar to which the cube was added must be moved one space to the right. As you continue to move cubes one at a time, adjust the sticky notes accordingly.

Changes in the Mean

Notice that the mean only defines the center of a set of data and so by itself is not a very useful description of the shape of the data. The balance approach to the mean clearly illustrates that many different distributions can have the same mean.

Especially for small sets of data, the mean is significantly affected by extreme values. For example, suppose that another toy with a price of $20 is added to the six we have been using in the examples. How will the mean change? If the $1 toy were removed, how would the mean be affected? Suppose that one new toy is added that increases the mean from $6 to $7. How much does the new toy cost? Students should be challenged with questions such as these using small sets of data and either the balance or the leveling concept.

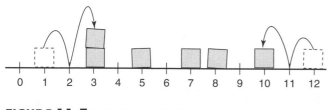

FIGURE 11.3 •

Move data points in toward the center or balance point without changing the balance around that point. When you have all points at the same value, that is the balance or the mean.

In NCTM's *e-Standards,* the applet "Comparing Properties of the Mean and the Median" shows seven data points that can be dragged back and forth along a number line with the mean and median updated instantly. The applet allows students to see how stable the median is and how changing one point can affect the mean.

Graphical Representations

How data are organized should be directly related to the question that caused you to collect the data in the first place. For example, suppose that a Scout troop wants to know how many merit badges they have earned. Each Scout writes down the number of badges and the data are collected.

> **STOP** **If your students were considering the data in this situation, what are some ways that you might suggest they organize and graph the information? Is one of your ideas better than others for answering the question about merit badges? Think about this before reading on.**

If a large bar graph is made with a bar for every Scout, that will certainly tell how many merit badges each Scout has. However, is it the best way to answer the question? If the data were categorized by number of badges, then a graph showing the number of Scouts with two badges, three badges, and so on will show the number of badges most commonly earned and how the number of badges varies across the troop.

Students should be involved in deciding how they want to represent their data. By third grade, students will have had some experience with the various methods of picturing data. However, they may not be aware of all the options that are available. Sometimes you can suggest a new way of displaying data and have children learn to construct that type of graph or chart. Once they have made the display, they can discuss its value. Did this graph (or chart or picture) tell about our data in a clear way? Compared to other ways of displaying data, how is this better?

The emphasis or goal of this instruction should be to help students see that graphs and charts tell about information, that different types of representations tell different things about the same data. The value of having students actually construct their own graphs is not so much that they learn the techniques but that they are personally invested in the data and that they learn how a graph conveys information. Once a graph is constructed, the most important activity is discussing what it tells the people who see it, especially those who were not involved in making the graph. Discussions about graphs of real data that the students have themselves been involved in gathering will help them interpret other graphs and charts that they see in newspapers and on TV.

What we should *not* do is get overly anxious about the tedious details of graph construction. The issues of analysis and communication are your agendas and are much more important than the technique! In the real world, technology will take care of details of graph construction.

There are two equally good possibilities you may consider when planning to have your students construct graphs or charts. First, you can simply encourage students to do their best and make, by hand, charts and graphs that make sense to them and that they feel communicate the information they wish to convey. This is not to say that children do not need guidance. They should have seen and been involved in group constructions of various types of graphs and charts. This provides them with some ideas from which to choose for their own graphs. This informal approach may be best in order to get students to be more personally invested in their work and not distracted by the techniques of technology. Care should be taken not to worry about fancy labeling or nice, neat pictures. The intent is to get the students involved in communicating a message about their data.

The second option is to use technology. The computer has provided us with many tools for constructing simple yet powerful representations. With the help of technology, it is possible to construct several different pictures of the same data with very little effort. The discussion can then focus on the message or information that each format provides. Students can make their own selections of various graphs and can justify their choice based on their own intended purposes. As just one example, Figure 11.4

FIGURE 11.4 • • • • • • •

Four graphs produced with *Graph Club* software.

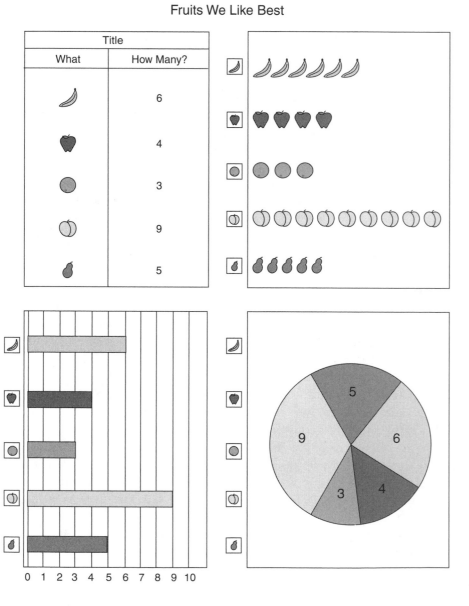

Chapter **11** EXPLORING DATA ANALYSIS

shows four graphs produced by *The Graph Club* (Tom Snyder, 1993). When two or more graphs are being created from the same data, it is possible to see all graphs change accordingly. How does a pie graph show information differently than a picture graph?

Bar Graphs

Bar graphs and tally charts are among those graphing techniques students have been exposed to in the primary grades. These graphs remain important tools throughout the grades and are frequently seen in newspapers and on the TV news. In grades 3–5, two qualitative differences in their bar graphs can be developed. First, students can easily use centimeter grid paper to construct their own graphs with little guidance. Students can decide on their own scales for their graphs. Labeling of graphs should be less a matter of teacher direction and more a matter of making a graph that communicates and answers the question that is being asked. Students' graphs can be constructed and discussed in terms of what they tell us and whether the labeling is adequate or how it might be improved. An easy idea for a quickly constructed class graph is to give each student a sticky note to use as graph elements. Sketch columns or rows on the board or on a chart. Students come to the graph and place their sticky note in the appropriate row or column.

A second element of progression may involve using a single tally or picture element in the graph to represent more than one count. For example, if a graph were being made to show how many seconds different students required to run around the gym floor, using one square of the grid to represent 10 seconds may be useful. A graph showing the number of cars passing through a busy intersection at three different times of the day might use drawings or cutouts of cars instead of squares or tallies. If the numbers are large, each car may stand for 25 actual cars.

Once a graph has been constructed, engage the class in a discussion of what information the graph tells or conveys. "What can you tell about our class by looking at this shoe graph?" Graphs convey factual information (more people wear sneakers than any other kind of shoe) and also provide opportunities to make inferences that are not directly observable in the graph (kids in this class do not like to wear leather shoes). The difference between actual facts and inferences is an important idea in graph construction and is also an important idea in science. Students can examine graphs found in newspapers or magazines and discuss the *facts* in the graphs and the *message* that may have been intended by the person who made the graph.

Interpretation

Making the graph or computing mean or median does not help me understand what it tells me about the data. There are a number of ways to get at interpretation. For example, several graphs and statistics for the same situation and data can be presented. "Suppose you were a newspaper editor. Which of these statistics and graphs should you use in your story? Explain your selection. Are any of these statistics of no value to the message?" In this type of interpretation, several options are provided, and the choice is based on the intended audience and purpose. There is no need actually to compute the statistics or create the graphs.

Another idea is to provide graphs and statistics for two related situations: your class and the rest of the school, your state and the rest of the country, hamburgers at

McDonald's and hamburgers at Burger King. What can be determined for sure from these data? What inferences can be made? What would help you make a decision about _____ that you cannot determine from the information gathered? How could you use this information to argue in favor of_____? How could you use the same information to argue on the reverse side of the issue?

Students in grades 3–5 should begin to make their own graphs of information gathered independently or by a group. Assign different data collection tasks to different groups of children. The task is to gather the data and decide on and make a graph that displays as clearly as possible the information found.

Stem-and-Leaf Plots

Stem-and-leaf plots are a combination of a table and a graph. They are actually a form of bar graph in which numeric data are plotted by using the actual numerals in the data to form the graph. By way of example, suppose that the American League baseball teams had posted the following record of wins over the past season:

Baltimore	45	Milwaukee	91
Boston	94	Minnesota	98
California	85	New York	100
Chicago	72	Oakland	101
Cleveland	91	Seattle	48
Detroit	102	Toronto	64
Kansas City	96	Texas	65

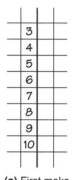

(a) First make the stem.

If the data are to be grouped by tens, list the tens digits in order and draw a line to the right, as in Figure 11.5(a). These form the "stem" of the graph. Next, go through the list of scores, and write the ones digits next to the appropriate tens digit, as in Figure 11.5(b). These are the "leaves." The process of making the graph groups the data for you. Furthermore, every piece of data can be retrieved from the graph. (Notice that stem-and-leaf plots are best made on graph paper so that each digit takes up the same amount of space.)

To provide more information, the graph can be quickly rewritten, ordering each leaf from least to most, as in Figure 11.5(c). In this form, it may be useful to identify the number that belongs to a particular team, indicating its relative place within the grouped listing.

Stem-and-leaf graphs are not limited to two-digit data. For example, if the data ranged from 600 to 1300, the stem could be the numerals from 6 to 13 and the leaves made of two-digit numbers separated by commas.

Figure 11.6 illustrates two additional variations. When two sets of data are to be compared, the leaves can extend in opposite directions from the same stem. In the same exam-

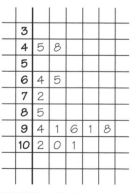

(b) Write in the leaves directly from the data.

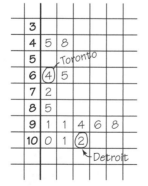

(c) It is easy to rewrite each leaf in numeric order. This puts all of the data in order.

FIGURE 11.5 ● ● ● ● ● ● ● ● ● ● ● ● ● ● ● ● ● ● ●

Making a stem-and-leaf plot.

Test Scores

Mrs. Day		Mrs. Knight
4	5	
	•	9
2 3	6	
7 7 8	•	5
3 0 4 2 4	7	1 0
7 9 5	•	8 6 9 9
3 4 1	8	4 0 1 3 1 2
5 8 7	•	9 5
	9	3 1 0
9 6	•	7
0 0	10	0

FIGURE 11.6 •

Stem-and-leaf plots can be used to compare two sets of data.

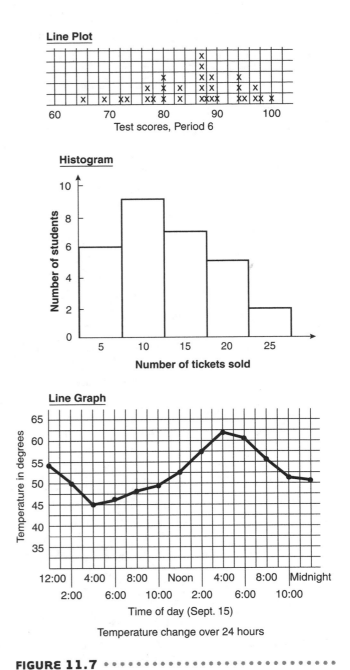

FIGURE 11.7 •

Three approaches to graphing data over continuous intervals. Notice that the horizontal scale must show some progression and is not just a grouping, as in a bar graph.

ple, notice that the data are grouped by fives instead of tens. When plotting 62, the 2 is written next to the 6; for 67, the 7 is written next to the dot below the 6.

Stem-and-leaf plots are significantly easier for students to make than bar graphs, all of the data are maintained, they provide an efficient method of ordering data, and individual elements of data can be identified.

Continuous Data Graphs

Bar graphs or picture graphs are useful for illustrating categories of data that have no numeric ordering—for example, colors or TV shows. When data are grouped along a continuous scale, they should be ordered along a number line. Examples of such information include temperatures that occur over time, height or weight over age, and percentages of test takers scoring in different intervals along the scale of possible scores.

Line Plots

Line plots are useful *counts* of things along a numeric scale. To make a line plot, a number line is drawn and an X is made above the corresponding value on the line for every corresponding data element. One advantage of a line plot is that every piece of data is shown on the graph. It is also a very easy type of graph for students to make. It is essentially a bar graph with a potential bar for every possible value. A simple example is shown in Figure 11.7.

Histograms

A *histogram* is a form of bar graph in which the categories are consecutive equal intervals along a numeric scale. The height or length of each bar is determined by the number of data elements falling into that particular interval. Histograms are not difficult in concept but can cause problems for the students constructing them. What is the appropriate interval to use for the bar width? What is a good scale to use for the height of the bars? That all of the data must be grouped and counted within each interval causes further difficulty. Unless your district curriculum specifically indicates an understanding of histograms, it is reasonable to skip over this type of graph. By middle school, students will have access to graphing calculators that make histogram construction rather easy.

Line Graphs

A *line graph* is used when there is a numeric value associated with equally spaced points along a continuous number scale. Points are plotted to represent two related pieces of data, and a line is drawn to connect the points. For example, a line graph might be used to show how the length of a flagpole shadow changed from one hour to the next during the day. The horizontal scale would be time, and the vertical scale would be the length of the shadow. Points can be plotted and straight lines drawn connecting them. In the example of the shadow, a shadow did exist at all times, but its length did not jump or drop from one plotted value to the other. It changed continuously as suggested by the graph. See the example in Figure 11.7.

Students have a tendency to graph discrete data using continuous data graphs like the line graph. For example, consider Figure 11.8, in which a student has graphed the number of siblings of each of his classmates using a line graph. The arrows have been added to the graph, highlighting the problem with displaying this type of data with a line graph. Every point on the line should have a value. What are the values where the arrows are pointing? A more appropriate choice would be a bar graph or a circle graph.

Circle Graphs

Typically, we think of circle graphs as showing percentages and, as such, these may seem inappropriate for students before the fifth grade. However, notice in Figure 11.4

FIGURE 11.8 ·

A line graph is used inappropriately to graph discrete data. What would the values be for the points indicated by the arrows?

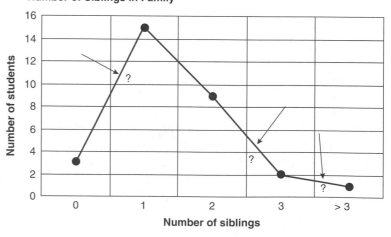

Number of Siblings in Family

that the circle graph only indicates the number of data points (in that case, students) in each of five categories. Many simple graphing programs will create a similar graph. An understanding of percentages is not required when the computer creates the graph. The circle graph in Figure 11.4 could also be constructed using common fractions. There were 27 students. The 9 who chose peaches represent $\frac{1}{3}$ of the students. As fraction concepts are developed in the third and fourth grades, making circle graphs is a good way to integrate different aspects of your curriculum. Furthermore, the fact that many fractions are a bit "messy" to deal with (e.g., $\frac{4}{27}$) is a good rationale for percents—make all the denominators 100 and round off the numerators.

Circle graphs show information that is not easily available from other graphs. For example, the peach and pear category accounts for a bit more than half of the class, whereas the apple and orange groups are about one-fourth of the class.

When comparisons are made between two populations of very different size, the circle graph offers visual ratios that allow for these comparisons. In Figure 11.9, each of two graphs shows the percentages of students with different numbers of siblings. One graph is based on classroom data and the other on schoolwide data. Because pie graphs display ratios rather than quantities, the small set of class data can be compared to the large set of school data. That could not be done with bar graphs.

Easily Made Circle Graphs

Even without technology, there are a variety of ways that circle graphs can be made easily. Circle graphs of the students in your room can be made quickly and quite dramatically. Suppose, for example, that each student picked his or her favorite basketball team in the NCAA tournament's "Final Four." Line up all of the students in the room so that students favoring the same team are together. Now form the entire group into a circle of students. Tape the ends of four long strings to the floor in the center of the circle, and extend them to the circle at each point where the teams change. Voilà! A very nice pie graph with no measuring and no per-

EXPANDED LESSON

(pages 337–338)

The expanded lesson for this chapter has students construct pie graphs without use of decimals or percents. Percents are explored as an extension.

centages. If you copy and cut out a hundredths disk (one is in the Blackline Masters) and place it on the center of the circle, the strings will show approximate percentages for each part of your graph (see Figure 11.10).

Another easy approach to circle graphs is similar to the human pie graph. Begin by having students make a bar graph of the data. Once complete, cut out the bars themselves, and tape them together end to end. Next tape the two ends together to form a

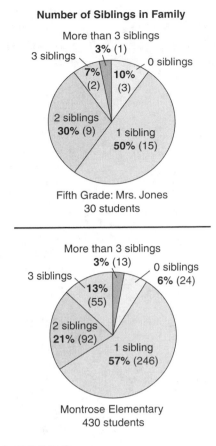

Number of Siblings in Family

More than 3 siblings
3% (1)
3 siblings — 0 siblings
7% (2) **10%** (3)
2 siblings **30%** (9)
1 sibling **50%** (15)

Fifth Grade: Mrs. Jones
30 students

More than 3 siblings
3% (13)
3 siblings — 0 siblings **6%** (24)
13% (55)
2 siblings **21%** (92)
1 sibling **57%** (246)

Montrose Elementary
430 students

FIGURE 11.9 • • • • • • • • • • • • • • •

Circle graphs show ratios of part to whole and can be used to compare ratios.

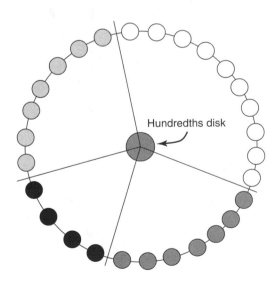

Hundredths disk

FIGURE 11.10 • • • • • • • • • • • • • • •

A human pie graph: Students are arranged in a circle, with string stretched between them to show the divisions.

circle. Estimate where the center of the circle is, draw lines to the points where different bars meet, and trace around the full loop. You can estimate percentages using the hundredths disk as before.

From Percentages to Pie Graphs

If students have experienced either of the two methods just described, using their own calculations to make pie graphs will make more sense. The numbers in each category are added to form the total or whole. (That's the same as taping all of the strips together or lining up the students.) By dividing each of the parts by the whole with a calculator, numbers between 0 and 1 result—fractional parts of the whole. If rounded to hundredths, these numbers are now percentages of the whole. Rounding may cause some error. With a copy of the hundredths disk, students can easily make a pie chart and never have to mess with degrees and protractors. Trace around the disk to make the outline of the pie. Mark the center through a small hole in the disk, and draw a line to the circle. Start from that point, and use the disk to measure hundredths around the outside.

Assessment Note

As you evaluate students in the area of graphing, it is important not to focus undue attention on the skills of constructing a graph. It is more important to think about the choice of graphs that the students make to help answer their questions or complete their projects. Your goal is for students to understand that a graph helps answer a question and provides a picture of the data. Different graphs tell us different things about the data. If you make all of the decisions about what type of graphs to make, how they should be labeled and constructed, all that students are doing is following your directions. Students who are simply not good at graphic arts are likely to do poorly drawing graphs even though they may have exceptional understanding of what their graph shows and why they chose to make that particular type.

Students should write about their graphs, explaining what the graph tells and why they selected that type of graph to illustrate the data. Use this information for your assessment.

EXPANDED LESSON

Bar Graphs to Pie Graphs

GRADE LEVEL: Fourth or fifth grade.

MATHEMATICS GOALS
- To introduce the use of a circle or pie graph to represent data.
- To informally explore the concept of percent.

THINKING ABOUT THE STUDENTS
Students have previously made a variety of graphs such as bar graphs, line plots, and tally charts but have limited or no experience with circle graphs. They have not been introduced formally to the idea of percentage. If students have explored the connections between decimals and fractions, the lesson can be used to both expand that connection and also introduce the concept of percent.

MATERIALS AND PREPARATION
- Make copies of the hundredths disk (Blackline Master 17) and 2-centimeter grid paper (Blackline Master 7) for each student. Also make transparencies of the grid paper and the hundredths disk. Cut out one of the hundredths disks for use with the class.
- Students will need access to scissors, tape, and crayons.
- Five pieces of yarn or string, each about 10 to 12 feet long. You will also need a heavy weight such as a brick or large book. The ends of the string will be anchored to this weight as the center of a class-sized circle graph. (See Figure 11.10, p. 335.)
- You may want to do the "before" portion of the lesson somewhere other than the classroom so that there is room to form a circle of all your students.

lesson

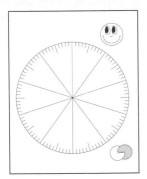

BLM 17

This lesson may take two days. Prior to this lesson, students must have gathered data to answer a question of their own. This can be a common data set for the class or individual students, or groups can have data sets from different questions and gather their own data. Use questions that lend themselves to being grouped in three to five categories. The following are only offered as examples:

- What are the favorite _____ (e.g., TV shows)_____ of students in the fourth grade? (Gather data by listing four shows and "other.")
- What are the populations of the top 50 cities in our state? (Get data from the Internet. Group the data into three categories.)
- How many students buy lunch at our school on each day of the week? (Get data from the cafeteria staff.)

BEFORE

Begin with a simpler version of the task:
- Ask a question in which each student will have one of three to five choices. For example: What are the colors of our eyes? Write the choices on the board (brown, blue, green, other).
- Quickly make a bar graph on the transparency, coloring in one square for each student as he or she tells you the color of his or her eyes.
- Have the students form a human bar graph by aligning themselves in rows for each color. Next help the students rearrange their rows into a circle formed of all the students in the class. In the center of the circle place the weight with the strings attached. Extend a string to be held by students between each different color of eyes (between the brown and green, the green and blue, and so on). To explore the idea of percents, place a hundredths disk at the center where the strings come together. With the strings fairly straight you can estimate the percentage of students in each category.

The Task
Decide on an appropriate way to graph the data gathered earlier to answer the students' question(s).

Establish Expectations

Students are to make one or more graphs to illustrate the data they collected to answer their question. Allow students to use whatever graphing technique(s) they choose.

DURING

Discuss with individual students or groups how their graphs will help others answer their question. Keep their focus on good ways to answer the question.

AFTER

- Have several students or groups display their graphs and have the class decide if the graphs help answer the question the data were collected to answer.
- If students have not made a bar graph of their data, have them do so. Each bar should be colored differently or marked with pencil to distinguish the bars. Have students cut the bars from the graph and tape them end to end to form a long strip. The two ends of the strip are then taped together to form a loop. This loop is similar to the circle of students made at the start of the lesson.
- Have students place the loop on the paper with the hundredths disk and form the loop into a circle. The center of the circle should be the center of the disk. Next they draw straight lines from the center of the disk to the divisions between the different bars, as they did earlier with the strings in their human graph. If the loop is smaller than the disk, extend the lines to the edge of the disk. Demonstrate all of this on the overhead projector using the transparent disk and one of the students' bar graph loops. Show how the first line drawn should align with one of the major subdivisions on the disk.
- Examine the transparent disk and note that it has ten large subdivisions each with ten smaller divisions for a total of 100 sections. Each is *1 percent of the whole.* Explain that 1 percent is the same as $\frac{1}{100}$.
- With this information, students can now label their own circle graphs as another representation of the data they collected. Have a discussion about which graph, the bar or circle graph, is best for answering their question.

ASSESSMENT NOTES

This is an example of a lesson in which students are introduced to a new convention. The circle graph does not arise out of a problem or task. Rather, you are showing students how such a graph is made.

- Since you are introducing a convention—how to make a circle graph—you are mainly looking for students who are having difficulty understanding how the graph is made. Students who need help making their graphs should be given help freely.
- Once the circle graphs have been made, see how well students seem to understand how the circle graph represents the data.

. . . .

- You may want to have students estimate the fractional amount of the data represented by each group on the circle graph. Portions of the graph can be likened to circular fraction models. For example, a portion that is about 25 percent will approximate the size of a one-fourth fraction piece.
- Have students find circle graphs in the newspaper and write about what the circle graph tells about the information shown.

- If you are ready to begin percents, further graphs can be made in which students first compute the percentage of data in each category and then draw the data directly on the hundredths disk.

next steps

EXPLORING CONCEPTS OF PROBABILITY

References to probability are all around us: The weather forecaster predicts a 60 percent chance of snow; medical researchers predict people with certain diets have a high chance of heart disease; the fine print on a lottery ticket states that you have a 1 in 5 million chance of winning the lottery this week; or airlines, in an effort to ensure the public's confidence in air travel, calculate the chance of a person dying in an airplane crash is 1 in 10,000,000, while being hurt in a car accident is 1 in 75. Simulations of complex situations are frequently based on probabilities and are then used in the design process of such things as spacecraft, highways and storm sewers, or plans for reactions to disasters.

Because the ideas and methods of probability are so prevalent in today's world, this strand of mathematics has risen in visibility in the school curriculum. By grade 3, most children have abandoned childlike notions about luck and probability that make games of pure chance so appealing in kindergarten and first grade. Now is the time for students to wrestle with

big ideas

1 Chance has no memory. For repeated trials of a simple experiment (e.g., tossing a coin), the outcomes of prior trials have no impact on the next. The chance occurrence of six heads in a row has no effect on getting a head on the next toss of the coin. That chance is still 50–50.

2 The occurrence of a future event can be characterized along a continuum from impossible to certain.

3 The *probability of an event* is a number between 0 and 1 that is a measure of the chance that a given event will occur. A probability of 0 indicates impossibility and that of 1 indicates certainty. A probability of $\frac{1}{2}$ indicates an even chance of the event occurring.

4 The relative frequency of outcomes of an event (*experimental probability*) can be used as an estimate of the exact probability of an event. The larger the number of trials, the better the estimate will be. The results for a small number of trials may be quite different than those experienced in the long run. For some events, the exact probability can be determined by an analysis of the event itself. A probability determined in this manner is called a *theoretical probability*.

5 Two events are either independent or dependent. If the occurrence of one event does not influence the occurrence of the other event, they are called *independent*. For example, the first flip of a coin does not influence the second flip of the coin. If eight heads in a row come up, the chance that the next toss of the coin will be a head remains exactly $\frac{1}{2}$. Two events are *dependent* events if the occurrence of one has an impact on the occurrence of the other. For example, if chips are drawn from a bag without replacing them, the probabilities for drawing the second chip are changed because there are now fewer chips in the bag.

some of the big ideas of probability, such as the difference between long-run and short-run results or the way that one event can affect another. In grades 3–5, the explorations should involve students in a variety of probabilistic situations, but the emphasis should be on exploration rather than rules and formal definitions. If done well, these informal experiences will provide a useful background from which more formal ideas can be developed in the middle and high school years.

Probability on a Continuum

The big ideas you just read can provide a fairly good sense of how you might expect to develop students' ideas about probability. An understanding that chance has no memory can only come with experience and through discussion with peers. Many adults still do not believe this. For example, many select lottery numbers because they have not come up recently. However, this is a critical idea if children are going to abandon their naïve ideas about chance and become more analytical in examining outcomes.

Before students attempt to assign numeric probabilities to events, it is important that they have the basic idea that some events are certain to happen, some are certain not to happen or are impossible, and others have different chances of occurring that fall between these extremes.

From Impossible to Certain

As a brief introduction to a discussion of probability, it is a good idea to discuss the extremes of chance situations—those that are impossible and those that are certain. Between these extremes are events that are possible but not certain. Have students suggest future events that fall into these three categories. As examples, you might have them discuss some of these:

- It will rain tomorrow.
- Drop a rock in water and it will sink.
- Trees will talk to us in the afternoon.
- The sun will rise tomorrow morning.
- Three students will be absent tomorrow.
- George will go to bed before 8:30 tonight.
- You will have two birthdays this year.

The key idea to developing chance or probability on a continuum is to help children see that some of these possible events are more likely or less likely than others. For instance, if a group of students has a running race, the chance that Gregg, a really fast runner, will be first is not certain but is very likely. It is more likely that Gregg will be near the front of the group than near the back of the pack.

The use of random devices that can be analyzed (e.g., spinners, number cubes, coins to toss, colored cubes drawn from a bag) can help students make predictions about the likelihood of an event. The following activity is a game of chance with unequal outcomes. However, students will not readily be able to predict which result is most likely, so it provides a good opportunity for discussion.

Add Then Tally

Add Then Tally										
2										
3										
4										
5										
6										

FIGURE 12.1 •

A recording sheet for "Add Then Tally."

ACTIVITY 12.1

Add Then Tally

Make number cubes with sides as follows: 1, 1, 2, 3, 3, 3. Each game requires two cubes. Students take turns rolling the two cubes and record the sum of the two numbers. To record the results, run off tally sheets with five rows of ten squares, one for each sum 2 through 6. (See Figure 12.1.) They continue to roll the cubes until one of the rows is full. They can repeat the game on a new tally sheet as long as time permits.

It is important to talk with students after they have played "Add Then Tally." Which numbers "won" the most and the least often? If they were to play again, which number would they pick to win and why? Furthermore, all of the outcomes, 2 through 6, are possible. A sum of 4 is the most likely. Sums of 2 or 3 are the least likely. However, since few if any students will analyze the possible outcomes, their predictions for future games will tell you a lot about their probabilistic reasoning. Students who observe that 4 comes up a lot and, therefore, is the best choice to win have abandoned earlier subjective ideas about luck or of chance having a memory.

Assessment Note

Remember that students' ideas about chance must develop from experience. An explanation from a teacher will likely provide only superficial understanding. It is important to have discussions with students after playing simple games of chance. During the discussions your task is to elicit their ideas, not to explain or offer judgment. The main idea that you are looking for is a growth from a belief in pure chance or luck to one where students begin to understand that some results are clearly more or less likely to happen than others regardless of luck. When you sense that this sort of growth has taken place, a significant milestone has been reached and you will know that your students are ready to move on and begin to refine their ideas of chance a bit more.

The Probability Continuum

To begin refining the concept that some events are more or less likely to occur than others, introduce the idea of a continuum of likelihood between impossible and certain. Draw a long line on the board. Label the left end "Impossible" and the right end "Certain." Write "Chances of Spinning Blue" above the line. Call this a "probability line" or a "chance line." Next, show students a spinner that is all white. "What is the chance of spinning blue with this spinner?" Indicate the left end of the probability line as showing this chance. Repeat with an all-blue spinner, indicating the right end,

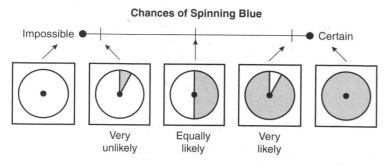

Chances of Spinning Blue

Impossible ●————————————————● Certain

Very
unlikely

Equally
likely

Very
likely

FIGURE 12.2 •

The probability line or "chance line." Use these spinner faces to help students see how chance can be at different places on a continuum between impossible and certain.

labeled Certain. Next, show a spinner that is half blue and half white. "What is the chance of spinning blue with this spinner?" The discussion should develop a consensus that it is about *equally likely* that blue will come up as not blue. Place a mark exactly in the center of the line to indicate this chance. You may want to note that this represents a chance of $\frac{1}{2}$ or 50 percent, although the position of the mark alone is actually sufficient.

Repeat the preceding discussion with a spinner that is less than $\frac{1}{4}$ blue and with one that is nearly all blue. Ask students where they would put a mark on the line to indicate the chance of spinning blue for each of these. These marks should be close to the ends of the line. (See Figure 12.2.) To review these ideas, show the spinners one at a time and ask which marks represent the chance of getting blue for that spinner.

In the next activity students design random devices that they think will create chances for various designated positions on the probability line. The activity suggests that students use a bag of colored tiles or cubes, which is a bit different than spinners. Even if the idea of drawing tiles from a bag seems new to your students, do not provide additional hints to help them with their reasoning.

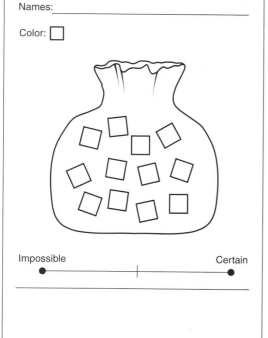

Names: _____

Color: ☐

Impossible ●————————————● Certain

_____

FIGURE 12.3 •

A possible recording sheet for the "Design a Bag" activity. Students mark a point on the line between impossible and certain. Then they color the tiles in the bag to create a mix that will produce the estimated chance of the designated color being drawn.

ACTIVITY 12.2

Design a Bag

(Note that students must be introduced to the idea of a probability line as described in the paragraphs preceding this activity.)

Provide pairs of students with a copy of a worksheet similar to that shown in Figure 12.3. This can be sketched by hand. Be sure there are 12 squares drawn on the bag. On the board mark a place on a probability line at roughly the 20 percent position. At this time do not use percent or fraction language with the children. Students are to mark this position on their worksheet probability lines. Alternatively, you could mark the worksheets before making copies. Students should color the square indicated by "Color" at the top of the page. Explain that they are going to decide what color tiles should be put in bags of 12 total tiles so that the chance of drawing this designated color is about the same as the chance indicated on the probability line. Before students begin to design their bags, ask for ideas about what colors of tiles might be put in the bag if the mark were very close to the middle of the line. Show how the real bags will be filled based on the design on the page. Demonstrate with tiles, a bag, and a completed worksheet. Emphasize that the tiles will be shaken up so that which particular squares on the bag design are colored makes no difference.

At the bottom of each sheet (and on the reverse if needed), students explain why they chose their tiles. Give them an example: *We put in 8 red and 4 of other colors because _____.*

The "Design a Bag" activity provides useful information about how your students conceive of chance as appearing on a continuum. More importantly, however, you should follow up "Design a Bag" with the following related activity.

ACTIVITY 12.3

Testing Bag Designs

Collect and display the designs made by the students in "Design a Bag." Discuss the ideas that students had for the number of designated colors to put in the bag. (Expect some variation.) Some students may think that the colors used for the other tiles make a difference, and this point should be discussed. Do not provide your opinion or comment on these ideas. Select a bag design that most students seem to agree on for the 20 percent mark. Distribute lunch bags and tiles or cubes to pairs of students to fill as suggested. Once filled, students shake the bag and draw out one tile. Tally marks are used to record a Yes (for the designated color) or No for any other color. This is repeated at least ten times. Be sure that students replace each tile after it is drawn.

Discuss with the class how their respective experiments turned out. Did it turn out the way they expected? With the small number of trials, there will be groups that get rather unexpected results.

Next, make a large bar graph or tally graph of the data from all of the groups together. This should show many more No's than Yes's. Here the discussion can help students see that if the experiment is repeated a lot of times, it is clearer that the chances are about as predicted.

EXPANDED LESSON

(pages 356–357)
A complete lesson plan based on "Testing Bag Designs" can be found at the end of this chapter.

The dual activities of "Design a Bag" and "Testing Bag Designs" can and should be repeated for two or three other marks on the probability line. Try marks at about $\frac{1}{3}$, $\frac{1}{2}$, and $\frac{3}{4}$. You may want to assign a different mark to different groups so that a discussion can include comparisons of different designs and outcomes. To compare results it is useful if the total number of trials for each design is about the same.

"Design a Bag" and "Testing Bag Designs" are important activities. Because no numbers are used for the probabilities, there are no "right" answers. The small group testing of a design shows students that chance is not an absolute predictor in the short run. The group graphs may help students with the difficult concept that the chance tends to approach what is expected in the long run. However, this latter idea involves comparing ratios in the small trials with ratios in large numbers using the accumulated data. Do not be surprised or concerned if students do not see this as clearly as you might hope.

As another variation of "Design a Bag" have students design a spinner instead of a bag of tiles. This will allow you to revisit the concept at a later time without being repetitious. With spinners, students can see the relative portion of the whole given to each color or outcome, a visual indication of the probability. Depending on the activity, that may or may not be an advantage. A clear advantage is that spinner faces can easily be made to adjust the chances of different outcomes. Transparent plastic spinners can be purchased that have no partitions. Paper spinner faces that suit your current needs are

FIGURE 12.4 •••••

An easy way to make
a spinner.

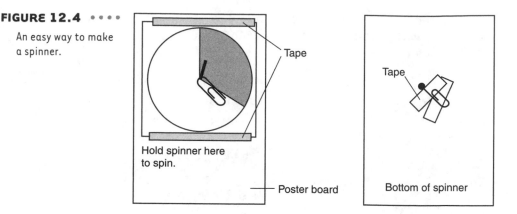

Draw spinner faces and duplicate them so that you can easily make lots of
spinners. Cut these out and tape to poster board. Students can color the
sections of the spinner. Make a small hole in the spinner center. Unbend
one end of a sturdy paper clip and poke this upward from the bottom of the
spinner. Tape the paper clip to the back leaving a paper clip post sticking up
in the center of the spinner. To use the spinner, students put another paper
clip on the post to act as the pointer. Hold the spinner flat to spin fairly.
Spinner faces can be changed easily.

taped to the bottom of these spinners and can be changed later. Transparent spinners
can also be used on the overhead projector. Use an overhead pen to mark the sections.
There are also several methods that can be used to make a spinner. One is shown in
Figure 12.4.

Sample Spaces and Probability

So far in this chapter, we have focused on the basic idea that some events may
be more or less likely than others. Calculating numeric values for probability has pur-
posely been avoided. As a readiness for probability calculations, students were asked to
locate the likelihood of an event along a continuum from impossible to certain. In
order for students to determine a numeric probability, it is important that they can
identify all of the possible outcomes of an experiment and consider their relative
chances of occurring.

The *sample space* for an experiment or chance situation is the set of all possible
outcomes for that experiment. For example, if a bag contains 2 red, 3 yellow, and 5
blue tiles, the sample space consists of all 10 tiles. The *event* of drawing a yellow tile has
3 elements in the sample space and the event of drawing a blue tile has 5 elements in
the sample space. For rolling a single number cube, the sample space always consists of
the numbers 1 to 6. However, we might define several different events that split up the
sample space in different ways. For example, rolling either an odd or an even number
splits the sample space into two equal parts. Rolling either 5 or more or less than 5
splits the sample space into two unequal parts. When rolling a number cube, each
number from 1 to 6 has an equal chance of occurring. Therefore, the chances of rolling
an odd or an even number are equal. However, the chance of rolling a 5 or 6 is less
than the chance of rolling a number less than 5.

One-Stage Experiments

Students should initially explore experiments that require only a single device such as a number cube, a spinner, or drawing a tile from a bag. These can be referred to as *one-stage* experiments because there is only one activity to determine an outcome. Drawing tiles from a bag as in "Design a Bag" was an example of a one-stage experiment.

The next activity allows students to define events within a given experiment. In addition to experiencing the relative chances of different events occurring, the activity allows you to see how well students comprehend the concept of a sample space.

ACTIVITY 12.4

Create a Game

Two students are given a bag with different colored tiles. For example, the bag might have 6 red, 2 green, 1 yellow, and 2 blue tiles. The task is to separate the possible outcomes into two lists, one for each of the two players. For example, Player A might be assigned red tiles and Player B green, yellow, and blue. This should be recorded. The players take turns drawing a tile from the bag and then replacing it. When players draw a tile of their color, they win one counter. If it is not their color, the opponent wins a counter. Start with ten counters. Players take turns drawing and replacing tiles until all ten counters have been won.

Repeat the activity with different tile combinations so that you can observe how students divide the events and on what basis. Try situations such as 2 red, 3 blue, and 7 yellow, where there is no possible way to create a fair game. Will these bother students? What do they believe about their chances of winning? For a 2-3-5 bag of tiles, will students separate the three colors to create a fair game? Allow students to replay the game with the same tiles but with a change of how the colors are divided.

Instead of drawing tiles from a bag, try playing "Create a Game" with different spinners. Provide a variety of spinner faces and see how students divide up the possible outcomes. Some examples are shown here but do not feel restricted to these.

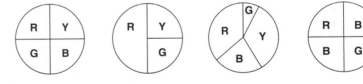

Assessment Note

In "Create a Game" watch for students who omit an outcome from the two lists. Allow them to play the game anyway. When the omitted outcome occurs in the game, listen to how students handle the situation. Remember, you want them to realize that all outcomes are possible, even those that have small chances.

The other thing to watch for in "Create a Game" is the manner in which the outcomes are sorted between the two players. Do they seem to understand the relative chances of each and try to make the game fair, or do luck and "favorite colors" influence decisions?

Two-Stage Experiments

Flipping a penny is a one-stage experiment, and the sample space has only two elements: heads and tails. Flipping two pennies is a two-stage experiment. What is the sample space for two coins?

 Imagine flipping two pennies 100 times. About how many times would you expect to get one head and one tail? Jot down your predictions before reading on.

For a one-coin toss, you would confidently predict that about half of the trials would result in heads and half in tails. For tossing two coins, it is quite common for people to observe that there are three outcomes: both heads, both tails, and one of each; so they predict that a head–tail combination will occur about one-third of the time. (What did you predict?) After conducting the experiment, they are surprised to find that the head–tail combination occurs about *half* of the time. To understand the results it is useful to reexamine the sample space.

Although both coins are pennies, they are different coins. We could identify them as the first and the second penny. They could be tossed by two different people or in sequence. There is only one way that two heads can occur and one way that two tails could occur. But one head and one tail can occur in two ways: first coin heads—second coin tails, and first coin tails—second coin heads. The sample space has four—not three—equally likely outcomes: HH, HT, TH, and TT. The event of a head and a tail makes up two of the four outcomes.

Rolling two dice and adding the two results is also a two-stage experiment, even though the two dice may be rolled at the same time. (Think about a red die and a green die.) The sample space really has 36 outcomes, not just the sums 2 through 12. Figure 12.5 shows the results of a large number of dice rolls recorded in two ways—first by the sum and second by the result of each die.

By third grade, students should begin to explore two-stage experiments. However, an accurate analysis by third- or even fourth-grade students of all of the elements of the sample space (as in Figure 12.5) is not very likely without some guidance. What is more important than explaining to students how to interpret these two-stage sample spaces is to allow ample time for students to explore experiments and to think about why the results turned out as they did. An experimental approach—actually conducting experiments and looking at the outcomes—is important for a number of reasons.

- It is significantly more intuitive. Results generally make more sense to students than an abstract rule.

- It diminishes guessing at probabilities. Initial estimates of probabilities can and should be made on the basis of experimental results.

Sum of Two Dice

2	𝍇 I
3	𝍇 𝍇
4	𝍇 𝍇 𝍇 IIII
5	𝍇 𝍇 𝍇 IIII
6	𝍇 𝍇 𝍇 𝍇 𝍇 IIII
7	𝍇 𝍇 𝍇 𝍇 𝍇 𝍇 𝍇 IIII
8	𝍇 𝍇 𝍇 𝍇 𝍇 𝍇 IIII
9	𝍇 𝍇 𝍇 𝍇 𝍇
10	𝍇 𝍇 𝍇 I
11	𝍇 II
12	𝍇 𝍇

(a)

Red Die

Green Die	1	2	3	4	5	6
1	𝍇	𝍇 I	𝍇 III	𝍇 II	𝍇 IIII	𝍇 II
2	𝍇 IIII	𝍇 III	𝍇 I	𝍇 𝍇	𝍇 III	𝍇 II
3	𝍇 𝍇	𝍇	𝍇 III	𝍇 II	𝍇 𝍇 II	𝍇 IIII
4	𝍇 II	𝍇 𝍇 II	𝍇 IIII	𝍇 𝍇 II	𝍇 𝍇 II	𝍇 III
5	𝍇 IIII	𝍇 𝍇 II	𝍇 𝍇 II	𝍇 III	𝍇	𝍇 IIII
6	𝍇 III	𝍇 IIII	𝍇 III	𝍇 II	𝍇 IIII	𝍇 III

There are six ways to get 7.

(b)

FIGURE 12.5 •

Tallies can account only for the total (a) or keep track of the individual dice (b).

- It provides a background for examining the theoretical model. When you begin to sense that a head–tail combination occurs about half of the time rather than a third of the time, the explanation seems more reasonable.

- It helps students see how the ratio of a particular outcome to the total number of trials gets closer to a fixed number as the number of trials increases. (The way that results converge in the long run is explored later in the chapter.)

- It is a lot more fun and interesting! Searching for the explanation is challenging, especially when the result is different than expected.

The next two activities in this section each involve two-stage experiments. For most students, the results of their experiments will be different from their initial expectations. Refrain from explaining the sample spaces. Rather, encourage students to accumulate results from an even larger number of trials. If you have students who you think may be able to construct the sample spaces for these experiments, by all means challenge them to do so.

ACTIVITY 12.5

Twelve Chips

This game for two players is played with two number cubes. Each player needs a game board with 13 numbered columns (0 to 12) and 12 chips that can be placed in the columns as in Figure 12.6. Before beginning play, each player places his or her 12 chips on the columns of the game board. These can be placed in any of the 13 columns. More than one chip may be placed in a column if desired. Some students may even wish to put all of their counters in one column, although spreading them out from 2 to 12 is a common approach. After placing their chips, the players roll to see who goes first. A turn consists of rolling the two number cubes one time and adding the two numbers that come up. If the result indicates a column in which the player has a chip, one chip is removed from that column. After one roll, it is the other player's turn. Play continues in this manner until one player has removed all 12 chips from his or her board.

After students have had several chances to play the game, discuss where they placed their chips and why. Which numbers are possible (2 to 12)? Which are impossible (0 and 1)? Do some numbers come up more often than others (yes)? Why do you think that happens?

Allow students ample opportunities to play "Twelve Chips." See if students have noticed that some numbers seem to come up more often than others. Students will undoubtedly notice that 2 and 12 are "hard to get." Exploring that observation may lead to students noticing that there is only one way to get each of these numbers. A natural question then is "How many ways are there of getting other numbers?" Students may not think about the fact that a 2 and a 5, for example, can happen two different ways. You might increase the likelihood of this observation by having students use two different colors of number cubes.

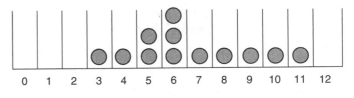

FIGURE 12.6

Game board for "Twelve Chips." Each player places 12 chips on the board. On a player's turn, he or she may remove one chip if the sum of the two number cubes is equal to a column number on which there is a chip. The first player to have an empty board wins.

SAMPLE SPACES AND PROBABILITY

Match

In this game for two players, tiles or cubes of two different colors are placed in a bag. Before playing, one player is selected to be Match and the other is Not Match. Each player reaches into the bag and draws out one tile. If the two players' tiles match in color, Match scores a point. If they are different colors, Not Match scores a point. The tiles are then returned to the bag for the next turn. The player with the most points after 12 turns wins.

Match should be played often with different combinations of tiles. Begin with 2 tiles of 2 colors (e.g., 2 red and 2 yellow). Then let students try other combinations of two colors, but use no more than 6 total chips.

The key question to ask about the "Match" activity is this: Is this game fair? That is, does each player have the same chance of winning? For the 2-and-2 version (two chips of each color), students may be surprised to find that Not Match seems to win more often than Match. This version of "Match" will, in the long run, favor Not Match twice as often. Many students will attribute this result to luck but others may want to find a way to make the game fair by changing the tiles in the bag. Still others may want to discover why the game seems to be fair for some combinations and not for others.

This is a good example of allowing students to explore a problem to an extent compatible with their interest and ability. At one level, students will enjoy playing the game and perhaps trying out different combinations of colors. At the other extreme, students will be eager to find a logical explanation for the results.

Possible results for first draw.   Possible results for second draw.

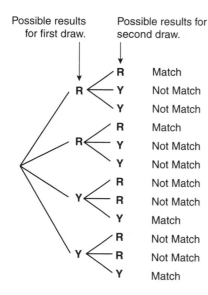

Before reading on, see if you can determine all of the elements of the sample space for the situation with 2 tiles of each color and explain why Not Match will win more often. As a hint, the sample space has 12 elements, each of which is equally likely.

For those students who are interested in why the "Match" activity is not fair for the 2-and-2 version, a good suggestion is to introduce a tree diagram as shown in Figure 12.7. The first branches of the tree show all of the ways that the first tile can be drawn. The second branches show the ways that the second tile can be drawn. Note that the second branches depend on what was drawn first. If a red chip is drawn first, then there is only one way—one red chip—that the second player has to get a match and two ways—two yellow chips—to get a not match.

A tree diagram is a good method for young students to analyze two-stage experiments as long as there are not too many outcomes for each stage. In the 2-and-2 version there are 4 outcomes for the first stage and 3 outcomes for the second. This produces a total of 12 (4 × 3) outcomes for the combined experiment. If there are 6 tiles in the bag, there will by 6 × 5 or 30 elements in the sample space. This is about as large a tree diagram as is reasonable to draw.

In "Match" the outcome of the second stage or second tile drawn depends on the outcome of the first. These are called *dependent* events. But when two number cubes are thrown, the result of each cube is independent of the other. These are known as *independent* events. Even if students played

FIGURE 12.7 • • • • • • • • • • • • • •

This is a tree diagram analysis of drawing two successive chips from a bag with two red and two yellow chips. Each complete branch shows one outcome in the sample space. There are 12 branches each resulting in a Match (both chips same color) or a Not Match (different colors).

"Match" by themselves, drawing two tiles at once, the results remain the same as if drawing one tile and then drawing a second. However, if the first tile is returned to the bag before the second tile is drawn, then the two draws are independent of each other; the contents of the bag are the same for each draw. The results of "Match" are much more predictable for the replacement version because any bag with the same number of tiles of each color will be a fair game. Other combinations will not be fair. (Can you tell why?)

Tree diagrams are most easily used when the outcomes of the experiments are equally likely. For example, consider the two-stage experiment of spinning this spinner and tossing a coin.

If you draw a tree for which the first branch represents the result of the spinner and the second branch represents the result of the coin toss, the branch for red is twice as likely as the branch for yellow or blue. In this case you could make two branches for red and the diagram would be correct. In the upper grades, students will learn to assign probabilities to each segment of a tree diagram and multiply these to obtain probabilities for each complete branch.

Theoretical Probabilities

The probabilities for many experiments can be determined by examining the experiment. For example, we are completely confident that the probability of tossing a fair coin and getting a head is $\frac{1}{2}$. This probability can be referred to as the theoretical probability. The *theoretical probability of an event* is the proportion of the sample space that is defined by the event. The theoretical probability is determined by an analysis of the event itself without any reference to experiments that may have been conducted. When all of the events of the sample space are equally likely, we can define the theoretical probability as

$$\frac{\text{The number of outcomes in the event}}{\text{Number of outcomes in the sample space}}$$

Your fourth- or fifth-grade curriculum may require students to use fractions to describe the probability of an event. Using a fraction to describe the probability of an event is an obvious application of fraction concepts. The number of outcomes in the sample space is the whole and the number of outcomes in the event is the part; the probability is the corresponding part/whole fraction. Being clear about the elements or outcomes in a sample space and the number of those elements in a particular event is a critical step in being able to describe probabilities as fractions.

In "Twelve Chips," we saw that the sample space for rolling two number cubes has 36 elements. The event that the sum is 7 has six of those 36 outcomes. Therefore, the probability of rolling a 7 is $\frac{6}{36}$ or $\frac{1}{6}$. There are only five outcomes in the event of rolling a 5; the probability of rolling a 5 is $\frac{5}{36}$, a bit less than $\frac{1}{6}$.

The tree diagram for "Match" (Figure 12.7) has 12 separate branches, each of which is equally likely. Therefore, the sample space has 12 outcomes. The event of getting a match has only four outcomes; the probability of a match is $\frac{4}{12}$, or $\frac{1}{3}$. The probability of getting a not match is $\frac{8}{12}$, or twice as much. This is a numeric explanation for why Not Match will win about twice as often.

We can also determine the theoretical probability for some experiments that do not have equally likely outcomes, such as a spinner that is one-half red and one-fourth

SAMPLE SPACES AND PROBABILITY

each green and yellow. This is because we can measure the proportion of the spinner for each color. For a single spinner, the probability of spinning a particular section of the spinner is equal to the fractional part of that section of the spinner.

It should be reasonably easy for students to determine the theoretical probabilities for one-stage experiments, such as drawing a tile from a bag, spinning a spinner, or rolling a single number cube. As we have already seen, determining probabilities for two-stage experiments is often more difficult. The main problem lies in articulating all of the outcomes in both the sample space and in the event under consideration. The following are two more two-stage experiments you may wish to have your students explore. As always, students should gather real data by conducting the experiments before they attempt to determine a theoretical probability.

A bag contains 10 tiles: 1 red, 2 yellow, 3 green, and 4 blue. The experiment involves drawing a single tile and rolling a standard number cube. What is the probability of drawing a yellow tile and rolling a number greater than 2?

You are a prisoner in a faraway land. The king has decided to give you a chance to escape. He shows you the maze in Figure 12.8. At the start of each fork in the path, you must spin the spinner and follow the path that it points to. You may request that the key to freedom be placed in one of the two rooms. In which room should you place the key in order to have the better chance of freedom?

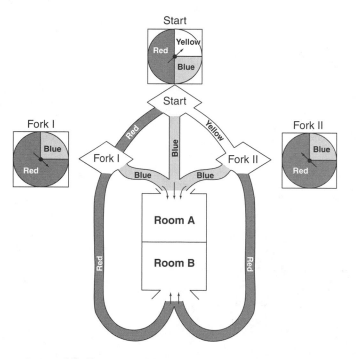

FIGURE 12.8

Should you place your key to freedom in Room A or Room B? At each fork, the spinner determines your path.

Both of these problems are two-stage experiments. One involves dependent events and the other independent events.

> 🛑 **Determine the sample space for each of the problems just listed. A tree diagram is suggested for each.**

A tree diagram for the tile and number cube experiment technically has 60 equally likely branches. However, it is not really necessary to draw all of these. If the first branches represent the 10 tiles, only the 2 yellow branches are important for the desired event. Each of the remaining 8 branches will have 6 more branches but none of these will belong to the event of drawing a yellow and rolling a number greater than 2. In all, there are 60 complete branches. On each of the 2 branches beginning with yellow, 4 will end in numbers 3 or more. Therefore, there are 8 out of 60 outcomes in the event of drawing a yellow cube and rolling a number greater than 2. The probability for this event is $\frac{8}{60}$ or $\frac{2}{15}$.

Chapter 12 EXPLORING CONCEPTS OF PROBABILITY

For the prisoner problem, a useful suggestion may be to think of all of the spinners as divided into fourths. In that way a tree diagram can be drawn with equally likely branches, one branch for each fourth of each spinner. This method of looking at the sample space will produce a total of 16 equally likely branches. Notice that a first spin of blue goes directly to room A. However, in order for all of the branches to be equally likely, it is necessary to think of an all-blue spinner—4 fourths—following an initial blue spin. The chances for the two rooms are very close: $\frac{7}{16}$ and $\frac{9}{16}$.

Short-Run Versus Long-Run Results

Suppose that you have conducted the experiment of tossing a coin 100 times. In your experiment, heads came up 56 times and tails 44 times. The relative frequency of heads for your experiment is $\frac{56}{100}$. The *relative frequency* of an event is

$$\frac{\text{The number of observed occurrences of the event}}{\text{The total number of trials}}$$

If you toss the coin another 100 times, the relative frequency may even drop below $\frac{1}{2}$, perhaps to $\frac{93}{200}$. If you toss it 1000 times, you would expect that the relative frequency would be very close to $\frac{1}{2}$, although you might be surprised if it was exactly $\frac{500}{1000}$. The fractions $\frac{56}{100}$, $\frac{93}{100}$, and $\frac{489}{1000}$ can be compared as ratios of a part to the whole, although each of the wholes is different (100, 200, and 1000). Note that the number of heads for each successive fraction is further from one-half (4, 7, 11). However, the corresponding ratios are closer to one-half (56 percent, 46.5 percent, 48.9 percent).

Experimental Probability

The relative frequency of an event is also called the *experimental probability* of the event. The more trials that are conducted, the more confident we can be that the relative frequency or experimental probability is close to the actual probability for that event. Conversely, if the experimental probability is based on only a small number of trials, we should not be very confident that this ratio is close to the actual probability.

Spinners, dice, and tiles in a bag are only used to develop ideas about probability. In the real world, probability is often used to express the likelihood of situations such as the chance of a tornado, the rise of the stock market, or the number of hours a lightbulb will burn. For "muddy" events such as these, experiments are typically run a large number of times and the relative frequency or experimental probability of the event is used as an estimate of the actual probability.

These definitions of relative frequency and experimental probability involve ratios. The ratio for 10 trials is compared to that for 100 trials and for 100,000 trials. The comparison of ratios for different-sized wholes (here the number of trials) requires proportional reasoning—an idea that research has indicated is not at all easy for young students. Typically, it is developed in the middle school years and only then with appropriate meaningful experiences. In contrast, fraction concepts are developed based on the idea of a single whole or *one*—one circle, one candy bar, one segment, or one unit on the number line.

Comparing Results as Numbers Increase

A visual comparison may help students understand how the relative frequency of an event gets close to a fixed probability as the number of trials gets very large. The next two activities are designed to help students with this difficult idea.

BLM 40

ACTIVITY 12.7

Checking the Theory

Make a transparency of the Blackline Master 40, "What Are the Chances?"

Provide pairs of students with a spinner face that is half red and half blue. Students should agree that the chance of blue is one-half. Mark the $\frac{1}{2}$ point on the Impossible–Certain continuum and draw a vertical line down through all of the lines below this point. Then have each pair of students spin their spinner one time. Make a tally chart for Red and Blue results and tally these first spins. Collect the results of additional spins until you have a total of 20 spins. Mark the result of the 20 spins on the second line. For example, if there are 13 Blue and 7 Red, place a mark at about 13 on the 0-to-20 number line. If the result of these 20 spins was not exactly 10 and 10, discuss possible reasons why this may be so.

Now have student pairs each spin their spinners 10 more times. Collect these results and add them to the tallies for the first 20 spins. Your total should be a multiple of 10. Mark the total in the right-hand box of the third line and indicate the number of Blue spins on the line as before. Repeat this at least two more times, continuing to add the results of new spins to the previous results. Each time, enter the total in the right-hand box to create a new number line but with the same length as before. If possible, try to get the total number of spins to be at least 1000.

The successive number lines used in "Checking the Theory" each have the same length and each represents the total number of trials. When the results are plotted on any one number line, the position shows the fraction of the total spins as a visual portion of the whole line. If you try to be fairly accurate with your marks (perhaps measuring with a centimeter ruler) successive marks will almost certainly get closer and closer to the $\frac{1}{2}$ line you drew earlier down the page. Note that 240 Blue spins out of 500 is 48 percent, or very close to one-half. This is so even though there are 20 more Red spins (260) than Blue. To be that close with only 100 spins, the results would need to be 48 and 52. For even larger numbers, the marks should be extremely close to the line you have drawn. If you draw much longer lines—say 2 meters each—on the board, the results of "Checking the Theory" will be more dramatic. It will be clearer that the ratios are closing in on one-half.

For students who have begun to study percent or decimal equivalents to fractions, "Checking the Theory" provides an excellent opportunity to use these new representations. Rather than list a common fraction on each number line, students can express the results as decimal fractions and/or as percents. These numbers are much easier to find on the number lines. As the number of trials increases, the changes from one line to the next may only be in the second or third decimal place, which will barely be noticeable on the line. This provides you with an opportunity to discuss place value in a real context.

A spinner is suggested for "Checking the Theory" because it is the easiest for determining the theoretical probability. However, spinners sometimes are less than accurate due to spinning techniques, bent spinners, and so on. The same experiment can and should be conducted with other devices. For example, bags with two each of four colors could be used with the probability of each color marked on each line. Rolling a number cube with the event being an odd number is also a good idea.

Technology Note

Software is readily available for exploring probability concepts. It can generally be described as computer-animated random devices. Graphics show students the coins being flipped or the spinner being spun. Most allow different speeds. In a slow version, students may watch each spin of a spinner or coin flip. Faster speeds show the recording of each trial but omit the graphics. An even quicker mode simply shows the cumulative results. The number of trials can be set by the user. With some programs the random devices can be adjusted (e.g., the number of colors on the spinners or the numbers on the dice). Among others appropriate for grades 3–5 are Scott Foresman's *E-Tools* (2004) and Edmark's *Probability* (1996).

The advantage of these tools is found primarily in being able to generate results of a large number of trials very quickly. However, your students must accept that these results are just as good as actually conducting the experiments physically. Computer programs such as these should never be a complete substitute for students conducting real experiments.

The following activity is similar to "Checking the Theory" except that the theoretical probability cannot be determined.

ACTIVITY 12.8

Experimental Probability

The purpose of this activity is to estimate the probability of an event where the theoretical probability cannot be determined. Students will gather data on how often you can expect a dropped thumbtack to land with the point straight up. Each pair of students will need five thumbtacks and a small box with a cover or lid. All the tacks in the room must be the same.

Use the same Blackline Master as you used for Activity 12.7. Demonstrate the two possibilities for a tack to land on a flat surface. After exploring their own tacks briefly, let students decide about where on the top line of the worksheet they think the probability of point up should fall. Next, have four students shake their boxes of tacks and report the number of point-up results. Tally these as in the previous activity and mark the corresponding point on the 0-to-20 line. Have students get data for 10 more tacks—two tosses of five tacks. Tally and record on the third number line. Continue to gather data on more and more tacks, recording accumulated data on successive lines.

It should not take too long to get 1000 total tosses and it is not unreasonable to continue to 1500 or even 2000 tosses. At this point, discuss with students where they think the correct probability mark on the top line should be and why. Draw a vertical line from this point through the other number lines. The marks near the bottom of the page should be very close to this line.

The difference between Activities 12.7 and 12.8 is the ability to determine a theoretical probability. In the first of these activities, the observed results are compared to the expected result—the theoretical probability. In the second, the results of more and more trials should converge or get closer to a single value, which is an estimate of the actual probability.

Instead of tossing thumbtacks, you might want to explore "Experimental Probability" by experimenting with the ways that these items land when tossed: small plastic portion cups or medicine cups (side, open end up, upside down), plastic spoons (bowl up, bowl down), or marshmallows (side or end). (Note that large marshmallows produce different results from small marshmallows.)

This approach of repeating an experiment a large number of times can be applied to other situations. For example, students can open phone books to any page, randomly point to a name on the page, and count the number of letters in the last name. What is the probability of a name having five or fewer letters? Another experiment involves tossing a paper airplane and determining the probability that the plane will travel at least 15 feet. To gather data, make multiple identical airplanes and try to have all students throw them in the same manner.

Discuss with students how this method could be used with events that happen over time but are difficult to recreate in the classroom. For example, what is the chance of getting hit by lightning? What is the chance of having to stop at the next stoplight? What is the chance of the phone ringing during dinner? In all of these cases, data can be collected over a long period of time by observing what happens rather than by conducting experiments. Researchers interested in answers to questions such as these often use polls to gather information from lots of people rather than wait for the data from one source over time. That is the same as pooling data from the students in the class. The point of this discussion is to bring the science of probability into the real world.

Assessment Note

An important idea to develop is that long-run results are better predictors of probabilities than short-run results. However, it is difficult to ask questions about this idea without students playing "guess what the teacher wants you to say." Instead, pose the following situation and have students write about their ideas.

> Margaret spun the spinner 10 times. Blue turned up on three spins. Red turned up on seven spins. Margaret says that there is a 3-in-10 chance of spinning blue. Carla then spun the same spinner 100 times. Carla recorded 53 spins of blue and 47 spins of red. Carla says that the chance of spinning blue on this spinner is about even.
>
> Who do you think is more likely to be correct: Margaret or Carla? Explain. Draw a spinner that you think they may have been using.

In the students' responses, look for evidence that they know that even 10 spins is not very good evidence of the probability and that 100 spins tells us more about the chances.

> Recall that the first big idea in the chapter was this: Chance has no memory. Toward the end of your probability unit, you may want to see if students have developed this idea to any extent even though the activities explored have

not explicitly addressed this idea. Have students either write about or discuss the following:

> Duane has a lucky coin that he has tossed many, many times. He is sure that it is a fair coin—that there is an even chance of heads or tails. Duane tosses his coin six times and heads come up six times in a row. Duane is sure that the next toss will be tails because he has never been able to toss heads seven times in a row. What do you think the chances are of Duane tossing heads on the next toss? Explain your answer.

In this case you are looking for the idea that each toss of the coin is independent of prior tosses. As noted earlier, however, do not be surprised if students are as convinced as Duane is about the next toss being tails. As noted, many adults would agree with Duane as well even though they would be in error.

EXPANDED LESSON

Testing Bag Designs
Based on: Activity 12.3, p. 343

GRADE LEVEL: Third to fifth grade.

MATHEMATICS GOALS
- To refine the idea that some events may be more or less likely than others.
- To explore the notion that for repeated trials of a simple experiment, the outcomes of prior trials have no impact on the next.
- To determine that the results for a small number of trials may be quite different than those experienced in the long run.

THINKING ABOUT THE STUDENTS
Students have been introduced to the idea of a probability line as described in the text before Activity 12.2, "Design a Bag." They must have completed Activity 12.2 with all students using the same mark on the probability line. In this lesson, that mark is assumed to be at about the 20 percent location.

MATERIALS AND PREPARATION
- Collect and display the designs made by the students in "Design a Bag."
- Provide a lunch bag and color tiles or cubes for each pair of students.

lesson

BEFORE

Estimate
- Have students share their reasoning for the number of each color they put in their designed bag for "Design a Bag." Some students may think that the colors used for the other tiles make a difference, and this point should be discussed. Do not provide your opinion or comment on these ideas. Select a bag design that most students seem to agree on for the 20 percent mark and instruct them to fill the bag as suggested.
- Ask what they think will happen if they draw a tile from their bag and replace it ten times. How many of the designated color do they think they will get? Encourage a discussion of their thinking.

The Task
Students are to test a bag designed to create the chance of drawing a designated color about 20 percent of the time. (The mark on the probability line is an indicator of the targeted percent.)

Establish Expectations
Once students fill the bag according to the design, they shake the bag and draw out one tile. If a tile of the designated color is drawn, a tally mark is recorded for Yes. If a tile of any other color is drawn, a tally mark is recorded for No. The tile should be replaced in the bag and the bag shaken. This process is repeated ten times. Students should be ready to discuss their results.

DURING
- Make sure that students are replacing each tile before drawing another tile.
- Are students appropriately recording as they draw tiles?
- Ask students questions about what is occurring with their trials. For example, what do students think when they retrieve the same color tile repeatedly?

AFTER

- Discuss with the class how their respective experiments turned out. Did they turn out the way students expected? With the small number of trials, there will be groups that get rather unexpected results.
- Use results from students' small number of trials to discuss ideas such as how drawing a red tile seven straight times affects the chance of drawing a red tile the next time.
- Make a large tally graph of the data from all of the groups as shown here. Stop and discuss the data at several points as students give you their results. There should be many more No's than Yes's. Here the discussion can help students see that if the experiment is repeated a lot of times, the chances are about as predicted. If students have discussed percents, stopping after data have been collected from 10 students (100 trials) or from 20 students (200 trials) might be useful because the total numbers lend themselves to simple percentage calculations.

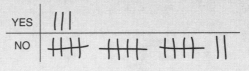

ASSESSMENT NOTES

- The small-group testing of a design suggests to students that chance is not an absolute predictor in the short run. How do students react to results that are unexpected?
- The group graph may help students understand the difficult concept that chance tends to approach what is expected in the long run. However, this idea involves comparing ratios in the small number of trials with ratios in the large number of trials. For example, the result for 15 trials may be 36 out of 150 total. It will be difficult for students to compare this with 3 out of 10 trials or 43 out of 200.

- -

- The dual activities of "Design a Bag" and "Testing Bag Designs" can and should be repeated for two or three other marks on the probability line. Try marks at about $\frac{1}{3}$, $\frac{1}{2}$, and $\frac{3}{4}$. You may want to assign a different mark to different groups so that a discussion can include comparisons of different designs and outcomes. To compare results it is useful if the total number of trials for each design is about the same.

- If you feel that students need to revisit the ideas highlighted in this lesson, have them design a spinner instead of a bag of tiles. This will allow you to revisit the concept without being too repetitious. With spinners, students can see the relative portion of the whole given to each color or outcome, a visual indication of the probability.

next steps

APPENDIX A

PRINCIPLES AND STANDARDS FOR SCHOOL MATHEMATICS

Content Standards and Grade Level Expectations

Source: Reprinted with permission from *Principles and Standards for School Mathematics.*
Copyright © 2000 by the National Council of Teachers of Mathematics. All rights reserved.

NUMBER AND OPERATIONS

STANDARD

Instructional programs from prekindergarten through grade 12 should enable all students to—

Understand numbers, ways of representing numbers, relationships among numbers, and number systems

Understand meanings of operations and how they relate to one another

Compute fluently and make reasonable estimates

PRE-K–2

Expectations

In prekindergarten through grade 2 all students should—

- count with understanding and recognize "how many" in sets of objects;
- use multiple models to develop initial understandings of place value and the base-ten number system;
- develop understanding of the relative position and magnitude of whole numbers and of ordinal and cardinal numbers and their connections;
- develop a sense of whole numbers and represent and use them in flexible ways, including relating, composing, and decomposing numbers;
- connect number words and numerals to the quantities they represent, using various physical models and representations;
- understand and represent commonly used fractions, such as $\frac{1}{4}$, $\frac{1}{3}$, and $\frac{1}{2}$.

- understand various meanings of addition and subtraction of whole numbers and the relationship between the two operations;
- understand the effects of adding and subtracting whole numbers;
- understand situations that entail multiplication and division, such as equal groupings of objects and sharing equally.

- develop and use strategies for whole-number computations, with a focus on addition and subtraction;
- develop fluency with basic number combinations for addition and subtraction;
- use a variety of methods and tools to compute, including objects, mental computation, estimation, paper and pencil, and calculators.

GRADES 3–5

Expectations

In grades 3–5 all students should—

- understand the place-value structure of the base-ten number system and be able to represent and compare whole numbers and decimals;
- recognize equivalent representations for the same number and generate them by decomposing and composing numbers;
- develop understanding of fractions as parts of unit wholes, as parts of a collection, as locations on number lines, and as divisions of whole numbers;
- use models, benchmarks, and equivalent forms to judge the size of fractions;
- recognize and generate equivalent forms of commonly used fractions, decimals, and percents;
- explore numbers less than 0 by extending the number line and through familiar applications;
- describe classes of numbers according to characteristics such as the nature of their factors.

- understand various meanings of multiplication and division;
- understand the effects of multiplying and dividing whole numbers;
- identify and use relationships between operations, such as division as the inverse of multiplication, to solve problems;
- understand and use properties of operations, such as the distributivity of multiplication over addition.

- develop fluency with basic number combinations for multiplication and division and use these combinations to mentally compute related problems, such as 30×50;
- develop fluency in adding, subtracting, multiplying, and dividing whole numbers;
- develop and use strategies to estimate the results of whole-number computations and to judge the reasonableness of such results;
- develop and use strategies to estimate computations involving fractions and decimals in situations relevant to students' experience;
- use visual models, benchmarks, and equivalent forms to add and subtract commonly used fractions and decimals;
- select appropriate methods and tools for computing with whole numbers from among mental computation, estimation, calculators, and paper and pencil according to the context and nature of the computation and use the selected method or tool.

NUMBER AND OPERATIONS

STANDARD

Instructional programs from prekindergarten through grade 12 should enable all students to—

Understand numbers, ways of representing numbers, relationships among numbers, and number systems

Understand meanings of operations and how they relate to one another

Compute fluently and make reasonable estimates

GRADES 6–8

Expectations

In grades 6–8 all students should—

- work flexibly with fractions, decimals, and percents to solve problems;
- compare and order fractions, decimals, and percents efficiently and find their approximate locations on a number line;
- develop meaning for percents greater than 100 and less than 1;
- understand and use ratios and proportions to represent quantitative relationships;
- develop an understanding of large numbers and recognize and appropriately use exponential, scientific, and calculator notation;
- use factors, multiples, prime factorization, and relatively prime numbers to solve problems;
- develop meaning for integers and represent and compare quantities with them.

- understand the meaning and effects of arithmetic operations with fractions, decimals, and integers;
- use the associative and commutative properties of addition and multiplication and the distributive property of multiplication over addition to simplify computations with integers, fractions, and decimals;
- understand and use the inverse relationships of addition and subtraction, multiplication and division, and squaring and finding square roots to simplify computations and solve problems.

- select appropriate methods and tools for computing with fractions and decimals from among mental computation, estimation, calculators or computers, and paper and pencil, depending on the situation, and apply the selected methods;
- develop and analyze algorithms for computing with fractions, decimals, and integers and develop fluency in their use;
- develop and use strategies to estimate the results of rational-number computations and judge the reasonableness of the results;
- develop, analyze, and explain methods for solving problems involving proportions, such as scaling and finding equivalent ratios.

GRADES 9–12

Expectations

In grades 9–12 all students should—

- develop a deeper understanding of very large and very small numbers and of various representations of them;
- compare and contrast the properties of numbers and number systems, including the rational and real numbers, and understand complex numbers as solutions to quadratic equations that do not have real solutions;
- understand vectors and matrices as systems that have some of the properties of the real-number system;
- use number-theory arguments to justify relationships involving whole numbers.

- judge the effects of such operations as multiplication, division, and computing powers and roots on the magnitudes of quantities;
- develop an understanding of properties of, and representations for, the addition and multiplication of vectors and matrices;
- develop an understanding of permutations and combinations as counting techniques.

- develop fluency in operations with real numbers, vectors, and matrices, using mental computation or paper-and-pencil calculations for simple cases and technology for more-complicated cases;
- judge the reasonableness of numerical computations and their results.

ALGEBRA

STANDARD

Instructional programs from prekindergarten through grade 12 should enable all students to—

Understand patterns, relations, and functions

Represent and analyze mathematical situations and structures using algebraic symbols

Use mathematical models to represent and understand quantitative relationships

Analyze change in various contexts

PRE-K–2

Expectations

In prekindergarten through grade 2 all students should—

- sort, classify, and order objects by size, number, and other properties;
- recognize, describe, and extend patterns such as sequences of sounds and shapes or simple numeric patterns and translate from one representation to another;
- analyze how both repeating and growing patterns are generated.

- illustrate general principles and properties of operations, such as commutativity, using specific numbers;
- use concrete, pictorial, and verbal representations to develop an understanding of invented and conventional symbolic notations.

- model situations that involve the addition and subtraction of whole numbers, using objects, pictures, and symbols.

- describe qualitative change, such as a student's growing taller;
- describe quantitative change, such as a student's growing two inches in one year.

GRADES 3–5

Expectations

In grades 3–5 all students should—

- describe, extend, and make generalizations about geometric and numeric patterns;
- represent and analyze patterns and functions, using words, tables, and graphs.

- identify such properties as commutativity, associativity, and distributivity and use them to compute with whole numbers;
- represent the idea of a variable as an unknown quantity using a letter or a symbol;
- express mathematical relationships using equations.

- model problem situations with objects and use representations such as graphs, tables, and equations to draw conclusions.

- investigate how a change in one variable relates to a change in a second variable;
- identify and describe situations with constant or varying rates of change and compare them.

ALGEBRA

STANDARD

Instructional programs from prekindergarten through grade 12 should enable all students to—

Understand patterns, relations, and functions

Represent and analyze mathematical situations and structures using algebraic symbols

Use mathematical models to represent and understand quantitative relationships

Analyze change in various contexts

GRADES 6–8

Expectations

In grades 6–8 all students should—

- represent, analyze, and generalize a variety of patterns with tables, graphs, words, and, when possible, symbolic rules;
- relate and compare different forms of representation for a relationship;
- identify functions as linear or nonlinear and contrast their properties from tables, graphs, or equations.

- develop an initial conceptual understanding of different uses of variables;
- explore relationships between symbolic expressions and graphs of lines, paying particular attention to the meaning of intercept and slope;
- use symbolic algebra to represent situations and to solve problems, especially those that involve linear relationships;
- recognize and generate equivalent forms for simple algebraic expressions and solve linear equations.

- model and solve contextualized problems using various representations, such as graphs, tables, and equations.

- use graphs to analyze the nature of changes in quantities in linear relationships.

GRADES 9–12

Expectations

In grades 9–12 all students should—

- generalize patterns using explicitly defined and recursively defined functions;
- understand relations and functions and select, convert flexibly among, and use various representations for them;
- analyze functions of one variable by investigating rates of change, intercepts, zeros, asymptotes, and local and global behavior;
- understand and perform transformations such as arithmetically combining, composing, and inverting commonly used functions, using technology to perform such operations on more-complicated symbolic expressions;
- understand and compare the properties of classes of functions, including exponential, polynomial, rational, logarithmic, and periodic functions;
- interpret representations of functions of two variables.

- understand the meaning of equivalent forms of expressions, equations, inequalities, and relations;
- write equivalent forms of equations, inequalities, and systems of equations and solve them with fluency—mentally or with paper and pencil in simple cases and using technology in all cases;
- use symbolic algebra to represent and explain mathematical relationships;
- use a variety of symbolic representations, including recursive and parametric equations, for functions and relations;
- judge the meaning, utility, and reasonableness of the results of symbol manipulations, including those carried out by technology.

- identify essential quantitative relationships in a situation and determine the class or classes of functions that might model the relationships;
- use symbolic expressions, including iterative and recursive forms, to represent relationships arising from various contexts;
- draw reasonable conclusions about a situation being modeled.

- approximate and interpret rates of change from graphical and numerical data.

GEOMETRY

STANDARD

Instructional programs from prekindergarten through grade 12 should enable all students to—

Analyze characteristics and properties of two- and three-dimensional geometric shapes and develop mathematical arguments about geometric relationships

Specify locations and describe spatial relationships using coordinate geometry and other representational systems

Apply transformations and use symmetry to analyze mathematical situations

Use visualization, spatial reasoning, and geometric modeling to solve problems

PRE-K–2

Expectations

In prekindergarten through grade 2 all students should—

- recognize, name, build, draw, compare, and sort two- and three-dimensional shapes;
- describe attributes and parts of two- and three-dimensional shapes;
- investigate and predict the results of putting together and taking apart two- and three-dimensional shapes.

- describe, name, and interpret relative positions in space and apply ideas about relative position;
- describe, name, and interpret direction and distance in navigating space and apply ideas about direction and distance;
- find and name locations with simple relationships such as "near to" and in coordinate systems such as maps.

- recognize and apply slides, flips, and turns;
- recognize and create shapes that have symmetry.

- create mental images of geometric shapes using spatial memory and spatial visualization;
- recognize and represent shapes from different perspectives;
- relate ideas in geometry to ideas in number and measurement;
- recognize geometric shapes and structures in the environment and specify their location.

GRADES 3–5

Expectations

In grades 3–5 all students should—

- identify, compare, and analyze attributes of two- and three-dimensional shapes and develop vocabulary to describe the attributes;
- classify two- and three-dimensional shapes according to their properties and develop definitions of classes of shapes such as triangles and pyramids;
- investigate, describe, and reason about the results of subdividing, combining, and transforming shapes;
- explore congruence and similarity;
- make and test conjectures about geometric properties and relationships and develop logical arguments to justify conclusions.

- describe location and movement using common language and geometric vocabulary;
- make and use coordinate systems to specify locations and to describe paths;
- find the distance between points along horizontal and vertical lines of a coordinate system.

- predict and describe the results of sliding, flipping, and turning two-dimensional shapes;
- describe a motion or a series of motions that will show that two shapes are congruent;
- identify and describe line and rotational symmetry in two- and three-dimensional shapes and designs.

- build and draw geometric objects;
- create and describe mental images of objects, patterns, and paths;
- identify and build a three-dimensional object from two-dimensional representations of that object;
- identify and build a two-dimensional representation of a three-dimensional object;
- use geometric models to solve problems in other areas of mathematics, such as number and measurement;
- recognize geometric ideas and relationships and apply them to other disciplines and to problems that arise in the classroom or in everyday life.

GEOMETRY

STANDARD

Instructional programs from prekindergarten through grade 12 should enable all students to—

Analyze characteristics and properties of two- and three-dimensional geometric shapes and develop mathematical arguments about geometric relationships

Specify locations and describe spatial relationships using coordinate geometry and other representational systems

Apply transformations and use symmetry to analyze mathematical situations

Use visualization, spatial reasoning, and geometric modeling to solve problems

GRADES 6–8

Expectations

In grades 6–8 all students should—

- precisely describe, classify, and understand relationships among types of two- and three-dimensional geometric shapes using their defining properties;
- understand relationships among the angles, side lengths, perimeters, areas, and volumes of similar objects;
- create and critique inductive and deductive arguments concerning geometric ideas and relationships, such as congruence, similarity, and the Pythagorean relationship.

- use coordinate geometry to represent and examine the properties of geometric shapes;
- use coordinate geometry to examine special geometric shapes, such as regular polygons or those with pairs of parallel or perpendicular sides.

- describe sizes, positions, and orientations of shapes under informal transformations such as flips, turns, slides, and scaling;
- examine the congruence, similarity, and line or rotational symmetry of objects using transformations.

- draw geometric objects with specified properties, such as side lengths or angle measures;
- use two-dimensional representations of three-dimensional objects to visualize and solve problems such as those involving surface area and volume;
- use visual tools such as networks to represent and solve problems;
- use geometric models to represent and explain numerical and algebraic relationships;
- recognize and apply geometric ideas and relationships in areas outside the mathematics classroom, such as art, science, and everyday life.

GRADES 9–12

Expectations

In grades 9–12 all students should—

- analyze properties and determine attributes of two- and three-dimensional objects;
- explore relationships (including congruence and similarity) among classes of two- and three-dimensional geometric objects, make and test conjectures about them, and solve problems involving them;
- establish the validity of geometric conjectures using deduction, prove theorems, and critique arguments made by others;
- use trigonometric relationships to determine lengths and angle measures.

- use Cartesian coordinates and other coordinate systems, such as navigational, polar, or spherical systems, to analyze geometric situations;
- investigate conjectures and solve problems involving two- and three-dimensional objects represented with Cartesian coordinates.

- understand and represent translations, reflections, rotations, and dilations of objects in the plane by using sketches, coordinates, vectors, function notation, and matrices;
- use various representations to help understand the effects of simple transformations and their compositions.

- draw and construct representations of two- and three-dimensional geometric objects using a variety of tools;
- visualize three-dimensional objects from different perspectives and analyze their cross sections;
- use vertex-edge graphs to model and solve problems;
- use geometric models to gain insights into, and answer questions in, other areas of mathematics;
- use geometric ideas to solve problems in, and gain insights into, other disciplines and other areas of interest such as art and architecture.

MEASUREMENT

STANDARD

Instructional programs from prekindergarten through grade 12 should enable all students to—

Understand measurable attributes of objects and the units, systems, and processes of measurement

Apply appropriate techniques, tools, and formulas to determine measurements

PRE-K–2

Expectations

In prekindergarten through grade 2 all students should—

- recognize the attributes of length, volume, weight, area, and time;
- compare and order objects according to these attributes;
- understand how to measure using nonstandard and standard units;
- select an appropriate unit and tool for the attribute being measured.

- measure with multiple copies of units of the same size, such as paper clips laid end to end;
- use repetition of a single unit to measure something larger than the unit, for instance, measuring the length of a room with a single meterstick;
- use tools to measure;
- develop common referents for measures to make comparisons and estimates.

GRADES 3–5

Expectations

In grades 3–5 all students should—

- understand such attributes as length, area, weight, volume, and size of angle and select the appropriate type of unit for measuring each attribute;
- understand the need for measuring with standard units and become familiar with standard units in the customary and metric systems;
- carry out simple unit conversions, such as from centimeters to meters, within a system of measurement;
- understand that measurements are approximations and understand how differences in units affect precision;
- explore what happens to measurements of a two-dimensional shape such as its perimeter and area when the shape is changed in some way.

- develop strategies for estimating the perimeters, areas, and volumes of irregular shapes;
- select and apply appropriate standard units and tools to measure length, area, volume, weight, time, temperature, and the size of angles;
- select and use benchmarks to estimate measurements;
- develop, understand, and use formulas to find the area of rectangles and related triangles and parallelograms;
- develop strategies to determine the surface areas and volumes of rectangular solids.

MEASUREMENT

STANDARD

Instructional programs from prekindergarten through grade 12 should enable all students to—

Understand measurable attributes of objects and the units, systems, and processes of measurement

Apply appropriate techniques, tools, and formulas to determine measurements

GRADES 6–8

Expectations

In grades 6–8 all students should—

- understand both metric and customary systems of measurement;
- understand relationships among units and convert from one unit to another within the same system;
- understand, select, and use units of appropriate size and type to measure angles, perimeter, area, surface area, and volume.

- use common benchmarks to select appropriate methods for estimating measurements;
- select and apply techniques and tools to accurately find length, area, volume, and angle measures to appropriate levels of precision;
- develop and use formulas to determine the circumference of circles and the area of triangles, parallelograms, trapezoids, and circles and develop strategies to find the area of more-complex shapes;
- develop strategies to determine the surface area and volume of selected prisms, pyramids, and cylinders;
- solve problems involving scale factors, using ratio and proportion;
- solve simple problems involving rates and derived measurements for such attributes as velocity and density.

GRADES 9–12

Expectations

In grades 9–12 all students should—

- make decisions about units and scales that are appropriate for problem situations involving measurement.

- analyze precision, accuracy, and approximate error in measurement situations;
- understand and use formulas for the area, surface area, and volume of geometric figures, including cones, spheres, and cylinders;
- apply informal concepts of successive approximation, upper and lower bounds, and limit in measurement situations;
- use unit analysis to check measurement computations.

DATA ANALYSIS AND PROBABILITY

STANDARD

Instructional programs from prekindergarten through grade 12 should enable all students to—

Formulate questions that can be addressed with data and collect, organize, and display relevant data to answer them

Select and use appropriate statistical methods to analyze data

Develop and evaluate inferences and predictions that are based on data

Understand and apply basic concepts of probability

PRE-K–2

Expectations

In prekindergarten through grade 2 all students should—

- pose questions and gather data about themselves and their surroundings;
- sort and classify objects according to their attributes and organize data about the objects;
- represent data using concrete objects, pictures, and graphs.

- describe parts of the data and the set of data as a whole to determine what the data show.

- discuss events related to students' experiences as likely or unlikely.

GRADES 3–5

Expectations

In grades 3–5 all students should—

- design investigations to address a question and consider how data-collection methods affect the nature of the data set;
- collect data using observations, surveys, and experiments;
- represent data using tables and graphs such as line plots, bar graphs, and line graphs;
- recognize the differences in representing categorical and numerical data.

- describe the shape and important features of a set of data and compare related data sets, with an emphasis on how the data are distributed;
- use measures of center, focusing on the median, and understand what each does and does not indicate about the data set;
- compare different representations of the same data and evaluate how well each representation shows important aspects of the data.

- propose and justify conclusions and predictions that are based on data and design studies to further investigate the conclusions or predictions.

- describe events as likely or unlikely and discuss the degree of likelihood using such words as certain, equally likely, and impossible;
- predict the probability of outcomes of simple experiments and test the predictions;
- understand that the measure of the likelihood of an event can be represented by a number from 0 to 1.

DATA ANALYSIS AND PROBABILITY

STANDARD	GRADES 6–8	GRADES 9–12

STANDARD

Instructional programs from prekindergarten through grade 12 should enable all students to—

Formulate questions that can be addressed with data and collect, organize, and display relevant data to answer them

GRADES 6–8

Expectations

In grades 6–8 all students should—

- formulate questions, design studies, and collect data about a characteristic shared by two populations or different characteristics within one population;
- select, create, and use appropriate graphical representations of data, including histograms, box plots, and scatterplots.

GRADES 9–12

Expectations

In grades 9–12 all students should—

- understand the differences among various kinds of studies and which types of inferences can legitimately be drawn from each;
- know the characteristics of well-designed studies, including the role of randomization in surveys and experiments;
- understand the meaning of measurement data and categorical data, of univariate and bivariate data, and of the term variable;
- understand histograms, parallel box plots, and scatterplots and use them to display data;
- compute basic statistics and understand the distinction between a statistic and a parameter.

Select and use appropriate statistical methods to analyze data

GRADES 6–8

- find, use, and interpret measures of center and spread, including mean and interquartile range;
- discuss and understand the correspondence between data sets and their graphical representations, especially histograms, stem-and-leaf plots, box plots, and scatterplots.

GRADES 9–12

- for univariate measurement data, be able to display the distribution, describe its shape, and select and calculate summary statistics;
- for bivariate measurement data, be able to display a scatterplot, describe its shape, and determine regression coefficients, regression equations, and correlation coefficients using technological tools;
- display and discuss bivariate data where at least one variable is categorical;
- recognize how linear transformations of univariate data affect shape, center, and spread;
- identify trends in bivariate data and find functions that model the data or transform the data so that they can be modeled.

Develop and evaluate inferences and predictions that are based on data

GRADES 6–8

- use observations about differences between two or more samples to make conjectures about the populations from which the samples were taken;
- make conjectures about possible relationships between two characteristics of a sample on the basis of scatterplots of the data and approximate lines of fit;
- use conjectures to formulate new questions and plan new studies to answer them.

GRADES 9–12

- use simulations to explore the variability of sample statistics from a known population and to construct sampling distributions;
- understand how sample statistics reflect the values of population parameters and use sampling distributions as the basis for informal inference;
- evaluate published reports that are based on data by examining the design of the study, the appropriateness of the data analysis, and the validity of conclusions;
- understand how basic statistical techniques are used to monitor process characteristics in the workplace.

Understand and apply basic concepts of probability

GRADES 6–8

- understand and use appropriate terminology to describe complementary and mutually exclusive events;
- use proportionality and a basic understanding of probability to make and test conjectures about the results of experiments and simulations;
- compute probabilities for simple compound events, using such methods as organized lists, tree diagrams, and area models.

GRADES 9–12

- understand the concepts of sample space and probability distribution and construct sample spaces and distributions in simple cases;
- use simulations to construct empirical probability distributions;
- compute and interpret the expected value of random variables in simple cases;
- understand the concepts of conditional probability and independent events;
- understand how to compute the probability of a compound event.

APPENDIX B

A GUIDE TO THE BLACKLINE MASTERS

This appendix contains thumbnail sketches of all of the Blackline Masters that are referenced throughout the book. Those introduced in the Expanded Lessons appear at the end and are numbered separately. Each master can easily be downloaded as a PDF file at www.ablongman.com/vandewalleseries. Once downloaded, you may print as many copies as you need. Keep the files on your computer.

Tips for the Use of the Blackline Masters

When a Blackline Master is to be used either as a workmat for children or will be cut apart into smaller pieces, the best advice is to duplicate the master on card stock. Card stock (also known as index stock) is heavy paper that comes in a variety of colors and can be found at copy or office supply stores.

Workmats such as the ten-frame mat and the place-value mat are best if not laminated. Lamination makes the mats slippery so that counters slide around or off.

With materials that require cutting into smaller pieces, we suggest that you laminate the card stock before you cut out the pieces. This will preserve the materials for several years and save valuable time in the future. Here are some additional, specific instructions for certain masters.

- Little Ten-Frames (BLMs 3 and 4): Make the full ten-frames on one color card stock and the less-than-ten sheet on another. One set consists of the ten cards of each type, cut from a strip of ten on the master.
- Assorted Shapes (BLMs 20–26): Make each set of seven pages a different color. Otherwise, it is very difficult to tell to which set a stray shape belongs.

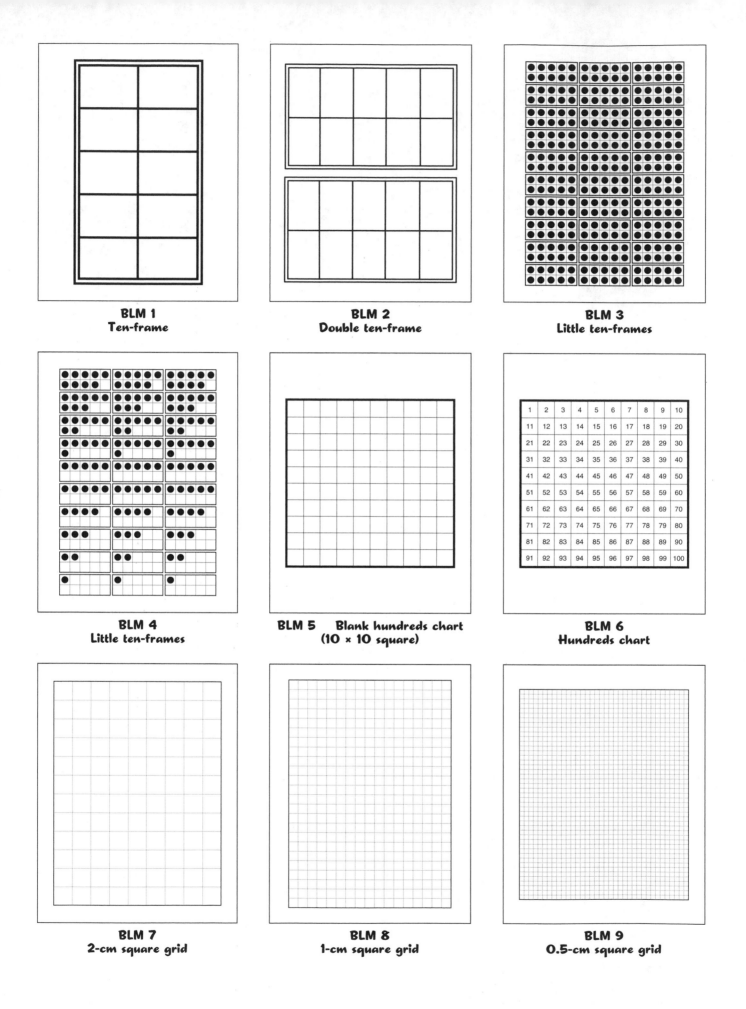

BLM 1
Ten-frame

BLM 2
Double ten-frame

BLM 3
Little ten-frames

BLM 4
Little ten-frames

BLM 5   Blank hundreds chart
(10 × 10 square)

BLM 6
Hundreds chart

1	2	3	4	5	6	7	8	9	10
11	12	13	14	15	16	17	18	19	20
21	22	23	24	25	26	27	28	29	30
31	32	33	34	35	36	37	38	39	40
41	42	43	44	45	46	47	48	49	50
51	52	53	54	55	56	57	58	59	60
61	62	63	64	65	66	67	68	69	70
71	72	73	74	75	76	77	78	79	80
81	82	83	84	85	86	87	88	89	90
91	92	93	94	95	96	97	98	99	100

BLM 7
2-cm square grid

BLM 8
1-cm square grid

BLM 9
0.5-cm square grid

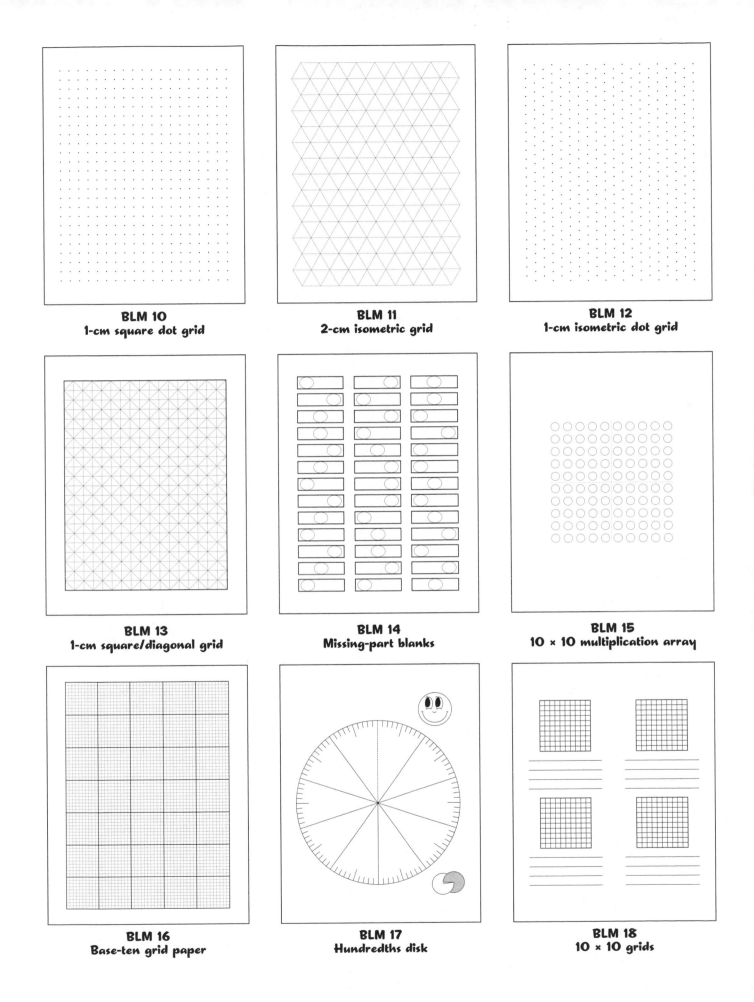

BLM 10
1-cm square dot grid

BLM 11
2-cm isometric grid

BLM 12
1-cm isometric dot grid

BLM 13
1-cm square/diagonal grid

BLM 14
Missing-part blanks

BLM 15
10 × 10 multiplication array

BLM 16
Base-ten grid paper

BLM 17
Hundredths disk

BLM 18
10 × 10 grids

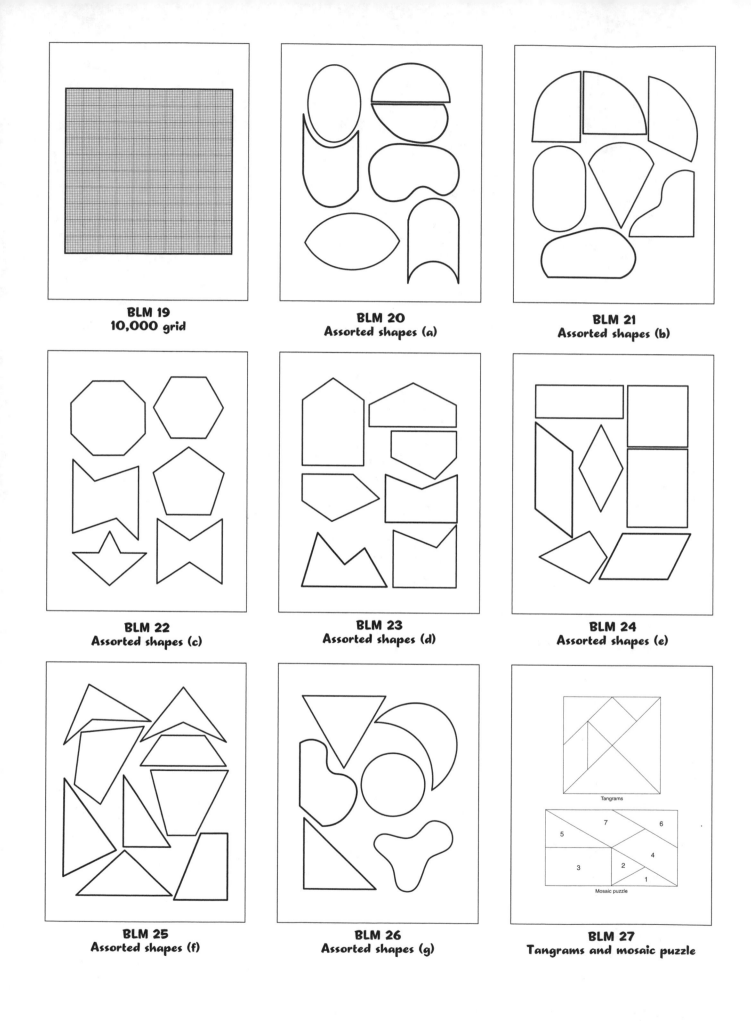

BLM 19
10,000 grid

BLM 20
Assorted shapes (a)

BLM 21
Assorted shapes (b)

BLM 22
Assorted shapes (c)

BLM 23
Assorted shapes (d)

BLM 24
Assorted shapes (e)

BLM 25
Assorted shapes (f)

BLM 26
Assorted shapes (g)

BLM 27
Tangrams and mosaic puzzle

Tangrams

Mosaic puzzle

7   6
5
4
3   2
1

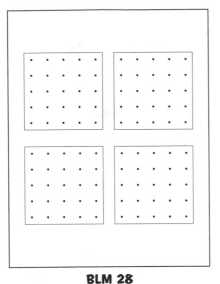

BLM 28
Geoboard recording sheets

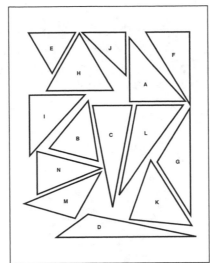

BLM 29
Assorted triangles

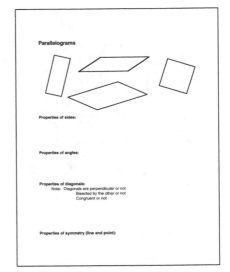

BLM 30   Property lists for quadrilaterals (parallelograms)

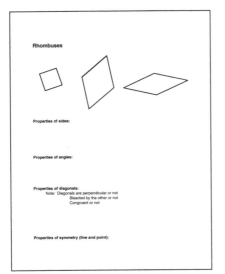

BLM 31   Property lists for quadrilaterals (rhombuses)

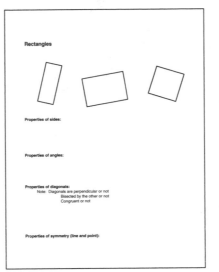

BLM 32   Property lists for quadrilaterals (rectangles)

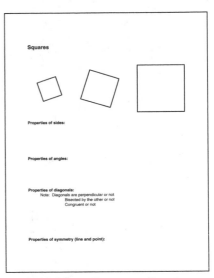

BLM 33   Property lists for quadrilaterals (squares)

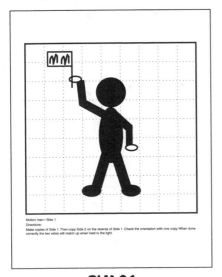

BLM 34
Motion Man (side 1)

BLM 35
Motion Man (side 2)

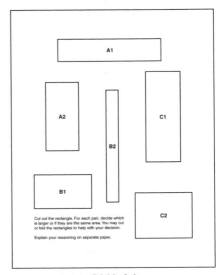

BLM 36
Rectangle comparison

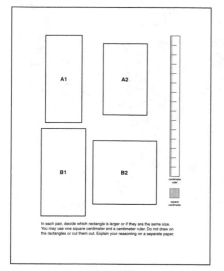

In each pair, decide which rectangle is larger or if they are the same size. You may use one square centimeter and a centimeter ruler. Do not draw on the rectangles or cut them out. Explain your reasoning on a separate paper.

BLM 37
Rectangle comparison—units

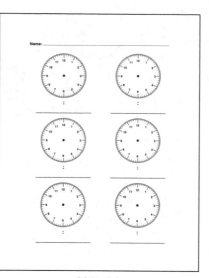

BLM 38
Clock faces

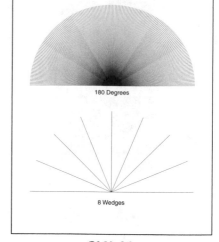

180 Degrees

8 Wedges

BLM 39
Degrees and wedges

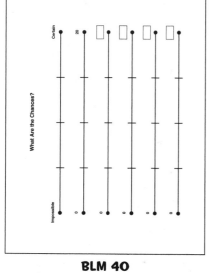

BLM 40
What are the chances?

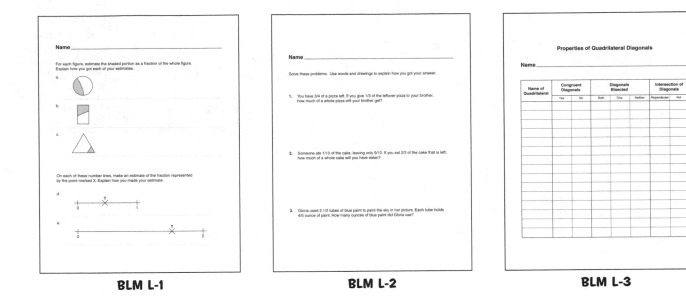

Name _____

For each figure, estimate the shaded portion as a fraction of the whole figure. Explain how you got each of your estimates.

a.

b.

c.

On each of these number lines, make an estimate of the fraction represented by the point marked X. Explain how you made your estimate.

d.

```
    ?
0 --X---------- 1
```

e.

```
              ?
0 ----------X---- 2
```

BLM L-1

Name _____

Solve these problems. Use words and drawings to explain how you got your answer.

1. You have 3/4 of a pizza left. If you give 1/3 of the leftover pizza to your brother, how much of a whole pizza will your brother get?

2. Someone ate 1/10 of the cake, leaving only 9/10. If you eat 2/3 of the cake that is left, how much of a whole cake will you have eaten?

3. Gloria used 2 1/2 tubes of blue paint to paint the sky in her picture. Each tube holds 4/5 ounce of paint. How many ounces of blue paint did Gloria use?

BLM L-2

Properties of Quadrilateral Diagonals

Name _____

Name of Quadrilateral	Congruent Diagonals		Diagonals Bisected			Intersection of Diagonals	
	Yes	No	Both	One	Neither	Perpendicular	Not

BLM L-3

Name _____

Rectangles made with 36 tiles

Rectangle Dimensions	Area	Perimeter

BLM L-4

Windows

Name _____

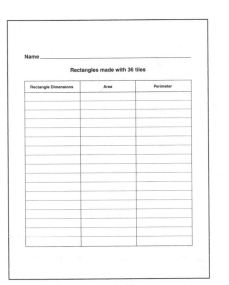

Step	1	2	3	4	5	6	7		20
No. of stiks	4	7	10						

Describe the pattern you see in the drawing:
_____
_____

Describe the pattern you see in the table:
_____
_____

Describe how you can find the number of sticks in the 20th step:
_____
_____
_____

BLM L-5

Predict How Many

Name _____

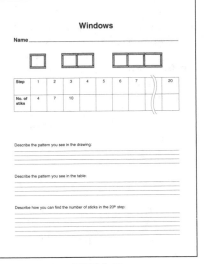

Step	1	2	3	4	5	6	7	8	9	...	20
No. of stiks	2	6	12	20						...	

Describe the pattern you see in the drawing:
_____
_____

Describe the pattern you see in the table:
_____
_____

Describe how you can find the number of sticks in the 20th step:
_____
_____
_____

BLM L-6

REFERENCES

Backhouse, J., Haggarty, L., Pirie, S., & Stratton, J. (1992). *Improving the learning of mathematics*. Portsmouth, NH: Heinemann.

Baek, J. (1998). Children's invented algorithms for multi-digit multiplication problems. In L. J. Morrow (Ed.), *The teaching and learning of algorithms in school mathematics* (pp. 151–160). Reston, VA: National Council of Teachers of Mathematics.

Ball, D. L. (1992). Magical hopes: Manipulatives and the reform of math education. *American Educator 16*(2), 14–18, 46–47.

Barrett, J. E., Jones, G., Thornton, C., & Dickson, S. (2003). Understanding children's developing strategies and concepts of length. In D. H. Clements (Ed.), *Learning and teaching measurement* (pp. 17–30). Reston, VA: National Council of Teachers of Mathematics.

Battista, M. C. (1999). The mathematical miseducation of America's youth: Ignoring research and scientific study in education. *Phi Delta Kappan, 80,* 424–433.

Bresser, R. (1995). *Math and literature (grades 4–6)*. White Plains, NY: Cuisenaire (distributor).

Burger, W. F. (1985). Geometry. *Arithmetic Teacher, 32*(6), 52–56.

Burns, M. (1999). *Making sense of mathematics: A look toward the twenty-first century*. Presentation at the annual meeting of the National Council of Teachers of Mathematics, San Francisco.

Burns, M. (2000). *About teaching mathematics: A K–8 resource* (2nd ed.). Sausalito, CA: Math Solutions Publications.

Campbell, P. B. (1995). Redefining the "girl problem in mathematics." In W. G. Secada, E. Fennema, & L. B. Adajian (Eds.), *New directions for equity in mathematics education* (pp. 225–241). New York: Cambridge University Press.

Campbell, P. F. (1996). Empowering children and teachers in the elementary mathematics classrooms of urban schools. *Urban Education, 30,* 449–475.

Campbell, P. F. (1997, April). Children's invented algorithms: Their meaning and place in instruction. Presented at the annual meeting of the National Council of Teachers of Mathematics, Minneapolis, MN.

Campbell, P. F., Rowan, T. E., & Suarez, A. R. (1998). What criteria for student-invented algorithms? In L. J. Morrow (Ed.), *The teaching and learning of algorithms in school mathematics* (pp. 49–55). Reston, VA: National Council of Teachers of Mathematics.

Carpenter, T. P., Franke, M. L., Jacobs, V. R., Fennema, E., & Empson, S. B. (1998). A longitudinal study of invention and understanding in children's multidigit addition and subtraction. *Journal for Research in Mathematics Education, 29,* 3–20.

Carroll, W. M. (1996). Use of invented algorithms by second graders in a reform mathematics curriculum. *Journal of Mathematical Behaviour, 15,* 137–150.

Carroll, W. M. (1997). Results of third-grade students in a reform curriculum on the Illinois State Mathematics Test. *Journal for Research in Mathematics Education, 28,* 237–242.

Carroll, W. M., & Porter, D. (1997). Invented strategies can develop meaningful mathematical procedures. *Teaching Children Mathematics, 3,* 370–374.

Chambers, D. (1996). Direct modeling and invented procedures: Building on students' informal strategies. *Teaching Children Mathematics, 3,* 92–95.

Charles, R. I., Chancellor, D., Harcourt, L., Moore, D., Schielack, J. F., Van de Walle, J., & Wortzman, R. (1998). *Scott Foresman—Addison Wesley MATH* (Grades K to 5), Glenview, IL: Addison Wesley Longman, Inc.

Clements, D. H., & Battista, M. T. (1990). Constructivist learning and teaching. *Arithmetic Teacher, 38*(1), 34–35.

Clements, D. H., & Battista, M. T. (1992). Geometry and spatial reasoning. In D. A. Grouws (Ed.), *Handbook of research on mathematics teaching and learning* (pp. 420–464). Old Tappan, NJ: Macmillan.

Cobb, P. (1996). Where is the mind? A coordination of sociocultural and cognitive constructivist perspectives. In C. T. Fosnot (Ed.), *Constructivism: Theory, perspectives, and practice* (pp. 34–52). New York: Teachers College Press.

Davis, R. B. (1986). *Learning mathematics: The cognitive science approach to mathematics education.* Norwood, NJ: Ablex.

Dietzman, C. M., & English, L. D. (2001). Promoting the use of diagrams as tools for thinking. In A. A. Cuoco (Ed.), *The roles of representation in school mathematics* (pp. 77–89). Reston, VA: National Council of Teachers of Mathematics.

Edmark Corp. (1996). *Probability.* Redmond, WA: Author.

Empson, S. B. (2002). Organizing diversity in early fraction thinking. In B. Litwiller (Ed.), *Making sense of fractions, ratios, and proportions* (pp. 29–40). Reston, VA: National Council of Teachers of Mathematics.

Fosnot, C. T., & Dolk, M. (2001). *Young mathematicians at work: Constructing number sense, addition, and subtraction.* Portsmouth, NH: Heinemann.

Fuys, D., Geddes, D., & Tischler, R. (1988). The van Hiele model of thinking in geometry among adolescents. *Journal for Research in Mathematics Education Monograph, 3.*

Gag, W. (1928). *Millions of cats.* New York: Coward-McCann.

Geddes, D., & Fortunato, I. (1993). Geometry: Research and classroom activities. In D. T. Owens (Ed.), *Research ideas for the classroom: Middle grades mathematics* (pp. 199–222). New York: Macmillan.

Greenes, C., & Findell, C. (1999). *Groundworks: Algebraic thinking.* Chicago: Creative Publications.

Hiebert, J. (1990). The role of routine procedures in the development of mathematical competence. In T. J. Cooney (Ed.), *Teaching and learning mathematics in the 1990s* (pp. 31–40). Reston, VA: National Council of Teachers of Mathematics.

Hiebert, J., & Carpenter, T. P. (1992). Learning and teaching with understanding. In D. A. Grouws (Ed.), *Handbook of research on mathematics teaching and learning* (pp. 65–97). Old Tappan, NJ: Macmillan.

Hiebert, J., Carpenter, T. P., Fennema, E., Fuson, K., Human, P., Murray, H., Olivier, A., & Wearne, D. (1996). Problem solving as a basis for reform in curriculum and instruction: The case of mathematics. *Educational Researcher, 25* (May), 12–21.

Hiebert, J., Carpenter, T. P., Fennema, E., Fuson, K., Wearne, D., Murray, H., Olivier, A., & Human, P. (1997). *Making sense: Teaching and learning mathematics with understanding.* Portsmouth, NH: Heinemann.

Hiebert, J., & Wearne, D. (1996). Instruction, understanding, and skill in multidigit addition and subtraction. *Cognition and Instruction, 14,* 251–283.

Hoffer, A. R. (1983). Van Hiele–based research. In R. A. Lesh & M. Landau (Eds.), *Acquisition of mathematics concepts and processes* (pp. 205–227). Orlando, FL: Academic Press.

Hoffer, A. R., & Hoffer, S. A. K. (1992). Ratios and proportional thinking. In T. R. Post (Ed.), *Teaching mathematics in grades K–8: Research-based methods* (2nd ed.) (pp. 303–330). Boston, MA: Allyn & Bacon.

Howden, H. (1989). Teaching number sense. *Arithmetic Teacher, 36*(6), 6–11.

Huinker, D. (1994, April). Multi-step word problems: A strategy for empowering students. Presented at the annual meeting of the National Council of Teachers of Mathematics, Indianapolis, IN.

Huinker, D. (1998). Letting fraction algorithms emerge through problem solving. In L. J. Morrow (Ed.), *The teaching and learning of algorithms in school mathematics* (pp. 170–182). Reston, VA: National Council of Teachers of Mathematics.

Janvier, C. (Ed.). (1987). *Problems of representation in the teaching and learning of mathematics.* Hillsdale, NJ: Erlbaum.

Kamii, C. K. (1985). *Young children reinvent arithmetic.* New York: Teachers College Press.

Kamii, C. K. (1989). *Young children continue to reinvent arithmetic: 2nd grade.* New York: Teachers College Press.

Kamii, C. K., & Clark, F. B. (1995). Equivalent fractions: Their difficulty and educational implications. *The Journal of Mathematical Behavior, 14,* 365–378.

Kamii, C. K., & Dominick, A. (1997). To teach or not to teach the algorithms. *Journal of Mathematical Behavior, 16,* 51–62.

Kamii, C. K., & Dominick, A. (1998). The harmful effects of algorithms in grades 1–4. In L. J. Morrow (Ed.), *The teaching and learning of algorithms in school mathematics* (pp. 130–140). Reston, VA: National Council of Teachers of Mathematics.

Kenney, P. A., & Kouba, V. L. (1997). What do students know about measurement? In P. A. Kenney & E. Silver (Eds.), *Results from the sixth mathematics assessment of the National Assessment of Educational Progress* (pp. 141–163). Reston, VA: National Council of Teachers of Mathematics.

Key Curriculum Press. (2001). *The geometer's sketchpad* (Version 4.0). Berkeley, CA: Key Curriculum Press.

Kulm, G. (1994). *Mathematics and assessment: What works in the classroom.* San Francisco: Jossey-Bass.

Labinowicz, E. (1985). *Learning from children: New beginnings for teaching numerical thinking.* Menlo Park, CA: AWL Supplemental.

Labinowicz, E. (1987). Assessing for learning: The interview method. *Arithmetic Teacher, 35*(3), 22–24.

Lamon, S. J. (1996). The development of unitizing: Its role in children's partitioning strategies. *Journal for Research in Mathematics Education, 27,* 170–193.

Lamon, S. J. (2002). Part-whole comparisons with unitizing. In B. Litwiller (Ed.), *Making sense of fractions, ratios, and proportions* (pp. 79–86). Reston, VA: National Council of Teachers of Mathematics.

Lappan, G. (1998). Capturing patterns and functions: Variables and joint variation. In *The nature and role of algebra in the K–14 curriculum: Proceedings of national symposium* (pp. 57–59). Washington, DC: National Academy Press.

Lappan, G., & Mouck, M. K. (1998). Developing algorithms for adding and subtracting fractions. In L. J. Morrow (Ed.), *The teaching and learning of algorithms in school mathematics* (pp. 183–197). Reston, VA: National Council of Teachers of Mathematics.

Learning Co. (1994). *TesselMania!* Mahwah, NJ: Author.

Lesh, R. A., Post, T. R., & Behr, M. J. (1987). Representations and translations among representations in mathematics learning and problem solving. In C. Janvier (Ed.), *Problems of representation in the teaching and learning of mathematics* (pp. 33–40). Hillsdale, NJ: Erlbaum.

Liedtke, W. (1988). Diagnosis in mathematics: The advantages of an interview. *Arithmetic Teacher, 36*(3), 26–29.

Lindquist, M. M. (1987a). Estimation and mental computation: Measurement. *Arithmetic Teacher, 34*(5), 16–17.

Lindquist, M. M. (1987b). Problem solving with five easy pieces. In J. M. Hill (Ed.), *Geometry for grades K–6: Readings from the Arithmetic Teacher* (pp. 151–156). Reston, VA: National Council of Teachers of Mathematics.

Ma, L. (1999). *Knowing and teaching elementary mathematics: Teachers' understanding of fundamental mathematics in China and the United States.* Mahwah, NJ: Lawrence Erlbaum.

Mack, N. K. (2001). Building on informal knowledge through instruction in a complex content domain: Partitioning, units, and understanding multiplication of fractions. *Journal for Research in Mathematics Education, 32,* 267–295.

Martin, G., & Strutchens, M. E. (2000). Geometry and measurement. In E. A. Silver & P. A. Kenney (Eds.), *Results from the seventh mathematics assessment of the National Assessment of Educational Progress* (pp. 193–234). Reston, VA: National Council of Teachers of Mathematics.

Mathews, L. (1979). *Gator pie.* New York: Dodd, Mead.

McKissack, P. C. (1992). *A million fish . . . more or less.* New York: Knopf.

Mokros, J., Russell, S. J., & Economopoulos, K. (1995). *Beyond arithmetic: Changing mathematics in the elementary classroom.* Palo Alto, CA: Dale Seymour Publications.

National Council of Teachers of Mathematics. (1989). *Curriculum and evaluation standards for school mathematics.* Reston, VA: Author.

National Council of Teachers of Mathematics. (1995). *Assessment standards for school mathematics.* Reston, VA: Author.

National Council of Teachers of Mathematics. (2000). *Principles and standards for school mathematics.* Reston, VA: Author.

Nelson, R. B. (1993). *Proofs without words: Exercises in visual thinking.* Washington, DC: MAA.

O'Brien, T. C. (1999). Parrot math. *Phi Delta Kappan, 80,* 434–438.

Pothier, Y., & Sawada, D. (1983). Partitioning: The emergence of rational number ideas in young children. *Journal for Research in Mathematics Education, 14,* 307–317.

Resnick, L. B. (1983). A developmental theory of number understanding. In H. P. Ginsburg (Ed.), *The development of mathematical thinking* (pp. 109–151). New York: Academic Press.

Riverdeep. (1996). *Tangible math: The geometry inventof.* Cambridge, MA: Author.

Rowan, T. E., & Bourne, B. (1994). *Thinking like mathematicians: Putting the K–4 standards into practice.* Portsmouth, NH: Heinemann.

Scott Foresman. (2004). *E-Tools.* Chicago: Author.

Scheer, J. K. (1980). The etiquette of diagnosis. *Arithmetic Teacher, 27*(9), 18–19.

Schifter, D., Bastable, V., & Russell, S. J. (1999a). *Developing mathematical understanding: Numbers and operations, Part 1, Building a system of tens (Casebook).* Parsippany, NJ: Dale Seymour Publications.

Schifter, D., Bastable, V., & Russell, S. J. (1999b). *Developing mathematical understanding: Numbers and operations, Part 2, Making meaning for operations (Casebook).* Parsippany, NJ: Dale Seymour Publications.

Schifter, D., Bastable, V., & Russell, S. J. (1999c). *Developing mathematical understanding: Numbers and operations, Part 2, Making meaning for operations (Facilitator's Guide).* Parsippany, NJ: Dale Seymour Publications.

Schroeder, T. L., & Lester, F. K., Jr. (1989). Developing understanding in mathematics via problem solving. In P. R. Trafton (Ed.), *New directions for elementary school mathematics* (pp. 31–42). Reston, VA: National Council of Teachers of Mathematics.

Schwartz, D. (1985). *How much is a million?* New York: Lothrop, Lee & Shepard.

Schwartz, D. (1989). *If you made a million.* New York: Lothrop, Lee & Shepard.

Schwartz, S. L. (1996). Hidden messages in teacher talk: Praise and empowerment. *Teaching Children Mathematics, 2,* 396–401.

Smith, J. P., III. (2002). The development of students' knowledge of fractions and ratios. In B. Litwiller (Ed.), *Making sense of fractions, ratios, and proportions* (pp. 3–17). Reston, VA: National Council of Teachers of Mathematics.

Taber, S. B. (2002). Go ask Alice about multiplication of fractions. In B. Litwiller (Ed.), *Making sense of fractions, ratios, and proportions* (pp. 61–71). Reston, VA: National Council of Teachers of Mathematics.

Tahan, M. (1993). *The man who counted: A collection of mathematical adventures* (Trans. L. Clark & A. Reid). New York: Norton.

Texas Instruments. (1994). *Cabri geometry II* [Computer Software]. Dallas: Author.

Thompson, P. W. (1994). Concrete materials and teaching for mathematical understanding. *Arithmetic Teacher, 41,* 556–558.

Tom Snyder. (1993). *The graph club* [Computer Software]. Watertown, MA: Author.

van Hiele, P. M. (1999). Developing geometric thinking through activities that begin with play. *Teaching Children Mathematics, 5,* 310–316.

Winter, M. J., Lappan, G., Phillips, E., & Fitzgerald, W. (1986). *Middle grades mathematics project: Spatial visualization.* Menlo Park, CA: AWL Supplemental.

Wood, T., & Turner-Vorbeck, T. (2001). Extending the conception of mathematics teaching. In T. Wood, B. S. Nelson, & J. Warfield (Eds.), *Beyond classical pedagogy: Teaching elementary school mathematics* (pp. 185–208). Mahwah, NJ: Lawrence Erlbaum.

REFERENCES

INDEX